GREENPORT, C.I.

By Brian Gay

DISCLAIMER

Long Island, NY including the townships or villages of Greenport, Oceanside, Massapequa are all real places. There is a Mafia in New York, but none of the characters herein are based on any real persons. The names of some individuals may be borrowed from real people but as portrayed herein have nothing in common with any characters. In all respects this novel is a work of fiction. Names, characters, places, and incidents are either the product of the author's imagination or used fictitiously. Any resemblance to actual persons, living or dead, or to actual events or locales is unintentional and coincidental.

AUTHOR'S NOTE

It has been many years I have worked on this novel and several more that will be coming out in the forthcoming months and I am finally happy to move my work from a few beta readers to the reading masses.

First, I would like to point out that all errors, exaggerations or misstatements of facts are entirely of my own making. This includes any technical data of information provided by former shipmates, friends and acquaintances who took an interest in my work.

Much of this novel was written while seated at my desk at home, but more often than not, while sitting on my boat or at a diner or restaurant in South West Florida.

And now here goes my thanks. First, Karen without whom I could not get this project completed. Karen proofed and reproofed the manuscript, made numerous suggestions to improve the "flavoring" of the story line, including making the love scenes "lady friendly" and more. The novel would not exist without her.

To my many friends who took the time to read the manuscript and make suggestions and helpful corrections to technical jargon, medical procedures or grammatical changes I thank you. If I missed you here, I apologize.

To Barbara and Nick Castronova, Barbara first exclaiming "Brian wrote this?" were invaluable in their critiques and suggestions for a more readable novel.

Karen's parents, Harry and Audrey Herrmann, now deceased, who took the time to print in 14 pt font or larger and place the pages into a loose-leaf notebook so other "mature" friends could read the novel was greatly appreciated. May they both rest in peace.

Karen's sisters Jenny and Krissy, who held no punches after they read the manuscript here and several other manuscripts. Their suggestions improved the story line.

To my lifelong friend Roseann Thompson-Falcone, who gave me invaluable feedback and always tried to make my writing or me softer and more likeable rather than the coarse and acerbic man I sometimes am.

My dear friend Alicia Purple, who also was surprised I could write and who thoroughly enjoyed this manuscript.

To my dear friend Thomas Ehlert who provided a valuable critique of my character development and a smooth storyline.

And to all the others out there whose names escape me, I thank you.

TABLE OF CONTENTS

CHAPTER 1

"Billy. You guys come in from the northwest with Chief. Mikey is in the tree line covering the front of the buildings. Kev has the west side covered from the ridge. We'll go in like we planned. Echo in five to our close-up positions. Let me know when you're ready to go. Report anything you see."

I got clicks and acknowledgments over my radio.

We'd come upon a village. In fact, the outskirts of a village, a farm at the beginning of a village. A family compound of buildings with mud, concrete, and stone walls, huts with rough plank doors, a stable, a barn-like building, and a workshop spread over several acres of land squeezed between three mountains. This house was a nice home, the owner having made improvements by installing some modern windows and an idle generator. We'd been tracking ten men for two days. Our intelligence put six of them in this compound, including their leader, who was a high-priority target, though no one saw anyone yet. Smoke wisped from the little pipe-like chimney. We could smell horses, goats, and humans nearby.

It was mid-January, and I had long ago stopped getting cold in the Afghan mountains. The temperature hovered around five degrees. We were somewhere about 8000 feet above sea level in the Hindu Kush range northwest of Parun, which is several small villages tucked into a valley along the Parun River in Nuristan Province. We, an eight-man SEAL squad, an Afghan interpreter, a four-man Afghan Army Special Forces fire team, and I were tracking a group of Taliban insurgents wanted for setting IEDs, beheadings, shootings, and killing an entire

1

Afghan family two weeks ago. I feared whoever owned this compound would die, too, by the same methods and means.

It was 0352, and it was cold. My exhalations froze on my beard and mustache as I waited and listened. The wind blew the falling snow sideways. Our surveillance showed several human heat plumes in the buildings. Possibly twelve or more humans in the main house, four to six humans in the stable with several horses and oxen or cows. The building farthest from us up the mountain was cold, but owing to its size, the distance, and the heavy falling snow, we couldn't be sure. Several stone and mud walls stood between us and the building.

We had tracked this group of insurgents since the night before last. The group of ten had split up. I chose to follow the six who moved toward the village and not chase the others who I felt were leading us over a mountain and around another to avoid the villages and reduce the chance the entire group would be caught or to confuse us as we tracked them while they escaped to Pakistan. As we came upon the compound, we heard other human noises but didn't see anything except heat plumes. Most of the human forms appeared horizontal, on the floors or beds, though some were sitting in chairs per our IR scopes. I felt that we'd come upon a larger group than anticipated. I sent two men—the interpreter and a shooter—into Ishtewi, the northernmost village, to raise the village elders to find out what they knew about this family compound. This village is believed to be friendly, but you just never knew. Two weeks ago, a "friendly" Afghan soldier opened fire on Army Ranger troops.

We'd sit for four minutes before we'd move in closer. I had snipers covering two sides of the building from high hides on the mountain. Everyone was looking and listening. Perhaps I'd have some intel from the village leader before we assaulted. I wouldn't wait, as I didn't want a daylight gunfight.

I got some alpha clicks on my headset.

"LT. I just spotted a face looking out the west window," Kev reported.

"Weapon, man, woman, child, anything else, Kev?" I said.

"Man, I think. Nothing else, LT. The fire is going in there, but not casting enough light. He wiped a fogged window. Who'd be looking out a window at 0400?"

"Right. Okay to move, Kev?"

"Clear."

"Close it up to our selected positions. Move!"

Nine men and I moved in. We were close on three sides. I had Billy covering the exit route in case the bad guys ran, which wasn't an *if*. They always ran once they knew it was us.

An alpha-click in my headset.

"Hami. What is it?"

"Sir. We spoke with the village tribal leader. He claims that a family of ten lives there. Five young children, an older daughter, two older sons, and the parents. The daughter is seventeen years old. The oldest boys are fifteen and sixteen years old. The father is feeble, having crushed his arm with a stone several years ago. They have been beneficial to our cause and were paid in American dollars. He says they have two horses, a few cows, and a small herd of goats and sheep."

"Hami. Get back here. We have too many adults and too many horses."

"We come at once, sir. The villagers will help us if it is your wish."

"I'd prefer they set a security perimeter to prevent these guys from entering the village."

"Roger, LT."

"Advise and return. We'll go in ten. Everyone checks. Anything yet?"

"Nothing. Mark, why not hold until they come out?"

"Chief, I suspect the wife and daughter are not being treated well, and if they find dollars in there, they'll kill them all. Any movement in that far building?"

"Nothing, sir."

"Echo in nine. Watch it and get ready."

I was in my fourth year at Cornell University when we were attacked on 9/11. That seemed like a lifetime ago. I graduated college in May 2002 and was sworn into the Navy the same day. I travelled to Newport, Rhode Island, for Officer Candidate School, where I was commissioned. Following OCS, I was shipped off to California for BUD/S, followed by jump school, then SQT or SEAL Qualification Training, then language training in Pashto, Dari, and Farsi; I already spoke Spanish and Arabic, which I'd taken in high school and college, then close quarters combat training, unit training, and more training, and I've been at war ever since as I moved up through the teams. I'd received word that I'd been selected for lieutenant commander. I was likely on my last mission, but who knows?

A movement caught my eye. I looked through my Night Force NXS scope and then looked with my Thermoset scope, which I had attached to an auxiliary rail on my MK12Mod1 rifle to sight on heat sources. The heat blob I saw was a group of goats and sheep pressed together in a walled pen. They'd moved past a hole in the wall. The property had lots of walls.

My only breaks from this crap had been for advanced language training, team training, and the Naval Post-Graduate School. I was currently filling a billet as the Special Operations Officer for the Joint Task Force, preparing me for an executive officer tour, having punched all the tickets my seniors and detailer wanted me to punch. I'd been selected for lieutenant commander on my first look. I have been awarded two silver stars, three bronze stars, and three purple hearts. Pending this tour, I was headed stateside to a staff position that would further prepare me for executive officer, joint duty, and commanding officer of a SEAL team. My superiors liked me, and I got the job done. I'd cut my teeth in Iraq, catching most of the shit that SEALs were involved in there: Basra, Al-Fallujah, and Al-Ramadi. I'd worked for some impressive SEAL officers, and they'd taught me a lot. I liked being a SEAL officer, but I was tired of war.

Three minutes until someone would die.

"LT, Hami. We are in position."

"Shrek. Check-in."

"I'm here, LT."

"I want you in close, shooting over our shoulders from the western ridge. I just have a feeling. Watch that goat pen. Keep an eye on that goat pen and far building. Surfer. You ready?"

"Yes, Mark."

Surfer was a brand-new lieutenant. He joined the team a year ago, and, well, the CO wanted me on this mission for his own reasons, and the commander of the JOC okayed it. Missions were slowing down, though I figured we were headed back to Iraq and Syria to fight ISIS and al-Qaida. Surfer is a good SEAL. His officer leadership needed some help, and that was the CO's intent in assigning him to me. I'd had Surfer initially plan and direct most activities with the guys, but now this assault would be on me.

"Gladiator one, this is Emperor one zero. Over."

Shit! JOC ops.

"Emperor one zero, Gladiator one. I'm about to be very busy. Over."

"Roger, Gladiator one. Standing by. QRF is briefed and standing by. Over."

"Roger, Emperor, one zero. Gladiator one about to make contact with the enemy."

"Roger, Gladiator one. Emperor one zero standing by. Over."

Leave it to JOC ops—my people—to come up on the comms minutes before we went in. I'd already called in within the window. They were monitoring our communications. Our QRF, or Quick Reaction Force, was comprised of a SEAL platoon, a Marine platoon, a four-man Navy EOD detachment, an Air Force para-rescue team, a Marine K-9 unit, four Army MH-47E Chinooks and two MH-60M Black Hawks from the Night Stalkers of the 160th SOAR, and four Marine AH-1Z Viper gunships from the Gunfighters of HMLA-369. An Air

Force AC-130 Specter gunship circled overhead. Still, the doctrine would call for it to leave at daylight while an Army MC-12C ISR (Intelligence, Surveillance, and Reconnaissance) aircraft loitered above, providing command with a picture of our situation. Finally, two RQ-170 Sentinel drones, operated by the CIA and the Air Force, flew near our position monitoring intelligence. This was the same drone used to verify that Osama bin Laden was where the CIA thought he would be when one of our teams went in to ruin his day. Hopefully the QRF would not be called away to another unit in contact with the enemy. We were truly a joint force.

"Two minutes. All clear?" I said.

I got "clear" responses from all members.

I checked my weapon. We were going into the house from two sides from the west corners since it was a large building. I'd be the second man through our door. Breachers would destroy the doors, and we'd toss in flash bangs, then yell. Anyone holding a weapon or standing would be killed.

"One minute and we go," I said.

I rehearsed in my head what I'd do, like a hundred times before. As my weapon came up, my heart rate and breathing slowed. My breath smoked in front of me and blew back into my face as I stood like the Budweiser Clydesdale horses exhaling streams of steam through their noses as they pulled a sleigh in their Christmas television commercials.

"Five seconds!" I said. I looked through my NVGs and saw my team in slow motion, readying to attack as they stood.

"Move. Now," I said. Eleven human forms converged on the building. Two to the door in front of me.

"Position... clear. Blow!"

The breachers exploded the doors and tossed flash bangs. The noise and light were startling. We yelled, "Down! Down!" in Pashto, Dari, and Farsi as we entered the building. Noise exploded around us as automatic weapons fired. I shot three men to my right in rapid succession and swept right.

"Clear, right," I said while Talbot fired his weapon to the left, killing several men as I swept the room.

"Clear," Talbot yelled while he checked his kills, putting security rounds in two.

"Clear," yelled Chief from the rear of the house over the radio.

"We got squirters. Oh, shit! The far building and goat pen. Set up! RPG! RPG!" Surfer said.

I heard a whoosh, and the wall behind me exploded. Something hit me in the back.

"RPG! RPG!" Surfer continued to yell as automatic weapons fire erupted all around us. I heard a second and third whoosh, and the wall in front of me exploded.

I looked around as we set up to defend. I flipped up my NVGs. The old man was dead. He'd been shot in the head some time ago; the entrance wound and exploded exit wound had already coagulated. The daughter was tied to the lone bed in the room. She'd been beaten and raped but was alive. Her mother was moving to untie her. I saw the older boys dead—their throats cut. The younger children huddled in fright in the corner. I cut the older girl loose. In Pashto, I ordered them to hit the floor.

"Hami, tell them all to take cover. Kev, what do we have?"

"Fifteen to 20 bad guys. Another RPG!" Kev yelled.

The RPG exploded at the corner of the building, raining stone and dirt on us.

"Set up, guys. We'll go out the southwest door. Surfer, what do you see?"

"In the goat pen. Maybe eight men. RPGs and AKs"

"Okay. You and Hami's guys sweep right around the building. I'll come out my door and engage them. Chief, take your guys and Hassan's team and fill in behind Surfer."

"Aye-aye. We're headed out the door. There's a bunch of them, Mark," Chief said.

"Roger!"

Grenades and automatic weapons fire sounded all around us. One of the enemies seemed to be firing his AK weapon continuously on automatic. I poked my head out and saw what Surfer had described. I readied two grenades. I let one go. It landed in the pen. Sorry goats. I tossed the second one just before the first exploded as bullets chewed up the wall next to me. The second grenade exploded. I heard the cries of dying men and the bleating of dying goats and sheep. Talbot and I dashed out the door and swept toward the pen, weapons up. I could hear Kev, Shrek, and Mikey communicating on the radio, shooting targets smoothly and calmly as they'd been trained. Chief was shouting orders to his fire team and the Afghan fire team.

"LT! They're coming around to your side!" Surfer advised.

Shit. The guys had not swept right fast enough.

"How many?" I said.

"Twenty! Look out, LT!" Surfer, Chief, and Kev warned at the same moment. Talbot and I looked at each other, and as we turned, some twenty Taliban came running from around the building and walls. We fired at the same time as we dropped. Talbot and I both were hit. We continued firing.

"LT. We're coming. Mikey, from behind! LT, we're coming; hang on. . . More are coming from the far building. Set up, guys. Cover our flank. Shrek, Billy, Hassan, Aarif, Chief," Surfer said.

"I got two more," Kev said as a Taliban's head exploded in front of me.

Another Taliban fell. Two more went down. The sounds of small weapons firing were all around me. The intensity of the gunfight was unbelievable. I was firing from the ground as I struggled to get up. I replaced my MK12 mag, and then I swung my shotgun up, firing twelve rounds. I got off eight more rounds, emptying my twenty-round weapon as a round slammed into my chest armor, knocking me down. Four Taliban insurgents fell just feet from me. I raised my MK12 as I rose to my knee and fired as half the remaining Taliban insurgents scattered right, and the other half charged us. I got hit by several rounds and knocked back, my MK12 blown from my hands. I reached for my SIG Sauers, pulling both from their holsters. I fired just as an insurgent stepped up to shoot me. Talbot was still firing his H&K with one hand and his SIG with his other. He was shooting them within feet of us. Both of us were on our backs in the snow, shooting at the insurgents from three to fifteen feet away. I shot another and another—I just kept shooting. Fuck! God help me! They were all over us. I leaned up in the snow to shoot and got off several more shots as three Taliban charged me. I was hit again, and I went down for the last time, a vision of my mother standing before me.

CHAPTER 2

"Good morning, commander. How are you today?"

"I'm okay, doctor. I'm ready to go home."

"Well, you are ready. Your recovery almost seems like a miracle. You're a lucky man."

"Yeah. Like I've won the fucking Irish Lottery, doctor."

The doctor looked at me. He was a retired U.S. Navy doctor who now worked as a Veteran's Administration doctor.

"Look, Mark. It's going to take some time. I won't sugarcoat what's happened to you, but you're a good guy. You're young, what, just thirty-two. You have your whole life ahead of you. You've healed up remarkably well, physically. I read where your gastroenterologist will keep you on a special diet for a while. You'll see me at least once a month for now or more if need be. Physically, you're cleared, and mentally, I've cleared you. Emotionally, you will heal. You need time to grieve, but that grief must begin so it can end. You'll be okay. Look, you have your grandfather and grandmother waiting for you. Your grandfather is a tough old guy. He's been there. He'll be there for you. Talk to him. He told me when you were a little boy you used to sit on his lap and pick his ribbons off his uniform. He did four tours in Vietnam during his first ten years in the army. He's your grandfather, a retired general. He'll help you, but, and I think this is more important, Lauren needs you. You are all she has. Go home and take care of her. Let her get to know you again. Losing your parents is just as hard or harder on her."

"I know, doctor. I'm just so . . . freaking angry! Why? With all I've been through... Why? Why did it have to turn out like this?"

"I can't answer that, Mark. I've written you a prescription for something to help you sleep if needed. You must work hard to lose the anger and begin to get through your grief. We've spoken of this. Your mother didn't save your life for it to be angry and hollow. Your mother was full of life. Live your life for her and Lauren. Lauren tells me the home is all ready for the two of you to settle in. Take care of her. Put her first, and you'll find you'll be better off."

"I'll be okay. My uncle is anxious for me to get to work at the firm, but I'm not sure if I'm ready, though."

"Then don't work yet. It's April, almost May. The weather is unseasonably warm, and it's terrific outside. Greenport is beautiful right now. Lauren said your grandfather put the boat in the water. Fish. Relax. Think about what you want. Take care of Lauren. She needs you."

I smiled. It seemed like I hardly knew her.

"Okay, doc. Let me go before The General starts barking orders."

"You'll make it, Mark. You're one of the good guys. I'll see you in two weeks."

"Fine. Thanks, doctor."

#

I walked out of my suite at the Veteran's Transition Recovery Center at the VA Medical Center in Northport, Long Island, New York. Waiting for me were my grandparents,

13

Lieutenant General William H. MacKenzie and Martha R. MacKenzie, USA, who retired. I hugged my grandmother.

Grandma is a slight woman of seventy-four years, although she looked like she was in her late sixties. She stood about five feet, five inches tall, having shrunk a little with age and the burden of loss on our family. Her hair was various shades of gray and silver that she kept pulled back in a bun or clipped in a short ponytail. Her bright blue eyes sparkled with love, though not as brightly as in years past. Sadness and grief had taken their toll. She hugged me tightly.

"Oh, Mark. I'm so glad you're coming home. You look good, son," she said.

"Thanks, Grandma," I said as I looked at my grandfather.

He looked very happy and pleased to see me. My grandfather is 75. He stands just over six feet tall and weighs about one hundred seventy-five pounds. He's in good health. He has most of his hair, though it's powder white and a little wispy now, but he keeps it combed and perfectly trimmed as if he were still in uniform. His blue-grey eyes and penetrating look still command respect. He appears to be a warm and loving man, but he always seemed tentative about expressing emotion to my father and me.

"Sir. How are you?"

"How are you, son? You look great. Don't I get one of those, too?" he said.

I hugged my grandfather, which I'd not done since I was a child.

"Let's take you home. Lauren took today off and is making a wonderful lunch for you. It's so nice out. We can sit on the porch overlooking the bay," Grandma said.

"Sure. Let's go."

I took my grandmother's hand and my grandfather's arm, and we walked out of the building to their car. I assisted my grandmother into her seat, and I took a seat in the back.

We took NY-25A headed east to Greenport. It would take a little over an hour to get home. We could take the Long Island Expressway, or L.I.E., but we were in no hurry.

Greenport is a small town—a village—in the north fork of eastern Long Island, New York and is part of Southold Township. The main commercial activities there are agriculture, fishing, and tourism. My parents had a four-bedroom beach house on the bay. My mother, Elizabeth, was a designer in New York City, and she'd decorated the home in a modern style but with a British West Indies flare. I'd seen pictures of the remodel, and it looked nice. My father, William MacKenzie, Jr., was a securities broker. He ran the brokerage house that my grandfather started with a few other guys almost twenty years ago. My parents were killed in a motor vehicle accident last year. It was a hit-and-run crash. No one was arrested. I wasn't past losing them.

I looked out the window as we drove along, not speaking. My grandmother was hurting with the anniversary of my parents' deaths just a few days ago. She needed this visit to the beach house with Lauren and me more than I did. My whole family suffered the deaths of my parents. Grandma loved my father, her son, with all her heart, and, if it was possible, she loved my mother even more. My parents were childhood sweethearts and inseparable. While my grandfather ran around the world to war, Grandma settled the family on Long Island. Grandpa is from upstate New York, and Grandma is from the city. Grandpa graduated from West Point, having dated my grandmother while he attended the Military Academy. They married after he graduated in 1961.

My father was born in 1962. Grandpa went off to war and to wherever else the Army sent him, but they hung onto the Oceanside house they'd purchased in 1961. The whole family returned to live there periodically. My father, aunt, and uncle all graduated from Oceanside High School. So did I. My father didn't physically qualify for the military, so he went to NYU, took a securities job for a while, and then got his law degree from Fordham Law. He went back into securities. After twelve years in the business, he joined my grandfather's new firm.

My mother graduated from Oceanside High School, a year behind my father. My parents married early, and I was born while Mom was in college. Mom started an interior design firm and did very well. My Aunt Lorraine, Mom's older sister, graduated from Oceanside High School and now lives in the city. My maternal grandparents live in Miami.

My uncle Matt is three years younger than my dad. He also went to NYU, but he got a job brokering stocks and stayed there for several years, eventually joining my father and grandfather at the firm. Matt is married but has no children. Matt currently runs the family brokerage firm. His wife, Betsy, is a nurse at a hospital in Nassau County. She, too, was a great help in my recovery.

My aunt Missy attended Hofstra University and received a liberal arts degree. Missy is six years younger than my dad. She got her real estate broker's license, started a real estate company, and is very successful selling real estate in New York City. Missy is in her late forties, but she looks like her Glamour Shot photo. She has no children and has had very few husbands, just two thus far. Missy periodically appears on the society pages of the New York Times in the arms of older, affluent gentlemen, but she doesn't seem to want to marry again.

I looked out the window.

"How has Lauren been?"

My grandmother turned in her seat to answer me. Lauren has lived with my grandparents since my parents' deaths. Lauren is my fifteen-year-old little sister. Lauren was my parents' surprise baby. I was at Cornell when she was born. My mother had her tubes tied, but apparently not very tightly tied. Lauren, to me, has been something of a different little sister. At first, while I was at college, a sort of play toy or a pet when I was on break from school. By her second and third years, she'd developed a terrific personality, and she was a lot of fun and made me laugh. I'd take her out on my surfboard at the break in Long Beach or out on the boat. She was a baby magnet when she was with me. Then I went off to war. However, each time I returned, I made a special effort to see her, and over my time in the Navy, I got to see her several times each year. I never missed her birthday or holidays, and I'd send her gifts and pictures from faraway places, and I'd call her wherever I was for each holiday. Now, I'd be responsible for raising, protecting, and teaching her into adulthood. I was scared shitless!

"I think she's doing very well, Mark. You coming home and getting better has helped her. She's had nightmares, but she's convinced that her big brother, her hero, can protect her, and she'll make it. Mark, you both need each other. You know she kept every letter and card you sent her. She worried about you as much or more than your mom and Cathy."

"Thanks, Grandma. I haven't thought of Cathy in a week."

"Oh, don't be so whiny. I never thought that would last, anyway."

Only the wife of a general could call a SEAL "whiny."

Cathy, my lovely wife, decided to fool around with other men while I was at war. First in Virginia Beach, where we had a home, then back here in Long Island. She got caught, apparently, by everyone except me. I found out on social media, if you can believe that. She came to see me in the hospital; she brought the divorce papers with her. She signed away all her rights, took some of our money, our vehicle, and our furniture, and disappeared to Hawaii or California with her African-American boyfriend. I think she sells undercoating for new cars at a Kia dealer. As liberal as Long Island can be, that set of circumstances didn't play well. She was sort of run out of town when she appeared in Oceanside with her paramour. Cathy and I dated on and off through high school. She was a year behind me. We married after I returned from Iraq. She didn't have the backbone, honor, and compassion to stick it out. The separations were difficult, but she is a weak, immature, and immoral person. I was trying to forget her but could no sooner forget Cathy than I could forget Lauren. I'd known Cathy longer than I've known Lauren.

My grandfather just smirked.

"So, what will you do when you don't have Grandma around to pick on you?"

"I thought I'd do nothing. I've read every book, prospectus, sales document, and annual report for every company Matt is carrying securities for and several others. You know I passed all the series exams?"

"Yes. Matt told us. Missy said you passed the real estate licensing exams. Are you going to do that, too?" Grandpa asked.

"I doubt it. Missy wants me to join her, but I don't know. Missy is okay, but that other one, Sabrina... If you tossed a bucket of water on her, there'd be nothing left but a pointy, black hat."

My grandfather laughed.

"Oh, she's not that bad," my grandmother quipped.

My grandfather rolled his eyes.

"I miss my parents a lot. They loved you two very much," I said.

My grandmother nodded her head in agreement. Tears formed in her eyes and rolled down her cheeks as she turned away from me and looked out the window. I put my hand on her shoulder. We didn't speak for the rest of the ride home.

#

We pulled into the long driveway and drove toward the house. My grandfather's restored 1989 Jeep Grand Wagoneer in bright red was parked there. My grandparents have a house on Long Island Sound in Rye, New York, which is upstate near the Connecticut border. They get a little more snow there, so Grandpa has had the Jeep since it was new.

Our house sits on about a square acre of land, not counting the beach and long driveway. The original property consisted of some twenty-six acres and was subdivided into twenty-four one-acre lots, give or take, plus the beach and right-of-way between the beachfront and street-front houses. The twelve lots along the shore are accessed by long driveways, and the twelve lots along the road access the beach by long paths. Imagine water dippers placed alongside each other, alternating driveways and beach access paths. All the homeowners had beach access and piers if they built them. The more desirable lots were along the water. My sister and I owned the house, and five more lots, four of which were on the water; the other lot was in front of our house along the road. We sold one other lot that had an old beach cottage on it, which also accounted for more land since it was peninsula-shaped and jutted out into the bay. The new owners promptly died, and nothing had happened to the property but languish in probate. The original 26-acre parcel was bought by my great-great grandfather in the 1920s.

We have a separate three-car garage and a two-car carport next to the house. We stopped under the carport. I opened my door and grabbed my bag. I got to my grandmother's door and helped her out of the car. We started toward the stairs as Lauren came bounding down, launching herself at me. I dropped my bag and caught her.

"Be careful, Hun, you might hurt him," my grandmother said.

"I can't hurt Mark. Right, Mark?" Lauren said.

"Right. How are you, Squirt?"

"I'm good. I'm also too old for that nickname."

"I guess you are. You look like a young lady. You look like Mom, and you're even more beautiful," I said as I hugged her.

"Come on. I made your favorite things. C'mon, Mark!" Lauren excitedly said as she took my hand and led me up the stairs into the house.

The house is a shingled-style beach cottage. It's three stories, the first floor being the storage, unfinished room, den or extra bedroom and an entire bath floor. The home is up on stilts, so to speak, pilings or piers are the correct terms to describe the stilts. The second floor is the main floor where the kitchen, living room, dining room, den, half-bath and four porch decks are located. The third floor is comprised of a master bedroom suite and two more ensuite bedrooms, one with hallway access to the bathroom and a laundry room. The property was once part of a bay-front farm and estate. Currently, most of the farming to the west is comprised of vineyards, hops, flower, and berry farms.

"Mark. You've not been here since mom redecorated?" Lauren said.

"No. Very nice. Very modern. I like it. It has an island feel to it. Wow. That looks like an outdoor living room. The pictures I've seen didn't do it justice."

"Look!" Lauren pushed three, eight-foot-tall sliders into a hide-away space joining the living room with the outdoor living room.

"Very nice. I just noticed how mom painted all the trim dark. That's so different but so nice. I love the mahogany shutters and mahogany kitchen cabinets. Don't lie now, Lauren . . . you helped, didn't you?"

"Every step of the way. Mom and I shopped together for every piece of furniture, too."

"Well, I'd say you've done a terrific job, sis. I'm very proud of you."

"It's what I want to do when I'm older. You know we haven't sold Mom's loft?"

"I know. I guess we need to work on getting you into the NYU School of Design so you can use that loft."

"Oh, Mark, can we?"

"I think so. We'll figure out something. Who knows, I might want to work full-time again. We can both use the loft apartment."

"Come on. Let's sit and eat. I made you unsweet iced tea with lemon. C'mon."

Lauren grabbed my hand and pulled me toward the kitchen. My grandmother was very happy watching Lauren lead me by the hand. We took a seat around a huge bar-height, silver-grey-white, quartzite-topped center island that Lauren had already set while she grilled some pastrami and Swiss cheese on marbled rye bread for us. Sauerkraut on the side, spicy mustard, dill pickles and Charles Chips. I ate two servings of everything, but I went easy on the sauerkraut and mustard I wasn't supposed to eat.

The rest of the day we just relaxed. For dinner, we had beef brisket, on toasted French bread, salad, and French fries, also prepared by Lauren.

#

I parked myself on the outdoor couch and I watched the boats go by, which made me think of our boat tied at the end of the pier. I'd check it out tomorrow.

My grandfather sat across from me and handed me an on-the-rocks glass with bourbon over ice. He tilted his glass to me.

"Welcome home, son."

"Thanks, Grandpa."

I sipped my drink that I should not be having. Grandma and Lauren joined us, Grandma sitting on my right side and Lauren to my left. Both brought blankets since it was a little chilly, as April nights can be. Lauren snuggled in close to me.

"You have a lot of decisions to make, Mark. Lauren knows all this, so it doesn't matter that we talk about it in her presence, but you're her legal guardian now."

"Does that mean I get lunch and dinner like this every day?"

"No, but I'll try some recipes on you. Grandma and Mom taught me well."

"I'll have to be careful I don't eat too much. First, I want to know about school. There's still two months left, right?"

"I'm already enrolled at Greenport High School. I met my teachers. They're all so nice. I can play softball, but everything else starts for me next year," Lauren said.

"You're in ninth grade?" I said.

"Yes. My grades are good enough where I could skip a grade like you did, but I don't want to. I did well in Oceanside and fabulous in Rye. This school here is smaller. I know some of the kids from summers here. I've known Kim for like nine years," Lauren said.

"Good. That's handled," I said.

"We've talked some about the estate and the insurance. The houses, condo, and loft are owned free and clear. You two were added to the deeds several years ago. Lauren, in trust and you outright. For the most part, your parent's accounts were jointly held and either one or both of you are joint owner with right of survivorship, so most properties avoided probate. There is some tax liability, but it's minimal. The boat is titled in your name, Mark. You'll have to get a car. Matt got your parents' second car since he needed one following an accident he had. It was a nice gift from the estate. Besides, you're too young to be riding around in a Mercedes-Benz S Class anyway.

They had a life insurance policy on your dad's life at work. Matt and Missy each got $1 million, the firm got $5 million, you each got $1 million, and your mother got $1 million, which passed to the two of you. Your parents each had a marital policy for $2 million, double indemnity. You each got $2 million from each parent for a total of $4 million to each of you as the only beneficiaries of that policy. The $5 million that went to the firm funds an annuity for the two of you.

You inherited all their investments, valuables, and their stock in the brokerage house. Your parents owned 37% of the firm's shares. Matt owns 25%. Grandma and I own 18%. The other 20% is owned by a few other shareholders. One of the guys works there. He's interesting, about your age, maybe a little older. NYU and Wharton Business School. He's sort of an ass, but you'll see. You've got a good head on your shoulders; you're intelligent and perceptive. You will take over the business as president. Matt will not oppose it," Grandpa said, looking at Grandma, who turned away.

"I don't have to worry about this now, though, right? I mean the business is doing okay?" I was not in a hurry to go to work. My grandfather, Matt and Missy had said there was no hurry for me to get to work. Yet it seemed there was always an urgency each time we spoke of the firm.

"Things could be better, but it's okay. Your father was a good leader. He'd have made a good military officer like you if it wasn't for his back. We'll talk. You two are okay. Take some time off. Go get a new car, decide what you want to do, go fishing, or something. Grandma said you're divorced now. I didn't know she'd sent you the divorce papers."

"Yeah. It's done. She leased the Virginia Beach condo to a friend of mine for now, but she signed a quit claim deed to me. She's gone," I said.

"Well, I'm sorry. You'll find another girl soon enough," Grandpa said.

"I'm in no hurry. I do have a question though?" I said and paused. They all looked at me. "Where are my weapons? If I'm her legal guardian, I'll have to screen any gentlemen callers, won't I?" I deadpanned.

"Don't you go scaring off any potential boyfriends. I'm a good girl, right, Grandpa?"

"I'll show you where the guns are later," Grandpa said, and he laughed.

CHAPTER 3

I awoke from my usual nightmare. I was lying in the snow, covered in blood, and I began to sink into the snow as several insurgents shot at me. I was supposed to write down my nightmares so I could act them out in therapy. I could act out this nightmare and receive an Oscar. I wouldn't be able to sleep again. I had all the issues with post-traumatic stress disorder: nightmares, insomnia, elevated blood pressure, hypervigilance, hearing things, and the assumption that danger lurked around every corner. My physical wounds had healed. I thought I was in good enough shape to go back on active duty, but once they have rearranged your guts and taken parts out, it was not allowed.

I am thirty-two years old, divorced, recently orphaned, and I didn't know what I wanted to do in life. I'm not whining; just recognizing the facts. After more than ten years of war or preparing for war, it was all I knew.

When I saw the attack on the World Trade Center, I knew what I had to do. I'd avoided going to West Point or Annapolis, having been under considerable pressure through high school to attend one of the academies. I could have gone to any one of them, having been accepted to both the Naval Academy and Military Academy. Still, I chose Cornell with an idea of either going to medical school or into a securities and stock brokerage career. I got into Cornell at a young age, having been accelerated one grade in grammar school. I did well.

I was a good student and athlete in high school and college, playing nearly every sport—excelling in all. My size and athleticism helped me. I'm almost six feet three inches tall, and I've regained my weight back to a solid 230 pounds, though I graduated high school at about 195 pounds. I was thinner, nearly half my current weight at one point during my recovery. I have blond hair, blue eyes and I get ruddy tan in the sun. In addition to team sports, I surfed year-round. Mainly at the breaks in Long Beach, but I'd go to Rockaway, Jones, Tobay, and Gilgo beaches to surf and compete in contests.

Following 9/11, I had a mission. I met with the Navy recruiter and a SEAL mentor. I trained to become a SEAL officer for the next eight months, attacking my studies, swimming miles and miles each week, working out, running for miles each day, and shooting. I purchased several pistols and rifles that were copies of military weapons, without the automatic feature, that my SEAL mentor told me about. I probably shot a ton of ammunition in that eight-month period prior to swearing into the navy.

I did well at *Knife and Fork* school or officer boot camp. I did very well at BUD/S. I didn't embarrass the officer corps and I was the top graduate in my class. I was at war a few months later.

I walked downstairs and started some coffee. I hardly recognized the house. Imagine all warm browns, taupes, tans, and natural mahogany with off-whites in several shades, along with beautiful dark wood floors covered with rugs and runners of matching colors. It was sort of New York City modern meets the Caribbean Islands. It seemed to me so absurd. Here I was at war all that time, and my mother and sister were redecorating the house.

I poured some coffee and walked outside onto the porch deck. The sky was becoming light in the east. It was perfectly still out. The bay was flat. I heard the gulls cawing and terns tweeting as they flew across the bay. I looked at the lights across the bay on Shelter Island. Fishing boats were leaving Deering Harbor and the harbor at Greenport just northeast of our home. Some boats were coming in after a night pulling trawl nets for whatever they caught this time of year. Some of the boats would continue to Riverhead at the west end of the bay, but many would offload their catch here in Greenport or further west at Southold or Mattituck.

It was late April and warm for this time of year. Around here they'd say it was due to climate change, which was correct—the climate always changed. I noticed the light at the end of our pier casting a halo of gold light over the water. In the past, I'd toss a cast net over the spot and bring in a lot of bait—spearing, we called them. Great for fishing for almost anything around here, especially for bluefish. I missed fishing.

I wondered how Lauren was doing. Our entire life together had been nothing but fun. At least until I was shipped back to the states via an air force medevac. I'd been severely wounded in my final engagement in Afghanistan. I'd taken some shrapnel and had been shot three times as two of us were overrun by a group of Taliban insurgents. Talbot and I were down to our pistols shooting the insurgents who were overrunning us. Fortunately, Surfer, Chief, Billy, and the Afghan team came to our aid and they, along with Kev, Mikey, and Shrek, our snipers, took out the Taliban. Surfer called in the QRF, and they got the remaining Taliban insurgents who squirted. This was all related to me weeks later, but I remember most of it like it was yesterday. That movie plays several times a week in my head.

What I recall was that at the time it was happening I was angry and fought as hard as I could Now, in my nightmares, I'm afraid.

I was stabilized at Bagram Air Base then flown to Germany. I was there for a few days then flown to Dover AFB and transported to Walter Reed National Military Medical Center. The doctors put me back together, and apart from missing a little bit of my small intestine, my appendix and some of my liver, I'm as good as new I'm supposed to stay on a strict diet for a year or so, and I must eat more frequently to get all the nutrients I need, but I'm good to go. No very spicy foods and no raw seafood or raw meat for at least a year. I could live with that.

I heard someone in the kitchen clink a cup or dish on the counter. A moment later my grandmother, Martha, a grandma name if ever there was one, came outside and sat with me. She wore a quilted white and blue robe over what appeared to be men's or boy's green and red Scotch plaid flannel pajamas. My grandmother was never one to follow all the rules or conventions. She said that she did just enough to help my grandfather make lieutenant general and no more. It's why he didn't make general because Grandma retired is the family joke. She is a terrific woman and I liked being around her.

"Good morning, Mark."

"Good morning, Grandma "

She sat next to me on the couch as she sipped her coffee. She looked out over the bay and sighed. "I always love the bay in the morning. I used to sit out here with your mom, and we'd watch the world wake up. It's changed so much here in the last forty years. More homes, but more wildlife, too. Deer ran by yesterday morning, and I regularly see foxes and raccoons—even a bobcat. Seals swim in the bay now, too. I'd say the wildlife has done well out here despite the increase in the number of houses."

"I think you're right. Will Lauren go to school today?" I sipped my coffee.

"That's up to you, isn't it? She wants to go, but she doesn't want to leave you alone."

"I'll tell her to go. I'm fine. I'll just hang around here and get used to the house again. I can't believe it's the same house."

"Your mother did a fine job on it. You should come to see our house. She redid it, too. She had new windows put in, the porch decks redone; it's all painted nice and has all new or refinished furniture. Your mother was quite talented. I miss her so much."

"I do, too. I thought I'd go by and put flowers on their grave this week."

"That would be nice."

"How does Lauren go to school here? It's not that far away."

"There's a bus stop two blocks over, but why don't you take her. You can drop her at the side door by the semi-circle drive-up. Go in from the west entrance so you don't go against the direction of the buses. You can drive out onto Moore's Lane and then back onto Front Street. The traffic is getting worse. The entire block across from the school was rezoned to allow retail stores and eateries. A bakery coffee shop is there, along with a sandwich shop, a luncheonette, a barber, a dress shop, and a florist. It's nice. They widened the street, and you park diagonally.

I still remember the day your mother called me and said she was pregnant with Lauren. She knew the baby would be a girl . . . she'd had a dream. We were all so overjoyed. Lauren has brought a lot of happiness to our lives. Help keep her happy, son."

"I will. She does make you smile. I expect she's popular with the boys?"

"Her phone never stops ringing. She's been on a few couple's dates, to the movies, the mall, school events and to the beach, things like that. She's a good girl. She'll choose to do right. Just remember to devote time to her every day and be very generous with compliments and encouragement. Recognize the smallest thing she does. And don't fix everything she talks about. Ladies just like to talk. It's how we bond. If we want a problem fixed, you'll know it."

I smiled at my grandmother. "I assume you'll be just a phone call away should I need your counsel?"

"Of course, but you'll do fine. You have a good heart like your mother. It's still healing, but you have a good heart. Let me get breakfast started. Your grandfather will be up soon. Go wake Lauren and tell her to go to school."

"Yes, ma'am."

We walked to the kitchen together. I refilled my coffee then walked upstairs to Lauren's room. I heard my grandfather showering. I knocked on Lauren's door and then opened it.

"Hey kiddo, time to get up for school."

Lauren awoke yawning then she smiled. "I thought I'd stay with you today since Grandma and Grandpa are leaving."

"No. I'm fine. You should be in school. Besides, I'm sure you're excited to be going, aren't you?"

"To be honest, I am. You don't mind?"

"No. Not at all. I'll drive you today and we'll talk about the rest of the year—bus, walk or drive. You don't get your learner's permit until next year?"

"That's right."

"Get ready. Grandma is making breakfast."

"Mark?"

I turned back to Lauren. "Yes."

"I love you. I'm glad you're home."

"Me, too, Lauren. Me, too."

#

I walked down the stairs to the kitchen. I took a seat at the counter. I was incorrect when I said I'd thought I'd just poke around a little and do nothing. I would food shop after I dropped Lauren off at school. I'd grill some London broil for dinner. I'd also arrange parent-teacher conferences to make sure Lauren was on track to get into NYU or wherever she wanted to go.

I was technically the parent of my little sister, and I had a steep learning curve to absorb. I'd sit down with Lauren tonight and learn about her likes and dislikes. She'd just turned fifteen in March, but she looked like she was of age. Lauren got the best of both of our parents. She got her height, at about five feet nine inches, from our father, but she got her beauty from our mother. Lauren has sandy blonde to light blonde hair, deep blue eyes, a sprinkling of freckles across her nose that were lightening some. She tanned in the sun, our part German heritage helping there. She is athletic looking and shapely. She reminded me of one of the cute women in the musical group *Celtic Woman*—the beautiful blonde who dances around playing the violin—just taller. She will be a heart breaker. I'd have to keep an eye on her.

"Here you go, Mark." Grandma placed a plate of scrambled eggs, bacon, toast, and jelly in front of me. I heard my grandfather coming down the steps. He appeared in the kitchen.

"Good morning, dear. Mark . . . How are you?"

"Morning, Grandpa. I'm good."

My grandmother kissed him. "Good morning, dear. Come sit. Breakfast is ready."

"Has your grandmother been giving you the how-to-take-care-of-a-girl lecture?"

"A little, I suppose. Why?"

"Because I got the same lecture about a year ago. I figured you'd get it, too. I thought it funny because I recall that I raised two sons and a daughter," Grandpa said.

"Revisionist history, Bill. You were off playing soldier most of that time," Grandma said rolling her eyes. My grandfather frowned.

"I'll be all right. Lauren is a good kid and you two are just a phone call away. Are you taking the Bridgeport ferry today?"

"Yes. Anything to avoid that mess in the city. You'll be okay without us, won't you?" Grandpa said.

"Sure. I'll get into a routine."

"Good morning," Lauren said as she walked to Grandma and kissed her, then to Grandpa and kissed him.

"Sit, dear. Breakfast is ready. Who knows what you'll get after I leave," Grandma joked.

"I was thinking left-over pizza for breakfast," I said.

"I love pizza for breakfast!" Lauren said.

Grandma didn't look very happy.

"We'll say good-bye now, sweetheart, since we'll be gone when you return from school. You'll be okay with Mark. We're coming back for Memorial Day weekend, right William?"

"Yes. I think so. If Mark has made it through his first month of being a parent."

I looked at my little sister. "We'll be just fine, right Lauren?"

"Yes. I'm ready," Lauren said.

I looked over and noticed that Lauren had finished her toast and eggs, but she ignored her bacon. I snatched it and shoved it into my mouth.

"I'll be back. Anything I need to know about that Jeep?"

"No. It runs like new," Grandpa said.

"Good-bye," I said.

"Good-bye, Grandma, Grandpa. I love you guys," Lauren said as she kissed and hugged them both then ran out the door with me in tow.

#

We got into the Jeep. I looked it over then stuck the key in the ignition and started it. We pulled out and drove to the school just a short ten blocks away.

"I'll speak with you more tonight, but I'll set an appointment to meet with your teachers over the next couple of weeks. I'll food shop later. Is there anything you need?"

"Yes. Five spiral-bound notebooks. The three-subject type. Oh, and Playtex super tampons."

"I think I can remember that. Anything else?"

"Grapes. White seedless grapes. And I need a pack of colored pencils, too. Oh, get paper towels. I put the last roll in the dispenser last night." Lauren smiled at me.

We pulled up to the school entrance and were directed into the driveway that led to Moore's Lane. I stopped at the drop-off point and Lauren leaned over and kissed me then got out. A teacher, perhaps a gym teacher, nodded at me as I rolled by. I wondered if he thought Lauren was my daughter?

I drove out of the school drive onto Moore's Lane then crossed Front Street to the new shopping area. I watched the activities of the kids, parents, and teachers. The school is primarily a three-story affair. I thought the enrollment was a little over three hundred students and covered grades seven through twelve. The district had over six hundred students. The school's colors were purple and yellow. Lauren would become a cheerleader next year. She played volleyball, basketball, softball and swam. I'd have to setup my schedule to be sure I could get her around to her activities. Fortunately, Greenport is a small village, though Southold township covers some distance.

I arrived home to find my grandfather loading his car.

"She run okay?" Grandpa said about his Jeep.

"Yes. I feel like I should be driving on a large estate."

"Ah. Well, you'll find something soon. Next time we come we'll have you pick us up at the ferry and we'll drive back in the Jeep. Listen, Mark. I didn't want to leave you with the impression that you need to jump into a job at the firm right away. Take time off. Just call your uncle and make a few visits to the firm to let them know you're around."

"Grandpa. What was going on with Dad? The last few times I saw him he was . . . distracted—worried even. I know he was worried about me, but by the third month I was solidly on the mend. It was as if the worry and distraction at that point would have been more appropriate three months earlier."

"I don't know. I felt it, too, but didn't ascribe anything more than your condition to the cause. I don't have a good answer. Maybe Matt knows?"

"There you are! I was afraid we'd leave without seeing you," Grandma said as she descended the stairs.

"Mark, your jewelry box, files, and memorabilia are in the downstairs bedroom. Your weapons from Virginia Beach are in the safe your mother had installed in the garage. I left your temporary access code on your bed. The safe was upgraded to a fingerprint and combination access like the safe in Oceanside. Once you log in you control who else accesses it. I'm the only one who currently has access," Grandpa said.

"I'll take a crack at the safe later. Pun intended."

"Good-bye, Mark. Call us if you need us. Call your Aunt Missy, too. She misses you. I think she'd like to have you at her firm because you're so good-looking. You'd attract all the rich old biddy widows from the upper-west side to list their homes with her," Grandma said.

"I don't see that happening. I'll call her and Matt. Maybe I'll go into the city next week."

"You only have one thing to do—take care of Lauren," Grandma said as she looked from me to my grandfather.

"Don't worry. I will. Bye now."

I kissed my grandmother, I hugged my grandfather, then helped my grandmother into the car. I watched them drive away.

It was just 8:00 a.m. I climbed the stairs and entered the house. I poured a cup of coffee and sat down to finish writing a shopping list. I'd have to go to Riverhead for the sports equipment and Cutchogue to food shop. Unless things had changed around here while I was away, King Kullen was it. I decided to do food shopping on the way back from Riverhead. I'd start at the school.

#

I walked into the high school and checked with the hall monitor. She pointed me to the office. A secretary greeted me.

"Good morning. Can I help you?"

"Good morning. Yes. I'm Lauren MacKenzie's guardian. She just started here today. I was wondering if I could make appointments to meet with her teachers to say hello?"

"Why certainly, sir. Let me pull up her schedule. I'll print a list of her teachers with their email and telephone contact. Can I see some identification first, please?"

"Of course." The secretary copied my license and handed it back to me.

"Here you go, Mr. MacKenzie. This is her schedule, her locker number, her gym locker number, and the list of her teachers. Email the teachers to arrange a conference. Here is our handbook that you might find helpful. There is more information on our website, too. Lauren is in ninth grade so there isn't much left for her to do this year."

"Thank you." I turned to accept the papers as she came around the counter. At that moment a very nice-looking woman entered the office.

"Good morning, Ms. Menduni."

"Good morning, Mrs. Harris. How are you?"

"I'm good. Ms. Menduni, let me introduce you to Mr. MacKenzie. He's . . ."

"Lauren's father?" Ms. Menduni said as she looked at me in surprise.

"No, ma'am. I'm her brother, her legal guardian." I smiled at Ms. Menduni. She seemed confused. Mrs. Harris jumped back in.

"Mr. Mackenzie intends to contact each of Lauren's teachers to set up conferences," she said helpfully.

"Oh. I'm sorry. I was caught off-guard because of your age. Certainly, I'm Lauren's English and Creative Writing teacher. It's very nice to meet you," she said as she offered her hand. I took her hand as we looked at each other, both of us hesitating a moment before continuing.

"It's a pleasure to meet you. I guess I'll just email you to set an appointment?"

"I'm on break. I was going to walk across the street for coffee. Do you have time now?"

She looked down at my left hand for a ring, no doubt.

"Sure. That would be fine. Thank you, Mrs. Harris. You've been very helpful."

"You're welcome, Mr. MacKenzie."

I followed Ms. Menduni out, and I opened the main entry door for her.

"So, you just moved here? I'm shooting blind. I briefly spoke with Lauren. I'm her homeroom teacher, too."

"Sort of. We've owned the house and the property around it for many years. It's been the family's summer home for a long time. I'm just moving back after serving in the navy."

"Where are your parents?"

"They passed away about a year ago."

We walked to a little coffee shop bakery. I opened the door for her. As she stepped over the threshold, I found myself drawn to her figure. I recovered before she noticed me looking. We ordered our coffees, my fourth of the day.

"I'm Haley."

"Mark."

"I gathered from what you said you're no longer in the navy?"

"Correct."

"Did you leave because your parents passed away?"

"No." I sipped my coffee. Ms. Menduni looked at me for further explanation.

"I always ask my students to expound on their answers. Do I need to ask you, too?" she poked.

"I'm sorry. I . . . I'm just not used to talking about it. I was wounded in Afghanistan. I was medically retired." She studied me as if searching for signs of a wound.

"What did you do in the navy?"

"I was a SEAL officer."

She made a funny face again as if verifying my statement by visually inspecting me.

"I read the story about you in *Newsday* last spring when that admiral pinned those medals to your pillow at the hospital. I'm sorry. I shouldn't be talking about that." She looked embarrassed.

"No. It's fine. I'm fine. It's . . . well, that's why I wanted to touch base with you all. We lost our parents right after that article came out. I just want to keep an eye on my sister. I was at Cornell when she was born so we have a bit of an age difference between us."

"I understand. Well, Lauren appears to be intelligent and outgoing, and her looks and athleticism will help her, I'm sure. I reviewed her grades for the past three years. She has shown no deficiencies. I don't think your parents' deaths affected her academically. I'll keep an eye on her. Look, Mr. MacKenzie . . ."

"Mark, please."

"Okay, Mark. If there is anything I can do, please call me."

"Thank you. I will. I've never raised a child. I'll have all of you on speed dial," I said.

Haley laughed. Haley is a beautiful woman. I liked talking with her. She has perfect teeth and soft, almost clear blue eyes. Her hair is blonde and may have had a little help from a bottle; I couldn't be sure. A ring was absent from her left hand. She wore a watch, a tennis bracelet, a gold Christian cross, and a gold heart on a chain around her neck. She noticed me looking at her.

"Nice cross and heart. I was trying to read the inscription," I covered.

"It says 'To Mommy, Love, Paulie.' It's from my son. He's seven."

"My turn to be surprised. You don't look old enough to have a seven-year-old."

"Thank you."

I looked again for a ring and got caught.

"No ring. I'm trying to get divorced. It's been over three years since I filed. We've been separated almost five years."

"I didn't mean to pry," I said, then wondered why I said it. She volunteered the information.

"So, you attended Cornell. You're okay in the smarts department, I take it?"

"I'm okay."

"What will you do now?"

"I'll eventually go to work for my family's securities firm. I'll take the summer off, take care of Lauren . . . or let her take care of me." I laughed at my joke, but so did Haley. She has a great smile. Her fingernails were nicely polished, and she was dressed very well. Haley smiled at me.

"I need to go back in a minute, but please call me. We can talk about Lauren or maybe get another coffee."

"Sure. I . . . well, sure. That sounds cool." *Cool? What a boob!* Haley smiled at me.

We finished our coffees.

What a fool—cool? Where did that come from? Cool? Jeez! Smooth operator. I walked Haley to the curb across the street.

"I'm parked over there." *More brilliant dialogue from a Cornell grad.*

"You are? I suppose you'll go there now?" Haley said, smiling and now picking on me.

"I guess. Look, Haley, I will call you. Have a nice day."

"You, too, Mark."

I watched Haley walk into the school. Probably giggling to herself. If Haley answered the phone when I called it would be a miracle. *Cool?* I got into the Jeep and drove to Riverhead.

#

I had the sports store guy load everything on a large cart and I shoved it out the door and into the Jeep. Nice sporting goods store near the Tanger Outlets. I drove to the food store and got everything on my list. I arrived home and put away the perishable food. I nearly ate the whole bag of white grapes while I put away the food. I'd need to get more grapes.

I went to work assembling the sports equipment. After two hours, I was finished. Now I needed to buy some weights. I looked at my watch. Almost time to get Lauren. I ran upstairs and washed up, put away the rest of the non-perishable groceries and carted off the cardboard boxes. I made a high protein shake since I'd not followed my diet today. I prepared the London broil and put it back in the refrigerator to dry marinate.

I arrived at Lauren's school, driving into the pick-up lane. Five minutes later Lauren came out with four other girls. Good. She was making friends. The girls said good-bye, like teenage girls say good-bye, and Lauren hurried to the Jeep smiling at me as she got in.

"Hi, Mark. Today was great. I'm so glad I went. I met a few new girls and we're gonna get together this weekend. Can we grill hot dogs? We'll do salad, too, and ..."

I smiled. I could do this. Lauren continued to tell me about her day and plans—commas, periods and semi-colons omitted; just one, long, run-on sentence. We pulled out of the school's lot onto Moore's Lane and drove home.

"So, softball practice tomorrow. I'll need new cleats. I have something to wear this week, but maybe this weekend, when we go shopping, I can get a new pair."

"Sure. I was just at the sporting goods store today."

"You were? Why?"

"Let me show you." I led Lauren to the workout area.

"We can work out here! Oh, thank you, Mark. I love it. I get creeped out working out at some gyms. When it was my friends and me, I couldn't concentrate when some guys came in."

"Is that why you wanted to live here instead of Oceanside? Guys bothering you?"

"Partly, yes. There was one guy. He was older, and he would follow us around the gym and outside. Some of the football players were asses, too. I wish we were closer in age because my girlfriend, whose brother was a senior, had no problems. With me getting taller and then these things sprouting overnight, I got too much attention."

"Well, your big brother is back, and I pack a hell of a lot more wallop than a football player." Lauren hugged me.

"C'mon. Let's go eat some grapes."

"Uh . . . oops, I think I'll need to get more. I already ate half."

"Fine. Tell me about your day," she asked as we walked to the kitchen. She opened the refrigerator fruit drawer. "Oh. You bought white and red grapes. So long as they're seedless, either one is fine."

"I met Ms. Menduni today."

"Isn't she nice? I think she's my favorite. We only have four teachers plus coaches."

"I know. I have your schedule and their contact information."

"I'm glad. Oh, London broil. Perfect."

"With a really cool salad and . . . By the way. Is it okay to say "cool" nowadays?"

"Yeah. Most young people say sick, which replaced cool."

"Oh, well, I'll stay with cool then." *Sick wouldn't make it. Grandma, that dress looks sick. Yeah, I'll stay with cool.* "I'll make some garlic-roasted mashed potatoes, too."

"I think I'm going to like having you home. I usually do my homework when I get home from school if I don't have sports. I assume you'll check it?"

"Yes. Hopefully, I'll understand it. You don't strike me as someone who has trouble with homework."

"Not usually. I know you're a genius at math, English and history and that you're good in most sciences, too. You learned Arabic, Pashto, Dari, Farsi and some other Iraqi dialects and Spanish. I take French so you'll be limited help there."

"Ah, but my command of the English language will allow me to help you understand written French."

"I don't have much problem with French. I cheated and bought the software."

"Dinner will be ready about 5:30 p.m."

"Perfect. Did you get the notebooks?"

"On your bed with your girlie supplies. We can call your grandmother later and you can give her a good report on me." Lauren smiled at me and ran off to her room.

Favorite teacher. Mine, too, but anyway.

I set about preparing dinner. While dinner cooked, I glanced at a few automobile brochures I'd picked up over the past month. I wasn't sure—car, truck or SUV. I liked the GMC Yukon Denali XL, but I also liked the new Dodge Challenger Hellcat SRT-8.

"What are you doing?" Lauren said as she approached me with a bottle of water in her hand.

"Trying to decide on a new vehicle."

Lauren looked at the Challenger and Yukon brochures. "They're both nice, but for different things. One can haul people comfortably, and the other is a very cool hotrod. If I were you, considering what you like to do, I'd get both."

"Is that your vote?"

"Yes. In black. After all, this is New York, capitol of wearing black year-round."

"I may just do that."

#

"So, how did you like Ms. Menduni?" Lauren said as we sat down to eat.

"Very nice." I forked a bite of London broil into my mouth.

"That was a short answer. You had coffee with her."

"How do you know that?"

"I have my ways. I spoke to Kim. Her friend, Janet's mom works at the coffee shop bakery. She knows Ms. Menduni and said she had coffee with a good-looking guy who was new to the neighborhood. She described you."

"I'll have to make sure I don't run any stop signs in town."

"She's nice. Do you like her?"

"We had a cup of coffee. She bought her own. I met her in the office and Mrs. Harris introduced us. She was going on break, so we knocked out our meeting. That was it."

Lauren scanned my face then smiled. "There's more to it. You're going to ask her out, aren't you?"

"What are you trained in interrogation by the CIA? She sort-of made it clear that I should ask her out for coffee, and I sort of made it clear that . . ." I took a bite of my London broil.

"Well?" she shouted.

"That I would. There. You got it out of me. We don't need CIA in Afghanistan, just a bunch of fifteen-year-old girls to do the interrogations."

Lauren smiled at me. "Good. I think she's nice."

CHAPTER 4

I awoke from a bad dream. I was sliding down a mountain in snow, mud, and ice while Taliban insurgents shot at me. I finally got past the shooting when I suddenly slipped off the mountain and was falling into space. This was a new twist on an old theme—sliding down the mountain. I wrote it down in my notebook. I was up now. I went to the bathroom. I showered the night before, so I looked in the mirror and decided a two-day growth of beard was fine. I got dressed and went down to the kitchen to make breakfast for Lauren. I figured out I'd better ask what she likes for breakfast. Lauren didn't eat the bacon yesterday.

I started coffee. Then decided oatmeal with blueberries and strawberries. I could make it after she awoke. I poured a coffee and clicked on my tablet to locate the nearest GMC dealer. There was a Buick-GMC dealer in Riverhead who had several Denali's—three in black. I'd be there at 9 a.m.

I refilled my coffee and walked outside. No wind. It was perfectly still. Growing up I liked to sit on the beach and look up at the stars. I'd sit for hours studying them. Finding the constellations and navigational stars. My favorite time was early morning. I was good at identifying stars. I had not been out to check the boat yet. I walked to the end of the pier where the light pointed at the water. Bait fish, no doubt spearing, splashed about eating whatever they ate. Every now and then a bigger fish ate the spearing, which pretty much summed up life—eat or be eaten.

I looked over the bay. It was usually cooler this time of year. The weather forecast was for 62 degrees. It would warm up some more today. Rain was forecast for tomorrow, which would likely be our last chilly rain before the May warm-up. The weather here on the North Fork was different than the rest of Long Island. It was almost Mediterranean-like, which probably accounted for all the vineyards. After living other places for years, I liked coming back to Long Island.

I needed to check out the Oceanside home and the city loft. I like the Oceanside home. It was a new American-style remodel that my parents had done while I was in high school, and they updated from there. It has five bedrooms and an extra-large room over the detached three-car garage, which was used as an attic. My parents bought the house from my paternal grandparents. Years later, they bought the crappy house next door and knocked it down. From there, the old garage went away, the current garage went up, and the house was torn apart, expanded and improved, all under my mother's supervision. When it was all finished, it looked like a brand-new house. During my last two years of high school I bounced from room to room as construction progressed. Now we have a very cool, very big house on two lots, 160 feet of waterfront dock overlooking the bay, a boat house at the end of a pier, a boat lift, and a heated, in-ground pool.

I checked the time. Another half hour before Lauren needed to get up. I'd call Uncle Matt today and see about going in next week. I'd call Aunt Missy, too, and have lunch with her while I was in the city.

I sipped my coffee and wondered about my future. I'm 32-years-old. I have a VA retirement, investments, and real estate.

In seven years, Lauren would finish college. I could do whatever I wanted to do then. I just had no clue what that was. I'd just have to figure a way where I didn't have to work every day while I took care of Lauren. Since Lauren and I owned the most stock in the firm and I held authority for Lauren's shares combined with either my uncle or grandparents, I held controlling power. I'd work how I wanted to work.

I was out of coffee. I walked back to the house and awakened Lauren. I prepared Lauren's breakfast and cut the tops off the strawberries while I looked out over the bay. The house is built on what amounts to a sand-covered rock and topsoil hill. At least the rocks were everywhere I ever had to dig for my father during my youth. The back part of the house was over sand and lawn, followed by fifty feet of bull weed, sea grass, and sea oats, then a sandy beach. The further out you went into the bay it changed from sand to mud and rock mixed with sand.

"Looks good, Mark. Thank you." Lauren popped a strawberry in her mouth.

"I didn't mix it up for you. Tell me what you like."

"Like this." Lauren took a spoonful of raisins, a spoonful of brown sugar and a knife-spread of butter and mixed it in her oatmeal.

I made myself a bowl, adding butter, fruit and a scoop of vanilla protein powder. Lauren watched me then she added a spoonful of protein powder to her oatmeal.

"You eat a lot of protein, don't you?"

"I must to heal and maintain. Once I start to lift heavy weights, I'll need to eat more. For now, I eat enough to feed and repair my body."

"How tall are you?"

"Six feet two and three quarters."

"That's what Dad was, right?"

"Dad was six feet two, Grandpa six foot. Matt is six feet one inch."

"I'm taller than Mom."

"You are by at least an inch or so. I expect that you are done growing. Girls grow faster than boys, but boys can grow until they're in their twenties. I was a sleek guy when one day I awoke and noticed that I was bulking up all over. I was stronger and faster. We're just built differently. We're built to fight, and you're built to have babies."

"What if I wanted to become a SEAL? What would you think about that?"

"I would not think it a good idea."

"That was short and to the point. Why not?"

"You're not equipped for it. There's no equal opportunity on the battlefield. War is not a social experiment."

"But what if . . ." Lauren began.

I put my hand up. "Lauren. You're my baby sister. I just spent more than ten years at war or training for war or recovering from the wounds of war. It's terrible and horrible. No man should see it and certainly no woman should have to see it. Our society is desensitized enough. Our women folk should not have to defend their homeland so long as there are men available." I ate my oatmeal. Lauren watched me.

"I'm sorry, Mark. I didn't mean to upset you."

"You didn't upset me, but you just demonstrated another reason why you were put on this earth. You women have more empathy and can sense when things are wrong in a family better than men. I just feel we have our roles. Come on, let's finish up so we can get you to school. And don't stop asking questions of me just because they're close to home. I was a liberal once and challenged convention. What's that saying? "If you're twenty and not a liberal, you don't have a heart . . . if you're thirty and not a conservative, you don't have a brain." I think that is a fair statement. I quit being a liberal when I watched the towers come down on our friends and neighbors and realized that our government failed us. Now the same government that failed then is failing again in the other direction. The wars should be over. C'mon, we should go."

Lauren nodded and smiled at me. "Thanks for treating me like an adult, and don't worry, you and Grandpa represented our family well in the armed forces. They won't get me."

She sure did make me smile.

#

I dropped Lauren at school. Fine. I pulled over to watch the children being dropped off by their parents, the children running into the school. This was normal. This is what it was about. This is why I went to war.

I drove home, cleaned up the kitchen and started the wash. That all started, I poured a cup of coffee and got into the Jeep and drove for the GMC dealer.

#

I drove directly to a black Yukon Denali XL. I was not inconspicuous in a reconditioned, red, and wood-paneled 1989 Jeep Grand Wagoneer. A salesman approached me.

"Nice SUV," he said.

"That's why I'm here. I'd like to test drive it."

"I meant your Jeep. Will you be trading it in?"

"Only if I had a death wish. No. I'd like to test-drive this one. I'll be paying cash."

"Let's go, sir."

An hour later I was driving away in the Yukon Denali XL. I drove toward Oceanside. I needed to check my wardrobe and collect a few things to bring out to the Greenport house. I pulled up to the house in front of the middle door of the garage. It looked nice. I assumed we had a gardener. I opened the middle garage door and walked inside. I saw Lauren's mountain bike. I removed the front wheel to fit it in the SUV. I looked at my gun safe but decided to get my things from the house first.

I went inside and got my suit bags from the closet. I grabbed all my suits; I only had eight suits that fit me. I put them in the SUV. I gathered up several dress shirts, a handful of ties, a box-full of dress socks, belts, several pairs of shoes and placed all into the SUV.

I walked through the house. Everything looked fine until I entered my parents' bedroom. The file draws to the desk were open as if someone ransacked through them. The nightstand drawers were in the same condition. A small flip-down secretary was open, and its drawers were open. The walk-in closet shelves were in disarray. I wondered whether Matt or Missy left it like this looking for my parents' wills?

I walked past my sister's room on my way to the study. I saw her nightstand drawers open and rifled through. Her closet had been gone through. My sister would not have had my parents' wills or any documents. Why would someone go through her drawers?

I saw pictures around Lauren's room that made me happy and sad. A picture of Lauren as a little girl with our parents on the beach. Another of Lauren on my shoulders, which had to be taken during my last year of college. Then I noticed her collage of pictures of all of us. I collected them all up and put them in the SUV. I walked to the study and found it had been gone through. I took pictures of each room with my smart phone. End of life documents would not be in a little girl's room. Something was very wrong here.

I walked to the garage and opened my gun safe. Inside were my shotguns, several rifles, and pistols. My mother's and my father's jewelry boxes were also in it. Another box caught my eye, sitting on the bottom shelf. It was a thick, polished aluminum equipment case like the Pelican boxes we used in the teams to protect our equipment. I withdrew it from the safe. It was heavy. I opened it. Inside were packets of one-hundred-dollar bills—$10,000 per packet. I counted $2 million, which accounted for the 44 pounds of weight. I closed the case and put it back. I entered the code for auditing who had been in the safe. It showed just two other codes. My grandfather's code and my father's code. My father was in the safe last, having accessed the safe five times during the last four weeks of his life. I mentally inventoried what was in the safe. A pistol was missing.

I pulled open the flat drawer in the safe. Inside were several manila-colored, clasp-envelopes that were large enough to hold several letter-sized documents. I opened one. Inside were bearer bonds. The envelope held ten, each with a face value of $100,000. I counted 18 envelopes, glancing inside each. The total value of the cash and bonds was $20 million!

I put everything back into the safe. I removed a SIG Sauer P226 pistol, inserted a magazine, put two more magazines and the weapon in a pancake holster, and put it on my waist at the small of my back. I locked up the safe. I had a feeling, and it wasn't a good one. I set the house alarm and the one for the garage. I programmed my HomeLink in the SUV to open the middle garage door.

I got into the SUV and drove to the highway. Why was $20 million in my safe? I checked my six o'clock. I was just being paranoid. I took Merrick Road to the Meadowbrook State Parkway and drove south to the beach. I continued down Ocean Parkway to Robert Moses Causeway. There would be almost no traffic and I could spot a tail. I sped down the highway and got on the Robert Moses Causeway. It was nearing 1:30 p.m. I called Matt.

"Hello?"

"Uncle Matt."

"Mark. How are you? Getting settled in out there?"

"I suppose. I'm learning about taking care of my sister."

"Oh, she's a sweetheart. She's easy. When are you coming to work?"

"You don't beat around the bush, do you?"

"I could really use you. I know you need to figure things out, and Lauren is the priority, but we could use you. Frankly, I need an ally."

"I'll be in next week to say hello. Tell me who I'm supposed to scare."

"I have that picture of you and your guys on a mountain in your combat gear on my desk. It gets lots of questions."

"Good. Matt, I wanted to ask you, was my father acting weird in the weeks before he died?"

"Well . . . now that you say it, I guess he was. Elizabeth said something to Betsy, too. I didn't think anything of it. I thought maybe they had a spat, but he was abrupt with us, and he wasn't paying attention when I spoke with him. It was like his mind was elsewhere."

I resisted asking more.

"Well, I'm thinking Monday I'll come in. I want to have lunch with Aunt Missy."

"Good luck. The market's picking up. She's busier than a one-armed wallpaper hanger, but call her. You always were her favorite nephew."

"I'm her only nephew."

"So, I'm right then. Hey, call me. I gotta take a call. I need you, Mark. Bye."

"Bye, Matt."

I got on the L.I.E. I wondered about the money. Where did my father get $2 million in cash and $18 million in bonds? And why was it in my safe? This added a whole new dimension to my parents' deaths. I picked up my phone and pressed a number on my speed dial.

"Sergeant Pluhowsky."

"Good afternoon, sergeant. I'm calling for Sergeant Cicola."

"Yeah, sure. I'll transfer you."

After some clicking and a pause, I heard, "Sergeant Cicola."

"Good afternoon, sergeant. Mark MacKenzie. We spoke following my parents' deaths in a MVA on the L.I.E. about a year ago? I don't have the case number . . ."

"I remember you. Securities broker and his wife. BMW seven series. Hit and run. What can I do for you?"

"I was wondering if you had learned anything else on the case?"

"Actually, we have. I'd rather not discuss it on the phone. Can we meet?"

"Sure. When? Where?"

"How about tomorra at 1 p.m. at Jay's Luncheonette across from the courthouse in Westbury, on Old Country Road. I gotta couple of cases dare tomorra."

"Okay. At 1 p.m."

"Your first name is Steve, right?"

"Yeahr. Okay, Mark. I'll have the file. We'll talk den."

"Okay. Bye Steve."

"Bye."

I punched another number.

"Hello."

"Joe."

"Mark. What's doing?"

"I'm getting around. You on duty?"

"No. I go on tonight. What's up? You sound like you want to talk."

"Not on a cell. I'm on the L.I.E. just past MacArthur Airport. Can you meet me later or tomorrow?"

"I'm in Patchogue now. I was just looking at a fixer upper I was thinking of buying. Get off on Medford Avenue and drive about two miles south. On the left is the Metropolis Diner. Across from the car wash. I'll meet you there in 15 minutes."

"Thanks, Joe. See you in 15 minutes."

I looked at the GPS screen. I was seven minutes away. Now, what could I ask him? What could I tell him?

I got off the L.I.E. and drove south on Medford Avenue. I saw Metropolis Diner. I pulled in and parked.

"Lunch for one?" The hostess asked.

"Two. Coffee, maybe some pie."

"This way, sir."

She sat me at a table and gave me a menu. A few minutes later I watched Joe pull up in his Expedition and park next to my SUV.

Joe is a Suffolk County cop. He's a detective sergeant who works financial crimes involving fraud, racketeering and organized crime. He was recently with the Joint Organized Crime Task Force in the city with NYPD and FBI but was promoted off the team when he was selected for sergeant. Joe is my height. Like most Long Island men, he'd played every sport growing up and in college, then quit, got a wife, a dog, and a beer gut. He just lost 120 pounds via divorce he likes to say, but he did trim down his gut. He needed to trim some more. We grew up together in Oceanside, but, like most of my friends, he couldn't afford to live there so he got a job as a Suffolk County cop and moved *out on the island.* We've known each other since before kindergarten. Joe entered the diner, saw me, and just pointed to let the hostess know where he was sitting. I stood up.

"Hey, Joe."

"Hey, Mark." We shook hands, did the guy-hug thing, and we sat.

"You order yet?"

"No. I'm getting coffee and apple pie."

"I'll get the chocolate cream pie with coffee. You look great. Better than me, and I ain't been shot."

"I'm okay. I worked hard. I have to eat more."

"Shit. I gotta eat less. I eat like shit since Myra left. What's doin?"

"I can't go into too much detail, mainly because I don't know much yet, but it's about my parents' deaths. You know they ruled it hit and run. That and the tire marks and skid marks led Nassau PD to rule it hit and run. Sergeant Cicola and his special team even said it was almost a purposeful flip, like police might do to stop a fleeing driver. I'm meeting with Cicola tomorrow. He says he has some info he'd like to share with me."

"He say what?"

"He did not. He didn't want to talk on the phone. I'll see him tomorrow at 1 p.m. Let's say something has come up that causes me to question my father's . . . well, his last days before he died. He wasn't himself. He was nervous, distracted, jittery. Uncle Matt and Grandpa both agree with my assessment. Remember I was still mostly bed-ridden but improving. That's not all. I went to the house today. You knew I was living in Greenport, right?"

"Yeah. You said you'd go there. Lauren wanted to live there, too."

"Right. Well, I went back to the house and picked up some stuff. Oh. That's me there in the Yukon."

"Wow. Nice SUV. Navy SEALs pay well."

"I went into my gun safe just to check it out. One pistol is missing. However, I found other things. My parents' jewelry boxes were in there. I also found bearer bonds and cash. When I walked around the house after loading my suits and ties, I walked into my parents' room. The drawers to their nightstands and dressers were open or closed, with papers still sticking out like someone had rifled through them in a hurry. Here."

I showed Joe the pictures on my phone.

"First, I figured Matt or Missy had been looking for my parents' wills or other documents. Then I found the same thing in Lauren's room that you see there. My gun safe has a fingerprint and numeric code system with an audit feature. Only my father, grandfather, and I have access. My grandfather was in it a month before my parents died, but my father was in it five times in the four weeks before he died."

"Well, you didn't tell me the amount . . ."

"Twenty million total. Two million cash and the rest in bonds." The waitress poured our coffees, and we ordered our pie. Joe shook his head.

"Where'd your father get that?"

"I don't know. They were worth several million between investments, real estate, and the business. I suppose he could have saved it, but he wouldn't have that much cash sitting around not working for him. The totality of the circumstances gives me pause. I have all my father's financial records. His accounts are all joint with my mother and Lauren or me. Most of their estates passed outside probate. All the investments, stocks, mutual funds and even his firm's stock were jointly owned with right of survivorship with Lauren and me. Joe, I just have a gut feeling about this. Dad knew something might happen and he put the valuables away to protect them."

"Well, he . . . you said five times he was in the safe, and you found two jewelry boxes, bonds and cash. That's four things and the missing pistol. Five reasons to be in the safe. He could have put them there all at once. What was the money in?"

"A water-tight, insulated aluminum equipment case. Like a weapons case."

"And the bonds?"

"Eighteen flat, manila envelopes containing ten certificates each."

Our pie came. Joe contemplated what I said.

"What did the bonds say?"

"I didn't read them all. I recall an electric co-op or something similar."

"That will help us identify them. Even if we can't ID the purchaser, we can ID the corporation and issuance dates and trace money transfers from the purchasers."

"Can you pull the banking information for the firm?"

"I'm supposed to have a reason."

"The incoming president has concerns about the possibility of illegal conduct by some of the firm's employees?"

"That'll work. Give me a few days. That stuff okay where it's at?"

"Yeah. That safe is hardened steel, locked, bolted down and alarmed."

Joe finished his pie then looked at his watch. "Shit! Call me tomorrow after you see Nassau. I gotta run."

"I got this. Yeah. I gotta get Lauren from school. Thanks, Joe. I'll call you tomorrow."

We stood. I put a twenty on the check-plate, and we walked out of the diner together.

"That's a nice SUV. How's Lauren doing?"

"Good. I think she likes having me around."

"Good. Call me, Mark."

"I will. Thanks, Joe. Bye."

#

I drove to Greenport. I forgot my SIG was still in my waist band. I'd applied for a concealed carry permit, but New York is a liberal, less constitutional state than most other states and it requires a reason for someone to carry a concealed weapon and *just because* isn't one of them. I had an attorney write up that my background as a SEAL killing lots of terrorists made my family and me a target. I'd hopefully know in a few weeks. Meantime I put the weapon in the center console.

I parked across the street from the school at the coffee shop-bakery and I walked toward the doors Lauren would exit. Cars were already lining up and the buses were lined up in the semi-circle drive. The bell sounded when it dawned on me. *Duh! Softball practice.*

I walked around to the field. I stood by the outfield fence and watched. There she was. Like when I played baseball, Lauren played third base, too. She has an arm for a girl. My father was a baseball nut. Between Dad and me, Lauren got a good dose of baseball. Practice would take more than an hour. I could either run home or I could get another cup of coffee and read the paper and wonder about the money and bonds.

I walked to the coffee shop. It was a beautiful day, the temperature unseasonably warm. The buses were gone. I entered the coffee shop and ordered a coffee. The lady who took my order smiled at me. I wondered if she was the tattletale? I paid for my coffee and took a seat at a table. I was 20 minutes into the newspaper when the woman topped-off my coffee.

"Thank you."

"You're welcome. Ms. Menduni just walked out."

"Oh. That's okay. I'm not waiting for her, but thanks." My tattletale, for sure. Haley was walking toward the coffee shop. I picked up my coffee and walked outside. Haley was about to get into a late model Acura sedan when she saw me.

"Hi, there." Haley closed her door and walked toward me.

"Hi," I said. *Man of masterful salutations.*

"What are you doing hanging around after school?"

"I forgot Lauren has softball practice. Would you like to join me?"

"Uh . . . okay. Sure."

"I have to warn you that we're being reported on."

"Oh? What do you mean?"

"I think the lady at the counter has a girl in school who knows Lauren or Lauren's friend Kimberly. They got the intel on us having coffee yesterday."

"Oh, did they?"

I held the door for Haley. She ordered a mocha something or other and I paid for it.

"It's nice out. Can we sit outside?" Haley said.

"Sure. It'll make it easier for the spies to report our whereabouts."

Haley smiled as we walked outside. I again found my eyes dropping to a very nice . . . well, anyway. We took a table with a view of the exit doors Lauren would depart from.

"What did you do today besides come to pick up Lauren too early?"

"I bought a new vehicle."

"What did you get?" Haley looked around, her eyes settling on my SUV.

"That's it right there."

"Wow. It's big. Nice looking. Are you going to tow a house with it?"

"Just a boat. Saturday, I'll take Lauren and several of her friends to the outlet mall."

"I bet it has a large carbon footprint?" I looked at Haley, who burst into laughter. "I think I got you."

"Actually, I think it spits coal out the tailpipe," I came back.

"It's very nice. Lots of SUVs around."

"Where is your son?"

"His father got him, or I should say his paternal grandmother has him. He'll be brought back later tonight or whenever his father feels like it," Haley said, resentment in her tone.

"Don't you have a schedule or court order?"

Haley laughed. "Yes, but he never follows it. He expects to take him when he wants to and drop him off with me any time he wishes. It's frustrating. I'm sorry. I shouldn't have reacted so harshly. It just gets old."

I wanted to say something smart to fix it, but I detected that wasn't what she wanted to hear. "I had a friend whose ex did the same thing to him. It's all about control, I think."

"It is, and the children suffer."

We sipped our coffee as Haley looked over my shoulder down the street.

"Speak of the devil," Haley said.

I turned to see a black Lincoln Navigator slowing as it turned into a parking spot four down from Haley's car. The back door opened, and a little boy got out. He looked upset. He had his backpack with him. From the other back door emerged a guy about my age. Italian descent. He wore a dark suit with a white shirt open at the collar. He exuded attitude. The boy came running to Haley.

"Mom. He brought me back . . . Grandma said you were still here . . ." the boy said, pausing as he noticed me.

His father, I presumed, came over. His attitude followed him.

"What are you teaching my boy? He's disrespectful, and he don't listen," he said.

"You don't listen, and you break the law, so why would he listen?" Haley shot back.

"Don't you fucking come at me with that shit . . ." he trailed off suddenly, having become aware of me sitting there.

"Listen, c'mere," he said as he reached out and yanked Haley off her chair.

"Let go of me, you're hurting my arm."

"Let her go, Dad," the boy said.

"Let me go, you're . . ."

"Excuse me, friend. The lady said to let go of her arm. You're setting a poor example for your boy," I said as I stood up and stepped toward the man.

He looked at me, incredulous that I'd said something, looked me over and apparently didn't like what he saw.

"Who, the fuck, are you?" He asked.

"It doesn't matter, but I won't ask again." He was about four inches shorter than me and a pig as far as his physical fitness.

"Look, maybe you don't know who I am, but . . ."

I cut him off by putting up my hand. "You're her soon-to-be ex-husband, but I don't care. If you don't release her, you'll be picking yourself up off the sidewalk."

"Mark. It's okay," Haley said.

I took a step closer at which point two guys got out of the front seats of the Lincoln Navigator. Haley's husband still had her by the wrist, but his grip had relaxed, and she yanked her arm away from him and stepped back with her son toward me.

The larger of the two men walked toward me. He was perhaps an inch or two taller than me, and he had me by at least sixty pounds, but they were soft pasta-pounds.

"Is there a problem, Mr. Menduni?" The big guy asked as he eye-balled me.

"Yeah. I was talking to my wife and that guy butted in," Menduni complained.

The big guy looked at me. "It's time for you to go, mister," he said as he walked toward me and reached with his right hand for my left shoulder, I assumed, to turn me around.

"Don't!" I said.

He hesitated then stepped into me and touched my shoulder. I deflected his right arm with my left and gently hit him with a right just below his Adam's apple, so I didn't seriously hurt him, as I swept his feet out from under him, and he fell on his back with a loud thud from his head and back striking the sidewalk. He lay there struggling to breathe. Haley's husband looked at me in disbelief.

"I don't like to be touched!" I said.

The driver, a guy about Menduni's size, started for me.

"Don't or you'll not be as lucky," I said.

He stopped then looked at Menduni for guidance. Menduni shook his head.

"No. Let's go. Pick up Monty. Listen to me, mister; I'm gonna walk away today, but don't let me catch you alone."

"You have a nice day," I said as they collected Monty from the sidewalk and departed.

I looked over and saw Lauren hesitantly walking toward us from across the road. I nodded to her to come over.

"Mark, that was amazing, but, well . . . it's too late. You don't know his family, do you?" Haley asked. Lauren walked to us.

"What happened, Mark?" Lauren asked.

"The gentleman was impolite to Ms. Menduni and the other one didn't follow directions well. To answer your question, Haley, I'll assume he doesn't have a regular job," I said.

Haley laughed. "No. He has a regular job. He owns a restaurant. It's his irregular stuff he and his family do that's a problem. You be careful. He doesn't like to lose."

"What are you two doing here?" Lauren asked.

I smiled at Lauren. "What's the matter? Your network fail to advise you yet?" I said.

#

It was almost 5:10 p.m. Haley was comforting her son.

"Where's the Jeep?" Lauren asked.

"At home. That's our ride." I pointed.

"Wow. You got it. C'mon. Let's go," Lauren said.

"You up for eating at the Soundview?" I offered.

"Sure. Why don't you invite . . ." Lauren said as she nodded toward Haley and her son?

"Okay. Uh, Haley. Would you and your boy like to join us for dinner at the Soundview?"

Haley thought for a moment. Her son was onboard with the idea. "Okay. Mark, I'm sorry about all that . . ." she said as I put up my hand.

"Don't worry. I've already forgotten about it," I said.

#

We drove to the Soundview Restaurant.

"This is very nice, Mark. I like it." Lauren said as she ran her hand over the leather.

"So, you and Ms. Menduni. She's nice and she's beautiful," Lauren said.

"Agreed."

I pulled into a parking spot at the restaurant. Haley pulled in next to me. We entered the restaurant together.

"Four for dinner?" The hostess asked.

"Yes. Along the windows, please," I said.

"Yes, sir."

The hostess led us to a table with a view of Long Island Sound and the beach. The sun was low in the western sky casting a reflective golden glow across the sound. I assisted Haley into a seat, and I was about to pull a chair out for her son when Lauren said, "Here. Sit with me, little guy," which caused the boy to sit next to Lauren leaving the chair next to Haley open for me. Smooth move, sis.

"I'm sorry about that, again," Haley said.

I nodded not wishing to talk about it in front of the children.

"Lauren, how are you adjusting to school?" Haley asked.

"I like it. I have lots of friends from my summers here so that makes it easier."

"I guess so. I hadn't thought of that," Haley said as our waitress appeared.

"May I take your drink orders?" The waitress said.

"I'll have a cola, he'll have an unsweet iced tea with lemon," Lauren said pointing at me. "What do you want, Paulie?"

"A cola with a cherry for him and iced water with lemon for me," Haley said.

"I'll be right back with your drinks. Tonight's specials are swordfish, broiled, baked, or grilled or strip steak, grilled to order. Our soup of the day is New England clam chowder or minestrone. The soups are fresh-made daily," the waitress said.

"So, tell me about yourself. You just bought a new SUV, Lauren is in school here, and you're recently discharged from the navy. You were at Cornell when your sister was born. What else?" Haley asked.

"You're his sister? I thought he was your father," Paulie said to Lauren who smiled.

"I was the surprise baby for my parents and my brother, Mark," Lauren said.

"Are you ready to order?" The waitress asked as she served our drinks.

I looked at Haley, then to Lauren.

"Yes!" Paulie said.

"Start with the lady, please," I said.

They ordered their meals and I ordered steak which was my go-to meal out.

"You were asking about us. I—we—grew up in Oceanside. Our family home is still there, but Lauren and I decided to live out here. I'll go to work at my family's securities brokerage in the city at some point, but I'm in no hurry. I'll just take care of Lauren and watch her grow up and make up lost time. Our paternal grandparents live in Rye, New York. Our maternal grandparents live in Miami. Our paternal uncle runs the securities firm, his wife is a surgical nurse, and my paternal aunt sells real estate in the city. Our maternal aunt is a buyer for a department store chain. I think that's it," I said.

"We wanted to live out here because it's not as busy and we love the house," Lauren added. I nodded in agreement as I watched Paulie, straw in mouth, trying to spear his cherry at the bottom of his glass of cola.

"Tell us about you living here and . . ." I looked at the boy, ". . . you know," I said.

"Sure. I grew up in Glen Cove. I went to CUNY and Hofstra. I'm working on my doctorate in education at Hofstra. I've been teaching for nine years. I've taught here for four years. I started in Uniondale School District then we separated, and I found this job and moved here. We love it, right Paulie?" Haley said.

"Yes. I get to go fishing all the time with my grandpa," Paulie said.

I looked at Haley for explanation.

"We live with my parents. I couldn't afford to buy yet. My parents want me to build a home next to them. They have what amounts to two lots on the bay near Southold. Where is your home?" Haley said.

"On the bay. It's called Fanning Point. My family owned the land around the home then sold most of it. We own six lots total so it's private and quiet," I said.

72

"It sounds nice," Haley said as our dinners arrived. Paulie's eyes got big as he saw his fried shrimp dinner. The waitress placed our plates as we oohed and aahed over the food.

Lauren assisted Paulie when, out of the blue, he said, "I'm glad you knocked down Monty. He's mean to me."

I looked at Paulie and then to his mother. I didn't encourage further discussion about Monty.

"So, securities, huh? Going to enter the rat-race?" Haley asked.

"I guess. I'll go visit next week. I'll have lunch with my aunt while I'm there. She'd like me to join her selling real estate. I won't work full-time until Lauren enters college," I said.

"That will be a lot of commuting for you," Haley said.

"I'd stay at our loft apartment in the city some nights. Our mother was an interior designer. Our parents owned a design studio and apartment in SoHo. If I did go in to work, I'd stay over some nights," I said.

"You could work out of your home, too, couldn't you?" Haley said.

"No. The only work that goes on at home is homework and that's Lauren's job. I like the peacefulness and tranquility of our home," I said as I speared a bite of steak. Haley smiled at me. It dawned on me that I'd not yet told her I was divorced but decided not to bring it up now in front of her son.

"I think that's a nice plan. I do lots of work at home, but I'd never get all my grading done if I didn't. But I don't consider my job work. I love teaching and I love the children. They keep me grounded," Haley said.

I watched Paulie. He'd eaten his shrimp and only had potatoes, vegetable medley, and salad left. He was looking at our plates.

"Would you like to try some steak, Paulie?" I said.

He shot a look at his mother who nodded.

"Yes. I like steak."

I cut off a piece, placed it on his plate and carved it up for him.

"Thank you. He loves his meat and fish. I try to get him to eat his vegetables, but he's at that age," Haley said.

"You know how I got like this and learned to fight so well?" I said to Paulie.

"No. How?"

"By eating all my vegetables growing up. I'd eat all of them, especially carrots, zucchini, broccoli, and cauliflower," I said which included every vegetable on his plate. Paulie looked at his mother for assurance then he dug into his vegetables. Haley and Lauren smiled.

"I remember a similar lecture from you when Mom put out salad for me to eat when I was about his age," Lauren said.

"It worked, too, didn't it?" I said.

"Yes, but back then, I worshiped you and did everything you suggested."

"What? You don't worship me anymore?" I feigned insult.

"I guess I still do. So, you'll take us shopping in the *tank* Saturday. There will be seven of us. And when we come back, we'll grill hot dogs and sausages for dinner. We'll make salads, too. We decided to bake some chocolate layer cakes. You just need to make sure we have the ingredients. I'll make a list later. Okay?" Lauren said.

"Sure. All I do is shop," I said as I took my last bite.

"But you won't have anything to do except watch the grill. So, you'll have plenty of free time to tend to your guest, Ms. Menduni."

I looked at Lauren in surprise, then to Haley. *What the heck?*

"Would you like to join me and seven fifteen-year-olds for an afternoon of, well, you heard the itinerary," I said.

Haley looked at her son.

"Oh. Wait. Paulie. Would you like to come over and eat hot dogs?"

"Yes!" Paulie said as he smiled at his mother.

"Okay. That sounds like fun. What time should we be there?" Haley said.

I looked at Lauren.

"We'll be back from shopping after 1 p.m. so we'll start making a mess about 2 p.m. You want to help make chocolate cakes, Paulie?" Lauren asked.

"Yes, and eat them, too," he said.

The waitress cleared away our plates and asked about dessert. The vote was for it. I went with coffee.

"So, tell me about your Manhattan apartment," Haley said.

"You tell her, Lauren. I've not been there since it was redone."

"It's beautiful. It's three bedrooms on the eighteenth floor plus a master bedroom loft, a wrap-around balcony and a roof-top deck. The seventeenth floor is where my mother's studio and office are located. Mark said it will be mine since I want to become a designer. I worked with my mom on the big projects and some small ones, too. The apartment is all woodsy-modern. It has a huge kitchen that I love. All wood, European smooth-faced cabinets, in light mahogany, black granite counter-tops, and a Miele coffee-expresso machine. The living room is totally sick with a wall of ten-foot-tall sliders that can be completely opened to the balcony. The roof-top garden and deck are beautiful. There's a gas fire pit on the roof and a fireplace in the living room. We love it," Lauren said.

"It sounds nice," Haley said.

"I'll have to see it sometime," I said.

"Next week when you go into the city," Lauren said.

"Perhaps," I said.

We finished our coffees and desserts. I asked for the bill.

"Thank you very much, Mark. Lauren and you made a nice ending to our day. Right, Paulie?" Haley said.

"Yes, sir. Thank you for dinner, Mr. Mark, and thanks for knocking down, Monty," Paulie said.

I looked at Haley for the explanation, but she seemed as confused by Paulie's statement as I.

"You're welcome, Paulie," I said.

We walked to our vehicles.

"Oh. Let me give you our address," I said.

"Text it to me. You have my number," Haley said.

"I'll send it later," I said as I opened Haley's car door for her.

"Thank you, Mark."

"You're welcome. I'll text my address then you'll have my number." *Master of the obvious, I was. Brilliant statement.*

"I will. Good night," Haley said smiling and giggling, too.

"Bye."

Lauren and I got into the Yukon.

"I like her a lot, Mark."

"She's very nice." *I was wondering if I'd ever be able to formulate a coherent thought around Haley other than obvious observations and monosyllabic replies?*

#

We drove home. Lauren showered then began her homework. At some point, Lauren called our grandmother because she called me.

"Hello."

"Hello, Mark. It's Grandma."

"Hi. How are you?"

"I'm good. How are you?"

"I'm good. Things are going well with Lauren."

"Oh, I know that. What's this about dinner with her teacher?"

"Word sure travels fast."

"Well? Do you like her?"

"We had dinner, Grandma, but, yes, she seems very nice."

"I'm told she's beautiful."

"She's very nice-looking, yes."

"You should take her for a walk on the beach, Saturday. That would be special."

"Grandma. I have an idea how to do this. I think you and Lauren need more to do."

"No. We barely get our two or three daily calls done now."

"Good-bye, Grandma. I love you."

"Good-bye, Mark. I love you, too."

Jeez! I texted my address to Haley. I walked toward my room and stuck my head into Lauren's room.

"Do you talk with Grandma two or three times a day?"

"Well, yes. It used to be once or twice a day except while I lived there, but after Mom died, we spoke more with everyone. I talk with Missy, Grandma Emily, and Betsy almost every day, too. Lorraine isn't as regular, but I talk to her several times a week."

"You do?"

"Of course. You just said to me we have our purposes in life. We women talk and keep in touch a lot more than men. It's how we take care of the family. Cathy was part of all that, too, then her calls got shorter and less frequent. That's how we knew."

I shook my head in amazement. "I'm getting a shower if you need to update anyone."

#

I use the master bedroom. It takes up the back half of the third floor if you include the master bath. It has a nearly full-width balcony deck, too. The master bath has a shower that contains two shower heads and a picture window with a bay view. Lauren has the next largest suite and then there's the third suite, a laundry room, a wide hallway, a linen closet, and attic access to finish off the third floor. The fourth bedroom is a first-floor family room with an attached full bath. It's huge and could be made into two bedrooms. The house is almost 100 years old but was state-of-the-art when our great-great grandfather built it. Since then, the piers have been replaced by lifting the home off the old piers and installing new piers that are ten times the strength of the old piers. The house was stripped to its skeletal frame and completely redone. My parents took ownership in the 1990s, and they upgraded all the systems and dumped all the 1970s solar crap that never worked right. Then my mother and Lauren redid it in a major refurbishment less than two years ago. I like the Oceanside house, which is certainly handy to get into the city, but being at our Greenport home makes me feel like I'm on vacation.

I showered, dried off and put on my cut-off sweats and a T-shirt. It was cooler now that it was dark. I noticed my SIG Sauer sitting out on my nightstand. I put it away. Lauren was not a concern, but her friends would be over this weekend along with Paulie.

CHAPTER 5

I awoke to the sounds of the gulls cawing outside my window. It was just 5:10 a.m. No nightmare. That was good news. I had another busy day ahead of me. I had to meet with Sergeant Cicola at 1 p.m. I decided to move all the valuables from the Oceanside home to safe deposit boxes. I'd bring my mother's jewelry box back here for Lauren. I had a hidden safe in the walk-in closet where we stored our valuables and a huge gun safe in the garage. I had to call Joe afterward, too. I had one more thing to do. I sent emails to Lauren's three remaining teachers to set up conferences.

I needed to check the boat. The boat is a few years old and has some mileage on it. The one complaint I recall hearing was from Missy, who said the boat was "Spartan on comforts." Fine for the boys to fish for striper off Montauk or further out for tuna or marlin. It was okay for bay fishing, too. We left it at our Oceanside house most of the year but moved it to Greenport for the summer. I was seriously considering upgrading. The boat was almost twenty-years old. While I was in the hospital, I flipped through all the yachting books. I was torn between a nice long-range center console, a convertible sport fisherman, or a cruiser that would comfortably carry my whole family. Of course, I was looking for a boat at the worst possible time of the year for price.

I started coffee and then walked to the new work-out area. Twenty minutes of calisthenics, 15 minutes of skipping rope, followed by 20 minutes on the heavy bag and speed bag. I was soaked with sweat and wiped out. My first work-out since leaving the hospital. I walked up stairs and knocked on Lauren's door.

"Wake up, Lauren."

She stirred, then sat up and smiled at me. "Good morning. Did you just do a workout?"

"I did. What do you want for breakfast?"

"That melon, a bagel with cream cheese, and OJ please."

"Sounds good. I'll be down before you."

I showered, dressed in dress slacks, a light-blue button-down Oxford shirt, a blue blazer, Cole Haan slip-ons, and a matching belt. I wore my Tudor Heritage Black Bay watch.

I prepared Lauren's breakfast and poured myself coffee. Lauren came bounding down the stairs and sat at the counter.

"Looks good. Thanks," she said as she reached for the cream cheese. "You have the list for Saturday? I think we should double the cake ingredients."

"Oh? Expecting an army for dessert?"

"A couple of us thought, maybe, if it's all right with you, we could have a few boys over Sunday for dessert. You know, an ice cream and cake social," she pleaded.

"How many boys?"

"Maybe seven. I'll know today and that's with seven girls so fourteen of us. The girls will stay over Saturday night. They'll bring sleeping bags and we'll just use downstairs and my room," Lauren advised, informed, pleaded, and asked permission all in one statement.

"Fine. Don't wreck the house. No boys until Sunday afternoon. Understood?"

"Thank you. I'm so excited."

"Finish your breakfast. We must go."

"Why are you almost in a suit?"

"I have a meeting to go to and some business to attend to."

We got into the Yukon, and I drove Lauren to school dropping her out of sequence by pulling over to the bakery.

"Good-bye," and she was off to the school. She waved at me. Lauren sure was upbeat.

#

I drove down the highway. I brought a briefcase with me suitable for the bearer bonds. My bank had a branch a mile from my Oceanside home, another in Mineola and another in Riverhead. I'd obtain safe deposit boxes at each branch and split up the bonds, money, and jewelry at each of these banks over the course of the day.

An hour and thirty minutes later, I pulled into the driveway at the Oceanside home. I opened the middle garage door with the HomeLink button and pulled in. I opened the safe. I placed the bonds in the briefcase after looking inside each envelope. As I assumed, 10 in each envelope, $100,000 in bonds for a total of $18 million. All the bonds were issued by an energy company. I placed the jewelry and money into the Yukon, along with three pistols, then took the three garage door remotes from the work bench, removed their batteries, and locked them in the safe with my weapons.

I drove to the UPS store and made copies of each of the bonds. I drove to the bank. The manager led me to the safe deposit box area then left me alone. I placed the bonds in the safe deposit box with a SIG Sauer P226 pistol. I locked it up and drove to the bank in Mineola. There I placed the money in a larger safe deposit box with a P226. By now, I needed to get to Westbury for my 1 p.m. appointment.

After I got into the Yukon, I looked at what was in my mother's jewelry box. Lots of diamonds, a couple of beautiful watches, a lot of gold and what I assumed were emerald, ruby, and sapphire jewelry, and lots of pearls. I had no idea what Lauren liked. I closed the box. I looked in my father's jewelry box. Some nice gold, but many nice watches. I took a Breitling Superocean and an Omega Seamaster and closed the box. I'd lock it up at the bank in Riverhead.

#

I drove to the luncheonette on Old Country Road to meet Sergeant Cicola. I wondered what he'd tell me. I wondered more about what he wouldn't tell me.

My parents were returning from an affair in New York City the night they were killed. It was a chilly, wet, April night, and they were driving home to Oceanside. For whatever reason, they remained on I-495 to the L.I.E. instead of dropping south on the Cross-Island Parkway. What we do know is at the off-ramp to Meadowbrook State Parkway their car was hit, and it lost control and rolled several times until it struck a concrete bridge embankment. The car, a newer BMW 750Li, was moving quite fast. They died having never fully regained consciousness.

I pulled into a parking lot at Jay's Luncheonette and went inside. I took a booth table in the middle of the restaurant along the wall. A waitress came to me. I asked for coffee and a menu since I didn't know whether Cicola would eat. The luncheonette was clean and modern. It smelled of French fries, onion rings and hot dogs. The local court, government, and pedestrian traffic shuffled through.

I had my parents MVA file with me. I'd read each document in it several times. I hoped I'd get more information today. I wondered who hit my parents and left them to die? I looked up just as Sergeant Cicola entered the luncheonette.

"How you doin?" Cicola said as he extended his hand. I stood and we shook hands.

"I'm okay."

"You sure look a lot better than when I first seen you. You put on some weight?"

"I did. I'm back in fighting shape. I'm healthy. You want to order something?"

"Yeah. I only got an hour, and I gotta be back," Cicola said as the waitress approached us.

"You ready to order?" The waitress said.

"Yeah. Gimme a bacon cheeseburger, rare, with fries, rings, and a Coke. Ketchup on the side, will ya?"

The waitress turned to me.

"Two tuna on toasted oatmeal bread and a pickle. Unsweet iced tea with lemon."

She wrinkled her nose at me. Perhaps I should have asked her to deep-fry the sandwiches?

"You eat healthy, too. I gotta lose weight, my wife tells me. What have you been doing?"

"Just relaxing, taking care of my sister. We're staying in Greenport."

"Nice."

The waitress placed our drinks and our orders.

"That was fast!" Cicola said.

We chatted about baseball while we prepared our food. Cicola took a bite of his burger and washed it down with a swig of Coke.

"We found some interesting things. First, we lifted several fingerprints and a handprint off your parents' car." He pulled out two pictures from a file and placed them in front of me. I didn't recognize either man. "'Dis one is a muscle guy for the Calabrese family. His handprint was on the left rear quarter panel like he'd put his left hand on the car as he bent over." Cicola took another bite of his burger with a handful of fries. He chewed a moment, sipped his soda then placed a picture of a tracking device on the table. "This was found in the wreckage, crushed up under the left rear fender well." Cicola paused while sipping his soda. "The prints of the other guy were found on the trunk, in the trunk, and on the inside front passenger door. We also found wool threads on the jagged edge of the passenger door. The glove box and trunk were pried open with a metal object." He placed another split picture showing damage to the glove box and trunk lid. "As you know, we didn't find a briefcase in the car. All of you confirm that your father always had a briefcase with him. It's possible your father didn't have it with him that night because it was a formal affair they'd attended. However, your Uncle Matthew said your father left the office with his tan briefcase earlier that afternoon to meet your mother at the Manhattan apartment to get ready for their evening. From that affair, they drove home toward Oceanside, but we all agree, not by his usual route." He took another bite of his burger. I took my first bite of my sandwich and contemplated what I'd just learned.

"Have you talked to these two guys yet?"

"No. We want more on them, but we, with help from the Organized Crime Task Force in the city, have been watching them. Here . . ." He placed a picture of a Lincoln Town Car with the guy in the first picture sitting in the driver's seat. ". . . is a picture of the first guy picking up his Town Car from a well-known Lincoln repair and body shop in Brooklyn two days after the accident."

"I don't get it? How did you get this picture when you hadn't done anything to investigate the accident yet?"

"Sharp. The OCTF got it. They routinely tag these guys with GPS trackers even though both the New York Court of Appeals and United States Supreme Court say we need a warrant. We say, 'We didn't know?' and the courts call it a "good faith exception." When it showed that the car was put in the shop just two hours after your parents MVA, they put a surveillance unit out there the following day. They got this picture the next day. The GPS tracker shows that the car was at the scene of your parents' MVA and that it followed them from Manhattan, where the device was placed on your father's car. We think your father saw them and decided to take the long way home to be sure. Based on the movement of the Lincoln, the GPS tracker we found in your father's car, and the BMW GPS, we know he moved suddenly to get off the L.I.E. at the interchange with Northern State Parkway and Meadowbrook State Parkway. These guys figured he was running and nailed them," Cicola said as he stuffed the last of his burger in his mouth and washed it down with his cola.

"Don't you have enough to arrest?" I said.

"Oh, sure. We can get an indictment. That's easy. Proving it in court is another thing. This ain't federal court. We must prove our case in state court. We can put the car there. We can put them at the scene in the car at some point. A slick-dick, shyster lawyer will say the one bent over to check your mother and his suit got hung up. He'll say he thought she was dead. Other people showed up and called 911 along with the crash notification system in your father's car. Witnesses identified these two at the scene, but said they left after several people stopped to help. It's doubtful we can even get leaving the scene of an accident since no one said they caused the accident, and plenty of other people were there rendering aid. The body shop owner and tech told us the Town Car was beat up, but no pictures, no insurance claim and it was a cash repair. They know we know, but what can we do?" He stuffed a handful of onion rings in his mouth. "Circumstantial at best, is what we have. What I need is a motive. What was in your father's briefcase? Or what did they think was in his briefcase? 'Dat's what I want to know."

I finished my sandwiches and sipped my tea. Cicola studied me before saying what I expected him to say.

"You have any idea what they were looking for?"

I'd learned enough about interrogation to identify deception. I also know that telling a similar answer to the truth covers deception.

"I'd guess something to do with the firm. Investment information or financial documents dealing with trades, bonds, and purchases, perhaps?"

"It could be. Your uncle said that your father's firm is a brokerage that it mainly took orders to buy and sell securities. Is that right?" Cicola said.

"I'd say that's mostly true. Most people are familiar with stocks and commodities because those products have huge exchanges, but a security is any form of commercial paper. They're traded through the brokerage houses and at some banks. Think of it like a real estate broker or freight forwarding broker. My father's firm found people with securities to sell and people who wanted to buy them. Depending on the relationship, they would provide advice as to the discount rate for the security."

"And your father's firm got a commission on the sale?"

"That's correct. In a nutshell, that's what they did. You're correct, they would not sit down and advise you how to invest your money no more than a real estate broker would advise you how to invest in real estate," I said.

"You know this because of your family's firm and because your aunt has a real estate firm?"

"Mostly, yes, but I've just recently obtained my securities licenses to sell securities and my real estate license, too."

"Did your father hold the securities—the actual paper?"

"At times, yes, as an escrow agent. Most of the time another escrow agent held the paper and didn't close the transaction until it had the money in its accounts. Now, with software programs, the transactions happen quickly, so the physical paper may not go to an owner for weeks or months. It may be traded four or five times in a day as investors seek to capitalize on their buys and sells."

"Would your father have a reason to carry the paper home with him?"

"I don't know. Taking it home doesn't make sense to me. Taking it out of the office perhaps to meet a buyer to deliver it with a personal thank you? Maybe. I just don't know. I know my father and Matt would service accounts by taking them to dinner, throwing parties or, one year, Dad chartered a jet and flew some clients to a hotel in the Bahamas, but I've not worked there, so I could not answer your question any better than that."

"When will you be going to work there?"

"My plan is to start part-time while I take care of my sister. I'm going into the city next week to meet the group. Once I'm acclimated, I'll be made president."

Cicola nodded. "So why did you call me?"

"To find out what you knew. I was at the Oceanside home to pick-up some things and that trip reminded me to call you."

Cicola nodded again. "You ever dealt with the Calabrese family before?"

"Not that I know of. Why don't you give me some names, addresses, and contact info for those two," I tapped the photos, "and their associates, and let me run them through our computers at the office? Maybe there's a connection?"

"I thought you'd ask. Here's a list of those guys and their associates. Ruggerio Calabrese was the boss. He died a while ago. His brother-in-law took over. He's out of Queens. Anyway. All the contact information is in there. If you learn something, you'll contact me. I didn't give you that," Cicola said with a smile.

"Can I have those pictures?"

"Sure," he said as he passed the package to me. "Call me when you learn something."

"I will. Thanks."

"I gotta go to court. Oh, miss, check please."

"I got it. I'll be talking to you," I said.

"Thanks. I'll be seeing you."

I sat there looking at the file. The flow of people into the luncheonette had reduced to a trickle. I needed to get to one more bank and out to Greenport to get Lauren, but I had something to do first.

#

It was nice and sunny. The wind blew a slight breeze across the long expanse of green before me. The well-manicured grounds and trees lent to the quiet and tranquility of the place. It was as if the cemetery was made for the living not a place to bury the dead. A peaceful place to come and be with a loved one no longer of this world.

It was just over a year ago when I first visited this place. It was a chilly, overcast day following several days of rain. My family rented a van to help me get to and from the funeral home, church mass and cemetery. I remember sitting in the wheelchair in my dress blue uniform wearing a wool navy watch coat, a black scarf around my collar instead of the usual white scarf, wondering: *Why? What had I done to deserve all this heart break?* Ten months prior to my parents' deaths, my wife confirmed what was all over the Internet—she was an adulterous slut. Then I nearly got killed in Afghanistan the January just past. Now this—my parents' deaths. Lauren was in tears while I held her hand during most of the service. Our grandparents, both sets, stood to either side of us, each of them there to bury their child. I didn't cry that day. I was angry at the world—at God. My family knew it.

The priest recited some prayers. He said some nice things about my parents. I'd heard them all before at the memorial, at the funeral home and during their lives. I knew my parents as the funny and loving human beings they were. They did everything together from high school until their deaths. I don't think my father ever spent a night away from my mother after they married until I was brought back shot up. They were as in love on the day they died as they were on the day they married.

I'd scanned the crowd that day. I remember all the faces of the attendees. There were many people who I didn't know, but they introduced themselves to me or my Uncle Matt introduced them. There were several people at the cemetery who I did not meet. Seven men and one raven-haired woman wearing unnecessarily large sunglasses on such an overcast day. I pointed them out to Joe who didn't recognize them either. I surveyed the crowd that day to see who was looking at the burial service and who was looking at the crowd. Cicola was one who was looking around at the crowd. A New York State Trooper was another. Nassau police recorded every license plate of every car that appeared at the funeral home, church, and cemetery. I don't know what that produced—I forgot to ask Cicola.

I stood at their grave. They were side-by-side in death as in life. I was saddened that I'd missed so much time with them. I was saddened for Lauren missing so much more with them. I'd at least attained adulthood with their support. Lauren had suffered the childhood tragedy of being orphaned.

At the end of the burial service while the crowd departed, I stood up and, holding Lauren's hand, walked to their caskets. I said a prayer aloud that only my parents and Lauren could hear. Then I swore I'd find who'd done this to them. Today, I knew I'd be able to keep that promise.

"Mom, Dad . . . I just want you to know that Lauren and I miss you. Lauren is okay. She will make it, and I know that is what you want. I'll protect her like you would have protected her."

Tears rolled down my cheeks. It was time for me to begin to mourn their loss. I put flowers in the pot on the flat, black granite ground stone.

"Mom, Dad, we love you. I'll return when I'm done." I walked away.

#

"Joe. Mark."

"Hey. What do you have?"

"A bunch. Look. I'm running out of time. I gotta get Lauren in an hour and I'm by Brookhaven. Can we meet later?"

"I'm off tonight. Why don't I come out to your place?"

"Works for me. When?"

"Why don't we say 6 p.m. You can grill me a steak."

"That's fine. I'll see you at 6 p.m. You remember where it is, right?"

"I'll never forget. That's where I lost my virginity to Donna Demetri that summer."

"That's right. On the beach and my mother and father knew about it."

"I don't remember that part," Joe said, feigning ignorance.

"See you then. Bye."

I sped to the bank, opened a safe deposit box account, placed my Dad's jewelry box in it, less two watches, along with a SIG Sauer P226.

I rolled up to the school and noticed Haley out directing children to buses or cars. I observed her. She is quite beautiful. I moved to a spot in front of the bakery where Lauren would see me. The pickup line took too long and, while necessary for little kids for security, not required for high schoolers. I watched for Lauren, but mainly I watched Haley. After a few minutes, Haley spied me leaning against the Yukon. She smiled and waved. I did likewise. As Haley turned around to continue to direct traffic, Lauren walked past her. Haley said something to Lauren, who smiled and nodded her head. Lauren continued walking to me.

"Hi. Nice day." Lauren said.

"Yes, it is. And yours?"

"Great. Ms. Menduni said you look great in slacks and a sport jacket."

"Oh, she did, did she?" I turned around to look at Haley, who smiled and waved. I smiled and nodded at her. Lauren and I got into the Yukon and we drove off.

"What are we doing tonight?" Lauren said.

"Dinner, for one thing. Joe is coming over. We're going over a few things together. Oh. I brought that for you," I pointed over my shoulder with my right thumb to the back seat.

"Mom's jewelry box!"

"Yes. Go through it and see what you want, for now. I'll put the rest in a safe place for whenever you want it. Some of the jewelry is too formal or adult for you, but it's all yours."

"It's ours."

"Somehow, I think the pearls and diamonds Mom wore will look nicer on you than me. They're yours. There are rings in there from when our grandmothers were children. You get to protect them. When you have children, they can wear them."

"Your children, too. You're a lot closer to having children than I am."

"Oh, really?"

"Yes. I have at least ten years. You must get started soon, old man."

"'Old man?' I do a nice thing and I'm called 'old man.'"

Lauren leaned over and hugged my arm. "I don't know if I'll wear those watches. We use smartphones nowadays."

"You won't carry a smartphone wearing a formal gown. You'll wear a beautiful Patek Phillip watch covered in diamonds is my guess."

"Good point. Did you get Dad's stuff?"

"Yes. I already put it away except for these two watches." I showed Lauren the watches.

"Nice. You already have some nice watches, too, like the one you are wearing."

"I do. Dad had a few more," I said as we pulled into the driveway.

"Can I go to a movie tonight with Kim and a couple of other girls?"

"Sure. I need to know all the info. Who, what, where, time, what you're seeing, whether boys will be in the theater or not . . . that type of stuff."

"You're so strict," Lauren kidded.

"I'm new at this and I was once a boy your age."

"I have to call Kim for the time."

#

My phone buzzed.

"Hello."

"Hi. It's Haley."

"How are you?"

"I'm good. You looked nice in your suit today."

"So, I heard. Now I'll never take it off."

"Really?"

"Really. I haven't washed my left cheek since second grade after Barbara Verali kissed me on the playground."

"You began dating in second grade?"

"Not really, but I'd give her my cookies at lunch."

"How sweet. I was calling to ask you what you're doing? My father and son are going fishing tonight and my mother is playing cards with her friends so I'm all by myself."

I quickly thought. "Come over. I'll grill you a steak and you can interrogate my childhood best friend about me giving away my cookies in second grade."

"Are you sure?"

"Yes. I was just beginning to marinate the steaks. Lauren is going to the movie with her posse. Do you like beer, wine, or bourbon?"

"All three, it depends."

"Great. I know you ladies always worry about what to wear, so I'm wearing jeans and a V-neck pullover sweater over a T-shirt. Enough information?"

"Oh? I thought you were wearing the suit?"

"You're quick."

"What time?"

"My friend will be here at 6 p.m. but come over when you're ready. I'll start cooking the steaks at 7 p.m. Lauren is not eating with us. Their movie begins at 7:30 p.m. so I'm making her supper now. The girls will be back at 10:30 p.m.

"Okay. I'll be over in a bit. Bye."

"Bye."

I pulled another steak from the refrigerator, cut up more potatoes, and readied more salad ingredients from the crisper. Lauren's supper of grilled ham and cheese with side salad and glass of milk was waiting.

"Hi." Lauren said as she entered the kitchen.

"Perfect. Thank you. Look what I'm wearing?"

I saw a gold chain and a locket around her neck.

"I remember that. Who's inside there, you and me?"

"Yes. I'll put pictures of Mom and Dad in there this weekend."

"I think Dad gave that to Mom when they were in high school."

"Correct. On the back, it says, *'To Liz, Love, Will. June 1978.'* Dad was sixteen and Mom was fifteen—my age!"

"Wow. It's an antique," I said, ignoring Lauren's emphasis on age.

"You know Mom and Dad were pretty young when you were born," Lauren observed while biting into her sandwich.

"They were twenty and twenty-one years old. Dad had just graduated college and he was working in the city. Mom was in her last year of college. I know the whole story."

"So do I. Grandma and Mom told me. We were sitting around the table here when we came out for a long weekend after we saw you. You had finally begun to improve. Mom was talking about you. She was so worried. You had just gotten over another infection. I think it was the third or fourth one. Mom cried while she told us how happy she was after you were born."

Lauren paused as she ate some salad. I listened saying nothing.

"Grandma began telling her story about how they found out Mom was pregnant with you. Mom told everyone she was pregnant. They married right after Mom graduated high school, what, not even a month later. Grandmas Stuart and MacKenzie said they always knew Mom and Dad would marry. Did you know Mom and Dad wrote letters to each other while Dad moved around with *The General* as Grandma calls Grandpa?"

"No. I didn't. I knew that after a few years of moving every year Grandpa got out-voted on where they would live. Grandpa was gone four times to Vietnam. I think each time he deployed they moved back to Oceanside."

"Not each time, but when Grandma found out she was pregnant with Missy, she came back while Grandpa was in Vietnam. But Mom just cried as she told us how much she was in love with Dad and you. I learned a lot that day. While you were away, Mom would talk about you all the time, but when the news came on television about the war, she'd become quiet. Dad told me that when you were in Iraq, and there were all those terrible battles, that Mom would sit and cry because she knew you were there. I was too young to understand why she cried. I just hugged her, and I'd sit in her lap when the news was on. Then you got shot the first time. Dad had to tell Mom that you were fine. I guess she didn't understand that it wasn't as serious as they were first led to believe. Mom was trying to book a flight to Iraq."

I didn't know all of this.

"When you finally called her, she was fine. Both Grandmas supported Mom and helped a lot. When you were shot the last time, it was the worst. We got very little information at first. We were all crying. We were told your team had been overrun and even Dad was shaken by that news. We recalled the story about that other Long Island SEAL officer whose team was overrun."

"Murphy."

"That's right. We congregated at the Oceanside house and waited for news. The next day we were told you and some of your guys were being "worked on" at Bagram Air Base. I always thought that such a cryptic term—*worked on*. Mom was ready to fly there. Cathy wasn't with us, but she got better details from your command at Dam Neck Naval Base, and she would pass them along. It wasn't until Mom saw you at Walter Reed National Military Medical Center that she stopped crying."

Lauren ate more sandwich. I didn't know about these events, either.

"Mom loved us a lot. We're a part of her. Mom was very worried when she first saw you getting moved into the intensive care ward. We stayed at a hotel just a short distance away from the hospital, but Mom only showered and changed there, spending all her time with you. We drove there so Mom could relax a little since she disliked flying. We arrived a few hours before you. It was another two hours before we could see you. You were unconscious. Mom held your hand the whole time. For the first week, they tried to fight that infection and they operated on you again. I think that was when they removed part of your liver?"

"I think so."

"Anyway. It wasn't until you finally awoke, looked at Mom and said, 'I didn't expect to see you when I woke up?' that Mom knew you would be all right. Dad and I flew down that night. We'd been going back and forth for work and school," Lauren said as she took her last bite of salad. "I wanted you to know that story and how much Mom and Dad loved us."

"I know. I was out there today."

"I want to go again soon, too."

"We'll go in May. I'll take you."

I heard a car pull up outside. Lauren ran off to brush her teeth. I walked to the door. Kimberly came running up the steps.

"Hi, Mr. MacKenzie. Is Lauren ready?"

"Brushing her teeth and . . ."

"Hi. I'm ready," Lauren said appearing at my side.

"You have your phone?"

"Yes. I'm good."

"I'll see you at 10:30 p.m. or before?"

"Yes. Bye. Thanks."

"For what?"

"Caring," Lauren said as she kissed my cheek then she and Kimberly ran down the stairs. I followed to reacquaint myself with Kimberly's mother.

"Hi. I'm Mark, Lauren's older brother. We met several summers ago."

"Oh, yes, of course. You live here now?"

"Yes."

"I'm Judith Schwartz. It's nice to see you again. Thanks for taking them tomorrow. That's a chunk out of your day."

"It's no problem. Just call if you need anything."

"I will. Ready girls? Bye, Mark."

#

Haley pulled up at that point.

"Hi. Was that Lauren and her entourage?"

"It was. Come on. I must check the potatoes."

"This is beautiful. I have always admired this home—all of them along here."

I showed Haley into the house. My phone was buzzing.

"Hello."

"I'm on my way. I got caught up. I'll be there in thirty minutes."

"Who is this?"

"Funny man. Bye," Joe said.

"Is that your friend?" Haley asked.

"Yeah. He's a Suffolk County cop. I didn't say while you were on the phone, but he and I will take a little time later to go over a project we're doing. Lauren will be back by then. I didn't want to bring it up on the phone because I didn't want you not to come over."

"Oh? Well, I think I'm flattered," Haley said.

"Can I get you something to drink?"

"Sure. What are you drinking?"

"Unsweet iced tea."

"Oh? You said beer, wine, or bourbon on the phone. May I have wine?"

"Sure. I was going to open a bottle of red for dinner. I have red or white?"

"May I have white now and red later?"

"Yes, you may."

I removed a bottle of white from the under-counter wine cooler, uncorked it and poured her a glass.

"Here you go." I handed the glass to Haley.

"Thank you. Now you can show me around your house. It is so nicely decorated. I remember when the outside was being painted, and the decking and roofing done."

"I'd seen pictures, but four days ago was my first time seeing it since my mother and Lauren redid it."

"Lauren worked with your mother on this? That's cool."

I'm okay with using cool.

"C'mon. We'll begin the tour upstairs." I showed Haley the third floor, beginning with the guest suite, then Lauren's room which looked like a bomb had gone off in it, then the master.

"What a view. Oh, my, look at that shower! That is so nice and it's huge. This is all so nicely decorated and it all goes so well. I like it," Haley said as she scanned the room. She walked out onto the balcony. "This is very nice. It's just gorgeous. What a view up and down the beach, too."

I looked at Haley looking out at the bay. It was nice to do. Both were very easy on the eyes. She turned and smiled.

"Show me the rest."

"Follow me." I led Haley to the first floor and showed her the huge bedroom and den area. While we walked through the unfinished room Haley noticed the work out area.

"Did you build that?" Haley pointed at the heavy bags.

"I did. It helps keep me in practice. I never know when I'll need it."

"I didn't even see you move last night. It was like he stepped toward you then he was on the ground. Did you learn that type of fighting with the SEALs?"

"No."

Haley looked at me with *the look* that I'd seen before.

"There you go again not completely answering my question."

"I've done martial arts and kickboxing my whole life. I've been to several hand-to-hand combat and close quarters combat courses while in the navy. What I did the other night I knew before I joined the navy."

"See? That wasn't so hard, was it?"

I smiled despite my attempt not to.

"C'mon. Let's go tour the main floor." I was still smiling as I took Haley's hand and led her up the stairs to the second floor.

"Oh my, this is beautiful. I love the living room . . . and look at that you can connect the room to the deck by opening the doors. This is gorgeous. Your mother liked full-length curtains, but it so works in all these rooms. The rugs are terrific."

"When Lauren gets home you can ask her about the decorations. She'll give you the minutiae that 'straight men overlook,' as she says. She can tell you what everything is made of, by whom, and why it was selected over something else." I walked Haley to the outdoor living room.

"That's your pier and your boat?"

"Yes. The pier was placed there so the view would be clear in front of the house."

"That's the boat you want to replace that you spoke of last night?"

"Yes. You've been on boats. What do you like to use a boat for? I'm asking because you are a woman."

"That's easy. To cruise, relax, suntan, enjoy the company of family and friends, explore the coast—things like that."

"I didn't hear fishing and your father fishes?"

"Fishing is fun, but if I got a boat that would be the last consideration. I mean, you can stick a pole over the side of any boat. You're talking about offshore for tuna or marlin fishing, I assume?"

"Yes. We'll have to explore this more because, well, I'm just not sure what I want."

A knock at the door announced that Joe had arrived. I walked toward the hallway.

"Come in, Joe," I yelled.

"Hey. Wow, is this nice? This is the same house?" Joe said as he walked back to the deck. He saw Haley. "Boy, your Mom even decorated the place with a beautiful woman. I'm Joe and big boy there hasn't said a word about you."

Haley flushed, then smiled.

"Haley, this rude man is my childhood best friend—the emphasis on *child*. Joe, please meet Haley. She's one of Lauren's teachers," I said.

"What? Did you get detention already?" Joe cracked.

"I think I mentioned that Joe is a cop. We played cops and robbers as children. Joe took it literally. Can I get you a beer?" I said.

"Sure. Nice looking steaks. So, I'm new to this whole dating game. Did he ask you out or did you ask him?" Joe said. I smiled, Haley blushed again.

"It sort of happened, but I asked her out for dinner with the children last night . . ."

"I'll skip that type of date. Go on," Joe said.

"And I invited her here this evening so she could see where most of Suffolk County's tax dollars are going with you as exhibit 'A,'" I said.

"I assume you are recently divorced?" Haley said.

"I look pretty good for a guy who just lost 120 pounds, don't I?" Joe cracked.

"You look fine," Haley added.

"Just fine, huh? Not like super SEAL over there. Look at him! Hard to believe he took four bullets, got stabbed, and was blown up, huh?" Joe said.

Haley gave me a concerned look.

"I'm fine. It wasn't as bad as he makes it sound."

"I read that story in the paper. It sure sounded bad," Haley said.

"It's the past. Joe, I was just asking Haley what's important in a boat? What do you like in a boat?" I said. Haley looked at me, nodding, acknowledging my subject shift.

"Well, I think mainly plenty of room for ice, fishing equipment and room for the wife or girlfriend or both to stretch out and suntan," Joe said.

I rolled my eyes. Haley smiled at me.

"This place is really nice. It was pretty much a sandy beach cottage when we were kids. Your mother did all this?" Joe said.

"With Lauren's help."

"Where is Squirt?"

"At the movies. She'll be back before you leave," I said.

"Who said I was leaving? With as much of your beer and bourbon I will drink, it would be against the law to drive. I hear Suffolk County cops are real dicks, too."

"I need to start the grill. How do you like your steak, Haley?"

"Medium, please."

"Joe, you still a well-done guy?"

"No. Go with medium."

"Sure."

I adjusted the fire for the steaks and turned off the oven. The salad was ready.

"Joe, did you decide to buy that house?" I said.

"I did, but my partners are still reviewing it," Joe said.

"Joe buys houses to fix and flip," I said to Haley.

"I thought that sort of slowed down again?"

"It did. What a deal, right? I make it through all the financial BS brought on by the government and the big banks, then the next time I need to do some more, the market tanks again. It picked up this month It'll work out. So, tell me, are you divorced?" Joe asked.

"I'm trying. It seems my husband's lawyers are dragging it out. I'll be finished this year. My lawyer finally told my husband's lawyer that he settles for X or he goes through the business with auditors," Haley said.

"What does he do?"

"He has a restaurant. Tito's Italian Eatery," Haley said.

Joe furrowed his brow, then looked at me, then back to Haley.

"What's your last name?" Joe asked.

"Menduni," Haley said, then looked at me.

Joe looked from Haley to me, then back to Haley.

"Menduni, as in Calabrese family Menduni?" Joe said which caught my attention after my talk with Sergeant Cicola.

"Yes," Haley somewhat reservedly responded as she looked at me.

"You tell him you're married to the mob?" Joe asked Haley.

"Hold that thought. I should check the steaks. Joe, I know. Be nice." I flipped the steaks and turned down the temperature. "Okay. I'm back. First, we're just getting to know each other. Deep dark secrets are scheduled for confession next week. However, I met her soon-to-be ex-husband yesterday. He acted impolitely with Haley and, well, you know me, I said something. His gorilla came at me and . . . I think he's still icing parts of his anatomy."

"No shit?" Joe said.

"Yeah. It was nothing, really. Right, Haley?"

"Joe. I was standing right there. Monty stepped toward Mark and then he was on the sidewalk on his back trying to catch his breath. It happened so fast."

"Back to the husband. Your husband is Paulie Menduni of the Calabrese crime family?"

"Yes. I was a late bloomer. I didn't realize. I thought I was marrying a restauranteur."

"Does he know about the connection?" Joe said.

"I'm standing right here, Joe. I know he's a mob guy based on what I saw yesterday. That's all I know. Calabrese . . . they're related to the Gambino clan. Right?" I said.

"Yes. Menduni is great Grandpa Calabrese's wife's maiden name. I think the old biddy is dead, too, but her brother, old man Menduni is around and let's say when Menduni and Calabrese married everything became related. The old man who died controlled both sides under Gambino until he died. He even had his other brother-in-law whacked about thirty years ago. When old man Calabrese died, his brother-in-law, Romeo Menduni, took over. He's semi-retired. His son, Vincenzo Menduni, runs most of the businesses as far as we can tell. Paulie is his son. You won't mind what I'm about to say, Haley, but your soon-to-be ex-husband is a very minor lieutenant. You were the brains in the marriage, I have no doubt. What'd ya let some young girl, low self-esteem thing allow you to make a bad choice?" Joe said.

"You're very blunt, but you're pretty close. He was a nice guy. We met in college. His family was very nice. After a few years and all these single guys start hanging around and, well, that and our lousy marriage," Haley said.

"Jeez, Mark—I don't mean this as a reflection on you, Haley—but you can pick them. First Cathy, now this," Joe said.

Haley looked at me.

"My ex-wife dumped me while I was away at war. She embraced the diversity thing too literally and she took off to the west coast with an African-American gentleman. I learned about the relationship on social media while in Afghanistan," I said.

"That is terrible. I don't like this whole social media thing. It's gotten stupid," Haley said.

"C'mon. The steaks are ready," I said. I placed the salad and potatoes in front of us at the counter family-style, then I placed a steak in front of each of us and took a seat next to Haley.

"Let me begin with telling you that none of what we talked about makes a difference to me and, while Joe is a little rough around the edges, he has no issues either. He knows I'm a big boy and can take care of myself. To make it fair and even, Haley, maybe Joe should tell you about the night he lost his virginity on my beach and my parents caught him," I said.

"Jeez! I thought that story died a long time ago," Joe said shaking his head smiling at Haley.

#

We had a nice dinner. I got to know Haley better. I liked what I saw, but was it too soon? Joe . . . well, Joe is Joe. I just needed to keep him from getting drunk until we'd discussed the information I had.

"I'd like to have a shot of bourbon and to sit out on the outside living room couch. We have over an hour before I don't know what will happen, but fifteen-year-old girl bombs will fall. Haley, I have a blanket you can curl up with and a sweatshirt," I said.

"Thank you. It's such a nice room out there. I'll have a shot, too."

"Okay. I need not ask Joe." I poured three heavy shots and put them on the table. I got out three blankets just in case and carried them to the couch.

"Grab a shot. Oh, Joe. If you want a cigar there's a humidor full in the living room. I don't want one." I walked outside with Haley.

"You don't smoke cigars, do you?" Haley said.

"I do, but I'm currently not supposed to. Note, I had half a glass of wine with dinner. I'm not supposed to drink at all, but the doctors know that's not possible for a SEAL so I'm allowed one or two, but on a full stomach after plenty of other liquids."

We took a seat on the larger part of the U-shaped sectional couch. I sat near the corner of the couch with Haley next to me.

"Why do you have all the restrictions on alcohol?" Haley said.

"I had part of my intestines removed and rebuilt, and part of my liver removed. So, I can't drink like a fish, not that I ever did, and I must eat more often and take supplements. It's all mostly healed. It took a few tries to get it right. I just left the VA rehabilitation center this week. I've been in or around a hospital since a year ago January."

"Is it all right if I ask what happened?" Haley said.

"Yes. I was in a gunfight, and I took some shrapnel and got shot three times."

"Joe said four times."

"I got shot about eight years ago in a battle in Iraq a few months after I was stabbed by an insurgent while we busted into houses looking for bad guys. I got blown up in another battle over a year later in Iraq. A mortar landed near me, and the concussion blew me into a wall. I got peppered with rock, shrapnel and concrete but I kept fighting."

Haley looked at me with concern. "You know the people don't hear about all this you guys go through. If they did, we'd stop going to war."

"Well, I doubt that because history has shown that the people in our government do not care about us—citizens or military. I agree we should have been done a long time ago. We create bigger problems by staying too long and violating other country's sovereignty. That's a discussion for another time."

Joe came out with a cigar. "Nice Cubans. Where'd you get these?" Joe asked.

"Uncle Matt. He knows a guy," I said.

Joe sat on the other part of the couch and put his feet up. "I can't believe what your Mom did with this place. It's very nice. What will you do with the Oceanside house?"

"Keep it. It will remain a family home too. Once Lauren figures out her place in adulthood she and I will decide. If she does the design thing in New York, then she'll get the SoHo apartment and studio. I'll probably go to Oceanside once I start to work more, but maybe not. We'll see. I'll never sell this place. I might build another house next door, but further back," I said.

"What about the Miami condo?" Joe said.

"Now hold on here. Your name is MacKenzie, right, not that other billionaire, real estate mogul from New York City? How many homes do you own?" Haley asked.

"Lauren and I own four properties. The Manhattan apartment and studio, this house, and the lots here, the Oceanside house and a Miami Beach condo. I also own an oceanfront condo in Virginia Beach which is currently leased to a fellow SEAL officer and his wife."

"You seem to be okay then?"

"I'd prefer my parents to the real estate," I said.

"I'm sorry. I didn't mean for it to sound like that," Haley apologized as she placed her hand on my thigh.

"I know you didn't, but back to Joe's question. We'll keep them all until we decide what's doing."

At that moment Lauren came in with Kimberly.

"Hi, Ms. Menduni. Hi, Uncle Joe. How are you?" Lauren said.

"Hey, Squirt. I've missed you," Joe said as he hugged Lauren.

"Hi, Lauren. How was the movie?" Haley asked.

"Good," Lauren said.

"Mark. Can Kimberly stay over?" Lauren asked.

"Sure. Do I need to talk to her mother?"

"Yes," Lauren said as Kimberly passed me her phone.

"Hello."

"Hi. It's okay if she stays then?" Mrs. Schwartz said.

"Sure. It'll be a dry run for tomorrow," I said.

"Okay. You have my number if you need anything. They're good together. Kimberly is happy Lauren moved here full-time," Mrs. Schwartz said.

"Good. I have got them covered. I'll talk to you this weekend at some point. Bye."

"Bye, Mark."

"Ms. Menduni. Let me show you the house," Lauren said.

"The home is beautiful," Haley said as she walked off with Lauren and Kimberly.

#

"So, what did you learn from Cicola?"

I explained to Joe what Sergeant Cicola had told me as I handed him the documents.

"You look at this yet?" Joe said.

"No. Not yet. I haven't had a chance."

"Look at the name second from the bottom," Joe said passing the list to me.

It indicated Paul Menduni. My jaw clenched as I looked up at Joe.

"The question is what will Nassau do?" Joe said.

"He wants me to run the names. I believe he thinks that my father and these guys got mixed up in something. Here. Those are copies of the bearer bonds. They're issued by energy corporations. I haven't researched them thoroughly yet. Short, brief summaries were included in the material Matt provided me about the firm transactions. For instance, Michigan Energy Resources is just a buyer and seller of electricity. They produce nothing. Consumers sign up with them to get cheaper electricity and they enter into contracts with energy producers. They pay one bill to the producer thereby reducing the cost of servicing the accounts and collections, but the corporation, Michigan in this case, also buys cheap electricity from all over the country and moves it into the various markets. It competes in the ten regional electric power markets. It's like saying to the producers of electricity, 'I'll buy your excess energy and reroute it to other areas that need it,' then through power-sharing and distribution arrangements, controlled by these regional electric markets and independent system operators, the energy is moved though the major transmission lines. These companies buy and sell the electricity just like pork bellies and orange juice. The purpose is to bring down the cost of power to the consumer by fostering competition rather than relying on utility regulators. It got big after the California electricity crisis of 2000 and 2001. The Federal Energy Regulatory Commission, which is an independent agency under the Department of Energy, regulates the interstate transmission of electricity, natural gas, and oil."

"How do you know all this shit?" Joe said.

"I read. Anything to do with my father's business, I read about it. Just like other commodities, energy, electron flow measured in megawatts and gigawatts, is sold around the country. The firms that do it need capital to run and grow so they issue bonds. Sometimes small municipalities get together with one of these companies and issue bonds so the corporation will go out and buy them sufficient energy for their communities. These bonds are backed by agreements to sell and move energy around the country."

"Damn. I'm flipping houses to pad my retirement. What are we going to do?" Joe said.

"You're going to pull those records. I'm going to work on Monday with Uncle Matt."

"What about these two?" Joe said indicating the two men whose prints were on the car.

"I'll figure out something."

"Mark. Don't do this alone. I'll be there for you."

"I'll let you know when I need you. Can you get this stuff?" I handed Joe a list.

Joe nodded his head. "It'll cost a little bit though."

"How much?" I asked.

"Six or $7000."

"Be right back." I got up and walked to my room. I returned a couple minutes later with an envelope and handed it to Joe. "There's $10K in there in case I need more. I'll spend the next few days researching. I'd want to start surveillance by mid-week."

"You going to take these guys out?" Joe asked.

"I don't know yet."

"Hi!"

I turned to find Haley standing there. "Hi," I said as Haley scanned over the stuff on the table as Joe put it away in the file.

"Lauren said we're having ice cream."

"Oh? Okay. Where's Lauren?"

"Coming down. I can start dishing it," Haley said.

"Sure." I walked to the kitchen to put out the ice cream, chocolate syrup, and scoop, as Haley ran the scooper under hot water. Joe handed me the file.

"I'll get that from you later. Now what do we have here?"

CHAPTER 6

I awoke to the sea birds shrieking outside my window. I dragged myself into the shower. We stayed up late chatting away. Joe had too much to drink. He was asleep in the guest bedroom. Kimberly and Lauren were asleep in Lauren's bedroom. Haley went home. She had a good time. She'd be back with her son later today. I turned the water on and looked out over the bay. A nice sunrise was in progress. The weatherman had called for rain, but I thought not today.

It was still and calm on the bay except for the occasional wake left by fishing boats headed out for a day of fun or a day of work. I let the hot water fall on me while I woke up. I shampooed and lathered up to shave while the water fell on my back. Five minutes later I was toweling off. My day would be easy. I'd drive the girls to the outlets, shop for the things on Lauren's list, and spend the rest of the day at home.

I started coffee and took out eggs, pancake mix, and sausages and started the cook top griddle. I started frying the sausages and heating the griddle for pancakes. I knew Joe would eat about eight. I poured eight pancakes then heard a groan. I turned to see Joe rubbing his face.

"Coffee?" I said.

"Yeah. I can't drink like I used to," Joe said. I put a cup of coffee in front of him.

"Over-easy eggs?" I said.

"Yeah," Joe said as he sipped his coffee and looked out over the bay. I cracked four eggs into the pan and removed the pancakes from the griddle and plated them for Joe. I poured eight more pancakes. I placed Joe's pancakes in front of him with syrup and butter then flipped his eggs, removed them, and put them in front of him with the sausages.

"Go ahead. The girls won't be down for a bit." Joe dug in. I made some scrambled eggs for me then removed the pancakes from the griddle. I joined Joe at the counter. "You think over what we discussed?" I said.

"Yeah. I'm trying to figure out a way to make this easy. You want the top guy, don't you?"

"Yes. Those two take orders from someone. The car belongs to that bigger guy, and we know the other guy was at my parents' car. We don't know who else was in the car, if anyone. I want the person who ordered the hit. I have no doubt my parents were murdered now."

"You'll have to be careful. These guys are technologically sophisticated, too," Joe said.

"Hence the shopping list. I'll track and check their habits. I mean these clowns spend their days and some nights working for their boss, but they don't live there. I'll visit them at home at night. I'll get the answers I need."

"You be careful."

"I will. I'm in no hurry."

"I was thinking. You know Robert and Tony went into the computer security business. They started a tech company in Westbury. They get contracts to do DOD, CIA, and NSA work.

I spoke with Rob at your parents' funeral, and I saw them a few months later at a tech show. They might be able to help get into the computers these guys are using. They do stuff like attack the Chinese and Russian computers for those agencies I mentioned. Heck, they may be monitoring us now for all we know," Joe said as he looked around to emphasize his point.

"I'll call them."

"I'll copy all that stuff you gave me at the Copy & Print up the way. I'll drop it back by here after. I looked again last night. Cicola gave you a lot of information. The home addresses for those guys are in there," Joe said.

"We know where the boss is, and we know where they hang out. By tagging them with a GPS tracker I'll learn and verify all without exposing myself. The FBI is part of your old team?"

"Yeah."

"The surveillance run on the mob would come from the OCTF?"

"Yes. Why do you ask?"

"I don't want to be monitored by them, so I'll have to be very cautious and, frankly, I'm pretty sure DEA and Homeland Security are watching them, too, because of all the import business they do."

"That may be, but they're supposed to run everything through the FBI. Homeland has no function when it comes to organized crime and DEA, well, we all know about DEA. Don't forget, NYPD has their own special unit, too. Anything to do with organized crime, terror, or computers they go after. Most of these guys live in one of the boroughs. You know the old man has a big place up on Oyster Bay. His son and a couple of capos have big places too. The two who killed your parents live in Queens. Your girlfriend's husband lives down in Freeport Harbor. I Googled the address last night. He's right at the beginning of a wide canal on Baldwin Bay. Nice place for a young guy. His two goons are on the list, too. I'll get better pictures sent to you. You got a junk email address?"

"No emails. Too many details and a trail. Just print and courier the items to me. No trail."

"That's better. Good idea."

"Can you get me a dossier on Menduni and his goons?"

"I'll get one for all of them. I requested your firm's banking records. I'll likely have them Monday or Tuesday. You need to get your parents' cell phone records for the months before their deaths."

"Okay. What else?"

"You carrying?"

"Not legally. I applied for a concealed carry and the application is pending."

"I'll call and push it. Suffolk helps Southold do concealed carry. How long has it been?"

"Six months. I hired an attorney to write the application, too."

"I'll call and push it. Probably a couple of days."

I poured Joe more coffee. I heard some footsteps on the stairway. A moment later Lauren and Kimberly appeared.

"Good morning, Mark, Uncle Joe. Breakfast smells great."

"Give me a minute and yours will be ready. How many pancakes?" I asked.

The girls each indicated three. Joe put up four fingers. He was still hungry.

#

By 8 a.m. the girls began to arrive. By 8:30 a.m. all were present. I met the mothers or fathers of each girl. We exchanged cell numbers. I got the look-over by the parents as they thought me young for a father of a fifteen-year-old until I explained I was Lauren's brother. By 9 a.m. we were on the road to Riverhead. Joe had gone to copy the file.

Driving through the Long Island wine country was always nice. I could see the vineyards were in bloom along with the flower fields adding to the beautiful scent in the air as we drove highway NY-25. The winemakers, vintners, or grape farmers, I could never recall the difference between them, were out doing whatever they did to their vines. The flower farmers were cutting flowers. The sunflower fields were growing, though not yet in bloom. I loved this area. The drive was about 22 miles but would take about forty-five minutes due to the speed limit and traffic.

I drove into the center mass of stores and parked. "We leave here at 12:45 p.m. I will food shop during the last hour we're here, so I will have perishables with me so we cannot dawdle after that. Everyone stay together. You all have my number."

Lauren was smiling at me.

"What?"

"You're so not a parent, but you care. We'll get you trained up, big brother," Lauren said.

"Bye, Mark," they all said in unison as they departed the Yukon.

So not a parent? What did that mean? I needed to talk to Haley or Mrs. Schwartz to figure some of this out. I walked to a coffee shop and got a medium black coffee. I thought about the Dodge dealer we'd passed on the way here. I got into my Yukon and drove to the Dodge dealer. They had what I wanted per their website. I strolled into the dealership and was met by a salesman.

"Hello. Can I help you?"

"Yes. I want to check out the Challenger Hellcat," I said.

"Yes, sir."

He showed me to a black one in the showroom then we took an orange one for a ride. It ripped. It had an eight-speed ZF transmission and all the bells and whistles. It's a big car so it was fun in the corners, but on the highway, it moved out. We returned to the dealer and wrote up a deal for the shiny black one in the showroom. They'd detail it and deliver it to the house for me.

I drove back to the mall, purchased another coffee and took in the sights. It was just 11:30 a.m. I sat while people-watching as they went about their day. My phone buzzed.

"Hello."

"It's Joe. I'm done with the copying. I put the file back in the house. I'll call you later with what I get. Bye."

"Bye."

I sipped my coffee wondering where I'd go with the information about my parents' deaths. I watched the people go by as I zoned for a bit before I shopped. I walked to the food store. Fifty-five minutes later I was out of there loading the back of the Yukon. A moment later my phone buzzed.

"Hello."

"Can you pick us up by the J.Crew store?" Lauren said.

"I'm on my way. Did you get everything you needed?" I asked.

"Yes. We'll see you in a minute. Bye."

"Bye." I drove around to the J.Crew store. As I pulled up, the girls came out each carrying bags in their hands. They climbed in and we were on our way.

Arriving at the house was a bit of a free-for-all. I directed the girls to the grocery bags before they ran off. It was nearly 2 p.m. so I left out the hotdogs, sausages, and salad ingredients. I started the water boiling for their potatoes and pasta.

The girls came into the room as one large chattering group and they set about their tasks. They chatted, used their cell phones, tried on clothing, or showed off what they bought. They were fascinating creatures to watch.

A knock at the door produced the detailer kid with my red and black key fobs for my Challenger.

"Thank you for delivering it. It looks nice," I said.

"It's a sick car, mister. It really moves," the kid said.

"Thank you. I appreciate your help," I said as I tipped him.

"If you ever need it or that Yukon detailed, please call. I'll do a good job. Here's my card," the kid said.

"I'll call you."

"Bye."

Lauren came down the steps and saw the car. "It's hot. Two very cool vehicles in one week. Do you have extra pillows in your closet?" Lauren said.

"I don't know. I'll look. How many do you need?"

"Just two."

"I can scrape that up, I'm sure. Go do your cooking. Let me know when to start the sausages and hotdogs. I'll toast the rolls. I have some olive oil and butter for that, too."

"Ooh sounds good. I think we'll be ready in an hour or so."

"You're the boss."

I was about to walk upstairs when I heard Haley pulling up in her car. She parked where I'd directed her to yesterday. Haley and Paulie got out and came up the stairs.

"Hi," I said.

"Hi. Looks like you made it through a seven girl shopping trip," Haley said.

"I managed. Hey, Paulie. How are you?"

"Good. I caught a big fish with my Grandpa yesterday."

"You did? What did you do with it?"

"We cleaned it and we'll eat it someday. It's in the freezer with the other fish."

"Good for you."

"Who's new car?" Haley said.

"Mine."

"Nice hotrod. Can I go for a ride in it?"

"Sure. I'll take you later, perhaps. C'mon in. Would you like something to drink? I picked up a few nice North Fork wines today," I said as Paulie ran into the house.

"A little later. I'll just have iced water with lemon if I may."

"Sure." I escorted Haley into the house. Paulie was already the center of attention with the girls. I squeezed in and got iced water with lemon and an unsweet iced tea for me. I brought Haley her drink while all the girls said hello to Haley—Ms. Menduni to them.

"All I will do is grill. The chatty bunch will handle everything else. We can relax."

"Terrific. My mother knew your mother."

"Oh? How?"

"There used to be an artists' sidewalk show as part of the Maritime Festival years ago in Cutchogue that turned into a designer, artists, and sculptors show, too. Your mother participated, and my mother hired her to redo her house. That was almost five years ago. They spent over a month redoing it. Not a major renovation. Just new cabinets, counters, and appliances, new paint, décor, furniture, windows, and flooring. I wondered about it when I was here last night. Your Mom's use of area rugs, the cool trim colors, and the clean, uncluttered cabinets. She designed a lift-up garage for the counter appliances for my Mom. My mother didn't know about your mother's passing. She expresses her sorrow at that news. They were the same age. She told me how your mother told her she was so worried about you. This was after you'd been shot the first time. My mother was against the war by then and your mother said she had a hard time believing it was still necessary for it to be going on so long. Anyway, I just wanted to let you know. My Mom feels like she already knows you."

"Good. I'm glad to know my mother has happy clients."

"Your mother was very talented."

"She was."

"I can't get over how nice this house is," Haley said as we sat on the outdoor couch.

"I received a package in the mail today from my lawyer. Paul signed the property settlement. He didn't want to sell the Freeport house on Prospect Street, so he must pay me half of its value. Per my attorney, Paul stupidly paid it off four months before we separated. He must pay child support for Paulie, and he must pay all the bills. I should get more than enough to build a house on the lot next to my parents. I will also get a one-time payment of $900,000 for the business by the end of September. Oh, and he must pay for my attorney and college for Paulie. His father would do that anyway," Haley said.

"Tell me about the house. It's in Freeport?" I said.

"Yes. On the water. It's on two lots down by those older waterfront homes just a few blocks or canals over to the west from the Nautical Mile with the seafood markets and restaurants."

"That's Baldwin Bay he's on. My Oceanside house is on Parsonage Cove just around the peninsula to the west. Good. When will you be divorced?"

"I go to a hearing in Mineola next week."

"Good for you. Sounds like a long time coming."

"It has been. It's been tough with Paulie, but his father is a sociopath. You saw. You were right last night when you were speaking about the boat and us women. I was blind. It took a few years to see what was going on, the late nights, the women, the drugs—selling, not using, the men always around. My father-in-law and grandfather-in-law tried to talk me out of the divorce. His sister threatened me. I just needed to get away."

"Did you ever see any bad things?"

"No. I'd hear things that bothered me. I didn't know enough to tell anyone."

"I'm sorry you had to go through that."

"Can I ask you something, and will you be honest with your answer?" Haley said.

"Yes, if I can, with due regard to national security."

"Last night, I saw a picture on the table. I recognized the man. He's one of my grandfather-in-law's guys. Why did Joe have his picture or why was he showing it to you?"

"National security question. I don't think I can honestly speak to you about it."

"But . . . you don't work . . . why would Joe have that picture here, or did you have it?"

I contemplated what I could say. My gut instinct said to speak with Haley about it while my logical brain kept saying *operational security*.

"Haley, I barely know you, but what I do know of you I like very much. I don't want to lie to you, and I don't want you to lie to me. Look, I never thought I'd even be interested in spending time with a woman this soon after my last marriage. Then you came along and pleasantly disrupted that whole thought. If I'm honest with you, will you be honest with me?"

"Yes. Mark, I wasn't looking either. When I walked into the office the other day, I nearly fell when I saw you. When you smiled at me my heart skipped. I won't lie to you, and I'll answer your questions."

"Hold on. Lauren. How long before I start cooking?" I said.

"We're a little behind. An hour, maybe?"

"Okay. Haley and I are going to take a walk on the beach."

"Okay."

"Come on." I reached my hand out to Haley, who took it, and she followed me down the steps. We walked across the low dunes to the beach. There was a slight breeze blowing, but it was nice and sunny, the sun midway to the horizon in the western sky.

"Haley, my parents didn't die in a car accident. They were murdered. The evidence, and don't ask me what and how, is very strong that the man you saw in the picture and another man ran my parents off the road. Joe and I, on our own, are investigating. Next week I'll start digging. Joe is helping on his off-duty time. The Nassau officer has given me enough leads to run an intel op on these guys. At least two men killed my parents, but neither of them ordered it. Someone else did. I'm going after that person."

"I am so sorry, Mark. You just put a face on all the whispers and rumors. I feel so bad for Lauren and you."

"It's not your fault," I said as I squeezed her hand. Haley pulled me to her and reached up to kiss me. I held her to me and kissed her back. It was a good first kiss for both of us.

"Mark. I'll tell you whatever I can. I don't know much, but just ask away."

"Do you still have a key to your old house?"

Haley looked at me, searching my eyes for something. "Yes. I do. I have keys for everything, even his restaurant. If he didn't cooperate, I would have turned them over to . . . well, I don't know to whom? My attorney, I suppose."

"Does he know you have them?"

"The house, of course, but not the restaurant or his storage spaces. I have a key to his father's house, too, but there's always someone there."

"I'd like to borrow them. I take it you've been in your father-in-law's home?"

"Many times. It's on the water in Glen Cove. It's on a fifty plus acre island called Dosoris. He owns the island."

"What about the grandfather's house?"

"I don't have a key, but I've been there many times. His home is a huge mansion on Oyster Bay not very far from his son's home. The property is comprised of many properties that were subdivided then the grandfather purchased them one after another until he'd assembled a huge parcel of land with many homes, even other mansions sitting on the land."

"Grandpa Menduni is the patriarch since Calabrese and Gambino died those years ago?"

"Yes. It's a little complicated, but as I understand it, Calabrese, with help from the Menduni clan, took over the Gambino and another family's business, as they euphemistically refer to it. When old man Calabrese died, he had no sons who were alive. My husband's grandfather, Romeo, who was married to old man Calabrese's sister, took over. Then, his son, my father-in-law, took over most of the businesses. Vincenzo Menduni runs the day-to-day things and, I think, all the legitimate businesses. The big issues still go to his father, but I don't know much more. I do know that Vincenzo and his father, Romeo, do not agree on much, and they have a strained relationship. Romeo is in his late seventies. He golfs every day, exercises, fishes on his boat and he frequently hangs out at Paulie's restaurant and another restaurant in Queens. There's a huge corner table at Tito's that is always reserved for them."

"The guy in the picture . . . I'll show you what I have later . . . who does he work for?"

"Romeo Menduni."

"Are you able to identify the old man's lieutenants?"

"Most of them. They're all middle-aged guys who have been with him a long time. Some have been to prison then a few years later they're back."

"This is going to be easier than I thought."

"What are you going to do?"

"I'm going to go in and get evidence that they killed my parents," I said.

"Oh, Mark, that will be dangerous."

"I know. Let's go hang out with the kids. We'll talk some more this week. Why don't we plan on going out for dinner on Wednesday night? Just you and me. Lauren can watch Paulie if need be."

"Okay. Casual or dressy?"

"Dressy. I'll wear a nice suit."

"Ooh! I can't wait," Haley said.

CHAPTER 7

"I may be home late. Mrs. Schwartz said she'll drop you off tonight or you can stay with Kimberly. I'll call you as soon as I'm near home. Okay?"

"Don't worry, Mark. I've been by myself before," Lauren said.

"Ah, but that was while in the care of experienced parents. I, my dear, have never even changed a diaper."

"You never changed mine?"

"Nope. By the time you were left alone with me you were potty-trained. Heck, you were walking at ten months of age."

"Okay. Nice car. I like," Lauren said. I pulled to the curb and let Lauren out. Haley was directing cars. Lauren walked past Haley and said something. Haley turned toward me, smiled, and waved. I waved back. I was already smiling.

I drove down NY-25 and headed to Manhattan because I like to do stupid things. The plain fact of the matter was I wanted to be able to get going when I wanted to. I was in no hurry. It was 8:30 a.m. when I entered Manhattan. I drove to the firm near Wall Street, but it's still far enough north that it's not in the real mess. I valeted the car today only because I wasn't sure where to park. Parking was *free* to our employees, but we paid for it in our lease. I took the elevator up. I brought along a briefcase in case Uncle Matt gave me some more reading material. I got off at the eighteenth floor and walked to the receptionist's station.

"Good morning. I'm here to see Matthew MacKenzie," I said.

The lady smiled then did a double-take.

"Are you Mr. Mark MacKenzie?"

"I am."

"Just one moment, sir." She spoke into her headset. A moment later, a very nice looking, young woman came out.

"Mr. MacKenzie. Right this way, sir." I followed her through a cypher-locked door down a hallway to my uncle's office.

"Mark. How are you doing?" Uncle Matt said as he stood to hug me.

"I'm good."

"Coffee or something?"

"Coffee is fine. Black."

"Margie. Black coffee for Mr. MacKenzie."

"Yes, sir." I noticed Matt watch her leave. He caught me watching him.

"I can look, right? Sit. Sit. Did you drive in?"

"I did. I won't all the time, but today it was fine."

"I'm glad you came in. Dad, your grandfather, has plans for us, but you know that. You have an office, your father's old office. If you want to change anything, just ask Margie. We use a designer who apprenticed or interned—whatever they call it—with your mother. Your mother designed all this."

"Then my father's office would be specially designed by mother. I'll order a new chair since Dad and I are different builds, but that's it."

"All right. Already saving the firm money."

Margie returned with my coffee. I stood for her and accepted the coffee.

"Thank you, Margie."

"You're welcome, sir," she said as she departed.

"At 10 a.m., I'll introduce you to the rest of the officers and the brokers. Some of them will love you. Some will not. Mostly, they loved your father. There were a few who were lukewarm, even hostile, but they all did what they were supposed to do," Matt said.

"Who gives us problems?"

"Allan Rizzo is a bit of a problem. He's brought in a few bad deals. He's brought in some deals that were outright fraud. Rizzo is head of the faction that owns 20% of the firm's stock. It may be that they're not all model citizens. When your grandfather's old partner died, we agreed to allow his widow to sell his shares to Rizzo and his family group. We did our due diligence, but we should have done more. It happened right after the bottom fell out of the real estate market. Then all that other too-big-to-fail BS with the big banks and insurance companies on Wall Street. I think it was in 2009 or 2010 they bought in. Rizzo came in here a young fellow . . . NYU, Wharton . . . good academic creds. He was young with no background good or bad. He came right out and said he was buying eight percent of the shares. The other twelve percent would be purchased by his family members, but that he would buy them out after a few years. Grandpa's friend's wife vouched for them, and things were fine until about three years ago. Rizzo suddenly gets sloppy in a deal. Your father covered it. We have good reserves and good E&O insurance so we're okay for the most part. Your father had a talk with the kid. I learned later that there was a meeting, and some of Rizzo's family members who owned the shares came. I wasn't there. Secretaries told me. I don't know what happened, but Rizzo wasn't fired. Then it happened again. Then, another deal came in that was pure fraud. Will caught it and had it out with Rizzo. Rizzo pushed your father. Now, we're not little guys, but your father held back and walked away. That was about two years ago. I've been through the records, and I can't find anything wrong. None of the deals in the past year have soured so I can't say, but I'm not my brother. Your grandfather and two other guys built this business, but your father made it work and produce. He was sharp, and he could sell. Will liked to show the flag, and he made people feel comfortable. Your dad made us the top or next best brokerage house. However, something happened that you need to figure out. Look, Mark, I'm not president material. I'm smart enough to recognize my limitations. Grandpa is too old, and Grandma wouldn't let him come back anyway. I'm doing it, but I'm killing my health. I'm over 300 pounds, I have high blood pressure, and I don't sleep worrying about the business. It's not the day-to-day shit I worry about too much. As I said, I know my limitations. There is a problem that is strategic in nature, and I'm unable to put my finger on it."

I just listened to my uncle talk. He continued after sipping his water.

"Mark, you already know you'll be made president. Grandpa will remain chairman of the board for a little while longer. You have a seat on the board. I have a seat on the board. We have a few advisory members of the board, but they're a bunch of old guys Grandpa has known a long time. They get to come to the city every quarter with their wives for dinner, a hotel room, and a meeting. It's perfunctory, and they always do what Grandpa wants. All their seats expire in September. They've been automatically renewed all these years. Will wanted to curtail all that old-school stuff. Grandma wants Grandpa off the board, and I think he's ready. You're his hope since Will died. Grandpa is just thinking of his legacy— MacKenzie Securities, Inc.—is what I think, but so what. You can do what you want to do. We gotta go to our 10 a.m. meeting. Anything to say about what I said?"

"Not yet. Let's go meet the team," I said.

"Okay. Thanks for coming in today."

#

We walked into the conference room. Standing before the table were seven men and a woman.

"Everyone, please sit. This is my nephew, Mark. Some of you have met him over the years, but for clarity, I'll introduce each of you. Starting to my left is Jason Aarons, our Chief Marketing and Media Officer. Next to him is Steven Frank, our Chief Information Systems Officer. Next to him is Marsha Collette, our HR and Administration Officer. Seated next to Marsha is Ira Goldman, Chief Broker; at that end, there is Allan Rizzo, broker; Harry Train, broker; then Harvey Silver, broker; and finally, Michael Marino, broker. Davis Middleton and Paul Campari are on vacation or training. Mark, this is the team."

I observed each person look at me as they were introduced. They smiled as I nodded, except Rizzo and Train, who were putting on an air of arrogant indifference. Rizzo is a little older than me and Train is my age. Everyone else was much older, in their late forties to sixties. All the Jewish guys were Matt's age, mid-fifties or older. Collette was a nice-looking, blonde woman who appeared more professional in dress and manner than the rest of the group. Collette seemed very familiar to me. I was friendly with Goldman, Silver, and Frank as they'd been around since I was in high school. We'd been to Ranger, Mets, and Knicks games together.

"Mark will be visiting and working his way into the driver's seat over the next few months. I know he doesn't mind my saying he just left the hospital after more than a year of recovery from a few bullet wounds. Mark was a Navy SEAL," Matt said.

Everyone looked at me. I stood.

"Thank you for your welcome. I've been impressed with what I have seen and read about over the past year or so. I look forward to working with you all. I'll meet with you after I've reviewed your work product. I'm doing this not to check you but to check me. I will look over every transaction so I can get a feel for how we do business. I'm sure my review will cause me to ask questions. Again, that is so I can learn. I hope I can be half as good as my father was here. I've reviewed the past quarter's sales statements and you folks are impressive. I appreciate it. Matt appreciates it and I know my Dad would appreciate it, too. Thank you. I've taken enough of your time. Have a good day," I said.

Rizzo and Train were not smiling, but the others were all smiles. Mr. Aarons approached me and shook my hand.

"Welcome aboard. I'm an old navy guy myself," Mr. Aarons said.

"It's great to meet you, Mr. Aarons." Mr. Silver and Mr. Frank came over and we shook hands.

"Good to see you again. You look terrific," Mr. Frank said.

"Thanks. Nice seeing you guys again," I said.

The rest of the group filtered by, and we made small talk, except for Rizzo and Train who left the room. I followed Matt to his office. Ms. Collette joined us.

"Marsha. Who do you want to be Mark's secretary?"

"I was thinking Bernice if she'll do it," Marsha said.

Bernice was my father's secretary.

"And as his assistant?" Matt said.

"Clara. She's sharp and she knows who here lies. Bernice and Clara together have knowledge of everything," Marsha said.

"How many in total are we?" I asked.

"Sixty-eight full-time employees and two part-time, disabled employees who are primarily used in mail, bulk copying, printing and binding," Marsha said.

"How long have you been with the firm, Marsha?" I said.

"Your mother made your father hire me as his secretary a couple years after he got into the business. When he moved jobs, I went with him," Marsha said.

"She 'made' him hire you? There's a story there," I said.

"Your mother and I were close friends. We grew up together, though I'm younger by three years. I knew your father, too. I was pregnant and unmarried at the time. You were a little guy then. I had no education beyond high school, no prospects, and no medical insurance. Your Dad hired me. I love your Mom and Dad so much. They're loss broke my heart," Marsha said.

"Marsha has been here longer than me. She and Bernice are our old timers," Matt said.

"Well, I appreciate it, Marsha. So, you're a trusted henchman. I'll meet with you when you have a moment. I saw Bernice at the funeral," I said. Marsha looked at Matt.

"It's okay, Marsha. Mark. You didn't see Marsha there because she was so heartbroken. She couldn't go to the funeral or burial. She spoke to me about it beforehand," Matt said.

"That's fine. We all handle grief differently. After what I have experienced, I have no interest in judging how another person grieves," I said.

"You're taking a late lunch with your aunt, Missy. Do you want to meet Bernice and Clara now?" Matt said.

"Sure, if they're available."

"C'mon. I'll bring them to your office. Follow me."

I followed Marsha to my father's office. Except for not one paper in sight, Dad's office looked like it did the last time I was here about ten years ago. I was on leave after SQT. I made the rounds in my dress blues, Dad showing off his Navy Officer son. There was a picture of my mother and father on the shelf by the window. I picked it up. They were on an anniversary cruise. They left me at home by myself for a week. My mother said my father was a nervous wreck. All I did was surf, eat out every night, and work on my car in the new garage. I think I was sleeping in the living room during that time because of construction inside the house. Joe and I surfed every day and I bought him dinner each night. My parents had each given me $500, unbeknownst to the other. Joe and I ate good that week.

"Hi, Mark."

I turned to see Bernice.

"Hi, Bernice. How are you?" I said.

"I thought I was good but seeing you there . . . you look like your father," Bernice said with a note of sadness to her tone as I took her hand. Bernice is in her late fifties.

"Sit down, please," I said as I helped her into a chair. I sat on the corner of the desk. "Will you be my secretary, Bernice?" I asked.

"Yes. I'd be very happy to be. I'd be honored."

"Nonsense. I'd be honored. I'll need a lot of help, but I won't be full-time for a couple of years, perhaps longer. I'm taking care of Lauren."

"I know. What will you do?"

"I will likely work a couple of days a week. I don't want to telecommute because I don't want to work at home."

Clara walked in. Clara is a few years my junior. Her title would be administrative assistance to the president, my *Girl Friday*. Clara worked for my father for almost a year before he died.

"Hi, Clara. I'm Mark. Please sit."

Clara sat next to Bernice. I looked at Clara then to Bernice, who nodded affirmatively.

"Clara. Will you be my administrative assistant?"

Clara looked at me with surprise, then to Bernice who smiled.

"Yes, sir. I mean, absolutely," Clara said.

"Okay. My job is to learn to lead this firm. I've spent the past year reading anything and everything I could about the business and this firm. I have two goals. First, to be able to earn enough money for everyone to get paid, save for retirement, and receive regular pay increases and bonuses and, second, to have a nice place to work where people want to be here. I'll need you two to help me and educate me. Okay?"

Both women nodded.

"I'll be very part-time for the next few months, one or two days per week, maybe more. I won't work from my home, but I will communicate with you two. Matt is the boss. I'll take my orders from him until a change is made. For now, the only changes in this office will be a new chair and from the looks of it a new computer and telephone. Can you arrange that, Bernice?"

"Certainly," Bernice said.

"I presume you'll take the ante office there, Bernice, and Clara, you'll have that office off to the side, correct?"

"Yes," they said together.

"I know while I'm transitioning, you'll do some other things, perhaps what you're doing now. Wherever you're comfortable, but I want you to keep what you do for me separate and distinct from other work. Moreover, I want it kept confidential. That means while working for me you'll be up here. We call it OPSEC and need-to-know in the navy. Understand?"

They nodded.

"Bernice. What do you do now?" I said.

"I supervise the production of the various documents and booklets each broker drafts, I supervise the secretaries and receptionists, and I assist Marsha. I'm next in line under Marsha on the HR and Administration side of the house," Bernice said.

"What do you do, Clara?"

"I'm the special assistant to the president and vice-president. Barbara is your Uncle Matt's long-time assistant. I've been doing things that cover a wide range of subjects," Clara said.

"What's your degree in?" I said.

"English—liberal arts. I started work on an MBA in finance but quit after six months. My time here was more valuable. Your father taught me more than I learned in school."

"Are you research savvy?"

"Yes," she replied.

I looked at Bernice.

"I am, too. I'm good on computers," Bernice said, then laughed.

"It's almost your lunchtime. . ." I trailed off as the ladies shook their heads.

"No. We go at 1 p.m. We cover here while the others are at lunch," Bernice said.

"Oh. Then tell me what concerns you?"

Bernice looked at Clara who looked up while she thought.

"I think we're being monitored," Clara said.

Bernice nodded in agreement.

"We don't know who is doing it. We didn't ask your uncle because we don't know whether he ordered it or not," Clara said.

"What makes you say so? Just a second," I said as I turned on the radio and the TV.

"Go ahead."

Clara looked at Bernice.

"People have gone through our desks and have been on our computers. I feel like we're being watched," Bernice said.

"Someone put keystroke logger software on my computer and on Barbara's computer," Clara said.

"How do you know?" I said.

"I've done computers my whole life. I could have gone into IT, but I got a more useful degree in my opinion," Clara said with a smile.

"You checked with IT to find it?" I said.

"No. I found it myself. When I looked it up on my home computer my suspicions were confirmed. When I told IT

144

something was wrong, my computer was slow, they said nothing was wrong. Sir, they should have found the software by one of several ways," Clara said.

"Do they know you know computers?" I asked.

"No."

"Let's keep it that way and between us. Did Mr. Frank tell you there was nothing wrong with your computer?"

"No. Jeff Taylor did. He's one of the techs. We were hired around the same time."

"Go on about your day. Do you both have smartphones?" I asked.

"Yes, but we're not to use them during work hours per firm policy," Clara said.

"Bernice, draft a memo to my uncle from me. Re: cell phone use by you and Clara while I transition as it benefits our limited time together, blah, blah, blah. Give me your numbers. Here's mine. Bernice, Clara, I want you to text me anytime you see something wrong or odd."

Clara nodded and wanted to say something.

"What, Clara?"

"Can you come to Matt's office right now?" Clara said.

"Sure. Why?"

"I'm pretty sure someone is watching him from across the street."

I looked out the window. Matt's office is on the other corner of the building, but on the same side. I found my father's binoculars.

"Same floor?" I said.

"Yes. Three windows from the building party wall," Clara said.

The angle was almost too great, but she was right. There was a telescope or telephoto camera lens near the window.

"How long have they been there?" I asked.

"At least six months, but I'm not sure," Clara said.

"Did you tell Matt?"

"Yes. Matt said, 'They'll have a long, boring day watching me,'" Clara said.

"Is that a business building?"

"It is, but the building information board lists that office as vacant."

"You're quite the investigator. I'd like IT to install my computer. Bernice, would you arrange that for me, please? I'd like a nice new computer and two flat-screen monitors. Let me know if they send Taylor. Can you tell me the name of the closest and best pizza delivery?"

"That's easy. Mario's Palermo Pizza," Clara said.

"Thank you. See you in an hour or so," I said.

#

I walked to my uncle's office. I confirmed that someone was looking at the building.

I rode the elevator to the first floor, got out and crossed the street. I entered the building. The information board indicated two vacancies on the eighteenth floor. I called Mario's and ordered a large pizza to go. It'd be ready in ten minutes. I rode the elevator to the eighteenth floor. I located the door to the vacant office. There was no sign on the door. I could hear breathing and I smelled cigarette smoke. I thought they banned cigarette smoking in New York City along with large soft drinks?

I departed the building for Mario's. I paid for the pizza, and purchased a black T-shirt and ball cap. The T-shirt had a chef holding a large pizza on the front and the ball cap simply stated *Mario's Pizza*. How cheesy!

I returned to the building, rode the elevator to the eighteenth floor, put the T-shirt on over my suit and put the ball cap on my head pulled down low. In front of the vacant office, I announced in a loud voice, "Hey. Anyone want a discount pizza? Some dope stiffed me." I knocked on the door. "Hey, any of you secretaries want a half-price pizza? Eight bucks." I made sure I was facing away, but the guy could see the hat and shirt. I heard the door unlatch and he partially opened the door. "Hey, you want a pizza?" I said as he opened the door all the way, and too late, realized his mistake. I kicked him in the groin and shoved him into the office. I hit him in the solar plexus and knocked him out with a right jab just below his left ear. It appeared he was alone. I placed the pizza on a table then quickly tied his hands and feet with the window blinds sash cord. I stuffed his handkerchief in his mouth. After making a security sweep of the office, I searched the guy and found a Beretta 9mm. I walked to his observation post. Let's see, a Nikon digital camera with telephoto lens, a tablet computer, a smartphone, a pack of cigarettes, a lighter and an ashtray. I checked his jacket and found a bifold wallet with credit cards, a New York Driver's license, some cash, a few other cards. I tossed his wallet on the table. I plugged in the cord for the camera and downloaded the pictures to the tablet then wiped the remainder of the camera's memory. I took the smartphone and removed the battery and placed both in my pocket. I grabbed a slice because it smelled so good, and I have no willpower when it comes to pizza. I removed the handkerchief from his mouth and laid him out on the floor. I found a coffee mug and filled it with water. I took off the T-shirt, soaked it in water. While doing so, I noticed a plastic trash can next to the sink. I filled it with water.

I finished my slice and rejoined the guy. I poured the cup of water on the guy's face. As soon as he began to spit and sputter, I covered his face with the wet T-shirt and clamped it over his face and nose with my left hand.

"Now, I'm not going to fuck around here. Who do you work for?" I said.

"I don't know. . ."

I clamped down harder while I poured more water on the T-shirt over his mouth and nose. He struggled, but it was useless. After about thirty seconds I stopped and released my grip.

"Now, let's try this again. Who do you work for?"

"Please. I don't know. . ."

I clamped down over his nose, and this time, I dipped a cup of water from the garbage can and slowly poured it on the T-shirt over his mouth. He struggled and flailed about. That's why strapping the interviewee to a board was less taxing on the interviewer. Hence the name *water-boarding*. After a long, slow pour, I stopped. He was crying now, the pussy, after just two tries. He wouldn't even make air force survival school.

"Last chance," I said as he gasped and choked. After a moment, he spoke.

"All I know is I get instructions by email. I photograph and report what I see and what I'm told to photograph," he gasped.

"Who were you told to photograph?"

"The guy in the office on the eighteenth floor, in the corner office, across the street."

"How long have you been doing this?" I dribbled water on him to remind him.

"No. Don't. This is my seventh or eighth month. It's in my tablet; look at it."

"How are you paid?"

"A $10,000 package of cash each month to my post office box."

"Have you done this work for this individual before?" He hesitated. I dribbled water on him as I clamped down on his nose.

"No. Wait, ugh. . ."

He was getting very whiny now. I'd do this for 40 seconds this time so he would learn. I enjoyed SERE school. I was water-boarded, and it can be scary, but one must just relax and think they will not die and not struggle. The instructors won't kill you. I released my grip.

"Now get it together. You're going to give yourself a heart attack and since you smoke, shit, anything can happen. Have you done this work before for this individual?"

"Yes. I photographed the other guy. In the other corner office and, the same guy and his wife, I figure, at a loft in SoHo," he gasped out.

"When did you start and stop photographing the other man and woman?"

"About Christmas time two years ago, and I stopped about a year ago this month. I guess I watched him for five or six months. It's in my tablet."

His answer matched with my parents' deaths.

"What do you do for a living?"

"Is that a trick question? Dis is what I do."

"Why do you have a weapon?"

"Because, as you can see, it sometimes gets dangerous for me. Are you going to kill me?"

"I'll ask the questions. Have you ever worked for this entity before, photographing the other guy and his wife?"

"No. I do mainly catching people screwing off on their spouses or faking disability claims. I don't know what they're doing with these two, well, now one. The other guy ain't been around since last year, but both are clean. They never touched another woman."

That was nice to hear.

"Here's the deal. I'm going to let you live. You'll keep doing this, but I'm going to periodically contact you and you'll make a report to me. If you lie. . . well, let's see, Anthony De Benedetto, look at all the ways I can find you, credit cards, driver's license. . . Oh, you commute from Brooklyn. I hear traffic is a bitch on the Brooklyn Bridge. I'll find you and we'll do this in a toilet bowl next time. Any questions for me?"

"No, sir."

"Now if you mention this to anyone, same thing—I kill you and you'd be easy, too. Just one cup of water. Think about that when you brush your teeth each morning."

"I got it. Yes."

"I didn't see a concealed carry permit in your wallet. I'm going to save your life by keeping your weapon. You could have been shot with it today. You'd be just another statistic for liberals against the Second Amendment. If you cooperate, I'll return it to you in a few months. Oh. I'll send your tablet and smart phone back by runner in about an hour. Will you be here?"

"Yes."

"I'll have them delivered. Be careful opening the door. Always know who is there. I'll have the runner say, 'Delivery from Mr. Smith.' Fair enough?"

"Yes."

"How'd you get into this place?"

"They mailed me a key for this office and another empty office on the other side of the building."

"How do you advertise?"

"Yellow Pages, word of mouth."

"The pizza is free since I ate a slice."

I pulled out my Swiss Army knife.

"I'll cut you loose. Do not move for five minutes. If you do, well, you know."

I began to pour water on him as I clamped his nose shut. Just ten-seconds. He struggled and flailed about. He was scared. I wiped the cup clean, dropped the ball cap, cut the cord, and walked out. I was in the elevator in 14 seconds. I took it to the top floor, got out, walked across the building to the other side and took another elevator down. I was on the street and walking to the firm, thinking, *I should have grabbed another slice.*

#

I entered my office. Someone was installing a new computer.

"Good afternoon, Mr. MacKenzie."

"Good afternoon. Who are you?"

"Jeff Taylor."

"What do you have for me?"

"Your computer. It's brand new with two monitors as you requested."

"Anything special I need to know?"

"No, sir. I can show you how to log on . . ."

"Is it standard stuff?"

"Yes."

"What's my temporary log-in password?"

"The last four digits of your social security number."

"How long is the temporary good for?"

"Thirty days or five days after you log in. It will prompt you to change when you log on."

"There is no special keystroke logger or spyware on it, is there?"

Taylor hesitated a second. "No, sir."

"How about the phone? No copying or software tracking the telephone numbers dialed other than the provider's billing? No digital recording of the phone calls?"

"I don't think so, but I only installed it."

"Thanks. I appreciate the fast service. You finished?"

"I am. Uh, okay, I'll be seeing you, sir."

"Bye."

As soon as Taylor departed the room, I unplugged the computer and phone. I walked to Bernice's office.

"Aren't you going to lunch?" I said.

"No. I brought mine, but I'd stay for that show I just heard any day. Right, Clara?"

"You were great," Clara said.

"He'll be back in a bit. I unplugged the phone and computer."

"Your sleeve is wet," Clara said.

"Bathroom accident. Why aren't you at lunch?" I said.

"I saw you come in then heard you talking with Taylor."

"Ah. Would you call Uncle Matt and ask him to come to my office, please?"

"Yes, sir." I walked back into my office and looked around. I looked at the TV, and old-style cathode ray tube television on an entertainment center. Using my Swiss Army knife, I proceeded to dismantle the TV. As I removed the last screw on the TV, Matt walked in.

"What are you doing?" Matt said.

I pulled the back cover off and looked inside. Where a second speaker should have been, there was a digital, wireless camera with its own battery backup which was spliced to a DC wire to maintain a charge. I ripped the camera out. I walked to the radio and turned it on.

"Sit, Uncle Matt." I pointed at a chair. I sat on the corner of the desk.

"Matt, someone is watching you. They are also watching and listening all over the firm. I just found that camera. I'm sure keystroke logger software is on your computer. A tech, Taylor, was just here installing my computer. I asked him point-blank if there is keystroke logger software on the computer. He denied there was. I'm sure we'll find some.

I just spoke to the gentleman across the street who has been photographing you for seven months. Prior to that he was photographing Dad and Mom, at the office and at the loft. I have his phone and tablet. I'm going to download them to my tablet. Who could be doing this?" I said.

"How did you get the guy to talk to you?" Matt said.

"I waterboarded him."

"That's funny. No really?"

"I waterboarded him. You're good, by the way. He said you and Dad don't cheat on your wives."

"Mark. I don't know. Clara told me about the guy. I thought it was just a guy shooting pictures for a day. I see people with telescopes. . . I don't know."

"Well, in a few minutes Taylor will knock on the door because I disconnected the computer and phone. I have a few techs coming over to sweep our offices then I'm going to have a talk with Mr. Frank. Who hired Taylor?"

"I don't know. It will be in the file. . ." Matt said.

A knock at the door interrupted us. "Don't say a thing, Matt. Let me handle it."

I opened the door.

"Yes, Mr. Taylor?"

"Uh, sir, well, your computer is not sensing the server," Taylor said.

"Oh? Just a second." I closed the door. "Bernice. Would you ask Mr. Frank to come to my office, please? Clara, please join me after calling Barbara. Ask her join us, too," I said.

"Yes, sir."

I went back into my office and opened the door. "Mr. Taylor. Come in, please." Clara and Barbara followed through the main door behind Taylor. Mr. Frank appeared as I turned around.

"I'll be blunt." I tossed the camera to Mr. Frank. "I found that in the TV. After Mr. Taylor installed the computer, I unplugged it. It seems he may not have told the truth about keystroke software on Clara's and Barbara's computers. He point blank told me it is not on my computer. After I disconnected my computer, Mr. Taylor appeared at my door stating my computer was not 'sensing the server.'"

Mr. Frank flinched.

"That of course, is incorrect, right Mr. Taylor? Clara. Check my computer for keystroke software."

Clara plugged in the cord and turned on the computer and monitors.

"What's your temporary log-in, sir?"

"Zero-eight-three-two."

Clara logged in then she accessed the registry. A minute later she turned the screen around for all of us to see. The cursor sat under a file name.

"That's it, sir. The software is created by a company out of San Francisco," Clara said.

"Mr. Frank?" I said.

"I don't know what to say. It's not authorized by me or Matt. Mr. Taylor. Why would you deny such software was on the computer unless you checked? Had you checked you would have found it," Mr. Frank said.

"Mr. Taylor?" I said. He was leaning against the wall with his arms crossed.

"Mr. Taylor, you have one minute to explain yourself or you're out of a job and we'll note the reason why on our website. You'll never get a job," Mr. Frank said.

Taylor was being defiant.

"Who's paying you, Taylor? Clara, Barbara, please excuse us. Would you step out and close the door?" I said.

Taylor looked confused. As the door shut, I swept Taylor's feet out from under him and hit him in the gut as he landed on the floor. I bent down and pressed a point on Taylor's rib cage.

"I can hurt you all day long without leaving a mark. Who paid you to do this? Who's giving you orders?" I said.

"I . . . I . . ."

I hit him in the gut again.

"Who?" I said.

"I . . . I . . . don't know who," he said.

I hit him in the gut again, and now he was dry heaving.

"How are you paid? Cash each month at a post office box?"

Taylor took a moment to breathe.

"Yes. How'd you know?"

"Am I going to have to persuade you anymore?"

"No. No. Please. I'll tell you what I know," he gasped.

"Sit up. Now act like a man. I'm going to bring the ladies in and we're going to take all this down. When we're done, we'll decide your fate," I said.

"You mean about my employment?"

"That, too. Now shut up and sit down. Mr. Frank. Please ask Bernice and the ladies to join us with a steno pad." Taylor was sitting on the floor. "Take a seat," I said.

Taylor struggled into a chair. Bernice came in followed by Clara and Barbara, who were both wide-eyed as they looked at me then to Taylor.

"Bernice. Please take this down. Mr. Taylor who hired you?"

"Your father."

"Who pays you by mail?"

"I don't know. I get $5000 in cash each month."

"How long have you received that payment?"

"Since I've worked here."

"Who is listening in on the firm?"

"I don't know. I was given the several Internet Protocol Addresses to enter in the various software. When the computers back up, they send to those IPAs."

"Are you telling the truth?"

"Yes."

"In a few minutes I will have two techs here who take down Chinese websites for NSA. What will they find?" I asked.

"Keystroke logger software on most computers, microphones on many computers, video cameras in computers—I didn't know about the TV—and assorted digital eavesdropping devices like you correctly asked about in the phones."

"Are there any other devices in this room?" I said.

"I only know about the phone and computer. "

"How do you receive directives?"

"By email."

"How were you initially contacted for this position?"

"By a mutual friend who was told someone was needed to do this here."

"Who is that person?"

"Mr. Train?"

I looked at Matt and Mr. Frank. A knock at the door produced Matt's secretary, Margie. She looked quizzically at our group.

"Reception has Messrs. Anguilo and Cotton to see Mr. Mark MacKenzie? Should I show them in?"

"Yes, Margie. Please show them to my office," I said.

"Taylor. These guys are experts, but you will assist them," I said.

"Yes, sir."

"If you don't, I'll ask the ladies to leave again. Am I clear?"

"Yes, sir."

A knock at the door. Robert poked his head in and looked at me like, WTF?

"Hey, Robert. Come in." I said.

"What's going on?" Rob said as he walked in followed by Tony.

"Hey, Tony," I said.

"Hey, Mark," Tony said.

"Guys, we have some security issues with cameras, microphones and software. Mr. Taylor has volunteered to assist you. If he lies to you in any way, please let me know."

"Jeez, Mark. You sure know how to start a new career," Tony said.

"And I need this tablet and phone copied, too. Do that right away. I promised the guy I'd get it back to him today. Clara?"

"Yes, sir."

"Please have a runner deliver the tablet and smartphone to our friend across the way. Make sure the runner announces, 'Delivery from Mr. Smith.'"

"Yes, sir," Clara said, smiling.

"Mr. Taylor, I must run, but I'll be back. You will check out with me today. Am I clear?"

"Yes, sir."

"Now get to work with these guys. Rob, you'll get a check from . . ." I said as I looked at Matt.

"Come see me. I'll issue a check. I remember you two. Mark's old friends," Matt said.

"Yes. We should get to work," Rob said.

#

I caught a cab to my aunt's real estate brokerage office. I was a few minutes late which was easy to blame on the cabs. Mostly, Muslims controlled the movement through the city via Yellow Cabs. I got to Missy's building and rode an elevator up to her office.

"Mark. Oh, my, look at you! You're so handsome," Aunt Missy said as she hugged me.

"Come on in. Let me show you off."

Missy is gorgeous. She's the only real estate broker I'd ever seen who looks better in person than in her pictures. We walked into a large open office with low glass-walled workspaces through the center of the room and glass-enclosed offices along the outer perimeter.

"Hello all. This is my nephew Mark back from the wars. Please try to convince him to work with us," Missy said. The room was full of beautiful women and handsome young men.

"I'll show him around today, if you like, Ms. MacKenzie," one pretty, young woman said.

"Not today, Hillary. Next time, right Mark?"

"Sure. Nice meeting you all. C'mon, I'm hungry. All I've had since breakfast is a slice of pizza and I had to torture a guy to get it," I said.

"Okay. We'll go. It's just a few blocks over. How are you? Well, you're okay physically. Lauren and I talk almost every day," she said.

"I just learned about the MacKenzie lady chat-line. I had no idea you all talked that often," I said.

"Honey, if we didn't, we'd talk your ears off, and we know how little you men talk when you're together. If it wasn't for us speaking by phone, you'd get nothing done. I thought Matt might come?"

"He's cleaning up an IT problem."

"Oh. Good. I'll have you all to myself. Besides, Matt should skip a few lunches. I don't know what Betsy is feeding him, lard sprinkled with sugar? The man is a balloon. Don't tell him I said that."

"Should we go get a cab to lunch, Aunt Missy?"

"Oh. Yes. I'm coming," she said.

#

Two and a half hours later, I made it back to the firm with a case of tinnitus.

"How's Missy?" Matt asked.

"Fine. How did it go here?"

"They're still at it. Mr. Frank, too. What I don't get is Taylor said Will hired him."

"Yeah. I figured that. Look, I don't have all the answers, but Dad may have been forced to hire him, I suspect. I'll be poking around, and I'll make some recommendations to fix some things here. Taylor is history. We can't bluff his handlers, and they can't keep getting our information. I'll just take him out in the boat off the North Fork and shoot him. They'll never find him," I said.

My uncle looked like he would have a heart attack.

"I was joking, Matt."

"Jeez! I can't tell with you anymore. I thought you were serious about killing him."

"I was. I was joking about the boat. I can shoot him and leave him in the basement."

"Stop it. You're scary. They teach you guys some shit. Can your friends put in protections so we don't get hacked?" Matt said.

"Yes. They'll install hardware and software along with encryption software. That will prevent unauthorized access. I don't know Mr. Frank's level of up-to-date knowledge on this stuff, but I asked Tony to get with him and to train him and whomever else on his team. Let me call Lauren. I'm going to be late."

#

"Hey."

"Hi, Mark. When will you be home?"

"A little later than I expected. Are you okay?"

"Of course. I'm fine. I'll eat with Kimberly and I'll stay so we can do our homework."

"I'll be on my way in a little bit. Aunt Missy says hi."

"I know. I just spoke with her."

Of course.

"I'll be there in a couple of hours. I love you, sis."

"Love you, too, big brother. Bye."

"Bye." I'm late on my first day. I would have to do less, but who knew today would turn out like this?

#

"Lauren is good. She already spoke with Missy." I said to Matt.

"I know. They talk almost every day. Betsy talks to them every day, too. Your friends are coming up to make a report. I'll hire them to fix us and bring us up to the latest and best security. You want Mr. Frank or me to fire Taylor?"

"I'll do it. It will set the tone, and it will allow for others to react to me," I said.

"I see." A knock at the door produced Robert, Tony, and Mr. Frank.

"Come in, please," Matt said.

"Well?" I asked.

"We found and eliminated everything you described. I think Taylor was truthful with us. We will track down the receiving computers via their IPA. We'll start now because they'll recognize a problem soon if they're monitoring. You want us to do a sweep, too?" Rob said.

"Yes. You're hired to do the whole deal that we discussed. Mr. Frank would like you to bring him and his techs up to speed on this. Take the time you need to do it right. Is it the government watching?" I said.

"I doubt it. Lack of sophistication. That's why they needed Mr. Taylor. The software he used is a couple of years old. Very easy to detect. We even got the credit card number used to pay for the key logger software. We'll learn more by this time tomorrow after we've gone through everything. But you have someone else inside here doing things. The camera in the TV and things Taylor didn't know about tell us that," Rob said.

"We know. I'm working on it," I said.

"Okay. We'll get to work. We're still on for Friday though, right?" Rob said.

"Yes. I'll talk with you some more. Have you finished with Taylor? Because I'm going to give him the boot if you are," I said.

"Yeah. We downloaded his phone, tablet and laptop, then wiped each of the firm information. I also installed software on each to send us a report of what he does. He could find the software if he looks, but I doubt he will," Rob said.

"Thanks guys. I'll be talking to you," I said. Rob and Tony left Matt's office. "Mr. Frank. Let's bring Taylor to my office. I already drafted a discharge agreement," I said.

"Oh. Good. I was just going to call Marsha to sit in," Mr. Frank said.

"Do that. Bernice and Clara will witness," I said.

#

"Mr. Taylor. You're terminated effective immediately. This discharge agreement lays out the background and facts related to your termination. It is for cause. Should you defy or resist our agreement here then I will turn over the evidence I have of your wrongdoing to NYPD and FBI. The agreement contains a confidentiality clause. Abide by it. Sign here. Marsha has your paycheck through today," I said.

Taylor looked around after signing the agreement. Bernice and Clara witnessed it and Margie notarized it after I signed it. Copies were made and Taylor was given a copy.

"Mr. Taylor. Good day," I said. One of the other techs escorted Taylor from the firm. "Thank you, Clara, Bernice, Barbara, Margie. You're free to go," I said.

Clara hesitated and caught my eye.

"Yes, Clara?"

"Sir, that guy is still across the street," she said.

"I know. He works for me now."

Clara smiled. "Yes, sir! Good night."

"Bye."

#

The ladies departed except for Marsha.

"You had a hell of a first day, Mark," Matt said.

"Look, I'll be back Thursday. I understand your desire to have me here full-time, but I can't just yet. I'll talk with Grandpa. I'm sure he already knows or has called someone."

"He has. I'll fill him in. Good work today, Mark. We still have the issue of who was watching and listening, though, and then there's Train," Matt said.

"I'll work that. Keep an eye out and let's see what happens. Leave Train alone for now. I want to see what happens. Matt, I think a new vetting needs to be done for these employees," I said as I handed a list to Matt and Marsha.

"Want to say why these six?" Matt said.

"No. Not yet. The report should go to just you two," I said.

"Mark. Who do you think is behind this?" Matt said.

"For now, they're bad guys. We'll talk Thursday. I don't mean to be cryptic, but I have more to do to be sure," I said.

#

I picked up Lauren at 7:20 p.m. It was a long drive from Manhattan to Nassau County. Once I hit the Suffolk County line, traffic thinned out some.

"Hi, Mark. Did you eat yet?" Lauren asked.

"I drank a protein drink on the way home. I ate late with Missy. I'll eat when we get home. How was your day?"

"Great. I got an A on my first math test today," Lauren said.

"Terrific. Keep up the good work."

"Problems at the firm?" she asked.

"Nothing we can't fix. I just feel bad that on my very first day I wasn't back to get you."

"That's okay. I'm sure the first few times it will be an adjustment. Did you call Haley?"

"Well, no. I thought I'd call her after I got relaxed and in bed. I'm a little tired after today," I said.

"Good. You're not going to work tomorrow, are you?"

"No. I'll meet with Joe and do a few things around the house. The pier builder will be out to take another look at installing the PWC lifts."

"Oh, cool."

We pulled up to the house and went inside. I got a shower then made a pan of leftover sausage and scrambled up some eggs. I picked up my tablet, my plate of food, the mail, the

Calabrese file and headed to my bedroom to take up residence in my bed. I dialed Haley's number.

"Hi, stranger. Tough first day?" Haley asked.

"I've had tougher," I said.

"You sound tired. Are you okay?"

"I am and I am. You?"

"I'm good. I had a nice weekend, Mark."

"I did too. Are we still on for Wednesday?"

"You bet. I have the perfect little black cocktail dress, too."

"Good. I'll confirm a time tomorrow. Okay?"

"Sure. Mark, please be safe."

"No doubt there. Good night, Haley."

"Good night, Mark."

I called Joe on my father's old phone.

"Hello?" Joe cautiously answered.

"It's Mark."

"Hey. I'm on duty so I might have to cut you off. Get the pictures?"

"I'm looking at them now. I had an interesting day at the office. All the computers were bugged and a guy across the way has been photographing Uncle Matt for seven months. Before that he was photographing my parents."

"You have been busy. Did you bring in Rob and Tony?"

"I did. They're doing everything. I fired a tech who was being paid to spy and install monitoring software. He said my father hired him. I'll get into the files myself and see what's doing. What do you have?"

"The banking records came in. I'll stick a copy in the box to courier to you tomorrow. We're still on for Friday?"

"Yeah. Rob and Tony will be here, too. Look, I've been talking with Haley. She still has access to the house and restaurant."

"That certainly allows for more possibilities. I got the list of equipment you wanted. I'll courier it to you tomorrow morning. I put a few extra things in there for you. Oh. Our joint task force guys say they're the only law enforcement watching the family. They're not watching everyone, but they're on the old man, the son and some capos and top lieutenants. They're watching the restaurant in Nassau and another in Queens," Joe said.

"Do they still have a tracker on the Lincoln Town Car?"

"They do. They just tagged it with a new one a day ago. I put the code in the box for you."

"Okay, Joe. I'll be talking to you."

CHAPTER 8

I was up at dawn. I felt good after eight plus hours of sleep. I dressed and headed out for a five-mile run. I'd swim in the bay later. I needed to swim out the cobwebs. I hadn't been in saltwater in more than a year, which is unusual for a SEAL.

I returned from my run dripping sweat. I went inside and started some coffee and took out the extra eggs I cooked up last night. I sliced up some mild Italian sausage, left over steak, and breakfast sausage and put all in a pan with the eggs on low heat for Lauren. I'd cover it with cheese just before I served it to her. I woke Lauren. I showered up, dressed in board shorts and a T-shirt, and ran downstairs to check breakfast. It was nearly ready. I popped some bread into the toaster as Lauren appeared.

"Smells good," Lauren said.

"Good."

"Milk or juice?"

"Milk. So how is Ms. Menduni?"

"Fine. I'm taking her to dinner and a show at the Suffolk Theater."

"Where are you taking her to dinner?"

"The Lobster Roll. It's close, you can dress up or not, it's not pretentious, the food is good. We'll be wearing black. She's wearing a nice black cocktail dress."

"Are you wearing Varvatos or Zegna?"

"Varvatos, I thought."

"Open collar or tie?"

"I was thinking tie, but . . ."

"Go open collar if you're wearing a white shirt. Cuff links, pocket square and those Varvatos boots you have, too. Blue pocket square to make your eyes stand out."

"Yes, ma'am."

"And roses. Deep red roses. She'll love them, and her parents will be impressed."

"You sure know a lot about this."

"It's what we women live for, dummy. Romance. The sight of a nice-looking guy like you rolling up in a hot chariot—take the Hellcat—dressed to the nines with a bouquet of roses, it's the best. We will always remember it. Wear that Dolce and Gabbana Light Blue cologne."

"You're just full of advice, aren't you?"

"Yes. I just need my book bag and I'm ready."

#

I dropped my fashion adviser off at school. Haley was at the drop-off zone. We waved. I drove home, dressed in my spring suit, and dove off the pier for a swim. I'd swim a mile out and a mile back. I adjusted my mask and snorkel and tightened my fins. The water was a little chilly, but once I was moving, I warmed up. I returned to the pier and climbed the ladder to find Mr. Jeffrey, my dock builder, sketching or writing on a drawing board.

"Hey, there," I said.

"I thought that was you. The water's a little chilly for a swim," Mr. Jeffrey said.

"About 53 degrees. It's not bad. So, are we good to go with the county?"

"Yes. It shouldn't be a problem. The PWC lifts there and there, a twenty-five thousand pound covered lift there, and a T-pier addition large enough for a 100,000-pound yacht. What are you getting?"

"A family boat. I'll move that Parker to Oceanside. I'll get a center console to fish and a big family cruiser that everyone can enjoy. A fifty to sixty-five-footer, I suspect," I said.

"That lift will hold any center console that I know of. The pier will accommodate a large yacht. Good luck in your search. The permits should issue this week."

"Great. Do you need me?"

"No. Just a few more pictures and measurements and I'll be finished."

"Okay, Mr. Jeffrey. Bye."

I jogged to the outdoor shower next to the house and rinsed off and stowed my gear. I toweled off and walked upstairs, dressed in jeans and a T-shirt and broke out the files on our friends.

A knock at the door produced a courier with a large box. I tipped him and brought the box into the kitchen. I opened the box and found several large envelopes on top. I opened the first and it contained surveillance and satellite pictures of several properties. I guess the Menduni and Calabrese homes. Next, I found FBI dossiers on what looked like everyone in the family including the women. I lingered over Haley's, though it was less than a page with several older pictures attached. I separated the pictures of the Town Car driver and his pal and laid them aside. The next envelope contained information about the restaurant owned by Paul Menduni, a restaurant owned by Vincenzo Menduni, and a restaurant owned by Romeo Menduni. It included builder's drawings for each restaurant. The last envelope contained pictures of several of the men around town or getting in and out of vehicles with narratives about what they were doing and where they were when the pictures were taken. Most were of my current favorites, and Romeo and Vincenzo. There was one of Paul walking with a striking young woman who wore large sunglasses. She seemed familiar to me. She was not identified in the picture. I found several of Romeo Menduni on his boats. One, a small center console, and the other, an 85 to 100-foot yacht, a late 1990's vintage Burger, I thought. A lone piece of paper with an Internet website address and a series of letters and numbers told me that was for the GPS tracker for the Town Car. I tapped on my smart phone, enabled the encryption software Robert had installed yesterday and logged in. I entered the code and voilà, I had a scalable satellite view of a street map with a red dot. The vehicle was parked and by tapping the spot twice it showed that it was parked at the Nassau County restaurant of Paul Menduni. A Rockville Center address was indicated between Merrick Road and Sunrise Highway where the two roads nearly converge.

My phone buzzed.

"Hey, Joe."

"You get that stuff?"

"I did. I was just going through it. Guess where the Town Car is right now?"

"Where?"

"The restaurant in Rockville Center."

"Want to go look?"

"Sure. I'll pick you up?"

"I'm ready."

"See you in about an hour."

"Bye."

#

I dressed in a black button-down shirt over my T-shirt, and pulled on a pair of black, grey and blue light-weight boots. I put a Sig Sauer P220 in my pocket. I took my Swiss Army knife; I placed my electronic eaves-dropping kit with GPS for a car and two homes in a roll up bag. I packed my pistol lock-opener and picks. I grabbed my phone, the files for the two men, the restaurant and Freeport house files, my tablet, and the Yukon fob. I headed out to Babylon.

#

I pulled up to Joe's. He must have seen me coming as he walked out of his house before I called him. Joe climbed in and we departed. I drove toward Southern State Parkway.

"What's the plan?" Joe said.

"I'd like to get a microphone and camera in the car and put a kill switch on the ignition."

"That'll take a while, won't it?"

"Less than five minutes if no splicing is involved. It's not that bad. If the OBDII port is somewhat hidden I have a plug-n-play unit."

"They teach you all this in the navy?" Joe said.

"Uh-huh. Now we have remotely operated detonators so we can stick them on a terrorist's vehicle and blow the vehicle when we need to. That would draw attention here."

"Are we going to run to their homes?"

"I want to confirm that Dopey is with him. If so, we'll do the car, then run to Queens. The Freeport house will be easy. I'll have the keys tomorrow."

"You okay with her?" Joe said.

"Yes. She's fine. She hates him. Her divorce will be final next week. I guess you want to know do I trust her? I do."

"Okay. I just . . . the fewer the better."

"I know. She won't know anything we do. No, no. I'll still enforce OPSEC. Okay. I'll get off here. Just like we're headed home. How are your mom and dad doing?"

"Okay. The divorce was a surprise to my father, but not to my mother. She figured that since we had no children on the way we weren't doing well. My sister Annie has three kids so that keeps my mother happy. I think you make a right up here and it should be on the left. Yeah, I see it. Whose Tito, anyway?" Joe said.

"Fuck if I know. All right. I'll drive around it once. Look for the Town Car."

"I got it. It's not in a bad spot. We should look for cameras. Parking spaces are open on either side."

"I'll take a slow drive down Merrick Road and come in behind the building. Here's a monocular. Look for cameras in the lot or on the building." I slowly drove past on the right then pulled over on the right, so Joe could look.

"Nothing here that I can see. There's something at the door, but it's a robbery camera pointing at the exit door. Swing around so I can look at the front part."

I drove up the street and turned in front of the restaurant. "Anyone walking around the lot or side alley? Any employees out there smoking?"

"No one," Joe said.

"I'll pull down the street. You'll take the wheel. I'll sit behind you. Pull into the spot on the passenger side of the Town Car. Go in and get a couple of sandwiches to-go, and look to see if Dopey is with the driver. See who else is there. Haley said they have a large corner table reserved for them."

"All right. I'll talk on my phone like I'm having a real telephone conversation. I'll let you know what I see."

"Okay. Let's switch." I pulled over on Sunrise Highway and got into the back seat while Joe moved to the driver's seat.

"You ready?" Joe said.

"Yeah."

Joe swung around and drove into the parking lot pulling into the spot next to the Town Car on the north side of the parking lot.

"Leave the keys."

"I'll call you after I order."

"Bye."

Joe got out and walked to the restaurant. I got out with my kit, slim-jimmied the Lincoln's passenger's door, put the pistol key into the ignition and turned it to keep the security system from sounding. I slipped the ignition remote disconnect into the OBDII port under the dashboard. I pinned a microphone to the sun visor. I got under. . . my phone rang.

"Yeah?"

"You're good. Veal parmesan or meatball hero?"

Is he fucking kidding?

"Meatball."

"Go to work. I'm going to talk. You don't have to. Okay. . . Okay? Did you hear me?"

"Joe! I'm busy!"

"Right."

I got under the dash, set the camera to angle up to the driver, I quick-spliced the power wire and ran a hair-thin antenna along the underside of the dash with clear tape. Shit! Four minutes. I put another camera on the rearview mirror that would give a fisheye view of the car's interior. It snapped in and was held with double-back tape. Only the rectangular lens box showed which looked like part of the mirror. I checked my work. I looked in the glove box and found nothing unusual. I checked the ashtray. Bingo. It looked like a spare key to the car and the house. I took them. I opened the center console and found cash and about thirty bags of cocaine. I hid two bags in the vehicle owner's guide in the glove box. I hit the trunk button and exited.

"Joe. Okay there? Is anyone coming out?"

"No, dear. I don't think he's coming out and they all are having such a gay time at the corner booth. All eight of them. I think his grandfather is there, too . . ."

Jeez! Had I only known.

I lifted the trunk lid and looked inside. Some tools, the usual things, well, except for the shovel, but if you watched Goodfellas a shovel would be usual. Then I saw my father's briefcase under a blanket and winter coat. I looked around and all was clear. I removed the coat and blanket then opened the briefcase. Inside were various papers and things, but nothing odd. Enough to show me it was my father's briefcase if the engraved initials by the handle were not enough. I snapped a few pictures, put the briefcase back under the blanket and coat and closed the trunk. I jumped into the Yukon.

"Done," I said to Joe.

"A few more minutes and I'll be out."

"I'll pull up to the door."

"No, no. I can walk. It would be good for me since people may be walking by. I'm on my way, sweetheart. Okay. I'll call later, bye."

Thank God the call ended. I watched Joe exit the restaurant followed by four guys none of whom were our heroes. I pulled out my Nikon and snapped a few pictures through the back window. I recognized Paul's driver and his henchman, Monty.

Monty was moving a little slow. I looked to my left and spied the Navigator. Joe got in.

"I got you ice water. No tea was brewed yet."

Joe set the food and drinks down and I drove off.

"'Do you hear me? A gay time?' Jeez! Turn that tablet on and let's see our pictures. The camera and microphone numbers are on the masking tape, 'Mr. Gay Time.'"

"I get nervous sometimes and just say stuff. Okay. I got the wide angle or fisheye, I guess. Where'd you put that, in the middle of the windshield?"

"Rearview mirror."

"Okay. I can see part of a steering wheel and the headliner. Oh. This is aimed up at the driver. Good. I don't hear anything, but nothing to hear since they're not in the car."

"My father's briefcase is in the trunk and they're into drugs. I found about thirty packets of coke in the center console. I hid two in the owner's manual in the glove box so there's a find for drugs from a CI report to pull them over."

"Good thinking. You should have been a cop. I got you veal anyway. Better for you and easier to eat while driving," Joe said.

I shook my head. Only Joe would say a veal parmesan hero is better for me than a meatball hero.

"Look what else I got?" I showed Joe the keys to our guy's home.

"Damn. You have been busy."

We ate while we drove to Bayside, Queens.

#

George Castellano lived by himself in a moderately sized, Queens-style townhome. It was two stories over an unfinished basement. It contained three bedrooms, two-point-five baths and a cat that ran away upon our entry. Out back stood a small garage that would barely hold a golf cart. Joe looked downstairs while I checked upstairs.

I placed a camera in the bedroom ceiling vent and microphone at the headboard by the nightstand that had the phone. I found his weapons stash under his bed in a suitcase where the cat was hiding. I opened the suitcase. Shit, he had some stuff. I photographed each serial number. Two .22 caliber pistols lacked serial numbers. Mob guys use a firearm once for a job. Sometimes they'll even drop the firearm at the scene or in a surviving witness's lap.

I checked his dresser and chest. The usual things. I ran through the other rooms and found a closet full of women's clothing in somewhat recent styles. Maybe a girlfriend? I snapped some pictures. I looked in the bathroom. I found drugs in the DEA's preferred hiding spot in the toilet tank. Didn't these guys watch Cops? I ran downstairs.

"Everything is cool upstairs," I said.

"The guy's a pig. Look at this kitchen?" Joe said.

"Anything?"

"No."

I plugged a jump drive into George's computer and opened the program. His password was his house number. I downloaded the files from his hard drive and installed monitoring software, a compression program and set it to send periodically to an anonymous Cloud account. I installed a wireless transceiver to transmit audio and video from the cameras and microphones.

"Did you check the freezer and oven?" I said.

"No."

"Go check."

Joe opened the freezer. I heard him moving things around. I finished with the download. I reached over and opened the oven.

"Joe. There's his bank." Joe reached for it. "Don't touch. Don't they teach you guys anything? It could be rigged with an IED. Just take a picture. We're not taking it with us. If we need it, we can come back. We can call in a CI report, too, if need be. He has a stash in the toilet tank upstairs, too. It looks like at least a pound of coke," I said.

I closed the oven. I placed a microphone inside his landline phone, and I placed a camera on a bookshelf and aimed it at his favorite chair in the living room. I rifled through his desk. I found an address book. I took it. I snapped a few more pictures.

"Okay, Joe. Nine minutes. We're out of here in one."

Something shiny in a cut crystal glass bowl on the coffee table caught my eye. I picked it up. It was a gold chain necklace with a scrolled banner plate with a small diamond on each end. It was inscribed, "Mom, All My Love, Mark. Christmas 1993." The heat of anger coursed through my veins.

"Mark. Mark! What is it?" Joe took the necklace from my hand. "Shit! Where was this? Mark. We gotta go. We'll get this back. C'mon. Put this back."

I placed the necklace back in the bowl and we ran out of there.

#

We didn't speak during the ride to Dopey's apartment. It was in the Rego Park section of Queens which I found odd as it's a predominantly Jewish neighborhood though it's changed a little over the years and has a mix of people now.

"Joe. We got to do this one faster. In and out in five minutes. I'll set up in the master and living room. You go through the kitchen and just photograph what you find. If anything looks bad, say so and we're out of there."

"You're going to kill them, aren't you?" Joe said.

"Pay attention to the op, Joe, we can't be distracted." We pulled up to the building. It is a fifteen-story residential building in a cluster of eight buildings of various heights. "Joe. If people get nosey, you'll flash that badge to chase them away. It will be busy I expect."

"We'll be fine. In and out of the apartment in four minutes," Joe said.

I circled the apartment complex before finding a parking spot across the street from the back entrance. Cameras would be everywhere, but it was unlikely our guy would complain. I just had to pick two locks in a short time.

We parked. I put on a blacked-out New York Yankees hat and Joe a monochrome blue New York Mets hat, which demonstrated one of our differences growing up. We wore dark shooting glasses and a two-day growth of beard. Heck, Joe, being mostly Italian, always had a two-day growth of beard.

"You ready?" I said.

"Let's do it." We walked to the building entrance. We entered the building.

"Camera left and ahead," I mumbled. I hoped the elevators were not the secured card-wipe style. They were not. We got on the elevator and I punched the button with my knuckle.

"Camera, ceiling, right corner," I said.

"Got it."

We got off on the eighth floor and followed the arrow to apartment 832. It was around the corner. We turned right and I spotted the door halfway down the hallway. I pulled on my tactical gloves and withdrew my pick and pistol-grip lock pick. I opened both locks in less than a minute.

A quick look around showed no alarm which I didn't expect to find. Who'd break into a wise guy's apartment? We went to our tasks. I placed a camera in the bedroom. It was a one-bedroom apartment. I attached the jump drive to his computer, bypassed the log-in and began to download his hard drive. That took just seventy seconds. I installed the upload software and placed a microphone and camera. I listened to his old-styled telephone answering machine while I worked. Nothing of interest. I found his weapons stash in a suitcase under his bed. I photographed each weapon's serial number. I looked in his closet and found eighteen suits. The guy had more suits than me. I flipped through until I came to one that matched the description given by a bystander to the accident and the color provided by the sample Nassau PD took from my Dad's car. I pulled out the suit. The right sleeve had a jagged pull and rip. I photographed the suit and the tear, then clipped a sample of the material from beneath the liner. I put the suit back. I closed the door and walked to the kitchen.

"Anything, Joe?"

"The freezer is empty, but same thing in the oven. These guys must not cook much."

I looked in the oven. I estimated $40,000 and a brick or kilo of cocaine.

"You photograph all of this?" I asked.

"Done."

"Let's go."

We walked out. I locked the doorknob, pulled it shut and locked the deadbolt in a few seconds. We were out of there.

We walked down the hallway toward the elevators, Joe behind me and to my left. As we rounded the corner four men were exiting the elevator. One of them was Dopey.

"You dink dem Yankees are gonna choke dis year?" A man said as we walked past.

I paid attention to Dopey, committing his details to my memory. I was sure we'd see each other again. He ignored us, but as we reached the elevator another guy eyeballed us.

I punched the button. Shit! I was still wearing gloves. I crossed my arms.

"You know those two?" I heard a man say.

We stepped into the elevator, and I pushed the button.

"If they call someone our best bet is to badge our way out," I said.

"No problem."

We exited the elevator and went through the exit doors. We got into the Yukon and drove off.

"Look back. Anyone interested in us?" I said as I drove down Booth Street.

Joe scanned with the monocular. "Nothing."

"Check it. See what we have," I said.

Joe tapped on the tablet and accessed the cameras and microphones. The eighth-floor height would extend the RF range, but with the transceiver and Internet on the computer we could get it anywhere.

"Got them. Let me tap the microphone."

I suddenly heard voices. Joe played with the tablet as I pulled over to park.

"They're still talking baseball. It sounds like someone. . . let's see? It must be Dopey is doing something in the kitchen. He didn't seem like the entertaining type."

"They're taking out the drugs," I said.

"I think you're right. They're talking about a delivery tonight."

"We'll pick up their conversations and, if need be, we'll flip the information to NYPD. I need more evidence to prove who ordered my parents' deaths, but I'll be happy to pick apart their organization. I just don't want to raise any suspicion that we're on to them. Let's get to your place and check their computer data. Who knows what that will show?" I said.

"Don't expect much. We usually got cryptic emails, but sometimes we'd get lucky."

I drove Queen's Boulevard to Jackie Robinson Parkway, which became Grand Central Parkway then to Northern State Parkway.

"We got a tail," Joe said.

"Can you see inside the vehicle?" I said.

Joe turned and looked with the monocular.

"I see two guys. The black Suburban. A driver and one guy in the passenger seat. I can't see anyone else."

"I'll lose them."

"Why? Let's drive to Wantagh State. Get off south to Southern State. If they're still with us we can just pull over and let them pass. I'll call in the plate," Joe said.

I drove toward Wantagh State Parkway while Joe made a call.

"You sure? Thanks. Shit! Feds. We must have been spotted at one of the places. Signal and pull over at the next off-ramp. I'll talk to them."

I slowed and pulled off the parkway right onto a side road in Old Westbury. I made a left turn onto Jericho Turnpike then left on Guinea Woods Road to the Old Westbury Diner and pulled in. The Suburban followed us. Joe got out with his badge in his hand. He walked to the Suburban. It stopped several lengths behind us as Joe approached the passenger door. The window came down and Joe spoke with the men. After a few minutes, Joe nodded his head. The Suburban pulled over and parked. Two men in suits got out and walked toward the diner. The driver was about our age and the passenger in his mid-forties. Joe walked to my door.

"Fibbies. They want to talk. We'll get a table inside."

We entered the diner. The FBI agents already had a corner booth. Joe pointed at their booth to let the waitress know and we took seats opposite the special agents.

"I'm John Stayton. This is Dan Carter. We're special agents with the FBI."

"As I said, I'm Joe Mott. Suffolk County PD and this is Mark MacKenzie," Joe said. John nodded.

"Tell me, what business do you have with the Calabrese-Menduni family?" Stayton said as he looked at me. I remained silent. The waitress appeared. John and Dan ordered coffee.

Joe ordered coffee and pie for both of us.

"What business do you have with the Calabrese-Menduni family? I recall your name now, Mott. You promoted off the JOCTF just before I got there," Stayton said.

"That's right," Joe said.

"You're not a cop are you, Mr. MacKenzie?" Stayton said.

"No. I'm not."

"What do you have to do with this?" Stayton said.

"We believe the Menduni family or persons involved with them caused a hit and run MVA that killed his parents," Joe said.

John looked at Dan, who got up and walked away with his smartphone in his hand.

"Isn't Sergeant Cicola in Nassau heading that investigation?" Stayton asked, again looking at me.

"He is," Joe said.

"Well, why don't you leave that up to him?" Stayton said still looking at me.

"I have some free time. I thought I'd see what I could stir up," I said.

John looked up as Dan approached the table. The waitress appeared with our orders. I sipped my black coffee while the others prepared their coffees. Stayton looked at his phone.

"Mr. MacKenzie. I understand that you're a recently discharged naval officer. What did you do for the navy?" Stayton said.

"I think you know," I said.

"Yes. I'm just doing the control questions to check whether you're telling the truth. I learned that you were at the restaurant. You were at the Queens homes of Marco Palami and George Castellano. I know those two were involved in the MVA with your parents. Nassau County thinks they caused it. Whatever you do, you are on your own. Don't mess with our investigation. What do you want to tell me about what you learned?" Stayton said.

"I'll tell you something after I have what I need to nail the persons responsible," I said.

Stayton looked at me trying to gauge my statement with my facial expression. I took a bite of my apple pie and put down my fork.

"Look. I have enough evidence for you to take out those two. I've arranged to flip them to you at any time of my choosing. Give me a few weeks and I'll help you out. I want no interference. If you or your people see me, ignore me. I'll contact you when I need to, and you'll have your evidence. I think your time is better spent checking up on my reliability as a CI," I said.

"Then let me ask you, are they into drug distribution?" Stayton said.

"Yes," I said.

"What else?" He asked.

"I have my suspicions. I'm collecting the evidence. I'll know more this week."

John looked at Dan then back to me. I ate my last bite of pie.

"Are you going in to get the old man?" John asked.

"I'm going to take down the persons responsible for my parents' deaths," I said.

John nodded. "How do I reach you?" John asked.

"Give me your number. I'll call you," I said.

"Before we go, what's the connection between your father's death and the Calabrese-Menduni clan? Why'd they do it?" John asked.

"If I knew that answer you'd be making arrests. If you have something you want me to do to prove my reliability as a CI, contact Joe. I won't give you those two guys or their bosses, but if you want to cull the herd, let me know. I'll get what you need," I said.

John again looked at Dan who nodded. "Okay. Do you know Monty Fiorelli?" John asked.

"He's the bodyguard to Paul Menduni, the owner of Tito's," I said.

"That's correct. You've done your homework. We think he's been running young girls and, perhaps, young boys in a sex slave ring. We don't know if it's sanctioned by the family or not. Last week two girls turned up dead. We think the buyer refused them because they were not what he wanted. We suspect Monty Fiorelli killed them. The bodies were found in Hempstead Lake. I want him," John said.

"Give me an email where I can contact you," I said.

John wrote an email and telephone number on a blank business card.

"Do you have agents on him?"

"Yes, but he just seems to have a way of leaving either the restaurant, Paul Menduni's house or his own house undetected. We're trying to get someone inside the restaurant, but they're carefully screening our people. They haven't hired anyone we've sent them."

"I'll get something. Anything else?" I asked.

"That's it for now," John said.

"You don't know how he moves the kids?" I said.

"We're not sure. In one case, a fourteen-year-old girl was pulled off the street. The witnesses described several versions of a truck, SUV or van. We don't even know what color the reports were so confusing. We haven't found her. If you connect the family to this I want to know right away," John said.

"Roger that."

John looked at Dan and they rose together.

"We'll be seeing you," John said as he tossed some money on the table. They departed.

♯

"Well? Monty Fiorelli was at the restaurant, and his house is in Merrick. It's 2 p.m. Shall we go hit the house?" Joe said.

"No. I'll take care of that. His car is likely at Paul's house or the restaurant. I'd like to get into both places along with Monty's car and house. I need to do the restaurant after 3 a.m. Paul's house I'll do in the early evening when we know he's not there. I'll have the keys tomorrow night. C'mon. I have some planning to do. We'll skip working at your place. I'll just drop you off. When do you go to work?" I said.

"At 6 p.m."

"Okay. I'll let you know. I suspect our smartphones will be monitored. In the SUV, I have both my parents' old phones. I'll give you one of them until I'm sure Rob or Tony can protect all of us with encryption. Until then we'll talk shop on the old phones," I said.

"Okay."

I paid our bill and we departed. No one followed us. I dropped Joe at his home, and I drove Sunrise Highway toward Riverhead. No one followed me with a car. I wasn't sure they didn't use a satellite.

#

An hour and twenty minutes later I arrived at Lauren's school. I parked at the coffee shop-bakery and got out. The buses were pulling up by now. I went inside the coffee shop. The nice, nosey lady was working the counter.

"Hi," she said.

"Hi. Medium black coffee, please."

"I just made it. How about a cheese Danish, Linzer tart, or black and white cookie?"

"No thanks. I already had dessert today."

She handed me my coffee. I paid for it, walked outside, and took a seat. Then it dawned on me. Softball practice! I waited to be sure. I needed to recall this stuff faster. Haley walked out of the school, saw me, and walked over.

"Hi," she said.

"Hi. How are you?" I said as I stood.

"Great. No bus duty today. New month. I don't have a class either this late on Tuesdays. I saw you, so I came over to give you these." Haley handed me a set of keys. "The red colored keys are for the restaurant, the silver keys are for the house, the blue are for Vincenzo's house. The little brass one is for his mini-storage. The last big brass one I don't know. Probably his girlfriend's place. Here's the alarm code."

"Thank you."

"Oh. My attorney delivered the agreement. It's done. He deposited the $900,000 into my attorney's trust account. Another $500,000 must be paid by June 1. The child support will begin in June. I'm done dealing with him."

"I'm sure that's a relief. When does construction begin?" I said.

"Not for a long time. I don't even have a plan yet."

"Well, take your time and do what you want. On another note, I'll pick you up at 5:30 p.m. Between travel and all, I don't want to rush our dinner, but after dinner, we have someplace to be," I said.

"I'll be ready. Come by at 5 p.m. so my father can give you the third degree."

"How hard can that be? You married a mobster," I kidded.

"He's a lot tougher now. Of course, since he knew your mother, it won't be hard."

"I'm sorry. Would you like a coffee or something?" I said, remembering my manners.

"No thanks. I must run in and pick up my papers, then go get Paulie."

"Haley. How long has that big guy, Monty, been around?"

"Since before Paulie was born. Why?"

"No reason. I just want to get a feel for these guys. Paulie said he's not nice to him. Has he ever hurt Paulie?"

"Odd that you ask. Paulie just said that Monty smacked his friend and yelled at him. Paulie said it was because his friend Jason yelled at Monty for touching his sister, Erica. I think she's fourteen or fifteen. Jason is nine. They live a couple of houses down from Paul's house.

"He touched her, how?" I asked.

"Paulie said he grabbed her arm and pulled her onto his lap and touched her chest."

I nodded. "I see."

Haley looked at me, searching my eyes. "What's wrong, Mark?"

"Just something bothered me about what Paulie said the other night." I sipped my coffee. "What do you know about Paul's family businesses?"

"They have the restaurants and auto repair shops. They have a trucking company. They have a boat yard in Bellmore. They're into drugs and I'm sure they're into pornography on the Internet. They're into bootleg movies, betting, the horses, gaming, and other things. They have apartments, hotels, commercial buildings, a concrete company, a big funeral home, auto leasing companies. Vincenzo pretty much runs all their legitimate businesses. Why do you ask?"

"Just looking at what's there to check out."

Haley continued to search my eyes for something. She found what she wanted.

"I have to go."

Haley stood as did I. She pulled me to her and kissed me. Not a full-blown passion kiss, but one that would leave me thinking of her. She pulled back smiling.

"See you tomorrow at 5 p.m. Bye."

"Bye, Haley."

I watched her walk to the school. I hadn't noticed the buses leaving. I wandered over to the fence to watch Lauren. She was in line for batting practice. I sat on a bench along the fence and watched her practice. Parenthood!

#

I got Lauren home at 5:45 p.m., prepared dinner and we ate. Lauren was more excited about my date with Haley than I was, and I was very excited. Lauren had a lot of homework to do.

I called Joe with my mother's old cell phone.

"Hello," Joe said hesitantly.

"Hey. I just wanted to let you know that Monty is a chomo. He grabbed Paulie's friend's sister and touched her. Paulie told his mother. I'm concerned for the girl. She's fourteen or fifteen per Haley. I got the keys. I'm going in tonight to see what I can find. When he snatches the girls, he must hold them somewhere. I want to learn where. I'll hit Monty's place, Paul's house, and the restaurant. I got the keys for the homes and Paul's SUV. I'll do the houses and restaurant for sure. If I can, I'll get the Lincoln SUV."

"You're not going into Vincenzo's place, are you?"

"No."

"Be careful. I'll be off by 3 a.m."

"I'll be doing the restaurant then. I'll call when I'm finished."

"Okay. Be careful. Bye."

#

My smartphone rang.

"Hello."

"Hey, Mark, Matt."

"Hey, Uncle Matt. How goes it?"

"Your friends found more problems today. Are we monitoring Rizzo and Train?"

"We are. Are you in the office?"

"No. I'm in my car. I just got off the train. Rizzo came into my office wondering why we didn't contact him before firing Taylor and going through all the computers and software."

"Sort of ballsy, but I thought he might have an issue. Rob and Tony will look through all their communications. Where are you?"

"I'm just a few streets up from the house."

"Don't lose control of your car. Dad and Mom were killed."

"I know. Hit and run . . ."

"Hold on, Matt. No. They were targeted. Dad had to do something, or they were trying to force him to do something. He didn't do it, or he screwed them on whatever it was. I already know who did the actual attack. I don't know who ordered it or why it was ordered. I'm convinced that Rizzo and some or all the others are involved. I think 20% of the firm is owned by the mob." There was a long pause before Matt spoke.

"What will you do?"

"I'm already doing it. The office is clean. Those six on the list are being closely monitored. Once I get something I'll put more surveillance on whomever and we'll track them. You worry about keeping the firm operating. I'll work on connecting the bad guys. We'll know more Thursday and we'll talk."

"Okay. Watch Rizzo. He's already talking smack about you per the secretary line."

"What's their 20% valued at?"

"Thirty-five million to $38 million, maybe. If the firm was liquidated, less. We're valued at $175 million to $200 million at market. Our corporate reserves and investments are around $59 million. Why do you ask?"

"I'm trying to figure out how to handle it when I nail Rizzo. We can dismiss him from the firm. As majority shareholders, we can force things a minority shareholder might not like."

"When your father took action against Rizzo the silent shareholders got involved."

"That's what I'd like to do is have a talk with them. The shareholder agreements call for a forced sale of the shareholder's shares if the shareholder takes any action against the firm or that is injurious to operation of the firm including criminal conduct. If I show that Rizzo and the silent shareholders acted illegally and against our corporate interests, we can freeze them out, lock up their shares or repurchase them. Understand me?"

"I do, but these are some pretty scary guys."

"I'm scarier. Don't worry. Let me do my thing. Talk to no one about this. I'll see you Thursday. I'll be in touch. Bye, Matt."

"Bye, Mark."

#

"Lauren. You'll be asleep when I run out very late tonight. I'll be back before you wake up. I just didn't want you to wake up and not see me here."

"That's fine. I know you're doing something because Grandma and Betsy spoke, and I spoke with Grandma who's friendly with Bernice. Don't you just love her? Anyway. You shook up the firm and, I guess, it has something to do with Mom and Dad. I'm fine. Aunt Missy wants you to come work for her, she said."

"I don't think so. I'll have enough to do at the firm. I'm going to lay down and get three hours. You'll likely be asleep when I get up. Good night." I kissed Lauren on the top of her head. She hugged me.

"Mark. Please be safe. I want you to do what you're doing, but I want you more."

"I'll be safe. Good night."

CHAPTER 9

I dressed in black and charcoal grey. The weather was nice outside, the temperature mild, but I put on an Under Armor long sleeve T-shirt and a lightweight black and dark grey motorcycle jacket, and lightweight motorcycle boots. I wore my black and grey, leather and suede tactical gloves. I put my little SIG P220 in the jacket's inside breast pocket. I made up surveillance kits. I rolled each kit in a paper bag. I placed the kits in my saddle bag on my BMW 1600GTL sans the tour pack. The motorcycle was custom painted a flat charcoal where it was originally black, with blackout accessories and engine. I had all the silver parts painted flat charcoal. I did it to be different after inflicting serious scratches and dents along the fairing, gas tank and side cover with a piece of metal I was tossing away while cleaning out my garage. I tossed it right at the bike forgetting it was there. The paint scheme would be helpful tonight. I just needed to insert my switchable light fuse which would allow me to turn my lights on and off with a flip of my thumb. I already had a 007, flip-up, license plate courtesy of sport bikers who'd invented that handy little feature.

I drank a Coke, ate six Oreos, drank a protein drink and popped four Excedrin to keep me awake. The time was 11:10 p.m. Lauren was asleep. I estimated six hours to do the op including travel. I got on my bike and headed to Merrick.

I set the GPS for Monty's house. I wore a full-face flat charcoal grey and flat black helmet. It was very difficult to see me at night dressed as I was which was my intent. The GPS would speak to me via a Bluetooth speaker. No lights from the

GPS would show. I could listen to my iPod the same way. You couldn't hear the BMW running standing next to it. I flew down the road. I cruised at three miles per hour over the speed limit. I jammed to REM along the way. It was nice to be out on a bike.

#

I arrived after an hour and sixteen minutes. I tried the lights-off feature and kicked up my speed to near one hundred miles per hour to feel the bike. I parked on the sidewalk by some bushes a few houses up and around the corner from Monty's house. The house is a standard Merrick, Levitt owner styled home with a basement and a two-car, detached garage out back. I pulled on a pair of night vision goggles and my blacked-out Yankees ball cap over top, backwards. I flipped the NVGs up in standby. I observed the home and walked around it. No alarm, lights or dogs. I used the pistol-grip lock pick on the basement door. I was inside in less than a minute. I flipped down my NVGs and swept the basement. What jumped out immediately were the two sets of twin bunkbeds and mismatched couches arranged in a U-shape. I flicked on my black-light penlight. Organics were all over the room and the furniture. I wasn't prepared for this. I'd have to improvise. I walked upstairs. Of note, I found the door locks to the basement door reversed. I was locked in. I opened them within a few seconds. I found a hasp in place on the kitchen side of the door, but no lock installed. The door was a metal, solid core, fireproof door sealed with a rubberized, magnetic strip like you'd find between a garage and house.

I walked through the kitchen then the hallway to the master bedroom. The rooms were tidy but old and dated. In the master, I found a king bed, a dresser, two nightstands, a bureau, and a chair. On a corner desk was the computer. I attached my equipment, and I downloaded the files. I placed a camera and microphone by the bed. I moved into the closet. Men's and women's clothing. Monty was divorced and lived alone. Whose clothes were in the closet? I looked under the bed. What, was it a bad guy thing to store weapons in a suitcase under a bed? I photographed all as I'd done in the other homes. I found several pistols and a sawed-off shotgun. I also found ten sets of handcuffs which I found unusual. I pounded the firing pin over in the shotgun. Now he couldn't fire it. I put all away and headed to the kitchen and living room. I placed some cameras and microphones. From under a kitchen cabinet, I grabbed some plastic bags. I ran to the bathroom and found some Q-tips. Then I thought about what might be upstairs.

I walked up the stairs. I found a bathroom at the head of the stairs. To the right was a neat and organized guest room. I opened the door to the left and my heart shuddered. It contained just a full-sized bed covered in a dark sheet. Nylon rope, or line to us U.S. Navy types, was looped around each leg of the bedframe and to a metal ring hanging from the ceiling. Organics were everywhere. I walked to the linen closet and removed a clean washcloth then wet it with fresh water. I flipped off my NVGs and using my black-light pen for illumination, I dabbed a spot with water then rolled the Q-tip end in it then placed it in a plastic bag. I repeated this seventeen more times. I got another cloth, wet it and headed downstairs.

I searched the kitchen. His bank and stash were in the freezer. I found eight nearly five-inch thick bundles of money wrapped in white deli paper in addition to at least two kilos of cocaine. I estimated he had $800,000 in the freezer.

I walked to the basement and took eighteen more samples of organics. I photographed the room with my smartphone. I departed the house.

I walked to the garage. It was unlocked. Inside I found a dark blue or blue grey Ford van. It was rusty and dirty. On the side was a large sign with a white background indicated South Shore Fryer Service. Inside I found a futon mattress, more nylon line, rags, and newspapers. Five-gallon buckets filled the back of the van along with what I assumed was equipment to clean deep fat fryers. I took some photographs. I bagged the rags and closed the door and placed a GPS tracker on the rear roof by the commercial roof-rack. I placed a camera in the rafters to view the van as it departed and entered the garage. I memorized the license plate. I looked around. The garage was a drive through type with a back door. I looked out and saw tire tracks across the property behind Monty's garage. I knew how he evaded the FBI surveillance. The right side of the garage was full of tools, a work bench, and stacks of lawn chemicals. I thought the pallet of lime excessive, especially for his postage stamp lot. South Shore Long Island lawns are usual high in ph requiring the addition of sulphur not lime.

I was finished. I was way behind, but it couldn't be helped. I departed the garage. A dog barked. I stood still and listened. I walked to my bike, took off my NVGs and cap, and put on my helmet. I got on and took off for Paul's house. I was very concerned about what I'd discovered.

#

I arrived at Paul's house. I wondered how far I was from Erica's house. I put on my NVGs and ball cap. The house is a large Mediterranean-styled house with a decidedly Italianate flare. Lots of tile, masonry, pea gravel, stone, and bricks. Hardscape was everywhere. It had a pool and a three-car, side-load garage that you entered from Prospect Road. The house was built on the two lots at the point of Prospect Road and Fairview Place. Several lights were on inside.

I walked to the garage and peered inside through the window. There was a late-model, red Corvette, some kid's toys, and boating equipment. The far-left spot was open, and I assumed it was for the Navigator SUV. I used the key Haley provided to gain entrance. I placed a camera where it viewed the open parking spot and door. I looked around, but nothing interested me.

I left the garage headed for the back door. I saw two cameras, but they viewed the walkway from the side yard gate and walkway from the dock. I was walking in between their fields of view. I opened the door with the key and looked for the alarm pad. I found it on the wall. I nearly entered Haley's code, but suddenly realized the system would record who entered the log-in. I quickly entered M-o-n-t-y and was rewarded with access. Perfect. I went to work. I placed cameras and microphones in the master bedroom, study, and kitchen since I figured that's where Paul's men hung out by the looks of the place. I got into his computer in the study, downloaded the files, and uploaded the software that would send new files and keystroke information to the Cloud account.

I walked through the rest of the house. Nice place. I was finished. I reset the alarm and departed by the way I came. I gained some time on my schedule. I walked past the garage then thought I'd check something.

I noticed a center console boat, two PWCs and a go-fast boat of perhaps thirty feet in length tied up at the dock out back. The bay was flat and calm. The go-fast boat was black and had a pair of outdrives on it. I climbed down into the go-fast boat. I affixed a GPS tracker near the mechanical interference near the stern-drives. The boat had a short windshield, a small cuddy cabin, a compass, a VHF marine radio, an AM/FM/CD stereo, and a mounted GPS. I placed a canvas seat cover over the GPS unit and turned it on. I tapped through the history to the last voyage. The last time the boat went out it traveled to a point twelve-miles south by southwest off Jones Inlet across from Point Lookout. That voyage was taken after midnight last Monday. There is no legitimate reason for a black go-fast boat to be out at that hour. I photographed the display, downloaded the history to a jump drive and turned the unit off. I had a very good idea how the children were transported off the island. I was caught between disabling this boat or leaving it alone. I knew about this boat. I didn't know about an alternate plan, so I let the boat be. I memorized the boat's registration and the registration of the center console.

I put the seat cover back and got out of the boat headed for my motorcycle. I took off for Rockville Center. The time was 1:48 a.m.

#

I arrived at the restaurant. I drove up and down each street to get a feel for the area. I came into the rear of the rear parking lot which is shared with other businesses. I'd already turned off my lights and flipped up my plate. I saw the Lincoln Navigator parked, backed in, near the median strip between the north and south sides of the lot. The restaurant occupied an L-shaped piece of land with the front doors facing Park Avenue to the west, the restaurant being between Sunrise Highway and Merrick Road. The back doors led to the parking lot. There was a public entrance and a kitchen access from the parking lot.

I parked my bike near the end of the lot in a park of trees by Morris Avenue to the east and walked toward the Navigator. I stood next to the Navigator, closed my eyes and pressed the key fob button. The locks popped and I got into the driver's seat. I put the key in the ignition and turned it on accessory then to off. I sensed the lights go out and opened my eyes. I went to work. I downloaded the vehicle's data from its computer via the OBDII port then I plugged in the camera and kill switch. I set a microphone in the head rest behind the back seat where I'd observed Paul sit. I placed another camera on the rearview mirror as I'd done on the Town Car.

I went through the glove box, console and ashtray. I saw a ministorage scan-card in the ashtray. I got out of the vehicle and placed a GPS unit just under the roof rack. It was 2:14 a.m.

I rode off on my bike while I let time pass. I cruised to the Atlantic Ocean and back on Long Beach Road. I would have gone to my home in Oceanside, but I didn't want to draw any attention to me riding down my street.

I rode back to the restaurant. It was approaching 3 a.m. I pulled up to the parking lot and parked nearer to the restaurant, behind another business. I removed my FLIR scope and observed the restaurant. Thirty-six cars remained in the lot, some, perhaps, belonging to people who owned a nearby business. I didn't know how many employees worked at Tito's, but I assumed many if the restaurant sat two hundred people. I also didn't know if Paul closed the place or left that to someone else?

I watched people leaving. I noticed employees leaving and by 3:20 a.m. the lot held just twelve cars. I watched the doors open again and seven men depart. Paul, Monty, the driver, and four other men who all looked familiar. I realized I was looking at Vincenzo Menduni and three of his men. Paul walked to the Navigator. Monty and the driver walked to Monty's Impala, and Vincenzo and his men walked to a Mercedes-Benz S Class LWB. Had I paid attention I could have tagged Vincenzo's car, too. I needed to brush up on planning for my black bag ops.

After five minutes of talk the men departed. I waited and watched for nearly thirty minutes before walking to the back door. I used the key and got inside. I flipped down my NVG but decided I didn't need them due to the light coming from under the swinging doors from the bar and dining room. I found the office and accessed the computers. One was for HR and administration, and the other appeared to be a server for the point-of-sale terminals. I downloaded the files from both. I placed a camera aimed at the row of three desks. I departed the office for the reserved table Haley had described. I placed microphones at six different locations and placed three decoy chirpers to be found if someone looked for microphones. I placed four cameras in the artwork and plants along the walls and dividers near the table. I was finished.

I hustled to my bike, placed my equipment in a saddle bag, put away my NVGs and cap and put on my helmet. I jumped onto the bike, put the iPod on to Autograph's Turn up the Radio. I blasted the music while I hit the throttle heading down Sunrise Highway. It was just before 4 a.m. I cruised Sunrise Highway until I came to the Massapequa Diner where I pulled over. I was ravenously hungry. I went inside and took a small booth. The waitress appeared.

"Coffee?" she said.

"Yes. I want six eggs, scrambled, eight pieces of bacon and toast with strawberry jam."

"Yes, sir."

I called Joe on my mother's cell phone.

"Shit man, it's about time. I've been wondering. I was about to drive there," Joe said.

"Oh? You were worried about me? I got all four targets. If I had my shit together I could have tagged Vincenzo's car. Stayton is right about Monty. His basement is full of bunk beds and couches. Covered with organics. But upstairs it's a den of horrors. The left side bedroom has just a bed, nylon rope around the bedframe and it's splattered with blood. And, get this, I found an older, black, go-fast boat behind Paul Menduni's house. The last time the GPS indicates it was used for a trip twelve-miles south by southwest off Jones Inlet and back. The boat had the same nylon line. I found a van in Monty's garage with a mattress in it, more nylon line, and a bunch of five-gallon buckets. The van had a sign on the side that indicated it was a commercial fryer cleaning service."

"Shit. We gotta do something."

"I took samples of the organics. I have thirty-six samples in plastic bags. I need to get this to Stayton. I put a tracker on the boat."

"What are you doing later?"

"I'll take Lauren to school and take a nap. I'll freeze the samples. Stayton is right to worry about this guy."

"Maybe Dave has some radar data on shipping off Jones Inlet that night," Joe said.

"What's Dave doing now?"

"He's Officer-in-Charge of the Coast Guard Sector New York Command Center at Staten Island. He runs boats along the coasts of New Jersey and Long Island. They do board and search, but the HQ has the radar history for the Captain of the Port," Joe said.

"Okay. Call him. The plot placed the furthest point twelve miles out at just after midnight. I'll text the longitude and latitude to you later."

"Shit. You done good, sailor boy."

"I'll call Stayton after I get up. I want Monty off the streets. I wonder who else is in on this enterprise? I don't see the old man nor Vincenzo doing this."

"I agree, but what do we know. We need to look at the computer data and those swabs. Those two girls they found last week . . . they'd been repeatedly raped. Their hands and feet were bound at one time."

"I'll copy the jump drives for Stayton. I'm at Massapequa Diner. By the time I'm home, I'll need to get Lauren up. Knowing my body, I'll crash for a few hours right after I drop her at school. Let me get three or four hours sleep before you call. I'll be ready then."

"Okay. I'll call Dave. I'll call you after 10 a.m."

"Thanks. Bye."

I gobbled my food. I asked for two crumb buns and two bacons, egg, and cheese on toasted hard roll sandwiches to go. I paid, packed and got on my bike. I was okay. I turned on my music and blasted down the highway headed for Greenport.

#

I arrived home after 6 a.m. I popped the sandwiches in a frying pan to warm and toast-up the rolls, and I put the crumb buns in the microwave oven. I started coffee. I walked upstairs.

"Hey, you. Get up. Time for school," I said.

Lauren awoke with a smile, then noticed how I was dressed.

"How'd it go?"

"Great. I'm warming sandwiches and crumb buns."

"Oh. Good. I'll be right down."

I ran to my room, shed my clothing, showered, put on some jeans and a T-shirt. I ran downstairs to the kitchen. I placed the organic samples in a brown paper bag and into the freezer.

"Hi," Lauren said.

"Morning." I punched the microwave switch to warm the buns. I flipped the sandwiches onto plates and put one in front of Lauren then poured her a glass of milk.

"You stopped at a diner."

"I did." I placed a crumb bun in front of her. "This is okay for breakfast?" I said.

"It's great. You look tired. Take a nap before you go out tonight."

"I will. In the war, we would be just getting back about now. Sometimes they'd bring us breakfast. We'd eat, wash off the war, clean our equipment, post it in our ready boxes, prepare our uniforms for the next shift and go to bed until late afternoon. We'd get up between 1500 and 1530 hours to eat, do some things, maybe a short work-out, and eat some more. I'd have to be at a brief by 1800. We'd plan or finish planning the night's work, get ready and do it all over again.

"How are you though?"

"I'm good. C'mon. We should go. Red roses? Who has the best?"

"The old florist in Greenport. Order them and tell them you'll pick them up later."

#

I dropped Lauren at school, then I drove to the florist where I ordered two dozen red roses. I drove home and collapsed into my bed. I was thankful that my mother put long, lined drapes on the windows in the bedroom.

CHAPTER 10

I awoke at 11 a.m. I showered again to wake up. I reheated some coffee. I made a protein shake and I added all sorts of ingredients to it. Even a scoop of vanilla ice cream. Lots of protein and likely 1600 calories, but I needed it.

I went to work on the computers. I put Monty's jump drive in. I looked at the file list and realized that not only did he have mail files and document files, but he also had picture files of child porn. I downloaded the emails for the past month and scrolled through them. He didn't work with Paul on this I could glean from the emails. Let's see, "Hamas Hammod" was listed, which was no doubt an alias. The email contained a longitude and latitude which nearly matched the one I got off the GPS. I'd seen enough then another email caught my eye. I read it. It was about the children found dead last week. It seems that "Hamas Hammod" rejected them, and he disposed of two more that he was not pleased with. I was thoroughly sickened. I called Stayton.

"Hello?"

"MacKenzie here. You need evidence on that Monty guy?"

"I do."

"Can we meet? I'll be honest. I don't want to drive to the city. I got in very late and just got up," I said.

"Busy night?" Stayton said.

"Yes. I have his data on a jump drive. There are emails about the two girls last week and two more girls. There are organics all over his basement and an upstairs bedroom. I took thirty-six samples. They're in my freezer. He's ducking you guys with a black go-fast boat behind Paul Menduni's house and a dark-colored van. The last trip was a week ago Monday night around midnight, to a point twelve miles off the coast from Jones Inlet. Can we meet here?"

"We're on our way to Mattituck Airport. I'll call before we arrive at your home."

"Bring a computer. I'm afraid to look at this stuff on mine."

"Got it. We're leaving now. Bye."

I called Joe.

"Hey. I was just about to call you. Dave is working on locating the surface shipping data for that night. He said if FBI asks, he can spend more time on it. He's swamped right now."

"Stayton is flying out to Mattituck Airport on his way here. I can't send you everything on Monty because I don't want it on my computer."

"That's fine, Mark. We want just the financials anyway so just pull those files."

"Oh. Right. I haven't gone through the other two guys' computers yet. I'm going to copy them because FBI wants those, too, I suspect. I'll send all except Monty to your Cloud account."

Okay. I have your concealed carry license. They overnighted it to my office. I'll send it to you via courier now. Don't forget to register all the trackers, microphones, and cameras you placed last night."

"I'll do that now. I'll call you."

"Okay. Be cool," Joe said.

#

I activated most of the cameras and microphones on my tablet. I entered the tracker details for Paul's SUV. The SUV was at his house. I entered the GPS tracker details for the go-fast boat. It was still at the dock. My phone rang.

"Hello."

"Yes. Mr. MacKenzie. Your flower order is ready for pick up."

"Thank you. I'll be down in a bit."

I better check my suit.

I ran upstairs and pulled my John Varvatos suit off the bar. Good to go. I had a freshly starched and pressed white shirt that looked crisp and nice next to the jacket. I readied my cuff links, a tie just in case, a blue silk square as I'd been instructed, my black leather boots, also by John Varvatos, and matching belt. I pulled out a SIG P226 pistol, loaded it and placed it in a black leather pancake holster. I was good to go. I went back downstairs.

I copied the jump drives for all but Monty's computer to Joe's Cloud account. I began to review the data for the original bad guys. I managed to kill the last half hour researching. I dressed in jeans and a button-down blue shirt. I made coffee and some unsweet tea. My phone buzzed.

"Hello?"

"It's Stayton. We're rolling up in two vehicles."

"Fine. Just come on in, the door is open.

"Bye."

Several minutes later I heard the vehicles pull up. I heard six doors close so there were at least six of them. A knock at the door.

"Come in," I yelled.

The door opened. First in was Dan Carter, who nodded at me, then John Stayton.

"Mr. MacKenzie, please meet special agents John Driscoll, Ron Wyckoff, Bill North and Melissa Shepard."

"Hi. Coffee anyone?"

"Sure. Thanks," John said.

"Who's the techie?" I asked.

"Shepard and Wyckoff," John said.

"You may set up on the counter there in the kitchen. Electrical outlets are available under the counter," I said as I poured coffee. Wyckoff and Shepard set up laptops.

"This jump drive is from Monty Fiorelli's computer. Take it with you. I don't want it in the house. These here . . ." I pulled the bag of organics from the freezer. "are the samples of organic material, mostly blood, I took from the locations marked on the bags. John, something terrible has happened in that house."

John nodded and Driscoll took the samples.

"Here is a sample of the line I took from his van."

"His van? What van?" Dan asked.

"A dark blue or grey Ford Econoline. I'm not sure what year. New York plate MDS-7743. It has a sign for a fryer cleaning service on each side," I said.

Dan took notes then got on a phone.

"He was driving a blue, late model Impala last night. New York ZTS-4971. Okay. Ask away. What do you need to know? I assume Monty is your most pressing issue," I said.

"He is. Describe what you found," John said.

I described the events of my previous night with precise details. The special agents periodically stopped me to inquire further and to, no doubt, check the accuracy of my intel. After an hour, they were out of questions.

"Hold on, Mr. MacKenzie. What do you want to do, John?" Stayton said to Driscoll.

"Stony Brook is our best bet," Driscoll said.

"How long?" Stayton said.

"The rest of the day for all samples. I detect organics. It might work," Driscoll said.

"Mark. We need to land a helicopter on your lot next door," Stayton said.

"Do it," I said.

"Dan call them over. Melissa what do you have?" Stayton said.

"At least seventeen of the missing children. Mr. MacKenzie are the mismatched couches set up in a U-shape?" Melissa said.

"Yes. With twin bunk beds behind."

"Do you recognize the furniture in this picture?" Melissa asked.

It was a picture of a little girl, perhaps nine or ten years old, naked on the center couch. She'd been beaten and she was bleeding from various parts of her body.

"Yes . . . that's the basement set up," I said.

"And this. Is that the other room you mentioned?" Melissa asked.

The picture showed a young girl of fourteen or fifteen years, tied to the bed, naked, beaten and bleeding. My blood temperature rose.

"Yes. It is," I said. I looked up at John Stayton who'd been watching me as I sat down in the adjoining den. I could feel the heat of anger shoot through my veins after looking at those pictures. I'd seen a whole lot of death and injury in my life, but those pictures I'd just seen . . .

"What else do you need?" I said, my nerves on edge.

"The data you collected. Where is it?" Stayton said.

"Right here. Numbers one and two, the red jump drive, came from the homes, numbers three and four, the yellow drive came from the business and the blue drive, five and six, the two guys I pegged the day we met."

I heard a chopper coming in and could hear the turbine engine straining as it hovered and landed.

"John. Do what you need to do. Melissa. You don't need to be here," Stayton said.

"Yes, sir." Melissa unplugged her computer. She handed jump drives to Stayton.

"I copied them. There is all manner of evidence in there. Emails, pictures, texts, Twitter, Facebook, and Instagram files. I'll match the players and the children to the photos," she said.

"Fine. Get going. You heard our confidential informant's statement. Get warrants ready to go to the district court in Central Islip," Stayton said.

"Yes, sir."

The chopper landed and powered down. Boy, would I be getting some questions from the neighbors. After a few minutes the chopper powered up and took off with the two agents.

"Okay, Mark. We'll go through all this. We'll contact you with our questions. We will have more. Anything else?" Stayton said.

"What I'm about to tell you I got from a seven-year-old boy. Monty grabbed Paul Menduni's neighbor, Erica. A fourteen or fifteen-year-old girl per Haley Menduni. I didn't get a last name," I said.

"How did you get that information?" North asked.

"Last week I went to my sister's school to set up parent-teacher conferences. I met Ms. Menduni who is a teacher there. Ms. Menduni, who will be granted a divorce next week, was on break so we had our conference over coffee across from the school. The next day my sister had softball practice, so I waited for her across the street at the coffee shop. Ms. Menduni came out and we had coffee together. While we spoke, her husband drove up with her son, Monty, and the driver. He spoke with

Ms. Menduni then roughly grabbed her by her arm. She protested and I stepped in. Monty tried to intimidate me, and I put him on the ground. Later, Paulie, the seven-year-old, thanked me for knocking Monty down because he said, 'He's mean to me.' After you mentioned that information about Monty, I asked Haley whether Monty had ever done anything to Paulie. She conveyed to me what I just said to you," I said.

"You had an altercation with Monty?" Stayton said.

"Yes. He put his hand on my shoulder on Paul's order. I put him down on the ground. Paul called off his dogs and they departed. Haley and I have since begun to date," I said.

Special Agent North was shaking his head.

"But you got into this because of your parents' deaths, right?" Stayton said.

"Correct. I met with Nassau PD. I learned enough helpful information that allowed me to identify Castellano and Palami. I did this with Monty only because you guys asked. I would never have bothered with Monty unless my investigation led to him. I doubt it would have since the two I'm looking at work for Romeo Menduni," I said.

Stayton nodded. "I'm good with this. Thanks for telling us," he said.

"Are you going to watch this creep?" I said.

"I expect we'll arrest him by this time tomorrow. I hope your DNA samples show some connection, too. We're going to get out of your hair now. We'll be in touch. Anything else folks? Thanks, Mark."

I walked them to the door. They departed. Shit! I had to shower, shave, pick up flowers, and pick-up Lauren. Crap!

#

I flew up the road to the school to get Lauren.

"Hi. You're not dressed," Lauren said.

"I know. I gotta get the flowers. Come on."

I drove like a madman to the florist, ran into the store, grabbed the flowers, and a small bunch for Lauren, paid, then hurried out to the Yukon. I jumped in and we took off.

"Here. You've been a pretty sweet little sister lately."

"Thank you, Mark. Now when you get home you have to get ready."

"Thanks for pointing out the obvious."

We pulled into the driveway. I put the roses in the back seat of the Hellcat, ran upstairs and got into the shower. A knock at the door.

"Yes?"

Lauren came into the bedroom.

"And shave, too," Lauren said.

"I am. Thanks. I've done this before."

"Not really. You dated Cathy mostly since high school. You knew her in grade school," Lauren said.

"Can we do this another time?"

"Oh. Yeah. I'll come back once you're decent," she said.

I finished shaving. No bleeders. Good. My hair was way too long for the navy, but it looked fine. I toweled off, put on all the lotions and liquids that Esquire says I need, and I dressed.

"Okay in there? Lauren said.

"You can come in now, if you must."

I tucked in my shirt and looked at myself in the mirror. With the boots on I was more like six-foot five-inches tall. I put on my father's Omega Seamaster, linked the cuffs with the cuff links and squared away the pocket square. Some hand lotion stuff and Dolce Gabbana Blue something squirted on me, and I turned to my sister for approval.

"Okay?"

"You are a rock star! She's gonna love it. Now don't forget to compliment her. And escort her. She'll hold the crook of your right arm."

"Lauren. I know all that. What's that?"

"A courier delivery for you I found at the door."

I opened it. My concealed carry permit. I stuck it in my wallet. Cash? I walked to my dresser and took out some cash and put it in my pocket. I grabbed my SIG off the bed and placed it at the small of my back. I ran downstairs. Lauren walked out of the kitchen.

"You look great. Here's your phone and auto charger. Anything else?"

"No? Right?" I said.

"Sunglasses?" Lauren said as she twirled them on her finger.

"Oh. Thanks." I kissed my sister's cheek.

"Bye."

"Bye. Have a nice time."

"We will."

I got in the car and floored it out of there. I punched it as I hit the highway. I had four miles and ten minutes. I relaxed at one mile away. I wondered if I should have told Lauren about the helicopter landing? I slowed to turn onto Haley's street. I drove about two blocks and I pulled up to the door in the semi-circle driveway. I looked at my watch which would have informed me of the time had I set it. I looked at my phone. One minute to go. I grabbed the flowers and walked to the front door. I pressed the doorbell.

Haley's father came to the door.

Shit—I mean shoot. What is his sir name? I didn't ask Haley.

"Hello. You must be Mark? I'm Haley's father."

I wondered how many sharp-dressed men appeared at his door with flowers? Then I decided he was just responding to my arrival.

"I'm John."

Come on. Just a little bit more.

"John Shore," he said.

"It's nice to meet you, Mr. Shore," I said.

"Please. Come in. Haley will be down in a minute. Nice car. I had one when they first came out."

"Oh. A 2008?"

"No. A 1970."

"Oh? Yeah. That's right."

"Your car looks special."

"It is. The SRT-8 Hellcat version."

"Sharp. Oh. This is my wife, Evelyn."

"Hello, Mrs. Shore. It's nice to meet you."

"It's very nice to meet you, too. You look very nice tonight."

"Thank you."

"Please. Come in," Evelyn said. I followed them through the entry foyer to the living room.

Their house is a New England Cape Cod, but on a grand scale. I could see my mother's touch. The house was large and airy. My Mom went with a blue and white theme with other primary colors here and there to draw interest.

"Very nice. I'd have recognized the style even if Haley had not mentioned that you hired my mother," I said.

"I loved your mother. I'm so terribly sorry. I didn't know until Haley told me. I feel so bad," Evelyn said.

"You shouldn't. You have a nice home and the memory of redecorating your home with her. You'll have to come see the beach cottage. Mom did everything to it. She taught my little sister who helped and, well, Lauren can tell you all about it," I said.

"Maarrrrkk!" Paulie yelled as he ran to me.

"Hey. You been eating your vegetables like I said?"

"Yes, sir. Every day. Right Grandma?"

"He has ever since you spoke to him," Evelyn said with a smile.

"Mark has big muscles, Grandma. I want mine to be big, too. I'm going to my Dad's tonight. I wish I didn't have to go," Paulie said. I looked at Evelyn and John who tried to keep their facial expressions neutral without much luck. I smiled at Paulie and messed up his hair.

"That's all right, Paulie. You'll go fishing with your grandpa again soon, I'm sure." Turning to Mr. Shore. "I understand you have a fishing boat?" I said.

"Yes. A Grady White. It's twenty-eight feet with twin Yamaha F250s. It's a walk-around cuddy cabin model," Mr. Shore said.

"I understand you go out often," I said.

"A few times a week. I don't golf, so fishing is my past time," John said.

"I can golf, but I'd rather fish. I—we—the family have an old Parker twenty-eight pilot house with twin F250s. Nice but rugged. I've decided to get a larger family cruiser so the ladies can go out. I've been polling everyone. Mrs. Shore. What do you like or prefer in a boat?"

"Oh. Well, two things. A comfortable bathroom and a kitchen where a real meal can be prepared."

"Good points. And you Mr. Shore? What should a family boat have?"

"I'd have to add the space where the family can be together and sit and not have to be sitting in folding beach chairs, and good electronics since valuable cargo will be aboard," Mr. Shore said as he hugged Paulie to him.

"What are you looking at getting?"

"A boat between fifty and sixty-five feet. I'm having our pier enlarged, lengthened, and strengthened to hold a larger boat just because my Dad taught me to over-build things," I said.

"Hi!"

I turned at the sound of Haley's voice.

"Uh, Hi. Wow. You look nice," I said.

"Thank you," Haley said as she smiled and looked at her mother.

"Oh. These are for you," I said as I passed the roses to Haley.

"They're gorgeous. Thank you. They smell so nice. I should put them in water."

"I'll do that for you," Evelyn said.

"Thank you, Mom."

"Why do men have to give ladies flowers?" Paulie said, which I found funny. His grandfather answered first.

"It's so she'll go out with you again," John said.

"No. It's to show the lady that you admire her and think she's special," Evelyn said as she turned her gaze to me.

"Do you admire my mom, Mark?" Paulie asked.

I smiled at Haley.

"Yes, Paulie. I admire your mom. She's special. But we'd better get going or she'll be special and late, too," I said.

"Oh. Bye. Paulie be good. Thanks, Mom, Dad. Let's go, Mark," Haley said.

"It was terrific meeting you all. I look forward to the next time. Bye," I said.

I opened the door for Haley, and we departed. She took my right arm for the walk to the car. I opened the door and helped Haley into her seat. I ran around the other side, jumped in and we were off.

#

"Hi. You look very nice, too. That's a nice suit and the blue square and cuff links work," Haley said.

"Thank you. I thought they'd work well together."

"Sure, with help from Lauren."

"What? Are you already in on the ladies' telephone line?"

"Not completely. Lauren and I talk at school, and she did call me about the suit you're wearing. She mentioned that you looked nice in black with a touch of blue."

"There are no secrets with you ladies."

"No. That's Led Zepplin playing Good Times, Bad Times?" Haley said.

"It is. You like Led Zepplin?"

"I do. My mother has their vinyl albums. My mother likes rock. Dad does, too."

#

We zoomed to the Lobster Roll with Led Zepplin as background music. We parked and walked inside. They led us to a table for two. The service was great.

"This is so nice. I never thought it was so intimate and classy. The name is misleading," Haley said.

"I guess so. I suppose if they called it the Lobster Bisque it might seem classier. Lobster Roll is better sounding than the other New England favorite."

"The Clam Roll?" Haley said.

"You got it."

"What are you getting for dinner?" Haley said.

"I will get a piece of beef and the lobster tails. And you?"

"I think lobster for me with the vegetables. I think salad and soup come with our dinners."

"Good. I'm hungry. How was your school day?"

"The usual. Oh. Did a helicopter land in your yard today?"

"The lot next door." I sipped my water. After a pause, Haley spoke.

"You know, Mark, this works better if you tell me the whole story," Haley said.

"Oh. I was just answering your question."

"Can you say why a helicopter landed on the lot 'next door' to your home?"

"Can I take a rain-check on that and tell you in a couple of days once it's done?"

"Yes. You know, for a part-time securities broker, you sure are Mr. Cryptic Mysterious."

"How'd you know that was my call sign—Cryptic Mysterious?"

"Was that really your call sign?"

"No. I was given the nickname Night Eagle."

Haley squinted her eyes as she tilted her head in thought.

"I like that. It's different. Someone gave you that name?"

"Yes. A more senior officer during my first tour. He gave me the name during the first battle of Al-Fallujah."

"Here are our drinks. Will you have a glass of wine during dinner?"

"Sure, but what goes with beef and lobster?" I grinned.

"A nice Zinfandel. We'll get that. I noticed that you eat mostly proteins, fats and vegetables in the afternoon and evening."

"That's right. I eat carbs in the morning before or after exercise.

"I'm ready."

We placed our orders with the waiter.

"You look beautiful. How bad was I when I first saw you?"

"Not too bad. You recovered well. But thank you. It's been a long time since a man looked at me like that."

"You're a teacher. No one wants to think of a teacher that way. Well, except for twelfth-grade jocks in Florida."

"Isn't that's terrible?"

"Now hold on. You're an eighteen-year-old hero jock and you knock off a twenty-two-year-old honey who looks like that teacher looks. There's no damage. He's high-fiving in the locker room while society is figuring out how damaged he is and how to protect him. It's BS. I'm not saying what she did is right. She should be fired, but I'm also not saying how they're handling it is right. She's a sex offender? Come on?"

"I see your point. What if it was an eighteen-year-old girl and a twenty-two-year-old man?"

"That's different. I still don't believe it's a sex offender crime though with the ages that close. As an eighteen-year-old you can choose to go to war. You can kill another human being because the government says it's okay, but you cannot have sex with a twenty-two-year-old or have a drink? It's silly."

Our salads came with bread.

"Bread?" I offered.

"Thank you. I see your point. Now make it a seventeen or eighteen-year-old girl and a forty-year-old man."

"Big difference. Now you have a fully-grown man who shouldn't be with anyone but his wife or, at least, a woman his age. See, that girl belongs to her family. Another man should have taken responsibility for her before that could happen. No men older than Lauren will spend time with her unless they're vetted by me. I'm responsible for her."

I ripped up some bread and slathered it with butter now that our government said it was okay to eat butter again. Our soup arrived.

"What do you think about when you're alone and not doing anything, Mark?"

"Of late? How my family got all mixed up in this problem? Why my parents died? How I was so afraid to be responsible for Lauren? Things like that."

"Are you still afraid to be responsible for Lauren?"

"Not so much. I'm still afraid I'll screw up, but I think she knows it. She tells me that she's fine knowing I care even though I don't know the ropes of parenting yet."

"What of the future? You don't have children of your own."

"I know. I thought I would by now then my wife pulled her stunt. I'd still like to have children. What about you?"

"I have a boy, but I'd like a few more."

"A few? In my family, a few is three or more."

"That's right."

"Oh."

"How old are you, Mark?"

"I'm thirty-two this past October. And you?"

"I turned thirty this past March."

"Oh. I thought you were older. Not by your looks, but by how you speak and act."

"I was raised almost as an only child. My older brother died when I was four. My parents never had any more children. I always wished for a sister or brother or that my brother would come back. What about you?"

"As a kid, I thought I was different because I was an only child. My mother had a medical problem. She wasn't supposed to have any more children—her tubes were tied. Lauren was the miracle baby. I think I was happier than my parents when I heard."

"Are you two close?"

"I think so. We're talking more. I don't talk too much about . . . well, I don't talk too much about anything. After my parents died Lauren took on the project of essentially saving me. Mentally and physically. My wounds caused several infections. I lost eighty pounds. I had a lot wrong with me. Lauren, my grandmothers, and aunts rotated being with me. If Lauren wrote a paper about what she did last summer, it would be about how she saved me. I had just begun to improve two weeks before my parents' deaths. I slid backwards after they died. But we talk about everything. I talk to her and treat her like she's an adult. We're close. She's teaching me about you women. That ladies' telephone chat line. That's my sister, my aunts, and grandmothers. They talk two or three times a day. There are no secrets in my family. I'd bet Lauren has spoken with both grandmothers, our Aunt Lorraine or Aunt Missy or Aunt Betsy today about our date."

Haley laughed. "That's because we're the glue that holds the family together. Lauren and I speak each day now. It's how we bond. Same with my mother and me. It looks like our food is coming."

The waiter brought our entrées and poured us each a glass of wine. As we started our meals Haley continued.

"What do you look forward to in the future?"

"I guess it's for a simpler life. Everything in my life is layers deep. I'd like just simple things. A problem presents itself and I fix it. Lauren needs help with homework, I help her. My grandparents want to visit, I arrange it. Right now, I don't have that. My life is unsettled, too complicated and not easily fixed. A nagging unknown is out there that I need to figure out or I fear my life will never be settled. I'll resolve it eventually, but I don't have that simplicity and, combined with my combat-related issues, I'm . . . I'm not right with the world. I'm not at peace."

I took another bite of beef and lobster.

"Do you have PTSD or depression?"

I nodded. Haley looked at me for more. I was beginning to recognize the look.

"I have a counselor at VA. I haven't had a nightmare since the day after I met you. That's good news."

Haley smiled at my revelation.

"Life is complicated, but I understand what you mean. What about work? Do you want to work in the city?"

"Yes and no. I feel obligated to my family and to the employees who have served the firm so well, but I feel a greater obligation to Lauren. I won't work full-time until Lauren is in college. I think I may have mentioned that"

"What's going on that you need to fix?"

"It all comes back to my parents' deaths. So, while I'm working a day or two each week at the firm, I'm working to resolve that issue, too."

"Can you resolve the issue with your parents' deaths?"

"As far as finding who did it? Yes. I'll figure that out if the cops don't beat me to it. Their deaths, them being gone, will always leave a hole in my heart. I'm still working on that issue. I may have just begun to grieve so I must get through that. I think I'll make it, but I'm . . . I'm . . . so angry and sad and depressed. I avoid it to survive—shove it back until I can deal with it the right way. I'm not over the five stages of grief so I've not processed it right. I know you've caught me doing that—shoving the problem away."

I took another bite of lobster.

"What about you? You love teaching and children . . . are you headed where you want to go?"

Haley paused as she finished chewing. She took another bite while she thought about her answer.

"I want to teach. I want to be with children. I'm partly on track. I'd like to have some more children. I'm behind there. I'd take time off from teaching periodically to do that, but I will always teach. I like being a mother. I like being a teacher. I liked being a wife and still would be if I'd married a decent man."

That was thorough and to the point.

"How's your dinner?" I asked.

"Good. Almost as good as the company. So, what are we doing after this?"

"Lauren didn't tell you?"

"No. She can keep some secrets."

"It's still a secret then. You'll see soon enough."

I looked at my watch. Oops. I still hadn't set my watch. I looked at my phone for the right time and set it.

"Your watch wasn't set?"

"No. I was a little disorganized this afternoon. It's my father's watch. It's automatic so it had stopped. I put it on and ran off and didn't realize until I was on my way to your house."

"Were you nervous about our date?"

"I'm still nervous. How am I doing?"

"You are doing just fine," Haley said as she smiled.

I plopped my last bite into my mouth and wiped my mouth with my napkin. I sipped my wine. Only my third sip. I drank my water and ate one more piece of bread with butter.

"You cleaned your plate."

"Oh, I eat everything. I had a big appetite to begin with. After all the surgeries and having to eat more, I could eat all the time. I manage."

"Do you receive VA disability?"

"Yes. I guess I'll get it the rest of my life. I've not thought about it. I was just discharged from the Navy on March 31st."

"Would you have stayed in the Navy if they let you?"

"I don't know. With the war going on so long, it took something from me each month. I was tired of war. I should have been somewhere else when I went on the last mission. I was a last-minute addition. They were my old teammates, but well, anyway, it worked out."

Haley looked at me trying to read me. Her eyes had a funny way of darting left and right while she looked into mine trying to reach and understand me. I liked that she tried to figure me out. Haley was easy to talk to.

"Has your attorney disbursed a check to you yet?"

"It's coming this week. I'll bank it, invest it for a while. I don't need anything just yet."

Haley took her last bite and laid her fork and knife along the top of her plate.

"How long were you married, Mark?"

"About seven years. Less than five if you count the cheating."

"That hurts, the cheating I mean, doesn't it?"

"Yes. It just guts you. The fact that she did it, how she did it, who she did it with and how my family and friends found out . . . anyway. I'm having a terrific time and I think we have just enough time for a little dessert before we must go."

Haley nodded as she smiled recognizing my subject deflection.

"Coffee and tiramisu for me. I'm going to the lady's room."

Haley stood up, as did I, placed her napkin on her seat and walked away. The waiter came by, and I ordered our dessert as the busboy cleared our table. Our coffee and dessert arrived just as Haley returned.

"I was thinking I should have pinned one of those roses to your lapel. You look so dashing in that suit, Mark. I like it on you."

"Thank you, but you win. That is the absolute best dress I've ever seen. Did you do fashion in New York before you became a teacher?" Haley smiled.

"Is that apple pie?"

"It is. It's my go-to dessert. This or chocolate, but most of the time I just go for apple pie. As corny as it sounds, the contractors in Iraq and Afghanistan made great apple pie. It made me feel a little like I was home. Just a break from the madness and stress of war. I could eat my apple pie and it brought me home to my family even as I sat in the mess with two hundred Marines and SEALs around me. I enjoyed having a slice with coffee for breakfast."

"For breakfast?"

"Yes. You could say I worked the late shift. Most of our missions were at night. We returned from our missions in the early morning, sometimes too tired to eat. When I awoke, it was late afternoon, dinner time, but I wanted breakfast. I'd eat apple pie with coffee for my breakfast."

"These are the anecdotes of war that people never hear," Haley said as she giggled.

We ate our desserts and hurried through our coffee. We needed to go. I waved the waiter over and handed him my credit card. He brought it right back, I tipped him, signed and we got out of there.

#

The drive was just a short distance to the theater. The Suffolk Theater seats between three hundred and nine hundred people, depending on the event, in cabaret style seating. The theater would not be full tonight. I reserved a table up front, center stage, directly in front of the proscenium arch, so we'd be alone. Tonight, a version of Cats was playing. I'd never seen it. I think my parents had seen Cats ten times. As we pulled up Haley smiled.

"A man with culture. How refreshing."

"I get it all from my parents. My mother loved the theater and arts, and she knew about all the shows in the city. She went to them all. My father knew nothing, but he was astute enough to know how important the arts and theater were to my mother. They took in a show every month, two or three in December. My father would tell me half of them he had no idea what was going on, but my mother would have tears in her eyes, so he knew he'd done good by bringing her."

I valeted the car and took the receipt. I escorted Haley into the building. The theater is a striking example of a 1930s art deco building. We checked in at the box office with my preprinted tickets. We were shown to our seats, and I ordered some champagne. "Cats" were already roaming around. The seats were perhaps 75% sold. As the theater darkened indicating the show would soon begin, our champagne arrived.

"To a wonderful show with a wonderful woman," I said, and we clinked our glasses together.

"What a thoughtful and wonderful touch," Haley said.

We sat next to each other as the attention music started. Haley took my hand into hers. The curtain went up. Haley's hand was warm and fit well in mine. It felt nice holding her hand. We sat like that until intermission. At intermission, we walked around enjoying the old styled art deco building. The attention music sent us to back to our seats for the rest of the show.

"That was so nice, Mark. Thank you. I had fun."

"Me, too. I liked it. Maybe I can interest the lady in a return engagement?" I said and laughed with Haley.

We walked to the valet while I thought about what I could suggest to extend the night since I didn't want it to end. Perhaps we could stop for coffee and a second dessert?

The valet pulled the car up and opened the door for Haley. I tipped him and got in my seat. I started to drive off, but I noticed my phone had several calls and Haley was looking at her phone, too, so I pulled over. We'd left our phones in the car so as not to disturb the show.

"Mark. My parents called several times."

Haley hit her speed dial. I saw that her parents called my phone several times.

"Mom. What's wrong? Is Paulie okay? Yes! Yes? When? Who? No. She called? They called an Amber Alert? Oh, my God. Yes. He's here. Okay. Yes. Yes. I'll call back. Okay. Bye.

Mark. Erica is gone! She didn't come home from school. Nassau County has issued an Amber Alert."

"Buckle up." I stomped the gas and got on the highway. I hit my speed dial.

"Joe. Mark. That little girl I told you about. She's missing. It must be him. Yeah. You're on duty, right? Okay. Here. Go into my computer through the access I gave you. I put a GPS on the black boat. Let Dave know. I'm heading to Merrick now. Yeah. Yeah. I'll call Stayton right now. They were getting a warrant today. They took all the organics I gave them to Stony Brook. Yes. Okay. Call me. Haley is with me. I just hit the L.I.E. Can you put out a notice that I'm speeding down the L.I.E. in an emergency so Suffolk County PD don't stop me? A new Dodge Challenger Hellcat, black with temporary tags. I just got on at Riverhead. Okay. Thanks. Bye. Buckle up tight and hold on Haley."

I punched our speed up to over ninety miles per hour. I pressed a redial button for Stayton.

"It's MacKenzie. That girl I told you about is gone. Yes. That Amber Alert. Since school let out. Joe is getting with our friend at Coast Guard to check the boat. I'd bet that black boat. The girl's house is just a couple houses away from Paul Menduni's. I'm driving to the Merrick house now. I'm speeding down the L.I.E. Get someone out looking for the boat. What? Joe has access to my trackers. He's going in to find them now. I'm getting a call. Do something, John."

I paused to look at the phone.

"Hello. Joe. Oh. Okay. Thanks. I see them up ahead. I hope they can keep up. Bye."

"What's that?" Haley said.

"Our escort. Suffolk will lead us all the way in to Merrick. Joe's calling Nassau and Coast Guard. Haley, I'm sure Monty snatched her."

"What does Monty's boat have to do with it?"

"I looked at his GPS history. The last trip that boat made was a week ago Monday night, around midnight, to a point twelve miles off the coast. Two days later they found those two dead girls in Hempstead Lake. I—we—believe Monty has been snatching kids, but he has help."

I throttled up behind a Suffolk County Police cruiser who increased his speed to ninety-five miles per hour. There were two more police cruisers in front clearing the traffic lanes and two police cruisers were following us. All the cruisers had their lights and sirens going. I noticed other Suffolk County units coming onto the highway to clear traffic. My phone buzzed.

"Yeah?"

"I got the boat. It's off Lido Beach doing about thirty-knots. Dave has a helo in the air and a cutter moving to intercept. Nassau Police are involved. Their chopper just took off. Mark, Nassau pulled over Paul Menduni. Monty and the other guy are off tonight. Paul is in custody at his house. The Impala is not there though," Joe said.

We turned south onto the Sagtikos Parkway.

"What's the Merrick address?" Joe asked.

"Sycamore. I don't recall the number. Trace the house number. Blue-grey house. Two car garage. Two up from the dead end," I said.

We turned onto Southern State Parkway. We ripped past the other cars that were pulling to the right. Nassau County Police had joined us in lead position.

"Joe. Check the GPS on the van. I'm getting another call. Call me."

"Bye."

"Yeah," I said.

"Stayton here. We sent units to the restaurant. Nassau has Paul Menduni at his home. The Coast Guard is chasing a boat off Lido Beach. The helo has it and the cutter is moving to intercept it," Stayton said.

"We don't have his Impala and Joe is checking the van now. Where does the other guy live? That needs to be checked," I said.

"We'll get on it. We're sending a team to Menduni's home. We'll run a search there to be sure. We're waking a judge for warrants."

"We're turning onto Wantagh State Parkway. I'll be at the Merrick house in a few minutes. Out."

"What's happening, Mark?" Haley said, concern very evident in her voice.

"You'll have to take Paulie. They have Paul in custody at his house. I'm not sure if he's involved. They'll search his house and property because Monty has access."

"Mark, Monty could not have been out in the boat that Monday night. He was at the restaurant with Paul and Paulie. Paulie told me. It was a special dinner for the head chef who Paulie likes."

"Then it's someone else involved with them."

My phone buzzed just as we got off on Sunrise Highway. We turned west.

"Yeah, Joe."

"Coast Guard has them. They also stopped and boarded a one hundred sixty-foot yacht. Coast Guard and Nassau have all in custody. A little girl was found on the black boat. No Monty though. I don't have the name of the guy they arrested. They don't have Erica yet!"

"Okay. The FBI is going to the other guy's house. Did you get the van on the GPS?"

"No. It's not there. No blinking dot for the van. It's not listed, Mark."

I thought a minute. The police pulled over not knowing exactly where I was heading. I took lead and turned south on Central Avenue.

"Joe the trackers were sequentially numbered. I installed them in order. The second to last one is the number. Activate that number. Okay?"

"Okay. I'll call you, Mark. Bye."

"Shit! I screwed up," I said aloud to myself.

I stepped on the gas pedal and took a corner screeching my tires. I turned onto Monty's street just off Central Avenue. I hit the brakes and turned the wheel as I one-eightied the car in front of his house and stopped. I saw the Impala in the driveway.

"Stay here!" I pulled my SIG Sauer P226 from the console and exited my car.

"Cover the rear and garage! I'm going in!" I yelled at the swarm of cops that exited their vehicles.

I ran to the kitchen door on the driveway side of the house and slammed through with my body weight destroying the lock, bolt, and jamb. I dashed through the kitchen to the hallway and living room to the stairway. I hesitated a millisecond then turned to head up the stairs, weapon up. I climbed the stairs. It was dark, I sensed danger. A slight movement caught my eye.

"Hold it right there. Drop your weapon," I yelled as a man swung around and raised a weapon and fired. I fired off three rounds striking him at least once in the head. I dashed up the remaining steps, kicking the weapon away from the guy on the floor. It tumbled down the stairs.

I kicked the left bedroom door open. Monty was getting up off someone on the bed. He came up with a weapon in his hand as he pulled his pants up.

"Drop it!" I yelled.

Monty swung the weapon toward me and fired mid-arch. I fired as the weapon came up in his hand. I fired again hitting him in the chest a second time, knocking him back. I fired again hitting him in the face, knocking him back. I fired again hitting him in the forehead and I fired again hitting him in the chest as he crashed backwards through the bedroom window and fell to the driveway below, the weapon still in his hand. I cleared the room. I went to the girl on the bed.

"Erica? I'm a friend of Haley Menduni, Paulie's mother. She's outside. You're safe now," I said. She burst into tears. I found her shorts and I pulled a towel out of the bathroom to cover her. I pressed my speed dial to Joe.

"Joe. I have her, Joe. She's alive. I'm at the Merrick house. Let the others know."

"On it, Mark."

I heard people coming into the house.

"Clear. I'm up here. I have the girl. Sweep the basement," I yelled. At that instant, I heard the basement door come off its hinges as the police went through it. I heard officers coming up the stairs.

"All clear officers. I'm Mark MacKenzie. My weapon is holstered."

"I'm officer Murray, Nassau PD. I'm coming up. You have the girl?"

"Yes."

A woman's head looked around the corner. She looked in the other room.

"Officer Murray. The woman in my car knows this girl. Perhaps we can get Erica out of here and to her."

"Let's do that." Murray holstered her weapon, pulled open a linen closet and pulled a blanket out to cover Erica.

"Erica. Come on sweetheart. Go with Officer Murray. Haley will be with you."

Erica nodded. Officer Murray looked at me questioningly. I shrugged. I didn't know whether Erica had been raped. She been hit several times; her face was swollen and bleeding. Officer Murray walked Erica down the stairs. I followed. The police were swarming the house. Several officers nodded at me acknowledging what I'd done as I walked to my car.

Haley spotted Erica. "Erica. Over here. Put her in the seat here," Haley directed. Murray got on her radio to get an ambulance. Haley hugged Erica. "Let's call your mother, okay?" Haley said. Erica nodded while she cried.

"Mark MacKenzie?"

I turned around.

"I'm Detective Sergeant Kowalski, Nassau PD. First, thanks. Second, what do you do?" he said.

"I'm a securities broker," I said.

Kowalski looked at me questioningly. "FBI is on their way, and I've been speaking with a Sergeant Mott of Suffolk PD. Can we talk?"

"Sergeant. We found a live one in the van in the garage," a patrolman said.

"Excuse me, Mr. MacKenzie," Kowalski said.

I nodded. I popped my trunk and took out some bottled water and put my weapon away. I passed two bottles of water to Haley and Erica. Erica was speaking with her mother on the phone.

I walked over to Monty in the driveway. He was sprawled flat on his back, his head and face mostly not there with three holes in his chest. It struck me that the last time we'd met I put him in this position. This time it was permanent.

I watched Kowalski walk the other girl out with another lady officer. An ambulance appeared, and the second girl was escorted to it. Haley watched me. I nodded at her then walked into the house to look at the other guy—my other kill. How many were there?

I looked at the body. Two in the head and one in the throat. He was dead when he hit the floor. It was Paul Menduni's driver. If the Mendunis were not involved, I suspected Paul was still in trouble with his family. I wondered who was driving the boat? I walked downstairs to the kitchen. I opened the freezer. It contained one more bundle than I saw yesterday. I pulled the cash out and put it in a plastic grocery bag I found on the counter. I left one bundle as evidence. I walked to my car and threw the bag in the back seat. It was at that moment my mission became crystal clear.

"Is her mother coming?" I said to Haley.

"Yes. She'll be here in a minute."

I took out my phone and called my Uncle Matt.

"Hello?"

"Uncle Matt. Sorry I'm calling so late. Can we get our best civil action and civil forfeiture attorneys together for a meeting tomorrow or Friday?"

"I think so. I'll set it up in the morning. What's up?"

"It's a long story. I'll be in later tomorrow. If we can set it up for the afternoon. Just you, Marsha and me."

"Okay. See you then. Can you tell me what's going on?"

"Not right now. I'm sort of busy. I'll explain tomorrow. Thanks, Matt. Bye."

"Bye, Mark."

Haley was watching me from across the roof of my car.

"What are you up to?" She asked.

"We'll all talk about it Friday. I haven't scared you away, have I?"

"I'll be honest. When I heard the gunfire, and the body came through the window I freaked at first then realized it could not be you since he wore no shirt. Here's her mother."

A Toyota SUV pulled up. Sergeant Kowalski walked over to speak to the mother and father. Erica's father stepped out of the SUV ready to hurt someone. Kowalski pulled him aside as mom ran to Erica sitting in my car. Kowalski showed Erica's father Monty's body. Mom and Haley walked Erica to the SUV. I sipped some water as I sat on the edge of my trunk. It would be another long night. I popped four Excedrin.

"Mr. MacKenzie."

I turned.

"This is Erica's father, Ken Cox. I gotta run," Kowalski said.

"Mr. MacKenzie. Thank you for rescuing my daughter," Ken said.

"Yes, sir. You're welcome."

Ken Cox looked to be about forty years old or so. He was a technician or engineer, was my guess. I looked him in the eye. "Mr. Cox. I have something for Erica. I'll tell you; I took it from that bastard on the ground there." I reached into my car and withdrew four bundles of money. "I took this from that man. That's part of what he was paid to steal your daughter from you. That should pay for college for Erica and her brother. I'll never breathe a word of this. It's blood money, but it's your daughter's blood. It will do more good with you than if the government took it," I said.

"Who are you, Mr. MacKenzie?" Ken said.

"I'm Haley Menduni's date. . ."

"He's not just my date, Ken. That's my boyfriend, Mark MacKenzie. Keep it, Ken. Get a lawyer and put a lien on this house, his bank accounts—all of it. Get the assets for the children," Haley said.

Ken looked at Haley then at me. He stuffed the bundles in his jacket pockets then held out his hand. I shook it. "Thank you, Mr. MacKenzie." I nodded.

Ken walked to his SUV, got in with his wife and daughter and they drove off for the hospital.

"Those other bundles are for the girl over there?" Haley asked.

"Yes. I just figured something out. C'mon. Let's get you to your son. I have something to do."

#

We arrived at Haley's former home. We walked up to the door. I'd put my Yankees ball cap on. Nassau County PD was there, FBI, Coast Guard, Customs and Border Patrol, and Suffolk County PD, too. I kept my head low mindful of the IR cameras I'd seen the other night. We went inside. Stayton saw us and walked over.

"I'm pretty busy. Can we talk later or tomorrow?" John said.

"Sure."

Haley and I walked around until we found Paulie.

"Mom. I want to go home with you," Paulie said.

"You will, Paulie." Haley said as she hugged him.

"Haley. I must do something. If anyone asks where I am, say I'm around here somewhere."

Haley nodded.

I walked out the back door past the cops and agents toward the garage. The Navigator was parked in the driveway. I got in, took out Haley's fob and drove off.

A few minutes later I pulled into a Freeport Mini Storage. I took the scan card out of the ashtray and, while ensuring my face could not be seen by the camera, scanned the card opening the gate. I drove through and located the unit number listed on the card. I pulled up just past the unit and sat there looking for cameras. I noticed just one camera all the way down the end of the driveway. I pulled my cap down low and put on shooting glasses, turned the interior lights off, pressed the button to release the rear door and exited the SUV. I walked to the storage unit door and opened the lock with the key Haley provided me. I lifted the door and entered. I lighted my mini LED light and looked around.

I saw baker's racks, shelving, boxes, piles of uniforms, huge pots and pans, a dough mixing machine and more. In the back of the unit were several steel file cabinets, the horizontal file drawer type with six-foot wide drawers. I walked to one and pulled open the middle drawer. It was heavy and no wonder why. I reached in and removed a heavy bundle. I slit open the packaging. It held $100,000 in $100 bills. I closed the drawer and opened the others one by one. The files were full of cash. I checked the other file cabinets. They mostly held packages of cash like the first cabinet. I made a rough count and came up with over $60 million.

Now I had a problem. I knew that the money weighed about 1330 pounds. I was sure it would fit in the Navigator, but it was too much for my Challenger. I looked around for something to carry the money away in. I found a stack of black or dark-blue cloth bags piled on shelves next to the file cabinets. I pulled one off. They were draw-string canvas bags. I began loading them. I fit about $3 million in each bag or about 67 pounds. I filled 21 bags. All totaled, I had $60,400,000 and change. I knew $1 million in $100 bills weighed about 22 pounds or 10 kilograms which I found funny. I loaded the money into the Lincoln filling the rear of the vehicle and the back seats with room to spare. The bags would not fit in my Challenger.

Now I had to put the money someplace. I looked at the near-by storage units, but all had locks on them. I shut the drawers, piled a bunch of boxes into the corner to hide the lack of bags and exited the unit closing the door and locking it. I closed the rear door of the SUV and drove off keeping my face well covered. I sped off to my home in Oceanside.

I backed up to my middle garage door. I got out and punched in the code to the wall-mounted keypad and the door opened. I backed in and quickly unloaded the bags of cash. I left seven bags in the Navigator to put in my Challenger for the ride home. I put the rest of the bags in the upstairs room of the garage. I closed the door and drove to Paul's house.

I had all the mob's cash money!

I backed up to the trunk of my car, hit the key fob for the trunk and opened the Navigator's rear door. In seconds I transferred the bags to my trunk, just squeezing in five bags. I placed a bag on the back seat and another on the floor behind the driver's seat.

I tapped my Bluetooth Dash Program and accessed the plug-in monitor and camera I'd placed the night before in the Navigator. I accessed the vehicle's CPU and I wiped it of all data so a smart bad guy would be unable to determine where the vehicle had gone. I manually wiped the history from the touch-screen GPS. I closed the Navigator's rear door and locked it. I left it there. I got into my car and drove down the street to Paul's house and parked in front.

I removed my hat and glasses and walked to the front door. I stood looking around. Some officers looked at me quizzically, but another officer recognized me and said something to the officers. They nodded at me as I walked by looking for Haley. I found her in the den with Paulie on her lap asleep. She was sipping a bottle of Starbucks Iced Coffee.

"Hi. It's late. Stayton will speak with me tomorrow. Is Paul still here or did they take him away?" I said.

"They arrested him and brought him to the Mineola building since this incident involved Nassau Police's First and Seventh Precincts. Freeport Police are involved, too."

"It's 12:45 a.m. Let's go. I'll tell Stayton we're leaving."

I went looking for John and found him.

"Excuse me, John. We're leaving. You know how to reach me. I know various jurisdictions will want to speak with me. I'd prefer if it was done at one time. I want my name kept out of the papers. I'll be in the city tomorrow."

"Okay, Mark. Thanks. I mean it. We have a lot to talk about. Our techs are at the house. You'll get your property back."

"Fine. It served its purpose."

"Your DNA sampling identified eighteen other children so far."

My heart shuddered. I thought about all those families. "I don't know if that's good news or not, John. Can you give me the list of names in case they pop up in my investigation?" I said.

Stayton looked at me for a long moment then nodded. "Sure. I'll send over all the names we have. By tomorrow our team will have taken more samples at the house, but you did great getting those samples. Thanks again."

"Bye, John." I walked to the den, picked up Paulie from Haley's lap and we walked out to the car together. I laid Paulie in the back seat, his head up against a bag of money, then buckled him in. We got in and drove off.

#

"I'll keep him out of school tomorrow, but I'll go in. He's upset and confused. He wondered what you did because he heard the men in suits mention your name, so he's confused and tired. They pulled Paul over with Paulie in the SUV on his way home from the restaurant," Haley said.

"Then recline the seat and take a nap on the way home."

"I can't. I'm wide awake. Where did you go?"

"It's still better if you don't know, but I righted a wrong."

"Mark, what you did tonight . . . it was . . . it was just amazing, but what I'm wondering about is how did you get involved?"

I got onto Southern State Parkway while I thought of how to tell Haley most of the truth.

"Haley, I'm working on finding the persons responsible for my parents' deaths. While doing that, I was assisted by certain government agencies. Anyway, I was advised of Monty's possible involvement with the disappearance and deaths of those two girls last week. I was asked to turn over to the FBI what I learned to assist them and to create a good history of being a reliable CI or confidential informant.

When they told me of their suspicions, I thought back to Paulie's comments. I thought it odd that an employee would be mean to his boss's son. I mentioned it to you. You, in a sense, convinced me Monty was the monster he turned out to be. I put my energies into going after Monty. He was too close to your boy, and it just wasn't right. If Paul is not involved, then he's turned a blind eye. The boat going out late at night should have raised questions. They'll learn things from their computers," I said.

"So, you're finished with this . . . this child sex ring thing?"

"I hope so. They'll want my statement, but I'm finished otherwise. I'm back to securities and my parents' deaths." We cruised along the L.I.E. at the speed limit in silence. Haley placed her hand over mine on the center console.

"I didn't scare you off with boyfriend, did I?" Haley said.

"No. I'm okay with that. I've been looking for a gumball machine all night to buy a decoder ring to give you when I ask you to go steady with me," I deadpanned.

Haley leaned over and kissed my cheek.

"I didn't call Lauren!"

"I took care of it. She knows. It's all over the news on TV and the Internet."

"Shoot. Bad parent, huh? I need to get better at this."

"You will. Don't worry, you're a good parent," Haley said.

#

We arrived at Haley's house. I carried Paulie inside to his bed. Haley's parents were up.

"It's a big deal on the news. Mark, they didn't identify you by name, but some have described you as an undercover policeman which is good. They said this group may be responsible for more than sixty missing children from Long Island alone," Mrs. Shore said.

"We'll let you go, Mark. Haley told us what you did. We're very proud of you, son," Mr. Shore said.

"Thanks. I should go," I said as I nodded at Mr. Shore.

"Yes. Yes, of course," Mr. Shore said.

Haley came into the room. "Paulie is asleep. I wanted to say good night." Haley pulled me to her and kissed me in front of her parents. "Good night, Mark."

"Uh . . . good night. Yeah. Good night, all."

I looked at Haley and she smiled at me. I let myself out. I got into my car and drove home. I guess the date was okay? She kissed me in front of her parents.

#

I pulled up into the garage and shut the door. I placed the bags of money in my two large fishing coolers and three storage containers. I was just able to fit the twenty-one million in the containers. I placed the coolers and storage containers up on the rafters to keep out prying eyes. I'd have to find another place to store all the money. I wondered how long before Paul Menduni would learn the money was gone. Once I had a list of victims, I'd distribute the money to them, but that wouldn't be all I'd do. I wanted to take it all for the victims of the mob's crimes. I had a plan.

I checked on Lauren who was sound asleep. I stroked her head and she stirred briefly, then settled back to sleep.

CHAPTER 11

"Mark. Wake up. Kimberly's mom will take me to school. I already had breakfast. I know you're going into the office. I'll be home before you. Don't worry about me. I'll have dinner waiting for you. I'm very proud of you, Mark. Grandma and Grandpa are coming over this afternoon. Everyone will be here for the weekend."

"All right. Bye. You have money for lunch?"

"I'm fine big brother. Bye. I love you."

#

At 11 a.m. A knock and doorbell chime woke me. I walked downstairs to find a limo driver standing at the door.

I showered, shaved, and dressed in a blue suit, white shirt, blue striped tie and was ready in twenty minutes. I collected up my phones, SIG P226, and my briefcase and walked out carrying a cup of microwaved coffee. "Let's go." I said as I got into the limo. I got on my phone and called Joe.

"Joe."

"Hey. You are a bona fide hero. Those Suffolk units that went to the house with you filled us in on what Stayton or Kowalski didn't say. Busting down doors, shooting bad guys . . . I've been a cop for ten years and I've only drawn my weapon twice."

"Are you finished?"

"Yes. Go ahead."

"It wouldn't have happened without you, too. And Dave's guys got that yacht and saved that girl. We did it. Now we are back to why we're in this."

"I've been looking at the firm's bank records. I've been looking at the statements since that new shareholder group joined the firm. I've flagged about thirty-nine groups of payments and several hundred deposits. I can't put my finger on it, but there appears to be many deposits made at one time with many checks, but all carrying the same transaction number. The amounts vary from as little as $5000 up to $500,000. They stood out to me because other transactions have just one check or money transfer per transaction whether it be for $100,000 or $10 million, but I'm no forensic accountant."

"Where did the deposits come from?" I said.

"The various buyers of bonds of several different entities. Michigan Energy, Missouri River Power Corp., Great Plains Micro Resources, companies like that," Joe said.

All the names on the bonds I found in my safe.

"I'll need to match them up with our client list. Those are the names on the bonds I found, too."

"That's right. I wondered about that, too."

"Okay. Big family get together at my house starting tonight. I don't know the details, I just found out. I think last night has something to do with it."

"Oh?"

"Our meeting tomorrow will be well-attended. Rob and Tony will be there, too. I'd planned for you, Rob, Tony and

Haley, but this may be for the better since the horses are getting out of the corral."

"I'll be there."

"Bye. See you tomorrow."

"Bye."

I called Bernice. "What time is the attorney meeting?"

"At 2 p.m. A half a dozen of them will be billing us. Your uncle said just he, Marsha and you will attend. I assume Barbara and Clara, too."

"Yes. What's the word there?"

"Rizzo is going berserk. He's a sociopath. He tried to bring in an outside tech to work on the computers and a new hire tech blocked him, told Matthew and Mr. Frank, and they kicked the guy out. Matt told Rizzo he had no authority to do anything but broker paper and, I quote, 'If you want a f-ing paper clip ordered, it goes through Ira and me, and it's checked by Margie and Barbara, am I clear?' or words to that effect," Bernice said.

"Good. I'm on my way in. Does my uncle know he's coming back to my house tonight?"

"Yes. That's why he sent the limo for you. Missy will join you."

"Okay. Please put me through to Clara."

"See you in a bit."

"Mr. MacKenzie?"

"Yes. What's going on?"

"Your uncle stiffened his backbone. Rizzo is on the war path. Even Train is staying away from him. There's something wrong with that guy."

"Pull his numbers for me. Are the broker's numbers in graphic form?"

"They can be. The ones that were promulgated are BS. Ira has been carrying Rizzo, but it's not Ira's fault. Ira's been crediting Rizzo with some of his deals."

"Really? How do you know?"

"Call logs, faxes, office times, notes to file, emails, closing documents and Ira told me when I questioned him. Ira didn't come out and say it, but Rizzo has something on him or has threatened him. Your father started me on that project. Matt is the only one who may know. I'm not convinced that Matt has gone through everything yet. Of course, now you know."

"Make four copies. Put my copy in a thin notebook binder. Rizzo's check is direct deposited?"

"Yes."

"I'd like a copy of all payments to Rizzo and another print-out of all payments to Ira. Can you transfer me to Marsha?"

"Sure. Just a second."

"Marsha."

"Hi. It's Mark."

"Hi. Only a few of us know about last night."

"Yeah. Don't talk about it. I'm calling to have you pull a list of payments made to everyone on the six-person list. How are their background checks going?"

"Rizzo has problems that occurred after we hired him. Train has several issues, many he failed to disclose to us. Train has a slew of DUIs and three domestic violence convictions. His wife, ex-wife and his mother."

"Charming guy."

"Both Rizzo's and Train's assistants have minor issues like drunk in public, public nudity, speeding, etc."

"Did we get the cell phone records for all of them?'

"We did."

"Make up three copies of those records. Tell Ira I'd like to meet with him at 3 p.m."

"Will you be finished with the attorneys by then?"

"Yes. The meeting will be short."

"Mind telling me what it's about since you want me there?"

"First, I trust you. Second, I want you to know what I am planning so you can advise me I also want you to hear what the attorneys say."

"You still haven't told me what it's about."

"It concerns two broad matters. One involves our shareholder agreement, and the other is about making people whole after they've been damaged by a defendant. I want to force the sale of the 20% of the shares that Rizzo and those other shareholders have, but I'm still doing that research. However, since I think Rizzo and some of these people are committing crimes that go against the firm's interest, the agreement allows us to order a forced sell-back. I just need to assemble the evidence. The other matter pertains to making plaintiffs whole who were injured by some people.

Tell Rizzo I want to see him in my office at 3:30 p.m. Clara is drafting me a document for that meeting. Finally, would you ask Bernice, Clara, and Barbara to put together the bond sales that Rizzo and Train did for all those Midwest companies from Rizzo's date of hire forward through the month of my father's death?"

"Sure. What's there, Mark?"

"I think the evidence of a pump and dump, money laundering and skimming scheme. I think Rizzo, in concert with other brokers from other firms, has been pushing these energy bonds around. I think they're not as valuable as they appear on paper. I want to bring the hammer down on them. Moreover, I think these bonds were originally issued by a criminal enterprise."

"You are as smart as your father."

"We'll see. I'll see you in a bit. Bye."

I flipped open the newspaper. Nothing about what happened last night other than the Amber Alert. I turned on WNEW radio for the midday news. They didn't have much. Just a story about police rescuing a kidnapped girl. Once a U.S. Attorney got his talons into the story he'd be dancing in front of all the cameras. It was the one part of what I had to do that I didn't trust. U.S. Attorneys are all politicians. For the southern district of New York, which comprises Manhattan and the Bronx among other areas, it was some show-boater they called "Preening Pete." In the Eastern District of New York, which comprises Long Island, Queens, Brooklyn and Staten Island, it was some newbie with just ten years of lawyering under his belt.

The limo pulled up into our garage. I got out with my gadgets and things and headed to the office.

"Good afternoon, Mr. MacKenzie."

"Good afternoon."

The receptionist buzzed me into the executive hallway. Clara greeted me.

"We're finishing up on the copying. Marsh spoke with me so I have everything you requested put together. Your uncle is waiting to see you."

"Thank you, Clara."

I dropped my things in my office then headed to Matt's office.

"Hello, Margie. I think he wants to see me."

"Go on in, Mr. MacKenzie."

I let myself into Matt's office.

"Hey, Matt, Marsha."

"Mark, I'm just hearing from the family about what you did last night. I, we, are very proud of you."

"Thanks. I'd like to keep a low profile on that. The press doesn't know who I am. I'd like to keep it that way, but I know the ladies will talk and Haley was there."

"What are you hatching? Marsha was talking to me a little about it."

"Matt, if I'm correct, Rizzo and brokers from other firms have been pumping and dumping bonds and, perhaps, stocks of various energy firms. What I think they do is they generate interest with their brokers, one or two other brokers, at several of the competing firms. They get the brokers in these firms to push these bonds. They push the value, the performance, the sales, the technology, what-have-you, around in a circle. Meanwhile they buy stock through friends, and relatives or strawmen in these businesses or they already hold stock in these companies purchased while the value was low.

All these companies, by the way, appear to be a form of energy company. These companies, at first, have no real capital to speak of and they produce nothing. They move energy around and consolidate billing for energy producers. With news that the firm is becoming cash rich, as more and more bonds are purchased and traded, the stock value climbs. What is essentially penny stock, is now valued at $10 or $20 per share over a reasonable period, perhaps eight to 12 months, this way they stay under the SEC's radar by gradually climbing. If we research it, we'll find that most if not all initial bond purchasers are related to each other by blood or mob affiliation. The companies appear to be flush with cash from bondholders' money. The crappy stock has increased in value and the original stockholders start to sell their shares. Corporate looks fine as they can buy back stock and help their books. The Big Seven Banks and their subsidiaries see this and they're fine with lending to these companies. More stock is sold, the price goes up and the stockholders sell."

"Mark. You're describing a market except for the insider trading and collusion that occurred."

"Hold on, Matt. What if I told you the bonds, for the most part, are fraudulent and are mostly issued by the mob? That the sales and transfers were a series of transactions with the same money being recirculated? The same money is being used to buy all the bonds."

"You're saying that someone buys bonds from Company X. That money flows through Company X pushing the value of its stock up. That same money is used to buy bonds from Company Y. That money flows through Company Y pushing its stock value up. That same money is used again to buy bonds for Company Z and so on?"

"That's it. The same money counts how many times? So, with a little initial investment how many companies do they start? They somehow move the money out in cash or loans. They market themselves as cheap or low-price brokers of electrical power. They enter agreements with power companies who are happy to reduce their bill-collection costs and have their excess energy sold. I recall Rizzo handling the sales on nearly all these deals. Dad and you caught him about to sell securities for a company in bankruptcy and the other transaction that turned out to be with a company out of a post office drawer for a farm in Nebraska.

Here's the other catch. They launder their illegal proceeds through this process. I think Rizzo's last deal closed with eighteen cashier's checks and money orders being deposited to our accounts. I know the excuses are different funds, different buyers, different banks, et cetera, but, if I'm right, they're making deposits to thousands of accounts. Cash of $2000 here, $7000 there, and so on. Those accounts are controlled by a few mob lieutenants and capos who keep their books like a lawyer keeps a trust accounting for his clients except in this case there are multiple strawman accounts that narrow in a reverse pyramid to just a few accounts all within a few days once the word is given to make the deposits. These are the funds that we, and I'll bet, the other brokerages are being paid with. The securities they purchased are exchanged and the sellers get paid. The bad guys now have laundered money in the form of securities and their stocks are increasing in value while they moved the same $30, $40 or $50 million around buying bonds from these same companies who now borrow more money from the banks that they will never fully repay."

I took a sip of coffee. Matt looked at Marsha. They both nodded.

"What do you need me to do, Mark?" Matt said.

"First, did Dad own, or the firm own bearer bonds or hold these bonds for these types of companies?"

"I don't know. I, uh, well, I suppose. We'd have to look at the books. I don't think Will kept the bonds here though. We've invested in bonds, and I think part of our reserves are in bonds, but municipal bonds, not energy companies. I'm not aware of us purchasing those bonds," Matt said.

"Can we learn what bonds these companies have issued?" I said.

"Yes. I'll have Barbara look it up," Marsha said.

"Next. How many firms like us exist in New York?"

"I'd say between 35 and 40 that are going concerns. Banks and business brokers sometimes take a piece of the business," Matt said.

"Can we find out which of them brokered sales for the same list of companies?" I said.

"Sure. We index and report them on our association website. Each of us involved have an abbreviation. Ours is M-A-C. Those abbreviations are listed on the bond exchange where you can also find that information. I can get that in a few hours," Matt said.

"Then can you call the presidents of each firm who participated in a sale involving these companies and ask them three questions. First, have they had a recent hire who did some sketchy or fraudulent sales attempts or mistakes; second, have these same brokers closed deals with multiple buyers' checks and wire transfers; and three, were they ever paid with or offered payment in bearer bonds from these energy companies?"

"Sure. If the questions are answered in the affirmative, what do we do?" Matt said.

"Ask them if they hold these bonds, whether they hold them for themselves or clients, and what the total face values are of the bonds they hold for each company? After that I'd like to set up a meeting with these presidents."

Matt nodded his head as he looked at Marsha who was nodding her head and looking at me. "Sure. What are you thinking?" Matt said.

"Of putting them out of business and taking their money."

"Who? These companies and the mob?" Matt said looking at me in disbelief.

"Yes."

"Oh, Mark, you got some brass."

"How will you do it?" Marsha said.

"These guys buy stock, mostly on margin. My plan is to talk up the companies, driving their stock price up, redeeming the bonds held by the bond holders, then publishing our finding about the bonds, the poor performance of these companies and their problems that we find following the bond redemptions, driving the stock prices to the ground. These companies will need to use their reserves and borrow to pay for the redeemed bonds, leaving them cash strapped. They will buy stocks on margin as the stocks appear to perform. When the stocks crash and margins come due, they'll have no wherewithal to pay their margins. The banks will move to seize their assets. The stock houses will cease business with them until the margins are paid. The banks won't lend since they've levied on the security. I expect this part of the plan to be accomplished in less than two weeks. But that's not the whole plan.

It dawned on me last night with all these guys going legitimate that they've formed companies, corporations and LLCs. Looking over some communications from one such employer, on corporate email no less, made me think of vicarious liability and respondeat superior liability. What's the number one affirmative defense to bad acts of an employee?"

"They were illegal and could not be in the employer's course of business or benefit," Marsha said.

"But what if the employer authorized these ultra vires acts in the course of its business? It would be liable as would its officers and those who participated in those acts. I'm almost there proving that Vincenzo Menduni with Romeo Menduni, the chairman of the board, authorized the murders of my parents. I think there are many other acts that were ordered. I've viewed several emails that give direction as to performance of illegal acts. We get our lawyers to start suing and filing lis pendens on all bank accounts, real estate, yachts, stocks, cars—whatever. After all, what's the compensation one can put on the murder of my parents? I'm talking about just the Calabrese-Menduni family. I'm sure the other four New York-New Jersey families are involved. I'll soon have a list of many plaintiffs. I want the Calabrese-Menduni family living on the streets. I want to take away all of it," I said.

Matt looked at Marsha who was smiling. "What's in it for the firm?" Matt said.

"I already explained, Rizzo out and 20% share buy-back. I think I'm holding $18 million dollars in bad bearer bonds that my plan will make good and which may not have been accounted for properly, and we get the good will from fixing this with the other firms."

"The downside?" Matt said as he looked at Marsha then back to me.

"Vincenzo and gang may have a problem with me once they learn I'm involved and try to kill me. What we uncover will go to FBI, NYPD and Nassau County. I'm good with them," I said.

"Okay. You have a meeting with Rizzo at 3:30 p.m. Should I be there?" Matt asked.

"Yes. Both of you and Ira who will be meeting with me at 3 p.m. We will dismiss Ira from the room just before Rizzo comes in. I will start on Rizzo then you two will leave. I have the place rigged to catch Rizzo threatening me should that occur. I will put him on probation for his poor sales performance. I will harp on his inadequacies as a businessman and broker. I'll let him know that all future broker splits must be approved by me. Ira is carrying Rizzo. It's because Ira is being threatened or being paid which I seriously doubt," I said.

"I can't believe Ira would sell us out. He's been with us . . ."

"I think he's being threatened. I watched him the other day in the conference room. Oh. Do we have other brokers we'd like to hire?"

"Well, yes. Two senior guys with fifteen years or more and a young buck with five years. All with books of business," Marsha said.

"Matt, I want to fire Train. He lied on his employment application. I'd like to bring in these new guys, performers who know the business. Ira should be managing not selling full-time and giving Rizzo credit. Train gone, Rizzo soon gone and Ira managing, that's three bodies."

"He's right, Matt. After Rizzo, Train is the worst performing broker," Marsha said.

"Marsha. Call all three men in. Ask them to come in tomorrow. I like it. What if Rizzo does threaten you?" Matt said.

"I'll control it," I said.

"Will you fire him?" Matt said.

"I will do everything I can not to fire him. I need him for my plan. I'd like him to pass the bad information we'll develop in our plan next week. I'll be neutral with him. We have a lawyer meeting in five minutes," I said.

#

"Welcome, ladies and gentlemen. My nephew, Mark, has joined the firm. What we will discuss today may not be usual firm business, but rather as a possible plaintiff in an action for damages. Are you all comfortable?" Matt said. The lawyers all nodded. "Mark."

"Hello. I'm Mark MacKenzie. All of you knew my father. Some of you knew my mother. Today I am raising my fifteen-year-old sister who was orphaned last April. Contrary to what you may have heard, my parents were murdered." I paused as surprise registered and the lawyers commented.

"I know who murdered them. I'll come back to that. You all are lawyers, I am not, so please bear with me. If a corporation's employees purposefully injured a plaintiff, even while doing corporation business, the corporation and its officers would not, could not be held liable under the doctrines of respondeat superior or vicarious liability, as the acts of the employee would be ultra vires—illegal and not in the scope of employment or the business of the employer. Correct?" The lawyers nodded agreement.

"But what if that corporation ordered the illegal act? What if its officers and board members, using corporate devices and communications, order illegal acts to be performed?" I saw some slow nods affirming what I was about to say.

"The corporation would be liable as would the individual officers involved and officers who knew or should have known of the illegal acts. What if I told you I have emails from several officers and board members discussing illegal acts and, in that discussion, a participant identifies someone as a problem for the corporation and they agree that the individual must be taken care of—killed? Think of that for a second. Now add to this that the corporation owns other corporations, real estate, bank accounts, investments—and the officers and board unanimously or by majority vote, order the death of this individual? Do we have a civil suit that is winnable?" The lawyers looked at each other as they thought. After a short pause an older lawyer spoke.

"Being a lawyer, I want to ask you more about the facts, but given your fact pattern you have a justiciable cause of action. Moreover, the court would permit a plaintiff to lock up and preserve the assets pretrial."

"Yes, ma'am," I said.

"I agree with Michael. I'll presume your father's death is what you refer to and the class of plaintiffs would include family and this firm. If life insurance was paid out for the death, then the insurer could maintain a cause of action, too. Of course, the damages would include compensatory damages and punitive damages."

I looked over at the senior attorney who wanted to opine.

"Yes, sir," I said.

"Proving damages to the firm might be tough. I won't go into all the problems but suffice it to say a dollar is a win that proves the other plaintiffs could line up. A court might consolidate the cases, too," he said.

"Let me spice this up. What if I had evidence that they had done this before? What if the corporation and its officers had a history of bad acts, that it was part of an acceptable way of doing business? I'll crawl further out on my limb. What if there were several corporations doing this business? Yes, sir." I gestured at a whitehaired lawyer.

"I imagine you could only be speaking of a drug cartel or the mob. Such an undertaking could be dangerous."

"My parents—my mother, innocent as can be—were killed by the mob because my father caught them cheating. They did nothing wrong. I'm a retired SEAL. I saw danger. I took bullets defending others. That's danger. This is protected communications between attorneys and a client. It cannot leave this room even if you hear it from another source you cannot speak of it. I killed two men last night who kidnapped, raped, sold into sex slavery, and killed young girls all from Long Island."

I let my words sink in.

"Those men were members of the mob. The same information I found and gave to the FBI and Nassau County Police, I have available that shows what these men have done. The case yesterday was solved because of what I learned from investigating my parents' deaths."

"You are the man who rescued those girls in Merrick?" The senior lawyer said.

"Yes, sir."

"Erica is my granddaughter. Thank you very much, young man. I'll do the suits," the senior lawyer said.

I nodded at him. The lawyers consulted and conversed. After several minutes, they turned to me.

"We'll do the cases," the senior lawyer said.

"I'd like you to research and ready yourselves. I'd like to have a strategy telephone conference Monday. By then I will be in receipt of thousands of documents. My parents' case is just the first of many. I have some things I'm doing to get this in place. When you file, I want you to lock up every asset the mob owns. There may come a time that law enforcement and government get involved. I want our plaintiffs first in line," I said as I slid a packet of documents to the senior attorney.

"That's background information on my family and the firm. I included information on the victims from last night. I'll be providing much more information and, unfortunately, more victim information. As information develops, I will pass it to you. The plaintiffs' contact list will be sent to you as it is made so you may contact them. Be as it may, I think there are more plaintiffs than assets. You are the experts. Tell me how to sue the bad guys to leave them penniless and on the street. Thank you for your time on such short notice. My assistant will speak with you to set a conference call time next week," I said.

Matt and Marsha pressed the flesh and chatted with the lawyers as they got up and shuffled out.

Ira came in. "Do you want to meet here?" He said.

"No. In my office, Ira."

#

Ira is an older man. Slight and slim with a thick shock of almost white hair in the style of Albert Einstein. Ira stands about five-foot seven-inches tall and may weigh as little as one hundred forty-five pounds. His eyes are grey-blue. We've been acquainted for years.

"Ira. Tell me about Rizzo," I said. Ira immediately became uncomfortable.

"What do you mean?"

"Why are you cutting him in on your deals? Why are you covering for him? Why haven't you shown him, or for that matter, Train, the door?" I said. Ira's eyes welled up as he looked at Matt then back to me.

"Mark. I'm sorry. It started subtly at first then it became more and more overt. After your parents died, I was afraid. I . . . I should have spoken up."

"Did you accept any money from him?"

"No. I would never do that. He threatened me. I was afraid they'd hurt my wife or me."

"Ira. I will fire Train today. I will counsel Rizzo and place him on probation. You will no longer cover for him. I will make it plain that you had nothing to do with his probation and I will make it equally plain that should I hear of any retribution I will come down on him hard. No more supporting him. Tomorrow, Uncle Matt and you will hire three more brokers. You will be the manager where you are supposed to be. Do you understand me?"

"Thank you, Mark, Matt. I've been so worried for months," Ira said.

"Go do your work, Ira. You'll be there tomorrow with Uncle Matt to meet some new brokers . . . Oh. Matt is indicating you already know these guys. They will be strong allies for you. Now let me deal with Rizzo," I said. Ira departed.

"Clara."

"Yes, sir."

"Can I get an iced water, please? Matt? Marsha?"

"No thanks," Matt said. Marsha shook her head. Clara brought in my water.

"Rizzo just walked in, sir. He has someone with him," Clara said.

"That's fine. Only Rizzo will remain. I'll handle it. Ask Mr. Rizzo to come in."

#

Rizzo entered the room followed by an older man.

"I'm sorry. I need just Mr. Rizzo," I said.

"I'm his attorney, Sal Shapiro."

"May I have your card?"

The attorney put down his briefcase and withdrew his business card from a case and passed it to me.

"Is this your telephone number on here?" I asked.

The attorney looked at me like I was touched in the head.

"Yes."

"Fine. I'll call it if ever I need Mr. Rizzo to have an attorney present to discuss firm business. Good day, sir. Clara. Please show Mr. Shapiro to the door," I said. Clara had trouble maintaining her neutral expression.

"Call me," Shapiro said to Rizzo.

"Mr. Rizzo. Please sit."

"I'd prefer to stand."

274

"I wasn't making a request—sit!"

Rizzo sat.

"I've been looking through your work history. I don't know why my father kept you around. I will be blunt and to the point. I'm putting you on probation. If I don't see a marked improvement in your sales performance, you are history. You will no longer ride Ira's coattails. You will produce your own work product. Ira is the manager, your supervisor. Competition will pick up around here beginning tomorrow as three proven brokers will be hired. I am doing this for you for one reason— Ira stuck up for you. I was going to dismiss you. You're the only one Ira stood up for. Now think about what I said. Go to work. Perhaps the book of business these new brokers bring with them will have a spill-over effect. Unless something comes up, we'll meet on June 2 which is five weeks away. Good day, Mr. Rizzo." Matt looked at me confused.

"Something else, Mr. Rizzo?"

"I'd like to speak to you in private."

"That's at the pleasure of the president," I said as I turned to Matt and Marsha.

"That's fine. Al, don't screw up a good deal with your mouth," Matt said as he and Marsha got up and departed my office.

#

"What is it you'd like to say, Mr. Rizzo?"

"I don't know who you think you are calling me out . . ." I put my hand up.

"Then let me tell you. I'm the majority shareholder and president designate of the firm. Matt is my boss. The rest of you work for me," I said.

Rizzo was getting ready to blow.

"Look for yourself," I said as I slid a book with his performance figures toward him. "You're a graduate of Wharton. Read it! You wouldn't be able to eat, but for Ira."

That did it. Rizzo stood up.

"I ought to . . . no one talks to me like this."

"Sit down! Talks to you like what? I told you the truth. You need to get to work and do what we pay you to do. Now you're wasting my time." Rizzo remained standing and simmering. He looked at me with rage in his eyes. "Good day, Mr. Rizzo."

Rizzo stormed out. I was betting for at least a chair kick or door slam. Bernice and Clara came into my office smiling.

"Oh, my God. You shut him up! Even your father couldn't do that with him," Clara said.

"It's just for a little bit longer. One more task. Have Mr. Train come to my office. Ask building security to come up. Train will leave with his jacket and no more. Ira's assistant will pack Train's things. He can wait in the building lobby," I said.

Clara smiled at Bernice.

#

I looked out the window wondering if Anthony was working. I grabbed the binoculars and looked. He was working. I tapped my telephone for Mario's Palermo Pizza.

"Yes. One regular cheese pie. Delivery." I gave them the address. "Make sure the delivery guy says it's from Mr. Smith. Yes. Credit card." I gave the woman the information. "Thank you." I'd like to be a fly on the wall for that delivery.

A knock at the door.

"Yes."

"Mr. Train is here," Bernice said.

"Thank you. Send him in."

#

"Mr. Train. Please take a seat." Train sat.

"I'm dismissing you for cause. You were inaccurate in your answers to our employment and security questions on your employment application. Here are the documents I relied on in making this decision. In addition, I relied on every other document in your work and employment file. If you list us as a work reference, we will give you a neutral reference. I don't need a response. Your final check is before you. Ira's assistant will pack your things. You may wait in the building lobby."

If looks could kill.

"But my performance is good," Train said.

"I won't debate this with you. Good day, Mr. Train."

"I'll sue you."

"That is your prerogative. Again, good day, sir. Clara, please show Mr. Train out."

Clara appeared with security. Train stood and departed.

#

I looked at the information Marsha and Clara had put together for me. I had a lot to do.

My phone buzzed.

"Hello."

"Hello, hero."

"Who is this?" It was Stayton.

"I'm sorry. It's special agent Stayton."

"Oh. I didn't recognize the voice. I don't like to advertise . . . Opsec you know."

"You'll be happy to know that the three girls are doing well. Erica was not raped. He was about to rape her. He slapped and hit her, but you got there in time."

"Small miracles."

"Look. I've copied our file on what we know of your parents' matter. Do I give it to Cicola or you?"

"Me. Can you put it in the mail to my house?"

"I'll do that now. I wanted to say we impounded the yacht, the go-fast boat, and the Impala from last night. The yacht belongs to a venture capitalist. We found physical evidence of at least six women or young girls on the yacht. His crew is singing like the Jackson Five as to what they know."

"Why are you telling me this?"

"I thought you'd like to know. I'll stick the contact info for the girls' parents and what we have on the defendants in the mail to you. Maybe someone will help them get an attorney to seize the venture capitalist's assets?"

Where was he going with this? "What are you getting at, John?"

"One of my agents reported that six tough civil litigators, one an expert in forfeiture law, were at your office today. I just thought maybe you'd help out."

I smiled. *I'd opened the flood gates.* "Send them all to me. From now on send me all the victims' contact information."

"I will. Oh. We will release Paul Menduni tonight. His lawyers pushed. We have nothing tying him to the girls. No DNA in his house, nothing else. We may have some other things that we took incident to the downloading of his computer. I'll send you your equipment from the Merrick house. We're done there. The neighbors want to burn the place down. We recovered thousands of pictures, clothing, organics and more. ICE and our team are hunting down the bad guys involved on the computers. We recovered a packet of money, one hundred grand, from the freezer. You stated you saw eight packets in there." Stayton paused for a long time.

"Was that a question or statement?" I asked.

"A statement. Anyway. I'll get all this off to you. Thanks again. I'll be in touch."

"Hold on. Why is an agent following me?"

"To keep an eye on you so no one kills you."

"Call him off. I work alone."

"Or with Joe."

"You know what I mean."

"I'll think about it. I'll be in touch. Bye."

"Bye."

#

Bernice and Clara came in.

"Sir, you are shaking things up," Bernice said.

"What's the scuttlebutt?" I said.

"The what?" Clara said.

"I know this. It's where sailors drink water. I guess a water fountain or something, and they pass along what they heard about the ship and crew," Bernice said.

"I'm impressed," I said.

"Word Trivia for years."

"Everyone seems to be happy. The women think you're hot. The men, especially the gay men, think you're rugged and stand-up. They like what you've done in such a short time."

"Good. Tomorrow three more brokers will join us if they accept. Matt will handle that.

Ira will manage again. I'll be taking this notebook with me. I'll probably be in on Monday. I will start to rely on you more as I start moving things along. This upcoming week may be busy. I may be curt with you. Please don't take it personally. I will be trying to formulate and operate at the same time. I'll apologize in advance. My family will be with me for the weekend, so I won't get as much accomplished as I wished, but that's all right. My family is more important. Clara?"

"Yes, sir."

"One day you will make me laugh when I shouldn't. That will be all right when it happens. Your facial expression today while trying to maintain your composure when Rizzo's attorney left was priceless." Clara smiled.

"I've never . . . I've never seen your style. I like it. Plus, you've gone after the right people, in my opinion, so you've validated and affirmed my beliefs as correct. I'd like to move up in the organization, too, some day," Clara said.

"Promise me you won't fire me," I deadpanned.

"Yes, sir, or no, sir, I won't fire you, but, well, you never know?"

We burst out laughing. Clara was comfortable in who she is. She is bright, professional, and quirky beautiful or maybe pretty is the word. She reminded me of Marisa Tomei's character in the movie *What Women Want*. Clara and I would get along fine.

Bernice would take care of me like a mother. She is bright, experienced, and held sway over most of the other employees at the firm. I'd be in good hands with Clara and Bernice.

#

I looked at the time. Shoot! Time to pack it up.

"Hi!"

I looked up to see Aunt Missy. "Hi, Missy." I stood up, walked to her, and kissed her cheek.

"You look like your father sitting there. So, big weekend at the house?"

"Who started this?"

"Who else? Your grandmother. After what happened last night and . . . What?"

"Operational security. Don't talk about it. I'd prefer to remain anonymous," I said.

"Oh. Sure. I get it."

No, she didn't, but that was Missy.

"We'll talk about it in the car," Missy said.

"Missy, we won't talk about it at all."

"Oh, don't be like that, Mark. You must tell us something. Either that or I'll tell about the time . . ."

"Thank you, Missy. Come on. Let's get Matt. We have a ride ahead of us."

#

We got into the limo, Matt and Missy sitting in the back seat and me sitting in the rear-facing seat next to the bar.

"Your nephew is doing great at the firm. He's cleaning house. It's fun to watch."

"Well, your nephew would have a nicer life-style working with me," Missy said.

This is how they refer to me, *your nephew*.

"Okay, you two. I'm sitting right here, so the whole third person reference is strange. I'm not even working full time so don't worry about it. Would you like a cocktail, Aunt Missy?"

"Sure. What do you have?"

The woman is in more limos in a month than I've been in my whole life, and she cannot recall that they're all virtually identically stocked.

"There's champagne, red wine, white wine, Scotch, bourbon, vodka, gin and rum. It holds eight bottles."

"Oh. I didn't know that. I'll have a vodka martini."

Without Dry Vermouth.

I didn't say a word. I poured vodka on the rocks, a splash of club soda, a twist of lime.

"Here you go."

She wouldn't know the difference anyway.

"Matt?"

"Bourbon, straight."

Matt would know. I poured him a nice double in an on-the-rocks glass. I had club soda with a twist of lime so Missy would know I was suffering with her, too. Two hours and twelve minutes later we rolled up to my house. Haley's car was there and one that I couldn't place in addition to my family's cars.

I carried Missy's things inside. I had no idea what the sleeping arrangement would be, but I was sure I'd be displaced from my bedroom. We have plenty of beds, true, but the downstairs bedroom and den were deemed least desirable. Grandma, Missy, and Betsy could fight over it. Tomorrow Joe would be here, too. No way would Rob and Tony stay here with the whole family around.

"Hi!" Haley said as she kissed me.

"Are you all right? They haven't drugged you or anything?" I asked Haley in all earnest.

"No. We've had a good time. We were making hors d'oeuvres and preparations for dinner. My parents are here. My Dad and your grandfather are chatting it up about fishing and boats. Betsy, Grandma, my mother, and I were having a good time talking about all sorts of things. I've been mum with most of the details about last night, but I had to tell them what I saw. I didn't mention anything you told me or what we spoke about. You'll have to say something."

"C'mon. I gotta change. It's the only chance we'll have to talk."

"Won't they want to say *hello*?"

"They'll just come into the shower and say hello. You're the only one in the house who hasn't seen me naked in the past year. Well, you and your parents." Haley laughed at me.

"Does this mean I'll see you naked?"

"If you're standing in the bathroom while I'm showering, yes." I placed my weapon on the nightstand.

"Don't you lock up your gun?"

"No. Oh, yeah, Paulie." I put the weapon in my lock box in the closet. I got undressed, hung up my suit and, with towel wrapped around me, walked to the shower.

"Damn! You're pretty buff for a wounded warrior," Haley said.

"Thanks," I said as I felt myself blush.

"Those scars look terrible. Let me see."

"You're just trying to get close to me to pull the towel off. I'm onto you. Let me shower. Besides, I'm self-conscious about the scars."

"You are not."

"Well, I could be." I smiled at Haley as I got into the shower. "I know you're looking."

"So, what. So, I was saying . . . Can you hear me?"

"Yeah."

"I was saying, Lauren called me. Well, first she said she'd call me, then she called me.

She invited us over. Lauren remembered my mom though she was just ten-years-old when your mother redecorated the house. Anyway, she told me what was up, what they all heard and talked about. They decided that we needed to have dinner and to get to know each other. I mean this is the first time I was ever on a first date and my man killed two guys," Haley said.

"Wait until you see what I do on the third or fourth date. Whatever *Esquire* or *GQ* say."

"What's that about?"

"Nothing. You were saying?"

"So, your Aunt Betsy and grandmother went shopping. They took your Yukon. Now your grandfather is pissed-off because your grandmother wants a Yukon instead of the Jeep. Anyway. They got almost everything for the whole weekend. Oh. They'll need the extra big cooler from the garage. It's up in the attic rafters. It was too heavy for us to move. Grandma and Betsy want to go pick up some fresh lobster tomorrow."

"Uh, yes. I know where it is. I'll get it later," I said. *They'd been able to get a lot of lobster if they'd opened that cooler!*

"Is everyone staying here, or will they send some of us to the old cottage?"

"I don't know what that is?" Haley said.

"The old beach cottage on the point. We don't own it anymore, but we use it. We sold the property, and they were going to knock it down and put up another home, but they all died. I offered to buy it back, but the estate lawyer hasn't billed enough hours, so he hasn't replied to my offer yet."

"I don't know. I didn't hear anything."

"You won't. They'll sneak it in," I said as I washed my hair. I rinsed off, toweled off, found some soft comfy jeans and put them on.

"No boxers or briefs?" Haley said.

"No. I'm a commando," I said looking serious. Haley considered this then I laughed at her. "It isn't a requirement at home, but in keeping with age-old, grandmotherly advice, we always wear clean underwear when we leave the house— usually." I pulled on a light, long sleeved V-neck sweater in dark grey over a T-shirt. I put on a watch to complete the look and I was ready. I grabbed Haley and kissed her again. "Well, are you ready? Last chance. There'd be no dishonor or hard feelings if you bailed out now. I can hear them sharpening the cutlery."

"Oh stop. They're great," Haley said.

"Wait until they've had a few drinks."

We walked down the stairs, Haley holding my hand. We walked to the kitchen-den-living room-back porch to a chorus of, "There they are."

"Hi. Bet you didn't miss me," I said.

"Don't I get a hug and a kiss?" Grandma asked.

"If I give you one, then I'll have to give everyone else one," I kidded as I hugged and kissed my Grandma. Of course, Betsy was next and so on until everyone got a hug or kiss or both. The men shined me on though. My grandfather handed me a beer. He wanted to talk. He invited Mr. Shore along for the walk to the pier.

"Mark. Mr. Shore, John, was in Vietnam with the Marines," Grandpa said which confirmed my belief that Mr. Shore was a few years older than Mrs. Shore. "We've been chatting away about last night. We know you'll keep it PG for the ladies. What were those guys doing with all those girls? One report said they were sending them overseas," Grandpa said.

"I don't know about that, but they intercepted a large yacht off the coast that belongs to a venture capitalist. He's in custody along with his crew. Three girls were rescued yesterday. They hope more will be found alive," I said.

"How on earth did you end up in this?" Grandpa asked.

I explained how I got involved with the FBI and the child-sex ring.

"How did you know where to find him?" Grandpa asked.

"I didn't. I just drove to his house. I put a tracker on his boat and Coast Guard and Nassau chased it down. I put another on Paul's car and another on Monty's van that I failed to

287

activate. Joe activated it while I raced to the guy's house. The computer indicated the van was there. FBI went to the other guy's house after we were advised that Erica was not on the go-fast boat. I figured other people had to be involved, but after my visit at Monty's home I knew he kept the children there before he moved them. We were lucky I got there when I did. Suffolk and Nassau escorted us to the house. It was interesting."

"Haley said you just crashed through the door, slamming through it with your body without knowing what was there, what danger, and you saved the girl's life. Mark that's incredible."

"Grandpa. We did that crap for years. We'd get intel and we'd kick down doors. First that deck of cards thing in Iraq. Then Afghanistan. We tracked down and killed or arrested bad guys most nights. I didn't see the sun for weeks it seemed. It was what we did."

"Yes, but you had a team there with you. Here it was just you."

"Yes, but I already knew who I was up against. Two pasta fat, dough-boys who probably had not shot fifty rounds in their lives. I was right," I said.

"Did he actually fall out the window?" Mr. Shore said.

"Yes. I shot him five times and it knocked him back and through the window. He swung his weapon toward me and fired. It turns out he also had a .45 ACP on the bed and a sawed-off shotgun alongside the bed," I said as I smiled thinking of the shotgun. "The other guy fired his weapon, but it seems he hit the ceiling he was so scared when he drew on me. I hit him three times on my way up the stairs. Erica was not raped, thankfully."

"An unbelievable story, son. I just wanted to . . ."

"Be briefed first, general? I know, Grandpa. Let's go see what shit Missy is stirring up. Oh. We gotta talk about the firm, too."

"I planned on it. I understand you've crashed through the doors there, too," Grandpa said.

#

We were each greeted by our ladies. Haley was very openly affectionate with me. All the women in my family expressed their approval.

"Hi. Giving the combat vets a briefing?"

"Perhaps. Do I have to cook anything?"

"No. It's all cooking. They have a huge roast beef going," Haley said.

"Where's Paulie?"

"Hanging out with Lauren and Kimberly in her room watching TV. Lauren and Kimberly made the dessert. How was your day at the office?"

"It was good, productive. We'll hire three new brokers tomorrow. I fired one broker today and put another on probation."

"You did? Gee, you hit the ground running," Haley said. Missy joined us on the living room deck.

"My nephew has a new girl!" Missy said to Haley as if I wasn't standing right there.

"Aunt Missy, this is Haley. Haley, Aunt Missy. I'll tell you now she has all the embarrassing stories about me. I think she made a fortune off Dad baby-sitting me between one to four years of age," I said.

"No, your dad was cheap. Your mother was much more generous. I used to change his diapers," Missy said.

"See, you're the only one who hasn't seen me naked."

"I just saw you in the shower!" Haley said.

"I knew you were looking," I said.

"I couldn't help it," Haley said as she winked at Missy.

#

We had a nice dinner. I may have mentioned one of the quirks of the house is that it has no real dining room, that it is an overflow bedroom-storage room at present. The den-family room that you must walk through to get to the kitchen was the country kitchen dining area. It now has a couple of chairs and a lounger in it. The bar-height counter seats six if we put the sixth stool at the end. The living room has five modern takes on what we called TV tray tables. The kitchen porch deck has a table that seats eight and, of course, we have the outdoor living room porch deck. We have several picnic tables on the beach level deck, on the lawn and beach for our lobster boils and barbeques. The extra room could be a dining room, but it's inconvenient to the kitchen. It will likely become another bedroom suite. I believe my mother had a plan drawn up to do that. We'd be spread out for dinner.

I ate outside on the porch living room deck with Haley, Matt, Betsy, the Shores, and Paulie. I was sitting in what had become my spot with Haley next to me. It was getting dark as the ladies took care of the dishes. We would take a break before dessert. It was very comfortable outside. I sat sipping my unsweet iced tea flipping through a Princess Yacht brochure. I was looking at a yacht thinking how nice it would be to have all of us on it for a cruise to Martha's Vineyard. The clanging of dishes, pots and pans died down and everyone moved toward the living room and living room porch. Matt poured drinks for the men and cordials for the ladies, for those so inclined to enjoy one, as they all took seats around me. As expected, they began to look toward me for the story. I headed them all off with what I wanted to talk about.

"I'm thinking about buying a boat. A boat large enough for our entire group to get underway on, be comfortable and safe. The last time I saw one of you ladies on the Parker was years ago and that was for a ride to Lido Beach. Gents . . . that's not a ladies' boat. It's a fishing boat. I've already asked some of you what you'd like to see in a boat. Grandma. I haven't seen you on a boat since I was a child. How would you like to cruise from Rye to here with the General?"

"Oh my, that would be nice. Well, I'd like it large enough for all of us to be able to relax together and have a kitchen large enough to prepare real meals. Oh, and a cabin large enough to have beds to sleep on," Grandma said.

"Grandpa?"

"I agree with Grandma. If it will be used to go to Rye or Martha's Vineyard, it would have to be large and safe enough for the transit. If for extended cruising for long weekends, a washer and dryer."

"Good points. Missy?"

"Well, all of that, but what about large enough to entertain clients? Enough cabins to sleep a sizeable group of us before resorting to sleeping on couches or dinettes," Missy said.

"Betsy. What do you like in a boat?" I said.

"I agree with everything so far. I know you, Matt and Grandpa would like to go off-shore deep sea fishing, but what I've heard so far wouldn't allow for that," Betsy said.

"I'm not including that capability since we can drop a few lines over the side for flounder or stripers, but no deep-sea fishing. Uncle Matt?"

"I like the idea of taking clients out, too, but that would entail a fairly large boat. A yacht. An occasional client appreciation cruise around Manhattan sounds nice. Where would we keep it?" Matt said.

"I'm having the pier extended and services put in. A fifty-foot, heavy-duty T-dock will be added to the end after the pier is extended further out into the bay," I said.

"You've been doing some planning," Matt said.

"I had a lot of free time in the hospital. You've already told me your ideas, Lauren, but how about you Kimberly?"

"Me? Oh, uh, well, I guess places to suntan and hang out, and plenty of USB plug-ins for phones and our music . . . cell phone service or a Wi-Fi hot spot. Oh, and a TV, too . . . and a hot water shower outside to wash the saltwater from our hair," Kimberly said.

"Very good points. So, I've been looking at old and new. I like a boat that has classic lines, but modern comforts. I also like the modern American and British take on the Euro-look." I opened the Princess brochure to the sixty-four-foot and seventy-two-foot yachts. "I was looking at the sixty-four, but with what you're saying maybe the seventy-two," I said as I passed out the pictures and blueprint drawing of the yachts.

"We could structure this as a business. You buy it with some factory financing, the firm leases it for the payment and maintenance costs and Missy sub-leases it for her usage. Write it all off," Matt said. My grandfather was nodding.

"Grandpa. What do you think?"

"It sounds good. Minimal cash out-of-pocket. Factory financing which would be easy to get with a lease contract in-hand. My only concern is the seventy-two might not be big enough for a client cruise. Maybe the eighty-two? We should take a trip to their New Jersey facility and talk to them," Grandpa said.

"That's not too much boat for us? I don't want to get killed with costs," I said.

"You'll never go anywhere over fourteen-knots unless it's an emergency. Let Matt give you a budget with what the firm can do. Hence the larger yacht, but it's still small enough where you can single-hand it into the dock here. We can put our heads together, but you're right, we've neglected our women-folk too long. They deserve a nice boat to relax on," Grandpa said.

"Okay. You've put us off long enough," Matt said.

"Lauren. Would you and Kimberly like to put a movie on in your room for you all and Paulie to watch?" I said giving Lauren a clear message.

"Sure. I think we should have dessert within a half hour," Lauren said which meant I better be done telling the story before then. Lauren, Kimberly and Paulie walked off to Lauren's room.

Haley and I told our stories. I thought Betsy, Evelyn and my grandmother would have heart attacks when I explained my view. I cleaned it up some and made it more PG.

After we finished telling our stories, Grandma, Evelyn, Missy, and Betsy got up to get dessert ready. The children came down at the sound of ice cream dishes clicking in the kitchen.

"You should think about limiting Paulie's contact with his father," Mr. Shore said.

"I know, Dad. It's very hard for all of us. It's down to one day a week and one weekend per month and some holidays. Hopefully, he'll go to prison," Haley said as she glanced at me. Mr. Shore followed her gaze and looked at me.

"That would be best for all," Mr. Shore said. He got up and walked to the kitchen to help with dessert.

"He is a criminal, and he has done some bad things. I find it implausible that he didn't know something about what his men were doing with those girls. Maybe the evidence is there?" Grandpa said.

"Maybe. Did Matt tell you what I did today?" I said.

"He did. I like your idea with the attorneys and lawsuits. I like the idea of the other brokerages getting involved. I've had my suspicions, but you've confirmed them. You are right about Rizzo. He's mixed up with them," Grandpa said.

Haley perked up. "Rizzo? Like Allen Dino Rizzo?"

I looked over to Matt and Grandpa for confirmation as I didn't recall his middle name.

"Yes. About thirty-four or thirty-five. Italian. Six foot tall, perhaps? Frumpy look, dark hair and brown eyes. Graduate of Wharton," Matt said.

"Yes. He's been to Paul's house at barbeques and other events. At the restaurant, too. He's been to my father-in-law's home and Grandpa Menduni's home. I knew him to be in stocks," Haley said.

"How did you know that?" Matt asked.

"He was talking with Paul and Grandpa Romeo Menduni about buying up some stocks. This was several years ago. I recall one conversation at the grandfather's house where Vincenzo and his father told Rizzo—Al, right?"

We nodded.

"They told him to buy a particular stock. I was standing below them on the patio playing with Paulie and his friend with the dogs. Rizzo was always at the grandfather's house even when I dated Paul," Haley said.

I looked at Matt who had a confused look on his face. "This might be easier than I thought," I said to Matt who nodded agreement.

#

Haley, Paulie, and the Shores departed after dessert. Haley would be back the next day. A late shopping trip was planned by the women. They'd take my Yukon into Riverhead after Lauren, Kimberly, and Haley got out of school.

Robert, Tony, their best tech, Matt, Grandpa, Joe, and I would meet to promulgate and finish my plan. I was sure Stayton would learn that all the guys were coming over. We'd meet at 4 p.m. The deal was we men would make dinner which meant I'd make dinner for all. I planned to make lasagna, salad, sausage, and meatballs. The sauce takes a while, so I'd start first thing in the morning after breakfast. It was getting late. Matt and Betsy took the downstairs bedroom, Grandma and Grandpa took their usual room. Lauren and Kimberly got Lauren's room. Missy got my room, and I got the overflow room or the couch. I took the couch. Someday I'd just go sleep on the boat at the end of the pier.

CHAPTER 12

I awoke to the clatter of dishes in the kitchen. My grandmother was up starting breakfast.

"Morning, Grandma."

"Oh? I'm sorry. Did I wake you?"

"No. I have to take Lauren and Kimberly to school. I also have a meeting set with two of her teachers. It should go fast. I guess I should throw on a suit."

"Nonsense. Wear some khaki pants with a light-blue shirt and a blue jacket," she said as she put a coffee in front of me.

"Okay," I said as I thought about the cooler. I walked out to the garage to do that before someone else tried to lift the cooler again.

I entered the garage, and, in a few minutes, I transferred the money from the fishing cooler to another storage container. I carried the cooler to the Yukon and placed it in the back. I put a layer of ice in the cooler from the ice machine we had in the garage. Grandma, Missy, and Betsy would shop in Greenport, Cutchogue and Southold today for the food and whatever else they'd buy. At 4 p.m. they'd be joined by Haley and the girls for a shopping trip to Riverhead. Matt would go into the office to interview the prospective brokers. Bernice and Clara would provide me with updates throughout the day. I parked the Yukon nearer to the house.

"I put ice in the cooler and put it in the Yukon," I advised my grandmother.

"Good. We'll get enough lobster for tomorrow night. If we don't buy today, I'm afraid the selection won't be as nice," Grandma said.

I sipped my coffee. I had some time before Lauren and Kimberly needed to be up.

"I like Haley and her parents. They're very nice. I feel bad for them being mixed up with that Paul Menduni. Will you be able to fix that?" Grandma asked.

My grandmother never beat around the bush.

"We'll see, Grandma."

"I mean it's obvious you love her."

"Wow. I hadn't thought of that yet, Grandma."

"Yes, you have. You just don't want to recognize it. Cathy hurt you and your sense of self. You're not complicated or hard to figure out in matters of the heart. You are a good man. That's why what's going on in your life now has you caught in various dilemmas, right and wrong, and ethical issues. You walk a very tight rope. The wisdom of experience and war have changed you. Haley is your savior, your grounding in what's good. She survived a very bad marriage and some ugly things. Evelyn said Haley is a different woman than she was five years ago. That man took a young, idealistic girl and almost ruined her. The Shores helped save her and brought her back." Grandma paused before continuing as she refilled my cup.

"You always stood up to the bullies when you were a child. Whether protecting that Autistic boy across the street or protecting Andrea Hutchinson down the street from those kids around the block. You weren't afraid. Most people aren't like you. Many people live in fear. Your father lived in fear the last few months of his life. I spoke with Grandpa. I think you are correct about your parents' deaths. Those men did that. Those same men made Haley afraid.

You said you wanted a big boat so you could take all of us out together. You value family and what is good about men and women in strong relationships. You did everything with your mother and father as a child. We thought you'd go into the arts, but later realized you just like doing things with and being around your family. As crazy and confusing as it can be with all of us around, you're happiest when we are. You have a good idea what the right thing is to do. It will become clearer to you; I have no doubt. But you are in love with Haley. All of us women saw it. Haley knows it, too. Make sure she is protected this time," Grandma said.

I sat there assembling what Grandma had said. I got it. I smiled at my grandmother as she grilled up some eggs for Grandpa. I walked to her and kissed her cheek.

"I will, Grandma. I will." I ran upstairs to wake Lauren and Kimberly. I entered my room quietly. I dressed in my closet and bathroom without waking Missy. Five minutes later I was ready. I walked back to the kitchen. Grandpa was already eating. Grandma put a plate in front of me.

"Morning, Grandpa."

"Good morning, Mark. What's on your agenda today?"

"I'll take the girls to school, meet with two of Lauren's teachers, return here to start the sauce and make the pans of lasagna to cover us men since we're supposed to make dinner tonight, then I thought I'd go shoot for an hour or so. I'm out of practice."

"I doubt it! Matt is going into the office. The ladies are going shopping. Pull out that Beretta for me. I'll go shoot with you. I haven't shot in a while and, unlike you, I am a little rusty," Grandpa said.

Lauren and Kimberly joined us. Lauren hugged me, then kissed Grandpa and Grandma. Grandma put a plate of food in front of each girl.

"I've been doing well with Mark taking care of me, Grandpa. He's getting pretty good at being a parent," Lauren said. I messed her hair up. She smiled at me. "He does forget about softball practices though, but he shows up early to get me which works out well since he gets to see me practice and to rescue damsels in distress. We have a game tomorrow, so you'll get to watch Kimberly and me play," Lauren said.

"We'll be there," Grandpa said.

"Okay, ladies, the bus leaves in five minutes. I'll take the Yukon since I'll be back in less than an hour."

#

I pulled up the Yukon to the edge of the carport as the girls came running down the steps. They jumped in and we were off. We pulled up to the school and parked. We walked inside together. The girls ran off to their homerooms and I walked toward the office. Haley was coming out of the office.

"Hi, sailor. You look preppy-nice today," Haley said.

"You look nice, too. You've made a nice impression on my family. They like you a lot," I said as I put my hand on Haley's shoulder.

"My grandmother said that I am in love with you, that I haven't yet recognized it, but that you already know it."

Haley smiled. "You are. It's obvious to all, but you. I think you just recognized it or at least acknowledged it. It's not just here," Haley said as she tapped my head. "It's in here, too," she said as she tapped my chest with her fist. "I can see it in how you look at me and by the way you act toward me. You have the kindest heart of any man I know."

"I think you're correct. Would you get in trouble for a PDA?"

"What's a PDA?"

"Military acronym. Public display of affection," I said.

"No. I don't think so, so long as it is tasteful."

I leaned down and kissed Haley.

"I love you, Haley."

"I know. I love you, too, Mark. I need to go. I'll see you later. Bye."

"Bye." I watched Haley walk down the hall. She turned to see if I was watching. She smiled when she saw that I was.

#

Twenty-five minutes later I was driving home. Lauren is doing well and is loved by her teachers. They agreed to periodically email about Lauren's progress. I'm glad Lauren hasn't gone wild teenager on us.

I pulled up to the garage. I needed ammo and the Beretta for Grandpa. I had to put the money away, too. I decided to find a mini-storage to hide the money. I put 500 rounds of ammo and the Beretta in a shooting bag and walked to the house. I placed the bag in my Hellcat. I walked back into the house. Everyone else was up.

"Hi, Mark," Betsy said.

"Good morning, Aunt Betsy."

"Did you eat yet?"

"Yes, ma'am. I'll just have more coffee."

Betsy poured me a cup. Grandpa and Matt were outside sitting at the kitchen porch table. Grandma was probably getting ready to shop. Missy had been down as I could see her coffee cup—the one with lipstick on it. I took my coffee outside to sit with Matt and Grandpa.

"I'm going in to meet with the new brokers at noon, so I'll have a car here soon. I'll be back by 5 p.m.," Matt said.

"Sure. You're sort of up to speed. I will begin without you. Joe will have some new information. It's Robert and Tony who must come through for us for all three prongs of the plan to work. Was that not interesting last night about what Haley heard about Rizzo?" I said.

"Yes. I've put together my call-list for the other firms. I'll call them today and ask them the questions you posed," Matt said.

"I'll put our assistants on researching and graphing a time-line on Rizzo's activities. I also want to coordinate with the other firms when we redeem the bonds. When we write our misinformation releases, I want to make sure we keep them as unofficial for internal use only so we don't get in trouble with the SEC or the exchange. We want the bad guys to buy lots of stock on margin. While we're driving the stock up in value, we'll redeem our bonds. The one thing I want to make clear is that we need to make sure the media releases are not actual releases so all that needs to have disclaimers on it like not yet for public release, awaiting the president's approval or similar safe-haven statements. I don't care if Rizzo tells his people because we owe no duty to people using insider trading. Anyone buying because the stock is rapidly climbing is making a bad choice and that's on them. So, we get the mob to buy the stock, we redeem our bonds in a predetermined order—perhaps by company is best. If they see it across all the companies . . ." Matt cut me off.

"I think we should all redeem on the same day. Next Friday. Any media releases will be lost over the weekend and when the companies announce Monday . . . well, now . . . What do you think? If we redeem Friday just before business closes, but after the market closes the week will start off with the media releases. We and all the other firms can write releases that state our lack of confidence in these energy companies and that we're not recommending bonds and securities from them," Matt said.

"I agree, Mark. One fell swoop Friday. Start just before the stock market closes. The companies will be forced to use their liquid capital and will be forced to borrow to cover the redemption of the bonds as the day progresses. When the stocks tank Monday and Tuesday, the banks will cut them off. The stock brokerage houses will call the margins due which the mob will not be able to pay because they won't have the liquidity," Grandpa said.

"And because the liens will be placed on their accounts that we know about, their real estate and so on," I added.

"There is one problem. These guys have reserves of cash," Matt said. My grandfather started to nod in agreement when he looked at me and saw something in my expression.

"Mark. I get the feeling that you have something to say," Grandpa said.

I looked around to be sure we were alone. "Let's just say the Calabrese-Menduni family isn't as cash liquid as they think they may be," I said.

"How do you know that?" Grandpa said. A smile spread across Matt's face.

"Let's say I found over $60 million and made it look like Paul Menduni took it."

My grandfather shook his head.

"Can they trace it to you?" Matt asked.

"They might figure out it wasn't Paul, but to me, I don't think so. Plus, I'm monitoring Paul's house, phone, computer, and car. I'll learn what he's doing when he does it," I said.

"Where is it?" Grandpa asked.

"In the garage here and in Oceanside. I'm going to lock it up elsewhere after the ladies leave. I'll get the rest from Oceanside later," I said.

"If we can get this in place by this Friday and pull it off by next Wednesday, we could bankrupt the mob?" Matt said.

"Yes. I just need to bury that money. They were talking about pulling that cooler out last night saying it was too heavy to move. The cooler was full of money," I said.

"Hi guys! What are you talking about?" Missy said.

Matt couldn't resist.

"How to bury $60 million."

"Oh, sure. Where would you get that kind of money?" Missy said. Even Grandpa had a hard time keeping a straight face.

#

The ladies departed. I made the meatballs and brazed the sausages and started the sauce cooking in the giant double boiler. I made the lasagna using thawed homemade sauce and placed the pans in the refrigerator. A limo took Matt to the office. I was just coming in from my run. I needed it. While I was out and sweaty, I put the money in my car. I locked the car and garage and walked into the house. My grandfather was sitting on the living room deck reading the paper.

I showered, dressed, and readied. I pulled out some lead wire seals I used to use for our ammo audits back in the day and I put a high security lock in a bag for the mini-storage. I put my SIG Sauer on and grabbed my gun-cleaning kit since the weapon would get a lot of use today. I ran downstairs with my gear bag.

"Ready?" I said.

"I am. You know, Mark, if you pull this off some people will be very angry with you."

"I don't see how they'll pin it on me. The rumors that we'll plant will help cover or distort that. I plan to cover that later today. We will leave a trail that leads to Menduni and Rizzo and the guys who killed Mom and Dad. Some of this money will be found in their homes, don't worry," I said.

"You know, I've seen some bad things in my life. I've seen man's cruelty to man. When I came home from Vietnam the last time, I swore I'd never go to war again. Then the first Gulf War happened and I was put in command of VII Corps that would lead the attack following the air war. For months, we practiced in the desert, got ready to go at least six times, only to stand down. Once we were given the go ahead, we rolled over the enemy like it was nothing. Our lead tank commanders were so far ahead and had killed so many enemy tanks and soldiers, I had to slow them down and move forward our reserve tanks because the lead elements were nearly out of munitions and fuel. It was so easy the young tank company commanders almost outran their supply line.

Why do I tell you this story? You are one of those front-line battlefield commanders. Make sure you don't out run your logistics. None of your team here has been with you in battle. You need to make a cohesive team that understands its mission and can adapt to changes in circumstances and things that will go wrong," Grandpa said.

I listened to my grandfather and heard what he said loud and clear.

#

We got into the Hellcat. I drove toward eastern Greenport.

"Where are we going?" Grandpa said.

306

"I want to see who is following us," I said.

"I'll just watch," Grandpa said.

I drove fast east, came to an intersection, and turned around and headed west. I kicked up the speed and passed the FBI agent who had followed me on my run that morning. I drove fast to lose him, and, in a few minutes, I found the mini-storage and turned into the driveway to the office.

I executed a contract in the name of Peconic Bay Technologies, LLC—I saw a sign for the bay on the way—and bought forty, two-cubic foot boxes and packing tape. I borrowed a ladder to install the video monitoring and signal monitor that would signal my phone if the door opened, or the lock was messed with. I plugged it in and ran the wire while Grandpa started taping boxes. Finished with my tech install, I began helping Grandpa tape boxes and load them with cash. We spread the cash out over several boxes. I marked the amount on each.

"You could buy a hell of a boat with this money and what you have in Oceanside," Grandpa said.

"We'll get a nice boat without it. I was thinking of putting the Parker in Oceanside. I got a line on a Deep Impact center console with twin Mercury 350s. It does sixty-knots. It's cheaper than my first pick an Invincible forty-two with triple or quadruple engines. I mean, we catch and release bill fish, but we keep the tuna," I said.

"What about the Hydra-Sports 34CC? It's funny we're talking about this. I wanted to discuss with you something like a center console to keep in Greenport. The best all-around center consoles seem to fall in the thirty-two to thirty-five-foot range," Grandpa said.

"Hold on. We're done here. Let's lock up and get out of here. We need to get to the range and get back on the grid before they look for us."

"You're in charge."

We locked up and drove to a McDonalds to get a coffee and to toss the bags in a dumpster. We drove to the gun club range a few miles away in Mattituck. I already had a membership in the club. I requested and received permission for rapid fire practice.

"You ready, Grandpa?" I said as we took our lanes and I put our batteries back into our phones. No one had tried to call us.

"Yeah. I'll start at thirty feet."

I set our targets. I liked to start long and dial in my eye short. I was just different. I found it made my short shooting better. I'd begin at fifty feet. My grandfather wore glasses. I put on shooting glasses, and we began shooting. I clicked off fifteen fast and took out the bull's eye in my target. Grandpa shot and placed almost all his shots in the black circle.

"They sure teach you guys to shoot funny," Grandpa said.

"Things have changed a little since you graduated West Point. As an entity, SEALs didn't exist when you graduated in 1961. We trace our roots pretty far back, but not until January 1, 1962 was the acronym SEAL officially used. But just before that we were involved in the Bay of Pigs invasion, we continued to train Cubans to invade Cuba until 1965. By then we were in Vietnam and it hasn't stopped for us since."

"True. Damn, time flies. I remember graduating West Point like it was yesterday."

We reloaded and shot more. After Grandpa shot his seventh magazine he was tiring, his shots dropping off to the right which is the tell-tale with right-handers.

"You're tiring, Grandpa. Not doing any good now," I said.

"No. I guess not. If I need to shoot more than ten at my age, I'm fucked," Grandpa said.

I smiled. My grandfather rarely cursed.

"Give me a few minutes." I filled six magazines, wiped them off with my oily rag and I set a target in our alleys and the several alleys on either side of us at twenty-five, thirty-five, forty, and fifty feet from left to right. I stood in the forty-foot alley.

"Okay. Time me. All kills, a full mag in each target. I must hit each target at least once before emptying my first magazine. All in one-minute thirty-seconds. This is for lunch," I said.

"You're on. What if you jam?"

"One-minute thirty-seconds. The enemy doesn't give you a time-out for a jam." I put my hearing protection on, put the weapon in my holster on my hip and lined up my magazines.

"You call it, Grandpa. Just say 'go.'"

The three people in the range and the range master stopped to watch me shoot.

"Go!"

I withdrew my weapon and as I brought it up I dotted the twenty-five, thirty-five, forty, and swept right to the fifty and emptied my mag into it. I reloaded and put three more into the fifty, and four into each of the others. I reloaded and put five into the twenty-five, thirty-five and forty. Last reload and I put five into the twenty-five, thirty-five and forty targets. I laid the weapon down.

"Time," I said.

"Damn, son. That was good!" Grandpa said.

The range master retrieved my targets. "Son of a . . . All kills, all inside the first ring," the range master said. The other shooters clapped.

"Let's go outside to clean our weapons at the picnic table. Then you can buy me lunch," I said as I wiped down my mags.

"That's some good shooting, son," Grandpa said.

"Thousands and thousands of rounds, Grandpa. Going through every course we did that. It becomes muscle memory. It saved Talbot's and my life in the last battle. It's all practice. I kept a pistol on my chest harness and my right thigh. I used both as we were overrun," I said.

We cleaned our weapons and put them away.

"What shall it be for lunch, Mark?"

"How about a bacon cheeseburger platter at O'Mally's?"

"You're on. Don't tell Grandma. Let's go."

#

We ate a terrific lunch and we were back at the house before 1:30 p.m. I waved at the FBI guy as we drove past. He waved back. We walked into the house. I checked the sauce. It was doing fine. Grandpa's phone rang. After what seemed like and endless chain of yeses, noes, uh-huhs and okays, he ended the call.

"They're on their way. Wanted to know if we needed anything," Grandpa said.

I poured us both a glass of iced tea and we found seats on the porch.

"Back to the center console. I like the Hydra-Sports 34CC. It seems like the most boat for the money in a thirty-two to thirty-five-foot range, and it has the joystick control system for docking and maneuvering," Grandpa said.

"What color?"

"Dark navy-blue or black hull, white and teak deck and dark T-top. The engines are the usual grey color," Grandpa said.

"Works for me," I said.

"Terrific. I know where we can get last year's model with twelve hours on it for seventy-five thousand off retail. The guy died and his wife wants it gone. It's in a lift at a marina by me in Rye. It's got everything. I'll call her in a minute. Halfies, right?"

"Fair enough you old scammer. The PWCs will be delivered as soon as I call. The lifts go in this weekend. Even the one I selected for the center console," I said.

"You were serious about getting some boats!"

"I am. I want Lauren to build some memories and learn to drive a boat. I figure with the PWCs, the Parker, and a center console, she'll have plenty of opportunity. I took the Parker out at age thirteen. The other boats before that," I said.

"But you're a good captain," Grandpa said.

#

The ladies arrived with the SUV full of food. They began giving orders to Grandpa and me to unload the vehicle which meant I'd unload it. I put the cooler full of lobster and clams in the lower level storage room with more ice. I didn't want the racoons and foxes to get them if I left it outside. I hauled in several armloads of food which confused me since I was under the impression they already shopped for the weekend. Naturally, all three women had to check my sauce. They seemed surprised that it was good. I watched my mother and she showed me a thing or two about tomato sauce or tomato gravy as it sometimes mistakenly called in Long Island if it lacks meat.

I walked to my room and collected my documents for my presentation. I heard a vehicle pull up. I walked downstairs and saw that it was the rest of the girls in Haley's car. Each kissed me as she walked by me, though Haley lingered longer.

"Hi. The sauce smells good. You do all right for a commando," Haley said.

"You should see what I can do with olive oil and rattlesnake."

"Eww! I don't like snakes. I guess we'll talk some more later?"

"You all will be back at 7:30 p.m. or so. Dinner will commence then. I'll be finished with my thing and you can have me all to yourself, with these other people and a couple more.

Just so you know, whenever we're together the rule is 'The more the merrier,' so if you want to invite your mom and dad and Paulie, do so. I'll try to remember to ask you, but I'm forgetful sometimes. We always had friends, neighbors, family, stray cats and dogs, on occasion, over to eat. I . . . Yes, Grandma?"

"Did you invite the Shores and Paulie for dinner?"

"I was just getting to it, Grandma. See what I mean!" I said.

Haley giggled and kissed me. "I'll call them. Dad may be taking Paulie fishing," she said.

"Let them know it's okay to say no. I just overheard them say my grandparents were likely staying this week, so tell your parents it's okay to say no," I said.

"We'll have fun shopping." Haley pulled me to her and kissed me hard and long. We broke apart.

"That'll keep you thinking of me while I'm gone."

"Come on. They'll be looking for us." I took Haley's hand and escorted her to the kitchen.

#

"Will there be any sauce left for the lasagna?" I said while the ladies continued to dip bread in my sauce.

"Oh, don't worry, you don't need much sauce for lasagna anyway, but it is good. Maybe as good as mine," Missy said.

"Oh? Do you cook?" I deadpanned. Missy slapped my arm.

"Such a fresh kid my brother raised," Missy said.

"Let's go girls," Grandma said.

I kissed Haley once more and sent them on their way just as Rob, Tony, and their tech pulled up. After ten minutes of, "Hi, how are yas," the ladies departed.

"Hey, guys. Joe is on his way. Come on in," I said.

Robert lived across the street from me growing up. Tony lived just down the block, and Joe lived across the street and down a couple of houses. We were very tight growing up. We did everything together: sports, cars, boats, surfing, jobs, girls and so on. We went to different colleges. I went into the navy, Joe became a cop, Robert did a stint in the army then went to NSA, and Tony went straight to NSA.

Robert is Irish-Italian, looks Irish except for the nose. He's got blond hair and blue eyes and stands about five-nine and one hundred eighty pounds because he eats like a computer geek. Tony is about five-eleven tall, one hundred seventy pounds, slim, athletic, brown hair and eyes and looks every bit Italian.

"Mark. This is Carl Morgan, our sharpest tech. We told you about him," Robert said.

"Hey, Carl. Nice meeting you," I said as we shook hands.

"Let's go in and have a beer and talk shit about Joe since he's not here yet. My grandfather is here somewhere. He'll join us. The men in my family know most of what we'll discuss. My new girlfriend, as I've explained, is married to the mob. That'll end next week."

"Nice. Shit, Mark, your mom really fixed up this place. Oh, look. The boat is still around. This looks like a new home. Your mom did a terrific job," Robert said.

"This is all yours now?" Tony asked.

"Lauren's and mine. We still own a few other lots. Those there and that one over there," I pointed.

"You'll take over as president of the firm?" Tony asked.

"One day. I'll be part-time until Lauren goes to college. We'll see. I must help my family and I want to do right. But yeah—you saw what had to be done there. Come on. We'll sit out on the porch. Hey, Grandpa. You know Robert and Tony. They grew up on the block," I said.

"Hey, guys. Yes, I remember. Robert. You went into the army, I recall," Grandpa said.

"Yes, sir. I did. I made captain then got out. I was in intelligence—DIA," Rob said.

"And Tony, I recall you did not," Grandpa deadpanned.

Tony, always very quick on the up-take, replied, "I knew I couldn't meet your high standards, sir, and I was over-qualified for the navy."

My grandfather smiled. "I can accept that."

"And this is their top tweeter, Carl," I said.

"Nice to meet you. I'll just sit here and listen. Don't mind me," Grandpa said.

We took seats on the outdoor living room couch. Tony, Rob and Carl pulled out large lap-top computers. I pointed at electrical receptacles in the deck. Settled in with drinks in hand I began.

"Gents, I have a problem. My problem began with the deaths of my parents. The problem we'll resolve began before that with the mob penetrating the firm. To make this go faster,

I'll just say my father did or didn't do something and the mob killed him and my mother. Getting the people who did that, from the guys in the car who drove them off the road, to the top guy who ordered it, is problem one.

Next is that a certain group has penetrated our firm, and I believe there are additional mob guys who have gotten into other firms . . . they have, essentially, gotten into everything to protect and grow their businesses. I have evidence showing that a bunch of those energy companies with innocuous names like Lake Michigan Energy or Iowa Electricity Technologies and more, are the same company and possibly fronts for other activities. Sure, they go out and bill customers and sell other customers a line about saving them money and they buy power from one company and sell it down the lines to municipalities and counties, but that's a front for their real purposes. I believe that my father caught on to their scam. These companies issued bonds, millions of dollars of bonds . . ." I laid down copies of a bond from each company, "all of them did it. But I'm sure that millions of dollars were created purely on the books of these companies. Company X issued X bonds which were bought up by bullshit entities owned by the mob or mob individuals. That money was returned and run through Company Y. That money was returned and used to buy bonds from Company Z and so on. I think anywhere from $20 to $40 million was circulated through these energy companies by the mob and recirculated to give the appearance of greater wealth. Now with this phony book wealth they did two things. They went public, hyping these companies by pointing at all the investors who purchased bonds and the companies entered strategic alliances to share discounts and the transmission of surplus electric power to protect their companies. With the faked proceeds from the sales of these bonds, millions of dollars—at least at face value—they looked good to investors who bought up stock and millions more flowed into these companies.

I don't have their books yet, but I'm sure they fudged the numbers on payroll, co-sharing of employees, and expenditures on corporate expansion and improvements and operating expenses. The co-sharing of employees means one employee is working for several of these companies at a time. The payroll of each company will show wages paid to an employee, though only one company pays that wage, making it appear as if more people are employed by these companies and more money is paid out in wages and salaries.

Now the Big Seven Banks will lend to them. They fill their accounts with loan money that mostly will not be paid back, or they have huge lines of credit available. That's problem number two. Are you with me so far?"

I got nods all around.

"Next, is the things the mob does to people. You heard about Wednesday night and what happened. The FBI is still working that case. Let's just say Joe and I were approached and with a wink and a nod they asked me what I could find out to prove my reliability as a confidential informant. I found out a lot. But for a little boy complaining to his mother and making an odd comment to me about his father's employee, we may not have saved those girls. There are many victims. Nowadays the mob is literally a corporation. I have evidence that they used corporate email, employees and assets to order the hit on my father. That makes the corporation and its officers liable. I have evidence that they've done criminal acts to others through the corporation hierarchy. I have some corroboration that other mob families or corporations knew about the child sex slave ring.

I want to do several things. I want to get all the men in the chain of command from these guys," I tossed a picture of Castellano and Palami on the table, "to this guy," I tossed a picture of Romeo Menduni on the table. "I want all the emails, letters, car movements, credit card, gas card records whatever shows them planning, ordering, or doing crimes, by whatever means you have available. I will take that information and parse through it and communicate with the FBI, Nassau County, Suffolk County, and NYPD. That's problem three.

This is the plan, and my firm will do a lot of this with our lawyers, but what I need is tech support and intelligence. I want to know everything about these men, and I want to chase the leads wherever they go. Once Uncle Matt and I have done our homework, we will begin releasing not ready for public release opinions about these companies that will be communicated past the suspected mob people in our firm and other firms. Hopefully, this will cause the mob employees to buy or order the purchase of the stocks of these corporations driving up the price. As the stock price increases, we'll orchestrate additional bogus releases that will never be publicly released. All the internal emails, memos, loose talk, maybe confidential president's eye's only memos and faxes will be sent past these guys. We think the mob will buy most of the stock on margin. We want them to do this next week. Once we've done this, and we think the stock has reached its pinnacle price, we will redeem our bonds. This will occur Friday after the stock market closes, but before the bond markets close. The companies will be forced to use their liquid assets to buy back these bonds or use their lines of credit since we know they do not have enough money to repurchase the bonds. We, all the firms involved, will follow that bond repurchase releasing poor opinions about these companies. We hope this action combined with the bond redemptions will drive the stock down—essentially, we want to crash the stock value. Things will be bad for the mob, but there's more. Beginning that following Monday, civil actions will be filed in state and federal courts on behalf of the victims and survivors of these corporations' bad acts. The attorneys will lock up all the mob's assets pending litigation. They will have no assets available to pay their stock margins, no security to pay the banks for the loans, and their bank accounts will be locked down by both the courts and the banks. Personal accounts, cars, houses, yachts, boats, what-have-you, will be locked up. They will be unable to borrow, unable to buy, and unable to trade.

All information obtained by whatever manner or means we will pass to the attorneys in sanitized form. We'll pass all criminal evidence to law enforcement, but I will become familiar with all of it so I can inform law enforcement of the criminal activities which will allow them the probable cause to obtain arrest warrants. That's what should have happened the other day, but the kidnapping of the girl accelerated other action."

A car door slammed announcing Joe's arrival. A knock and he entered.

"Just like old times. Hey guys!" Joe said as he hugged Robert and Tony and was introduced to Carl. Joe shook hands with Grandpa.

"I was just explaining the three prongs of the operation. Since we were or are government or military we must call it something. Being a SEAL and having just described the three

319

prongs of the mission I propose Poseidon's Spear with the first prong being called Operation Vengeful Eagle, the second prong Operation Trident—bonds, businesses and stocks, and the third prong Operation Restore Dignity—the civil actions against the mob."

A car rolled up announcing the arrival of my Uncle Matt. A moment later Matt entered the house.

"Hey guys. Joe, Robert, Tony . . . do I know you?" Matt asked Carl. Handshakes and guy hugs all around.

"You really want to turn your business over to this guy?" Tony said pointing at me.

"Someday. He's smarter than he looks," Matt kidded.

"I've just explained the three parts of the mission. This is how it will work. Vengeful Eagle will be led by Joe. He will work with one of you to gather intel on the chain of command and the other families. That op has already started. Direct action on that op will be withheld until Trident and Restore Dignity are completed or nearly completed. I will be overall in charge, but I will head up Trident with assistance from one of you and my staff at MacKenzie Securities. My grandfather will advise me during the op. Matt will lead Restore Dignity. An attorney and one of you will actively lead that while Matt conducts the day-to-day business of the firm. I want every piece of property found and identified. Bank accounts, boats, houses, businesses, investments, et cetera, must be found. You will research and assist the law firm. The attorneys will identify a need and you will fulfill it. Questions?"

"Use our resources to obtain whatever we can?" Rob said.

"Yes. I want you to gain access to every mob guy, associate, and their kids' computers. Here." I tossed Rob some jump drives. "The first two go with Vengeful Eagle. The third with Restore Dignity. Now there's some crossover information here. It's possible those first two drives have info for assets or about defendants. We will sue all companies, officers and employees who are liable for injuring others. The attorneys are already preparing actions against some on the lists. Rob, Tony. . . perhaps you can write a protocol for each group to use to disseminate the info as it is found?

You may hire who you need from your firm. We will have our staff available for Trident and Restore Dignity. There will be no extra eyes on Vengeful Eagle unless I approve it. That's a snoop only op to prepare all information for me."

"Mark. I think we need a little help. We're talking what, two weeks of work and, if we don't leave soon, hugs and kisses from Missy," Tony said.

We all laughed except Carl who looked bewildered. I reached into my mission bag, removed, and placed 10 packs of money in front of Tony.

"That's to get you going. If you need more let me know."

I handed five bundles to Joe. "That's to cover your expenses on your end."

I put another stack of 10 bundles in front of Rob. "That's for the op you'll do.

I think based on what you guys have said, that Rob, you should work with Matt and the lawyers. Tony with me which will mean every day in the office with or without me. My SoHo loft will be your home while you work the op in the city. My assistant, Clara, will arrange a car service for you. Rob, you'll take direction from Matt. Carl. I think you being the hacker extraordinaire, you'll take direction from Joe. Now where do we set you two up?" I said.

"Your Oceanside house. Most of what we'll do is computer searching and the guys we will monitor are all in Queens and Nassau. That puts us close. We can get a van to use if close up surveillance is needed," Joe said.

"Vengeful Eagle will operate out of my Oceanside home. Trident and Restore Dignity from the firm and loft," I said.

"Mark. We want to help, and we can't work for free, but we don't want to break you. We can't accept all this," Rob said.

I reached into my bag and removed four more bundles handing one each to Rob, Tony, Carl, and Joe. "It's not breaking me. The mob is financing their destruction," I said.

A smile burst across their faces.

"You always were good at breaking into shit," Tony said.

More car noises drew our attention to the front of the house.

"Must be the girls," Matt said.

I looked out and smiled. "Don't call these guys girls," I said as I walked to the front door. "You fuckers are late!" I said.

"Your shitty New York traffic!" Came a response.

Everyone looked surprised as six large men entered the house.

"Folks. Let me present the men who saved my life four times," I said.

"Fucking officers . . . it was five times!" Chief said.

"Right. Chief, there's beer in the refrigerator. Don't touch the food until the rest of the family gets home. Take a seat. Grandpa, Matt, Joe, Tony, Rob, and Carl, meet Petty Officers First Class Kevin McClellan, call him Kev, Michael Palmer, call him Mikey, Pierre Talbot, call him Talbot, Chief Petty Officer John Mason, call him Chief, Lieutenant Chuck Evans, call him LT, and Lieutenant Chris Sullivan, call him Surfer. These guys served with me over the last few years. All but LT were with me when I got shot up last time. Chief and I went through BUDS together and I've known him the longest. Guys, Joe is a Suffolk County detective, Tony and Rob are former NSA spooks who own their own spook company, Carl is their top geek. That's my Uncle Matt, president of our family's securities firm and my grandfather, who is a retired lieutenant general, U.S. Army. That's the same as a vice admiral, Surfer, if you're doing the math," I said.

Without missing a beat Surfer said, "So, that's sort of up-there, then?"

My grandfather smiled and said, "I'm sure it's true everything they've said about you guys."

I passed out drinks to all after the introductions and we got down to business.

"One SEAL will remain here. Another will stay at the Oceanside house, perhaps Surfer so he can get some sets in at the break in Long Beach. Another SEAL will be at the firm, one with Matt, and another at the SoHo loft. LT will coordinate and rove. How'd you get here LT?"

"Limo. We barely fit and it had shitty liquor," LT said.

"LT will be with me because he's kind of whiny. He will coordinate with you other five and move coverage should a threat develop. Now you all need to dress the part. In the city, out and about, and at the firm all of you in suits. Your cover at the firm will be special security techies who have been hired to review and test the firm's electronic and physical security. At the loft, I don't care what you look like. SEALs, in the city you'll have a car service. Whoever is at the loft will go back and forth to the office with these guys. Same for travel from Matt's house to the firm. SOP VIP stuff except you'll be solo or in pairs. You guys are on leave for three weeks, right?"

"That's right. We're do back three weeks from this Monday," Surfer said.

"Okay. Here," I handed each SEAL two bundles of cash.

"LT here's six more for tomorrow. You'll go to Riverhead and buy some suits for the job. We'll assign you guys this weekend. You'll stay in the cottage on the property over there," I pointed at the cottage, "but you'll join us here for your meals since the cottage has no cooking equipment or food. Joe. Questions, suggestions?"

"No. I think we're good. For Carl and me and whoever you assign with us, I think an SUV. That's a van and an SUV for Oceanside," Joe said.

"Okay," I pulled out another bundle and tossed it at Joe.

"I'm not clear on living arrangements," LT said.

"The SoHo loft and firm guys will stay at the SoHo loft. So, with Rob and Tony it's plus two SEALs with a car service. Whoever goes with Matt will stay at Matt's house. They'll travel by limo to and from the city each day, but have a SUV to get around in. Whoever stays here will have a SUV and another will rove. One SEAL at the Oceanside house will drive a SUV.

What else?" I said.

"What if a threat materializes?" Kev asked.

"I have twelve private security team guys, all former SEAL, Marine or Delta, ready to go at the touch of a speed dial. All men are New York residents with conceal carry permits. You guys will have whatever you like as a long gun with you. No concealed pistols, but rifle in the trunk or on a seat if not loaded is fine. You'll carry a mag with you. A pistol with the ammo separate is fine, too. Just don't carry a loaded pistol on you in Manhattan. Cool?"

"Got it, boss. When do we eat?" Mikey said.

"When the girls get home. Let me put out some pizza and hors d'oeuvres before you guys wither away. More questions? Rob, Tony, Matt—anyone?"

"Hey. Two SUVs just pulled up with a small sedan," Surfer said.

"That's the SUV for here and for whoever goes to Matt's house. Kev. Run out and get the keys, please."

"Right."

"You guys will use those SUVs this weekend. One final bit. The FBI is watching me. Not to bust me, but to protect me. I'm sure they're wondering what we're doing. The cover for all this is a reunion of childhood friends and wartime buddies with me since I just got out of the hospital. Cool?"

"Got it," LT said.

"I'd like to check out the boat just so we know it," Surfer said.

"Sure. The keys are in the toilet," I said.

Surfer, Talbot, and Mikey took a walk to the boat. I grabbed a beer and sat down on the outdoor living room couch.

"Well, Grandpa, Matt, what am I missing?"

"You continue to surprise me, son," Grandpa said.

LT came over and twisted the top off a beer.

"That was you who rescued those girls two days ago?" LT said.

Rob got another beer and sat down with us.

"Yeah," I said.

"Good on you, Mark. We'll learn more about them. Are you close to finding out about who killed your parents?" LT said.

"Joe and I identified two of them so far. He and Carl will find the rest."

My phone buzzed.

"Hello!"

"Mark. What are you doing?"

"Who is this?" I knew who it was.

"Special Agent Stayton. What are you and that posse of ten men doing out there?"

"It's a preplanned get together of my childhood friends and some wartime buddies to celebrate my return to good health. Why?"

"You ditched my guy and put both GPS trackers on your SUV. Not nice."

"I figured the FBI could follow the women in my family and they could drive someone else batty for a change."

"You and Grandpa went shooting today. What else have you learned?"

"Frankly, not much. Today's been a domestic day. Teacher conferences, picking up lobster, which reminds me, I need a few more. Anything else, John?"

"No. Keep it clean. Bye."

"Bye."

"We'll need more lobster. I have a hole in my plan. I almost out ran my supply line," I said as I looked at my grandfather.

Grandpa nodded. "You're doing just fine. Matt and I will take another cooler and get some more lobsters. I suspect we'll need more bread and dessert, too."

"Thanks, Grandpa."

Matt reached into my bag and peeled off twenty $100 bills.

"We'll be back," Matt said with a smile.

#

Matt and Grandpa took LT with them so he could become familiar with Greenport. I checked the sauce and continued rotating pans of lasagna in the ovens and bread in the warmer.

It was nearing 7:30 p.m. Dinner was all but ready. Rob helped me chop up the salad ingredients.

"Mark. What are you going to do when you get the evidence on who killed your parents?" Rob asked.

"I'll sanitize it, I'll personally verify it, and I'll inform the FBI and Nassau County," I said.

Rob looked at me searching for more.

"You know, Mark, you've developed a certain . . . I don't know, a hardness about you. You're more precise and guarded than you were growing up. I sure hope you pull this off and don't get hurt," Rob said.

"I'm with you there, bro."

I heard a vehicle pulling up to the house. I looked out and spied the ladies. I watched them get out of the Yukon. Missy noticed the other vehicles.

"We have company?" Missy said.

"No. It's family. C'mon in. Dinner is ready," I said.

Haley kissed me. "What's going on?" Haley said.

"The guys are here. You'll meet them," I said.

"My parents aren't coming. Maybe tomorrow. Dad took Paulie fishing."

"That's fine," I said.

I helped the women with their bags into the house. They saw Surfer and Kev first then the others standing on the living room deck.

"There are more good looking, rugged men in this house than in all of Manhattan! Who are these men?" Missy said.

Lauren and Kimberly immediately smiled when they saw Mikey and Talbot.

"Everyone. These guys are my brothers. They'll be visiting with us for a few days," I said. I made all the introductions.

"Where's Grandpa and Matt?" Grandma said.

"Getting more lobster, bread, and dessert. Tony, Rob, Joe, and I will start serving. Ladies first. Let's do this while everything is hot," I said.

Matt, Grandpa and LT returned. I put more bread in the warmer and we commenced dinner. Missy put her claws into Surfer who always enjoyed the company of older women.

Once everyone was served, I found Haley who was being doted over by LT and Kev.

"Watch it. Those two bite," I said.

Haley saved me a seat next to her on the outdoor couch. Talbot and Chief sat with Grandpa, Grandma, Tony, Carl, and Matt on the kitchen porch table. Betsy moved in and out making sure everyone had bread and drinks. Lauren and Kimberly giggled every time Mikey or Talbot spoke to them

"So, this is your A-Team?" Haley said.

"Part of it, yes."

"You'll tell me what's up later?"

"Yes. You'll work with Joe and Carl there. Robert will interview you later about mob assets," I said.

"You are really going to do it, aren't you?" Haley said as she looked into my eyes and put her hand on my thigh.

"We are going to do it, yes."

"I spoke with Erica's mother. She's doing as well as can be expected. She's home from school. Phyllis will home-school her for the rest of the year. Erica is afraid to be alone. Phyllis is afraid of what Ken might do to Paul. Ken is a computer software engineer, not a fighter, Mark. Would you speak to him? I don't want Ken getting hurt," Haley said.

"Sure. Why don't we call them in the morning or after the game?"

"What's the plan?" Haley asked.

I explained our plan.

"If all goes close to plan, I'll wrap it all up by Memorial Day," I said.

Haley looked at me, her eyes doing that darting back and forth thing as she tried to read me.

"Please be careful, Mark. I don't want any of you getting hurt," Haley said as she kissed me which I'd forgotten to warn her not to do.

"How would you rate that kiss, LT?" Kev asked.

"I'm not sure? She moved in slow, but it could have had a little more passion, perhaps?" LT said.

"I was thinking she should have put her hand behind his head and pulled him toward her more," Kev said.

"A valid observation," LT said.

Haley looked at me with a big smile. "These are your brothers, aren't they?"

"Yep! They are!"

CHAPTER 13

Haley left for home about midnight. Tony, Rob, and Carl departed then, too. Carl would begin to set up at the Oceanside house and Joe would join him. Tony and Rob began encrypting all our phones. Joe stayed over and would join us at the softball game. The SEALs would drive the two SUVs but would depart after the first game. The girls had a double-header.

Joe and I awoke first. We'd slept in the living room on the couches. Joe used the half-bath and showered outside while I started coffee and made a huge bowl of pancake batter. I put eight boxes of sausage on racks on cookie sheets and started them in the ovens. I broke open five dozen eggs into two large bowls. I placed two, eight-pancake griddles and a large, scrambled egg pan on the stove. I was ahead of the curve when Grandma walked in, looked around.

"I'll do this. It's what I do best to support my family," Grandma said and kicked me out of the kitchen.

Joe came in dressed and fresh. Grandma poured him coffee. I went outside and showered, too. I dressed in fresh jeans, V-neck T-shirt, and blue button-down shirt. I went back to the kitchen and Grandma poured me coffee. It was almost 7 a.m. and the game was at 9 a.m. Grandma started the pancakes. I woke Lauren and Kimberly.

I returned to the kitchen and found Betsy helping Grandma. I poured Joe and me another coffee and turned around to find a miniature man standing there smiling at me.

"Paulie? What are you doing here?" I asked as Haley walked in.

"I told him he could get breakfast with you and go to the softball game to watch Lauren and Kimberly play."

"Terrific. You want to be first to eat?" I said then noticed Joe was already eating. "Okay, second to eat?" I said.

"Yes," Paulie said.

"Take a seat right here next to Joe." Talbot and Chief came into the den area. Breakfast had officially begun, and Grandma was in her element. By 8 a.m. everyone was up and had eaten.

The guys put their toys in their SUVs. Betsy and Missy made a cooler full of sandwiches, snacks, fruit boxed drinks and bottled water for the games. We would all rendezvous at 4:30 p.m. for happy hour followed by dinner—a real New England lobster boil. Joe would spend the day with us. He ordered the vehicles they'd need at the Oceanside house. Carl was already in the Oceanside house and had already begun setting up, probing, and feeling out the bad guys' computers. The probes and attempts to access the mob's computers would look like the Russians did it. Amazing stuff. Tony and Rob were already in the loft setting up with their people.

I noticed a barge with crane being pushed up to my pier by pusher boat. Mr. Jeffries pulled up in his truck. I walked out to greet him.

"You're early," I said.

"You're all approved. I got the permits yesterday. The PWC lifts and boat lift we'll do today. Tomorrow, we'll begin placing the pilings to extend the pier."

"Then God is with us. My grandfather will pick up a new center console on Monday and the family is pining for a larger yacht. Let me know if you need anything," I said.

"Thanks," Mr. Jeffries said.

#

The family was ready to go. The ladies piled into the Yukon with Paulie. Grandpa, Matt, and Joe got into the Jeep with me. The team guys took their SUVs.

We pulled up to the school, off-loaded the chairs and coolers, and we got the ladies comfortably set up at the end of the stands along third base line since Lauren played third base. Lauren and Kimberly ran off to practice with their team. The weather was perfect for softball. The field was well-manicured, and the grass was lush. They even had true dugouts. The official's view box was behind home plate and a snack bar did a brisk business from a small concrete building between the stands also behind home plate.

The school's yellow and purple colors were everywhere. I think much of the extras I saw were paid for by donations. I noted two other fields under construction. The guys took a stroll around to check out the town around the school. The game would begin soon. I took a walk over to where the family was sitting. Haley was sitting between Betsy and Grandma. I watched how comfortable Haley was around my family. After a bit, Haley noticed me watching and smiled.

"Come sit. I can stand for a while," Haley said.

"Uh, no, ma'am. You stay right there. So, the lifts will be completed by tomorrow, Grandpa."

"Really? Then I'll deliver a check to the widow and have the boat towed here. It has a trailer we can just lock up on the lot next door," Grandpa said.

Grandma rolled her eyes.

"What, Grandma?" I said.

"I've been at him for years to get something nice. I'd like my husband to take me out fishing, too. I like to fish," Grandma said.

"If he doesn't, I will," I said.

"I want you to teach Lauren about boats like your Dad and this old guy taught you," Grandma said.

"It's already in the plans," I said.

Kimberly's father, mother and little brother arrived. They set up in our midst. Mrs. Schwartz got into a conversation with Missy and Betsy, and before long they were all carrying on like they'd known each other a long time.

The game began with Lauren playing third base and Kimberly pitching. The first pitch was a line-drive hit directly back at Kimberly, who caught it. The ladies went wild, clapping and yelling, and the game was on. Three up, three down. The girls got up to bat. Kimberly batted second and Lauren batted clean-up. Batter one singled to right field. Kimberly followed with a grounder that got between second and shortstop for a single while the runner advanced to third. Batter three flied out to center field. Lauren got up and the coach signaled for her to hit and run. Lauren hit the first pitch just right and drove it between center and right field. It bounced all the way to the fence for a triple with two RBIs. The ladies were going wild, jumping, standing in their chairs, yelling, clapping, and whistling. I smiled as I clapped and watched. Grandma was leading the cheer. Grandpa and Matt were on their feet yelling and clapping. The SEALs, abandoning all moderation, were whooping, and cheering for Lauren and shouting encouragement as she stood on third base smiling.

I heard Haley's phone ding. She answered it.

"Hello. Yeah. Okay. Don't worry. I'll handle it. I'll let you know. Bye."

Haley put her phone down then looked at me. "That was my mother. Paul stopped by looking for Paulie since he didn't get to spend time with him Wednesday, and I had him that night by default."

"Is it his weekend?" I asked.

"No. His scheduled weekend is next weekend."

"What do you want to do?"

"I don't want him to go with Paul."

"Then he won't go with him. Is he waiting for you at the house?" I said.

"No. He's coming here. Paulie told him he was coming to the game."

"That's fine."

"You don't know him, Mark."

"Don't worry, Haley. There is a policeman over there, Joe is a policeman with Suffolk County and then there's those guys and me. I don't expect a problem," I said.

"Thank you."

"Maybe he'll see that your car is not here and just leave. Relax and enjoy the game," I said putting my hands on her shoulders while standing behind her. Haley put her hands on mine.

The inning finished and our team was up by three, Lauren having scored on another single. The next two innings passed with each team earning a run. It was a nice game, and we were all enjoying it. I sipped a bottled water while watching Lauren pick up a grounder with her throwing hand, tossing the batter out at first. Dad taught Lauren to throw well. I wish our parents were here to watch Lauren play. Haley tapped my hand.

"He just pulled up," she said.

I looked at Joe and nodded at the Lincoln. I took out my phone and tapped to the microphone in Paul's SUV. I walked over to Joe so he could listen. We walked toward the SUV and listened to Paul ranting to his men. It sounded like at least two other men were with him. New guys I wondered? Then the background noise settled down and I heard Paul's voice clearly.

"That's her sitting over that with that group by third base. I don't know any of them. I'm going to just walk over and tell her to come talk to me with Paulie. If she gives me any shit, I'll just take Paulie. If she fights me just grab her while I put my boy in the vehicle."

As Paul spoke, I walked over to Haley with Joe, keeping the phone between us.

"Who's that, boss?" One of his men said.

"That's the fucker who butted in last time I was out here. She must have a thing going with him. I don't know the other guy. Look. We'll just walk over there. She won't answer her phone. Stay away from that guy. He laid out Monty and none of us seen it and we were standing right there," Paul said.

Joe smiled. The men got out of the SUV. I clicked the phone off.

"Excuse me," I said to Haley.

I nodded at Chief who saw what was developing. I walked directly toward Paul. Three men were with him. Joe got on his phone calling to get the cell number for the patrolman in the parking lot. Chief, Talbot, Surfer, and Kev appeared from behind the stands and walked towards Paul. Joe and I walked toward Paul in front of the stands from the third base side. Paul was parked behind the stands along the first base line. We intercepted Paul behind the stands.

"Can I help you?" I said.

"Fuck you!" Paul said but his expression changed when he noticed the guys. Joe had the patrolman on his phone.

"Haley asked me to tell you she doesn't wish to speak to you," I said. Paul and his men looked around sizing up the situation.

"What? You her errand boy or something?" Paul said to me.

"Or something. Now you fellas are welcome to stay and enjoy the game, but Haley doesn't wish to speak to you," I said.

At that moment, LT and Mikey appeared. To give a true sense of what Paul and his men saw, picture six men, all over six feet tall, in robust health who look, well, dangerous. Throw in Joe and me, and while Joe may not look in robust health, he looks dangerous.

"Look, you can't prevent me from speaking with her," Paul said.

"Ah, but I can," I said as I nodded at the two Suffolk County patrolmen walking our way. Paul looked at them then at me.

"You butt into my business too much, dickhead. One of these times you'll be alone," Paul said.

"Mr. Menduni. You are not welcome around Haley or her home. If you have an issue with that, take it up with me," I said.

"Is there a problem here?" A patrolman asked. Joe stepped forward to speak to the officer after quietly identifying himself. After a few minutes the patrolman turned to Menduni.

"Mr. Menduni. The lady does not wish to speak to you. Do not approach her on school grounds. She is an employee here. Harassing, threatening, or assaulting a teacher on school grounds is a felony. You may remain and watch the game, but once the game is concluded you must leave school property. If there is a problem . . ." the patrolman looked around, "after I pick you and your men up off the ground, I will arrest you. Am I clear?"

Paul looked like he would explode. He glared at me then turned and walked to his SUV. Joe thanked the two officers. I clicked back to the microphone on my phone and put it to my ear.

"Who the fuck were those other guys?" One of Paul's men said.

"I don't know. They ain't fucking cops or they would have just badged us," Paul said.

"What do you want to do, boss?"

"We'll sit here a while. Let's see what they do. See her over by the third base line sitting with those other women? I don't know any of those people," Paul said.

Joe walked over and I turned up the volume.

"We'll watch. Those must be his people," Paul said.

"Yeah, but who were those other guys? We would have been slaughtered," another of Paul's men said.

"Quit whining. Fuck, you guys piss me off," Paul said.

LT walked over. "Is that who I think it is?"

"It is. We're listening now. I have a microphone ten inches from his head," I said.

"Shit, Mark, you're good," LT said.

"LT, ask Chief to park an SUV in that open spot next to the Lincoln. I want to block his view."

"Aye, aye, sir," LT said as he ran off. The SUVs I'd rented were the Chevrolet Suburban 2500 model so they were higher than a standard SUV.

"Why are those two just standing there looking at us? What the fuck? Tell this asshole to move his truck," Paul said.

Chief had just backed in blocking their view.

"Fuck! It's one of them guys. He won't listen to us."

"That fucker told him to park there. Let's get out of here. This is bullshit. Let's go to my father's house. I ain't putting up with this shit no more. I need him to ask Grandpa to let me take her out of the picture. Let me call my father," Paul said. There was a pause in the conversation. "Yeah. Is my father there? Yeah, Paulie. Tell him we're on our way there. Yeah. Okay. He's there. Let's get a move on," Paul said.

"You should have done her before you handed over that money, boss."

"Shut up, you moron. It'll go to my kid, so I'll get it back when . . ."

I lost the signal.

"You get that, Joe?"

"I did. How do you want to handle it?" Joe said.

"Can Carl get into their phones?" I said.

"I'll call him right now. You stay with her," Joe said.

"I won't leave her side."

I walked over to Haley.

"Okay?" Haley asked.

"He's gone. We're covering it. Excuse me."

I walked over to LT and explained what we'd heard.

"You guys go get your shopping done and I'll see you guys at 1630 at the house," I said.

"Do you want to put Kev or Mikey at her house?" LT said.

"No. She'll be with me. I don't think Vincenzo is stupid enough to let Paul whack his wife the week of their divorce hearing. Especially after this little tête-à-tête. More likely, he'd let him rough up me, but they must first figure out who I am. Go have fun shopping and tell Chief no leather unless it's a belt or shoes. Oh. I just noticed something. Get the guys nice watches that won't make them look so obvious. Nice watches, LT," I said.

"Good idea. My wife is going to love you even more after she sees the suits, shirts, ties, and watch. We'll see you at 1630," LT said.

"Bye. And make the guys listen to the salesman. No Hawaiian tropical ties or blue seersucker suits. New York conservative, business attire."

LT nodded. I rejoined Haley and my family. Betsy handed me a ham and Swiss sandwich and an iced tea in a bottle.

We spent the rest of the morning watching the game. The girls split the doubleheader, but they were fun games. We took pictures of Lauren and Kimberly and several of the other girls. Grandma invited the Schwartzes to dinner.

#

"What's wrong, Mark?" Haley said.

She was already starting to read me. "Just thinking about the op to make sure I haven't missed something," I said.

"Thank you. Oh. My parents accepted your family's invitation for the lobster boil."

"Good. We eat out on the deck, on the lawn and beach. It's fun. We do all the boiling down there, too. Standard stuff. Grandma will put out all the leftovers and there will be lobster, clams, biscuits, corn muffins, potatoes, and corn on the cob. You won't go hungry."

"Good," Haley said.

We picked up our things to load into the SUVs. Paulie had a new friend in Kimberly's brother. They were both seven. He was coming back to the house with us. We fit all the ladies and boys in the Yukon. The men got into the Jeep, and we drove home.

"So? What was all that about with Haley's husband?" Grandpa asked.

"Paul got smart and left, but he's going to ask his father and grandfather for permission to take out Haley," I said.

"What?" Matt said.

"Don't worry. Vincenzo is no dope. He won't let him hurt her now, the week of her divorce. I'd expect that he'll let Paul and his guys rough me up instead."

"You don't look too worried," Matt said.

"He doesn't even know my name. It'll take him days to figure out who I am. We'll set up surveillance at the Shore's place to make sure. Any threat, we'll eliminate it."

"Did you recognize any of the three new guys?" I said to Joe.

"The one guy rang a bell. I took a couple of pictures to review. Carl is working on their phones. The number Paul called is Vincenzo's listed number. Carl is looking for his cell phone number, but Vincenzo is old school smart. He won't talk on it, but we just want to listen. He probably doesn't pull the battery so Carl might get into it. Paul's residence is already being monitored so Carl can get in there," Joe said.

"Oh. I'd like Carl to go into this mini storage video system and wipe out a few days of video. Start from the point just before Paul's SUV is seen pulling up there Wednesday night," I said as I wrote down the name for Joe.

"I'll call him," Joe said.

"Drop me off with the FBI agent so I can speak with him," I said. I got out of the Jeep and they continued to the house.

"Hi. You should know that Paul Menduni is headed to his father's place to seek permission to kill his wife. I don't know what capability you have there, but I thought you should know," I said.

"How do you know this?" The agent asked.

"My friend, Joe, that guy getting out of the Jeep, he's Suffolk PD. He and I overheard Menduni and his men discussing it."

"I'll pass it along."

"Oh, and you are kind of conspicuous here. Park back on my property or across the street. A car has never parked here in my memory. You are too obvious," I said.

"Thanks," the agent said.

I walked to the house. I could see the pier to my left. The PWC lifts looked like they were in. A guy was doing electrical work now. The barge and crane operators were sinking pilings for the boat lift. Interesting work. Haley was waiting for me.

"C'mon. Let's go get something to drink. I'll have to start getting things ready for boiling lobster and clams soon. Look, I'll tell you right now. I want to put a security monitoring system in your parents' house. This way we can detect Paul or his men there. I don't believe he's stupid enough to bother you there, but I'd feel better knowing that with a few clicks on my phone I can look at your driveway and see if he's pulled up there," I said.

"You're not just trying to keep an eye on me, are you?" Haley joked.

"No. The waterproof camera in your shower is for that," I came back.

I took her hand and we walked to the house.

#

I got a beer for me and poured a wine for Haley. The ladies were doing the basic dinner preparations, trying on clothes, and chatting about everything. Matt, Joe, and Grandpa were down on the pier looking at what the dock builder had done and was still doing because that's what men do.

"Looks like the boat and PWCs will fit fine," my grandfather said.

I was kind of anxious to get out on the water. It was warm with just a slight breeze—a nice spring day.

"C'mon. Let's take a ride," I said. Matt, Joe, and Grandpa declined my offer.

"Okay," Haley said.

We walked to the Parker near the end of the pier and I stepped aboard. I helped Haley aboard since it was low tide. I lowered and started the engines. I let them idle. I checked the fuel tanks, they were full. I took in the bow line then the stern line which were on fiberglass whips to keep the boat off the pier. I pushed the throttles forward and we got underway. I moved the throttles forward until the boat settled on a plane at a comfortable thirty knots.

"It's beautiful out today," Haley said.

"It is. I love being out on the water. I could be a fisherman, but just being out is great. It's been a long time since I was last out," I said.

Haley pulled in close to me. The wind blew her hair into our faces as it was buffeted by the pilot house. We headed west when suddenly Haley exclaimed, "I recognize where I am now. We didn't usually come up this far and when Dad goes fishing off Montauk, he goes below Shelter Island."

"I know where your house is by water. I used to explore that whole bay. I'd get up early and travel all over between the forks, to Orient Point, Shelter Island, down into Little Peconic and Big Peconic Bays. I'd chase the ferries. I'd get up early with the sun, pack a lunch and sodas, my fishing poles and equipment, bait, my radio and off I went. I wouldn't return until nightfall. We used to have a VHF radio mounted on the porch with a long antenna on the roof. My mother would call me to come get her. My dad worked a lot back then. I'd take Mom out. This was in 1996 or 1997. The boat was almost new."

"Where did you take your mother?"

"Different places. Out to explore the bay or to fish. I had to bait the hook for her. Every time she caught something she was so surprised by the act of the fish pulling on the pole she'd forget to reel it in," I said as I thought about those nice days with my mother.

"Did you spend the whole summer here?"

"No. We liked going to Long Beach, Lido Beach and even Jones Beach. I picked up a surfboard when I was nine or ten, so I did that, too. Out here we don't have surfable conditions most of the time and the south fork was too far. When we did go there, we had a long walk to get across the South Fork unless it was calm enough to anchor just off False Point by Montauk Point State Park. Joe and I once took our boards and drove the boat all the way around Montauk Point and anchored off the beach beyond the break. We surfed for hours as the conditions picked up and the waves got bigger. The afternoon wind picked up and the waves got huge. It got to the point that Joe couldn't get through the break to get to the boat. I just barely made it, but now I had to figure a way to get Joe without swamping the boat. I got aboard, started the engines, and pulled the anchor. I realized I had several one-hundred-foot anchor lines, so I attached a life ring, that one right there I think, to the line and threw it over. The waves brought it in to Joe. He grabbed it and I pulled him clear of the break."

"Sounds like it was dangerous?"

"No. We didn't think so. Joe and I have always kept our wits about us in the surf. When it comes to the ocean, I'm not afraid. It's my savior we're taught—all navy divers are taught that. I respect the ocean. I could never live inland like Iraq or Afghanistan or even Colorado. I've been to all of those places and after a few weeks of not smelling the salt air I miss it."

"I agree. My dad has had his boat for at least ten years. He had a few boats before that. I've driven them and I've been out fishing with him. I'll bait my own hook, by the way. But I've only been inland upstate, in Connecticut, Pennsylvania or Massachusetts. I would miss it, too. There are days in the winter I didn't care for it, but it wasn't the ocean I disliked, it was the cold. I've been to Florida a few times. I like it there. I think spring and summer here, winter in Florida," Haley said.

"Hard to do with kids and school," I said.

"Yes and no. Hard to do if working, but home schooling solves the school problem."

"Interesting. Let me ask you, if you could be anywhere in your life, and I don't necessarily mean only age or place, I mean station in life, where would you be?"

"Right now, on this beautiful spring day, cruising along the bay with a good-looking man, and you want me to say something else?" Haley said.

"I mean more than that. Let's assume for the question you and I are together. What would we be doing as a family unit?"

"I already said a few children. I would work on and off as a teacher, maybe even as a tutor . . ." I interrupted her.

"For the money or self-fulfillment?"

"More self-fulfillment, but I'd want to be able to devote most of my time to my family. So, I guess if I'm being totally honest, I'd be married to a decent man, I'd have four or five or more children and I'd live in a house like yours or the one I envision on my parents' property, and we'd have a house in Florida."

"That's nice, but I'm just a little concerned by that."

"Oh?" Haley looked at me with an expression of concern.

"I didn't hear anything about a boat." I hugged her to me.

"It goes without saying. Will your aunt and uncle go in on a boat with you? I mean, a yacht?"

"I suppose. We'll see after Matt gives me a budget. Missy and Matt were talking, but I saw Missy starting to become upset with Matt for whatever reason. I don't care if they do or don't. I'll get something myself between fifty and sixty-five feet. Grandpa had me talked into a new center console boat when he sprung the news on a year-old boat at substantially less than the new price."

"Are you okay with the growth plan—getting a larger boat than you planned?"

"I suppose. I've been to the New York, Miami, and Monaco boat shows. I've walked aboard a few. C'mon. We'll head back. I've been jabbering. We'll be at your place in a minute." I turned the boat around.

"My question to you is can you answer your question to me?"

"Yes. We, well you, touched on it the other night. I like kids. I'm just learning about them. I was a very independent child and always did for myself. I'll learn, and I am learning. I would want a few children, too. Where would I be? My station in life? I do not want to be a slave to the firm. Grandma knows it, Grandpa is learning it, and Uncle Matt fears it. Matt got thrown in the president's seat. He is not president material. He knows it. My Dad ran it. I wish my Dad had confided in Matt more. The current issues..." I drifted off in thought.

"Mark. Do you want to be president? Mark? Did you hear me?"

"What? Oh. Yes. Eh, uh, what did you say? I'm sorry. I was just thinking."

"I said, do you want to be president?"

"I think so. I'd like to get the firm fixed and work a power-share arrangement where Matt and I don't have to work every day or for several months at a time. I feel like I have an obligation to my family and a sense of duty to the employees."

"I know you do. I knew it after just a couple of conversations with you. You'll figure it out. You have time."

I bumped up the speed to get us back. I could see the pier and the crane now over the little peninsula that jutted out with the cottage on it which created a shallow cove along the four or five lots by the house. We rounded the point and I slowed, the boat's wake overtaking us as I waited for the water to calm before approaching the pier as I'd done hundreds of times before. I inched up under the mooring whips and hovered while I grabbed the bow line, affixed it to the cleat, then the stern line. I stopped the engines and raised them out of the water.

"Shall we?" I said. I climbed onto the dock and reached down and picked up Haley. We walked to the house holding hands.

The house was quiet while everyone relaxed. Grandpa was napping on the couch in the living room, Grandma sat nearby reading. Missy and Betsy were talking while they peeled ears of corn in the kitchen. I could hear Paulie and Barry Schwartz, Paulie's new best friend, playing under the house and out by the dunes. Lauren and Kimberly were sunning themselves on the western front porch. I guessed that Matt and Joe were napping somewhere.

I removed the large pot boilers from under the house and washed them out. I pulled the gas burners out along with the bottle of gas and the dual gas hose rig my father had made years ago that allowed us to run two burners on one bottle of gas. I set all up and turned on the gas. I tossed a match at the one burner. It ignited with a loud whoosh. I lighted the second burner with the same result. I adjusted the flames low. I placed the pots and began filling them with water from the hose. As I filled the first pot I tossed in a quarter cup of salt, a half cup of Old Bay, a few bay leaves and a handful of pepper all from a kit my father had made up years ago to hold the spices. I filled the pot to the two-thirds mark. My father put a mark there. Don't dare go past it. I used to over fill the pot on purpose in cahoots with my mother just to get a reaction from my Dad. He'd say, "Mark? Don't you know what that mark is for?" I'd say something like, "The fill line for when we do clams or is it steamers? I forget." My mother would be standing on the deck above giggling. My father would figure it out and either my mother or I got tossed into the bay. I thought about it for a minute. My mother liked to instigate things and pull me in the middle of them with Dad. I missed that. I started filling the second pot.

"What are you doing, Mark?" Paulie said.

"Starting the boilers for lobster and clams. This is where we'll cook them."

"Oh. Can I eat a whole lobster?"

"If you want to you can. How about you, Barry?"

"I want one. Can we chase my sister and Lauren with a lobster?" Barry said.

"Absolutely, but I must warn you, Lauren is not afraid of lobsters," I said.

"That's okay. Kimberly and my mom are afraid," Barry said.

I filled the second pot halfway to the mark then added the spices as before. I continued filling to the mark. I pulled the now three coolers of seafood out to the pots. I realized some people would enjoy grilled clams, so I searched for and located the little charcoal grill, charcoal and lighter fluid. I set the grill up next to the boilers. I loaded the grill with charcoal, but didn't light it until I received instruction from Grandma.

"What are you doing with that?" Barry asked.

"We'll grill clams on that. Some people like their clams cooked just in the clam's own juices," I said.

"Oh, so pisser clams, are cooked in their piss?" Barry said.

I smiled and thought about his observation. "Well . . . I . . . don't think so . . ." I heard giggling noises above me from the deck. I looked up to see Grandma and Haley observing us. "To answer your question, Barry, I don't think so. Have you ever dug for pisser clams?"

"Yeah."

"Then you know that they just squirt seawater, right?"

"So, they just keep all the piss in until you cook them?"

More adult laughter from above me.

"Well, no. I think the piss is already out by then," I said.

"Where does it go? When we put them in the bucket, I never see them piss in it," Barry said.

"Um, you see, when you dig them up, they squirt their piss . . ."

"You just said that was seawater. So, is it seawater they piss or piss that they piss?"

More giggling from the ladies.

"Barry, I think maybe you should have the boiled hard-shell clams."

"But won't they piss in the pot?" Barry said.

Now there was roaring laughter coming from the ladies who'd been joined by Betsy and Missy.

"Um, well, I don't know . . . Barry, maybe the best thing to do might be just to have ice cream."

"But I want to eat clams and lobster. Where do the lobsters piss? Do they piss in the pot, too?"

"Well, uh . . . I don't . . ."

Haley, Grandma, Betsy and Missy were crying with laughter.

"Have you ever seen a lobster piss?" Barry asked me.

"Uh . . . no, but I think with all the spices and fresh water you can't tell. You can eat whatever you want, Barry."

"Cool," he said as he ran off with Paulie.

I looked up at my peanut gallery.

"You did very well with him, and it was funny," Haley said as she tried not to laugh and wiped tears from her eyes.

"I shook my head and smiled. I went looking for the roaster pans and covers we put the cooked lobsters and clams in to put on the table. I found all the mallets, crackers, and pickers. Grandma would handle baked potatoes and melted butter.

We were twenty-two souls for dinner and there were seventy lobsters and a bushel each of soft shell and hard shell clams all in the medium range. I thought it was time for a beer.

Where were the boys? I didn't want them to run into the boilers. I saw them playing in the dunes. I thought don't let the Sierra Club see you destroying that dune, but if you're a feral horse taking a crap on a North Carolina beach dune it's natural per our government.

I walked upstairs to find a beer. Lauren and Kimberly were snacking on something.

"Are you afraid of lobsters, Kimberly?"

"No. I just don't like live ones touching me. They're like a big bug."

"Then you should pay attention over the next few hours."

Grandma giggled.

I found a beer and wondered where Haley was? I went looking for her and found her showering in my shower. She didn't hear me. I sat on my bed and, of course, I looked over. It's not my fault. God made us to look.

After a minute, I said, "One lobster or two."

Haley screamed then looked at me. "If the house wasn't full of people, I'd ask you to take a shower with me," Haley said.

"If the house wasn't full of people, I'd do more than shower with you. We should take off on them," I said.

"Okay. Now can I get dressed?"

"It doesn't matter. I got all that on video," I deadpanned.

Haley looked around then squinted her left eye and pointed at the door.

"Oh, all right, but I know at least one of your sizes now."

She hit me with a wet sea sponge. I let Haley dress while I walked around making enough noise to wake sleeping giants. Then I ran outside to the lower deck and sat with my beer.

"The potatoes and breads are all started, Mark," Grandma reported. I nodded and sat watching the bay.

"Mark!"

I looked up at the sound of Haley's voice.

"Yes."

"I have Phyllis on the phone. Erica's mom. Will you speak to Ken for us?"

"Yes. Drop me your phone."

"Hello."

"Hi. Is this Mark?" Phyllis said.

"It is."

"Ken is very angry. I saw him taking out his old guns in the garage. I'm afraid for him," she said.

"Was he in the military?" I asked.

"Yes. The air force, a long time ago."

"Okay. Let me speak with him."

I heard rustling then a door open and Phyllis call to Ken.

"Here he is," she said.

"Hello. This is Ken."

"Hey, Ken. Mark from the other night," I said.

"Yes. Hey, Mark. I want to thank you again. What's up?"

"I know what you are feeling about what happened the other day. If I were you, I'd be thinking the same thing. Do me a favor, don't do anything. I don't think you're trained for it and there are more of them then one man can handle," I said. I paused to let him speak. He didn't so I went on. "You do computers. You're a software engineer, right?"

"I do and I am."

"Who do you work for?"

"A small software company. We do government contract work for CIA, FBI, and Homeland Security. We write and test encryption software and check vulnerability of their computer systems and software," Ken said.

"Do you want to help put these guys away?" I said.

"Yes. What do you want me to do?"

"Do you have some vacation time you can take now?" I said.

"I'm off now because of what happened to Erica under the Family Leave Act."

"Good. I'll give you an address. It's in Oceanside. It's my house though I'm not there right now. Here's a telephone number, too." I gave him the address and Joe's number. "Call that number in ten minutes. You'll speak with Joe. He'll direct you. You'll be utilizing your expertise and talents with another guy. Don't do something that might make it worse for Phyllis and Erica. They need you. Do something that will help us put these guys away for good," I said.

"What do you do, Mark?"

"I'm a retired SEAL and I work for my family's securities firm."

"How did you get involved in this?"

"When it's done, I'll fill you in. Call that number in ten minutes, then go comfort your wife and children," I said.

"I . . . I will. Thanks."

"I imagine Haley and Phyllis will want to talk. I'll give the phone back to Haley."

"Okay."

"Joe. Catch this and give it to Haley, please," I said.

I tossed the phone up to him then I walked up the stairs to speak with Joe.

"Ken Cox, Erica's father, is going to call you in ten minutes. He's a tweeker like Carl. Former U.S. Air Force. Software testing and encryption. He wants to help. He has the time. Check him out, but I think he's good. Put him to work with Carl. I gave him the Oceanside address. He lives just a couple houses away from Paul Menduni."

"He and his home might be helpful. Okay. I'll run him and let you know," Joe said.

#

I heard two vehicles pull up. No doubt the guys. It was 1615.

"How's the water doing?" Grandma said.

"Good. I'll start the charcoal."

"I want to roast some corn on there, too."

"Yes, ma'am."

I tossed a match on the charcoal grill. I increased the heat to the boilers and put a cover on each pot. Kev came around the corner carrying a big cooler.

"What's that?" I asked.

"A few cases of beer to go with dinner. We bought ten gallons of ice cream, too," Kev said.

"Good. That will make you best friends for life with two seven-year-olds and a seventy-five-year-old," I said.

"We're going to look like we're out of GQ with our new suits. Just not as gay. LT thought six suits each would be enough. We each got a two dozen shirts and ties, and those handkerchief things . . ."

"Pocket squares," I said.

"That's it. We got six pairs of shoes, twenty pairs of socks, boxers, T-shirts, the works. We even got dress raincoats in case it rains. LT had us get new watches," Kev said as he presented me his new stainless-steel, Omega Seamaster Planet Ocean 600M.

"Nice, 007," I said.

Kev gave me a questioning look.

"That's the watch Daniel Craig wore in Quantum of Solace," I said.

"Cool. License to kill," Kev laughed.

"You guys are going to kill it. You should do a fashion show for the ladies."

Kev stood about six foot three inches tall and weighed about 205 pounds. Sinewy and lanky, he could run down a cheetah and outswim a shark. He could carry a hundred pounds of equipment strapped to him all day long without complaint. He has green eyes, sandy blond hair, and a ruddy tan. Kev is our best sniper. Kev is twenty-seven years old. I liked having him on my team.

"Commander. It's okay if we go into town tonight and explore a little, isn't it?"

"Yeah. Stay out of trouble. Don't get drunk and go with someone. Tomorrow we'll make the assignments. Chances are the two going to the loft will leave tomorrow. Whoever goes with Matt will leave tomorrow when he and Betsy leave," I said.

Talbot and Mikey joined us. Our other two snipers. Talbot is twenty-five. He's the baby of the bunch. He, too, is over six feet tall and very muscular. He is from Alaska and spent his childhood hunting and tracking all manner of wildlife. He joined the navy at age nineteen after two years of college at the University of Washington. He has brown hair and brown eyes. He can dress a pig for a barbeque in about fifteen minutes. Talbot was shot and injured with me. Fortunately for him and me, he was shot through the shoulder and the lower side, but no organs or major blood vessels were hit. Had he been shot as seriously as me who knows if we'd be alive?

Mikey is from Minnesota. He's twenty-nine, the oldest of the enlisted. He's our shortest six-footer at six one. He has his degree, but he doesn't want to be an officer because they'd eventually move him from missions. With everything winding down, that was likely true. He has blond hair and blue eyes and an average muscular build. The ladies liked Mikey a lot.

"Can we help?" Mikey asked.

"Absolutely. In a few minutes, I'll put some lobsters in the pots then we'll add some clams and put some clams on the grill. Oh. I need my basket scooper," I said as I walked under the house to find it.

"All right. We'll fit eight or nine lobsters in each pot. The idea is to slip them all in the pot within a minute but not to cool the boiling water too much. After they begin to turn red, I'll pull them out and put them in those big, covered roaster pans. They'll continue to cook, but we'll ice them to slow them down. We'll set up on that long picnic table, that old picnic table there that we'll move over here, and this one I'm sitting on. I'll put a fire in the fire ring over there later. We'll just eat, hang out, and eat some more," I said.

"Sounds like a good plan to me," Mikey said.

"Hi, chef. Can I help?"

I turned at the sound of Haley's voice.

"Yes. Ask Grandma or Lauren for the tablecloths and the stack of cloth napkins. We will eat down here. We'll set up over there and use these tables," I said.

"Okay. Anything else?" Haley said.

"No. Take Talbot with you. He can be your pack horse," I said as I clapped Talbot's shoulder.

"Start boiling, Mark," Grandma yelled down from the deck.

"Okay guys watch how I do it," I said as I loaded the pots. I got nine in one pot and ten in the other. I placed the clams on the grill surface. Haley appeared with Talbot and her mother, Evelyn, in tow. The ladies and Talbot began covering the tables with table clothes. Long cushions were placed on the bench seats while the guys moved the tables and six Adirondack chairs alongside three shorter tables. We had more than enough seats to allow us to eat together. After five minutes, we loaded the first two roaster pans with lobsters and a large wooden bucket with boiled clams. I covered all with ice to keep them from overcooking. Mikey and I refilled the pots with more lobsters and clams. Grandma sent Joe down with about thirty ears of pre-boiled corn, olive oiled and spiced, to roast on the grill.

"Ken called me. I'll run him later," Joe said.

"Good. Kev, put as many ears of corn on as will fit around the clams," I said.

The crowd had begun to move down to the ground level deck and patio. Missy was making sure everyone had a drink and that enough plates and utensils were available.

After thirty minutes, we were ready. Matt opened the wine, Kev set up the beer, Missy and Betsy seated everyone, so they'd mix with new friends. As expected, Paulie and Barry took this opportunity to chase Kimberly with lobsters. Once all looked satisfactory to Grandma she told us to start. It was a serve-yourself buffet. Grab a lobster, clams, corn, potato, vegetables, left-over lasagna, roast beef, muffins and take your assigned seat and eat. I sat across from Haley with Barry on one side and Evelyn on my other. Joe sat on Haley's left with Mrs. Schwartz sitting to Haley's right. Grandma sat at the head of our table, Grandpa at the head of the other long table. Chief sat at the other end with Paulie next to him and Mr. Shore to his other side. Chief had a pile of lobster in front of him. Paulie, Mr. Shore, and Chief were working together cracking their lobster.

I looked up from showing Barry how to crack a claw to see Haley watching me. Missy and Grandma floated around making sure everyone was happy. Matt and Mr. Schwartz were working on a pile of lobster together with Lauren, Kimberly, and Mikey. Missy joined LT and Surfer in the lobster fest. It was all chattering and cracking noises.

"You love this, don't you?" Haley asked me.

"Like nothing else in the world. I'd think about this while I was away. I'd be slugging through snow and mud climbing a mountain or running through a blistering hot desert city and I'd be thinking 'God, just get me back to my family for one more lobster boil.' I couldn't wait to do this," I said.

I was barely keeping up with Barry eating lobster as fast as I cracked it. I went ahead and cracked three lobsters and piled the meat in front of him.

"That's a lot of lobster," Barry said.

"Whatever you don't eat, someone else will," I said.

Mrs. Schwartz was watching me.

"You're very good with the boys," she said.

"Ask Haley and my grandmother about that," I said.

"Haley told me the story about the softshell clams. It was very cute," Mrs. Schwartz said as Haley, Missy, Betsy, and my grandmother began to laugh again. They began telling everyone else the story because they were laughing so hard. They reiterated my responses to Barry's questions and conveyed my facial expressions. When the ladies finished their story, Chief piped up and said, "Are we telling funny Mark MacKenzie stories?"

Aunt Missy and Uncle Matt said, "Yes."

Chief winked at me letting me know he'd keep the stories clean.

"Mark is a brand-new SEAL officer, still an ensign. I was a petty officer third class. We went through BUDS together. Mark killed it at BUDS, of course I had to push him to keep up since he was an officer." Everyone laughed. "We were sent through the training pipeline together. We ended up in Iraq on our first tour and we were in all that urban fighting that went on. We did many weeks and months of nighttime and daytime ops. This op was during the daytime on an oppressively hot day. We were all soaked through with sweat, and it dripped off us as we moved through the city. We're on this op to go grab some bad guys and we came upon some other bad guys. A whole bunch of them. Mark calls it in because we have our mission, and it was the Marine's job to get these other guys. We held our position, set up snipers in an overwatch, and we watched the Marines move in and engage the enemy who were spread across five or six city blocks of buildings. We estimated some two hundred insurgents are shooting at the Marines. First the Marines shoot mortars then the artillery starts. Mortars and high explosives are falling all around us, so you pay attention.

Mark initially called in the artillery, but now Marine officers are calling the artillery not Mark so we're nervous. Anyway, our building gets blown up by two shells, so we scramble out of the building and head for the street. Mark is screaming at the Marines over the radio to not drop on us. We've now taken up positions along two walls on either side of a small alley which provided us some cover. Suddenly heavy caliber machine gun fire erupts all around us. Lots of it. The bullets are striking all around us. We return fire and we must have had an effect because the machine guns stopped. Then another machine gun shot at us and their hitting high on the wall above Mark who's still trying to get the Marines to drop artillery on the enemy machine gunners instead of us. Suddenly the wall collapses above Mark and crumbles down on him. Two insurgents literally fall on top of him. Mark yells out various words that I cannot repeat in polite company. I don't know who was more surprised the insurgents or Mark. We swung around to cover Mark who has his pistol pointed at the two insurgents. Mark was lying on the ground, covered in concrete, rubble, and dust, all bloodied by the falling debris. The two insurgents put their hands up and surrendered to Mark. All you could see of Mark was his bloody face and his arm with his pistol sticking out of the rubble pointed at the insurgents. We all burst out laughing while we took down the two insurgents and cuffed them. We couldn't stop laughing for hours," Chief said who then laid on the ground sticking up his hand in the universal sign of a pistol.

Everyone burst out laughing. It took a while for them to stop laughing.

"What about when you blackened Mark's scope ring, Kev?" Chief said.

Kev looked at me and burst out laughing. "We were on another op in the last weeks of an Iraq tour. Mark put down his M-4 weapon with the night scope on it. He was busy doing something with a chart and coordinating with a unit of Marines as they moved through the city. I put black shoe polish around the eye piece of his scope. We were nearing the end of the night's work, so we needed a reason to get Mark to look through his scope. Another SEAL, Billy, I think, set him up by saying, 'I got an insurgent. Four hundred yards, in the pinkish building.' Mark picks up his rifle and locks. With Mark, it's fun because he'll use either of his eyes to look through his scope. For five minutes Billy played Mark getting him to look again and again before he declared, 'Never mind. Sorry. I think he's just another merchant opening and checking his shop.' We pack it up and we're all trying to not laugh.

We made it back to base and we reported to the boss, Commander Hart Steele. He's waiting for us. He acknowledges us as Mark makes his report to him. Steele never misses a beat. He took Mark's report then asked Mark if he felt okay. He told Steele he was fine. Steele says, 'You need a little rest. You're getting dark circles around your eyes,' and he tells us all to carry on. Instead of going to the showers first, Mark ran to the chow hall to eat. The civilian line servers and Marines told him about the black circles around his eyes," Kev said.

Grandpa was laughing, the kids were laughing, my aunts were laughing. It was all a lot of fun for them. I was laughing, too.

"He looked like Bandit on Johnny Quest," Chief said.

"What about the time that snake chased him?" Mikey said.

The guys burst out laughing while I grinned at them.

"We're training up at A.P. Hill before a deployment and we're slogging through the swamp after a night of the usual fun. We had a few miles to go and Surfer, who has no sense of direction ten yards from the ocean, was leading. We were crossing a swampy creek and Surfer screams 'Snake!' Mark tells him to be quiet. The sun is just cracking the sky, so we can see pretty well. Surfer throws a tree limb at this water moccasin, a big one, maybe six feet long. The snake went after Mark. Mark would smack it with a stick, and it would come back at him. After Mark made about ten attempts to get the snake to go the other way, Chief shot it with a shot gun."

Mikey is now standing and imitating me, smacking the snake with a stick.

"Mark is cursing his head off at Surfer for pissing the snake off. Surfer is saying, 'Sir. You're making too much noise,' which is pissing Mark off even more," Mikey said.

Joe, Chief, and Mr. Shore are crying they're laughing so hard at Surfer's antics who is now standing, pretending to hit an invisible snake with an invisible stick while pretending to yell at himself.

"You're a pretty good dude to put up with all the crap we pulled on you over the years, sir," Talbot said.

"It was all in good fun. You guys always came through when it mattered," I said.

"We're not finished yet, are we?" Joe said as everyone shook their heads no.

"Want to hear about the time he lost that boat?" Joe said as he pointed at the Parker which, of course, they all did.

"We took the boat out. It was fairly new. We were in Oceanside. We went out one day and returned to his dock. We took everything off, the poles, the line, anchor, cushions—everything and we thoroughly washed the boat and equipment down. Mark said to leave everything out to dry. The next morning the surf report said the waves are crushing it at Long Beach, so Mark says, 'Let's go.' We jump into the boat and arrive at the beach. All we have for line was the strings in our board shorts because the captain forgot to put everything back on the boat. Mark beaches the boat and says it'll be good. We run across to the beach and we're surfing for hours. It's huge. We come back, we've picked up a couple of girls no less, and no boat. It's gone. The tide came in and it floated away. We're looking up and down the beach. Finally, we spot it across the channel about a half mile or more away. It's stuck on a marsh island. The wind and tide took it across the main channel. Of course, it's after work hours so the channel is full of boats with more people coming out, but none are coming over where we are. Mark says, 'Wait here,' and he jumps into the bay and paddles away on his surfboard. It's late now. The girls have ditched us. I can't see Mark because it's getting dark. I'm thinking he got run over by a boat or eaten by a great white shark. After more than an hour, I see a boat, its bow lights, coming toward me. It's Mark.

We go home and washed the boat because Mark had to push it off the mud and he climbed in covered with mud. While we're washing the boat in the dock lights Mark's dad comes out, and I shit you not—oh, sorry kids—his dad says, 'You know, Mark, it's not a good idea to go out in a boat without an anchor.' I burst out laughing and Mark's swearing at me telling me to shut up and be quiet under his breath while his dad scolds him for leaving all the gear behind. So, I think Mark was always destined to be a SEAL, so he'd have a way to get to his boat," Joe said.

And everyone laughed again. My grandmother smiled at me and patted my hand.

"You were an adventurous boy," she consoled.

Everyone was still eating and laughing, but we were close to finishing up dinner. I'd reached my limit of lobster, corn muffins, beef, and salad. I refreshed everyone's wine and grabbed another beer. Grandma, Haley, and Missy began the clean-up organization, and the other ladies joined in. The men were still snickering at me, or they'd burst out laughing when I looked at them. My face hurt from smiling.

"Mark. You've been such a good sport and did all the cooking, you sit there with Grandpa. We'll clean up. Just direct the men where to put the pots and all," Grandma said.

"Yes, ma'am."

It was nearing 7:30 p.m. Time to get the fire ring going. Haley and Lauren grabbed a few of the guys to help carry up the items that went in the kitchen. Matt, Mr. Shore, and Chief began shelling the remaining lobster. There were quite a few left over. We'd enjoy lobster rolls tomorrow. All the clam shells got tossed on the pile, the tables were stripped, and the Adirondack chairs were set in a semi-circle around the fire ring. Barry, Paulie, and Mr. Schwartz helped me load the pit and we started the fire.

We set up Grandma's and Grandpa's chairs with a light blanket for Grandma. In what seemed like no time, everything was put away. We put a picnic table near the fire. All set to sit around and tell stories. Some of the guys were going into town. They'd be bored in an hour at this time of year. After Memorial Day, the village got a little busier.

Grandpa offered my cigars to all the men. We all eventually found a spot to sit, talk, enjoy the fire and digest our dinners. Mr. and Mrs. Shore were each given a chair to sit in and the Schwartzes were given the remaining Adirondack chairs. I thought I should buy six more chairs.

As if reading my mind, Grandma said, "Mark. I think we should buy six more chairs to put around the fire ring. Emily and Frank will be here this Friday," she said which was a not so subtle directive to me.

"Oh? When did that develop?" I said.

"Today. Emily wanted to come up last week, but they had medical appointments. They said the condo is fine. They had the gardener fix the gardens and replace some plants. We've decided that the dining room should be made into a bedroom so we can all fit," Grandma said.

"Are we still talking about the condo?" I said.

"No. This house," Grandma said.

I already knew who we were—Grandma, Missy, Betsy, Grandma Emily, Lorraine, and Lauren. I was out-voted all around.

"We think a small bump-out addition to include a bathroom would make it nice. With some of us getting older, having a bedroom suite on the living level would make it easier," Grandma said.

"True. When do 'we' start?" I asked.

"The architect and builder who did the rest of the house will be out Monday. Missy spoke to them," Grandma said.

"Do I get to pick the colors?" I deadpanned.

"No!" The women said at once.

Grandpa looked at me like, just accept what you cannot change.

"Lauren has all your mother's notes and drawings from when she first conceived the idea. Lauren will act as the designer just as your mother would want," Grandma said.

I looked at Lauren as she came down the stairs with Kimberly.

"She reminds me a lot of Mom," I said.

"Look at the picture album on the bookshelf. There are pictures of your mother when she was fourteen and fifteen. Lauren is the spitting image of your mother. Very beautiful," Grandma said.

"What?" Lauren said to me when she saw me looking at her.

"I heard you're doing the bedroom and bath remodel," I said.

"I am. I've been commissioned by Grandmas Stuart and MacKenzie to turn the leftover room into a suite. Naturally, I began with some ideas Mom penciled and we spoke about. You'll like it," Lauren said.

"I have no doubt," I said.

I was sitting on the end of the picnic table. Haley had taken a seat next to me.

"So, you see, around here it's a democratic process. The women decide, and the men acquiesce," I deadpanned.

"As it should be," Haley replied which got her verbal support from the women.

"Mark. You're still learning, but it's easier to agree. Right, John?" Grandpa said to Mr. Shore.

Evelyn looked at John who was a little slow with his answer.

"Oh. Yes. Of course," he said.

We spent the balance of the evening telling anecdotes and stories or talking about various design ideas for the bedroom suite. By 11 p.m. we'd pretty much wrapped up our night. Barry had fallen asleep in his father's lap and my new best friend Paulie had fallen asleep in my lap between Haley and me which all the women thought an omen that I was good father material.

Matt tossed the iced water of reality on the idea by stating, "The kid ate three lobsters, a plate of lasagna, roast beef, drank six sodas and ate a gallon of ice cream. He just crashed from the sugar high," Matt said getting him booed.

CHAPTER 14

We had agreed to sleep in late. My mind and body didn't. I awoke in stark fear, covered in sweat. I was running through the desert being chased by a camel that had a lion's head. I was running while an AC-130 Specter gunship shot at the lion-headed camel. Depleted uranium rounds were exploding just feet behind me. I had to keep running so I wasn't shot or eaten.

I got up and got a cold glass of water. I went to my room for my composition notebook to write down this new nightmare. How would I act this one out? I took my book off the dresser and quietly left the room. It was just 4:45 a.m. I went downstairs and sat at the kitchen counter and wrote down my dream. My notebook was half-full. My nightmares or dreams were diverse and very real in my mind. I was supposed to write them all down. I did what my doctor asked me to do—it didn't matter to me. I just wanted them to stop.

I drank my iced water as I sat back down on the couch.

"You okay," Joe asked.

I didn't know he was awake. "Yeah. I'm fine," I said.

"I heard you. You were talking in your sleep. You had another dream," Joe said.

"I did. It was new so I had to write it down," I said.

Joe knew I had PTSD and depression. From the time I'd been hurt until just before my parents died, I was in pretty much continuous pain and I had nightmares. I had lots of operations to repair my intestines, stomach, liver, to remove my appendix, to remove rotten or not viable parts of my guts, to strip muscles of infection, to flush my bowels of poison, to remove blood clots and rotting flesh. I was just getting to the point that I could get to the shower and bathroom by myself when my parents died.

I wasn't kidding when I said everyone has seen me naked. All the women in my family helped me in the shower under my mother's and Betsy's supervision. They changed my bandages, washed me, paid close attention to what the medical staff did to me. I remembered my mother would be soaked after helping me in the shower.

One time my stitches tore open on my back where they had to reknit together my muscles where the bullet had gone through. My mother helped hold me as I showered. When I thought I was through I turned to see her shirt and pants covered with my blood. She didn't even know until she saw me bleeding and followed the blood trail. After that I didn't want help because I feared what something like that would do to my grandmothers or Lauren. But the women kept pushing me back in there. My father, grandfathers and Joe, all pushed me back into that shower to make me wash every day.

I was never embarrassed. I was horrified that my pain, my nightmares, my wounds, would transfer to them. I don't think that happened. I hope it didn't happen. The day of the stitch blow-out, my mother wrapped my wound with a towel, sat me in a wheelchair and called the nurses. She simply stepped back into the shower and washed the blood off her clothing as I cried for what my family had to endure. I recall my mother telling me, "Mark. I bore you, my only son, and I suffered the pain of childbirth for you. That pain prepared me to take care of you now. God put me through that, so I'd be ready to care for my son again," and she did it. All the women in my family did. My sister, my aunts, my grandmothers working together which got easier for them at first as I wasted away from infection after infection, and my inability to take on enough nourishment. I was starving before their eyes until the third month when, led by my mother, the women of my family mounted a twenty-four, seven effort to force closer attention to the infections, fevers, and the nourishment I was getting. They marched into the doctor's office and demanded to know what was taking them so long to beat the infections and why was I not getting proper nourishment. An army colonel gastroenterologist looked at my chart and decided what needed to be done. I had surgery again for the last time on my intestines and that doctor fixed it.

I was finally getting better, and my family was so happy. Happy enough for my father to want to take Mom out. Dad asked me if he thought Mom was up for a night out and I said, "Yes." My mother asked me if she should go out. She didn't want to leave me alone for something as frivolous as a night out—I was more important. I told my mother, "No. You go out and have a good time with Dad, I'm fine, you saved me." She went out with my father to a wonderful formal affair—an annual event that she always enjoyed. She died that night alongside my father on a wet, chilly highway.

"I'll be okay, Joe. It'll just take some time," I said.

"You'll make it," Joe said.

"I hate them, Joe. They took my mother. I was finally healing after nearly three months of slowly dying in front of my family. My mother rallied the family and doctors and saved me. I told her to go out that night. Had I just said 'Mom, stay with me tonight, I need you,' maybe she'd be alive? Maybe they'd still be here?" I said.

"Mark. We talked about that before. What is—is! You can't change it. It's not your fault. I was there those months. Your mom did save you. I love her like my mom, too. You couldn't have known and it's not your fault. You must understand that. Who knows why it happened? You just saved the lives of three young girls. Maybe that's why your mom saved you? I can't answer it, but I do know you can't blame yourself. All these incidents, all these evil men would have happened whether you were shot or not. Maybe you were shot, and your parents died so you were put where you are to go save more lives and destroy these guys? Maybe Haley was put in front of you for you to love, to motivate you to do what you are doing beyond finding your mother's killers. And Lauren, too. Two people to give worth and legitimacy to your life.

I know you gotta do this, and we're in it until the end, but then you gotta live for them and you. You've kept this deep inside you and none of them think there's a problem, but I know and so does Grandma MacKenzie. I think finishing this and committing yourself to a family with that woman, who clearly loves you, and you'll be okay," Joe said.

I thought about Joe's words and my circumstances.

"Joe. Could you ever have imagined way back when we were children or when we played ball in high school, the five of us with Dave, Rob, and Tony, that we would be where we're at . . . at or in . . . this, this . . . this crap? I mean we listened to stories about wise guys and what they did, but now . . . now we're declaring war on them."

"No. I doubt I could have ever imagined this. I'm not sure what I thought the future would bring. I always thought that of all of us you'd be the one to do something extraordinary for someone else that was important. I hope you do, and I hope we all survive," Joe said.

I heard a noise, and my grandmother came around the corner. She looked at me and Joe then approached me. She hugged my head to her and kissed the top of my head as I sat on the couch.

"It's not your fault, Mark. Joe is right. You're doing something about it that is right. I told you you'd have choices to make, but that you'd make the right choices. You know what it is you must do to protect your family. You have the tools, and you have the resources. Now do what's right and be free of the burden you've carried because you need to live life. For Lauren, for Haley, for all of us," Grandma said as she patted my shoulder then walked to the kitchen.

I looked at Joe who nodded agreement.

#

I was up. I used the head then went outside to shower. I dressed in jeans, a black T-shirt and a grey-blue button-down garage shirt and returned to the kitchen. Joe followed my motions. He and Surfer would leave today for the Oceanside house to get set up with Carl.

Missy would go back to the city today. Two SEALs would accompany her. Matt and Betsy would go to their home. A SEAL would follow them to their home. LT would announce the assignments this morning, but he'd already informed me of the assignments.

I filled my coffee cup and walked out to retrieve the papers. The FBI guy was in my driveway. He nodded at me. They had three agents assigned. The agents would have a lot to report today. I retrieved the papers and walked back to the house. I sat on the back deck and stared off to the bay. The fishing boats were already underway headed out for the day's catch. I wondered what my life would be like had I become a fisherman. I sipped my coffee while my grandmother fried bacon and prepared left-over potatoes for home fries. Joe sat next to me with his coffee.

"That Ken guy is okay. He'll be at the house later today. Carl has already gotten into Vincenzo's computers, and he got into Vincenzo's and his wife's smart phones. Carl and Robert spoke. They think they'll set up a dedicated computer for each target group. I don't get it all, but bandwidth and speed have something to do with the amount of data they can record. They had your Internet provider upgrade your house to the best and fastest and they had two more lines brought in to better the speed and access. Anyway, your family room is set up with a dozen computers and they hung all your flat screen TVs on the walls and can project what they have on the computers onto the flat screen TVs. It looks like the Pentagon situation room," Carl said.

Robert and Tony have turned your loft into a downtown intelligence center. They've linked the firm's computers and telephones. Nothing goes in or out of the firm without them seeing it. They already got Train's and Rizzo's home computers and smart phones. They have already produced results. It looks like Train has gone to work with another firm. Luciens and Associates Securities, Ltd. Train is sending things to Rizzo, but Rizzo is communicating with someone at the grandfather's estate. Essentially, Carl, Rob and Tony have linked the players via email and texts, to the firms and the mafia families of New York and New Jersey," Joe said.

"That's good. We'll put it all together this week."

The others started coming down or up for breakfast. Grandma had breakfast well along and Grandpa was sitting down to eat. Matt joined us. Grandma put plates of food in front of each of us. It was almost 8 a.m.

"What are your plans this week, Grandpa?" I said.

"I'll have the boat delivered for one thing. It's been decided that we'll be staying here for now. With all you need to do, Grandma wants to be around, so you won't have to worry about Lauren getting to school and cooking. I assume you'll go into the office or elsewhere each day?"

"I think so. Thanks. That's very helpful," I said.

#

I assembled the troops. LT made the assignments. Surfer to the Oceanside house not just because of the surf, but because he would assist on the computers as he had a background and degree in computers, and he'd be able to learn more for the SEAL team. Surfer would leave with Joe. Mikey and Kev would travel to the city with Missy. They'd live at the loft. Kev would go with Tony to the office in the morning. Mikey would remain at the loft or travel to the office as needed. Chief would accompany Matt and Betsy home and travel with Matt to the office. Talbot would remain at the house, but would set up in the first-floor bedroom with LT. LT would rove where needed and coordinate coverage. He'd travel in the other SUV which would be his rolling command post.

Haley appeared after breakfast as everyone was packing. Before anyone left, I assembled everyone on the back deck.

"I want you all to just stop for a moment, get a coffee or juice, whatever, and take a seat outside on the deck," I said.

Once all were assembled, I began.

"We will be doing a lot of things this week and next. I'm the only one who knows the whole plan. Some of you know more than others. I don't know what the outcome will be, but success or failure rests with me. I don't plan to fail. I ask each of you over the next couple of weeks to keep me informed as to your whereabouts and that you pay attention to your surroundings. For my family, tell me if something is wrong. For the rest of you, tell LT. If I ask you to do something this week and next it is for your own good that I don't explain myself. I've prayed about this. Some of you have counseled and advised me. I want you to keep doing that. I know I've been a little cryptic with what I've said. I don't expect any problems this week. This week will be mostly intelligence gathering and planning. You all just go about your lives. Grandma and Grandpa Stuart will be here Friday. We'll all gather here this weekend as usual. If at any time I believe any of you are in danger, I will remove you from that danger. Listen to Joe or any of these men. I trust them all with my life. That said, don't worry, we have it covered. Don't talk about anything to do with what we're doing at all, anywhere. Just carry on your normal routines. I know you ladies talk frequently. Continue to talk as usual. Carry on your lives as normal since that's what it's all about. I love you all," I said.

"Gentlemen, it's a go," LT said and at that command the men moved. Surfer and Joe carried their bags to their SUV and departed. Missy's limo rolled up to the door. Mikey and Kev loaded their bags and Missy's bags and readied for departure. Missy stopped in front of me.

"Mark. I know you have a lot to do. I want you to know that your parents would be very proud of you. You've become the man and leader they would want as a son. I love you. Be safe," she said as she hugged me and kissed my cheek. Mikey got Missy's door and he got in after her with Kev and the limo drove off.

Matt and Betsy came over to me. "I'll see you in the morning, Mark," Matt said.

"Be safe, Mark," Aunt Betsy said. I nodded as she hugged me. Chief pulled up in his SUV behind the S550 and waited for Betsy and Matt to get in their car. They departed for Matt and Betsy's home.

I heard LT doing radio checks with all. I'd invested in a secured, encrypted satellite communications system and an encrypted, long-range FM/VHF/UHF radio system. All the SEALs, Joe, Rob, Tony, Carl, and I were up on both systems.

Lauren and my grandparents were sitting on the back porch. Haley came alongside me. She grabbed my arm and reached up to kiss my cheek. At 5 p.m. the op would begin in earnest.

LT set up two computers on the first floor for communications and to be able to see and copy anything the other groups sent us. Talbot had already set up the satellite antenna on a tripod on the kitchen deck and the VHF/UHF antenna in the attic. The same systems were set up or being set up at the other locations. Mobile sets with antennas were attached to the vehicles and the boat, and we had our headsets.

Carl was busy breaking into various computers. Each time he was successful, the breached system was assigned to Tony, Rob or it remained with Carl if it dealt with the people responsible for my parents' deaths. At 5 p.m. Clara and Barbara would begin working the telephones. They would contact the families of the victims of the bad acts of the Calabrese-Menduni family. They'd obtain details of the victim's and survivor's information to pass to the attorneys who had a team of lawyers and paralegals working this Sunday. As each injury came to light the attorneys, after being authorized by letter, email, or voice-recording, drafted a civil action against the responsible defendants. There would be many civil actions. I wanted all the victims compensated. Robert, Tony, and Carl had already identified thirty-eight corporations and over eighty individuals. They'd already linked the five New York-New Jersey crime families in criminal conspiracies. The attorneys would consolidate the civil actions, but the main goal was to shock with the sheer volume of civil actions filed then awe them with the number of assets seized.

My phone buzzed. It was 4 p.m.

"Hello."

"Mark. Joe. He's in. The old man is writing an email right now. It's amazing. I'm watching him type it. Anyway, two weeks before your parents were killed the old man sent Vincenzo and Castellano an email. It said, 'Get the documents back from WM,' no doubt your father and to, 'Make him go away.' He further said to them that it should look like an accident. Castellano wrote back that they, 'couldn't find the documents' and they 'didn't know where WM's wife was. She wasn't at the home.' That's because your mother was at the hospital with you. Romeo replied that he didn't care about the documents since they were worthless. Vincenzo wrote that nothing should be done and that he wanted nothing to do with anything. He wrote his father in another email and ordered him to knock off, and I quote, 'the stupid shit.' He said that he would not allow his father to hurt anyone over such a shitty deal and that he was abstaining and disavowing himself from his father's activities. Mark. That's a wrap. We have the emails. The old man states that they'll get a bonus from the company if they do it right. The emails are all on corporate or LLC email using company email addresses and officers' email addresses."

"I want to be sure, and I want them all. As info develops, let me know. That's four people. There must be more. Rizzo or the others at the firm did something. I want that, too," I said.

"No-no. We have emails that connect twelve of them and seven companies just in the conspiracy to kill WM. This is big-time, Mark," Joe said.

"I want them all. What other companies? Who else? Can we connect the other families to my parents' murders? Who else is involved in the sex slave ring and more? What does Vincenzo's abstaining mean?"

"It looks like someone petitioned Romeo to hit WM, but not in an email. This is just the order, and most addressees agree and state 'yes' to kill him. Vincenzo and another email address said they wanted nothing to do with this. Romeo blasts Vincenzo in several emails, but Vincenzo does not reply. Romeo did copy Rizzo and five members of the Bagatelli, Terrazzo, and Carlucci families. It's like a corporate discussion," Joe said.

"I need more, Joe. Let's identify the others involved, to whatever degree."

"Got it. I'll let Carl know. Ken Cox is here. He's a genius with this stuff. He's working with Carl and has started getting into bad guys' computers. I can't keep up," Joe said.

"What I need is a connection to the firm. Something from Rizzo or an acknowledgement from Rizzo to the old man and/or Vincenzo. I suppose I'm looking for motive, too, that will corroborate the emails and further identify WM. You get me?" I said.

"Yes. I'll have Tony scan your firm's data with search parameters including 'WM.'"

"Thanks. I'll talk with you later," I said.

\#

"Hey. Can you stand some company?" Haley said.

"Yes. That would be nice."

Haley ran down the stairs and joined me. We walked to the garage.

"What are you doing?" Haley said.

"I'm going through my routine," I said as I opened the gun safe. I exchanged my current pistol for another. I racked the slide, inspected the weapon, and wiped it off. I loaded it and put it in my pocket. I removed my M-4, with the fourteen-inch barrel, and went through it then laid it on the work bench. Haley looked at the weapons in the safe as I checked the scope and magazine. I removed my M-4 carbine and my AR-15s. Once I'd gone through them, I loaded all the weapons and made quick-service packs. I put a Beretta M-9 with five full mags in a shooting bag for my grandfather. I made up two more bags for my SIG Sauer P226 pistols and six mags. I checked two of my tactical shot guns and loaded them and attached a bandolier with ten more shells to each weapon. I wish I had the weapon I occasionally carried in Iraq and Afghanistan. Essentially it was an Americanized Russian AA12 short barrel, automatic shotgun with a ten or twenty-round capacity. My tactical shotguns were merely bad looking twelve-gauge civilian shotguns. I went through my M-40 sniper rifle, my H&K 614, which was an expensive and improved version of the M-4, and my H&K MP-5. I inspected and loaded each weapon.

"You don't fool around, do you?" Haley said.

"No. I guess I don't. Can you shoot?"

"No. I've never touched a gun," Haley said.

"That's good. You'll never have any ghosts following you," I said as I wrapped up my tasks and put things away.

"C'mon. It's time."

I placed a shooting bag with a SIG in my Challenger and another in the Yukon. I carried the shotguns and Beretta bag to the house. Haley looked at the shotguns.

"They look dangerous," Haley said pointing at the shotguns.

"They are. I'm placing them in my bedroom so I can get at them in a hurry," I said as we climbed the steps. I placed one shotgun in my closet, another under my bed and the shooting bag with the Beretta on the nightstand in my grandfather's room.

"Let's get an iced tea," I said.

My phone buzzed.

"Yeah."

"It's Tony. We're ready to go here."

"Okay. With Carl's okay, send out the emails, texts, and pictures. You're sure we're covered on this?"

"We're fine. As soon as they open them the Trojan will cause the old emails to populate the sent and received email history for the past sixteen months. There are a total of one hundred ninety-two emails and texts we created dealing with everything we discussed. Frankly, Mark, I expect that these guys will be at it in a few hours," Tony said.

"Okay. Do it," I said, and we ended the call.

"Mark. All teams checked in fine. We're up on all communications," LT said.

"Roger." I looked out over the bay and saw the dock builders testing the boat lift. Tomorrow a new center console would be in it. Life was amazing. I'd rather be out on the boat.

"Come on, Haley. Let's take a drive. Talbot should be finished installing the security system at your home by now," I said.

"He is. Dad just texted me. Talbot is on his way back."

"Good."

We got into my car and drove to the high school. I wanted to know Haley's location during the day so, if need be, I could send a response team to protect her and Lauren if something came up. I pulled into the school's semi-circle drive.

"Show me where you pull in and park each morning."

"Right there. I pull in like we just did."

"At what time?"

"About 7:15 a.m. Homeroom is just four minutes from 7:45 to 7:49 a.m. before the first period bell."

"What door do you use?"

"That one there," Haley pointed at the main door.

"Where do you go first?"

"The office where we met to check in then to my homeroom classroom on the second floor. It's the first room by the stairs."

"Stairwells are located at each end and each side of the building?"

"Yes."

"Tell me what you do after that."

"I'm off bus duty so I usually check in and go to my room then I go get coffee or water."

"Across the street?"

"Sometimes. For coffee, yes."

"Where is the school resource officer during arrivals and departures?"

"Normally he roves around. Sometimes he's in his car in the school bus drop-off area."

"Before you arrive here, you drop Paulie off at Southold Elementary?"

"Yes, but I don't get out of the car. I just drop him and continue here. Sometimes my parents take him."

"This week and next, I want you to stick with your routine. Call me if you change it. I placed a tracker on your car, and I entered software on your smart phone so I can track your location on my smart phone, so I can find you if need be. We're free for the rest of the day. What would you like to do?" I said.

"You mean free like just you and me?"

"Yes. Lauren is with Kimberly at her home. My grandparents are having wine and cheese with your parents at your house. Paulie is with Barry and the girls. LT is running to Oceanside to learn the route. Talbot is taking the boat out to familiarize himself with the route to your home by water. It's just you and me."

"Then take me home to your house. I want to make love to you," Haley said.

I grinned at her. "Really?" I said.

"Mark. I've wanted you for . . . I don't even remember. When I saw you in the shower it took all my self-control not to drop my clothes and join you."

We drove to my house. After we arrived, I made a quick search to ensure we were alone.

We dashed upstairs to my room and shed our clothes. Haley pulled me into the shower. We kissed passionately for a long time as we allowed the water from the shower heads to wash over our bodies. I explored Haley's neck, face, and lips with my kisses. She held my head as I kissed her breasts. We kissed and licked and touched each other as we discovered each other's body. I lifted her as she wrapped her arms around my neck, and I entered her as she let out a gasp and clamped her legs around me. After a while her breath came in rapid, short gasps as I made love to her. Haley pulled my face to her as I felt her shudder in a quiet climax.

I carried Haley to my bed and laid her down. I got in beside her, both of us wet from the shower and our lovemaking. Haley pushed me over onto my back and straddled me, lowering herself onto me. Haley rocked back and forth over me, her hands planted on my chest, her knees astride my hips as she moved up and down my length. It wasn't long before I was nearing the end. Haley sensed it and moved harder and faster. A moment later I pulled her to me as we finished together. After a few minutes of holding each other, Haley kissed me and rolled off next to me.

"I've been wanting you like that since we had coffee at the bakery-coffee shop," she said.

"Which time? First or second?"

"I'll leave that as a secret. I'll have to go see my doctor and get back on birth control."

"Oh? I . . . I could have worn a raincoat. I thought . . ."

"Don't worry. I'm regular."

"My wife was sort of, well hard to be around just before . . ." I said.

"I'm okay. I get emotional, but this time it was love directed at you. I don't get bitchy if that's what you're thinking. I don't need a monthly for that to happen," Haley deadpanned and I laughed.

"You don't appear to have wide mood swings, do you?" Haley said.

"No. I'm pretty even-keeled," I said.

"I spoke with Betsy and your grandmother. They said you were skin and bone at your parents' funeral but had started to get better just before that. The Newsday Sunday special only had a portrait of you in uniform that must have been a few years old, but the article showed a picture of your mother, grandmothers, Betsy, Lorraine, Missy, and Lauren standing around you in the hospital bed. I couldn't see your face well since it was in shadow, but the article described the battle and what happened. The doctor, an army doctor come to think of it, said you would heal and that they did something different to you that they'd never tried before. You were quoted as saying, 'I would have died except for my mother's care,'" Haley said.

"She did it. I mean my grandmothers, Lauren, Missy, Betsy, and Lorraine all were there, but my mother is the one who cried, yelled and forced me to get up each day. You can't imagine what it's like to be so physically gifted and healthy one day and the next you can't do anything without help—and to be aware of so much. I was in a medically induced coma for a while. I don't know how many times I was operated on . . ." I said as I trailed off.

"I noticed you do that a lot," Haley said.

"What?"

"You don't finish your statement. It's like you're suddenly reflecting on what happened and don't want to finish your thought or it's too painful to finish," Haley said.

"It is, in some ways. Sometimes I don't remember what happened. After I went down, I'd been shot twice already and had taken shrapnel from an RPG. Talbot was down, too. They just kept coming at us. I was shooting both my pistols because my rifle was shot out of my hands. I was blown back into the snow, and I was shooting them as they came at us. Talbot was ten feet from me when he went down. We just kept shooting. Then I got shot again by a guy standing over me. I went to shoot again, and I just unloaded my pistols, and all went black. I later learned that two of the Taliban fell on me and knocked me out. On top of all that happened, I got a concussion from the guy's head slamming into mine after I shot him.

The guys finished off the insurgents then pulled me into the building. They revived me and gave me water. Talbot had two bullet wounds, one through his left side and another to his left shoulder. Surfer didn't have a scratch on him. Surfer, an Afghan Special Forces sergeant, and Chief packed me and hit me with morphine while they called in the QRF. The next thing I can remember is waking up and seeing my mother holding my hand," I said.

Haley was crying. I reached over as pulled her close.

"I hope those are happy tears because that story has a happy ending."

"Mark, it does have a happy ending. I'm crying because of what you guys had to go through for our country's mistakes. I think if every Congressman, Senator, and the President had a son or daughter in the armed forces they would think before doing what they do. The wars would be over by now."

"You may be right, but that's all past me. Now I must protect my family," I said.

"We should get up before Lauren or your grandparents come home," Haley said.

"Or LT or Talbot who is pulling up to the pier now," I said as I looked out the window.

I got up and dressed then kissed Haley. "Take your time. I'll put out some hot and cold lobster rolls and salad for dinner," I said.

"I'm going to use that really cool bathtub," she said.

"Perfect."

#

I dashed downstairs to the kitchen and started pulling out food. A knock on the sliding glass doors announced Talbot's arrival.

"Come in. Hey, Talbot. Good run?"

"Yeah. I could do it at night if need be. I got a good feel for it. What's for dinner?"

"Lobster rolls. You want your rolls toasted and lobster warmed up with melted butter or cold lobster on a roll with mayo, ranch, or blue cheese dressing?" I said.

"Yes."

"That's what I thought." I toasted six rolls, stuffed them with lobster and butter and put them in the oven. I mixed up some lobster in mayo with Old Bay and olive oil and got out some plates. I pulled out a cold beer for Talbot and me that we sipped while we chatted about the boat and the new boat coming tomorrow.

"Hi guys," Haley said looking freshly scrubbed as she sat next to Talbot. I put a beer in front of her.

"Hi, Haley," Talbot said.

"Thank you, Talbot," Haley said.

Talbot looked at Haley strangely, then at me. "For what?" He said.

"For saving Mark," Haley said.

"Oh, no . . . no, no. He saved me, ma'am," Talbot said.

"You are some really incredible guys," she said.

The front door opened announcing the return of my grandparents and Lauren. Paulie was with them.

"Perfect timing. I have six lobster rolls in the oven, and I just made lobster salad," I said.

Grandma looked at what I had started.

"Give me a minute. Get your grandfather a bourbon and you all go sit down. Haley, Lauren, and I will finish this up. Now scat," Grandma said.

I got a bourbon for Grandpa; Talbot got another beer and I got an iced tea. We took seats out on the living room deck. I watched Haley working in the kitchen with Lauren as they chatted. Lauren said something to Haley and indicated with a tilt of her head toward me. Haley looked up at me and smiled. The woman had moved into my family and my heart.

CHAPTER 15

I slept well. My grandmother was up when I got up. I'd go in to the office today, but I'd stop at the Oceanside house on my way in. I showered, dressed, and went downstairs. Lauren could sleep a little longer.

"Good morning, Grandma," I said.

"Good morning, Mark. You remind me of how your grandfather looked just before he shipped out to Vietnam each time. Don't you worry or doubt yourself. You'll do the right thing. I know you will."

"I'm fine, Grandma."

I was never a big talker to begin with. As a mission came down to launch time, I was less talkative. I just kept going over in my mind what was going to happen and what could go wrong. I'd once been told that I couldn't be ready for everything, but I should be ready for the plan to go wrong. Good advice that had saved lives.

I sat down at the counter and Grandma placed a lobster omelet with toast and strawberry jam in front of me. I began to eat. Grandpa appeared.

"Good morning, Grandpa."

"Good morning, Mark," he said as he kissed Grandma. I liked that they were still in love after all these years. My parents were, too. The same went for most of my family—well, except Missy and me.

"Good morning, all," Lauren said as she kissed my cheek, my grandmother's cheek, and my grandfather's cheek.

Lauren was always happy it seemed. I smiled just looking at her. Grandma put a plate of food in front of Lauren.

"Wow, this is great. I won't eat it all though. I have PE first thing and we run today. When will I get to run with you again, Mark?"

"Any time you want. I'll be in and out this week, but I'll exercise some days," I said.

"Good. I want to kick your butt in a workout downstairs, too," she said as she ate her breakfast.

I smiled at Lauren as she smiled back at me. She truly was our family's miracle baby.

"Two PWCs will be delivered today, and Grandpa has arranged the delivery of a new boat, too. I want you to read that Rules of the Nautical Road pamphlet I gave you. I'll give you a test this week," I said.

"I read it last night. It seems a little much for operating a PWC that I can't even use at night."

"True, but if you want to move up to the boat you need to know it all," I instructed.

"I'll be ready. I already watched the PWC video. I suppose you'll put the limiter key on the PWCs while I learn?"

"That is correct. You'll do fine. Just remember, no one drives the PWCs unless I've checked them out," I said.

"Don't worry, I won't be going out unless you're around," Lauren said.

"Come on, sweetie. Time to get you to school," Grandpa said.

"Okay." Lauren ate two more bites then ran off to rinse her teeth and get her bag.

LT and Talbot appeared. Grandma started some omelets for the guys as I poured them coffee. "I'll go in today by myself. I'm going to Oceanside, first, then into the office. I'll check out the loft at some point while I'm at it." I looked at my grandmother before I continued speaking. "Anything I need to know?" I asked LT.

"Some email chatter and telephone calls from Jersey and the Bronx. The CEO, Mr. V is hot. The other corporations want a meeting with him about last week. It's working," LT said.

"Good. I want to know when and where," I said.

"You will."

"I'll call you when I'm on my way back."

"Aye, aye."

I kissed my grandmother and walked out to the Challenger, got in and off I went. I tapped the speed dial on my mother's cell phone for Joe.

"Hey. I keep forgetting I have this phone."

"Things, okay?" I asked.

"There seems to be a fight brewing because of the emails and what happened last week. The Carlucci family's patriarch is boiling mad because of the email that accused them of being behind the sex slave ring. He's directed a few of his lieutenants to find out who's behind it. It won't take long for them to figure out those two guys you killed worked for Paul Menduni. The third guy will be hard for them to figure out since he's in custody and the mob doesn't seem to know or care. Anyway. Dominic Carlucci sent an email to Vincenzo Menduni that they should meet in Manhattan and talk. The Bagatelli, Rapoli and Terrazzo families haven't responded yet, but they read the emails. They know," Joe said.

"Okay. Carl and company are identifying each email and account as this happens?"

"Yes. Carl already has what looks to be all the email addresses for all five families, most of their cell phone numbers and land line telephone numbers. We've passed the names to Robert along with assets that we uncovered. He and his guys are matching names and information to the assets. Rob already connected over five thousand banking transactions that moved money between these guys and we have the deposits, just like you said, multiple deposits pyramiding up made to these accounts just before they closed something with a securities firm including your firm. We'll have to match them up. Tony is working on that with them, too," Joe said.

"What about others involved in my parents' deaths?"

"Nothing else yet. Just the original four and the eight conspirators identified by email so far, but we think Vincenzo put out to his guys to not talk about what happened last week. Nothing has been said about it that we've found beyond Vincenzo discussing it with his *consigliere* and a couple of capos and lieutenants. Vincenzo and his people are meeting at the restaurant tonight in Rockville Center. Carl is ready to record the meeting.

Oh. We told you we got into Vincenzo's cell phone. We got into his wife's phone, too. Vincenzo doesn't talk on his cell phone much, but he must have it sitting on his desk or near where he works. His wife must keep her phone on her nightstand because we picked up Vincenzo cursing his head off about his son's request to whack Haley."

"He said this to his wife?" I said.

"No. To his *consigliere*, Michael Farina. Vincenzo had just finished working out and was about to shower when Farina went in to see him. Farina is in on the conspiracy to kill your father, too."

"What did Vincenzo say about his son?"

"I listened to it twice. He's not nice about what he thinks about Paul. He thinks Paul knows about what Monty did and about the sex slave ring. Vincenzo introduced that venture capitalist—Wilfred Manning—to Paul a year ago so Vincenzo is very suspicious. That said, it appears that the sex slave thing may not go up past Paul if it even involved him. However, someone above Paul or laterally to Paul had to know. Guys like Monty don't get introductions to guys like Wilfred Manning," Joe said.

"What did he say about Haley?"

"His language was polite, but he told Paul no way. Leave her alone that no one was to bother her. He told Paul he was a jerk to her so what did he expect. One of Paul's new guys is spying on him for his father. Vincenzo doesn't trust his son. Farina speaks with the guy a couple times a day. Farina has Vincenzo's ear. I checked Farina out. He's got an NYU and Fordham education. He has his bar license, but he rarely practices in court. He's Vincenzo's right-hand man—his *consigliere*. He controls the banking and the corporations—he's listed as president or vice-president on many of the companies."

"I have his bio in the file, don't I?"

"Yeah. He's in there. Hey, let me go. We're getting some heavy chatter. The Bagatelli family's boss just sent an email to Vincenzo. He wants to meet."

"Okay. I'll be there soon. Bye."

I was at the Nassau-Suffolk County line. I called Robert.

"Hey. It's okay to talk. We've encrypted all of our phones," Rob said.

"Good. I understand the weekend was fruitful?"

"Very. Matt just arrived at the office. We've taken over the little conference room, your office and the connecting offices. We can see everything that comes in or goes out of here. We can also see the same information from the loft. The loft looks like NORAD. We have seven techs with Tony supervising. The law firm has a lawyer here with me and another attorney with Tony. Tony and I can coordinate well. I know you said Tony with you on the *Trident* op and me with Matt on *Restore Dignity*, but with you in charge of all of it and they're so closely related while we gather intel, we're better off sharing and collating the intel now. Once you begin a dynamic operation that could change," Rob said.

"Tony's at the loft and you're at the office. Okay. Who's at the office with you, Mikey, or Kev?"

"Kev. He's looked around the entire office. Clara escorted him through the building. The car service has made three cars available to us with one at the loft and two here. Kev is roaming around and, while the ladies appear to be very happy to see him, Rizzo is not. Rizzo tried to engage him in conversation. Kev didn't say a word to him and pointed Rizzo to me. Of course, Rizzo knows who I am, so he walked away. Rizzo is on his email now."

"Okay. I'm stopping at the Oceanside house then I'll be in. Thanks, Rob."

"You got it. Bye."

I turned south onto Meadowbrook State Parkway. I looked at my tail. An FBI guy who's face I recognized. My phone buzzed.

"Hello."

"It's agent Stayton."

"Hello, John. What's up?"

"What are you doing?"

"I'm headed to my Oceanside house to pick up something before I drive to the office."

"What are your buddies doing?"

"Which ones are you talking about?"

"All of them."

"Well, John, I would have to be a psychic to know that. I know that my one buddy is going fishing in my boat today and another is going surfing at some point. Why?"

"Your friends all divided up and left your home in different vehicles over the weekend."

"That's how it works when you arrive in different vehicles, John."

"Mark. I don't know what you're up to, but so you know there has been an increase in email traffic between the five families. I know about your advice to our agent about you hearing Paul Menduni say he would ask his father for permission to whack his wife. Vincenzo said no. I just wanted you to know," John said.

"Then let me ask you . . . don't we have conspiracy to commit murder, a state and federal crime? Can't you take him down on that? As far as the state charge you have the overt act and you feds never concern yourselves with a lack of evidence when seeking a federal indictment."

"We could, but we want more. Mark, I think we should meet so I can give you a little more of the big picture. Why don't we meet tomorrow? I'll call you. You'll be in the city?"

"I will."

"I'll call you tomorrow. We'll meet at a restaurant for lunch."

"Okay, John. Talk to you then. Bye."

I always wonder what he's thinking when he calls. I got off Merrick Road then cut through Baldwin to lose the FBI agent via the backroads to Oceanside. Five minutes later I pulled into my garage.

Joe wasn't kidding. The house looked like a command center between the satellite antennas and VHF-UHF antennas outside, and all the computers and flat screens inside.

"Morning, Surfer," I said.

"Morning, Mark. I got in a nice session this morning. Nice right barrel wave. I like those retro boards you have in the garage," Surfer said.

"You'll appreciate the laid-back style here," I joked. "Sometimes the line-up looks like a boxing ring with the bloody noses fighting over the waves."

"No problems. I like the break."

"Good morning, Mark."

I turned to see Carl.

"Morning, Carl. I hear you've been very busy," I said.

"I think we've identified the men responsible for your parents' deaths. Joe told you that. We're also doing more checking and listening now and passing asset identification and possible plaintiffs to Robert and the attorneys."

"I want you to keep digging. Any connection between the conspirators and the other families yet?"

"I'm not sure. Follow me."

I followed Carl into the family room. Carl had hung a white board visual aid panel on the wall covering the windows and he'd listed several names in a pyramid form involved in my parents' deaths. Next to each name was a print-out of information about the person held in place by a colored magnet. There were twelve names, but four blanks with print-outs next to them.

"Mark. I don't have it all yet, but this blank here is likely Rizzo. We have circumstantial emails and telephone calls, but the only real evidence is an unopened email from Michael Farina to Rizzo. The email passes along the kill order for WM.

When I make an electronic cell phone overlay of Rizzo's and Farina's cell phone calls, it shows that just before and right after the old man, Romeo Menduni, gave the order to kill WM, Rizzo and Farina spoke. Rizzo is smart. There are 187 emails sent to him that he has not opened.

Farina has a bunch of unopened emails, too, but he uses several emails accounts. Farina has at least six aliases. The Atlantic City/Philadelphia family knows Farina as Michael Finelli. The Vegas family knows him as Michael Fetricelli. The Chicago family knows him as Michael Frucci. The local families know him as Michael Farina."

"What about these three blanks?" I said.

"That one there is someone in your firm. If I had to guess, I'd say a tech or an assistant. Whomever it is, they have access to several computers at the firm. I'm thinking male, about thirty-years-old, maybe younger. He knows tech, but never discusses fixes or tech jargon. His emails are cryptic and open. Things like 'How was your Easter? Ours was nice. Thank you for the present. Did you get the one I sent you?' He's very smart.

This second one is a floater. I can't be sure as he or she communicates to Vincenzo and Farina. Also, I found two emails to Paul and a couple of emails to others. I don't think he or she knows about Farina's aliases as he or she sent an email to Farina and in the email, asks who is Frucci?"

"What about this third one?" I said.

"I don't know. He sends very few emails. His emails do not coincide with cell phone calls with any of the other players and they are different. At first, going back more than three years ago, I'd say they were almost deferential and chummy. There are only twenty-two of them that I found so far. The last one was . . . well, here. You read it."

Carl tapped some keys and clicked his mouse to an email of April 30 last year. It read:

"You screwed up. I warned you. I'm out and if you bother me, I'll bring the house down on you and your bosses. Do not contact me."

"Where was this email sent from?" I said.

"It appears as if it was sent from overseas. It was sent to Farina and his aliases and copied to one of the phantom emails I just described, and to Vincenzo and Romeo Menduni. All the *Invisible Man's*, as I've nicknamed him, come via several means, usually from overseas. However, it's someone—a man, I'm sure—who is close to your firm and to Farina, Vincenzo, and Romeo. Mark, he's obviously writing about your parents' deaths. They were killed just over a week before the email was sent," Carl said.

"But why wait almost a week to send it? If Farina, Vincenzo, Romeo, and he were in on it together, why not send the email the next day or the day after that? And what was the screw-up? The order was given to kill my Dad. Was the screw-up . . . Hey, Joe. Does Joe know about this?" I said to Carl.

"Yeah."

"Well, this is sort of odd, Joe," I said.

"Mark. The guy starts off like a pussy, but over the years he begins to grow a set of balls. We only found twenty-two emails," Joe said as he looked at Carl for confirmation as Carl nodded. "His messages always speak of a subject, but they never identify the subject," Joe said.

I thought about what Carl and Joe said as I looked from Joe to Carl who handed me a cup of black coffee. I spoke out loud, more to myself than to the others.

"He's an outsider. He's not part of the family. Can I see the other emails?" I said to Carl. "He said 'your bosses' to Farina so he's either part of another family or something else.

Think guys, what did Romeo, Vincenzo and Farina have to gain by my father's death?"

"Self-preservation, maybe locating the documents and money, the bonds, staying out of prison, perhaps more . . ." Joe and Carl said.

"We're sure Rizzo is associated with the Menduni family. What happened in our firm involves the Menduni family. Killing my father had to help them some way. Romeo Menduni ordered my father's death. The Invisible Man didn't say they screwed up because they killed my mother. He's saying they screwed up because they killed my father. The Invisible Man didn't know of the kill order, right? You have no emails to him advising him of the kill order?"

"No. There are three that discuss killing WM, but the decision or kill order was not sent to the Invisible Man. Here are the other emails," Carl said as he brought up an email screen and printed the emails.

"Oh. There is never a reply to the Invisible Man's email. Not from anyone," Carl said.

I read the emails as I sat down. I passed each email to Surfer to read. A knock at the door produced Ken Cox.

"Hey, Mark," Ken said as he walked toward me with his hand out. We shook hands.

"Ken. I'm glad you're here. It feels good to do something, doesn't it?" I said.

"It does. Thanks. I owe you twice."

"No, you don't. Guys. This is our target." I pointed at the Invisible Man's blank on the VAP. "I need him identified. He may be part of another family, but I don't think so. Carl, Ken, find out who he is. Chase the emails, collate them with the dates, co-locate him with events, phone calls and answer this question: Why was killing my father a screw-up? Any questions?"

Ken and Carl looked at each other then turned to me.

"No," Carl said.

"Joe. Surfer. I need to speak with you. Let's go to the living room."

I poured myself another coffee and carried it with me. We took seats around the dining table instead.

"I want to cull Farina from the herd so I can speak with him," I said.

Joe looked at me funny then to Surfer who completely understood.

"Where does he live?"

"On Romeo Menduni's estate. It's about seventy-five acres. Menduni has owned it about forty years. It has several houses on the property. Farina lives in a five bedroom, five-thousand square foot waterfront home. The mansion is nearly thirty-thousand square feet. Farina's house is about two hundred yards from the main house. Farina's wife and daughter live there. His twin sons are away at prep school in Connecticut," Joe said.

"Can we get a blueprint or building plan for the place? Maybe an overhead shot of the lay-out?" I said.

"Hold on. I have a satellite view."

Joe walked off then returned holding several documents. He placed a satellite view of the estate in front of me. Surfer looked on. The picture showed the large mansion, six additional homes, a pool house, several garages, several sheds or maintenance buildings, a gatehouse, and a boat house. A second picture showed a public road that bordered the southern and western boundaries of the property and several connecting roads. To the north, the picture showed a road that traced the shoreline up through Mill Neck with additional mansions along that road. To the south and west of the main roads, smaller and newer *McMansions* were built on much smaller lots of one to two acres. The mansion was very Gatsbyesque, and it was at least one hundred years old. Farina's house was of a similar style.

"Who else lives there?" I said.

"One of his capos and Vincenzo's underboss, Bruno Pagano, lives in this house," Joe said as he tapped the house with his finger. "His wife and his Rottweiler live there. The gatehouse is manned by Romeo's men and several live there. Romeo has family living with him in the mansion. His wife's sister, an old uncle, and an aunt. All of them are assisted by nurses. The domestic help lives there in smaller houses and in rooms in the mansion. This house, here, has Romeo's girlfriend living in it. He must use a lot of Cialis because she's in her thirties," Joe said.

"How many men are on the property at night?" I said.

"Ten or more, plus domestic staff, plus Farina and Pagano," Joe said.

I looked at the satellite view. Surfer saw what I saw.

"Mark. You just want to snatch him and talk to him elsewhere, right?" Surfer said.

"Snatch and go. I don't want his family involved. What about his schedule? Does he leave the estate?" I asked Joe.

"He does. He goes to his office at a funeral home in Jericho. He also goes to church on Wednesdays and Sundays, but his family is with him. He goes to the Queens restaurant and, almost every day, he travels to Vincenzo's, usually at the end of the day, but he may spend the day there on occasion and on weekends. But his usual routine has him meeting with Vincenzo for dinner or after dinner. He drives to his home from there."

"Vincenzo's place is in Glen Cove. Farina must drive through Locust Valley to get home from Vincenzo's?" I said.

"I think so. He has an office in Locust Valley, but he rarely uses it," Joe said.

"This is what I want. Surfer. Call LT and Talbot. I want to run an observation on Farina. Joe. Does he travel with security?"

"No."

"Okay. Make an intel packet on this guy. We'll either snatch him on his way home from Vincenzo's house or we take him on his way home from the funeral home. Surfer. Let's get photos and cellphone intercepts today and tomorrow. Joe, is FBI watching him?"

"We were when I was there."

"We'll work around it. Get him watched and see if you can determine whether FBI is watching him. You, Talbot, and LT work it. We may have to go in our way," I said.

Surfer smiled. "Aye, aye, sir."

"Joe. You, Carl, and Ken work the Invisible Man. I gotta run. I'll be in touch. Surfer. We should do this tomorrow night."

"Yes, sir."

#

I arrived at the office. Kev greeted me with a nod as I walked past him.

"Good morning, sir." Clara said as I entered my office.

"Good morning, Clara. I hear good work this weekend. Thank you. Is Robert in the conference room?"

"Yes. Should I get him?"

"No. I'll go there. What are we doing in my office?"

"Brainstorming. I've written up some proposed bogus releases. Matt has spoken with many of the other firm's presidents. It appears that you were correct. At 2 p.m., Robert, Matt, Barbara, and I will meet with two of the senior attorneys. They have been working all weekend, too. I'll update you after the meeting," Clara said.

"Thank you. Let me see the opinions."

"On your desk. We're not emailing them until you give the say-so."

"Good. Thank you." I left my office for the small conference room. I found Robert inside with a few techs, Barbara and two women I didn't know.

"Hey, Mark," Rob said as he followed my gaze.

"Mark, this is Audrey McDermott, an attorney, and her paralegal Mary Cohen. They're culling assets and plaintiffs from the information we've provided them and sending that information on to their office to be included in the civil actions."

"Hello, Audrey, Mary. I'm Mark. Nice to meet you," I said.

Audrey was about twenty-nine or thirty. She had ginger colored hair, green eyes, and light freckling. Nice looking was an apt description of her. She wore a navy skirt suit with an off-white blouse, navy heels that made her legs look nice. She had a nice smile. She extended her hand to me and we shook.

"It's nice to meet you, Mr. MacKenzie. Mary is working with me while we read the raw data. She will be back at the office tomorrow at some point to coordinate with me."

"Audrey. Why don't you update Mark? So, you know, Mark is the boss," Rob said.

"Oh. At present, we have positively identified forty-nine corporations or limited liability companies as defendants. We're, essentially, doing two things. Determining causes of action and the parties involved. Once we have identified a cause of action with a plaintiff and defendant, we plug in other plaintiffs and defendants that meet the criteria for that cause of action. In some cases, plaintiffs have more than one cause of action. We separate those plaintiffs out and we will determine whether to file their civil action separately or with the other plaintiffs depending on the defendants involved. Our office has set up litigation teams to handle the review and drafting of the actual civil actions once they clear this team. The causes of action so far include wrongful death, assault and battery, RICO, embezzlement, involuntary servitude, rape, theft, fraud, and similar personal injuries. We hope to minimize the number of filings and we will put together similar plaintiffs and defendants because the courts will if we don't, especially the federal cases. We have identified one hundred sixty-two plaintiffs thus far. That's individuals and corporations," Audrey said.

"No corporations unless the business is a sub-chapter S, mom and pop without another cause of action or remedy."

Audrey looked at Rob. "You want primarily individuals to be made whole not companies?" Rob said.

"That's correct. Of course, maybe I'm too close to make that call? What have we identified as assets so far?

Robert and Audrey went to the computers. They looked at a screen then discussed what they read. "It looks like just over $9 billion," Audrey said.

"What? Where did they get that?" I said.

"Well, Mark, some of that will go away after you redeem the bonds and the stock crashes. We don't know how much in total yet but based on the current investments we guess that one billion to two billion could be lost after you pull the plug on the stocks and redeem the bonds. Perhaps more. There is no way to know since we are not sure how much stock they own. I am comfortable stating that over $5 billion will be available. I've excluded the assets involving the men arrested in the sex slave case. That list is growing, but so is the list of wealthy defendants. Wilfred Manning is worth over $2 billion himself," Audrey said.

"I agree, Mark. And we're not finished identifying assets. We have a lot left to do."

"This is just the New York families?" I asked.

"Just the Calabrese-Menduni, Bagatelli and Carlucci families. We're still working on the Atlantic City and other two New York families," Rob said.

"Have we tied these other families into these causes of action?" I said.

"Yes. All five so-called New York families have committed numerous personal injuries against that group of plaintiffs. The Atlantic City and Philadelphia families, which are one and the same family, are involved, too. We've connected them in on numerous criminal transactions. We have identified at least twenty-five causes of action against each family. I think we identified twenty-five plaintiffs against the other families unrelated to causes of action against the three families we have concentrated on," Rob said.

"Shit! Oh. I'm sorry. This just keeps growing. Okay. Include the corporate plaintiffs. I had no idea. The assets of the other families are not included in that total?" I said.

"No. Those families hold about seven to nine-billion in assets. Same thing, though. They will take a beating when you push the button on the bonds and stocks . . ."

"Hey, Mark."

"Oh. Hey, Uncle Matt." Clara followed Matt in.

"What's on your front burner?" Matt asked.

"Checking the troops on what the lawyers have done. It looks to be big and very thorough," I said.

"Terrific. I guess Robert and I will take the meeting or will you be there?" Matt said.

"No. You two have it with Clara. I want to go through our work and read the proposed releases. That will start Wednesday. Follow me to my office, Matt."

"What did you learn about the other firms?" I said.

"I spoke to the presidents of thirty firms. Of that group, twenty verified what you suspected. They have agreed to meet tomorrow. We will host in the large conference room."

"Who will be there?" I said.

"You, me, and our assistants. The other firms will include the president plus one. I have a buffet lunch being delivered. It's set for 1:30 p.m. to start to say hello and shake hands, but the meeting is at 2 p.m.," Matt said.

"Will they go along with it? I mean an *en masse* redemption of the bonds?" I said.

"I think so. You'll have to make the argument and sell them on it. So long as it's in their best interests, they'll do it. You'll need to deliver a great performance. I trust you will."

"What's the face value of the bonds they're holding?" I said.

"Between $15 and $50 million for each brokerage house."

"That's an average of $32.5 million each, That's $650 million plus interest. Jeez. We don't know what's being held by other bond holders?" I said.

"It appears that about a billion in bonds was sold by the various companies. Not a lot in the grand scheme. Enough to interest investors, but not enough to interest the SEC. It would hurt some of these companies and their investors if the bonds became worthless. Since the eighteen companies are probably one and the same, it's a billion dollar plus company. We don't know who else is holding those bonds. We'll find out Monday, I'm sure," Matt said.

"Matt. How are these firms holding the bonds and are they the investors or are they holding them in trust?"

"I'll know tomorrow, but I believe the firms own many of the bonds. As you know, we buy bonds, and we sometimes are given bonds in return for our brokerage services. We hold them and if we think the businesses will do well, we sit on them. We sell them if we think it's too much of a gamble."

"If we didn't know we had the bonds we wouldn't know if they were a good or bad investment. The other firms knew they had them, yet they kept them. Someone at each of those firms thinks these bonds are good investments or, like us, they have a Rizzo who is putting out bullshit opinions," I said.

"Some of these companies look good on paper. Due diligence would show them to be going concerns with decent, if not mild, balance sheets. Their value can be ascertained by their filings and the par value of their stock. So even good brokers might let them pass."

"Let's test that theory. Call Ira in here with our new brokers. Let's give them the companies to research and see what they come back with at the end of the day. Give each broker six companies to research," I said.

"Okay. I don't know what this will prove?"

"Humor me, Matt."

"You want to be there?"

"No. Let me clear my desk. I have something else to do. Let me know their findings right away. I'm going to run to the loft. Nothing about this goes to anyone remaining on that list of six, well, now five. Let me run. I'll be back in a couple of hours."

#

I called Stayton.

"Hello?"

"It's Mark MacKenzie. We'll have to move the meeting up tomorrow. My schedule was blown from 12:30 p.m. on, but I didn't check it before we spoke. Is that okay? Why don't we meet earlier and call it a brunch meeting at, say, 10 a.m.?"

"Fine. How about that diner over on 48th by 7th?"

Okay. 10 a.m. I think it's called Clarence's, isn't it?"

"That's it. Very good for a guy who's been out of town for so long."

"Everyone knows where you FBI guys eat. Should I bring a noisemaker to block listening devices?"

"Funny guy. Tomorrow at 10 a.m. Bye."

"Bye." What did Stayton want?

I got a cab to the loft. I knocked on the door, so Mikey didn't shoot me for just walking in. Tony opened the door.

"Forget your key?"

"No. Wow. Not only is the place gorgeous, I love what you guys have done with it. How goes the info gathering?" I said.

"Good. These guys, that's Todd and Jeremy, there, and that's Brandon and Kyle. They've been digging. Between Rob, Carl, and these guys, we will have assembled almost a terra byte of information for you. I know we've been parsing it down and managing it, but this is a major undertaking," Tony said.

"What do you think, Tony?"

"You always went big, Mark. Growing up, you were always the most careful and reserved of all of us but took the greatest risks after studying the problem. This is a big deal and we're confident that you've got a plan that will work. This is dangerous, but you're smart and I'd put our brain trust up against these guys any time. They're just sociopaths. I just hope no one gets hurt. All it will take is for one of them to figure it out which, as a practical matter, they cannot do."

"Oh. Why is that?"

"For one, none of our names will come up, but in one place, when you sue on your claim for wrongful death, you'll be in the company of hundreds of plaintiffs. I'm surprised they don't know about you from the other night. I think if they have anyone in Nassau PD or Suffolk PD, they'd be able to find out your name. Of course, the media is the greater danger. I think they will find out who you are. It's a hero story and too many people know. That said, since I don't think the mob owned that job nor do they want to be associated with it. You'll be fine." Tony paused, sipped his coffee then looked at me. "If they learned about this, what we're doing here, they'd go after you. This is big shit. Even after the assets are locked up they'll still try to figure it out. Once the criminal indictments start to fly— you know that Preening Pete character will not be able to keep his hands off this or stay away from the media—it's likely your identity will come out."

"So, are you saying I should quit, stay low, not participate when it gets going or what?"

"No. Wild horses couldn't pull you away and keep you from this. You must make sure you hurt them so bad that they realize it's not worth bothering you. But until that happens, you should be careful. Look, you know who is involved in your parents' deaths. You don't know why. I'm wondering if finding out will be worth it?"

I thought about what Tony said. I noticed Mikey looking at me. I looked at him and nodded. "Tony. Have you been updated on what Joe and Carl have learned about the people involved in my parents' deaths?"

"Yeah. We have twelve people identified, two probables, and two unknowns. I think the probables are who you think they are. I also think the other two are outside the Menduni family. One or both are close to your firm or your family," Tony said.

I looked at Tony nodding agreement.

"You've confirmed my thoughts. From this point forward, nothing leaves this room except through me. Let me qualify that. You, Carl, and Joe continue to do what you're doing. I'm going to isolate what goes to the firm. We have a meeting there tomorrow with the other firms. After that I think we'll scale down what we do at the firm. Did you read all the emails from the Invisible Man?"

"I did."

"Those emails didn't come from a mob guy. They came from an outsider. Someone in the business with them or someone who got involved—perhaps someone in government or business associated with them."

"My thoughts precisely," Tony said.

My phone buzzed.

"Yeah."

"It's LT. We're set up. I've already walked the property looking for my dog. I got to the pier before I was noticed. I walked right past Farina's house. I think we take him our way. Three play with two out front to cover our flanks. I spoke to your grandpa. Our chariot arrived today."

"It did, did it? Tell me, did you get caught on the property?"

"Yes and no. The gardener took my name and number. He'll call if they see my dog. There is no security from the north. It's all show at the front gate."

"We'll do a run through tomorrow night. We'll massage it from there. Two at the gate and three in the boat with me. Who's watching him now?"

"Surfer. Talbot will backup. Farina is at Vincenzo's house right now. Security is tighter there if for no others reason than there are more people there and it's practically an island with one road in. The old man's home is like a retirement home," LT said.

"Can we get a tracker on Farina's car?" I said.

"He has a beautiful new Audi A-8L. I'm looking at it now on my tablet."

"Good work. We'll talk later. Bye."

"Out."

Tony was smiling at me. "You know, Mark, you've become the embodiment of everything we used to pretend to be when we were kids and played secret agents and frogmen swimming across Zachs Bay, Jones Bay or Reynolds Channel to East Rockaway. I'm glad we're doing this," Tony said.

"Okay. Here are the releases. I've marked them up. Look at them. Tony, I'd like you to back me up at a meeting at 1 p.m. tomorrow at the office. Be in a nice suit. No sneakers."

"Damn. I was just starting to get comfortable. No problem."

"Are you comfortable here, Mikey?" I asked.

"I love it. The food is terrific and the view great. I worked out in the gym and on the roof. You have a cute neighbor named Melissa . . ."

"Thank you, Mikey. Just keep an eye out. I'm heading back to the office. Tony. What's your feeling about how long those unknown email authors have been around?"

"Mr. Invisible, for more than three years. The others . . . the earliest emails are just less than two years ago."

"Thanks. I'll talk to you later or tomorrow."

#

"Bernice. Would you ask Robert to come to my office please?"

"Certainly."

"And I'd like you to join us, too."

"Oh? Okay."

"Rob, we're going to close our circle of friends. I want you to take any info you get unrelated to plaintiffs and assets and keep it close. Do not discuss it around here with anyone. You'll only report to me from this point forward. If Matt or Marsha ask why, tell them my orders. As far as the plaintiffs and assets, you deal with Audrey and her firm. I will not speak with anyone but you, Tony, and Joe about that subject. Audrey will only report to you."

"We have a problem?" Rob asked.

"Perhaps. Bernice. Can I get a list of all employees who have been here . . .? Wait. That's it. Bernice. I want a list of all employees hired since Rizzo was hired. And I want a list of all employees hired by my father, Matt, or Marsha in the past five years. This will be between the three of us. No one else."

"Yes, sir. That will take me just a few minutes. Anything else, sir?" Bernice said looking unsettled.

"No. I'll go through my correspondence. Rob, would you ask Audrey to join me, please?"

"Sure. I'll send her in."

I turned on one of three white-noise makers I had with me and rebooted my computer.

"Hello, Mark. You wanted to see me?" Audrey said.

"Yes, Audrey. Please come in and take a seat." I stood until Audrey sat.

"Audrey, who are you communicating with at your firm?"

"Walter Aarons and Mary Fitzpatrick."

"Good. While you are here, I don't want you to pass the names of plaintiffs or defendants to anyone but Robert. No one else at all. If I need to know something, I'll get it from Robert. If anyone asks you about plaintiff or defendant identification, I want to know. Your excuse is attorney-client privilege," I said.

"Yes, sir. Is there a problem?"

"Yes. Too many people know too much. Thank you, Audrey." I stood and extended my hand. Audrey stood and shook my hand then departed.

Bernice came in with my lists.

"Will you be needing me any more today, sir?" It was already 5:10 p.m.

"No, Bernice. Thank you. I'll see you tomorrow." Bernice hesitated.

"Mark. How come you didn't fire Rizzo? Is he involved in your father's death?"

"Sit, Bernice, please." I got up and closed the door.

"What do you think, Bernice?"

"Oh, Mark, I don't know what to think anymore. I just have this awful feeling something is very wrong here. I don't know everything you are doing, but I trust you, your childhood friends and the silent, nice-looking men who walked in and out of here today. I don't know if I feel that way about some of the others. The firing of Train shook up a few people, but I don't trust Rizzo. He's up to something."

"Why do you say that?"

"Today, at lunch time, I saw him sitting at a secretary's station. He was on email, but it was Internet email or, oh my mind, Web-based email. It had purple and white background."

"Anything else?"

"Well . . . he knows I saw him. He walked to me and glared at me, then walked away."

"Are you in fear of him?"

"I don't know."

"I take it that if he was on that computer he logged in or a secretary failed to log out?"

"I watched him log in, but I could see into his office. His computer was on, and he was logged in there, too. It wasn't his secretary's station either."

"Did anyone else see him?"

"I'm not sure."

"Thank you for telling me. Go home. If you have any problems, let me know."

"I will. Good night, Mark."

#

I picked up my phone. "Ira. Can you come to my office, please?"

"I'll be right there."

I tapped Chief's number.

"Hey," Chief said.

"What did you do today?"

"I worked out, purchased additional clothes, and sat around your uncle's pool. Why?"

"Well, I'm confused. Why are you there and he here?"

Silence.

"I understood that I'd cover him and Betsy at home and when he asked me to go with him to the office. Matt told me he'd see me later here at the house. I'm sorry Mark if I got it wrong. I know you said accompany him to the office, but I thought he could modify that order as the boss?"

"You're fine. I wasn't clear to Matt. Tomorrow I want you to call me with the time he leaves. You have the kit I made up for you with you?"

"Yeah."

"Put a GPS tracker on the limo tomorrow. Use the pretext of checking the vehicle out to be sure it's safe and that no tracker is on the vehicle. I want to know if it's the same driver, too."

"What are you looking for?"

"I don't know. I want to catch anything unusual. I think we have a mole in our organization, and I know it's not you guys or my childhood buddies. I trust no one else."

"What are we doing up on the Gold Coast?"

"We'll talk tomorrow."

"Roger that. Bye."

I called my grandfather.

"Hello."

"Hello. It's Mark. I'm leaving now. I'll see you in a bit. Everything okay out there?"

"Other than your grandmother running me crazy, yes. Oh, two PWCs and a center console boat appeared today. I had them all fueled. They are in the lifts."

"Did we get a spec sheet or manual on the boat?"

"Sure. It has a two-inch thick notebook of operating and mechanical information. Why?"

"You know me, I like to read about things first."

"Well, I'll . . . hold on, Mark."

"Mark. This is Grandma." As if I'd fail to identify her voice standing next to my grandfather talking on his phone.

"Yes, Grandma?"

"I'll have dinner warming for you when you get home."

"Thank you, Grandma. I love you."

"I love you, too. Okay. Here's Grandpa."

"Bye. I'll see you in a little while."

"Bye, Mark."

A knock on my door produced Ira. "Come in. I know it's after knock-off . . ."

"Not for me. I stay to wrap up the day. I assume you want to talk about what the three new brokers discovered regarding those energy companies?"

"That is one item, yes. What did they learn?"

"Initially the companies appear to be fine, but William— he and I go back some ways together—has never liked these types of companies. Like many of the dotcoms that provided no real product, these companies exist on the blood and product of other corporations that produce something tangible. That said, we compared notes after our research. When I called to speak with HR at Michigan Energy, I had William call Ohio Micro Electric and Charlie call Iowa Electric Distributors. Part way through the phone calls we switched phones. The ladies on the other end got confused. They misspoke and while I initially called Michigan Energy, I requested information on Ohio Micro Electric. William and Charlie did the same thing. The woman eventually provided the information we needed, but we showed they had the information for all three companies at their fingertips. The telephone numbers are listed under different addresses, but when we looked at the geo-position information for the numbers the dots were on top of each other in a building in Detroit.

Then we called some of their customers. We got confusing information as to telephone numbers and billing addresses. I called Illinois Power and Light, one of the two big power producers in Illinois who uses one of these companies and I got yet another telephone number in Louisiana. Mark, I don't think these companies are separate entities."

"What would our brokers do about us holding millions in bonds for these companies?"

"Sell, sell, sell."

"Could there be value here. I don't mean to knock all these businesses but . . ."

"Mark. All—I mean every one of these companies—were incorporated in Las Vegas five years ago. I printed up the incorporation documents off the state website. Of the eighteen companies, only three names are listed. See for yourself."

Ira passed me some documents. The first one listed Michael Frucci. The second listed Michael Finelli and the third document indicated Michael Fetricelli. I was right.

"Thank you, Ira. Next. Rizzo was logged into someone else's computer today. What did he produce for you since I spoke with him?"

"Nothing. We introduced the new guys, got them settled in, showed them around and got them set up. Rizzo knows not to use other employee's computers. It's firm policy."

"Ira, I don't think Rizzo is long for this firm."

"Mark, he's up to something. I heard him on the phone today with some other brokers, but not anyone he was doing a deal with. He spoke with at least six other brokers, but when I listened in, I can cut in and listen to their sales calls for training, they were talking about a meeting. They were going out to an Italian place over on 5th at 8 p.m. tonight."

"Is that unusual?"

"Yes. It's not unusual for us to go toss a few so we can talk shit to our competition after a good deal, but we don't just meet and hang out—just one guy from each firm meeting."

"Keep an eye on him. Thank you."

"Yes, Mark. Bye."

#

I looked up to see Marsha standing at my door.

"Hello. I don't think I've seen you all day," Marsha said.

"What's up, Marsha?"

"You tell me. The attorney meeting go okay?"

"I suppose. Robert didn't say anything nor did Audrey. I haven't seen Clara or Matt."

"Oh. I thought Matt would have told you what was up?"

"I don't think there was much to cover. Audrey and Robert had a handle on it." Marsha just stood there looking at me. "Is there something else?"

"There is, but I can't seem to formulate what it is. I thought I knew, but now I cannot put my finger on it," Marsha said.

"When you do, let me know. I must run. Did you come in by train today?"

"I did."

"You're living in Nassau, right?"

"I am."

"Want a lift? I drove in today."

"Sure. Maybe I'll be able to verbalize what I'm feeling."

"Go get your bag. I'm ready."

#

"This is some car. I can feel it vibrating in my bones," Marsha said.

426

"It can move. Where do you live?"

"In Massapequa. We bought a place at Nassau Shores. My husband and I bought it about twenty-three years ago, right after we married. I got a little inheritance and we saved. He was in the Marine Corps, so we got a VA mortgage."

"You have children or at least one child you mentioned."

"Two. My daughter Priscilla, who Don adopted, and my son Brian, who was born after we moved into our new home. Priscilla is twenty-eight and Brian is twenty. He commutes to Hofstra. Priscilla is married and lives up in Huntington. She's a schoolteacher and her husband is a physical therapist. He was a medic in the army. He was in Iraq, too. He didn't get all shot up like you though. They have two children—twins. Clark and Lois."

I smiled at that news. "They have a sense of humor."

"Yes. I'm glad they didn't name Clark *Perry*." We laughed. "Or *Lex Luther*. Jeez, kids. What am I saying. You're just four years older, but you grew up fast. You don't remember me, I think, but when you were little, I'd watch you some days when Missy wasn't available. It was the crazy 1980s, big hair, lots of hair spray, all the rock bands wore spandex. It was a wild time. Then I got pregnant, and my life changed. Your mom and dad saved me, but it was your mom who made him hire me. Your father took a chance on me. Your mom saved my life," Marsha said.

I drove along listening as Marsha sobbed and wiped away tears.

"I miss your mom. She was truly an angel. I hope you get who killed her. Even if . . . Oh, I don't know. I miss Liz and

Will. I remember when your dad came to work after your mom told him she was pregnant with Lauren. Your dad was so happy and ditsy that week. Those were nice times. No wars, no terrorists, no deficits, no government listening to us on the phone or copying our email."

"Marsha. Is there something you want to tell me? Get off at Hicksville Road?"

"Yes. That's fine. I can't put my finger on it, Mark. I just have a feeling something is wrong."

"When you think of it, please tell me. I'll take Sunrise Highway?"

"Yes. Turn right on Ocean Avenue after the Massapequa Diner, then left on Merrick Road. It's three lights up on the right, on Bay then just drive to the bay."

"I have an old friend, my first commanding officer, who got shot up and retired who has a home at the end of one of those roads in Massapequa. Anyway. What does Don do?"

"He works for a trucking company. Logistics. He's been there the whole time we've known each other. I earn more than him, now, but that's just been in the last few years. We have a nice life. Our grandchildren are always over. They're four years old. Don is teaching them to fish. Clark is fine with it, but Lois is a little squeamish. It's fun watching them. It's the green one there on the left of the cul-de-sac."

I saw a nice, old, big blue-green, 1960s split-level rancher with an attached two-car garage on a very nice lot with a beach and a pier out back. Very nice.

"It's nice being on the water."

"It is great. Do you like it in Greenport?"

"I love it."

"I was out there for a cocktail party right after your mother finished redoing the home. Your mother was still waiting for some furniture pieces, but the home was finished. Liz and I sat on that wonderful living room porch, and we had a great time. I wish I could sit with her again on that couch," Marsha said as her voice cracked.

"Marsha. You are welcome to come out and sit on that porch any time. Lauren would love you to. I'll see you tomorrow."

"Thank you, Mark. Bye."

Marsha got out of my car, and I drove off. What is it she wants to tell me? I picked up my phone and tapped Haley's number.

"Hey, sailor. Where are you?"

"I'm getting on Merrick Road. I just dropped off our HR department head at her home in Massapequa. I still have a bit of a ride ahead of me. What did you do today?"

"School, fun with Paulie, deposited a check for $900,000 into my account. My hearing is Wednesday. I guess I'll get the divorce on the spot."

"Well then, we can celebrate. Oh, wait. Sorry. I opened my mouth without a plan. Let's plan a me-and-you night for Friday? Is that okay?"

"Sure. What do you have in mind?"

"It's a secret."

"No plan yet, huh?"

"It's a secret."

"I heard from my mother that a boat and two PWCs appeared at the house."

"You are on the MacKenzie ladies chat-line?"

"Somewhat. My mother is. Lauren told me. I'm about to eat with Paulie. Call me later."

"Sure. Bye."

"You know, it's okay to say it."

"Say what?"

"I love you."

"Well, I do."

"Bye."

"Bye." I picked up speed and took Southern State Parkway to the Sagtikos Parkway to the L.I.E.

#

I pulled into the garage as my phone buzzed.

"Hello."

"Hey. It's Joe. I'll call you back. Later. Bye."

That was cryptic. My mother's phone buzzed with my dad's number in it.

"Hey."

"Hey. They know."

"What do they know, Joe?"

"They know the money is gone. Paul pulled in there with two of his men and tore the place apart. Carl got rid of the video. Paul told Vincenzo who is very angry. I mean pissed off. Paul is shitting bricks. Tomorrow, Paul must be at his father's house to explain.

Next item. The war is on. Vincenzo and his guys got emails that point at the Bronx boys taking a big haul from Nassau. Nice work, by the way. The Bronx guys called bullshit and forwarded some emails from Newark that say something else. Vincenzo and Farina are going berserk. Vincenzo ordered Farina and Pagano to get to the bottom of it. Paul will be there tomorrow. The meeting is at Vincenzo's at 8 p.m. Another meeting that was to occur with all the families was cancelled. The Bagatellis told Vincenzo to stuff it after they got emails from Vincenzo, sent to others, wherein Vincenzo blamed the Bagatellis for the missing money. Of course, all those emails were sent by us. Vincenzo's guy checked out the mini-storage then he searched Paul's house. Terrible when a father doesn't trust his own thug son. Oh. There is something not right between Vincenzo and his father Romeo. Romeo said to his guy via email that he wants Vincenzo and Pagano checked out. He thinks Vincenzo took the money."

"No trust there at all, is there? Joe, did you get anywhere on the Invisible Man?"

"No. Carl linked a two-year-old email from overseas to a computer café in Jersey."

"How about the last email?"

"They're working on it."

"Make that a priority. We'll talk tomorrow which will be a long day."

"Gotcha. I'll talk to you in the morning."

"Bye." I walked to the house and noticed my SUV and BMW motorcycle were parked in front of my house.

"Hi, Mark." Lauren said as she came bounding up to me, kissing me on the cheek.

"Hi. You're chipper tonight."

"I got an A on my history exam today."

"Terrific. Very good. How was your day?"

"Great. And yours?"

"Long. Busy. Productive." I walked back to the kitchen area. Talbot and LT were eating.

"Hi, Mark. Come sit down and eat," Grandma said.

"Where's Grandpa?" I asked.

"Checking out the new boat," Talbot said.

I poked my head out the door and looked out on the bay. Nice boat. Black and white. I noticed the notebook on the table. LT pointed at a page. I looked at what he was referring to. The range in nautical miles was up to 450 miles at twenty-five miles per hour or 225 nautical miles at fifty-five miles per hour. I took a seat at the counter and began to eat. Lauren sat next to me.

"You know, Grandma and I can tell when you're planning something," Lauren said.

"Then in the interests of operational security you should keep that to yourself," I said as I poked her in the ribs which both tickled and irritated her.

"Stop!" Lauren shrieked.

"This is terrific, Grandma. What's the plan for this weekend?" I said.

"Emily and Frank will arrive Friday. We should clean out the extra room since they will start on that job any day. The builder was out today. Your mother already had a plan and permit approved, but it expired a few months back. They'll renew the permit after the township inspector looks it over. We'll remove the stuff from there to the garage and down to the first level. You'll stay in the room and Emily and Frank will get your room. Once the work is approved and they make a hole, you'll go to the couch," Grandma said.

I looked at Talbot and LT. "See? I'm master of my universe here."

"Oh, don't whine in front of your men," Grandma said.

Talbot burst out laughing.

LT smiled. "They ought to make *grandmother* a rank in the navy," LT said.

I ate my dinner and guzzled down my iced tea. I looked at my watch which indicated 8:10 p.m. almost dark or nautical twilight. "Come on. Let's go take a ride. Grandma, Lauren, put on a jacket. Get Grandpa's jacket, too. We're going to take a ride in the new boat," I said.

"In the dark?" Grandma said.

"Yes. You might be surprised to know, Grandma, but we do most of our work in the dark. Let's go guys." We walked out to the pier and boat. Grandpa saw us approaching.

"What a piece of engineering marvel . . . What are we doing?" Grandpa said.

"Taking a ride," I said. I checked out the boat, familiarized myself with the safety equipment and systems while Talbot followed along behind me. I went through the electronics and turned on all the navigation systems. Check, check and recheck.

"Come aboard," I said. The guys helped Grandma and Lauren get aboard. Grandpa and LT took a position near the portside of the helm. Talbot stood off to the starboard side. Grandma and Lauren sat on the transom bench seat. I pressed the fob to lower the lift and started the engines as they submerged in the water. When the lift reached the stops, I motored off at bare steerageway. Once I was clear of the lift, I moved the throttles forward.

"We'll need screens," LT said pointing at the two navigation displays on the console. I noticed the console instrumentation lights were red to protect our night vision.

LT, reading my mind, said, "We can put a dimmer switch on the navigation lights."

I nodded as I compared the magnetic compass direction with the GPS. All systems operated properly.

"You guys planning something, son?" Grandpa said.

"Not tonight. This is just a shakedown cruise. Everyone ready?" I asked.

"Yes," yelled Lauren from behind me.

I moved the throttles forward. Nine hundred horses very quickly moved us up to speed and on plane. I watched my radar. We had a clear shot for the next few miles. No one was around. I throttled up some more as the GPS indicated forty-five miles per hour.

"You okay, Grandma?" I asked.

"Fine. This is thrilling," she said.

"Okay. I'm taking the throttles all the way up now," I said as I moved the throttles forward. We were running at WOT and hitting fifty-five miles per hour. Fast enough for our work. I brought the throttles back to a thirty-five-knot cruise.

"You gonna run the fish over with the boat?" Grandpa joked.

"Grandpa, would you like to take the wheel?"

"Not tonight. I need daylight so I can see and practice."

"Talbot. Take the wheel," I said. Talbot took the wheel and checked his instruments. I punched in a course on the chart plotter for Talbot to follow. Talbot followed the course perfectly. I looked at LT.

"Four and two. Run it. If it's right, we do it," I said.

"It's a whole lot more time to plan than we're used to," LT said.

"You guys going somewhere?" Grandpa asked.

"Yes. See that waypoint? That's our pier," I said. Talbot brought us to the pier and put us in the lift. Talbot is a good sailor. We debarked and walked toward the house.

"Come on. It's dessert time," Grandma announced.

#

Following dessert my grandparents and Lauren said good night. I got out some bourbon and poured a shot for each of us.

"LT, your assessment?"

"We pick him off when he gets out of his car at his house. Let me show you."

SEAL officers initially plan all missions, but all SEALs have input and are involved in tweaking and modification of the final plan. The truth is most of the operations are planned by the senior enlisted. I was sure LT had already discussed the plan with the others. LT laid out a satellite photo of the estate.

"Four men in the boat. One stays in the boat covering with an M-40 or MK-12. The other three set up here, here, and here. Two guys at the front of the property with M-4s, H&K-416s or M-40s to cover and distract if need be. We can have them toss flash bangs to distract. I'm thinking because Farina parks here, these three spots make the best sense. Bring an injection kit just in case, hood him, cuff him and gone. Time to walk that driveway to the pier was seventy seconds. Three men with a body running should cover it in in half that time. It's a straight shot to the Long Island Sound here. I presume water will be used. The boat has a hose wash-down. We strap him to a board, upside down, dunk him in the Sound for effect then do the rest with the hose," LT said.

"Talbot?"

"I agree. If by chance a boat or police boat come along, we gag and bag him and put him in the console, but with radar, a mostly black boat, running dark or with dimmed navigation lights we're good. I'll install a dimmer on the lights tomorrow. We bring our NVGs and full wet gear. What do you want to do with him after we talk to him?" Talbot said.

I was thinking I wanted to tie a cinderblock to his neck and feed him to the fish.

"We'll put him back," I said.

"How?" Talbot asked.

"Knock him out, spill whiskey on him, force him to swallow a few large gulps—don't waste the good stuff on him. Leave him on a beach near the house."

"What if we're seen on extraction?" LT said.

"Then we'll just run along the coast while we do our business then dump him anywhere along the coast," I said.

"I agree. Snatch him, extract him, get the info, scare the crap out of him, dump him and we sip good bourbon and smoke nice cigars on the way home," LT said while Talbot nodded.

"Okay. He will be at a meeting at Vincenzo's house at 8 p.m. We will need to be in place by 9 p.m. We can loiter off the coast if we're early. The shore team will tail him and report when he's on his way home. That means underway by 7 p.m. for a two-hour ride at thirty-knots. LT, pick a direct course west to a point north of Oyster Bay. We'll stay just off the coast due to sand bars and small boats then turn to port and run right into the bay. Oyster Bay will be full of small craft and mooring buoys. Talbot, you'll have the conn. The buoys have reflective material on them and show up on radar, but don't count on every one of them being seen by the radar. There is a course through the mooring basin. LT pull the chart up on the Internet."

"I'll get it. Who else do you want with us?" LT asked.

"I'd like Chief, but I need him where he's at," I said.

"He told me," LT said.

"That leaves the rest of us. We'll rent a SUV to get Mikey and Kev from the city and they can use that to cover as the shore team. You all meet tomorrow along the route and scope it out from Vincenzo's house to Farina's place. Run the route for time and get familiar with the estate. LT, walk it through with the comms. We'll do it tomorrow night if it feels good. Talbot is right, we bring our wet gear in case we must swim into the beach. Kev and Mikey will not enter the estate, but I want them to know what's there. The Organized Crime Task Force has advised that the gatehouse has a security team. You have confirmed what they suspected, north security is weak or non-existent. There is a Rottweiler on the property. ROEs . . . no shooting unless fired upon. Shoot to suppress and scare. We're much better than these guys. We shouldn't have to shoot. I don't want any interest in this by federal or county authorities. I will know more tomorrow. I will meet with the FBI tomorrow at 10 a.m. This op goes no further than the seven of us. No one else. Nothing discussed on phones. Use satcoms only. You two, Surfer and I will snatch him. Talbot, you'll cover either from the boat at the dock or from the beach if we swim in. You'll have to watch your six while we set up and take him. If any police or feds come around, we call it off. I'll talk to Joe and see what my friend knows about federal operations nearby. I may have to include Joe and our friend, Dave, in on some details. You all take care of the op planning and I'll handle the external details," I said.

"Roger that, sir," LT said.

"Aye, aye, sir," Talbot said.

"Good night, guys. We have a hell of a day ahead of us tomorrow," I said.

"The only easy day was yesterday, Mark," Talbot said.

CHAPTER 16

I awoke with a start. I jumped up and hurried downstairs. My grandmother was up.

"Morning. I'll be right back," I said. I dashed to my garage and assembled my wet gear. I went through my check-list, re-bagged everything, and placed the bag on top of my safe. I went through my weapons and bagged what I'd take with me and locked it back up in the safe. I walked back to the house. My grandfather was up and eating breakfast.

"Good morning, Mark. Are you going into the office?"

"I am. I'll eat breakfast now, then shower and change. I have a 10 a.m. meeting, but I need to check the night's work in Oceanside. We're getting results from our misinformation campaign."

"Oh, really?"

My grandmother put some oatmeal, fruit, and a Danish in front of me. I added protein powder to the oatmeal. Grandma turned up her nose at my oatmeal.

"Just drink more milk," she said.

Five minutes later I was in the shower. Shoot. I forgot to call Haley. I dried off. It was 6:30 a.m. I tapped Haley's number.

"Hello? What's wrong?" Haley said.

"Sorry. Nothing. I'm an idiot and forgot to call you last night. I'm sorry. I love you. I'll talk to you later."

"You're sweet. I love you, too. I gotta go. Bye."

I put on a dark blue Armani suit with a white shirt, regimental tie and black leather slip-ons and belt. I said good-bye to my grandparents and Lauren and jumped into the Hellcat and took off for the highway. I dialed Joe.

"Hey. I'm en route."

"I'll call you."

"Joe, wait. Rob has encrypted all the phones."

"That's right. Okay. Someone got beat up last night behind a restaurant over on 5th Avenue. We picked it up on email and heard it on the police radio. Your guy Rizzo is involved. Some broker was badly beaten and was hospitalized. Check out Rizzo when you get to the office.

That last email from the Invisible Man was traced by Carl and Ken back to China and it sort of dead-ended there. Carl called the company who operated the server in Shanghai. They told Carl the email came from an IPA in New Zealand. Anyway, what I'm getting to is the email came back to an Internet café in Manhattan. It traveled through sixteen countries before it went to Vincenzo, Farina and Romeo. Someone knows email."

"There's no chance that the Internet Café has a video of the day the email was sent?"

"I'll check. I may take a run down there myself. What else do you need?" Joe said.

"We're going to talk to Farina tonight. I'd like you available to run interference with anyone who might happen along in your kind of work. I'd also like to let Dave know that his folks should not be in our op area tonight."

"I see. You are just going to talk to this guy?"

"That's right. Your swim buddy will join us. Only the current swim team of seven, Dave and you would know."

"I'll be back in touch. Oh. We think all the assets have been identified. All that's left is money in mattresses or buried in mayonnaise jars in their backyards. We've passed along everything to Rob. I've been advised I should speak to only Rob, Tony, and you."

"That's right. I feel like we have leaks and I narrowed it down to the professionals. All questions should be referred to me."

"Gotcha. No need for you to come by then. I see our friend is packing. I guess he got the word. I'll be in touch. Bye."

"Bye."

#

I stayed on the L.I.E. to the city. I was tempted to check out the op area, but I had trusted and capable operators for that. I drove into the city with six hundred thousand other people.

I parked in my parking space, entered the building, and got onto the elevator with many other people. Just as the door began to close, Rizzo stepped in. I stood in the back corner of the elevator behind several people and Rizzo did not notice me. I looked at Rizzo's head and face. I saw no evidence of a fight until Rizzo reached out and pushed the door-close button. His knuckles were cut and bruised. The elevator stopped at each floor letting people off. We reached the eighteenth floor and Rizzo stepped off and turned right toward his office. I stepped off and went left toward the receptionist.

"Good morning, Mr. MacKenzie," the receptionist said.

Rizzo stopped in his tracks and turned toward me and was startled to find me looking at him. I nodded at him. He walked away in a huff.

"Good morning. Please have Robert see me when he gets in."

"Yes, sir."

I entered the hallway that led to my office. I needed to finish my review of the internal press releases that we would begin to promulgate today within our organization. There were twenty-six releases to be disclosed by various forms and methods. I sat down at my desk and began to go through the releases. I polished several—okay, all of them—because naval officers can never not change something sent up from a subordinate. After forty minutes, I was finished.

"Morning, sir."

"Good morning, Bernice."

"I'm getting coffee. Would you care for some, sir?"

"Yes, please. Thank you."

A moment later Bernice returned with my coffee. "Here you are."

"Thank you. How are you today?" I asked.

"I'm good. Did that list I gave you help?"

"It will. I will work on that today. I have a 10 a.m. appointment at Clarence's Diner. Don't tell anyone. If they look for me, I'm out. I will be back for the 1 p.m. meeting."

"Morning, Mark, Bernice."

"Morning, Robert. Mark, you have a meeting with Ira and the new brokers in twenty minutes to go over final acceptance on their contracts," Bernice said.

"I need to use this computer schedule I have here, don't I? Sit down, Rob."

"It's working."

"What's working?"

"The emails we sent out. The families are fighting."

"Yes. The emails do seem to be causing them problems. I'm told we're at our end-point on asset identification?"

"I think so. Now we could look more on the other families, but for the five New York families we're there. I think with all five families the total value of assets exceeds $19 billion. The plaintiffs have been identified. Over 580 of them. You said you may have some more today?"

"It's possible. I'll bring it up at a meeting I have at 10 a.m. Has anyone approached you for information?"

"That Rizzo guy tried to do the paesano to paesano, help-me-out thing, but's that's all. Kev creeps Rizzo out for some reason, just so you know," Rob said.

"That's great. I'll post Kev in the hallway by Rizzo's door. Carl traced that Invisible Man's email to an Internet Café in Manhattan. Is there anything we can do?"

"Unless there is a video, no. This is what will eventually make this business hard. Wi-Fi hot spots, free Internet access, and encryption. It will shut the government down. It's too big."

"And you worked at NSA?" I said.

"That's why I quit. I saw what the government was doing to us and decided some of us had to be smart enough to curtail the government's ability to monitor *We the People*. Just like the Navy lied about the Soviet threat to build more submarines during the Cold War, NSA is lying to get more money to spy on Americans while saying they're not spying on Americans."

"Well, one battle at a time. I'd like you and Tony to assist with identifying the other guys on that list. If Audrey needs help or I get a list of new plaintiffs, you'll go back to helping her."

"You have really stirred it up this time, buddy-boy. I hope it works. Let me run."

"Thanks, Rob," I said as Rob left the office.

#

I had my meeting with Ira and the new brokers. We reached agreements on compensation and expectations. I was happy to see them come aboard. All three new brokers had deals close to terms, so I was extra happy. Ira was beaming with the news.

"Bye, Bernice. I'll be back for the big meeting. Hey, Clara. Is the presentation ready?"

"It's finished. I'll load it and all will be ready, sir."

"Thank you. I must run."

#

I got a cab to Clarence's. I had a white noise maker-jammer with me and my SIG P226 which I was sure someone would notice. The cabbie dropped me in front of the diner. I entered and spotted Stayton sitting at a booth in the back. Dan was with him and so was the guy sitting at the counter and the guy following behind me.

"John. Do you have your men follow me just for fun or what?"

"You lost my man yesterday after we spoke on the phone."

"Oh? I didn't notice. Maybe you guys should buy Dodge Hellcats?" I deadpanned.

"Are you eating?"

"Yes."

A waitress came over and poured our coffee. Dan left to report on me. The other two agents stood around being obvious.

"What do you want? Oh, first, our philanthropy. Do you have more names of victims or their survivors?"

John passed me a two-page document containing forty-six names. Most had asterisks indicating they were deceased, and the victim's survivor would be the plaintiff.

"The others were found?" I asked.

"We rescued some already. The crew of that yacht was very helpful. So was the government of a foreign power. It'll come out soon in the media, but it will take a few days. You will be mentioned in the Merrick case, but not by name or what exactly you did. I insisted on that, but your name is bound to come out somehow. A dozen cops and the neighbors saw you," John said as he slid a picture across the table to me. It was a picture of me standing next to my Hellcat, pistol in hand, as I put the weapon in my trunk and took out water for Haley and Erica.

"That's an Esquire, Dodge or John Varvatos advertisement if I ever saw one," John said.

I nodded.

"I spoke with my superiors in Washington. They're concerned about a La Costa Nostra blow-up here. It seems a fight is brewing among the New York families. Part of it has to do with that child porn thing in Merrick."

John placed a paper in front of me. I looked at it. I picked it up to read it, but the waitress came over. It was one of our fake emails.

"Are you ready to order?" She asked.

"I'll have the cheese omelet with bacon, toast, jelly and hash browns," John said.

"Eight eggs scrambled soft, six pieces of bacon, shred some cheddar cheese on the eggs, toast, jelly, and coffee. Shake some oregano on the eggs for me, please," I said.

"Oregano on eggs? I'll have to try it sometime. So, what have you learned?"

"That spices can enhance the flavor of eggs," I deadpanned.

"Mark. I need something."

"John. I told you my deal. I don't give you them until I have them all. Progress reports are fine. I've linked twelve men to my parents' murders. There are four more. If you want me to toss some scraps to you, I'll do that, but my mission is getting the people who killed my parents. It comes first. I don't work for you and once I get them and flip them to you and Nassau County, I'm done."

"You and I both know you won't be *done*. What are we looking at for a time frame?"

"For what, John?"

"To pass these guys to us."

"Look. I have a lot of good people working on this all of whom are contributing. I got twelve men identified so far. There are four more. Once I can put the info into usable bytes that you can understand, you'll be the second to know. I have uncovered more. I can tell you about how meth is coming into the Bronx. I can tell you all about how cocaine is coming in from Florida, Texas, and Arizona. I can tell you who killed that underboss in Chicago."

John's eyes got large at that revelation.

"I can tell you which container ship will leave with 150 stolen luxury automobiles headed for another continent via certain other countries. If I give you all this now it disturbs my goal. Just pay attention. I want you to pull DEA and Homeland off the big guys."

"Why?"

"Because they want to meet, but they're too concerned with all the people watching them.

The boobs at DEA and Homeland have their own agendas and, frankly, they're bullshit agencies that really get in the way of you guys and what I need to do."

Our order came. We fixed our food then started to eat. I caught the waitress as she turned to leave.

"A slice of apple pie, too, please."

John looked at me questioningly.

"I have a baseball bat, but no mom," I said.

John nodded. "What will these other families provide?"

"In addition to what I've previously discussed, adult sex slaves, kidnapping and rape, social security fraud, insurance fraud, Medicare and Medicaid fraud, and about fifty doctors and chiropractors who are full of shit from Maryland, Delaware, and New Jersey. Oh, and I wouldn't buy a timeshare in Miami. It's likely not there." I took a bite of my eggs. John ate his food.

"Do you plan to hit anyone?" John said.

I looked John dead in the eye. "No. If I must protect life I will kill, but I have no interest in assassination. When I hit them, they'll know it and they'll get to think about it for a long time. I don't plan to become well known, John. I'm Warren Zevon, a one-hit wonder. I risked discovery last week only for a little girl's life. This next op won't require that, I hope."

John ate and thought. "What will you do with that list?" John asked.

"It will be handled. You'll hear something, I'd guess, before Memorial Day."

I finished my second breakfast and started on my apple pie.

"Mark. I'll see what I can do about DEA and Homeland. Don't kill anyone."

"John, if I wanted to kill them, they'd already be dead, and I'd have tortured the other four names out of them. I'm a warrior not a cop. I don't work within civilian rules. If I was going to kill, I'd kill. This isn't a battlefield. I'm just using some skills I learned there to help me get where I need to be." I forked a bite of pie into my mouth.

"You eat a lot of apple pie, Mark."

"It's a long story. I'll tell you some time." I sipped my coffee. I looked at the time.

"Need to be somewhere?"

"Not yet. I already told you. Big meeting. The other brokerage houses get to meet me today. You know, finger sandwiches, punch, and petit fours, that type of crap," I said.

John sipped his coffee while he thought of another question.

"What are all your SEAL buddies doing here? Don't say reunion. That happened already."

"They are here to provide security to my family while I walk out to the pointy end of the spear to go after my parents' killers. They'll be gone in a couple of weeks to go back to train for more war."

The waitress refreshed my coffee and offered John who waved her off. I sipped my coffee. This date started out interesting enough, but it was quickly becoming dull.

"John. My ADHD is kicking in. Anything else, because I got a boatload of shit to do, and I only have so many hours in a day."

"What happened over on 5th Avenue last night at Ruggeri's?"

"I wish I knew more. I heard several brokers were meeting for some drinks. I'll meet the presidents or CEOs of some of those firms today, but I don't know any brokers outside of my firm. Anyway. I heard there was a fight, and a broker got his nose broken," I said.

"Mark. The guy died."

I know I was surprised at that news, but I didn't show it. "I didn't hear that. Shall I ask around?"

"Keep an ear out. The guy was beaten then stomped. He died just a few hours ago. We think these guys were related to the mob."

"I'll ask my broker-manager what he heard. Let me ask you was it about a deal? What caused that type of beating? Like I said, I understood it to be a drunken bar-brawl between a few securities brokers."

"We don't know. Witnesses described to NYPD a few men. NYPD is in process of trying to ascertain who the men are, and they'll be picked up for questioning."

Not good, I thought. I couldn't believe it. I had to protect Rizzo for a few more days to pull off my plan.

"I'll listen on the broker chat network, and I'll let you know if I hear anything."

"Okay. We're finished. You have a permit for that weapon, right?"

"That's a state matter, isn't it?" I replied.

Stayton was just letting me know he or one of his agents noticed my weapon.

"I'll be talking to you, John. Bye." I tossed a fifty on the table and departed.

#

I got back to the office at 12:10 p.m. due to traffic. Clara and Bernice had not gone to lunch yet. I sat down to try to think about which way I wanted to go first during my presentation when Matt walked in.

"You ready? This is your show," Matt said.

"I am. Did media produce that Power Point presentation for me?"

"It's all done and loaded on the computer, Clara said. They'll begin arriving soon so get yourself ready. Barbara and Clara will be near you if you need something. There will be twenty CEOs or presidents at the table. Their assistants will be sitting behind them along the wall."

"I'll be ready. Give me a few minutes."

#

Forty minutes later I was pressing the flesh with Matt introducing me to the presidents or CEOs of the twenty brokerage houses. My information showed that none of the firms were larger than ours, but with closely held companies that was hard to determine with precision. As a measure, our sales were 14% higher than the next closest firm. Some of these firms were only ten employee outfits. The total estimated combined annual sales revenue for the twenty-one firms was over $180 billion with estimated net profits of $5.45 billion.

I was not a schmoozer, but I knew I had to learn to become one to be in this business. Matt was a schmoozer. He had the affable talents of a used car salesman, a Jehovah witness and a

Girl Scout selling Do-si-dos all combined into one person. Matt could sell ice to Eskimos or sand to Arabs.

"Mark. This is Roland Gladwell. We went to NYU together. He's top dog at Gladwell Securities. That's his son over there at the buffet," Matt said.

"It's very nice to meet you, Mr. Gladwell. You have an impressive firm and you have really made this business what it is today," I said as we shook hands.

"I'm terribly sorry about your parents, Mark. Your father and I were competitors, but we were good friends. I'm very concerned about what you've discovered, and I hope we can fix it."

"I'll propose a fix today. Everyone here is in the same boat."

"I look forward to hearing your presentation, Mark."

"Thank you."

Matt moved me along to a woman who appeared to be about my mother's age. She had platinum-silver, blonde hair and she was well made up. She had a younger female assistant with her who was equally striking.

"Maggie. I want you to meet my nephew, Mark."

She extended her hand. "It's a pleasure to meet you, Mark. I can see your father in you," she said as she checked me out. "I've read over your syllabus for today. Interesting. I'd like to hear how you figured this out sometime. Where did you go to school before joining the navy?"

"Cornell."

"I see. Very nice. We miss your father. I'm sorry for you and your family."

"Thank you. Excuse me. Matt is moving me around. Oh. I guess I need to begin. Nice meeting you," I said.

"Welcome all. Please take your seats. Placards denote your place at the table."

The shuffling of chairs and people sitting was followed by silence and expectant looks at Matt. I stood to Matt's right. Clara and Barbara, who both, incidentally, looked stunning today, no doubt a securities firm fashion show thing, stood behind us. Tony stood off to the far right by the buffet, of course. At least he wasn't wearing sneakers.

"Thank you all for coming today. We spoke briefly about a dilemma we all share. You may thank my nephew for alerting us to this issue. Mark put together the evidence and I believe he came to the correct conclusion. We all share in this problem. Some of us are at greater risk than others. Mark has put together a plan. It will take cooperation from all of you to make it successful, but so long as we follow the plan, we will recover our investments and eliminate the risk of losing millions of dollars of our clients' money or our own money. Please let me introduce my nephew, Mark MacKenzie."

People clapped. I nodded and thanked them as I moved to the lectern. Clara turned on the flat screen TV behind me with the remote.

"Thank you all for coming. While learning my job here at MacKenzie Securities I stumbled across some information that didn't fit into the scheme of things. As you all now know after speaking with Matt, we share some uncomfortable characteristics. We hold various bonds issued by eighteen energy companies. They are listed on the screen behind me. The estimated value of the firms is indicated on the graph. While these companies are not Enron, WorldCom, or Madoff, when combined, and if left to their own devices, they can become a big problem for us, our investors and, I'd suppose, taxpayers if the past is an indication of the future regarding bailouts." I moved to the next graph.

"This is a hypothetical flow chart of what the evidence appears to show. Company X capitalizes with X dollars. I've indicated $30 million which is an educated guess at the low end of the scale based on deposit information that I've located. It could be more. That money from the initial bond holders—the mob—moved out the back door to the bond holders and was used to purchase bonds issued by Company Y. That same money moved out the back door to the original bond holders and was used to purchase bonds from Company Z and so on. That initial $30 to $50 million became $540 million to $900 million, perhaps more. Along the way, legitimate bond investors bought bonds and bonds were used as payment for closing services as some of you know. These companies began operations with this *seed* money. What these companies and their agents didn't do was disclosed shared employees, shared physical facilities, and shared officers. All these companies were incorporated in Nevada by the same man. This man." I put a picture of Farina on the screen.

"You all understand what these energy companies do. They buy excess electricity and natural gas and move it around the country to areas that require more energy which is a legitimate purpose. They have entered agreements with municipalities who, on their own, could not arrange for reasonably priced energy. These companies also took over billing for major energy producers. Here in Manhattan, for example, Consolidated Edison produces and distributes electrical power and natural gas to some 4.4 million customers. A company like Michigan Energy Cooperative comes along and says, 'We'll handle customer service, sign up new customers, bill them and pay you monthly.' Now over four million customer accounts become one account for ConEd. That's a savings of $24 million a year alone in postage assuming a monthly bill mailing. You can see how attractive this can be for large power companies. Their billing and associated personnel costs drop substantially. While not a dollar-for-dollar exchange since these energy companies make a profit, but all require on-line billing and if a customer does not agree to on-line billing, they're charged a service fee which more than covers personnel costs, postage and handling. These companies work both ends of the business. They sell surplus energy and reduce billing administration costs. What's not to like if you're ConEd or LIPA or another large power producer?

Back to the original bonds. You know what happened to them. They were sold—we sold them. Our due diligence showed revenues, bank accounts, contracts, and billing for millions of customers. Stock, while of little initial value, began to increase in value along with the frequency of trading and increase in financial strength of the companies. The stock is held mostly by the original incorporators and their families, though some is held by the public. The funds from the sale of the bonds still did not cover the value of the bonds issued that are out there. The interest paid on the bonds came from operations and borrowing and is being carried on their books as loan interest which is not in accordance with generally accepted accounting principles. To cover, they had to show good performance and increase the value of their stock. This would demonstrate to the Big Seven Banks what they needed to extend credit to these firms. Now with that credit line, redemption of the bonds could be accommodated without risk of the companies becoming illiquid. The companies could repurchase their stock, put enough into infrastructure and capital expenditures to appear to be growing. However, what one company did, so did the next and so on because there is only one company.

I've placed two letters on the screen. One from Iowa Energy and the other from Michigan Energy. I had a document expert look at the letters. Red circles highlight what I want to show you." I clicked to the next picture. "As you can see side by side the word *energy* on both letters was created by the same mechanical printing device." I clicked to a magnification of the same two letters to show the printing imperfections. "See the way the *e* is printed in each case. And on this Illinois Energy letter," I clicked to another letter and another and a last letter, "you can see that these six different companies printed letters on the same mechanical device though their mailing addresses are several states apart. I have examples showing similarities between all the companies letterhead."

I clicked to a picture of customer bills that showed the same similarities.

"Here are four bills from separate companies, yet they have the same imperfections."

I placed the incorporation documents on the screen with Farina's signature and the documents showing Farina's alias signatures.

"Mr. Farina has six aliases that we know of. Our investigation shows that bills, customer bill payments and business letters sent to each company go to post office drawers in various cities in different states. These drawers are emptied daily, the mail is boxed and overnighted to a location in Detroit. To this building," I clicked to a picture of the building, "that Mr. Farina purchased from the city of Detroit while it was in bankruptcy. Our investigators estimate that forty people comprise the workforce of the eighteen energy companies. Half are telephone sales staff who supervise contract telephone staff elsewhere around the country."

I put up a website picture with a white arrow pointing at the name of the website creator. "Niagara Media created this website." I clicked to the next picture showing another energy company website with a white arrow pointing at Niagara Media. "And this one, and this one and this one. All eighteen websites were created by Niagara Media." I clicked to a collage of all websites. "Our investigator spoke with the owner of Niagara Media. Farina was the sole contact for all companies.

Folks, we've been duped. I don't have to tell you how and by whom. You know by your discussions with my Uncle Matt. We all have people in our employ who work for the local crime families. I've compiled a list of those employees and we'll share that list once this operation is completed. I have identified the person or persons at each of your firms which I will pass to you as we begin the operation. Our goal is for our bond holders and us to be made whole. I have developed a plan that will permit us to recover our funds and put these companies into bankruptcy. It will take coordination on our part."

I clicked to another document.

"I drafted 20 some odd opinions as to our beliefs in the future performance of these energy companies. All the companies are listed. Notice the safe-haven and not-yet-ready-for-public-disclosure language in each opinion. These memos, advice notes and emails will be disclosed to the bad guys in each of our firms. No one else. I've compiled a creative list of means to get the word out. I expect that these people will disclose our opinions to their principles, and this will in turn cause them to purchase more stock driving the price of the stock upward. Most, if not all the purchases are made on margin. It being early in the month, it would not be unusual for large margin purchases. We will allow this to go on for three full business days. When the stock market closes Friday we will begin redeeming our bonds since that market remains open another hour based on Chicago's Central Time Zone. The companies will not have the liquidity to redeem all the bonds forcing them to use their reserves or lines of credit. But we will recover our funds. Over the weekend the chat rooms and financial boards will talk up what happened and by Monday we will all issue degraded opinions of these companies which will force a decline in stock value. The stocks will likely crash because of the combination of bond redemptions and poor opinion advice as they are traded and sold. The stock brokerage houses will call their margins due, and the banks will want their loans repaid. Of course, that cannot happen as the funds will not be there. The banks and stock brokerage houses will move to seize property securing the debts."

I paused and sipped my water. Whispering discussions took place. I remained quiet to allow them to formulate their questions. After a few minutes, they quieted down and looked at me expectantly.

"Now, I'll take your questions. Sir."

A distinguished looking, older gentleman stood. I put my hand up.

"I'm sorry. I don't know all of you yet. If you'd kindly state your name before your question, it would help me."

"Yes, sir. William Spalding, Spalding Investments. Won't these guys simply shore-up their accounts with their hidden cash and other accounts?"

"If they could. I think some of you may know this. The mob has been laundering money a little at a time. Most of your deals with these companies closed with multiple negotiable instruments—several checks, money orders and wire transfers. That money came from hundreds, perhaps thousands of accounts that were pyramid deposits up to the final accounts— all amounts less than $10,000. Most less than $5000. They couldn't react fast enough to cover those accounts. What about cash? Even if they had it they could not use that to shore up their holdings without suspicious activity reports being filed."

"This is all legal?"

"Of course. I just identified a problem with either your investment or your clients' investments. While you have no duty to protect yourself, unless you count your obligation as an officer to the other shareholders in your firm, you have an obligation to protect your clients. The distribution of internal disclosures of not-yet-for-public-dissemination opinions illegally used by criminals who are insider trading is also not illegal. Moreover, it helps us. It insures that the funds become available to support the repurchase of the bonds. Our public opinions as to the poor character of the companies are constitutionally protected speech since we'll have no stock in any of the companies. We'd be doing a public service and, what we'll say will be truthful," I said.

"What about the banks' money? I'm sorry. Patricia Barkley, P.B.B. Securities."

"What about them? They will have the property securing the loans and they can immediately freeze all the accounts related to these companies and their officers. The banks have E&O insurance and loss coverage insurance. Lastly, our government will bail them out if it got *too big to fail*. I doubt it will since we're only talking about several billion dollars. A big deal for us, but small potatoes for the Big Seven."

"What about the stockholders?" Patricia asked.

"The stockholders who purchase on insider information. So, what. Other stockholders? Well, they didn't do their due diligence. If they buy on the rapid climb of the stock, which is always a bad idea, then they assume the risk. Who else?"

"Ezra Skakle, Infinity Bonds. Who will coordinate this?"

"I will with my staff and some experts who I've hired with assistance from your firms. Perhaps these nice quiet people sitting behind you. Secrecy is paramount," I said as they all laughed.

Discussion ensued. I sipped my water and looked over to Barbara and Clara who were smiling at me. After several minutes a gentleman stood and raised his hand.

"Bill Montgomery, Billmont Securities. What's to prevent anyone of us from jumping the gun and selling before Friday's closing?"

461

"Nothing. Well, that's not exactly true. If we detect any of you selling before the planned time, I will notify the other firms. Obviously, our effect on the mob will be less, the energy companies could survive and many of us might lose money on the bonds. Should any of you breach our agreement, you would no longer enjoy doing business with this firm. I don't speak for the rest of you; however, I suspect there would be hard feelings. I did draft an agreement to bind our handshake. It contains a liquidated damages clause for failing to adhere to the agreement if that would make everyone more comfortable."

I placed the document on the table.

"Slide it over here young man. Manifest Destiny Securities is in."

"So is my firm."

And within a short time, every person in the room had signed the agreement. I watched Maggie sign the agreement. She turned and walked to me and handed me a card.

"This is my assistant's card. She'll work with your people. Here's my card. When this is over, call me. I'd like to get to know you over drinks and dinner some time," she said.

I'd never been afraid in my life, but now I knew the feeling.

"Thank you. I'm flattered," I said as Matt made big eyes like I'd scored a homerun. Tony saw and heard Maggie, too, and made his standard big eyes and goofy face. After another half hour of small talk and lining up contacts, they group departed. It was nearly 4 p.m.

#

462

"Bernice. Can you ask Robert, Clara, Barbara, Tony, Steve, and Ira to come to my office please?"

"Yes, sir."

"All right. We will be doing some things to protect our investments and to bring down some bad guys. Some of you know more than others. This will take some coordination." I passed out a sheet of paper with timelines and milestones on it. "At 5 p.m. today the operation begins. Steve. You and Robert will coordinate with this list of people here." I passed Steve a list of contacts for the other firms. "At 5 p.m. Clara will accidently include Rizzo as a blind copy of an email from Matt to me, Marsha, Ira and marketing. I will follow with a cautionary reply email saying *wait*. Barbara will accidently drop a copy of a memo next to the copy machine by Rizzo's door. It will be a proposed memo for public release as to the performance of two of the energy companies. Similar accidental releases will occur at other firms to their known moles. This will go on until Friday afternoon. These other two will have information disclosed to them by inadvertent slips of the tongue in their presence or a loose sticky pad note falling off a document in front of them or near their offices or desks. In all some eight to twelve disclosures will be made to these people.

Tony, with Steven's help, I want you to obtain all electronic communications about these disclosures. Ira. You need to make clear that any client advise about these companies does not leave the firm. We cannot bring in all the brokers and their secretaries and assistants, so you need to make sure you control what goes on the next three days."

"I got it, Mark. No problem," Ira said.

"Clara and Barbara, you will assist Robert and the other firms. Their questions or concerns pass to me immediately if you cannot fix it. The next six days will be scripted to make sure we're successful. Is everyone clear? Nearly a billion dollars rides on this part of the plan. Rob, are you good to go?"

"Yeah. Tony will back me along with the techs at the loft. We already had twenty of those plaintiffs from that list you handed me today. Audrey and her firm are drafting the civil actions. Most will be filed in Nassau County, and the rest spread over the boroughs and New Jersey. We will have a complete list Friday," Rob said.

"Tony. What am I forgetting?" I said.

"You got it. You could order some pizza. Oh. Kev and Mikey disappeared."

"They'll be back this evening. They had something to do."

"That's why I'm hungry. With those guys around, they're always eating," Tony said.

"Steve?"

"Good to go, Mark. We'll make it happen."

"Ladies are you ready?"

"We have our overnight bags with us in case we need to stay tonight to coordinate. Your office, the adjoining offices and the small conference room will be locked. They've been rekeyed. You, Bernice, Robert, Barbara, and I have the only keys."

"Good. Okay. Any problems you need help with, call me. Keep this secret. Good luck to all of you. I've got to run."

#

I got into my car and headed east. I put on my satellite communications and called LT.

"LT. What's our status?"

"We're ready. Land assets are in place. Route and location are familiar to all. Target is at home. He just arrived, having come from his office in Jericho. He's currently in his study on the phone. We've seen or heard several confirmations that a meeting will occur at Vincenzo's house at 8 p.m. Farina said so to his wife. Our transportation is up, fuel topped off and your coxswain has been practicing. We are ready to go in plus five."

"Fine. I'm enroute and my ETA is seventy-eight minutes."

"Roger. Dinner is started."

"Thanks. Out."

I called Joe.

"Hey. We good tonight?"

"Yeah. What will happen is if it goes shitty you let me know. I'll call my guy to tell him. The fact is they don't do much up there. Dave said nothing is scheduled up that way. If a problem materializes, we'll call him."

"Good. The FBI agreed to pull DEA and Homeland out of the area and away from the big guys. I expect a meeting any day now."

"Okay. You headed home?"

"I'm on the L.I.E. I just entered Nassau."

"Good luck tonight."

"Thanks. We'll be careful."

#

I pulled into our compound. An extra SUV and my BMW motorcycle were out again. I parked in the garage. I'd noticed the FBI guy parked across the street so that would make it easy for me to carry my gear to the house. I grabbed by bags and walked the beach to the house. I walked up the back steps, dropped my bags on the deck and went inside.

"Hello, Mark," Grandma said.

"Hi."

LT, Talbot and Surfer were already digging into plates of food. Haley walked up to me with Lauren and Kimberly.

"Hi, sailor. I'm told you're going fishing tonight."

"We are."

My grandfather rolled his eyes.

"Let me get you a plate," Haley said smirking at me.

"Thanks. I'm just going to change really fast."

"Okay. I'll wait for you," Haley said.

I dashed upstairs, undressed, and dressed in black and dark charcoal grey tactical clothing and lightweight boots. I checked my Sig Sauer P226, placed it in a tactical holster on my waist along with a tactical knife. I grabbed my blacked-out Yankee ball cap. I put cash, my license and a credit card in a waterproof container and put it in my pocket. I grabbed my grey camo jacket and combo LED light and headed downstairs.

"Hi. Looks good," I said as I accepted a plate from Haley.

She looked at me as if to ask a question and I shook her off. Dinner was pork loin, cornbread, baked beans, greens, and coleslaw.

"So, tomorrow is the day. You'll be a free woman back on the market," I said.

"I'll be divorced. I'm going steady with you even though I still don't have a decoder ring," Haley said as she smiled at me.

"What's a decoder ring?" Lauren asked.

"In the 1960s and 1970s they were rings with 3-D graphics, imprints, or other secrets stamped on or in them. They came in cereal boxes or from gumball machines. Young boys would give them to girls they liked, and it meant they were going steady," Grandpa chimed in.

"How do you know about decoder rings, Ms. Menduni?" Lauren asked.

"Mark said he'd get me one the other night, but I already knew about decoder rings."

I looked at my watch. Time to go. I guzzled a protein drink then, to Haley's surprise, a cola and I ate a few Oreo cookies.

"What's got into you?" Haley asked.

"He always eats a sugar fix just before . . . well, before we go out," Talbot said catching himself. Haley looked at me.

"You continue to surprise me, Mr. MacKenzie," Haley said. I winked at her.

"We will be back late so don't wait up. I'll see you in the morning, General. Let's go guys."

#

We loaded and were underway for the Long Island Sound. We had to first head east around Orient Point then west to our objective. LT had selected a waypoint at the intersection of the jurisdictional boundaries of Nassau County, Suffolk County and Connecticut as our turn bearing into Oyster Bay. Talbot was driving and doing well at operating the boat. We set a speed over ground of thirty-five knots. The voyage would take just over two hours. We passed from the bay into Long Island Sound between Orient Point and Plum Island. Talbot set the autopilot.

"Check your equipment. LT, contact Team Two and let them know we're enroute."

"Aye, sir."

I watched the helm while Talbot checked his equipment.

"We're ready," Talbot said speaking for himself and both officers.

"You have the conn," I said.

We were chasing the sun and the sun was winning as it sank further and further over the horizon. It was a terrific evening. I wished I was running the boat with Haley on a nice cruise.

We just had satellite communications up. We removed the batteries from our cell phones. I looked at my watch. An hour and a half to go before we arrived at our turn point.

In Afghanistan, we flew all over the country in Black Hawks, Sea Hawks and Chinooks. I always tried to get a 20-minute nap or *nooner* as we called them in the navy. I'd put ear plugs in my ears under my communication headset, pull my wooly-pully hat over top and take a nap. I'd be refreshed when I awoke. I'd pop four Excedrin and sip a bottle of water while in the helo, so I didn't use my on-board supply in my Camelback.

Long Island Sound was calm with just a slight breeze making small wavelets. The boat bounced in a slow, porpoising motion as we skipped over the slight, following swell. The wind blew from the southeast, so it was warming up. I withdrew a satellite picture of Farina's house to look at which had an architectural blueprint superimposed over it. Nice old house. I was hoping we didn't have to go in it. If Farina arrived home before we were in place or if we couldn't get into place as planned, we might have to go in to snatch him. If he was in his study, it would be easy, but elsewhere it would be a problem with his wife around. I wanted to grab him without anyone else knowing and release him before he was missed. I rehearsed the op in my head a hundred times like back in Iraq and Afghanistan. I looked at my watch again. Still over an hour to go. It was good to be back on the water. It's where SEALs are supposed to be. I closed my eyes for a quick nooner.

#

I awoke to a night sky. I looked at my watch. Almost time to turn. The night was a brown-grey-black. The shore lights of Connecticut to the north and Long Island to the south lighted our way to the huge glow in the south-western sky which was New York City. I imagined there where children living in New York who'd never seen the stars at night.

"Mark. Two miles to our turn," Talbot said.

"LT. Target status?" LT called Team Two.

I removed my FLIR monocular and looked around. Some small cruisers and fishing boats were some distance from us. A coastal crude carrier chugged along to the north by Belle Haven or Old Greenwich, Connecticut. If I concentrated, I could see my grandparents' home on the hill overlooking Long Island Sound in Rye, New York. That was our alternative escape point. We'd run northwest, swing into the small bay, anchor, and swim ashore to their house. Their home was less than eight miles from our next waypoint.

We reached the waypoint and turned south. Talbot took us off autopilot and dimmed the navigation and console lights as we entered the bay. I looked at our track on the GPS to the target's home. We were less than five miles away. In two miles, we'd slow, just maintaining a plane then at two miles out, just as we turned southwest, we'd slow to no wake. We'd hold about a mile from the dock we planned to use until we had confirmation that the target was leaving Glen Cove. The distance from Glen Cove to the house in Oyster Bay was about six miles as the crow flies or nearly eight miles by road, with a slow speed area through the village of Locust Valley.

Like many of the smaller homes on mansion grounds on the Gold Coast, this home's front facade faced the main mansion though it was closer to the water. A driveway traced along the outer edge of the property then curved around the house past a circular turnaround in front of the home, to a garage at the rear of the home. The garage faced the water. Farina's habit was to park parallel to the garage doors on the north side of the driveway. A hedgerow that grew along the driveway, northwest to southeast at that point, obscured a view of the bay. Another hedgerow to the west obscured the garbage can area and continued along to the pool deck to the west which also obscured a view of the bay. Basically, the way the hedgerows and spruce trees were placed, Farina's house was well isolated from the rest of the estate.

I searched with my FLIR scope looking at Farina's house now just two miles away. The light in the study was on. An upstairs light was on, likely the master bedroom. We knew from the OCTF file that Farina's wife usually went to bed at 9 p.m. but left the television on. Farina's daughter, a college graduate, drove a red BMW convertible. She came and went, as young adults of that age tend to do. Being a weeknight, she could be home with her mother or out with her friends. She parked her car in the garage next to her mother's car.

"Mark. They're still meeting."

"Roger. We'll wait where we planned. Talbot, you can hold it or place us on dynamic positioning and the boat will hold a position set on the integrated GPS."

"Aye, sir."

We were just making bare steerageway. The boat hardly left a ripple in its wake as it inched forward. The boat was so quiet I could not hear the engines over our breathing, radar antenna motor and the surrounding noise.

I counted forty boats swinging on buoys. Sailboats, cruisers, runabouts, speedboats, and fishing boats of every kind. On the east shore of the small bay were more boats swinging on buoys. I saw one small fishing boat going out. I made out three men aboard through my FLIR scope.

Surfer prepared the water board, a polypropylene plastic backboard used for an EMT stretcher. It had plenty of handholds and Velcro straps. We would immobilize the target, place him on the board, then strap him in.

471

I sipped a water. I noticed that the guys brought protein and energy bars for the mission. We wouldn't expend much energy if we did this right. We'd been hovering in position for the better part of an hour. My satcoms earphone sounded with Kev's voice.

"Paul Menduni and two guys are getting into a black Lincoln SUV. I heard Paul Menduni tell his driver to go to the restaurant," Kev said.

A moment later Kev made another report.

"The other guy . . . Pagano it looks like, is leaving. He's getting into a black Escalade SUV. He's alone like he arrived," Kev said.

That was good. Pagano lived in the house on the opposite side of the property. He'd be in his house by the time Farina arrived home.

"Joe just called. They heard Vincenzo say good night to Farina. The door just opened. I have the target in sight. He's getting into his black Audi; the same car he arrived in. No one is with him. I've confirmed eyes on target. He's alone. We're moving to our second OP. Confirm target moving and is headed east to Locust Valley," Kev said.

"Shall we?" I said to Talbot who took us off hover and we inched forward. The pier ran from northeast to southwest, perpendicular to the dock on the shore that ran from northwest to southeast. Our plan was to nose up to the dock, turn starboard side to, and hold our position. Surfer, LT, and I would debark and take our positions. Surfer would hide in the hedgerow by the wall. He would only be visible from Talbot's position on the boat. I would take a position next to the house near the garage.

I was the blocker if Farina went for the house. I would also provide the covering fire if we got a visitor coming up the road. LT would snatch Farina from behind while Surfer came at Farina in front. We covered our faces with black and green camo grease and put on our tactical gloves. I was wearing a SIG Sauer on my right thigh, my M-4 was slung over my shoulder. I had a shot gun loaded with rubber bullets in the event I needed to incapacitate someone. We each carried flash-bangs.

Talbot inched us to the pier and up to the dock with three of us wearing NVGs or an FLIR monocular looking and listening. We nudged the dock bumper. Three of us jumped the gunwale and ran to our positions. Surfer arrived first, LT second and me last as I had furthest to run. I dashed across the open driveway into the bushes by the side of the garage. I looked through a window into the garage. It contained just a Mercedes-Benz, Farina's wife's car. The daughter's BMW was out. I walked further out to the southeast to view the gate house and the back window of the master bedroom. The glow of a television lighted the bedroom. The gate house was lighted, but no one was outside it.

I returned to my position. I could see our boat and just make out Talbot with his M-40 sniper rifle. It was a little eerie looking at a sniper rifle roughly aimed at you. Talbot waved at me. Show-off! The move signal would be given after the door to Farina's car closed and locked. We didn't need to chance him seeing or hearing us then jumping into his car and sounding the alarm.

"Commander. I got a Rottweiler. It's a hundred yards to the west of the house. It's walking toward the house to the far west of the estate," Talbot said.

"Roger. Pagano's dog. Pagano will be here any minute, so the dog will likely run to him. Keep an eye on it," I said.

"Roger."

Just what one needs, one hundred forty pounds of muscle and teeth just as we snatch someone.

"Team two at second OP. Pagano is entering the estate. He's at the gate house," Kev said.

"Roger."

"He's rolling through the estate. He turned left after the gate house."

"Roger. Conn. Watch the dog," I said.

"He's got his head in the air and he's excited. He just ran toward the far west house."

"Roger. Keep an eye on him."

"Farina just got onto the straight away road to the west of the estate. I see headlights, too.

ETA to the gate house, one minute," Kev said.

There was enough light to see without my NVGs. A bright light from the mansion and other lights atop poles along the east fence line helped light the area but also hid areas beyond the light cast making that area darker. I looked through my FLIR scope at the gate. Two men were walking to the gate. It was open. I swept to the right. My view of the road Pagano had just driven was obscured by a hedgerow and the mansion.

I'd once read a novel where a gorgeous, naked, ginger-haired woman with perfect breasts, rode a white horse across a

Gold Coast estate like this one. I'd like to see that some time. Funny what you think of on an op.

"Target is pulling up to the gate," Kev reported.

"Roger." I had a visual on the target.

"Conn. Where's the dog?"

"I don't have it. I haven't seen it since the SUV arrived."

"Roger. Watch for it."

"Roger."

The Audi drove through the gate. I watched the gate slowly close, and the two security guys return to the gate house.

"Security has returned to the gate house," Kev reported.

"Roger."

I looked at my watch. 11 p.m. The Audi quickly covered the distance to the house.

"All clear?" I said.

"Clear."

"Clear."

"Conn, clear."

"Team Two, clear."

"The op is a go," I said.

The Audi swung around the road to the left fork. I could feel its headlights on me, sense the heat from its engine and smell the burn of diesel fuel. The car slowed and pulled to the right to his usual parking spot. It's brake lights burst on, illuminating the hedgerow and wall in red light. The engine stopped. Suddenly, it was quiet and dark. Just as suddenly, the door clicked open, and the car's interior dome light came on which I'd warned the guys to be prepared for so our night vision was not destroyed. The door slammed shut with a solid thud followed by the chime of the automatic locks.

Surfer and LT moved.

"Clear. No dog," Talbot said.

I moved to block Farina's escape to the house. LT came from behind Farina, knocking his briefcase from his hand and putting him in sleeper hold. Surfer hit Farina in the gut to expel the air from his lungs. Farina was down. I viewed the area toward the gate through my M-4 scope. The guys tossed Farina over Surfer's shoulder and hurried to the boat. I picked up the briefcase and ran after them covering our flank.

"Clear?" I said.

"All clear," Talbot said.

I heard them put Farina on the boat as the engines started. I looked off to the east as I ran north onto the dock. No one followed us. As I was about to step aboard Talbot suddenly raised his suppressed SIG Sauer at me and fired two shots. I heard a thwack and mush sound followed by a whimper. I turned to see the Rottweiler on the dock.

"Sorry, Mark. I didn't have time to warn you. It came out of nowhere," Talbot said.

"Shit! I thought you were shooting me. Hold on." I placed the briefcase and my weapons aboard. I picked up the dog and put it aboard. Talbot inched us away from the dock.

"Strap him in. Slow and easy out."

Surfer and LT strapped Farina to the board while I cut off the dog's collar and tossed it overboard next to the dock in case it carried a GPS. Talbot moved us through the buoy field.

"Team Two. Pack is in the mail. You are secured," I said.

"Roger. Wilco. Everyone okay?" Kev asked.

"Roger that."

"Roger. Team Two." We wouldn't need them the rest of the night.

LT pulled Farina's cell phone, downloaded the data, then removed the battery. I went through the briefcase as Surfer went through Farina's pockets. We were checking for signaling devices or GPS trackers. We tossed his pens, glasses, and jewelry overboard, just to be sure, then his shoes. Then we went through his jacket, pants, shirt and searched him. I dumped the contents of his briefcase onto the deck and tossed the briefcase overboard. Farina was completely immobilized on the board. We covered him with a black blanket to ensure no prying eyes in the sky could view him.

We exited Oyster Bay and traveled northeast at five knots, like most of the other traffic in the area which seemed to be fishing boats. Surfer looked west and north, I looked east and south. LT stuck a gag over Farina's mouth. Talbot increased our speed heading to a waypoint set on the chart plotter.

"Wake him," I said.

LT broke an ampule under Farina's nose. Momentarily he awoke, of course all he could do was hear and smell. I spoke to him in Farsi-accented English.

"We're far enough offshore. Stop. We'll dump them here," I said.

Surfer splashed the dead dog. Farina struggled and fought against his restraints clearly in a panic.

"Open the side door and we'll slide this one out."

The boat has a hull access door for swimming or pulling large fish aboard. Surfer tied a rope to the board and made it fast to a cleat. LT and Surfer slid the board through the door as I checked Surfer's knot to be sure we didn't lose our guest. They slowly slipped Farina over the water when the board suddenly upended and sunk headfirst into the Sound. Surfer only let it go up to the rope before he yanked it back up and we hauled Farina back aboard. Talbot kept an eye on the radar for approaching vessels.

LT and Surfer put the board head down at a forty-five-degree angle and removed Farina's gag. I held the saltwater washdown hose in one hand and a water-resistant digital recorder in my other.

"Do you wish to live?" I said in detached, Farsi-accented English.

"Yes, yes, yes. Who are you guys?" Farina said out of breath as LT covered his face with a wet towel and I turned on the water. Farina tried to struggle. It was much less taxing waterboarding someone with the guest of honor strapped to a board. I released the nozzle. Farina gasped and choked.

"I will ask questions. If you refuse to answer, we'll kill you and dump you into the sea like Pagano," I said.

"Yes. I'll tell you what you want to know," Farina said.

"What do you do for the Menduni family?"

"I'm an advisor and I'm listed as president or CEO of several of their companies. I'm Vincenzo Menduni's advisor or *consiglieri*."

"What was the meeting about at a Vincenzo Menduni's estate this evening?"

"His son, Paulie, lost over $60 million that he was supposed to safe keep for the family. We were trying to determine what he knew."

"What businesses do the Menduni's own?"

Farina rattled off about 50 businesses.

"Where are the family's financial accounts located?"

"All the top banks in the US, Canada, Switzerland, Grand Cayman, Nevis, Belize, Ecuador, Columbia and Singapore."

"How many people has the Menduni family killed in the past five years?"

"I don't know."

I nodded at LT who clamped the towel over Farina's nose as I squirt water on him. Farina struggled. I let it go on for a solid minute before I stopped.

"Let's try that again. How many people has the Menduni family killed in the last five years?" I said.

"I'm not sure. I can name 12."

"Name them."

Farina named my parents and ten more people.

"Who ordered the deaths of these people?"

"Romeo Menduni. Sometimes with the blessing of the council—the other New York families."

"All twelve?"

"Yes."

"Why were they killed? You named a husband and wife or brother and sister couple. William MacKenzie and Elizabeth MacKenzie. What did the woman do to get killed?"

"She didn't do nothing. That was an accident. Elizabeth MacKenzie was William's wife. We don't do that. That whole hit was wrong."

"Why?"

"MacKenzie may have double-crossed the family, but we, Vincenzo and me, had our doubts."

"What was the double-cross about?"

"We have some corporations that aren't exactly legit. Our guy tried to sell some bonds through MacKenzie's firm and MacKenzie caught him."

"How did MacKenzie double-cross you?"

"The bonds our guy tried to sell were supposed to be returned along with some cash to our guy and they were not. At least that's what they say. They think William MacKenzie kept them, but I'm not sure that's the right story because I wasn't in on the decision."

"Who is your guy?"

"I don't know who it is. Someone who's been at MacKenzie's firm for a while. Someone who knows about the bonds and the transactions."

"Is that person involved in the decision to kill the MacKenzies?" I asked.

"I think so. He was not consulted in the original discussion or by email, but it's clear he knew about it."

"Who else was involved in the decision to kill the MacKenzies?"

"About fifteen people were involved based on the emails I viewed. I don't know all the people involved, but it was fifteen email addresses and the sender so sixteen people."

"What are you talking about?"

"We operate like a corporation. The council, like a board, must approve what the boss wants to do especially for a civilian like MacKenzie. The case was made to the other families and Romeo ordered it. Though Romeo could order it on his own, but he is supposed to inform the other families."

"Did the other families agree?"

"I am not sure. I don't know who some of the email addresses belong to. What I do know is that eight other email addresses were included in the final order that don't belong to Vincenzo's or his father's family. They belonged to capos or lieutenants or others in the other families is my guess."

"Who? What families?"

"The Bagatelli, Rapoli, Terrazzo, and Carlucci families—the other New York families."

"Who gave the order to kill these two?"

"No one authorized the wife that I know of. I assume Romeo Menduni did since his guys did it. The order came from one of Romeo's email addresses."

"Who else outside of the officers were involved?"

"The two who did it. The two in the second car who followed the first car, and another guy at MacKenzie's firm."

"Name the board or council and the officers of each corporation involved."

Farina named them including Rizzo.

"All these people authorized these murders?"

"For the most part, yes. I've been talking about the MacKenzies, but the others were straight up business. I'm pretty sure the people involved here plus others authorized those hits."

"You didn't name Vincenzo Menduni. Why?"

"He abstains from all of that stuff. He's not involved as far as I know."

"Who do you work for?"

"Originally, Romeo Menduni. Now, mostly for Vincenzo, but Romeo has me doing things for him, too. It makes it hard because father and son do not agree on anything and have different visions as to managing the companies."

"If I kill you like I killed Pagano, then kill Romeo and Vincenzo, who takes over?"

"That would be hard to say. Dino Ferrara is a likely heir. He's a loyal capo, but not too good with some of the businesses. Paul Menduni would try to take over, but he's an idiot. He'd be lucky his grandfather doesn't make an exception and whack him. The smartest guy left is Rizzo. He's new school, educated and trusted by Romeo. He does the dirty work and business. The last name I gave you he did."

"You say Rizzo carried out a hit?"

"Yeah. He's done a few for Romeo. He made that last one look like a barroom brawl got out of hand. The guy died today."

"Why was that guy hit?"

"Someone is screwing around with our investments and email. They thought it was that guy."

"Who's they?"

"Romeo, his capo Frank Dinapoli, Paul Menduni, and Rizzo."

"Who does Rizzo work for?"

"Romeo Menduni. He used to do stuff for Vincenzo. He also takes orders from me for Romeo."

"I could drop you over the side like Pagano. Why should I let you live?"

"Look. I got three kids. My daughter just graduated college, and my boys are away at school. I've been trying to figure a way out of this business without getting killed. I've been trying to work for just Vincenzo, but the old man keeps working me. I don't trust none of the younger guys or Romeo. I think they'd kill my family. It's not like it used to be. There are no rules anymore with these young guys and Romeo is nuts. What do you want from me?"

I looked up at LT and Surfer. They smiled and nodded.

"You will work for me. I will contact you. Do not confuse me with the American FBI. I will kill you if you do not do as I ask as Allah wills it. Do you understand me?"

"Yes."

"If you breathe a word of this to anyone, I will come for you at night. You cannot get away from me. Am I clear?" Farina hesitated and I kicked him in the right side. Farina laid there gasping for air. I motioned to place him horizontally on the stern bench.

"No! No! I'll cooperate," Farina said.

"Quiet. I'm placing you horizontal. I'm going to put you back where we found you. Fuck with me and I will email our little conversation to the council. Tonight, you go home like nothing happened. If anyone was looking for you, you were sipping Scotch. You do drink Scotch? All you Infidels drink."

"Yes."

"You were drinking Scotch at the pier and fell in. If you don't do what I direct the children of that beautiful daughter of yours will never see their grandfather. You will be contacted. What are you doing tomorrow?"

"I have work to do at the funeral home. Then I'm to try to get the families together for a meeting. We had a meeting set then it fell through. I have additional business, but I'm not sure what that will be about, with some members of another family."

"Can you see people at the funeral home?"

"No. Too many people who don't work for me are there. I have an office in Locust Valley, but the feds bugged it and watch it. I have an office in the city, but I rarely go there to work unless we have something going on in the city. I work at home or at Vincenzo's house or the funeral home."

"I'll contact you." I nodded at Talbot who set a reciprocal course to the entrance to the bay.

"Hood him and take him off the board," I said.

LT and Surfer released Farina and sat him on the stern seat, hooded, and cuffed.

"Pagano is at his home alive. I didn't want you to act surprised when you see him. If I tell you to cooperate with the Americans, will you?"

"Yes."

"You will go about your business as usual. I will contact you. Double cross me and we'll take another boat trip but tow you behind the boat next time."

We entered the bay and motored slowly to the property making bare steerageway. The wind had shifted and was now coming out of the northeast. It was dark and becoming foggy. As we approached the dock, I put Farina's cell phone in his pocket with the battery.

"We will walk you to your driveway and release you. You will go into your home. Here are your keys." I put his keys in his pocket.

We gently nudged the dock bumper. We lifted Farina over the gunwale onto the dock and walked him to his driveway. I removed his cuffs.

"Don't take the hood off for five minutes."

"Company! A woman to the left," Talbot said.

The woman didn't see me until I moved, grabbed her, and clamped my hand over her mouth.

"Mr. Farina. Your daughter just happened upon the scene. Tell her it's all right. I have her in my grasp with my hand over her mouth. I don't want to hurt her," I said.

"Angelina! It's all right. Don't do or say anything. It may not look like it right now, but these men are going to help us get out of this. Don't say anything," Farina said.

I was looking into the frightened eyes of a beautiful, twenty-three-year-old woman.

"Angelina. I will release my grip. If you struggle, I'll disable you. I'm going to let your father hold you. You are to walk your father to the door. Do not look back. Nod your head if you understand." She nodded. I released my grip over her mouth and moved her to her father. Angelina looked me in the eye then at Surfer and LT. She was very frightened.

"Go inside. This never happened. Go!" I said. Angelina startled at my command. She hugged her father to her as she walked him to the door.

We were several hundred yards away, the boat moving quietly through the anchorage, when I saw the back door open, and Angelina look in our direction. We were into the fog as we motored away.

#

Team Two, Team One. Op secured. Romeo-tango-bravo," I said.

"Roger, Team One. Good work. Team Two, out."

"Talbot show these fine officers how to conn a high-tech boat like this and take us home. Good work guys. Talbot, I'm buying you one first. That dog would have hurt."

"Aye, sir," Talbot said as he increased the throttles and headed us east.

I poured four shots and passed out cigars. We had a nice run home. Good cigars, fine bourbon, and great buddies. We arrived home at 0345. We put the boat away and cleaned up a little before going to bed. I text Haley, *"All is good. Good luck today. Love M."*

CHAPTER 17

I awoke to the sounds and smells of my grandmother's cooking. It was nearly 8 a.m. I should have closed the curtains. I was still tired, but I got up, showered, shaved, dressed in my other Varvatos suit. I looked at myself in the mirror. I looked fine.

The other guys were still sleeping when I came downstairs.

"Good morning," I said.

"Well, look who's up?" Grandma said.

My grandfather looked at me over the paper. "Call Matt. He's wondering when you'll be in," Grandpa said.

"I will. I have everything covered."

My grandmother put a western omelet in front of me with toast and coffee.

"Mission successful?" Grandpa asked.

"OPSEC, Grandpa. We'll talk later."

"Oh, don't be such a fuddy-duddy. It's your grandmother. If they kidnapped her to extract secrets, they'd just send her back frustrated," Grandpa deadpanned.

My grandmother feigned indignation.

"It was successful. No KIA or MIA."

"Good. What's got Matt so hyper?"

"Matt. I cut people out of my coms because we have a mole at the firm."

"Rizzo?"

"No. Someone else. Our guest last night confirmed my suspicions and said specifically it was someone else."

"Could he have been lying?"

"No. I'm fairly persuasive," I said.

My grandfather nodded.

"I cut out all non-essential personnel and I'm the only one who knows everything."

"Can I ask what's the status of Op Trident?"

"It's begun. The other firms all signed on. The disinformation has started. Today should be an easy day for me since everyone else is doing what they should do."

"There's an SUV and a car parked across the street. FBI?"

"I guess. I think they'd like to know what I know. I just spoke with them yesterday."

I drank my coffee. I heard the guys coming up the stairs. Grandma started more omelets.

"Morning guys," I said.

"Morning, Mark. Good morning, General, ma'am," LT said for the three of them.

"My grandparents will pump you for details of what we did last night. Ignore them. I'm shopping for an assisted living home for them," I said.

Grandma laughed. Grandpa frowned.

"You guys know what you must do. I gotta go," I said.

"Okay, Mark. Bye," LT said.

I walked to my car in the garage and drove off. The FBI SUV followed me. I drove fast until the turnoff to Haley's house. I slowed, turned, and drove to her home. Her car was in the driveway. I pulled up next to it, parked, walked to the door, and knocked. Haley opened the door with a surprised look on her face.

"Hi. I was passing by and thought I'll be going by the courthouse in Nassau and the woman I love must be there today. Court is always stressful, so I thought that perhaps she needed my support more than anything else I needed to do. I'd like to be there for you, to have your back, while you go through that garbage."

Haley's eyes welled up with tears as she pulled me to her. "Thank you, Mark. Thank you," Haley said.

I saw Evelyn standing behind Haley.

"My mother was going with me, but I know she's stressing, too."

"Then I relieve you, ma'am. I was briefed by an attorney as to what will happen. You'll be asked questions, I'll be asked a few questions as your witness, and Paul will be asked questions. I can handle it," I said. Haley hugged me again.

"Mom, I have my white knight going with me," Haley said.

"Good. Thank you, Mark," Evelyn said.

"You're welcome. What time is the show? I thought it was a morning hearing?"

"It's been all over the clock. We were leaving in thirty minutes to be there early."

"Are you ready?" I asked.

"Yes."

"Let's go. We'll take a nice drive, and we won't be rushed," I said.

"Give me a minute." Haley ran into her house.

My phone buzzed. I stepped outside to take the call.

"MacKenzie."

"Mark. It's Stayton."

"You're like Mother Superior, always on my shit. What?"

"I just got some rumors and hints. You got something for me?" Stayton asked.

"I do, but as your underlings can tell you, I'm at my lady's house getting ready to take her to a court hearing to get her divorced from that fat Guido. After that I'll be heading into the office. Perhaps we can meet for coffee?"

"Yes. Let's do that. Can you give me a hint?"

"Yes. I have someone inside the family who is happy to help me out. I'll make you deputy director with what I have. Just give me some breathing room with my family."

"I'll call you after court. Bye," Stayton ended the call.

I turned to find Haley walking toward me.

"You know, you look very nice for someone going to court," I said as I snatched her up into my arms and kissed her.

"Come on. After court, you'll get to see what I do at work. Oh? Is that okay?"

"Yes. My parents will get Paulie. I'll go to the city with you. I took the day off."

#

We walked into the luncheonette on Old Country Road. We were getting coffee before court, but I was meeting Cicola, too. I saw Cicola already sitting at a booth.

"Mr. MacKenzie."

"Hey, Steve. Haley, this is Sergeant Steve Cicola of Nassau PD. He's lead detective in my parents' case."

"It's nice to meet you, sergeant," Haley said.

"Call me Steve. So, tell me, you got something?"

"I do. Almost the whole enchilada. I got twelve names for sure. That leaves four people, but I already know one of them and will likely figure out two more names today. I have a confession on digital media here, but I have so much more. Stayton wants to meet, but I owe you first dibs. I have someone on the inside in-the-know. I have plenty of crimes from murder to drugs to slavery to theft to racketeering to . . . pick a crime. I can give you what you want, or you can share with the fibbies."

"We got part of that Merrick case because of you. Tell you what. We want your parents' murders and any other Nassau County murder. I'll tell Stayton that. We can haggle over the rest. We'll give them their due with the RICO stuff."

I looked at Haley who looked like she swallowed an ice cube.

"Okay, Steve. I'll talk to Stayton. Then you two will talk. Plan on next week for your arrests to go down. Pay attention to the news. Oh. I cannot be in the press. That was a close call last week."

"You know it will come out—last week, I mean. I'll keep you a confidential informant here and I'll keep the Nassau guys quiet. I already spoke with Kowalski."

"Promise me you'll wait until next week to do anything."

"Cross my heart, hope to die," Cicola said as he crossed his heart.

"Here. Listen to that. You just made a promotion," I said as I passed him a jump drive.

"Thanks."

"Nothing until next week!"

"My word."

"Come on, Haley. Let's go get you divorced from the bonds of matrimony," I said as I pulled out money to pay for our coffees.

"I got dis," Cicola said.

"Thanks, Steve. Bye."

#

I took Haley's hand as we walked into the courthouse. We checked in to the proper court and Haley's attorney appeared, some fast-talking, jerky-moving, sweaty old guy. When he shook my hand, I thought I grabbed ahold of a warm flounder. He was about sixty or so, overweight, and slovenly dressed in a twenty-year-old suit. He told me they'd ask me questions.

"Who is they?" I asked.

"The court mostly, but opposing counsel may ask questions, too."

The lawyer briefly spoke with Haley then we sat down in a church-like pew bench seat. I always wondered why courts looked like churches since so much lying goes on in them, mostly from the attorneys and judges.

"I must wipe my hand. Where'd you find him?" I asked Haley.

"He was a neighbor when we lived in Glen Cove."

After the obligatory wait past the time set for the hearing, the judge and clerk came out and the case was called. We stood at the bench. A woman who looked to be about thirty-five-years-old appeared dressed as the judge. I wondered what pearls of matrimonial wisdom she could share with us? Paul wasn't looking very happy. I don't know if it was because of me or the divorce or the lost millions, but he didn't look well. Maybe he'd have a heart attack and save us all a lot of trouble? Paul looked at me with hate in his eyes.

Since Haley was the plaintiff, she went first. The judge asked her questions about the marriage, Paulie, and the property settlement agreement. Once the judge was finished asking questions, Haley's lawyer asked pretty much the same questions of her, then Paul's attorney asked almost the same questions. And lawyers wonder why we hate them.

The court cut off Paul's counsel finally admitting he was going over "old ground." She called Paul as a witness and after three versions of the same questions I was called as a witness.

"Have the parties been living separate and apart, without cohabitation and without interruption for more than a year?" The judge asked.

"Oh yes, ma'am. I can swear to that beyond a reasonable doubt," I said.

Paul looked at me like he wanted me dead. Haley blushed but was smiling. The bailiff and clerk were all but laughing, and the judge seemed amused.

"Is there any likelihood of reconciliation?" The judge asked.

"No, ma'am. Not while I'm around."

The bailiff burst out laughing while the judge and clerk lifted files to cover their expressions. Haley elbowed me.

"The witness is familiar with both parties," the judge said.

"I am." I wanted to say, *I shot his driver and his bodyguard*, but I didn't want Paul to know yet.

"Then I'll sign the order now. My clerk will mail copies to counsel and the parties. You're divorced. Good luck to you both," the judge said as she smiled at Haley and me.

We were free to go, but Haley's lawyer had part of an hour to bill so he chatted with her.

Paul walked past, leering at me. Once Haley's lawyer got her past the three-quarter hour mark, he released her. He must round up the quarter hour. Haley grabbed my arm, and we departed the courtroom for my car.

"You are such a wiseacre, but you were cute. Paul didn't look good. I wonder what's wrong?"

"Maybe he lost something?" I deadpanned. Of course, being a woman, Haley would immediately think I meant Paul losing her.

"Oh, how cute, but I don't think he believes he's losing me."

Like clockwork.

#

My phone vibrated as we got into my car. It was Stayton.

"Can we meet at Clarence's?" I said.

"Sure," Stayton said.

"I'm on I-495 in Long Island City. I can be there in 20 minutes."

"I'll be there. Bye, Mark."

#

"You sure spend a lot of time in diners and luncheonettes with police," Haley said.

"Not too much time. You heard what I said to Cicola. Now I'll do the Fed speech. As I mentioned, my goal is to be done with all this by Memorial Day," I said.

My phone buzzed.

"Yeah."

"It's Bernice. Rizzo just tried to throw a chair through the small conference room window. Kev and Mikey restrained him rather forcefully. After they let him up Rizzo threatened them then stormed off."

"Why was he so angry?" I said.

"He tried to get into the conference room. He had a key. Rob, Clara, Audrey, and Barbara took a late lunch. The key didn't work because Clara had the locks rekeyed."

"Why would Rizzo have a key? The conference rooms are controlled by Marsha."

"They are. Only Marsha's people should have access. Rizzo was either given a key or he took it."

"I'll be in soon. I just got into the city. I have another appointment. I should be there in less than two hours."

"Okay. We're good here. Kev made easy work of Rizzo," Bernice said.

"Rizzo went berserk throwing a chair at the conference room window. It seems some mobsters are stressed out," I said.

"I think you know why they're stressed out," Haley said.

"Maybe."

#

We pulled down the street by Clarence's. How nice, a fibbie pulled his SUV out of a parking spot to let us pull in it. I used a credit card for the parking meter. Odd. We walked inside. Six agents and Stayton, who didn't seem surprised to see Haley, no doubt having received a report that she was with me, sat in the same booth we'd occupied just a day ago. I pointed Haley into the booth, and I sat down next to her. Dan got up to make his report like last time.

"Haley. This is John Stayton. He's with the FBI."

"If someone told me I'd be sitting down with a Menduni to talk about taking down the Menduni crime family I'd have said they were crazy. Are you eating?" Stayton said as the waitress greeted us.

"What would you like, Haley?" I said.

"Grilled pastrami on marbled rye with mustard, iced water with lemon, please."

"Apple pie with coffee, please," I said. The waitress ran off to fetch our order.

"John, you must promise me that you will do two things. First, you will do nothing with any information I give you—no arrests—until next week. Second, you share with Cicola in Nassau. He wants the murders. He's not much into all the other stuff. I know you guys have your agreements. He helped me first—he gets my parents' case and the Nassau murders."

"Fine. Based on what you told me, I can't do a lot to disagree with you," John said.

I punched Cicola's number into my phone.

"Hello."

"Steve. It's Mark. John Stayton wants to say hello," I said. I passed my phone to John. "It's Steve Cicola."

"Hello. John Stayton, FBI JOCTF. We will cooperate on all we do, but I will yield to you on the murders in Nassau County by the various crime families specifically the Calabrese-Menduni family. I will. Thanks. We'll be in touch. Okay. He wants to talk to you."

"Yeah, Steve?"

"Is he for real?"

"Yes. No arrests until next week. Same for them."

"Thanks, Mark. I'll be talking to you."

"Bye, Steve."

Our food was delivered.

"I already agreed to your terms, but in return you have to tell me about you and apple pie," Stayton said. Haley giggled, and Stayton looked at her surprised. "You know?"

Haley looked at me and I nodded that she could tell the story.

"Mark worked the late shift in Afghanistan . . . well, I guess, in Iraq, too. The contractors cooked the meals for the troops. Mark and his team would return from missions while breakfast was served. They'd shower, clean their gear and get ready for the next night then go to sleep. Mark would wake up at between three and four o'clock in the afternoon and he'd be hungry, but not for dinner. He wanted breakfast, but all they had was apple pie. It reminded him of home. No matter how bad the days and weeks got, eating apple pie brought him home to his family. He'd eat apple pie before each mission," Haley said as she picked up her sandwich.

"You guys have some stories." John smiled.

I forked my last bite of apple pie and asked for another slice as the waitress refilled my coffee. "How do you feel about a top capo sitting down with you and telling you everything he knows about the New York crime families?"

John's eyes enlarged as two of his agents moved closer to better record us. I pressed the button on my noise maker to scooch them back.

"John. Save your batteries. I just turned on my jammer. Those two cannot hear anymore. Tell them to sit with us if they want to take notes."

John waved Dan over. My pie was delivered. "I'm all ears, Mark."

"Farina wants out. He seems to know quite a bit. He wants his family out, too. He will do as I say," I said then took a bite of my pie.

"How'd you . . ."

"I waterboarded him."

"Funny. No really?"

"No one ever believes me! Anyway. He said his job today was to try to set a meeting with the other families. He's working out of a funeral home, but strangers would be noticed there. He has an office in Locust Valley but doesn't use it since you watch it and he doesn't usually use his Manhattan office except when he goes into the city for Vincenzo. He's got a wife, two boys away at school in Connecticut, and a daughter who just graduated college living at home. I don't care what you do with him, but I care about his family."

"Why don't you care what happens to him?"

I took another bite of pie then reached into my pocket and pulled out the jump drive. I slid it across the table to John. "I don't recognize the voice of the one speaker, but the other person speaking is Farina," I said.

Dan grabbed the jump drive and ran off with it.

"Farina was part of the conspiracy to kill my parents. He identified twelve murders including my parents. I don't know

500

how many are Nassau murders, but the rest are yours. Remember I still have evidence of the Chicago underboss getting whacked, the slave ring, methamphetamine distribution, cocaine, money laundering, and all the other crimes I mentioned. Farina can help and your CI, me, is covered. Oh. Rizzo killed that guy the other night. I also learned that if they whacked the old man, Vincenzo, Pagano, and Farina, Rizzo is a likely successor. Not good. He's got anger management issues."

"Tell me, why don't you want to take them down until next week?" John said.

"Because I need Rizzo and a few other goombahs to pump some stock. After Monday, I don't care what happens to them. I'll take down Rizzo myself if I can dress like a Mexican Navy Commando when they take down the drug cartels. I just don't want to be in the news. Plus, I have a mole in my firm. I suspect he'll show himself or these guys will rat him out."

John smiled. I took another sip of my coffee. At that moment, Dan returned. He nodded at John. "He got him. Farina wants help," Dan said.

"Call the U.S. Attorney . . ."

I put up my hand. "John. Nothing until next week," I said.

"I'm bringing Farina in. Only a U.S. Attorney can offer immunity and witness protection."

I shook my head. "I don't trust U.S. Attorneys. They yap too much, spend most of their time lying, most have low self-esteem, and they cannot keep secrets. I mean, if we bring in Farina and he cooperates won't they grant immunity and witness protection anyway?"

"I'll give you a lawyer's answer—it depends. Farina is a lawyer. He won't deal unless he sees a U.S. Attorney in the room," John said.

I looked at Haley shaking my head. "Shakespeare was right!"

Haley giggled.

"Okay, John. If I hear one peep out of a U.S. Attorney from either district about this before Monday, I will visit him during the night at his home. Make that abundantly clear to them. You cannot get to Farina. I can. Am I clear?"

"Okay. I can keep the jump drive?" John said.

"Dan already copied it, but sure, I have more."

Dan looked at me sheepishly.

"You said you didn't know who it was talking with Farina in the recording?" Dan said.

"No. I said I didn't recognize the voice."

Dan nodded and smiled at me.

"Mark, we're going to work on this. I don't know all of what you're doing, but after Monday we can act—correct?"

"That's our deal. Go do what you need to do. I will be in touch with our man today. It needs to happen fast, I suspect. I mean Farina coming in."

"It will."

"And I don't speak to anyone but you two, clear? Oh, and this woman is never brought into any of it—she never needs to testify."

"Done. You'll be identified in the indictment as CI-1 most likely."

"I will not be put into a position where I must hide. I will make sure of that if you don't."

"Okay."

"Are you ready, Haley?" I said.

"I'm finished, yes."

I pulled out my wallet and put a fifty on the table. "We gotta go. Bye." I took Haley's hand, and we walked to my car.

#

The receptionist greeted us as we entered the executive hallway.

"Bernice. I'm here," I said.

"Oh, good. Hello. I'm Bernice. Mr. MacKenzie's secretary. Can I get you something to drink?"

"No, thank you," Haley said.

"Bernice. This is Haley Menduni, my girlfriend . . ."

"I'm Haley Shore, again," Haley corrected.

"That's right. She'll be hanging around my office while I put out some fires. Are Robert, Audrey, and company in the conference room?"

"Yes. Kev is there, too. Mikey is over by the broker area keeping an eye on Rizzo."

"Fine. Shit! Oh. Sorry. Bernice, Haley. I forgot or didn't think. Rizzo knows you and Paul. Paul has no idea what I do.

Rizzo has no idea I'm dating you. Just stay here. I'll be right back. Bernice. No one in my office."

"Yes, sir."

I walked to the little conference room. "Rob. How are we doing?"

"Great. They have taken the bait, hook, line, and sinker. The stocks have, on average, quadrupled in value. Lots of activity."

"Kev. Where's Chief?"

"I don't know. He hasn't been here."

"Contact him. Belay that. Kev, come with me."

"Hi, Kev," Haley said as we entered my office.

"Hey, Haley."

"Kev. Stay here. No one in my office except Bernice and Clara. Mikey is keeping an eye on Rizzo?"

"Yes. Looks like a lot of activity by Rizzo, too."

"Thanks. Listen, Rizzo is not to see her here. He knows Haley. I don't want her ex-husband putting this together," I whispered.

"Got it. I'd be happy to put him down again. Just give me a reason."

"Thanks, Kev. Bernice. Where is Clara?"

"With Barbara. They've been helping coordinate and communicate."

"In Barbara's office?"

"Yes. I'm going in to see Matt, but first I want to talk to Ira. So, I'll see Ira, Matt, then Clara."

"Yes, sir."

I walked to Ira's office. Mikey nodded at me as I walked past. Shit! Scatterbrain. I needed to call Chief.

"Ira."

"Mark. It's crazy. First our guys killed it yesterday and today. Thirty million in net income to us and some strong possibilities. Then Rizzo with the chair. The big guys put him down easy and are watching him."

"Did Rizzo make any sales?" I asked.

"No."

"I see he's doing everything but his job."

"Pretty much."

"Keep an eye on him."

"Steve and I have been watching him and his two assistants, too."

I nodded. I walked to Matt's office. "Hey, Matt."

"Hey, Mark. It seems the brokers are killing it."

"I saw. Where's Chief?"

"I haven't had him come in. We agreed to have him at my house. I thought more for Betsy and me after hours."

"He's to watch you all the time, Matt. You're most vulnerable while traveling."

505

"Oh. Sorry, Mark. I didn't get that. Anyway. So, the other stuff is good?"

"It is. We're on track and on plan. The lawsuits are all but ready."

"Great. Look, you'll get to take some time off to be with Lauren after this. Sorry, but, well, you sort of started it."

"No, Matt, I'm finishing it. Do you need me?"

"No. I'm just looking over last quarter's reports and taxes. They were emailed to you, too."

"Thanks. I'll look them over. I'm sure I'll have questions."

I walked to Barbara's office. And found Clara.

"We, okay?"

"So far all is well. The bad guys are talking it up and spending millions on the stock."

"You know about Rizzo's tantrum?"

"Yes. Good thing Kev and Mikey were here."

"Only Marsha controls the keys to the conference room, right?"

"Yes, but she delegates to others to open them when she's busy."

"But where did Rizzo get a key if it's controlled access?"

"Good question?"

"His assistants don't have access, do they?"

"Only if someone gave them access."

"Rizzo tried to get in with the old key. So, he got a key before you had the locks rekeyed. Rizzo and whomever gave him a key didn't know the locks were rekeyed. Someone has copied keys to the offices," I said.

"I bet you're right. Kev took the key from Rizzo. Here it is," Clara said as she handed me the key.

"Thanks. Call the locksmith. I want all door locks rekeyed ASAP."

"Yes, sir."

I returned to my office and called LT. "Hey. Did you speak with Chief today?"

"Yes. He's at the house. He did pass along that he got a tracker on the limo. Same guy driving each day. The software shows travel from home to the office and back. He stopped for liquor and some food shopping, but that's it."

"Okay. Tomorrow, I want Chief in here. You heard?"

"Yes. Kev and Mikey contained it."

"They did. Tomorrow let's have Chief and Surfer in here, too. You and I will go over with the team why I want them here, but it's beginning to get hot. Rizzo is bad news. I want to keep a closer eye on him. We must squeak by just a few more days."

"Gotcha. Did it go okay with the Feds?"

"Yes. I'll tell you more later. Where are you?"

"I just dropped your shirts at the cleaners. I took more shirts from your Oceanside house. Your grandmother and grandfather asked me to do it. Your grandfather's tailor is on his way to your office now to see you," LT said.

"What would I ever do without you and my grandfather?"

"It's the least I can do after you bought me a new wardrobe. Christine is going to love it. I'll see Chief in a minute when I stop by. Why don't we plan on Chief, Surfer, Talbot, and me coming in there tomorrow?"

"I think that will help. I'll be leaving here soon. Thanks. Bye."

"Bye."

"Mr. MacKenzie."

"Yes, Bernice."

"Your tailor is here."

Haley looked at me and laughed.

"I didn't do this. It was my grandfather."

"Well, good. Bernice and I can help you pick some suits."

"Send him in, Bernice. Thank you. It just seems so pretentious."

"You're busy and you have some means. You need to look good as the incoming president. How many will you get?"

"I don't know. I have seven or eight suits now that fit. How many do I need?"

A knock produced Bernice. "You'll need to authorize Mr. Del Duca to come in. Kev?"

"Oh. Right." I walked to the outer door of my office. "Sorry, Kev. I didn't know he was coming until a moment ago."

"Yes, sir."

"Hello. I'm Mark MacKenzie. I understand that you made suits for my grandfather?" I said as I escorted Mr. Del Duca to my office.

"I did, and for your father and uncle, and some of the brokers here, too."

"See, Haley. It's a tradition. Mr. Del Duca, how many suits did my father have?" I asked.

"I made him a total of eighty-four suits over the time I knew him. He purchased additional suits from my designer collection, too," Mr. Del Duca said.

Where would I put all those suits? "What do I need to do?" I said.

"Let me measure you. That's a nice Varvatos you're wearing, but you need a little help with my custom label, and some nice Brioni and Zegna suits . . . and what's with the four-color, regimental striped tie with a suit like this? I'll have to fix you."

Haley enjoyed every minute of the visit. An hour and twenty minutes later I was finished. Haley brought Bernice, Clara and Kev in to opine on the selections. Kev didn't even know what a pocket square was until this past Saturday! Anyway. I got fifteen suits, to start with, thirty custom shirts, fifteen of which were white, and fifty ties. Jeez!

#

Kev relieved Mikey watching Rizzo. Rizzo did seem to be spooked by Kev. At 5 p.m. Rizzo departed.

Rob, Audrey, and team wrapped up for the night. Marsha came into the office.

"Marsha. I'd like to make sure no one accesses the office tonight. Have our floor locked out, please."

"Certainly. I'll let building security know."

"Thank you."

I looked around my office for anything else that needed my attention. Clara and Bernice were gone and so were most of the other employees. Haley was occupied reading a magazine Bernice had given her. I sat at my desk for a moment to collect myself.

"You stay very busy here," Haley said.

"It's because of the other stuff. Once this is done, it will slack off and become boring for me."

"Do you worry about that? Things becoming boring for you?"

"I don't know. I have so many other issues that I don't need that one, too. I haven't thought about it. I suppose, maybe, but . . . being with the guys and having a mission is something I enjoy. I know I can't ever again go on real missions . . . I'm okay with that. I've done my share and I did it well. I suppose one day I'll give it some thought. Let me make a couple of calls then we're out of here."

"Okay."

I called Rob and Tony for updates then wrapped up my business day.

"Come on. We can leave. I'll make a couple of calls while we drive home."

"Let's go, sailor."

#

We entered the parking garage and my senses alerted. I scanned the garage for danger and saw nothing. I remotely started my car then walked to it while Haley waited near the door. I checked out the car and all was good. I looked around. I felt I was being watched.

"We're good. Come on."

I opened Haley's door and she got in. I got in and we drove off. I checked my rear-view mirror and saw the FBI detail following us.

"Mark. What will you do to keep Vincenzo from learning your identity?"

"I'm not too terribly worried, if he finds out, which he eventually will, sooner than later. He'll learn my identity today from your hearing. My concern is more as it relates to my family. Haley, I can take care of myself. I cannot cover Lauren, my grandparents, Matt, Betsy, or you twenty-four/seven for however long. These newer guys don't act normal. They are not old-school. I do not believe Vincenzo would hurt my family, but Paul and those other guys might. If these guys have a beef with me fine, go for me, but leave my family out of it. I do not think Vincenzo would order my family hurt, but the Montys and those guys, I don't trust them."

"What will you do if they were to go after your family?" Haley said.

My grip involuntarily tightened on the wheel. "I won't let any harm come to any of you. We'll get through this. Just a few more days." My phone buzzed.

"Yeah."

"It's Joe. The others in on the conspiracy are John Bonano of the Bagatelli family. He's an underboss for all intents and purposes. He may have just been moved up this past month since the old man over there trusts him. The other guy is a Joseph Paganelli. He's a capo with the Carlucci family, but probably the lowest regarded of the five they have.

Oh. We got Rizzo dead to rights on emails involving the planning of your parents' deaths. He has another account that he uses and somehow, he had the emails sent there without forwarding them from his other account. Rizzo confirms, agrees, and endorses the hit order and he opened and read all the conspiracy and kill order emails. That's all of them except for the Invisible Man," Joe said.

I thought for a moment. "Then we need to dig into those two families. I think Rob and Tony have linked the firms who employ the Carlucci and Bagatelli families."

"They have. All five New York families are involved. I'll forward the emails involving these guys. We located another email on Rizzo's account that was deleted. He sent it to Bonano. Mark. Rizzo is trying to double-cross the Menduni and Carlucci families. I'll send you that, too."

I thought about what Joe said while Haley looked at me.

"What is it, Mark?" Haley said.

I shook my head at her. "Joe. That's what this is about. I'll get back to you, Joe."

"Talk to you later. Call me."

"Bye." I punched Rob's number.

512

"Hello."

"Rob. Can you do ancestry research from the loft?"

"Sure. What did you have in mind?"

"I want to know the family ancestries of Rizzo, Farina, Pagano, Menduni and their relationship to the Carlucci and Bagatelli families. Check out John Bonano of the Bagatelli family and Joseph Paganelli of the Carlucci family. There is something there. Start with Rizzo, Farina and the last two I gave you. Check all associations like college, neighborhoods, marriages . . . look at Wharton, NYU, et cetera. I want all connections."

"Sure. Three of us will get on it now. Look Mark, we're way ahead here. I'm finished with the lawyers unless you come up with more plaintiffs or we come across more assets, so bring it on," Rob said.

"Thanks, Rob. Call me as soon as you have something. Oh. What family was that broker from who got killed yesterday?"

"The Carlucci family."

"Okay. Get on it. Thanks. Bye."

"Bye."

"What's going on, Mark?" Haley asked. We were passing the Queens-Nassau County line on the L.I.E.

"I think there is more to this than just what we've uncovered. I think there are some people either in the one family or people who have joined forces from the several families to take out the Carlucci and Menduni families. Hold that thought, Haley."

I tapped Farina's office into my phone. It rang several times before it was picked up.

"Hello. This is Michael Farina."

"This is a friend looking for some help with a funeral service," I said in Farsi accented English. Haley looked at me in wonder, my accent, no doubt. Farina responded nervously.

"Yes. I recall."

"I need to discuss what you can do for my family. Time is of the essence. Should I meet you there or can you meet me at the cemetery?"

"The cemetery. I was about to leave. Say twenty minutes?"

"I will see you then." I ended the call.

"Did I hear him answer 'Michael Farina?'" Haley said.

"You did. We're meeting him at my parents' cemetery. I have some questions for him."

"Where did you learn to speak like that?"

"I practiced with the locals while I was away. I guess you don't know. I can speak several languages."

"Which languages?"

"We need a few secrets between us, but several."

"You continue to surprise me, Mr. MacKenzie."

#

We pulled into the cemetery. I drove to a small parking lot near my parents' graves. Several minutes later I watched Farina pull into the cemetery in his black Audi.

514

"You stay here. I'm just going to talk with him."

"Mark. I know Mr. Farina. He always spoke with me when I was at Vincenzo's house or the grandfather's house. Of all of them he seemed the nicest."

"He's a spineless snake. As you know I flipped him. I need some answers. Stay here."

I walked into the cemetery and watched Farina pull into a parking spot fifty yards to my right. I looked over the other vehicles and they were empty. Farina got out of the car and walked toward the center of the cemetery to a crypt not one hundred feet from my parents' grave. I put on my dark sunglasses and blacked out Yankee cap while I waited for Farina. He walked past me without seeing me while I leaned against a wall. I came around behind him and in Farsi-accented English I spoke.

"Just walk. Do you recognize my voice?"

"Yes."

"Take a seat on the bench in front of you. Get comfortable."

I removed my scanner and ran the instrument over him from behind and got a cell phone.

"Phone, please."

He handed me his phone and I popped the battery out of it.

"Tell me about the plan to take over the Menduni and Carlucci families."

"What? I mean people are always waiting in the wings for an opportunity, but I know of no plan to take over both families."

515

"If there was a plan, who would be behind it?"

"Rizzo, Bonano, Paganelli, perhaps Bonano's brother-in-law Salvatore 'Skip-Skip' Solano and the Sciortino brothers in the Carlucci family along with Paul Menduni."

"Why were you so quick to name them?"

"They're all in their mid to late thirties, some in the forties, and they're ambitious and impatient. They have all been involved in bad businesses that we don't condone like that shit last week with the young girls. We don't do chomo crap. That's these new, amoral, vicious bastards. They are going into all sorts of crap, bothering the Indian casinos, setting up joint businesses with low-level members of other families without approval, kidnapping young women and selling them to rich guys or Muslim foreigners."

"Was Paul Menduni involved in that sex slave ring the other week?"

"Yes. Vincenzo doesn't know it, but he suspects Paul was. I know, and I've kept it from Vincenzo because his nephew is involved, too. He accepted money to turn a blind eye to what the other family members did. Was that you who killed Monty and the driver the other night?"

"I'll ask the questions. You have one of your men on Paul's security detail. Why?"

"Vincenzo wants to know if Paul is involved in the chomo ring, and he wants to know what happened to the $60 million Paul claims is missing. And he asked his father to whack his wife or now ex-wife, I think. I believe the divorce was granted today."

"Did Vincenzo order Paul to kill his wife?"

"No way. She's harmless. Vincenzo would not do that shit. He told Paul to get lost and either find the money or earn it, but that's an example how these young guys operate. No rules."

"Whose money did Paul lose?"

"Mostly Vincenzo's, but some of it was Paul's and Romeo Menduni's."

"Where did the money come from?"

"Corporate operations, payments by the companies, skimming from transactions involving bonds and securities, other legitimate businesses."

"What would Vincenzo do if he received proof that the individuals you named were planning to take over his businesses?"

"You already know what he'd do."

"He'd whack his own son?"

"If Paul planned to take out the old guard and install himself or Rizzo or one of those other guys—hell yes. Paul would be dead in two minutes. Recall, that's Vincenzo's guy on Paul's security detail."

"Tell me about Bonano."

"He's the oldest of the group. He's a cousin to Paganelli of the Carlucci family. A Napoli meets Sicily marriage. Bonano is in the Bagatelli family. He's the incoming underboss. He's taking over now. Of the three top guys in the Bagatelli family, Bonano is the smartest and most ruthless. The way I figure it, he'd take out the top leadership there and then old man Johnny

'Bags' Bagatelli. Paganelli takes out old man Carlucci and his sons. Paganelli is the recent *consiglieri* after years of being a soldier. Then Rizzo and Paul take out the Menduni leadership, which would include Pagano, all four of the capos, Vincenzo, his body guards, and maybe me. They might not whack Romeo Menduni since they think he's semi-retired, so long as he didn't act against them. Romeo isn't retired. He's got his own thing going and has taken or kept most of the shit Vincenzo refused to take over."

"Is that likely? Romeo doing nothing if Paul whacked his own father?"

"Unlikely. If someone whacked Vincenzo, Romeo would have to act so the council didn't think he whacked his son. He would have to do something especially since it's no secret that they don't get along."

"Even if Paul is the one who whacked his father?"

"Interesting question. If Paul could make a case for getting rid of Vincenzo, maybe not. But we don't do that. You retire your father. Old man Menduni is rarely consulted on anything except big deals or meetings with other families. It's a respect thing. If Vincenzo is screwing up, his son should be helping to fix it, not whacking his father. I'll be square here. Vincenzo is mostly on the up and up. That's why he and his father don't get along.

If you want my honest opinion, if Paul whacked his father, he'd be whacked within a few months by the others. He's stupid and he has little support from the rank and file or from the unions. I won't go anywhere alone with him. As you see I don't keep a bodyguard. Maybe I should hire you guys. You don't seem to be afraid."

"The U.S. Attorney is going over your case with the FBI. They know you want to come in. Do you have any concerns?"

"Yes. You are asking me about a scheme to knock off the family leadership which worries me. I should tell Vincenzo, but he'll want to know where I learned about it. I don't have a clue who you are."

"Don't involve yourself. If Vincenzo and his father are taken out, Pagano takes over?"

"At least at first. This has been Vincenzo's problem all along. His son is a dumb ass. I will not take over—I'm the business guy. Pagano could, but I don't think he'd be very effective controlling Romeo's guys, Paul and Rizzo. Pagano is a genius in business and logistics, but not with the leadership or the old stuff. I don't know about the other capos. If Paul and Rizzo just stepped up and took over and that other crap went on in the other families, the capos and lieutenants might leave it alone or they might not. Vincenzo has respect. Most of the capos and lieutenants don't know Rizzo and those who know Paul don't like him."

I thought for a moment. "Can you get your family out of town while this goes on?"

"Yes. If I must. Look, I'm not playing with my family in that house. They bring me in and put them somewhere safe is how it's played."

"Are they ready?"

"My wife and daughter are. My sons don't know yet. They're away at school. I had to explain what happened last night, but my daughter has been on us for months to do this."

"Are you able to take off Friday and be away without Vincenzo becoming concerned?"

"No. I can't go anywhere right now unless it's for business or forever. Not with everything that he's got me doing and all the crazy shit that's going on. We have things going on that I need to take care of, so they don't become suspicious."

"Tell me about Rizzo and his job as a broker," I said.

"We sent him to school. Smart kid. We groomed him to move into a firm doing stocks and bonds. He's been at MacKenzie for a few years now. Four or five, I think."

"What does he do there?"

"He's a bond broker, but his main purpose is to push around bonds for several companies I told you about, and to get insider tips. He helps me manage some companies."

"How is Rizzo connected to the family?"

"He isn't. His grandfather got whacked by old man Calabrese for stealing from him. That was back in the early 1980s."

There's a motive. "Why is Rizzo at MacKenzie Securities?"

"I'm not sure. Vincenzo said let it be. Somehow Rizzo got a foot in the door there. I know one of the firm's shareholders, Matthew MacKenzie, went to NYU when I was there, but I don't know him personally. The older brother, William MacKenzie ran the shop until his death. I don't know the connection."

"How were the other firms selected?"

"By a combination of means. Vincenzo or Pagano told me what firms we should apply to for positions. I'm not sure why they were selected, but when I checked they all showed to be a cross-section of the bond sellers from the best at the time which was MacKenzie, to a couple of small firms who would need the extra expertise and business we could provide them. Most of the guys work for Romeo and he put them there."

"How were those energy companies funded?"

"With thirty million in seed money provided by the five families. We added another twenty million, but we created the illusion that each company was capitalized with separate funds. We turned fifty million into nearly a billion five on paper in less than six months. Then we got lines of credit, issued stock, got more credit, resold the bonds or gave them in exchange for sales fees to the bond companies. All the families were involved. The other families agreed that we'd be lead since Romeo and Vincenzo put in the most money. By the second year the other families bought out Vincenzo who didn't like what was going on. Vincenzo sold his interest in the companies to the other families and to Romeo who bought fifty percent of Vincenzo's shares but hasn't paid him yet. I've stayed on managing the operation until Vincenzo is paid and I sell my shares. The companies are going concerns, but they are just under-capitalized, and investors were duped into buying the bonds after they were initially used to create the illusion of financial strength. Then there's the bank fraud."

"Can the companies pay the bond holders?" *I had to ask.*

"Probably, but it will be tight. But it seems the stock of many of the companies is climbing this week, so I think the bonds could be covered. They have lines of credit to cover bond redemptions and operating costs."

"You didn't make clear to me why William MacKenzie was killed. Romeo Menduni ordered it, but what you told me doesn't ring true. You said it was a mistake."

"Killing his wife was clearly a mistake. Me, personally, I think killing William MacKenzie was a mistake. I'm not convinced he did anything wrong. I think he was set-up if it did look like he did something."

"Set up how?"

"I don't know, but Rizzo stirred the shit on that one. I have no doubt that Rizzo or someone else he's close to invented the problem that he used to ask Romeo to whack MacKenzie."

"Why did you go along with it?"

"I wasn't in on the decision. I was told what would happen and I passed along some information. I didn't get a vote yes or no."

"Who wanted William MacKenzie dead?"

"Romeo Menduni, Dinapoli, Rizzo, Paul Menduni, guys in the Bronx and Newark families and some others. I named most of them last night. Look, Rizzo and them had to bring a case to get the authorization. I don't see that. Once they bring a case only Vincenzo or Romeo decide or the bosses of the other families if it comes from them. They might consult with the other families, too, to be sure they're not stepping on other people's toes. Whacking a civilian is not taken very lightly. Of all the murders I told you about, only the MacKenzies were not in the business. The others were all men, and all were in the business at some level. I need to go before I'm missed. Contact me tomorrow. I can meet here for a short time Friday. I gotta run."

"Go. I'll contact you on your cell."

"Right."

"Go!" Farina walked to his car. I watched him drive away before I walked to my car.

#

"So?" Haley asked as I got into the car.

"He thinks my father was set up. He said my mother should not have been touched. Come on. Let's go get some dinner."

"Mark. Why don't you just bring in Farina now?"

"Because I don't need to and the less that happens now the better."

"Haley. Is Paul capable of killing his father?"

"By himself? No! Vincenzo would tie Paul into a pretzel. Would he have someone else do it? I can see it. Paul used to get very angry with his father and say crazy things about him. Vincenzo is very smart. His wife is not. Paul is not his father, but Paul is ruthless. His sister is worse because she is brilliant. Vincenzo uses her in the business, too. She could take over the business, but the other families would not allow it because she's a woman. She was married, but her husband died mysteriously a few years ago. She wasn't too broken up over it. The rumor is she had him whacked for cheating on her, but who knows."

"Where does she work?"

"Either out of Vincenzo's house or out of her house which is on the edge of Vincenzo's property in Glen Cove. She had a nice big 6000 square foot modern Mediterranean built on the northwest side of the property right on the water," Haley said.

I pulled out the list of names who Farina said may have been consulted or who were on our list who conspired to kill my parents. I saw four Mendunis: Romeo, Vincenzo, Paul and Guido, the nephew. No female names at all.

"What are you looking at?" Haley said.

"The list of possible conspirators who killed my parents and those who may have known about it. No female names are on the list," I said as I passed the list to her.

Haley pointed. "She's on here. Al Rapano. Al is short for Alexandra. She still goes by Al Rapano, her married name. Mark, Alexandra is the *de facto* underboss to her father. That's why Paul would kill his father. Paul and Alexandra disagree about everything with the business. Vincenzo relies on his daughter like a chairman of the board relies on his president. She is as smart or smarter than her father when it comes to the business, and the men in the family respect her. She has engineered some good deals for the family. The other families have issues with her, but so long as Vincenzo is around, there's not much they can do about it. She's NYU, Wharton, and Columbia Law. With her at his side, Vincenzo can remain in power a long time. I think she and Rizzo were at NYU or Wharton together."

I had to get my head around this. "Where's your son?"

"With my parents. I told you they'd get him for me."

I tapped Joe's speed dial. "Joe?"

"Yeah. What's up. Mark?"

"I have Rob working on an ancestry tree on a few of the guys in the different families, but tell me, what do you have on Al Rapano?"

"Nothing, really. That list you gave me is the first time I saw that name. We have several emails to him, but they're unopened and an auto reply rejects the message. We haven't broken in to see if he's opened the email by other means. He's sharper than Rizzo. Nothing connecting him. No alternative emails. Nothing. Hold on a second. Carl. What do you have on Al Rapano?"

I could hear Joe and Carl talking but not make out what they said.

"Mark. I'm back. We're going to go back through this one. Carl and Ken just noticed the IPA for one of the Invisible Man's emails from Manhattan matches an IPA for an email sent a couple of years ago to this Al Rapano."

"Joe. What if I told you Al Rapano is Alexandra Rapano or, her maiden name, Alexandra Menduni?"

"Oh shit? I know that name. Right under our noses. That's Paul's older sister. We never had much on her at OCTF. She seems to have stayed in just the legal business side of the house for them. We don't have shit on her about criminal matters. I have her profile and bio."

"We're coming over. Order some pizzas."

"Already ordered. Who's we?'

"Haley and me."

"Bye."

"C'mon. We have work to do. Let me call Lauren."

"Hey, Lauren. Everything okay? You did? Great. I'm very proud of you. Tell Grandma I'll eat with Joe. We'll be at the other house. You'll probably be asleep when I get home. I love you, too, sis. Okay. Bye."

"I missed her makeup softball game. I didn't know about it because I didn't ask."

"Mark don't worry about it. Lauren understands. She sort of knows . . . knows what you're doing," Haley said.

"What?" I said surprised at Haley's statement.

"Mark. Lauren is or will be as smart as you. Don't you remember what you said at your parents' funeral? Lauren remembers every word. She wrote it down in her diary. You got out of the wheelchair and took Lauren by her hand and walked to your parents' caskets. You said a prayer, you promised to protect and care for Lauren, then you said you'd find out who killed them and that you'd avenge their deaths. You knew it was hit-and-run. All the women in your family know. At first, they were afraid you would just kill the people responsible. Now they understand that you're doing it legally. They were very afraid that once you came home that you would just go murder whomever killed your parents. They are very relieved that is not the case. Like you, they are surprised it's come to this. Your grandma said something I thought, well, interesting. She said to me, 'Please don't let him kill them all.'"

I thought for a moment about the statement. *'Please don't let him kill them all.'* I turned onto my street then into the driveway and pulled into the garage.

"Let's go see what we can find out. I'm a little confused right now. I need to think about all this. Lauren knows what I'm doing, but she and the rest of the ladies don't believe that I will just kill the persons responsible for my parents' deaths."

"Correct. None of us have any doubt that you'd kill to defend life—no one believes that you will just kill or assassinate these people."

"Good. Damn. You sure moved right into the inner sanctum," I said.

"Mark, your family has just been so worried about you. What you've done and shown them in the past couple of weeks has assured them that their grandson, nephew, and brother is fine and that he is back from the brink of hell that has been your life. Look sweetheart, I was there. I almost didn't make it because of that life, the trauma, the hurt that was my life with my ex-husband. My family saved me. Now we'll save you. Let's go do this. You said it would be done by Memorial Day. Do that. Finish this so peace can return to your life—to all of our lives," Haley said.

I looked at Haley and I knew in that instant she was right. I leaned over and kissed her. She kissed me back. "Let's do this," I said. We walked through the back door into the house. Joe, Carl, Ken, and Surfer were there. Ken hugged Haley and thanked her for everything.

"Okay, guys. We need to regroup. Rob's and Tony's end of things are going well. You guys have done great. Now we have all the conspirators, but one—the Invisible Man. We've learned that there is a possible power play going on with the five families . . ."

I was cut off by Carl. "Six families. We just connected the Rapoli and Atlantic City family to communications with Bonano, Rizzo and Paganelli. We're verifying an email confirming the Terrazzo family for a connection on this latest development," Carl said.

A knock on the door surprised all of us. Surfer got it; weapon drawn.

"Uh, Mark. You're wanted at the door," Surfer said.

I walked to the foyer. It was Stayton.

"What do you want, John?"

"To help. Can we come in?"

I looked at Surfer who walked off to tell the others and to secure the family room from prying eyes.

"Come on in, John, Dan and you are?" I said.

"Aldo Mariano. I'm an organized crime expert. I specialize in the northeast crime families. I was a special agent deep undercover for years with the Bagatelli family. I was pulled out five years ago after they tried to whack me. I'm still an agent and analyst with the FBI." Aldo walked in with a limp.

"What happened to you?" I asked.

"I got boxed in on the New York State Thruway and shot a couple of times by the Bagatelli family. I still have the weapon they shot me with. Oh, is it too late for me to throw my hat in as a plaintiff?"

I looked at Agent Mariano, nodded and smiled. Mariano was about forty-five years old, Italian in the usual respects, black to salt and pepper hair at five-foot ten-inches tall. I immediately liked him.

"We'll discuss that later. What do you want, John?"

"We know you saw Farina today. Based on the chatter and some things we learned or presumed, you are taking down the several New York crime families. You told me you know who killed and conspired to kill your parents. You have identified twelve of the sixteen people, but I think you have identified fifteen of the sixteen involved. One person remains to be identified in your email chains or communications. We don't know who that is either.

So . . . hey, Joe, Ms. Menduni. I was just explaining our perspective on what's going on. Is there any more pizza?" Stayton said.

"It's Shore. Haley Shore. She was divorced today."

"Oh. Good," John said.

"Come on. We'll eat in the morning room," I said. We moved to the round ten-person table in the morning room. Haley placed pizza, salad, and plates and we took seats.

"Thank you, Ms. Shore," John said.

"You're welcome. Please call me Haley, Special Agent Stayton."

"Okay. Haley. John."

Carl, Ken, Surfer and Joe joined us.

"Gentleman, this is Carl, Ken, and Surfer. They're researchers. You know Joe," I said.

"You should think about joining the FBI, Mark," John said.

"Sorry, John. My parents were married when I was born."

"Ouch!" John said.

Aldo laughed. "Great pizza," he said.

"John. Can we get to it? This isn't the SALT II treaty negotiations we're doing," I said.

"Fine. I'll tell you what we think you're doing. You are getting the information on the people responsible for conspiring to kill and who killed your parents. You have advised me that you will turn over the information on these people to law enforcement and that you are not going to assassinate them. I believe you. How am I doing so far?"

"Except for the additional co-conspirators, I told you all of this. Good notetaking, Dan," I deadpanned.

"Right. Stay with me on this, Mark. You are assembling evidence and drafting lawsuits—civil actions—to sue the various persons and corporations, owned by the mob, responsible for causing personal injuries to many people over the past several years. I am guessing because even with all the people involved, you do not know for sure how many suits will be filed, but I think you will file many civil actions and property seizure orders next week then add to them as new cases arise," John said.

"John. You gave me the names of the victims, guardians, or heirs. You learned of the attorneys meeting with me at my office last week. I told you to send me the names of all victims. I hope you didn't take up too much of the taxpayers' time figuring this out. Now tell me the rest," I said then took a bite of pizza.

"You are working a plan to pull a fast one on the mob's corporations by pumping stock value so the mob will invest so you can crash the stock and break their bank, but so you don't actually violate the law, you are issuing internal opinions, not ready for public dissemination that you hope Rizzo and guys like him who work at other firms will read and act on causing the mob to buy more stock driving the price up further," John said then took a bite of pizza.

"John. I told you pretty much all of that when I asked you not to arrest some people associated with local Italian crime families until next week. You've added some details hoping I will bite and fill in what you wish you knew, but I won't. I told you just about all you just told me, but what you just said is only part of the plan so you'll have to dig for the other part, so you earn your paycheck this week."

"Well, sort of. Now let me tell you what you're missing. Motive for your parents' deaths and you're wondering if there's about to be some coup attempts on the leadership of the various New York and New Jersey crime families," John said as he took another slice of pizza.

Haley watched with mild amusement. Joe gave away nothing. Carl ate his pizza and looked disinterested. Surfer was eating his fourth slice of pizza, and Ken studied a slice of pepperoni on his plate.

"John are you and your expert, Mr. Mariano, here for a purpose or to bait me into disclosing what I will not disclose?"

"Both. First, the U.S. Attorney wants to bring in Farina right away and use him to start making arrests. I know your answer. Look. His nickname is *Preening Pete*. I'd like to see if I can help there."

"You can't. We have a deal, John. Do you have his address? I will call on him and convey my position personally if you prefer."

"No. That's okay. I expressed to him that he'd have to wait. You win. Next. Can we get going on the Chicago murder while we await your operation?" John said.

I thought about the request and the possible effect on our operation.

"Who's requesting this?" I said.

"The Justice Department and the U.S. Attorney in Chicago."

"Can I ask why a dead guy is more important than the thirty women kidnapped in a sex-slave ring?"

"That was my next request. While I understand the importance of the Chicago case, I, too, think live people are more important. You already know that." John said.

I looked at Joe and Carl. "Will giving him that information interfere with our op?" I said.

"No. Carl and I already have a probability chart for locations of twenty-eight of the women kidnapped in the past two years. The bad guy bank accounts, yachts, and remote locations, too. I agree. We should pass that to them now. We just linked one case of an adult sex slave to a buyer of those children from the Merrick case," Joe said.

"You got it, John," I said.

"Can I bring in my team?" John asked.

I looked at Joe and Carl who nodded. "Yes. Make it clear there is no nosing around in the family room. They may set up in the living room or den." John nodded. Dan ran off to make a call.

"John. Same rules. We stay out of it. I'm your CI. I suspect you will use some of my old team to rescue these ladies on foreign soil. I will stand by to advise you on that if need be."

"Fair enough. Can we talk about the racketeering?"

"No. Not until next week. I'll give you a status, but none of my resources yet. Trust me when I say you will have it all laid out for you and you know why? I get first crack at the money and property for the victims," I said.

"Some U.S. Attorneys are balking at that . . ." John said, and I cut him off.

"John. I swear to God, I will hunt them down myself if I must. The victims get first dibs, or I will withdraw my cooperation. You know what? I don't have time for this right now. You get the attorney general on the phone or whomever in Washington, DC and we conclude a deal right now! I am not giving up one dime to the Feds until every victim is compensated."

"Okay, Okay . . ."

"John, we're done here. I need to hear and see an agreement signed by Justice or we'll just order more pizza and trade war stories," I said. *To my amazement, Haley spoke up.*

"Special Agent Stayton. I can provide a lot of corroborating information, too. I was about to assist Mark with that. I, too, will not help unless we receive an iron-clad guarantee that whatever Mark's team recovers, and his legal team obtains or seizes, goes to the victims."

"It goes without saying that I'd be of no help without this said guarantee. If you think you can obtain the information by a warrant, I'll lock it up in a Suffolk County investigation so deep your grandchildren will have to become FBI agents to ever see it," Joe said.

"I have saved nothing of value on the computers in that room and what is there is coded such that NSA couldn't break it without my cooperation so even if you seize the computers, you'd be better off buying them new from Dell Direct unless we get a guarantee the property will go to the victims," Carl said while Ken nodded agreement.

Surfer took another slice of pizza and glared at the special agents. John and Aldo smiled at us.

"John, I think they're some pretty stand-up folks. Perhaps we need to call the deputy director and get Justice on the phone," Aldo said.

Carl smiled as he took another slice of pizza.

#

Haley ordered more pizza pies while John, Dan, and Aldo contacted the people at justice and FBI who needed to sign off on the guarantee. I sat on the back patio overlooking the pool with a glass of Scotch. Haley came out and joined me.

"They're in there talking. It sounds like ten people in Washington on the phone."

"Thank you for standing with me in there earlier," I said.

"Mark. You are doing the right thing. You make it easy for us to follow you," Haley said as she sat with me. "I can see this is wearing you down. We're all behind you . . ."

"Mark. Okay." John came out with Dan, Aldo, and Joe.

"Yes, sir. He's right here. Let me put you on speaker, sir. Just a second." John tapped his phone and placed it on the table in front of us.

"Go ahead, sir. Mr. MacKenzie and Ms. Menduni have joined us," John said having forgotten Haley was now Ms. Shore.

"Commander MacKenzie. Ms. Menduni. Good evening. This is Director Markham of the FBI and I have with me Deputy Attorney General Kathleen Callahan and my Deputy Director Gary Morgan. First, I'd like to thank you for your help. I, we, don't have all the information yet, but I guess you're looking for a guarantee from us that the federal government will abandon all claims to the property of the various crime families . . ."

I shook my head at Haley.

". . . I assure you that . . ."

"Director. I don't mean to cut you off, but we have a lot to do, and many lives are at stake while we talk. Your SAC has already given me his word. I don't need your promise. I trust Special Agent Stayton. I do not trust the two local U.S. Attorneys or Justice. I want to hear and see Deputy Attorney General Callahan state that the United States will abandon all claims to property and assets of the five New York and New Jersey crime families—the Menduni, Carlucci, Bagatelli, Rapoli and Terrazzo crime families and the Atlantic City and

Philadelphia Colombo crime family—in favor of all victims or heirs of victims of the crimes of these criminal families. That's all, sir. Ma'am," I said.

Dan looked like he'd swallowed a pinecone. Aldo could hardly contain a laugh. John had to cover his mouth with his hand. Haley smiled at me while Joe nodded and grinned.

"Director. It's my show. I want the efforts of my operation to go to the victims. Failing in that I'll take my ball and go home," I said.

"Commander. This is Deputy Attorney General . . ."

I was beginning to think I'd just hang up.

". . . we could recall you to active duty and . . ."

"And what, ma'am? Send me off to war short half a liver and a foot of small intestine? Look. There are all manner of things you could do to me, but don't you want to help these poor people and get good press for a change?"

There was a long pause. I could hear a male voice speaking and Callahan responding.

"Commander. Excuse me. I wasn't aware of all the facts. You rescued those girls who were kidnapped last week in Long Island and provided the evidence which allowed FBI and New York police to track down the men involved in the child sex slave ring. I apologize. I was not aware of the extent of your help and involvement. The United States will abandon all interest it has in the property of the several crime families in favor of the victims. We'll fax and email you an agreement signed by me to that effect," Callahan said.

I heard some discussion on the other end of the call.

"Haley. Let's take a walk. I'd like to show you the neighborhood I grew up in."

Haley smiled at me as I stood and took her hand.

"Joe, John, you know what I need."

"Hold on, Mark." John said.

"Director. Are you finished with Commander MacKenzie?"

"No, John. Commander. Thank you. I'm sorry it came to this. You have my word. They're drafting an agreement. I'd like to meet you when this is all over," Director Markham said.

"Sorry, sir. I'm just a CI. My people and I will just disappear. Like when I was in the navy, we do the mission, we don't talk about it. Good night, sir. I have something important I need to do."

"Good night, Commander."

\#

"See that tree there?" I said to Haley as I pointed at a huge old sugar maple with a rope and tire swing hanging from it.

"Yes."

"Joe pulled on a rope I had in my hands while I was standing on that branch, pulling me right out of the tree. I landed spread eagle, flat on my gut right there. I was eight years old."

"Did you break anything?"

"Just my fall. I couldn't move for ten minutes, and I had a mouthful of grass and dirt, but I eventually walked away. Rob's sister Alice was in a panic and ran home to call our parents," I said laughing as I thought about it.

"Do you miss your old neighborhood?"

"Yes and no . . . not really. I like it here, but I could never have stayed. It's changed. It's different. I wonder what happened to all the kids. There was the first post-World War II phase of births in the fifties and sixties, then a second wave of births in the seventies and early eighties. Now, not so much. There needs to be more children. More families with children," I said.

"I agree. Should we head back to help?"

"No. Not yet. This is more important, even if it's only for a few more minutes. Look. A silver fox," I pointed for Haley.

"Wow. They're everywhere now."

"I hope she stays around so children can see her."

"How do you know it's a she?"

"She's carrying kits. Look at her belly."

"Mark, you're right. How nice. Let me ask you, would you have picked up your ball and gone home if the government didn't do what you wanted?"

"What do you think?"

"I think you would have figured a way to do it without the agreement. You'd have done it another way because of who you are and because you never quit," Haley said.

I nodded and smiled at Haley. "C'mon. I guess we have things to do, but can I ask you . . . can I take you on another date once my life is settled some?"

"I wouldn't miss it for the world."

"Good. I think I'd very much like that."

We walked together back to my house. Several more cars and SUVs were parked there.

#

I picked up a slice of pizza and a bottle of water.

"John. What or where do you want me?"

"They're going over the kidnap information now. I'd like to do two things. I'd like to get an outline of who, what and where and I'd like you to sit down with Aldo and Dan to go over the Menduni clan, first, then the other families."

"This is a two-way exchange of information?" I said.

"It is."

"Aldo. Tell me why Paul Menduni would whack his father?"

"Because he fears that the leadership of the family will pass to his sister, Alexandra, or a co-boss arrangement with Pagano. You already figured that out today is my guess."

"What happens next week when these guys have no money?"

"Well, at first, I suspect confusion and a lot of attorneys with names that end in *berg* and *stein* will be hired. They'll be okay for a few weeks, but as time rolls on and, of course, after they're busted by us and New York, the rest of them will be hunting for you. We want to get a jump on this because of that. They will pull out all stops to find who did this to them. They will find out eventually. It's too big for them not to find out."

"So, Aldo, John, Dan . . . what do I do?"

"You're doing it. You're in and short of going into Witness Security Program you're doing it. The fact is I don't think they'll be able to figure out you set this up. You're just one of many pieces of the puzzle. With the leadership gone, the rank and file will go back to work doing their thing. They'll hide their assets if they're named defendants in civil actions, but you'll—we'll take down the big players and dangerous players by the end of May or early June," Aldo said.

"Why did they kill my parents, Aldo?"

"I'm confused by that, too. I've gone through our files, Cicola in Nassau gave me the run-down. I've looked at Carl's information and Joe's file. You told John that Farina said it was a mistake. First, your mother. While clearly the mob doesn't usually take out the wives or girlfriends, here they did. Remember, your parents came from a formal affair. The car was valeted and brought to the main entrance of the venue your parents were attending. The bad guys were there and watching. They saw your mother get into the car. At that point, most wise guys know there is not much they can do. They had two cars, so they could have boxed your Dad in, shot him and dumped the gun on the seat next to your mother. Maybe that was the plan and they panicked when your father sped up and took off."

"But why? Why did they kill my father? Who did he double cross? What did my father do to get hit?"

"I can't answer that, Mark. Maybe they were told to hit your father, and someone told them to hit your mother for some reason?"

"Come on? My mother was as pure and honest and nice. Look there's Mary, mother of God, then Mother Teresa, then there's my mother. It is not possible that my mother could cause someone to want to kill her. She was beautiful, outgoing, charitable, giving . . . as her son I'd never been angry with her— ever. My father never had a cross word to say to her. She was an interior designer for crying-out-loud. I cannot conceive anyone being angry with her."

"We agree, Mark. We're as baffled as you," John said.

"So, let's concentrate on my father. He had some run-ins with Rizzo and the other shareholders aligned with Rizzo, but kill the majority shareholder? I'm not there. His shares would go to my mother who would give my grandfather MacKenzie or Stuart her proxy. She might even give my grandmother her proxy," I said.

"What about Matthew?" Dan said as he looked at Aldo.

"Not likely. First, he's not president material and the family knows it. Exercising a majority vote and running the business isn't Uncle Matt. So long as my grandfathers were alive, my mother would defer to their judgment."

"I don't know, Mark. Look. It's late. Let's pick this up tomorrow. We'll work here if that's okay. We want to prepare. Cicola will join us tomorrow. Can we have your murder file so we can prepare arrest warrants and get with the other jurisdictions?" John said.

"Sure. Ken."

"Yeah, Mark."

"Give these guys copies of the murder files. Everything we have. Sergeant Cicola will be here in the morning to work with?" I looked at Dan.

"Dana will handle it," Dan said.

"Give Cicola and Dana what they need, too. What of my meet with Farina Friday?"

"Set it up. We'll write up some questions for you to ask him. I must ask, why does it matter if we bring in Farina now? At best, he's the business brain. If he's out of the picture won't that hurt their business interest?" John said.

"Probably unless they have a backup plan if he goes missing," I said.

"Ask him," Aldo said.

"What if he doesn't know?" I said.

"I see your point. Well, it's after midnight. It's Thursday. Two more days of preparation. What's your plan for tomorrow?" John said.

"The office with a show of force to let the rank and file know we're serious about security, then business and perhaps I'll try to see Farina tomorrow instead of Friday. Then family time. I've spent no time with my sister. I've been a bad parent this week," I said.

Ken came out with the murder files. He nodded at Dana, and they walked into the dining room to work.

"I gotta go, guys. I have a drive ahead of me. See you tomorrow. Joe, I'm going."

"Okay, bro. We're here."

"C'mon Haley. It's after midnight," I said.

"Goodbye, John, Aldo, everyone."

CHAPTER 18

I awoke at 6 a.m. I jumped up wondering why I was jumping up so suddenly.

I got Haley home before 2 a.m. She napped on the ride. She had to be in class this morning. I didn't have to be at the office until I got there. I walked to Lauren's room. She was up and in her shower. I went downstairs. My grandmother was making breakfast.

"Good morning, Grandma."

"Good morning, Mark. You were out late."

"Yeah. I had to take a call from the director of the FBI and a deputy attorney general."

My grandmother looked at me with a puzzled expression on her face.

"You know. . . you are so good at deception I almost didn't believe you. What did they want?"

"It was what I wanted. *Operation Restore Dignity*—taking all the mob's property for the victims. I got the United States, oh, hey Grandpa. I was just explaining to Grandma how I had to get the government to release all claims to the assets of the mob, so they'd be available for the victims of the mob."

"Good for you and for them. Why did that come up?" Grandpa asked.

"Scummy lawyers. The local U.S. Attorneys are asses, one in particular, so I went over them."

My grandmother put a plate of homemade waffles and bacon in front of me.

"What else is going on?" Grandpa said.

"The FBI, Nassau County and my team have joined forces, if you will. We've started to educate them on what we know, but not how we know it."

"And the civil actions?"

"I'll have a list tomorrow. It's well over one hundred civil actions. I've turned over everything we had on the slavery ring. I suspect my brothers-in-arms are getting word about now to pack and deploy."

"Oh? Where to?"

"Africa, the Far East, Southwest Asia, and the Caribbean. I hope they kill the men involved," I said.

"How do you know your guys will go?"

"It's a contingency we and Delta train for. It will be a busy weekend. I expect the FBI's HRT will be busy, too, as three of the victims are likely being held in the U.S."

"Morning, all," Talbot said.

"Good morning," LT said.

"Hey. You guys look like you got some sleep," I said.

"We did. Once you decided to stay in Oceanside, Talbot went lights out. I thought, good idea and followed thirty minutes later," LT said as Grandma poured coffee for the guys.

"Good morning!" Lauren said as she entered the kitchen. She kissed Grandma then Grandpa then me. Grandma put a plate of waffles in front of Grandpa and Lauren and started more waffles for the guys.

"What does today bring us, commander?" LT asked.

"A muster at the office. They've seen Kev and Mikey, but not the rest of you. They're getting a little paranoid. I need to flush a mole in the organization. Rob, Tony, and Carl should have some leads. While you're walking around as eye-candy for the female staff, you'll be there to intimidate Rizzo and buttress the staff, so they know everything is under control. I will do a few things, but what began as what I believed to be an insurmountable operation has taken up less time and has managed to be easier than I thought. It's up to you, LT, but I thought Chief and Surfer could drive in from Oceanside and Baldwin and you two from here."

"Sounds good. Anything about the other op?"

"I'll decide today after I review the data. I need more intel from Carl and Tony. With the FBI in the room, it's not as easy for Carl to work," I said.

"So, you pissed off the Justice Department chick then she ended up apologizing to you. You are the Teflon SEAL my boy!" LT said.

My grandmother gave me *the look*.

"You talked to Surfer?"

"Yes," LT said.

"I think the FBI Director put her in her place. I got my way. The assets go to the victims."

#

I showered and dressed, picked up my cell and SIG P226 and said goodbye to my grandparents. Lauren was already at school. No softball today. Her next game was Saturday.

The SEALs were headed to the office, all immaculately dressed in new suits. The FBI, Cicola, Joe and team were parsing through the evidence for each FBI team to work. Joe had advised that Cicola was happy to learn that of the twelve murders, eight were committed in Nassau County, not that murder is a happy event. Cicola would bring in the county's special detail to assist and they would be seeking indictments tomorrow, but if not then, they'd obtain felony warrants once the affidavits were completed. Nassau would be ready to begin making arrests by Sunday night though they would wait until Monday.

The FBI and Nassau were working together on the arrests. The other murders occurred in Queens, Brooklyn, Staten Island, and the guy Rizzo hit, in Manhattan. NYPD would get lead on those cases. The RICO stuff, money laundering, Medicare/Medicaid/Social Security fraud were federal cases along with the drug cases that involved distribution which would go to DEA. Nassau and NYPD would assist in those cases. New York State, New Jersey State, and Connecticut State police were all interested in the financial crimes and, of course, the Securities and Exchange Commission was jumping in to show they were not irrelevant. All these agencies were waiting for the FBI to act, and the FBI was waiting for me. It was too big to remain secret.

I pulled into the parking garage. I saw three security officers walking around. They nodded at me. I took the elevator to the office and stepped out to be greeted by the receptionist.

"Good morning, Mr. MacKenzie."

"Hey, Mark."

"Morning, Surfer. Don't keep my staff from their duties," I said as I smiled at Jennifer.

"Oh, no, sir." Surfer said.

The receptionist is a cutie. The women would be heartbroken when the guys left. Jennifer buzzed me into the executive hallway. Mikey was standing outside the small conference room.

"Morning, sir. Great day."

"Good. You look like you're having an okay time?"

"Mark. If you need this type of security work again or after I retire, I'll do it."

"I'll see what I can do, Mikey."

"Good morning, Bernice."

"Good morning, sir. Coffee?"

"Please."

"I wanted to ask you, are there any fifty-year-old SEALs out there because I just saw two new ones who are gorgeous and, well, I was wondering?"

"I know one who's an admiral."

"I'd be fine with him," Bernice said as she giggled and walked off to get my coffee.

"Morning, sir."

"Good morning, Clara. It's quieted down. How's the misinformation operation going?"

"Great. The tidbits that have been dropped have been circulated. Robert backed off a little bit. He was concerned that it might be too much or too coincidental, so of the twenty-one firms, the false disclosures have been leaked at just eight firms so far. However, the insiders communicated the false information to the bad guys at each firm." Clara said.

"You might have my job someday. Terrific work. Clara, sit. I want to pick your brain."

"Yes, sir."

"Thank you, Bernice. You can stay, too. I'm trying to figure out why someone would want to kill my father."

"Gosh, sir. I don't know. Your father never screwed any one on a deal. He was always nice to people. You know about the altercation with Rizzo. I mean he caught Rizzo doing fraudulent things," Clara said.

"I agree, Mark. I can only think of Rizzo, but not why. I don't know a reason why Rizzo would want to kill your father," Bernice said.

"Here's the problem I'm having. I have information that Rizzo knew about and agreed with a conspiracy to murder my father, but we're not sure if he requested it. We think he did. Moreover, what would he have to gain by my father's death? With my father dead, the stock passed to my mother. She would have granted either of my grandfathers the power to vote her shares. Together that totals 55% of the voting shares. Rizzo is still out in the cold."

"But not Matt. He's easier to deal with," Clara said.

"I agree, but it's doubtful my mother would grant a proxy to Matt. She always did what my father said to do or what Grandpa Stuart or Grandpa MacKenzie said to do."

"Well, I don't know. Are you sure? How do you know that?" Clara asked.

"Because I was, my whole childhood, an only child. My mother talked with me. My mother always deferred to the senior men in our family. She told me it was their place and their job to protect the family, therefore she always listened to her father's advice. When my father asked her father permission to marry his daughter it was like a changing of the guard she said. My father became her protector, and she gained another father to advise her. My father gained another man to guide him and another woman to teach him. Recall that my paternal and maternal grandparents were friends long before my parents married. My mother had no reason to defer to Matt until my grandfathers passed away if my father was not around. Frankly, Mom and Matt were not that close. As liberal as my mother was, at home she relied on the strength of the traditional family hierarchy."

"I think you're right there. What if they went to Lauren? Who would control her shares during her minority if you were not around?" Bernice said.

"I don't follow, Bernice?"

"Mark. You were at war. When you returned, all shot up, I'll be frank, we didn't think you would make it. You looked like you were on your death bed. You only began to rebound just before their deaths. Most of us didn't know that since your father didn't speak much toward the end. He was withdrawn and aloof. What would happen if you died? Who would control Lauren's shares?" Bernice said.

"Oh, my God. I'm going to be sick," Clara said.

"What's wrong?" I said.

"Who would get the shares if Lauren died?" Clara said.

I was shocked to even think of that possibility. First my mother, now to consider someone going after Lauren. No. I could not believe that.

"Clara. Bernice. Say nothing of this to anyone."

A knock on the door produced Chief and LT.

"Good morning. All present and accounted for," Chief said.

"Very well, um . . ."

"What's wrong, Mark?" Chief asked.

"Just a minute, Chief. I . . ." I sat down. Chief came over to me.

"Mark. What's wrong? You look like you saw a ghost."

"Clara. Pull the shareholder agreements. All of them. Keep this close to your chest. Chief. You stick with Matt like glue. Tell him we have an increased threat level if he protests. Did he have the same driver this morning?"

"He did. Same limo. What's up?" Chief said.

"Hold on. Bernice. Clara. Go to work, please. Clara pull the shareholder agreements."

"Yes, sir." Clara and Bernice departed my office.

"I don't want to believe what I'm thinking," I said to LT and Chief as I explained the brainstorming session with Clara and Bernice.

"Mark, I'll cover Matt. What about your grandparents? They're shareholders. They're at risk," Chief said.

"We got it, Mark. Talbot and I will head back to the house now," LT said.

"Okay. Let me call Grandpa." I punched in the home landline.

"Hello?"

"Grandpa?"

"What's wrong, Mark?"

"I don't have the particulars right now. We have a generalized increase in our threat level. You have the Beretta handy?"

"Of course. Can you tell me what's up?'

"Our shareholder agreements. With my parents gone their shares went to Lauren and me. What would have happened if I didn't make it?"

"Lauren would have received all the shares in trust until she was of age."

"And if Lauren died?"

"I'm not sure. I guess the shares would go to all four of us grandparents, us, and the Stuarts. I don't know. Pull the agreements."

"I asked Clara to do that. If you grandparents didn't survive, where would the shares go?"

"I don't know that either. Likely to Missy, Matt, and Lorraine since they'd be the only remaining heirs."

"Where are the Stuarts?"

"On their way, here. They'll get a room in Delaware tonight and arrive here tomorrow."

"Does he carry?"

"No. I doubt Emily would allow that."

"Okay. Touch base with them today. Have them call you when they arrive in New York."

"Okay, Mark. I'll let you go. Call me when you can."

"Okay, Grandpa. Bye." I ended the call.

"Shit! My maternal grandparents are enroute to Greenport. They will be in town tomorrow. LT, Talbot, head to the house, please. Chief. Stick to Matt's side. Get me Surfer, please, Chief, then go sit with Matt. We'll all get on the satcoms. Shit! LT. When you get to Greenport, one of you cover Lauren at the school."

"Roger, that, Mark. Let's go Talbot."

"Get me Kev and Mikey, too, Chief."

"Aye, sir." Chief ran out of the office.

Mikey came hurrying in. "What's up, Mark?"

"Just a second, Mikey. Wait for Kev and Surfer." I said as they entered the room.

"Surfer. I need you to cover my Aunt Lorraine. I'm calling her now. Guys, I'm not sure, but I think an attempt may be made to wipe out my family this weekend." I punched up Lorraine's number. I got voice mail.

"Bernice."

"Yes, sir."

"Take this number down and call it until you reach my Aunt Lorraine. I must speak with her ASAP."

"Yes, sir."

"What about your Aunt Betsy?" Kev asked.

"She's one body removed from being an heir to shares. Matt would have to die first before Betsy was in line to become a shareholder. Lorraine is, too, but I recall something about her being named as a shareholder or controlling shares. Lorraine is my mother's blood. My mother was a shareholder. So, if I'm correct, my mother may have been targeted for a reason. Shoot! Missy." I punched Missy's number on my phone.

"Hi. You've reached Missy MacKenzie at MacKenzie Realty. I want to talk to you as soon as I can. Please leave your name and number or call my office at . . ."

Jeez, Aunt Missy. I'll be dead of old age before I get through your call greeting.

"Missy. Mark. Call me as soon as you get this message. Kev take the . . . hold on. You spook Rizzo, don't you?"

"He doesn't seem to enjoy my company."

"Okay. Mikey. Take the car service to my Aunt Missy's office. Stay on the coms."

"Aye, sir," Mikey said as he departed.

"Kev, stay on Rizzo. I want to know if he farts. You have a SIG with you and what else?"

"A couple of blades and a collapsible baton."

"Okay. He doesn't get near Matt. If Matt goes to his office, you and Chief are there."

"Mark. Rizzo has a guy in his office who doesn't look like a broker.

"Okay. Watch him."

"Mark. What's going on?" Matt said as he entered my office.

"Hey, Matt. I've got some security issues that have come up. Chief will always be with you whenever you leave your office or the house."

"But Mark . . ."

"Matt. Not now. I've been AWOL on this and I'm trying to recover. Do you have any reason to see Rizzo or any of his people?"

"I have an 11 a.m. with him and the other twelve percent shareholders."

"Whaaat? Why?"

"I'm not sure."

"What would you discuss with twenty percent of the shareholders that the rest of the shareholders wouldn't be a part of the discussion?"

"Anything, really. These people are Rizzo's family members."

Family members? I looked at my watch. It was nearly 10 a.m.

"Okay, Matt. I'll be in there, too. Chief will pat-down Rizzo and anyone else who goes into the big conference room."

"Mark, you need to slow down."

"Matt, don't. I can feel it. Just please do as I say. Chief. You have your orders."

"Aye, sir."

Matt glared at me then walked out of my office.

"Kev. Go."

"Yes, sir."

"Clara."

"I'm still looking for them, sir. The shareholder agreements were not in the safe. Marsha is looking for them," she said.

"Clara. Call my father's attorney for the agreements. Here is his number. Have them faxed over."

"Yes, sir."

"Clara. What are the names of the shareholders with Rizzo?"

"Just a sec, sir." Clara ran to her desk then hurried back.

"There are three names. Raymond Ferrara, John Sciortino and Michael Frucci."

"What? Wait a minute. Frucci is . . ."

"Sir, Lorraine on two," Bernice said.

"Thanks, Bernice. Aunt Lorraine. Where are you?"

"I'm just pulling up in front of my apartment. Why?"

"You're at West 100th Street, right?"

"Yes."

"Don't go in yet. Can you go to Missy's office until I can get a guy up there?"

"Mark. What's wrong?"

"Lorraine, I have some security concerns. Can you go to Missy's or to the SoHo loft?"

"Okay. Just a second, Mark." I heard Lorraine direct the cab driver to take her to the loft. "Mark. I'm going to the loft. What's up?"

"I'm sending Surfer up there. He will escort you home. Robert, Tony, and several techs are at the loft now. I don't want you alone until I tell you it's okay. I will speak with you once I know more. Surfer is on his way. I gotta go."

"Okay, Mark. Call me, please."

"I will. Bye."

"Go Surfer. I don't even care if she doesn't go home. She can stay at the loft for now." *The loft*! I called Rob.

"Yeah."

"Rob. Family tree ancestry."

"Got it. Let me pull it out."

"Rob. Tell me if Rizzo is related to Raymond Ferrara, John Sciortino or Michael Frucci?"

"No. Frucci is an alias of Michael Farina. John Sciortino is a second cousin of Paul Menduni on the mother's side. I don't know a Ferrara. He's not listed in any of the ancestry, certainly not related to Rizzo."

"Do you have Rizzo's ancestry there?"

"Yeah."

"Fax it over here along with the papers that connect Sciortino to Menduni. Right away."

"Roger. Bye."

"Bye. Clara anything from the attorney?"

"They're looking. He's in court."

"What about Barbara or Margie? Ask them."

"Mark, sir, I'm sorry, I've already asked them. Margie was sure she had copies in her desk, but she cannot find them."

"Clara, get Barbara and look on the computer for them."

"Sir. A fax just came in for you from Robert," Bernice said.

"Thank you." Shit! I punched Joe's number.

"Yeah."

"Joe. Mark. I think I got it. It has to do with the shareholder agreements."

"Slow down, Mark. What do you mean?" Joe said.

"My father owned twenty-five percent of the shares."

"Oh? I thought it was thirty-seven percent?"

"No. My mother owned twelve percent of the shares. Matt owns twenty-five percent and my grandparents owned fifteen percent each for a total of thirty percent. When Grandpa retired, Grandma sold twelve of her fifteen percent to my mother. She retained three percent that will pass to Lorraine. What happens to the shares when people die is what's important."

"It follows what the will says," Joe said.

"Not necessarily. The shareholder agreement may control, and it would trump the will. Anyway. My whole family will be in New York this weekend. Lorraine will be out at the Greenport house since her parents will be there. Recall what we discussed last night. There is no earthly reason to kill my mother unless they were trying to gain her wealth."

"What were her shares worth?"

"Twenty-five to $30 million."

"That's a reason. So, they kill your parents, but they still have you and Lauren."

"Recall I was almost dead last year. I'd just begun to improve, but, as Bernice pointed out, no one knew until the funeral that I was improving."

"So, three down, but then Lauren, your paternal grandparents, Missy and Matt."

"That's right. Lauren's shares or thirty-seven would be held in trust. At her demise they would pass up to my grandparents then to Matt and Missy. I just learned that Matt is about to have a meeting with the twenty percent shareholders. The names of the shareholders are Raymond Ferrara, John Sciortino and Michael Frucci," I said.

"Are you kidding me? What the fuck? You need to be in there. Do you think Farina will show up there?"

"He's never seen me, so I have no reason to think he won't appear. But I did learn that the twenty percent shareholders are not related. Moreover, I can find nothing where money changed hands selling the shares to these guys. You saw the accounts. The old shareholder sold his shares back to the firm and that was clearly marked in the books. But one of the shareholders is related to someone we know. John Sciortino is a Paul Menduni's second cousin. Other than that, there is no relationship so if shares were sold to them, they were not eligible to buy the shares since the agreement called for them to be related to Rizzo. "

"I don't like any of this. You have provided motive and connected the players. You have coverage there for everyone?" Joe asked.

"Yeah. Chief will be there, and we'll pat everyone down."

"Let me get with Cicola and Stayton. I'll fill them in so we can bat it around. If someone wanted to wipe out your family, this is the weekend. I'll call you back. Bye."

"Bye."

"Mark. Three more men just appeared at Rizzo's office. One about fifty-five to sixty, looks like a lawyer. Another in his late thirties, looks like a wise guy. The last one looks like Haley's ex-husband. Then the original creepy guy. Two guys are carrying."

"Kev, this is not good. Hold on. Chief. You getting this?"

"I got it. Kev, as they move to the big conference room, you tail them. I'll be with Matt already inside the room. Mark, you're carrying, too, right?"

"I am. I do not want a shootout. This is the plan. Chief, you'll be in the room with Matt. You'll check them at the door. Kev, you will cover, and I will appear at that point from the executive hallway. Gents this will be very dangerous. Rizzo is a hothead and so is Menduni. I don't think Farina/Frucci, the lawyer-looking guy, is a problem. I don't know about the other two. Hold on. Clara. How many security guys are in the garage?"

"Six, sir."

"Ask two of them to come up to reception and ask building security to send two security guards, too."

"Yes, sir."

"We'll post the uniformed guards at the conference room door and in reception. We'll move on your que, Kev. Chief, have Matt in the conference room five minutes before the meeting. Kev, I will handle anyone who acts up. You cover in case another weapon appears."

"Aye, sir."

"Sir. The security guards are here," Clara said.

"I'm coming out to brief them. Thank you."

#

I posted the guards. Four guards, three SEALs. No problem. It was 10:50 a.m.

"Sir, do you want me to accompany you?" Clara said.

"No, Clara. I want you out of the line of fire. If anything goes wrong, you sound the alarm."

"Shit, sir. I'm worried," Clara said.

"Don't be. It's just tight quarters if they go for their weapons."

"Mark. Audrey was on the phone with her boss. She's off. Would you like to speak with her now?" Bernice said.

"No, Bernice. After this meeting. Clara. Shareholder agreements?"

"We're looking, sir."

"Mark. We're moving to the conference room. Matt is not happy, and he looks very nervous," Chief said.

"Roger. Put him at the head of the table and take your position. Security is . . ."

"I got them. They see me," Chief said.

"Mark. Movement in Rizzo's office. They're standing up. They're coming out. Rizzo just avoided looking me in the eye. They're walking to the conference room. I'm behind them."

"I'm walking, too. I'll hold when Chief blocks then I'll enter the hallway," I said.

"Roger," Kev said.

"Excuse me. I need to pat you down. We've had a security concern today," Chief said.

I opened the door and walked toward the conference room. They were boxed in between us now. It was Farina with them. He looked at me without a hint of recognition.

"What the fuck are you doing here?" Paul Menduni said when he spotted me.

Rizzo turned to Paul. "You know him?" Rizzo said.

"That's the guy. He's the one who put Monty on his back and fucked with me at the softball game. Shit that fucker standing in front of us was there, too," Paul said as he pointed at Chief.

"I'm sorry. I don't think I've met all of you gentlemen. Mr. Rizzo, would you be so kind as to introduce your guests? But first things first. This is a no weapons office, gentlemen. We've had a security threat so we're checking everyone," I said. The two men I did not know looked around at Kev, Chief, the security guards then at me. The guards all stepped forward.

"Listen, MacKenzie . . ."

I put my hand up. "Mr. Rizzo. I'm the president designate of this firm, and you are my employee. I'm Mr. MacKenzie to you. Gentlemen. I apologize for that. I stepped forward with my hand extended to Farina.

"I'm Mark MacKenzie and you are?"

"Oh. Hi. I'm Michael Frucci."

"It's nice to meet you," I said as I almost crushed his hand as we shook.

"And you are?"

"Mr. Ferrara, Ray Ferrara."

"It's nice to meet you, Mr. Ferrara. Please pass your weapon to the uniformed guard. He'll hold it until you leave." Ferrara appeared surprised that I was aware of his weapon.

"You are?" I said.

"John Sciortino and what's with all this?"

"It's nice to meet you, Mr. Sciortino. You'll need to check both your weapons with the uniformed guard. My, my, what do you gentlemen do with all these weapons," I said.

Sciortino looked at me like he could kill. Menduni had had enough. "Listen, motherfucker . . ." I put my hand up and cut him off.

"Mr. Menduni, I don't know why you're here. Do you have business with my firm? I know you are not a shareholder. I was under the impression this was a meeting of the minority shareholders and the president," I said. Menduni looked at me then to Farina/Frucci who gave off no signals, then to Sciortino who was itching for a fight, but since he looked to be about five-foot-five, I didn't expect him to do anything.

"Yeah. That's right. It's a meeting with the minority shareholders and the president. You're not the president," Rizzo said.

"Mr. Rizzo, if you ever presume to tell me anything ever again, you'll find yourself on the street. Am I clear?" That was all it took. Rizzo swung at me, I ducked, came up and stepped into him and put him down with hard right jab to his solar plexus. Rizzo left his feet and flew backwards several feet landing on his back as he struggled to breathe. Paul Menduni stupidly took this opportunity to attack me. I slammed my left elbow into his nose, breaking it, and hit him with a right jab to his solar plexus, a left jab to his gut followed by a sweep with my left leg putting him down. Shorty went for his weapon. I stepped into him, grabbing his arm, twisting it up behind his back putting him in a sleeper hold.

"I'll snap your arm off and beat you with it if you persist. Clara. Please get Mr. Menduni a towel. Now if you wish to discuss something with us, gentlemen, we are available. Weapons please!" I said as I released Sciortino, one of his pistols already in my hand. Sciortino passed his other weapon to the guard, and I passed the weapon I took from him to the guard after ejecting the magazine and noting no bullet was chambered.

Kev and Chief observed with mild amusement showing on their faces. I looked at Matt and he looked sick. Clara and Bernice appeared with towels as a few employees looked through windows and doors.

"Kev, join Chief in the conference room. Security. Please escort Mr. Rizzo to his office. Mr. Rizzo. Mr. Rizzo. Are you in need of an ambulance or doctor?" I asked.

He didn't look good. I may have crushed his sternum or stopped his heart. Rizzo sat there attempting to breathe with the assistance of the guard who helped him sit up.

"Mr. Menduni. You don't look well. Do you require medical assistance, or can your driver take you to the hospital to have that nose checked?" I said. Paul was out of it. I turned to the uniformed guard who remained. "Would you escort Mr. Menduni to his SUV. It's a black Lincoln Navigator. His driver and security detail will take care of him." I turned and bent down to speak to Menduni. "Mr. Menduni. If you appear on this premise again, you'll be considered a trespasser. A bit of advice. If you ever threaten a family member, friend, or employee of mine again, all the plastic surgeons in New York won't be able to help you." Then I leaned down as I assisted him to his feet and whispered to him, "If you go near Haley, I'll kill you." I stood him up. The guards took ahold of him and walked him to the elevators.

"Thank you, officers. One of you please remain with Mr. Rizzo. Mr. Rizzo. Do not leave today without checking out with me. Of course, if you need medical assistance, we will obtain that for you. Thank you, officers. I'll be in the conference room if you need me."

#

I took a seat near Matt across the table from Farina/Frucci.

"I'm terribly sorry about that, gentlemen. Mr. Rizzo will be disciplined for his outburst. I'm not sure of your connection to Mr. Menduni, but I won't be filing charges against either man. Why are you gentlemen here?" I looked at Farina/Frucci as he was the obvious leader. Matt sat nervously observing the meeting.

"It involves some business we had with your late father," Farina/Frucci said.

"Firm business or personal business? I stand in my father's shoes on both accounts."

"Listen, sonny, knock off the bullshit. You know who we are and we have business with your father. We're here to collect," Sciortino said.

"I take it you expect me to understand what you're talking about from your little colloquy?" I said.

"A what? Listen. You might think you're someone here, but listen to me you fucker . . ."

"No. You listen to me, and you listen good, you little sawed off grom. I do know who you are. First, you are not family, nor are you related to Mr. Rizzo. Your fraudulent statement notwithstanding, that alone is enough for me to call a meeting of shareholders and put to a vote divestiture of your shares. I'm quite certain you did not pay for the shares so that means I pay you a percentage of nothing. If you'd like me to keep digging, I will. Now, Mr. Frucci, is it today, or should I call you Mr. Farina? I know who you are. I will speak with you to resolve any other issues. Mr. Ferrara . You are not related to any of these men, nor are you relate to Mr. Rizzo by blood, are you?"

"No. I am not."

"How much of your money did you put in to allegedly purchase shares of this firm?"

"You don't have to answer that," Sciortino said.

"Mr. Sciortino, do you purport to be an attorney now, too?" I said.

Sciortino looked at Matt then stood. "This ain't over, mother fucker," Sciortino said.

"Mr. Sciortino, how much do you contend you paid this firm for the shares?" I said.

"Twenty million dollars!"

"Fine. I have your social security number. I will issue a 1099 and suspicious activity report with the IRS and New York State Tax Department forthwith. You can explain to them where you got that $20 million. Where shall I send your copy?" I said.

"Fuck you. This ain't over."

"Mr. Sciortino, you are wrong. It is over for you. As Mr. Farina will tell you, not only do I have a quorum of shareholders present in the room by holding my grandparents' proxy," I tossed a copy to Mr. Farina, "I hold eighty percent of the voting shares with my uncle present. Accordingly, I hereby move to divest the so-called Rizzo Family, twenty percent shareholders of their shares in accordance with the shareholder agreement and bylaws of the firm, seconded and passed. But since you never paid any money to obtain those shares the motion is superfluous as the firm already owns those shares. I will have the minutes of this meeting memorialized, and copy forwarded to Messrs. Farina and Rizzo. Mr. Ferrara. Have you ever paid this firm any money?"

"No, sir. I did not."

"What is your connection to Rizzo? You don't look like a wise guy?"

"We went to school together," Ferrara said. Farina was looking at Ferrara .

"Mr. Farina. Do you have something to add?" I said.

"No. I don't. I would like to discuss resolution of this problem."

"Did you arrive together or in separate vehicles?" I asked.

"Separate vehicles," Farina said.

"Fine. Mr. Sciortino. It was nice to meet you. It will never happen again, for your own sake. You are a convicted felon. I will turn your weapons over to NYPD to be destroyed. If you wish to push the issue and create a scene, I will toss you out of here and explain to NYPD where I got the weapons. Good day, sir. You are not welcome in the office ever again. Should you cause a problem for my employees, I will take appropriate measures to neutralize you. Mr. Ferrara. Do you have a permit to carry that weapon?"

"No. I do not."

"Then leave an address with my receptionist where you would like me to mail it to as you leave. Good day, gentlemen." Sciortino and Ferrara got up. Sciortino started to say something, and Farina glared at him and shook his head. The two men departed.

#

"What is it you wish to resolve with us, Mr. Farina?"

"I'd like to speak with you in private," he said.

I looked at Matt who was sending mixed signals. I couldn't tell if he was relieved or concerned. "That's up to the president of the firm, sir. I will speak to you if he so desires," I said.

"Fine with me, Mr. Farina, is it? I don't know what business we could possibly do together. You may speak to the next president. He has my full authority. Good day." Matt walked out. Chief followed Matt out.

Boy was he good if he knows something. Who was lying, or did they not know each other though they were at NYU together? I nodded Kev out of the room.

"I guess you don't need a bodyguard the way you handle yourself," he said.

"No. I don't. What can I do for you, Mr. Farina?"

Farina looked out the window for a long minute before speaking. "I'm not really sure what you can do for me," he said as he studied me. "So, you'll take over the firm soon? You're a young guy."

"That's what my uncle said. Mr. Farina is there something you want from me?"

"There is. I need to ask a few questions first. Have we recently spoken to each other?"

The conference room intercom buzzed followed by Clara's voice.

"Excuse me. Yes, Clara."

"Mr. Frucci's assistant would like to speak to him. She's at reception."

"Thank you, Clara. Mr. Farina, shall I have her escorted here?" I said.

"Please. If you wouldn't mind."

"Clara. Please bring her to the conference room."

"Yes, sir."

"Now you were saying?" I said.

"You recently had a meeting with several other firms. It was set up as a light lunch to get to know you as the incoming president. My assistant, not the lady with me now, told me. Rizzo confirmed the short get-together . . ." A knock at the door and Clara entered with, of all people, Farina's daughter, Angelina. She walked to her father while looking at me like she saw a ghost.

"Hello. I'm Mark MacKenzie," I said as I extended my hand across the table to her.

Angelina stepped back then looked at her father who was crying. Angelina looked from her father to me.

"It's you, right? Please! I can tell by your eyes. Once I looked into them the other night, I knew you wouldn't hurt me. Can you help us? Please!"

I stood there momentarily lost as to what to do. I looked at Clara who was completely baffled. I sat down and indicated that Angelina should, too.

"Mr. Farina. Tell me what it is you wish me to do for you. I want to hear what you can do and what I can do."

"The other night. You asked me what I knew about twelve murders. You and other men, I don't know how many, snatched me from my home. You returned me there. My daughter had just returned home. You grabbed her. As she stated, she knew you wouldn't hurt her. She thinks you are real, that you were sent to help my family."

"Who knows you are here besides those four men?"

"No one. It's part of my work I do for some businesses."

"What happens if you come in now?"

"They will freak out. But what you asked about the other night is happening. Of course, you just took out two of them, so I don't know. I suggest both sides will be confused now," Farina said.

"Hold on." I tapped my cell.

"Yeah, Mark."

"It's starting. Look Joe, I can't talk. Is Stayton there?"

"No. Dan and a few of the others are here. Dan's in charge. Here he is."

"What's up, Mark?" Dan asked.

"Farina is in my office with his daughter. He wants to come in. After what happened today, I concur. He and his family should be brought in."

"I'm on it. Stayton is in town and may be headed there now. I'll check. Should we pick him up there?"

"Here is the problem. Hold on." I walked out of the room.

"Look, Dan. Can we bust Rizzo for murder?"

"We have enough, yes. It's NYPD's, but we could say it is part of the RICO enterprise."

"Okay. He's here. He's not feeling well. I had to put him down."

"What?"

"No time to explain. Dan, can you extract Farina's wife . . . hold on." I opened the door. "Where is your mother, Angelina?"

"At home."

"Can she leave the house unmolested?"

"Yes. Where should she go?"

"Hold on."

"Dan. His wife is at home, but she can leave. Where should she go?"

"Okay. Tell her to meet us at the Italian deli at the first intersection in Locust Valley, one block from her husband's office. We'll call her *Mary* when we approach her."

"Roger. I'll hold Rizzo. Get a warrant. I can hold him on an A&B for now. Get Stayton here ASAP. Bye. Angelina. Call your mother and tell her they will meet her at the Italian deli by your father's office in Locust Valley. They will call her *Mary*."

"Dad. Dad. I'm calling mom."

"Do it now, Angelina," I said. I spoke into my microphone. "Kev. Go pat down Rizzo and cuff him. They're getting a murder warrant now. Scare the shit out of him. The FBI is coming for him."

"Roger."

"Chief, tell Matt he needs to go. Now. It's not safe for him as there has been a particularized threat made on his life. Take him home. Now."

"I'll tell him. He seems pissed off about earlier."

"Fine. Tell him I'll speak with him when I have it under control."

"Roger."

"Clara."

"Yes, sir."

"Shareholder agreements?"

"Still looking. The Westbury attorney's office still hasn't responded."

"Where is Audrey?"

"In the little conference room."

"Ask her to get copies of the shareholder agreements from her firm. Ask Bernice to bring water and coffee to the large conference room, please."

"Yes, sir."

Kev waved me over to the door.

"Yeah."

"Rizzo is not doing well. I think we should call the EMTs," Kev said.

"Ask reception to call them. Crap. He's cuffed?"

"Yes. His secretary and assistant are acting funny, making calls, whispering and have been on the computers."

"I'll handle it. Thanks. Go cover him after you stop by reception to call the EMTs."

"Aye."

I walked to the brokers area. "Ira. Rizzo's assistants. Keep them off the phones and computers. Take their cell phones. Put them in the break room and tell they may not leave until they check out with me."

"Okay, Mark. Holy shit. What a day," Ira said.

"I'll chat with you later, Ira." My phone buzzed.

"Yes."

"It's Stayton. We're coming in. I have twelve agents with me."

"We're cool here. I'll let reception know. Rizzo is cuffed."

"We're on our way up."

"Clara. Tell reception I have twelve people coming up. Send them to the large conference room."

"Yes, sir.

I looked at Farina. He didn't look good, and I didn't hit him.

"Angelina. Did you speak to your mother?" I said.

"She is on her way. She was ready to go. We already packed our trunks with suitcases."

"I'm sorry this is happening to you. I wish it was different for you," I said as I noticed several FBI agents swarm the room led by Stayton.

"Mark. Terrific. We'll take it from here. Mr. Farina. Ms. Farina. I'm Special Agent Stayton. This is Deputy Marshall Phillips. She will speak to you and tell you what will happen over the next few days. Your father knows this, but initially, you, your mother and your brothers will go to a temporary location."

"I understand," Angelina said.

Angelina turned to me and hugged me. "Thank you, Mr. MacKenzie. I'll never forget you for saving my life. I wish you well."

"Goodbye, Angelina. Good luck to you, too," I said.

"Where's Rizzo?" Stayton asked.

"In his office with one of my guys watching him."

"What happened here today?" Stayton asked.

I related what had occurred today. "Their pistols are still in my custody. Farina says it's starting. The young guys are deposing the old guard," I said.

"We'll see. Let's go get Rizzo."

I led the agents to Rizzo's office. Two agents already had him. Rizzo looked pissed and in pain, as he still could not breathe right. They cuffed him with standard cuffs and walked him away. He'd be charged with murder and a slew of other crimes before the FBI and New York were done with him. I couldn't help but smile when Rizzo was marched past me. Kev saw it, too.

"Kev. Cover reception, please. Excellent job. Thanks," I said.

"Shit. You haven't lost your touch either. You thumped them. So, when do we eat around here today?"

"I'll send Clara over to take your order. Thanks."

I walked to the large conference room. Angelina, Farina, and Deputy Marshall Phillips were sitting at the far end of the table talking and going over some papers. Farina looked weak. Angelina was holding him. I wondered why a man would put his family through something like this. I sipped my coffee and noticed Ira and Steve trying to get my attention. I walked to them.

"My office, guys," I said as we walked to my office.

"What do you have?"

"Rizzo's secretary and assistant sent out some emails. I have them here. Essentially, they were notifying several other addresses that Rizzo was in cuffs and arrested by a big plain clothes officer. Kev, I suppose. They also got out that someone, they speculated that it was you, hurt Rizzo and Menduni. Here are the emails. Shall I have Marsha dismiss them?" Steve said.

"No. Not yet. Where are they?" I said.

"In the break room as you directed," Steve said.

"They know something. We'll let the FBI and NYPD speak to them before we dismiss them. Give the FBI those emails. Steve call Tony and pass them to him. Tell him to find out who they sent the emails to."

"Got it."

"Lock up their computers and desks. Do you have their phones?" I asked.

"Yes. Already downloaded them. Pass them to Tony?"

"Yes. Ira, the impact on your department with what you have going on amid all this?"

"We're okay. The new guys are killing it, and the established guys are going after them. Despite all this, if they keep it up, this could be the best week we ever had!"

"Keep it up, Ira. This is terrific. Do what you need to do to run your department. Rizzo's secretary and assistant are history. If you want more staff, do it."

"I have a few I'm thinking about. Marsha is already looking at two ladies now."

"Great. Thanks, gents. Great job."

Ira and Steve departed. It was nearly 4 p.m. Where did the time go? I went looking for John Stayton. I found him in a spare office someone let him set up shop in. I caught his eye and he waved me over.

"Yeah, Mark."

"I have Rizzo's secretary and assistant in the break room. I think you all should talk to them about these emails." I laid them on the desk in front of him. John read a few.

"They're part of it, too?" John said.

"On some level. They'll be dismissed for cause, but I thought you should know. I think they're part of my problem here."

"Well, that's it then. You got them all," John said.

"Nope. One left. The Invisible Man. I gotta go. Security will let you out and lock up if you stay late. Marsha and a few of Steve's people will be here to aid your people. What will happen to Farina's children?"

"They'll make some choices. I think that he should do some time, but that's not my call. His family will be okay. I think there's some puppy love there with Angelina toward you. You did a good thing. My other teams, New Jersey, New York, NYPD, and Nassau are getting ready. I guess your op is on track?"

"What are you talking about, John?" John looked at me and smiled. "OpSec!" "I have some things to do. I'll speak with you later or tomorrow."

"See you, Mark. Thanks. I mean it."

#

I called Missy first from my office. "Hello, Mark. I heard. I'm all safe here. Can I take him home with me?" My aunt always put a smile on my face.

"He'll escort you home. What are your plans for the weekend?"

"Well, Dad—Grandpa—ordered me to be out at the house so I've reorganized my schedule of open houses and my staff are covering me. I also organized a shopping trip for the girls for Saturday. Lorraine will be there, too."

"Good. Thank you. That alleviates some of my worry. Let me go. I have more to do."

"Thank you, Mark. We all appreciate your leadership," Missy said.

"I'll see you tomorrow. Goodbye, Aunt Missy."

"Bye, Mark."

I called Surfer.

"Yeah."

"You okay there?" I said.

"Yes. I've convinced her to stay here. She's taken the master bedroom, so she has privacy. Your Aunt Missy will come by with a car tomorrow and they'll drive to Greenport together. Your grandfather's orders." Surfer said.

"Okay. Joe, Carl, Ken, and Tony are all up looking and listening."

"They are. They're talking. I'll go back and get on a computer tonight and help. I've learned so much with them. Those guys are sharp. LT is up to date and Chief is back at

Matt's house. Betsy is there, too, home from work. Call Chief. Betsy and Matt had a fight and were arguing. Betsy said she was taking a few days off and going to Greenport. Matt told her no, that she shouldn't go, that he wasn't going since he had work to make up. Betsy is very angry with Matt. I mean the whole idea is to put your family together where we can protect them, right?"

"It is. I'll speak with him. Tell Lorraine I'll speak with her later and not to worry."

"I will. I'm told you haven't lost anything since you last kicked my ass?"

"I suppose. I'm just getting weary. I almost feel under more stress here than in the ops we did in Afghanistan," I said.

"It is more stressful. You're protecting your family. You'll be fine. We're here to help."

"Thanks, Surfer. Chat with you later."

"Clara. I forgot to ask. Do we have the shareholder agreements?"

"No and yes. We have not found the originals nor copies, but copies of them were placed in the notebooks we made for you while you were in the hospital."

"That's right. Good thinking, Clara. How is the op going?"

"Audrey said the civil actions are drafted, signed, and have filing fees attached. Service and media copies were made. Audrey wanted to know if you wanted to add a case for what happened today?" Clara said while giggling.

"No. We'll let that go to the victims. I only got a spot of blood on my cuff. You do make me laugh though," I said as Clara smiled.

"The stocks are still climbing. The purchases have slowed a bit, but nothing to be concerned with. I guess it depends on what the bad guys do to respond to what happened today."

"Thanks for reminding me. I need to make a call."

"Yes, sir."

I punched in Anthony's number.

"Hello."

"Hello, Anthony. This is Mr. Smith. Have you been getting the pizzas?"

"Yes. Thank you."

"You're welcome. What have you observed across the street since we last spoke?"

"Basically, lots of meetings with various people. He has some young, big guy with him sometimes, but I seen some other guys in his office. I can send you all my pictures. Something happened at his office today. I seen Feds show up then I seen EMTs and other shit go on. The guy left early like the young, big guy was making him leave just before all the Feds showed up. He must be a bodyguard or something," Anthony said.

"Good work. Put it all on a jump drive. A runner will come by and pick it up. The runner will announce 'Pick-up for Mr. Smith.'"

"When?"

"Within the hour."

"I'll be here."

"Anything else I should know, Anthony?"

"No. Until today, it's been quiet."

#

"Clara. I'm leaving. Please send a runner to the office across the street to pick up something for me. Ask him to say, 'Pick up for Mr. Smith.'"

"Yes, sir. I'll leave it on your desk."

#

I got into my car and drove east. I turned up an old Bad Company song my parents played a lot when I was young. I liked the old rock. I crawled along at twenty-five miles per hour out of Manhattan. I saw my tail, two of them now in a Suburban and an Impala. I crossed into Long Island City and could pick up speed to thirty-five miles per hour.

I needed to speak with Matt about several issues. I knew he was upset about today. I needed to know about the Farina-NYU connection, if there was one. I didn't see any recognition on Farina's or Matt's face today, but who knows? What's going on with Matt and Betsy? I needed to think. My phone buzzed just as I passed the First Calvary Cemetery.

"Hello."

"Hey, it's me," Haley said.

I smiled just hearing her voice. "Hi. How are you?"

"Just a little tired, but, well, what happened today? I'm told that Paul, my ex, is in the hospital. He'll be there for a few days, per my son, so he won't be getting Paulie this weekend. Unofficially, I'm advised that you put him there?"

"It's a long story, but yes. I didn't mean to, but, well, it happened."

"Mark, it's nothing to be ashamed about. I heard you clobbered Rizzo first and that he's been arrested for murder."

"True on both accounts. Farina and his family came in. They've gone off into witness protection."

"You had a very productive day."

"Tell me about it. Are we still on to do something when this is over because I really need it," I said.

"Yes, we are. Whatever you want. Oh, Missy called. I guess everyone will be out again this weekend. We'll all go shopping on Saturday. It will be fun," Haley said.

I thought it was like the war and my mother redecorating. Here I'm at war with the mob and Saturday is shopping day. I guess that's the point—keeping their lives normal.

"Good. I don't know what I'll be doing yet. I have to get through tomorrow."

"Well, I'm making dinner for Paulie. My mother is going to her bridge club. Dad wanted to work on a wood project with Paulie later, so I'd like to come over and hug my man if that's all right?"

"You know it is. You're always welcome. I'm in Queens. Traffic is bad. I'll be there in about two hours at this rate."

"I'll be there when you arrive. Bye. I love you."

"Me too, Haley. Thanks for your call."

#

I pulled up to the house at 7:20 p.m. The FBI guys pulled in right behind me. I wonder why there were so many of them. I put my car in the garage and walked to the house.

"Mark!" Lauren yelled as she jumped into my arms.

"That's a greeting," I said as Haley walked up and kissed me.

"Hi. How are you?"

"I'm good. Hungry," I said.

"Well, Grandma has plenty. Come on in. You look tired," Haley said.

"I know. Let me go say hello then I want to undress, shower, and get comfortable."

"Sure. Only Grandma is here. Grandpa is out in the boat. Talbot is showing him how to operate it. They're just off the beach. LT is with them. Did you see your neighbor's house?"

"No."

"Look out there. Out front on the left."

"What's going on?"

"They went to the Outer Banks two weeks early. The FBI rented their house. There are about eight agents living there," Haley said.

I wondered why?

"Hi, Grandma," I said.

"How are you, Mark?"

"Good. I'm hungry and tired. I just want to shower and change before I eat."

"Go do that. Lauren, Haley, and I will be here to fix you a plate. Dinner is ready."

"Thanks." I trudged upstairs to my room. Why were all those agents staying in that house? I needed a shower to relax. I undressed and as I stepped into the shower, Lauren and Haley walked in.

"Can't a guy get some privacy?"

"No. So what happened today? The rumor is you crushed Paul Menduni's face. We just heard that Rizzo was hospitalized with severe chest pains after he was arrested. Missy said . . ."

"Ah-ha!" I said.

"Anyway. She said that she was told you hit Rizzo so hard you knocked him ten feet and he never got up," Lauren said.

"Something like that."

"Paulie said his grandmother told him his father needs to have his nose and teeth fixed," Haley said.

"That so? I feel bad for little Paulie. Does he know I did it?" I shampooed my hair.

"No. They told him his father was in a car wreck," Haley said.

"Look. I must tell this story one or two more times. Can I tell you ladies something?"

They nodded.

"Even though they're bad guys and they deserved what happened, it rests on my conscious and it bothers me. I'm not picking on or criticizing you for being proud of me or happy that I defended and won on an attack. It's . . . it's the difference between me and them. They don't care who they hurt. I care who I hurt. That's all I wanted to say. You two make up two thirds of the three women with whom I'm closest too. Sometimes I just like to come home from an op, wash away the blood and the mission, and get on with my life. I just wanted you two to know so you'll understand why I withdraw or become solemn."

Haley and Lauren looked at each other and nodded. "I get it, Mark. We both do. Mark, we love you and we're glad we have you to defend us. We'll do our jobs better, too. Speaking of which, your VA doctor called looking for you. You missed your appointment. He asked how you were. I'm your sister so don't be angry with me. I told him I thought that you had finally started to grieve for Mom and Dad. He wants you to call him," Lauren said.

"Thanks. I would never get angry with you about that. As far as I can tell, I have no secrets in this family even my scars and birthmarks it seems." I smiled at Lauren and Haley.

#

"Mark, that boat is amazing. Talbot is very good on it, too. He's a fine captain. That hover or geo-positioning feature will be great for striper fishing," Grandpa said.

"I'm pretty sure that's why all you three and four-star officers wanted the GPS satellites launched into space, isn't it?" I joked, which got laughs from all.

I finished up my dinner. It was dark now. We took seats on the outside living room couch, me in my usual spot, Haley having displaced Lauren, so Lauren took the seat on to my left with Grandma and Grandpa seated across from us. I explained, as succinctly as I could, what went on today, advising that we took out three Mafioso today—two in the hospital and one in witness protection. I did not go into the shareholder motive. I still needed to read the shareholder agreements. I advised that due to the increased threat, I was circling the wagons around my family. I told them they were safe and that I hoped we'd be finished in four days. I answered some questions, but my family understood.

I sat on the couch as everyone got up to do whatever. My grandfather handed me a bourbon on the rocks. It was a nice, warm night. I needed to rest my brain, but I needed to think to plan. I told LT to make sure all the team guys were well rested. I just had a recurring feeling that we had more to do.

"Can I join you?" Haley said.

"Of course." I really liked Haley. I loved her, too, but I liked her next to me. She sat down on my left side this time and snuggled into me while covering herself with a small throw blanket.

"Will you teach me the stars?"

"Sure. I think I remember most of them. You don't mean tonight, right?"

"No. Another time. Maybe when you take me out on the boat, or we walk the beach together. Your grandfather sure likes the boat. Even at his age, men and their toys."

"We're getting an even bigger boat for you ladies."

"It's for everyone. Are you okay, Mark?"

"Yes. Right now, I'm more than okay. . ." I drifted off in thought.

"Mark. Mark!"

"I'm sorry. I need to work on that."

"No. You need to get past this and work on Lauren's future, your future and, dare I say, hopefully, our future. I still haven't seen a decoder ring. I don't know if I can just wait around like this," Haley said.

CHAPTER 19

I was up at 6 a.m. I thought that tonight I'd lose my bedroom to my maternal grandparents. Missy and Lorraine and, perhaps, Betsy would get the lower level since the extra dining room-cum-bedroom was under construction. They'd removed the siding, the deck railing, which would be put back, and the window, and the room was empty. The deck contour would bump out just like the bathroom contour would bump out from the house. A door between the bathroom and walk-in closet would lead to the deck. It would be a nice remodel. The architect and builder got the plan fast-tracked since it was previously approved. I noticed that holes had been cut and additional waste and sewer drain lines had been installed.

Talbot and LT would be back at the cottage. I noticed in my mail, that I'd neglected all week, a letter from the estate attorney accepting my repurchase offer of the cottage. I didn't tell anyone yet, though, because, unlike everyone else, I wanted to knock down the cottage and put up a nice new multi-story cottage. It was a nice lot that poked out into the bay with water on three sides, hence, bay views from three sides, yet it was higher than the surrounding land.

I pulled out my black John Varvatos suit and a bright red tie in shimmery silk with a matching pocket square. I put on cuff links that matched and my Tudor Black Bay watch. I decided to go with the Varvatos boots, too. I was ready.

I woke Lauren. "Come on, sweetheart. I want to drive you today."

"Okay. Wow. You look fabulous and confident."

"Thanks. Grandma is making breakfast so get a move on there."

"Aye, sir," Lauren said as she saluted me. She was such a MacKenzie.

"Good morning, Grandma."

"Good morning, Mark. You look nice."

"Thank you," I said as Grandma poured me coffee. In short order she placed a plate of eggs, bacon and toast in front of me. As I began to eat Grandma placed a slice of apple pie in front of me. I looked at her. I'd not told her that story. Grandma smiled at me.

"You came back every time after having a slice," she said.

I nodded at her. Lauren joined us taking a seat next to me at the bar. Grandpa joined us at his usual seat. Talbot and LT sat down as Grandma poured coffee for all. I looked up and noticed that they were looking at my piece of apple pie.

Breakfast was quiet. LT advised that the others were in place. Mikey would accompany Missy and Lorraine to the house. Check. Kev would hold down security at the loft. Check. Surfer would remain at the Oceanside house with Joe and a dozen FBI agents and Nassau County police. Check. Chief would cover Matt. Check. Betsy would drive to Greenport. Check. Matt went to the office to be there when the bond redemption began. Check. I'd already provided the bonds to Ira who would move the transactions along. Check. I finished my apple pie.

"C'mon, Lauren. We'll be late."

"Coming, Mark. Bye, Grandma, Grandpa, guys. I'll see you all later."

"Goodbye, sweetheart," Grandma said.

I got into the Hellcat which name seemed apropos to my mission. I pulled up to the steps and Lauren bounded down, her backpack on her shoulder. She got in and we were off. I pulled up to drop Lauren in front of the bakery-coffee shop. We exited the car.

"Mark. I love you. We all do. Be safe. I'll see you later. Promise me . . ." Lauren had tears in her eyes.

"Of course. C'mere." I hugged her to me.

"Don't worry. Easy day. Go do well in school." As I turned to get into the car, Haley came out of the bakery-coffee shop.

"Here," she said as she handed me a fresh coffee, "and this here is a fresh bottle of Excedrin and a couple of other things."

"Thank you, but . . ."

"I love you, Mark. All that matters is that you come home again. Nothing else counts if you aren't here."

"I'll be here." I held her close in a tight hug and kissed her. "I gotta go."

"I know. Aren't you supposed to be in white—my white knight?"

"I'm your white knight—black is the new white. I'll see you at dinner. Bye." I got into my car and drove down the street. I watched Haley in my rearview mirror waving at me. The bag contained a Coke, a pack of Oreo cookies and the bottle of Excedrin.

#

I hit my speed dial to Joe.

"Morning, Mark."

"Hey, Joe. What have you and Carl discovered?"

"First, John Sciortino and his brothers have been raising hell, but the old-school guard is not too upset or nearly as upset as John Sciortino and his family. The mystery seems to be, where is Farina? The Menduni family suspects foul play. They discovered Pagano's dog missing from old man Menduni's property and they found his collar sitting in a foot of water by the dock. Even better, they called in a stolen dog report and animal control called to advise that a Rottweiler was found dead on a beach by Oyster Bay with two bullet wounds in it. Nice touch. Surfer told me the story.

Vincenzo has called in his capos and lieutenants, Pagano and a muscle guy, but his dear daughter is in the thick of it. She told her father that Paul and Rizzo had a falling out on some double-dealing. She openly questioned why Paul and Farina had dealings with John Sciortino. She added that she thought her grandfather was behind all of it. She does not believe Paul's story about being mugged. Perhaps Paul, Rizzo, Sciortino, and Farina were up to no good trying to get that shareholder money from your firm? With Farina gone and Rizzo in the hospital . . . Oh, you caved in his sternum and bruised his heart. He has three broken ribs. I didn't remember you hitting that hard in the old days. Vincenzo doesn't know what to believe. Alexandra is in charge of finding out what happened while they bring in some lawyers, not for Rizzo, but to protect them from Rizzo and the grandfather.

Now, Bonano and Paganelli are going back and forth. They think Vincenzo hit Farina. Since they can't contact Paul, that has added to the mystery.

Sciortino is the most in the know. He just sent an email to Bonano, and he wants to meet, of all places, down on Mott Street in Little Italy. That will happen today. We're trying to figure out who all is going to be there. Only one email comes back to you, and it just talks about an appointment with Rizzo yesterday that Menduni was to attend. Alexandra Rapano has learned that. Vincenzo is going to the hospital to see Paul, but Paul has reconstructive surgery at 11 a.m."

"No one knows about me yet, then?"

"Not that we can tell."

"And the FBI?"

"Picture four hundred agents and detectives from FBI, DEA, SEC, Secret Service, NYPD, New York State, Nassau, and Suffolk getting ready. Dan didn't know the total, but they have over two hundred warrants between state and federal agencies. That's some shit, my boy. It will be an interesting weekend. First, can they keep the genie in the bottle? Then, can they take down the key people first? Here's Dan."

"Hello. Mark?"

"Yes."

"You will be happy to know that HRT and local police rescued the three women you identified who were still in the U.S. They rescued a total of six women in three raids. Two bad guys were killed. The others are being interviewed by several federal and foreign agencies. I thought you'd want to know. John already faxed their details to your team at the firm."

"Wow! You guys can be efficient when you want to be."

"Thanks. Look, we've maintained a Chinese wall here at the house between your guys and mine. You'll have to become familiar with the details Carl and Ken have found so you can advise us of the details as a previously reliable CI. All the warrants and affidavits are all but finished. Most are based upon your advice to us. We want you up-to-speed on the details."

"Fine. I can read it now. I can come by, or you can fax it to my office."

"Can you stop by now on your way in?"

"I'm about twenty minutes out. Dan, why are all the agents at my neighbor's home?"

"A precaution. The bad guys will get your name so until we get them, John wanted extra coverage on you. How would it look for us if our star CI got whacked after all this?"

"I see. Do you have anything on Rizzo's or Menduni's condition, or who knows about it?"

"Joe had our latest. No contracts have been put out on you that we know of," Dan said as he laughed.

"Thanks. I'll see you in less than twenty minutes." I looked behind at the Suburban following me. The passenger was answering his cell phone. No doubt Dan telling him I was going to Oceanside. I turned on WNEW News Radio for the half-hour news report. It announced that Allen Rizzo was arrested for murder and other offenses. Reporters would be digging now. I wondered how their investigation into Monty's death was going. I turned onto Meadowbrook Parkway. Five minutes later, I turned down my street and then into my driveway. Jeez. It looked like fifteen vehicles were in my driveway and on the street.

#

I got coffee and then went looking for Joe first. I found him with his coffee, wearing cutoff shorts, a torn T-shirt, and flip-flops. Carl was doing something on the main computer. Ken was at another computer. Dan was in the living room. The FBI had six computers up. I thought with all this and they'd never get Don Corleone since none of the business back then was on computers.

"Dan. Let me begin reading."

"That notebook there on the table. It's tabbed," Dan said.

I picked up a two-inch binder and walked to the backyard with my coffee. Before I began, I wondered what my mother would think about how her three beautiful homes had been turned into war rooms to help me track down her killers? I think she'd be surprised, and, in her usual way, she'd welcome everyone and ask them what they needed to make them comfortable. I missed my father, but my mother had my heart.

I noticed her silly bird bath in the back garden near the dock. On my first leave after I was shot—the first time—I moved that stupid bird bath around the yard a hundred times for my mother. It had to be just right and where she could see it from the patio where I now stood.

I put the binder down and placed my coffee next to it. I removed my jacket, hanging it on the back of a chair. I removed my cuff links and rolled up my sleeves. I walked to the bird bath and took the hose off the saddle in the garden. I flushed the bird bath clean and refilled it with fresh water. I rehung the hose then walked to the garage. I located the seed feeders and hummingbird feeders. I filled three seed feeders and four hummingbird feeders and carried them out to the gardens around the bird bath then hung them all on their poles and hooks. The birds had surely missed my mother.

I returned to the patio table, sat down, and sipped my coffee. The first bird appeared on a seed feeder. A sparrow. She sent out the call and before long many birds were pecking and arguing over the seeds. I decided I would not sell this home— ever.

#

Finished with my coffee and the binder, I went looking for Joe.

"Anything new?"

"Not yet. Go do your coordinating. So, when those bonds are redeemed, do we all get a finder's fee?" Joe asked.

"Not from the bonds," I said.

Joe smiled. He understood. Hey, they deserved it.

"I'm going," I said after I passed the binder to Dan. As I got into my car, I noticed the binder with the shareholder agreements that I needed to read once I got to the office.

I needed a second set of eyes on the books to advise me. No strangers would hold stock in the firm, but I'd consider an employee shareholder arrangement. I turned onto Southern State Parkway and tapped my speed dial for the office.

"MacKenzie Securities. How may I direct your call?"

"Marsha Collette, please."

"Hi, Mr. MacKenzie. Right away, sir. Bye." Jennifer put me through to Marsha.

"Marsha."

"Hi. Marsha. It's Mark."

"Good morning. What's up?"

"Who takes care of valuing our firm? Who tells us what our market value is?"

"Quarterly, our accounting firm who are checked and audited by an independent firm."

"So, the last valuation was done in April for the quarter ending on March 31st?"

"That's right."

"Based on what I did yesterday, the value of the firm changed if the accounting firm was under the impression that an additional twenty percent of our firm was owned by others?"

"I think so. I am not sure what the impact will be, if any. I read the minutes of the so-called meeting. Very interesting. Anyway, I sent that all over to the attorneys, along with the books for that time frame. There is nothing there showing any purchases of shares, only the buy-back of Mr. Baldwin's twenty percent. I confirmed the wire transfer repurchasing the shares. Our firm never received proceeds for the sale of that so-called twenty percent."

"Then how did the twenty percent shareholders become shareholders at all?"

"Mark, I can't answer that. I have searched all transactions since the year before the Baldwin repurchase. I found nothing."

"How about eighteen million in bonds purchased by the firm?"

"No. Nothing like that at one time. The fact is our bond purchases go through our investment firm who buys the bonds for us. We use that for the retirement accounts. The firm accepts bonds as payment for commissions earned, but in almost every case, we sell or redeem them within a short time. Your father preferred that we not sit on bonds. He likened it to a car dealership retaining their trade-in automobiles rather than selling them. The bonds used to pay our sales commission were substantially discounted from marketed bonds, so even if your Dad sold them a week later, we made money before we marked them up as the principal. He had no reason to sit on them."

"Were we paid with bonds on the sales of bonds for the various energy companies?"

"Yes. Up to five percent on each transaction as the agent, more if we were the principal. The increase was in the sales price. I went through the sales with Ira and Mr. Middleton. Matt went through it, too."

"What if we accepted two percent or two and a half percent, but the seller and buyer paid three or four percent and the bonds were left off the transaction?"

"You're saying the sale closed at less than three percent, but seller paid more than three percent and the difference was skimmed? I suppose that could happen. The closing documents and IRS documents would all have to be fixed or drafted to match. No big deal since it's done electronically in most cases.

I'll ask Ira to look. We'll check Rizzo's and Train's closings first."

"We're thinking alike. Next item. What was our valuation last quarter?"

"Just over two hundred fifty million."

"Wow. That's a little more than I was told. What are our reserves and liabilities?"

"Cash, stocks, bonds almost ninety million dollars. That is managed by our investment broker. Sixty-three million of that is the retirement reserve that pays the employee retirements."

"That's more than I was advised, too. So, one hundred sixty million dollars is the value of our book of business, notes and debts owed to us, fixtures, and goodwill?"

"And additional investments. The twenty percent of the shares owned by the firm is listed as a separate investment. Essentially if we sold the firm in an average market to a buyer, ready, willing, and able to buy, we should receive two hundred fifty million dollars."

"This determines the value of our shares upon which dividends are paid?"

"Yes."

"There never was twenty percent of the shares sitting out there owned by Rizzo and company after we purchased Mr. Baldwin's shares. How could that get past my father?"

"Your father did not handle that transaction. Matt handled it. Your Dad sold and instilled confidence. He took the firm from a strong going concern and made sales explode. Once the original guys retired, the tasks passed to Will, Matt, Ira and me.

Mark, I don't know where the so-called twenty percent came from. Matt handled Mr. Baldwin's repurchase and resale of shares to Rizzo and that group."

"I'm confused. I read or was told that Mrs. Baldwin recommended that Rizzo and his family members could buy her shares left to her by her late husband."

"Yes. Mrs. Baldwin was confused. She found the original stock certificates that Mr. Baldwin could not find. Mr. Baldwin executed an affidavit to that effect, and the buy-back was closed. The certificates Mrs. Baldwin held were worthless. Rizzo's neighbor told him about the stock. Hence his initial involvement. He walked through the door with the old stocks in hand, and he met with Matt a few times and once or twice with your father."

"Now I'm more confused. Farina said Rizzo was placed here. Well, I suppose, it could have been done that way, too."

"Mark. I don't want to speak out of turn, but I always thought something was wrong. It was only after your father's death that we reorganized to the point that I could see everything. I wanted to tell you when you drove me home that day. Those men, Rizzo and them, were never shareholders as far as I could determine."

"I think you're correct. Someone was skimming bonds from the transactions at closing. Our documents reported less paid in commission. It's the only thing that makes sense. I'd guess it all happened with the energy companies, so the 1099 filed with the IRS matched what these bogus companies filed. So, when we verified the bonds we held they were good because they were intended as payment for commission on the sale of many bonds. Someone was skimming them off the top, and my father found out and somehow intercepted the bonds."

"Yes. However, Matt had to know. You found eighteen million dollars in bonds. How many don't we know about? I'm sorry, Mark. I don't want to be disloyal."

"Marsha, you're not. I'm the president designate."

"I think your father found out in the months before his death. I think he approached Matt with it, or Matt ran to him scared. Will took what he could find or recover, and they found out.

Mark, you should know that your father has always taken care of Matt. Matt was a real screw off in the beginning. He bounced from firm to firm until your grandfather and father brought him in. Matt finally settled down a few years ago, but he spends his money without regard to his means. Betsy clamped down at home and she's paid very well as an organ transplant nurse. It's not a secret to us old-timers."

I had to think about this. My mother was killed because someone wanted her shares or because someone was incompetent and allowed the mob to steal from the firm. Now, who did what? Did my father cover and protect Matt and get my mother killed? This was too much for me to do right now.

"Mark. Mark!"

"I'm sorry Marsha. I was thinking. Draft a resolution for the board appointing me president of the firm. Separately, draw up a resolution accepting Matt's resignation as president and appointing him vice-president. I'll sign for Lauren and myself. I hold my grandparents' proxies, so I'll sign for them. I dispense with notice since it was already considered and passed by the board at the annual meeting in April. No one is to know of this until I speak to Matt."

"Yes, Mark. Thank you. I'll have the resolutions ready within the hour."

"How did Matt buy his shares of the firm?"

"From your grandfather and from earnings in the early years. Your grandfather sold and compensated your father with shares in the beginning then he did the same with Matt."

"Then my grandmother sold and gifted twelve of her fifteen percent to my mother, not her daughter, and arranged for Lorraine, also not her daughter, to receive the other three percent upon her demise. Why does that seem odd to me?"

"Your mother purchased the shares, and some were gifted. I'd have to look, but I think she paid about $1.2 million for the shares."

"Just $1.2 million for twelve percent of a $250 million firm?"

"Not exactly. The firm was worth about $125 million at the time."

"Okay. She multiplied her money more than twelve times."

"That's correct."

"Marsha. What am I missing in this family dynamic? It's apparent my grandmother thought my mother was special."

"I don't know all of it, Mark. Mark, we—you—have a lot to do to make this whole plan work. Get through your plan, become president, then tackle this. It's too much now. I'll speak to you and tell you everything I know, but you need to finish what you're doing to protect your family, yourself, and the firm. If you don't pull this off, you may never have another chance and I think some bad people will come looking for you."

"I'm pulling into Manhattan. I'll be there in fifteen minutes. Bye."

My God. What happened? My phone buzzed.

"Hello."

"Mr. MacKenzie. This Audrey McDermott."

"Good morning, Audrey. What can I do for you?"

"The civil actions are ready. The five boroughs, Nassau, Suffolk, six counties in New Jersey, and the federal district courts for New Jersey, The Eastern District of New York, and Southern District of New York. To have them ready for service on Monday, we must present them to the clerk today."

"Audrey. Why am I just now learning this?"

"Don't worry. The clerks will prepare them today. They will not be filed for public disclosure until Monday morning. They will go to special clerks in each court via hand delivery as a batch. We have a runner, a law clerk and a paralegal or new attorney ready to go to each court on your word. No one will know of the filings until they're noticed on Monday."

I thought back to the leadership axiom *"When in charge, be in charge."*

"They'll be filed with the court officially Monday, but you're presenting them today for clerical purposes?"

"Yes."

"File the civil actions. Service to begin by law after 8 a.m. Monday. Who will make service?"

"Private process servers for the state cases and federal officers for the federal cases. They will be served with the hearing notices. The attorneys will be before magistrate judges at 9 a.m. to enter the lien and *lis pendens* orders."

"Do it and may God protect us all."

"Sir, if I can say, this is so very exciting and historic. The causes of action—all of it. I'm very proud to be a part of this. The teams are already drafting motions and discovery. The top litigation partners are reviewing the law and cases in anticipation of the many hearings that will begin next week. We expect that additional actions will be filed."

"Thank you, Audrey."

"Sir, one more thing. Once the civil actions begin, we cannot update you . . ."

"I know all that Audrey. Attorney-client privilege."

"Then I'll speak with you later, sir. Goodbye."

"Bye."

I drove into the garage. The firm occupied most of one level of parking with the officers' parking spaces nearest to the door. I parked in the first spot closest to the elevator. I noted our security guards walking about. You couldn't miss them. With all that was going on it would make the staff feel safe. I noted Matt was not in yet. *Concentrate, Mark.* I exited the elevator and walked toward reception.

"Good morning, Mr. MacKenzie."

"Good morning, Jennifer." She buzzed me into the executive hall.

"Good morning, Bernice."

"Good morning, sir. Coffee?"

"Please. Good morning, Clara."

"Good morning, sir. You'll be happy to know that the stock of seventeen of the companies increased in value at opening and climbed some more this morning. The eighteenth company initially dropped, but it, too, is now climbing."

"Great. The order for redemption is set?"

"Yes. Ira and I, along with a representative of the other firms will coordinate. We launch in five hours and twenty-two minutes. At ten minutes to the closing bell of the stock market, between five and 10 million in bonds will be redeemed at each company. The geek boys think that will show positive on the algorithms and cause the stocks to bump up in value. The geeks think the stock will reach its apex late Monday morning or early afternoon. Based on today's closing, the price should jump Monday at opening."

"And the attorneys are sure about the ill-gotten gains bull crap? We can't just seize the stock and sell it when it hits the high?"

"Correct, because the companies and plaintiffs would benefit from insider trading. So even though a child sex slave victim could seize the stock and sell it, the SEC could come along and take it for itself."

"I should have thought of this when I spoke to the Justice Department."

"When did you do that, sir?"

"Oh, I don't know. This week is running together for me. I had to speak with them to ensure that all the assets went to the victims and not the government."

"Here's your coffee, sir." Bernice handed me my coffee.

"Thank you," I said as I grabbed from my in-box, checked the market on the eighteen companies, then I opened the binder to the shareholder agreements. Each agreement was some thirty letter-sized pages. I scanned the first one for survivorship. I found it on the second to last page. The sections were numbered with Roman numerals. I always wondered why lawyers did that? Why not use Chinese numbers, they were just as confusing? At section XXXVI or thirty-six I found it. There were six more sections to follow. I began reading:

XXXVI. Death of Shareholder and Survivorship

Should any holder suffer death or be legally declared as such by a court of competent jurisdiction, ownership of said shareholder's shares shall pass as follows:

As the shareholder elects by way of his/her last Will and Testament; or

As provided in any shareholder agreement providing for the purchase of the shares by other shareholders. Said purchase provision must be endorsed by the shareholder here, the contingent purchasing shareholder and the president of the firm. Such an agreement shall be attached herewith; or

As provided herein below to the named beneficiaries; or

As provided by New York State law.

I was reading my father's shareholder agreement. It referred to his will which I'd read. It passed his shares to my mother, or to his heirs at law if she predeceased him. She did not. She survived for more than an hour following the accident. My father died on impact. My mother died as she was placed in the ambulance having never fully regained consciousness. My father's shares passed to my mother upon his death then to Lauren and me upon her death pursuant to her will. A knock at the door.

"Come in."

"Here are the resolutions, Mark. If they're fine with you, sign where I've indicated. Have you spoken with Matt yet?"

"No. I'll do that later when he comes in. I understand he may not wish to come to Greenport this weekend. Betsy and Matt had a fight about it." I reviewed then signed the resolutions. "Copies for all and the lawyers get the originals?"

"Yes. They'll send over New York State Corporation documents, tax documents and SEC documents for you to sign. What is your first order as president?" Marsha asked.

"I want a lawyer to look at the shareholder agreements and answer my questions. There are five agreements that no one seems to be able to find, but all five—well, seven if you include the two phony agreements—are here in my binder." I withdrew them from the binder. The first fraudulent agreement was signed by Rizzo, Matt, and my father. The second one was signed by Ferrara, Frucci, Sciortino, Matt, and my father. The notary signed them on the same date. Matt and Farina had met just five years ago!

"Marsha. Look at what I'm pointing at." She followed my finger to Matt's signature then to Frucci's signature.

"I see it. So?"

"While Matt has not denied knowing Frucci/Farina, Farina has denied knowing Matt. Why would he do that? Yesterday, when they were in the conference room, they acted like they didn't know each other. Now I find out that my father and Matt signed a shareholder agreement with three men: a known felon, a mob lawyer, and a nobody. I understand Rizzo's getting by them, but what I cannot believe is these three. I cannot believe . . ."

"Please don't let him kill all of them." Why did that come to me now? What did that mean?

"Mark. MARK!"

"Sorry. I need an attorney to go over this with me. I don't think Audrey is qualified."

"I'll call over. They should have their copies by now. Perhaps a telephone conference."

"Fine."

"Mark. I want you to know I only suspected what I've learned over the past months. I would never have conceived of all of this."

"Marsha. After we sell the bonds and that's wrapped up, we'll talk."

"We will," Marsha said as she departed my office.

"Bernice, is Matt in?"

"Not yet, sir."

I called Chief.

"Yeah, Mark."

"Where's Matt?"

"In his office working when I last saw him. I just came back from a run. Surfer covered while I was out. His driver pulled up two hours ago, but Matt told him to come back at noon. Do you need to speak to him?"

"No. I'll see him when he gets in. Bye."

"Bye."

I took the jump drive the runner picked up from Anthony and put it in my computer, scanned it for viruses. Anthony saved the pictures in files by date. I began with the earliest date and set it for picture-show. I saw pictures of Matt with clients, the accountants, bond investors and others. I went through the days until I came to the day I fired Taylor. Rizzo was sitting down with Matt. A few pictures later, Rizzo was in Matt's face finger-pointing. Next, Matt had Rizzo by the arm, then the next picture showed them standing there looking at each other. I highlighted those pictures for printing. The next group of pictures I slowed down to look at was on the date after I fired Train and counseled Rizzo. Again, finger-pointing by Rizzo, anger, but this time another man, in his late fifties was sitting there unperturbed by Rizzo's conduct. He looked familiar, but the angle of the photograph didn't allow me to place him. I marked those pictures for printing. A few days later more people were in Matt's office. I recognized John Sciortino and another guy who could be his brother. A series of pictures showed Matt handing Sciortino documents and folders.

A day later, pictures taken in the late afternoon, showed my Aunt Lorraine standing in front of Matt's desk pointing at him. She looked angry. The series showed that she walked in with Barbara following, Matt pointing Barbara out of the office and Matt sitting down. Lorraine did not sit. She was yelling at him. Then she turned and walked out. What was she doing here?

I tapped my Aunt Lorraine's number. It went to voice mail. I'd see her later. I was hungry. I still didn't know the good nearby restaurants.

"Bernice. Who's nearby with good food and delivers?"

"We have a list here. I'll bring it to you."

"Thanks."

"These restaurants all deliver."

"Wow. How about if I want a large pastrami with Swiss on grilled rye, mustard on the side, pickle and chips?"

"Then I'd suggest Voltz's Deli."

"Okay. Did you bring your lunch today?"

"No. I was . . ."

"I'd like to buy you lunch then. Ask Marsha, Clara, Margie, and Barbara what they would like, too. I'd like to speak with all of you, so we can do it over lunch. Here's my credit card."

"Okay. They take about forty-five minutes."

"That's fine."

Bernice departed to place our orders.

"Sir, line seven. The attorney, Mike Schmidt," Clara said.

"Thank you. Hello."

"Good morning, Mr. MacKenzie. Mike Schmidt. I'm advised that you have questions about your shareholder agreements."

"I do. First, how many shareholder agreements are there?"

"Five. Mr. William MacKenzie, Senior, Mrs. William Martha MacKenzie, Matthew MacKenzie, you, and Lauren MacKenzie. You five are the only shareholders. Together you own eighty percent of the shares. The firm repurchased the remaining twenty from the original shareholder some six years ago. There were other repurchases prior to that when your grandfather and father changed some things, and the older guys retired. Those repurchased shares were purchased or issued as compensation to your family."

I wondered why I didn't call attorney Schmidt first. His rapid and direct answer was a stark departure from what I got around here.

"Tell me what happens to my shares if I die?"

"Based on your will they go to your sister Lauren. However, we included a provision that should you be married at the time of your demise, your wife would receive two-thirds of the shares and Lauren one-third. In the event you or we neglected to update your will, your spouse was protected, and it would avoid a lawsuit by your spouse asserting her marital election."

"I assume Lauren's is the same?"

"No. Her agreement spells out that the shares are held in trust by you as trustee and legal guardian. At her demise before age twenty-one, the ownership of the shares transfers to you. You are responsible for her and her shares until she attains the age of twenty-one years. The trust dissolves on her twenty-first birthday, and Lauren becomes a shareholder outright."

"If Lauren and I die, what happens?"

"Your shares pass to your lineal heirs."

"That's our direct descendants or up to our grandparents."

"Yes."

"Not to my aunts or uncle?"

"Correct."

"What about my grandparents' shares?"

"Your grandmother has elected to leave her shares to Lorraine Stuart-Collins. Her election is in her agreement. I cannot discuss her will with you."

"I understand. What about my grandfather's shares?"

"By will. Again, I cannot discuss that with you."

"Tell me about Matt's shares."

"Matt has a shareholder agreement permitting your father or grandfather to repurchase his shares at market minus forty."

"What does that mean?"

"Your father or grandfather may purchase the shares at sixty percent of market value."

"So, at Matt's death my grandfather or father have first right of refusal before the shares pass to my Aunt Betsy?"

"Mark, the repurchase may be exercised at any time."

What the heck? What's going on here?

"Mr. Schmidt tell me what happens if we all die except for Matt?"

"Well, I don't think I can without your grandparents' permission."

"Hypothetically, assume my grandparents' wills leave all to their heirs to share and share alike, and Lauren and I predecease them."

"Lorraine receives three percent of the firm's shares from your grandmother. At Lauren's and your demise, your shares would pass to you grandparents. Each would receive nine and a quarter percent or eighteen and a half percent to the Stuarts and eighteen and a half percent to the MacKenzies. At their demise the Stuarts's shares would go to Lorraine and the MacKenzies shares would be split between Missy and Matt."

"If someone wanted to get control of the firm by eliminating the shareholders and concentrating the shares in as few people as possible, how does the killer go about an expedient way to do that?"

"Like I just said. The surviving shareholders would own . . . Matt, 41.75%, Missy, 16.75%, and Lorraine, 21.5%."

"My Uncle Matthew would gain control of the firm."

"That's correct unless your grandfather exercised his right to buy back Matt's shares."

"How's that?"

"If your grandfather repurchased Matt's shares then died, Matt and Missy would each own 29.25% of the shares. Lorraine's percentage would not change."

"Did my father's right to purchase Matt's shares pass to me?"

"It did. The shareholder agreement is very specific in giving you that right."

"Mr. Schmidt, attorney-client privilege survives the death of the client. But I am allowed to use any and all information made known to me by my father or mother or contained in their documents that passed to me by succession. I know, as a matter of courtesy, lawyers refrain from discussing a deceased client's business, in any case. As president of MacKenzie Securities, I'd like to impose upon you as to any information I may obtain as to why my father did this?"

"Did you say 'president?'"

"I did. The corporate resolutions are being delivered to your office now. Effective today, I'm the president and Matt is the vice-president. No one knows but my administration department head and you."

"Then I have a package for you from your parents. I'll send it right over. Call me if you have any more questions. Is there anything else I can help you with now?"

"I take it the package will explain?"

"I cannot answer that because I don't know. My directive is to deliver the package to you when you became president of MacKenzie Securities."

"What if I didn't become president?"

"Then I was to deliver it to you upon your thirty-third birthday."

"Why?"

"I don't know."

"Please send the package to my office."

"Yes, sir. Goodbye."

"Bye."

"Mr. MacKenzie."

"Yes, Bernice."

"Reception just called. You have two visitors."

"I'm sorry, Bernice. I didn't check my calendar. Who are they?"

"They're not on your calendar, sir. It's Mr. Vincenzo Menduni and Ms. Alexandra Rapano."

Holy crap!

"Bernice. Ask Clara to show them to the large conference room, please. Offer them coffee, tea, or water. I'll be right in." *After I reload my weapon. Why are they here?* I tapped Joe's number.

"Yeah?"

"Guess who's in my conference room waiting to see me?"

"Who?"

"Vincenzo Menduni and Al Rapano AKA Alexandra Menduni."

"No shit? Can you wire the place?"

"It is. Call Rob or Tony and ask them to activate the large conference room."

"Will do. You okay there?"

"Yeah. They won't do anything here. If he kisses me on both cheeks, I'll let you know."

"Funny guy. I'll call them. Bye."

"Bye."

I looked at myself in the mirror. I looked good. My suit and shirt fit well. I walked toward the conference room. Clara was standing there.

"Do you want me to come in with you, sir?"

"No. I'll handle it."

#

I walked around the corner to the large conference room. I immediately recognized Vincenzo Menduni. It was he who had been in Matt's office with Rizzo in the picture. Vincenzo looked to be a young sixty years old. Black hair combed back in the style of Dean Martin, with some salt and pepper grey and greying at the temples. He stood when I entered the room. He was about six feet tall, perhaps one hundred and ninety pounds. He was tanned, fit, and he looked good. Women would find him attractive. I tried to recall if he had a media-given nickname like the *Dapper-don*, but nothing came to mind. His eyes were dark brown to black. He wore a ghost-striped navy suit that probably cost $4000.00, highly polished black shoes, with a navy blue, royal blue, silver, and white regimental striped tie and pocket square. So much for my tailor's advice on ties. He wore a gold wedding band and a Ulysse-Nardin gold watch. He smiled a white, toothy smile as I entered the room.

Alexandra—Al—was gorgeous with a Circe kind of appeal. Her hair was long, dark blue-black, in a semi-braided ponytail. She had sharp green-brown eyes that were striking, and a tan, café mocha Mediterranean complexion. She wore a skirt suit in a medium dark grey with a white silk blouse that may have plunged a little more than what is standard business office attire. She stood as I entered, too. She looked to be about five-foot eight-inches tall in her very nice stiletto heels. I don't think she wore stockings or pantyhose. She was shapely and endowed. She wore several gold bracelets on her right wrist, a lady's Rolex in gold and silver with a few diamonds on its face on her left wrist, diamond and pearl earrings and a double strand of Mikimoto pearls around her neck that changed direction right about the interest point of her chest finished off the look. I hoped I didn't squeal or smell like bacon when the meeting was over.

"I'm Mark MacKenzie," I said as I walked toward Vincenzo with my hand out.

"I'm Vincenzo Menduni and this is my daughter and corporate vice-president (*I'm thinking under-boss*), Alexandra Rapano."

We shook hands and I offered Alexandra my hand which she took as she smiled her red perfect lips at me. I guessed that she was in her mid-thirties, but I thought I recalled her profile stating that she was older. Her handshake was warm and firm.

"It's a pleasure to meet you, Mr. MacKenzie. Thank you for seeing us without an appointment," Alexandra said.

"Yes, ma'am. Please, sit. Can I offer you something to drink?"

"No, thank you," Vincenzo said.

I took a seat across from them at the mid-point of the table. "What is the occasion of your visit?" I asked Vincenzo while *Circe*, uh, Alexandra, looked at me.

"It seems we—my firm—may have had some business with your firm. By that, I mean my corporate counsel, Michael Farina, my son Paul Menduni, and some of his associates," he said as he looked to Alexandra.

I looked at Vincenzo, waiting for a question. Not getting anything from me, Vincenzo continued.

"I thought your Uncle Matt took over after your father passed away?"

"He did," *I replied wondering how many businesses announced the ascendancy of a new president for the first time to a mafia don?* "I'm about to take the helm here so I handle most business for the firm preparing for that role."

"You're a young guy. I remember reading about you in the paper about a year ago. You look pretty good for a guy who had been shot up like you were."

"Thank you."

"Thank you for your service. You were a Navy SEAL officer, weren't you?"

"You're welcome. I was. Mr. Menduni, I don't mean to be rude or disrespectful, especially in front of your daughter, but is there something I can do for you?"

"I heard that about you. You're direct. Your father was more of a schmoozer."

"It depends on the company, I suppose."

My comment produced a tooth smile from Vincenzo and quizzical smirk from Alexandra.

"Is Matthew here?"

"I was not advised as to my uncle's plans today. He is not here with me."

"Mr. MacKenzie, my father, and I are trying to reconstruct the business dealings of our corporate counsel (*You mean consiglieri?*) Mr. Farina. We are also trying to put together other business dealings of my brother, Paul, Mr. John Sciortino, and what any of that had to do with your firm. It appears they had business with your Mr. Rizzo. I believe he's a broker here?" she asked knowing the answer.

"I'm sorry. Mr. Rizzo is no longer with our firm. I dismissed him yesterday. I understand he was taken to a hospital with chest pains. My staff told me he was arrested for murder. I was rather shocked to hear that about Mr. Rizzo," I said.

"Mr. MacKenzie. We have some idea as to their business dealings. I believe it pertained to a shareholder agreement. If I have been advised correctly, Messrs. Farina, Sciortino and Ferrara are shareholders of this firm . . ."

I put my hand up. "Then you've been misinformed. The only shareholders of this firm are my family members and me. It has been some time since a non-family member owned shares of the firm. Surely you can appreciate the importance of a family owning a closely held entity?"

"I do. So, by way of your explanation, Mr. Rizzo, never owned shares of this firm?"

"Yes, ma'am."

Alexandra looked at her father who was cool, but she let it be known that news was a surprise. I think the boys have a problem with the boss now.

"Mr. MacKenzie. Can you tell us why my brother and those men met here yesterday?" Alexandra said.

"Truthfully, I cannot say because their appointment was with my uncle. That appointment did not happen because Mr. Rizzo was impolite and insubordinate, hence his termination."

Clearly frustrated, but still very cool, she continued. I could feel Vincenzo's stare burning into me, so I turned my gaze to him while his daughter spoke.

"Can you tell us what happened here at your office yesterday?"

"Ma'am . . ."

"Alexandra or Al is fine," she said.

"Ms. Rapano, why don't you ask your brother? He was here yesterday and would know."

"Mr. MacKenzie, Paul is having surgery to reconstruct his nose and upper palate. He has not been able to explain his day. Mr. Sciortino is employed by a competing firm and is unlikely to assist us. Mr. Rizzo is in the hospital having suffered a broken sternum and bruised heart. In any case, he is under arrest and unlikely to speak to anyone but his attorney. That leaves Mr. Farina who is missing, perhaps having suffered foul play. Mr. Ferrara is unknown to us, and we have been unable to locate him. We're trying to figure out what happened," she said.

I thought for a moment then replied. "Can you give me one reason I should help you if I know what you two know?" Her eyes flashed. A smile passed her lips, but it disappeared just as fast. I looked at Vincenzo. "Is there anything else?" I said.

Alexandra looked to her father, reading permission to continue she went on. "Mr. MacKenzie, we believe that your father or your uncle or both may have property of ours . . ."

I cut her off. "Ma'am. My father is dead. Whether my uncle has property of yours, it would be personal business, as I assure you this firm does not have your property. Is there something else?"

Clearly frustrated at not getting answers, she looked to Vincenzo.

"Mr. MacKenzie. I'm sure you are aware of what happened to Mr. Rizzo and Paul. I think you . . ."

"Mr. Menduni, I interrogated over one hundred insurgents and terrorists during my time in the service. Asking a litany of questions or making suppositions as to what I know and don't know wastes both our time. I'll give you five more minutes and then we're done."

That lighted a fire.

"Mr. MacKenzie, I go back some ways with your family. I met your father and uncle at NYU. Your father was already there when I started. Your uncle arrived while I was there. Does Matt still drink too much and talk too much? Be that as it may, Mr. MacKenzie, I'm interested in knowing whether my son was mugged or not?"

"I'll answer your question if you answer mine. Was my mother intentionally killed?" My question knocked him back into his chair. Alexandra was caught off guard, too. "Well?"

"We don't do that," Vincenzo said.

"Well, Mr. Menduni, I'm not sure why she's dead then if you don't do that? If you don't do that then perhaps you need to get control of your firm. Paul was not mugged. He stupidly attacked me in my place of business following Rizzo's attack on me. They lost," I said in a firm, calm and no mistaking my purpose tone.

"He's very lucky I disarmed Mr. Sciortino, or they all could have been killed. My actions yesterday were restrained and tempered, but do not believe for a second it is a sign of weakness. I am telling you both once, should a member of your so-called firm threaten, interfere with, or injure a member of my family or associates, that person or those persons will deal with me. I will make no distinction for gender," I said as I turned to Alexandra who seemed startled. "If you are part of a conspiracy to hurt my family, I will make no distinction when I come for you. Do I make myself clear?"

"Mr. MacKenzie, I don't know what you know, but I do not wish you or your family harm. I don't wish that my daughter suffer harm either. How or is there a way we can ensure that violence is avoided?"

"I already told you—get control of your employees. If any one of them harm my family, friends, or my employees, I will take out the leadership when I take out the person responsible. When a woman picked up a weapon to use against us in Iraq, Afghanistan or elsewhere I served, I made no distinction for her gender, and I killed her as ruthlessly and quickly as a man. If you employ such men and women in your firm and they harm my family, there is no way you can stop me. I will come for you in the middle of the night and the last thing you will see before traveling to Dante's Inferno will be my eyes!" *I looked at Alexandra who clearly got the message and was shaken up by my directness. No one had ever spoken to her like that before in her life.* "That is how you can prevent further violence. Is there anything else? Your five minutes are up."

Vincenzo nodded at his daughter.

"Yes. There is something. We are aware that a small group of junior associates from our firm, the Carlucci, the Bagatelli, the Rapoli and the Terrazzo firms are operating and coordinating activities that are not of our making and without our blessing and support. We disassociated ourselves from these men after we learned of their activities. I do not wish to die for the mistakes or unauthorized acts of others. My brother Paul is no longer part of the firm. His bodyguards and associates are not part of our organization. The activities of Rizzo, the Sciortino brothers, Mr. Bonano of the Bagatelli firm, and Mr. Paganelli of the Carlucci firm are without our authorization or blessing. If we learn of any activities directed toward you or your family, we will try to prevent it and we will advise you. . . Do you understand me?"

"Yes, but it won't save you if I learn otherwise," I said. *I didn't want to help these people. I empathized with Odysseus.* I stood. "I suggest you do what you need to do to prevent liability for their acts." Vincenzo stood and offered his hand. We shook. *I understood the Rolling Stones' song Sympathy for the Devil now.*

"You are direct and sharp. I'm glad our country has men like you in our military," Vincenzo said.

Now a compliment from the Devil. Alexandra stood and didn't know whether to extend her hand or not. I smiled at her. I didn't smell like bacon. I'd made it. I extended my hand.

"Good day, Ms. Rapano."

She took my hand and nodded her head. They turned then Alexandra turned back and asked, "Is there a way to reach you should the need arise?"

"Yes. Here is my card. My service can locate me."

"I meant a faster means. A cell phone, perhaps?"

"Yes." I wrote down my number on the back of my business card.

"Anything else?"

Alexandra looked at her father who nodded.

"We're glad you killed Paul's driver and bodyguard. We suspected they were involved in that activity but had no idea of the extent of the operation nor any evidence."

I didn't react.

"Paulie told me you're dating Haley. I noticed your car in the garage here. It is the same car that appeared at Monty's house the night he was killed. We wish you and Haley well. We know you put Monty on the sidewalk in Greenport a couple of weeks ago after Paul acted inappropriately with Haley. Paulie told us." She looked at her father before continuing. "Take care of Paulie. He's a good boy. We wish Haley all the best. She deserves a guy like you."

Okay, Circe, enough.

"I just wanted you to know."

"Yes, ma'am. Mr. Menduni, good day." I escorted them to reception and waited while they got on the elevator. Alexandra—Al—looked at me, smiled, and nodded her head as the doors closed.

#

"Mr. MacKenzie. I'll heat up your sandwich."

"That's fine, Bernice. I'll eat it as is. It's 1:40 p.m. Is Matt in yet?"

"No, sir."

"Clara. Ask Barbara and Margie to join us all in my office please."

"Yes, sir."

I swallowed a wedge of pastrami on rye after I dipped it in mustard. Seconds later the second half disappeared. I washed it down with water. I wolfed down the pickle and I followed that with a wedge of sandwich as Clara, Margie, Barbara, and Bernice appeared at my doorway.

"Come in," I said while chewing. I swigged down some water.

"I just had two visitors. Do any of you know who they were?"

They all looked at me like I was touched in the head. Barbara spoke up.

"Well, yes. Clara told us that Vincenzo Menduni was here and the woman, Alexandra Rapano, is his daughter."

"Have either of them been here before?" I asked.

Margie looked at Barbara then spoke. "Yes. Mr. Menduni has been here several times as recently as last week. I'd have to check the calendar for the other times," Margie said.

"Why was he here?" I asked.

"I don't know. I was going to tell you. I just didn't think of it with all that's been going on. Mr. MacKenzie, I've been Matt's secretary for over five years. Barbara has been around here nearly as long. We know you're the president and majority shareholder. Marsha, Bernice, even Ira will tell you, your uncle has spent more time here since your father died than at any time before. In the last two months, he has actively applied himself and he comes in almost every day, but there is something wrong, something going on. He drinks all the time. We dump it out when we find it in his office. He's lost his wallet three times in the last three months. He uses the car service so he doesn't get another DUI or into another car wreck, and so he can drink while commuting . . . I'm sorry Mr. MacKenzie . . . I don't mean to disparage Matt . . ."

"She's correct!"

I looked up to see Marsha standing at the door.

"Mr. MacKenzie. You need to rescue this firm and, maybe, save Matt, too. You coming to work has helped turn around the firm. Ira and I can show you what I mean, but we were the top firm and we're still up there. However, we've been in a nose-dive since your father died. The last two weeks the line has headed up almost as vertical as it can get on a graph since you appeared. They—these ladies, the brokers, Ira, Steve, and the techs, all the assistants—they need to know that you are the president and that you care about them. Moral is terrible but improving with you here. People have been abused, lied to, used, and more. The firm was slowly collapsing under Matt because beyond this hall he did nothing for them. The other people involved caused problems with the rest of the employees," Marsha said.

"Okay. I'll need a lot of help. I can move and manage people, but I have things I must fix and . . . I made a promise to my parents to take care of Lauren."

Ira, Steve, and Mr. Aarons joined us. I looked at each of them. I saw in each of their eyes, their faces, their souls, people who'd at one time were happy and supported, but who were now demoralized, down and unled. I looked at each person in the room and silently acknowledged their plea.

"Marsha. Ask the employees of MacKenzie Securities to assemble in the large conference room in five minutes, please."

"Yes, sir!"

"Excuse me folks. I have a telephone call I must make."

#

I called Matt's phone. I got his voice mail. I tried again. Ditto. I called Chief.

"Yeah, Mark."

"Is Matt there?"

"I think so. He's working in his office. He's been in there all day."

"Didn't you say the car was coming for him at noon?"

"He asked me to cancel it when it showed up. He's been on the landline phone all day."

"Go in and get him. I need to speak with him."

"Okay. I'm out by the pool. Just a second."

I heard the sliding door open then close. I heard Chief knock and call Matt. After two tries I heard a door open.

"He's not in his office. I'll check the bedroom."

"Chief, search the house then check the garage for a late-model silver Mercedes-Benz S550."

"No. Betsy took that car. She left him the Grand Cherokee."

"Fine. Check. I've called his cell. No answer."

"The Grand Cherokee is gone."

"Shit! Search the house for anything unusual. Look at what he was working on at his desk and in the computer. I'll call back. What did you hear when Betsy and Matt fought?"

"It was about his drinking and something about money. She is very angry with him. Mark, she said that you should fire him for what he's done, and he should go to jail."

"And what did he do?"

"I don't know. She didn't say."

"I'll call you in thirty minutes. Bye."

#

"Marsha. Lock down the bank accounts, please. Who has authorization and access?"

"Me, Ira, Barbara, Clara, Matt and you, depending on the accounts."

"Lock them down. No access by Matt at all. Lock him out. Why do Clara and Barbara have access?"

"Assistants to the president and vice-president. They're limited to $20,000. Ira for the closings and me for everything."

"Go lock out Matt. No access at all. Go. I'll begin without you."

"Yes, sir."

I entered the conference room, and it immediately became quiet. I looked around at each person. I wondered what they were thinking then I smiled.

"Good afternoon. Much has happened in my life over the past few weeks." I suddenly noticed Rob, Tony, Audrey, and two of their techs standing in the back. "Anyway. We have a job to do, and I'll need your help. Effective today, I am the president of MacKenzie Securities . . ."

They applauded, whistled, and yelled their approval. I put up my hand.

"We have a lot to do. I have a lot to do. I know you all have questions about many things . . . what happened yesterday, what happened today and what will happen. I'll answer all that as soon as I can. There are other things going on that I must tend to first, but I want you to know I will set an example—a moral and honest example—and I will do my best to make this a profitable and fun place to work. I'm just learning of some of what went on here. I will fix that. I'll lead you and protect you from anyone who attempts to harm you or intimidate you. Please go back to your work. I need that from you today. Many of you don't know what we're doing. When it's over and finished, I will tell you. Now please get back to your jobs and do them as the professionals you are. Thank you." With that I spun on my heel and walked out.

"Ira, Clara, Rob, Tony, Audrey, Steve, Barbara—small conference room, now, please." I hurried to my office to grab my water then walked to the small conference room. They were waiting for me.

"Ira. Are we ready?"

"All set. We'll have just over seventy-five minutes to do it. The schedule is set. If a tech problem occurs, Steve and his people will catch it and correct it. Once the bonds are cashed, confirmation emails will be sent to me. We will know though since we go first and we're last. We'll redeem fifteen million at ten minutes to the hour. Then, in order, the rest of the firms will redeem their bonds, until we go last with the remaining three million. It could all happen in as little as thirty minutes."

"Rob, Tony?"

"All security protocols are up. Nothing can stop a transfer or purchase. No one can get in to see or monitor us or the other firms. The transactions will be encrypted."

"Audrey?"

"Three hundred seventy-three civil actions were delivered to the courts and will be filed first thing Monday morning. Service of the actions will occur on Monday with the serving of seizure, protective and *lis pendens* orders. Service on corporate and registered agents will begin at 9 a.m. We've hired thirty process service firms and requested that service be completed by noon. Media copies will be faxed and emailed to all media in the tristate area."

"Clara?"

"We are ready to answer questions and respond to problems. Audrey will handle legal questions, I will take logistical problems, and Barbara will handle technical and third-party inquiries on entities who have been served protective orders and *lis pendens*. Ten security guards are posted in the parking garage and will remain there until you pull them."

Marsha walked around the corner and came in.

"Taken care of, sir. I had to clear a payroll list. It's payday," Marsha said.

"Do I get one of those or just the title?"

They all smiled.

"We gotta go, Mark," Ira said.

"Let's go folks. Thank you."

With that they scattered.

"Marsha. Matt is missing. I haven't called Betsy yet, but I don't know if I should be worried, glad or both."

"I understand. Call her. She understands."

"I will."

#

"Hello."

"Missy. It's Mark. Did everyone make it there?"

"Yes. The Stuarts arrived about 1 p.m. Lorraine came with me. Betsy came out by herself. Matt's not here. Betsy had a big blow-up with Matt."

"I heard. Can you talk right now?"

"Yes. They're all on the beach or the pier. We just began an early happy hour. Lauren and Kimberly are here, and Haley should arrive at any minute."

"Missy. What's up with Matt?"

"I guess you know if you're asking. He's a drunk, he may use drugs, and he associates with bad people. There's more to it that I don't know, even Betsy doesn't know, but, well, Matt seemed to improve after Will passed away. It was if he had to prove himself. He tried then failed then tried again. You didn't know because your father always covered for him, or Grandpa covered for him. Matt is a smart and competent man, but something happened and, well, you see. Again, I don't know what Grandpa knows or what Will knew, but something happened a long time ago that some people in our family know about. It has never been spoken of and you know me, I tried to get it out of them but got nothing."

"Missy. I took the presidency of the firm today. I wanted to tell Matt first, but he never came in and he disappeared. He took off on Chief, who was watching him."

"It doesn't surprise me. He'll be back in a few days, but I think Betsy has had it this time. If they divorce, Mom—Grandma—will keep Betsy and show Matt the door."

"Missy, why is that? Grandma transferred and gifted most of her shares to Mom. Mom paid a very low price for the shares. Grandma's remaining shares are set to go to Lorraine upon Grandma's demise. I don't know about Grandpa's shares because they're controlled by his will."

"I don't know, Mark. It's all been kept from me. Ask Lorraine and Grandma."

"What are you saying, Missy?"

"Grandma and Lorraine know, I'm sure. So, does Grandma Stuart."

"Can you catch Betsy for me?"

"Sure. I won't mention anything about this. Mark, I feel better knowing you're in charge now. Dad can retire for good. Oh. Did you look at the books and figure out the yacht thing? The numbers Matt was throwing around made no sense. Based on the boats you were looking at."

"What do you mean, Missy?"

"Matt said he'd pay two hundred fifty thousand per month for the boat and upkeep. Well, I called on that big eighty-two-footer. Fully loaded, if you don't act like an oil sheik, it can be had new for nine million."

"Missy, Matt told me the firm would pay seventy-five thousand a month, part of that from you and Grandpa."

"See! What was he going to do with the one hundred seventy-five thousand? He would have skimmed it? Here's Betsy."

"Hi, Mark. How are you?"

This would break my heart. "Aunt Betsy. Do you know where Matt is?"

"No, Mark. I left him at home. He said he had work to do and that he wasn't coming out this weekend."

I could tell by the stress in her voice that she knew what Matt said was not true. "Aunt Betsy, I love you."

"Mark. I love you. I love our family, too." She began to cry.

"Betsy. No matter what happens, you will never lose us— your family. I want you to know I'm president of the firm. Nothing will change for you, ever. You were there with Mom and Missy and Lorraine—you saved my life. You'll not lose your family."

"Thank you, Mark," Betsy said, crying.

"I'll find him and see what I can do."

"Mark, you are it. If you can't do it, he's done. Your father covered for him and, well, I just don't know."

"Aunt Betsy, go sit with Missy. She knows I know. If Matt cannot be saved, I think they're ready to go on with their lives with you. I'll see you later. I have some things to do."

"Okay, Mark. Thank you. I'll see you later. Bye."

"Bye, Aunt Betsy."

I felt so bad for her. No children or siblings, her parents are gone. How lonely would her life be without all of us?

"Mr. MacKenzie."

I looked up at the sound of Clara's voice.

"Yes."

"We redeemed the first $15 million in bonds. A transfer of $16,880,000 was deposited to our account which included interest. Three other firms have redeemed their bonds thus far."

"Great. I'll stay out of the way. I think I'll take a walk around the firm."

"Yes. You should do that, sir," Clara said as she smiled and went back to work.

#

I walked to the copying, binding, and mail area to see what was going on. Benny, who suffers from mild Down's Syndrome, and Marty, who has some limb deformities, do our bulk copying, mail distribution, and other functions. I walked in and Benny smiled at me.

"Afternoon, Mr. MacKenzie."

"Hi, Benny. How are you today?"

"I'm good, good. I'm happy for us that you're our boss. I heard you punched that bad man to protect us yesterday. Mr. Rizzo is not a nice man. He always made fun of Marty and me."

What type of person picks on people like Benny and Marty?

"It wasn't a big deal, Benny. You could have handled it. Thanks for the good job you and Marty do for us, Benny."

"You're welcome, sir, Mr. MacKenzie."

I walked off to the den of thieves as insiders call the brokerage area. They were all still at it on the phones and computers. I looked at the menu board. Revenue was up 68%

over last month. They were busy. Ira smiled at me and gave me a thumbs-up. I nodded at him and continued my tour.

I walked to the back office. They'd just closed out payroll and direct deposits were made by 4 p.m. These folks, five women and three gay men, worked for Marsha. I walked into their midst. I didn't know all their names, yet. I'd learn them.

"You folks did a terrific job today. Thank you. I'm glad you are here to help me."

"Well, don't we pay you something? I didn't see your name on the payroll list."

"I haven't done anything yet to earn a check," I said smiling at the woman.

"Yes, you have!"

I turned to look at the source of the voice. A young man. "What did I do?"

"You got rid of that sociopath who would push us around and call us names," the young man said.

I considered the faces of each of the men and women sitting in the room and nodded. "If anyone puts a hand on any of you again, they'll have a choice: termination, arrest, or three rounds with me. Seriously. I won't tolerate it. You come tell me."

"Thank you, sir."

"I'll let you get back to your work since it's Friday and you need to get out of here. Thank you, again."

I walked to the secretary area. The most dangerous area in the firm for a single guy.

"Good afternoon, ladies and gents."

"Good afternoon, Mr. MacKenzie," several of them said at once.

"We're glad you're our president and Cheryl wants to know if she can have a picture of you in uniform for her wall," a pretty, young woman said.

"Shush, Linda," another young lady said who must be Cheryl.

"I'm sorry, I'm fresh out. Perhaps a selfie sometime," I said which caused some excitement with the group.

"Thanks for the job you do. Enjoy your weekend."

I wandered back to the executive hallway and entered Matt's office. Margie and Barbara were doing their work,

"Ladies. Thank you for being honest with me today. I'm glad you both are unburdened by telling me. Still no idea where the shareholder agreements are?"

"No, sir. My guess is your uncle took them," Barbara said.

"I'll look into it. Thanks again."

I walked toward my office, pulled out my cell phone and called Chief.

"Hey, Mark. Nothing. He's gone. I looked at his desk. There are several files on it. The computer history shows he was looking at several documents on the office server in a hidden file. It says *Shareholder Agreement* on each of the files. He also looked at some other documents, maybe options contracts or bond contracts. It's too much for me to go through. He also printed off some contact information. All normal stuff to me."

"Okay, Chief. The bond redemptions are going well. What do you want to do since your done protecting Matt?"

"Sorry, Mark."

"Not your fault, Chief."

"Do you want me to stay here in case he comes back?

"No. Unless you want to."

"Not really. I can go to the city, the Oceanside house, or Greenport. I hear we've been bumped to the old cottage in Greenport."

"Don't feel bad. I might be, too. Your pick. I'm expecting a slow night unless Matt gets a DUI. Before you go, do me a favor. Pack up everything on his desk and forward to me all the files he looked at on the computer. I'll get the files from you later."

"Okay. It'll take me a few minutes. I'll see you out in Greenport tonight."

"Okay, Chief. Thanks. Oh, did you hear?"

"About the don visiting you? Yeah, I heard. I'm told his daughter is hot."

"Don't fall for it. She's like the Gorgon Medusa, men turn to stone when they look at her face, except, unlike the Medusa, she's gorgeous. She's a looker and, perhaps, a murderess. I'll see you out there later."

"Bye."

#

"Hello."

"This is John."

"John, who?" I knew who it was.

"Stayton. How goes the war?"

"I had two visitors today."

"I heard. What did they want?"

"Your pictures of her don't do her justice."

"I've heard she's a looker. I'm told the visit is on video?"

"It is. Rob and Tony will forward it to Carl later."

"So, why were they there?"

"Something to do with the amigos from yesterday. They think Farina suffered foul play. Paul Menduni told them he was mugged. They knew Rizzo was arrested and hospitalized. You'll see it soon enough. I forgot about the cameras otherwise I would have flipped you the bird."

"Great. Anything else?"

"Can you tell me whether my uncle is messed up with them"

"Do you really want to know?"

"Yes."

"We think he's involved in money laundering, teaching them how to skim money off firms like yours and skimming off transactions at your firm. Minor stuff until you add it all up. Of course, you'd have to complain to us for him to be arrested. We're not interested in him if you're concerned. You and your family have been through enough.

We have some information from one of our undercovers that movement is afoot to hit the leadership of the several families. We'll see what happens. Just pay attention, but I think it's all mob-on-mob action. So, tell me, did you put Vincenzo in his place?"

"You'll just have to wait for the movie. I gotta go. It's almost time. Bye."

"Bye, Mark."

I walked into the den of thieves. Clara looked over at me and smiled. Ira caught her gaze and saw me.

"It's done. We deposited $20,260,000 into our account just before the market closed. We'll let the lawyers and accountants figure out the tax issues, but frankly I think it won't matter much. You know Marsha and I found several transactions where the money was skimmed, right? We're not done, but it's a sizable amount over the past ten years."

"Matt?" I said knowing the answer.

"Him, Rizzo, and Train. Just Matt in the earlier years."

"How much?"

"I'm not sure since we're not done, but we're at $35 million thus far, but that's offset by what we recovered today. Mr. Middleton and I already put into place new procedures and all closings will be verified by Marsha and me. No broker will close his own sale anymore."

"Thanks, Ira. We'll recover."

"Oh. The stocks are up. They closed a buck and two bits higher just before the redemptions. The algorithm geeks called it. Now we'll see what happens Monday. Mr. Aaron and I will coordinate. We'll issue our first opinion at 7 p.m. tonight. By Monday afternoon most of the opinions and sell recommendations will be published. I wouldn't want to be standing on Wall Street when that rock falls. You could lose a toe."

"Great work, Ira. Look, I've known you a long time. Teach me, help me, and scold me when needed; I want to fix what needs fixing around here."

"I will. You know, you're a lot like your father. Will was more technical at your age, but you might be smarter and you're fearless," Ira said.

"Thanks."

"Well, the email reports are coming in. Success."

"Great, Ira. Thank everyone for this and for those numbers up there."

"I will, Mark."

I walked back to my office but stopped at the small conference room on the way.

"Great job, folks. Everything is done with the bonds. You did it."

"Thanks, Mr. MacKenzie," Audrey said.

"You're the star on Monday, Audrey," I said.

"Rob and Tony, too. They found lots of assets."

Audrey turned to look at her computer and I gave Rob the 'You gonna hook-up?' look and he nodded. Tony was making faces at Rob like when we were kids. I smiled at them.

"Well, I'm going to wrap it up. We're almost there, folks. Call me if you need me. Bye." I walked to my office to get my briefcase. Bernice was gone, but Clara was still here. "Clara. Did a package come for me from the attorneys?"

"I'll check. Do you need it now or should I courier it to the house?"

"Courier to the house. If it's not here, let me know. Attorney Schmidt said he'd send it over today. Good night. Great job, Clara."

"Thank you, sir. Good night."

#

Security was obvious in the garage. Just as I wanted it to be. I got into my car and headed east. It took twenty-five minutes to get out of Manhattan. As I entered Long Island City, I looked back at my FBI detail. Two SUVs today. I tapped my cell for Stayton's number.

"Hello."

"Why are two SUVs of agents on me?"

"We've increased security. With all that you've done today the chance of a leak has exponentially increased."

"Yeah, but it's too late to stop it."

"True, but not to send a message or seek revenge."

"I see. Any particularized threats?"

"No. Vincenzo and his daughter visited with their Carlucci family counterparts then they traveled to the grandfather's estate. They left there just minutes later. You think you have security coverage. They're traveling in three armored SUVs and an armored limousine. They have twelve soldiers with them. The Carlucci family, too. We think an underboss from the Atlantic City family may be at the old man's estate, too. A large group of men left the old man's estate for his restaurant in Queens. Notably, they are not traveling with as much security though we counted twenty-three men in all. Castellano and Palami are at a restaurant in Freeport owned by one of Romeo's capos. They've been there a few hours."

"Who's at the Rockville Center Restaurant?"

"No one. We're looking for about thirty-eight members or associates of Paul Menduni, the Sciortinos, Bonano, and a few others. Carl and Joe will tell you, it's quiet out there. The task force and our analysts think the young guns are hiding, but another theory is they're organizing. We're all listening and waiting for something to happen."

"Okay. I'm, well, you know where I'm going. I'll talk with you later. Bye."

"Bye."

As I passed the Nassau-Suffolk line my phone buzzed. It was Haley.

"Hi." I said, my mood instantly picking up.

"Hi. Where are you?"

"Suffolk county. I'll be there in less than an hour."

"You sound okay."

"I'm good. We're working it. What's for dinner?"

"Salad, calzone, pizza, and lasagna. We're just holding off a little waiting for you."

"Oh. If the pizza is there, don't wait for me. Start without me. I'll be there soon enough."

"You looked great in that suit today."

"Thanks. What's the scuttlebutt there?"

"The what?"

"The scoop, the rumors."

"Oh. The Paul and Rizzo thing has been thoroughly discussed and dissected to death. Now we just heard you had a visit from Vincenzo and Alexandra."

"True."

"Will I have to cross-examine you or torture the answers from you?"

"No. Just send in Lauren and her crew. You may not believe it, but Alexandra wished us well. Paulie bragged about me putting Monty on the ground out there. They figured out, perhaps when they arrived and saw my car, that I took out Monty and the driver. She said, and Vincenzo agreed, that you deserve a guy like me and that we should take care of Paulie."

"Wow. No. I don't know whether to believe it."

"I was watching her say it. I think she meant it."

"Paul's mother explained to me what Paul's surgery did today. He'll need a few more surgeries with an oral surgeon."

"What else?"

"The background discussion is about Matt. Betsy is vulnerable. Missy and Lorraine have been talking with her. You'll have to fill me in. I don't dare get involved."

"There's a lot more there to that. Oh, did I tell you . . ."

"That you're the president? No, but Missy told me. Betsy and Lorraine know."

"Who is there from my team?"

"Chief, LT, and Talbot. Mikey went back to the city. He had a date with a lady he's been working out with in your building. He said he'd be in the building early with some luck."

"I wonder if it's the third date?"

"What? Why?"

"Nothing. How did my maternal grandparents receive you?"

"Very well. They're sweethearts. I can see Lauren in your grandmother. Both sets of grandparents are very friendly with each other."

"They've known each other since the early 1960s. Is Paulie with you?"

"Not yet. He needed new soccer shoes for summer league, so my parents took him. My father just wanted an excuse to look at fishing equipment."

"I wish I could go fishing."

"They'll be back here later after dinner for dessert."

"Oh, what's for dessert? I've been a good boy."

"Cannoli, Linzer tarts, black and white cookies and, in your honor, apple pie and Oreos."

"You folks are too much."

"Mark, it's just so good to hear your voice."

"Yours, too. Let me run. I don't have my car's hands-free set yet."

"Okay. I love you."

"I love you, too, Haley. See you soon."

#

It was getting crowded in my parking area. I inched my way to the garage and tapped the HomeLink button and backed into the garage. I opened my safe, exchanged my weapon for another SIG. I removed my M-40 and placed it in my trunk along with a tactical shotgun, and my M-4 carbine. For added measure I put a .44 Magnum revolver in a holster and stuck it between my seat and the center console. I placed my tactical bag and wet gear bag in the trunk. I locked up the car and walked to the house.

Lauren and Kimberly spotted me first and came running. I got hugs and kisses from both. I must have moved up on Kimberly's list.

"How was your day, Mark?" Lauren asked.

"Good. We're in the fifth inning and we're ahead."

"Whatever that means. I have a little of everything in the oven for you. We're still eating," she said as Haley walked to us.

"Hi," Haley said then kissed me. "I told them you'd want to shower before you ate."

"I'll be back. I'm going to get a shower and change if you don't mind," I said.

"I'll let everyone know. Grandma and Grandpa Stuart are staying in your room. Missy, Betsy, and Lorraine are all set up downstairs. Your guys are at the cottage and all the comms work from there, I heard them say. You know about all the FBI guys so we're safe. Tomorrow, we want to take out the PWCs before we go shopping. I showed Kimberly how to operate them and she's been on one before with me."

"Sure. Thanks for the update, XO. I'll be in the shower if anyone needs an update."

I grabbed Haley's hand. "You can come with me. Have you had a shower today?"

"Yes, but I don't have anything with me . . . you're teasing me!" She slapped my butt.

I shed my clothing and stepped into the shower. I noted I'd been displaced from my room by my grandparents. I turned on the hot water and stood under the rainfall shower head.

"What did you think of Alexandra?"

"She's pretty and intelligent but perhaps playing for the wrong side. To be in her position she'd have to be charming and ruthless. Her looks make her more effective. I'm not sure I have a good read on her. I think something will happen this weekend. The factions are fighting. I think once the market opens Monday and the arrests begin, it will be all over for a while."

"What happened today?"

"We redeemed all the bonds. Those companies paid out about $1.09 billion, perhaps more if other bond holders got wind of the redemptions. That means those companies are operating on borrowed money. When the stocks dump, they'll be out of business."

"What will happen this weekend?"

"I think some wise guys will get whacked. I also think the feds and our military will do some hostage rescue operations to save the girls and women taken into slavery. I'd be stupid to think that the feds are not already taking down minor operations based on our information."

"What will you do?"

I walked out of the shower sans a waist towel drying my hair. "Me? Nothing. I mean, I'm doing it. I may go look for Uncle Matt to talk to him," I said as I dressed. "You're leering at me."

"Yes, I am. Why don't we escape for a few hours this weekend? You know, a hotel room, your garage, my bedroom, the back seat of your hotrod," she said as she took *ahold* of me and pulled me close and kissed me.

"Sure. We should build a house next door, so we can get some privacy."

"We'll find something," Haley said as she slapped down something of mine that suddenly awoke. After a moment, I dressed in boxer-briefs since both sets of grandparents were here, comfy ripped up jeans, a roomy T-shirt, cross-trainer shoes and a G-Shock watch. Total casual.

"Come on. I'm hungry and I'm sure the group is waiting. Is it cold in here or are you just glad to see me?"

"Oh, be quiet. You got me all excited. Let's go, you tease."

#

"Hello, Grandma," I said as I kissed her.

"Hi, Mark. I hope you're hungry," Grandma said.

"I am, ma'am," I said as Lauren and Kimberly put three plates in front of me—salad, calzone and pizza, and lasagna. I sat down and began to eat and looked up to see an audience had formed. I stood to greet my maternal grandparents, Frank, and Emily Stuart.

"Hi, Grandma. I've missed you."

"Oh, Mark, we've missed you so much," my grandmother said as she hugged me and kissed me. I kissed her back.

"Now, you have to let me go so I can hug Grandpa."

"No, I don't. He can wait," she said as Lauren joined us in the hug. By now everyone had entered the kitchen-living room-den area except the team guys. I shook my Grandpa's hand.

"How are you, sir?"

"I'm good. You look as solid and strong as you did last time you were on leave. You are twice the size you were at the hospital."

"Good genes and that German, Scottish, Irish stubbornness, sir."

Aunt Lorraine displaced Grandpa Stuart and she hung onto me as we hugged. Lorraine is the two-year older version of my mother. She's very much like my mother, but with the take-charge leadership that only first-born children learn by being born first.

"Oh, Mark, it's good to see you. Now we can relax with you here," Lorraine said.

"The other guys are pretty good and there's a houseful of FBI agents across the yard."

"Not what I meant. You're here safe with us now."

"Well, I'm glad we're all here, too. Wait a minute. Am I not supposed to be mad at you? You voted with the others to tear apart my home, didn't you?"

"Oh stop. It's just your home in title only because your name is on the deed. It's our palette and vacation home. Stop whining," Lorraine said as she took my pizza.

In the last few weeks every woman in my family had called me a whiner.

"Lauren, Kimberly, Haley, please bring Mark his dinner and a beer. He can eat out here while we gossip about his day," Grandma MacKenzie directed.

I sat and a grandma sat on either side of me. The grandpas took seats across from me and everyone else began to fill in around us. The girls put my food in front of me, but as I got further into answering questions and telling the story, my food seemed to disappear after each bite or two. My grandfathers, naturally, asked about the strategic issues. Grandpa Stuart wondered about all the FBI and what happened in the weeks before as I finished my *third* slice of pizza and third salad, having only eaten one of each.

The Shores arrived with Paulie, so we moved onto another subject. Paulie was introduced to my maternal grandparents and Lorraine. He was the perfect little gentleman.

"Can I call you Grandma and Grandpa, too?" Paulie said which delighted my grandparents.

I thought how odd it was that child of four generations of violence and here he was in our midst accepted as part my family. I knew that our families were on a collision course. Could Vincenzo and Alexandra control their family and the others, or would I be forced to act against them? I hoped for the former and prepared for the latter.

#

A call from Clara advised that a package had been delivered from attorney Schmidt. It went to Matt's office because it said president on the courier's address label and Benny delivered it before learning that I was the president. It would be delivered to the house tomorrow.

I didn't bring up Matt this evening. I sensed the family didn't want to deal with that subject yet. They wanted to circle the wagons and put each other at ease.

The Shores departed with Paulie after dessert. Kimberly and Lauren went to bed. My grandmothers and Betsy went to bed. Remaining on the deck with me were Missy, Lorraine, Haley, my grandfathers, LT, Chief and Talbot. We each had either bourbon, Scotch, or cordials.

"Congratulations, Mark, on assuming the presidency of the firm. I'm sorry it happened this early and under these circumstances," Grandpa MacKenzie said.

"Thanks."

"What can you add to what we were talking about earlier?"

"I think something will explode between the different crime family factions. I met with Vincenzo Menduni and his daughter Alexandra today. I made it clear to them that I would hold them responsible if harm or threat of harm came to my family or friends. They believed me."

"What will happen?"

"I think, one by one, the minor members of the rebelling coalition will be killed. Rizzo and Paul Menduni are safer where they're currently staying than on the street, but there are at least one hundred of them the Feds know of. Only forty or fifty of whom are what I'd call shooters. That's a lot of bad guys. One of them will learn something this weekend about the busts coming up that will occur on Monday and Tuesday."

"You won't have anything to do with any of the arrests, right?" Grandpa Stuart asked.

"Correct. I know you learned a lot today for the first time. I know the identity of fifteen people involved in the conspiracy. There is a sixteenth person, and we'll find him in the next couple of days. We're close. I've passed this evidence to the FBI as a confidential informant. I will leave the prosecutions of those people to the authorities."

"This sixteenth person is unknown. Will you continue to look for him even if it takes weeks or months?" Grandpa Stuart asked.

"Yes. I said I'd get them all. I promised that fifteen-year-old orphan upstairs and my parents that I'd find them all and avenge their deaths." I sipped my bourbon. Haley put her hand on my leg as she snuggled in close to me. I looked at the General who seemed to be drifting off into space. I saw Lorraine look at him and he came back. I looked at Lorraine who caught me looking and she turned away. Missy saw it, too.

"Come on, Lorraine. Let's get to bed. Big day shopping tomorrow," Missy said.

"Where are you going shopping, Missy?" I asked.

"The outlets in Riverhead and the mall. It will be just Lauren, Kimberly, Haley, Lorraine, and me. Betsy and the grandmas are going shopping in Greenport and Southold for groceries for the rest of the week. We'll take that nice new SUV of yours, thank you," Missy said.

"Then you'll drive, Haley. I don't want to lose my bumpers if Missy drives," I deadpanned.

"Such a fresh kid," Missy said.

"Good night, all," Lorraine said as she looked at me again.

"I better get going," Haley said.

"What? You're not staying with me tonight?" I said.

"Heck no. You're on the couch again. I'm going to my nice comfy bed, but . . . ." Haley kissed me again in front of the guys, "I'll see you in the morning," she said.

"Chief. I'd expect a little more from her kiss. Even I've heard her say she loves him."

"I agree, Talbot."

"Oh yeah? Watch this," Haley said as she laid over into my lap, put her arms around my neck and pulled me into a nice kiss to some applause from the guys.

CHAPTER 20

The house exploded with small arms fire. I bounded off the couch, reaching for my pistol, as I came alive then realized I was having a dream. I sat there with my pistol in my hand trying to calm down and catch my breath. It was 4:45 a.m. I clipped my weapon to the waist band of my board shorts and walked to the bathroom. I moment later I walked to the kitchen. My cell phone was on the counter indicating several missed calls. I started coffee then picked up my phone. I called Joe.

"Mark. You're in Greenport?"

"Yes. What's up?"

"This morning, Paul Menduni's guys got killed outside Tito's. Three of them. Shot with shot guns. They were shot walking to Paul's SUV at 3:30 a.m."

"Joe. He has just two guys who were his. Farina said the other guy was Vincenzo's man."

"You're right. John's people are there. I left them twenty minutes ago. It's a mess."

"Where were they staying?"

"As far as we can tell, at Paul's house."

"Perhaps they thought they were hitting Paul. Anyway. That's their problem. Joe, I'll call you back. I'm getting another call."

"Bye."

"Hello."

"Mr. MacKenzie?" It was Alexandra Rapano.

"Yes? You're calling a little early, aren't you?"

"I wanted to tell you we are not involved in the shooting at Tito's this morning. One of our men was killed, too."

"Why are you telling me this?"

"Mr. MacKenzie. I want to avoid even the slightest thought you may have that we're doing anything wrong."

"Ms. Rapano, that is such an absurd statement, I don't even know where to begin to respond considering what you've done."

"Mr. MacKenzie. I don't want you to kill me. I don't know what else to do. Something told me that if I let you know what I know, when I know it, you won't kill me."

"Then you didn't listen to me. I said to keep your people away from my family and friends. Why do I care if a bunch of criminals kill each other?" She was silent for a moment.

"You really hate us, don't you?" She said.

"You killed my mother! The most important person in my life. The woman who had just saved my life. You killed her simply because . . . because she was there. I will put you all in prison or in your graves. Goodbye!"

"Wait. I want you to know the truth. Your parents were not the target."

"You are without honor or integrity. I read the fucking kill order . . ." I shut up before I said more.

"Mr. MacKenzie, please. I don't know what your read. I'll meet you. I'll come alone. You tell me where and I will risk my life and come to you, just so you don't come and kill me anyway."

I could learn something, perhaps? "Fort Salonga, up on 25A. The Rusty Hinge Tavern. Four o'clock today. If you set me up, I'll blow you away before the first bullet hits me."

"I won't. I give you, my word. Thank you. Goodbye."

I poured my coffee and walked down to the beach. Now what? Three dead goombahs and now a lady underboss wants to meet with me. I sipped my coffee. What was the truth? The truth was Matt and, perhaps, my father got mixed up with Menduni. Matt pulled some shenanigans with those bonds and the cash and my father, somehow, took the bonds and cash back and hid them in the safe. Did they figure out that Matt or my dad had the bonds? Then they killed my father and mother? But Farina said it was a mistake. How? Shit, which death was a mistake? My mother's or my father's or both? Al Rapano says my parents were not the target. Who was? Matt? He had to be. He's the one meeting with Vincenzo. He's the poor money handler. He's the one suspected of money laundering and skimming. He's the drunk and drug user.

"Don't let him kill them all." What is my grandmother saying? She divests Matt and Missy of her legacy shares in the firm and sells them to my mother for pennies, then less than seven years later $1.2 million in shares are now valued at $30 million and Lorraine's shares are valued at over $7 million. What happened? Missy doesn't seem to be bothered that the shares went to my mother and will go to Lorraine, but she doesn't know the story, but there is a story.

My coffee cup was empty. It was 5:30 a.m. and the eastern sky was pink, orange, and golden. I saw the planet Venus, named for another mythical woman. I needed to figure this out. As I turned to walk toward the house, I noticed someone walking down the beach toward me. He walked with the self-assurance of a young man. I guessed he was a special agent. I had my weapon if he was not. He walked directly at me, but I could not see his face with the morning sky behind him. I didn't know him. He wore hiking boots and a light jacket.

"Badge! I don't know you," I yelled.

"What?"

"Badge! I don't know you!" I yelled again. He was within one hundred feet of me.

"What did you say?" He said as he reached under his jacket. I dropped my cup and came up with my weapon.

"STOP! BADGE!" I screamed. He halted.

"Hold on. I'm getting out my light so you can see me. Here's my badge."

I approached him and took his badge and ID wallet while I put away my weapon. "Well, Alan Hudson, are you fucking deaf?"

"Sorry. I didn't hear you with the wind blowing from behind me. Sort of jumpy, aren't you?"

"Is there a reason you're on my beach?"

"Yes. SAC Stayton needs you to call him."

"Give me your phone." He handed me his phone after he pressed Stayton's number.

"Hudson?"

"No. It's MacKenzie. We're on my beach and I didn't have my phone."

"Rizzo is dead," Stayton said.

"Was it something I did?"

"No. He was being prepared to be moved to the medical ward at the federal lock-up in Brooklyn. The cop outside his room walked two doors away to a bathroom. He was locked inside the room. Two .22 caliber Magnum bullets to the head sent Rizzo away. No one heard a thing. The weapon was left on the rolling table next to his bed. Joe said you know about Tito's."

"Yeah. Shit, John, if this keeps up, they'll have to retire your unit."

"Doubtful. Why are you out on the beach so early?"

"Same old nightmares, John. Thanks for the update."

"Don't you want to know our theory as to who killed him?"

"I think it's the work of the young guns. Rizzo is—was— a weaselly bully and he picked on weak and defenseless people. He would roll on them in ten seconds to save his own skin."

"That's our theory. We think they did the Tito's hit, too."

"I agree since one of the guys killed was Vincenzo's man. Who's watching Paul if his guys were off?"

"We think two other men from Vincenzo's group."

"Really?"

"His mother has been at the hospital almost the entire time. What are you doing today?"

"Trying to relax, figure things out, get this behind me."

"I read your releases. You stuck it to them. All the firms did."

"I'll chat with you later. Bye."

"Bye."

I passed Hudson his phone. "Thanks." I picked up my cup and jogged to the house.

#

"Let's go, Chief. Take it easy on me."

"Shit, Mark, I've sat around the pool sucking up beer and soaking up rays for a week. You take it easy on me."

We took off at about a six-minute pace to limber up. We ran east toward East Marion and Orient Point, running into the sun. The FBI special agent freaked when he saw us run by. Neither of us was armed, but that was fine. We were nearly three-quarters of a mile down the road when an FBI sedan passed us, and an SUV caught us and tailed us as we ran.

"Chief, I have a problem, and I need you to consider it. You know Matt is a problem. Many issues make him a problem. Let me add to it. He was at NYU while Vincenzo Menduni was there. My father started at NYU first in the late 1970s. Vincenzo showed up next, then Matt a few years later. I don't know the extent of their friendship or whether you could even call it that. Yesterday, Vincenzo asked me if 'Matt still drinks and talks too much?' He said it for a reason. I had just told them they had five minutes and I was finished. Vincenzo said it as a dig—an attack on my family. Matt the drunk. It was an emotional response to me, but it said more. What did Matt say when he was drunk?"

"Well, anything. Stuff about the firm, shit about Rizzo . . ."

"No. This was while they were at college. My father graduated NYU in 1982. Matt graduated in 1985. My father was there before Vincenzo, but Vincenzo was there before Matt. My father started early and graduated early then went to work. A few years later he attended Fordham Law. Vincenzo spent at least two years at NYU with Matt. If I figured it right, my father did a year by himself, Vincenzo showed up, then a year later Matt appeared. Two or more years of Vincenzo and Matt together without my father there. What I'm getting at, is Matt's statement while drunk could not have been made before 1981 nor after 1984. Matt was born in 1964. He started college at seventeen, turning eighteen that first fall semester. If the drunk statement was made, it had to do with an occurrence before college. Even if it was made the next year or the last year, they were together, it had to be dealing with something that happened in high school. Anything that happened at college would be known to Vincenzo since they were there together until Matt's last year."

"Maybe it had to do with girl conquests," Chief said.

"No. Think about it. Did we ever say anything about our conquests? We shit-talked, but have we ever said anything about the nitty-gritty?"

"Well, no. I guess not. We *hooked up* was all."

"Right. What Vincenzo was getting across was that Matt got drunk and runs his mouth. Remember that Personnelman Chief who'd get drunk and wanted to apologize all the time for stupid shit he did to screw up our guys' promotion points? He followed us around like a cry-baby looking for forgiveness for his screw-up whenever he was drunk. When he was sober, he was quiet as a church mouse. Vincenzo looks for weakness. He couldn't find one with me. My father is dead. My mother is dead though he wouldn't criticize my mother. So, he attacked me by using what Matt said and did based on his guilt for a past deed."

"That's a real long way to try to chink your armor, Mark."

"Maybe not. What if Matt had done other things, but Vincenzo doesn't know what I know? What if he doesn't want to associate himself with Matt's conduct? What if Vincenzo was a friend of my father's and he doesn't want to hurt his name or memory? Vincenzo's daughter said my parents were not the target. Vincenzo was in Matt's office last week. Matt's assistant says he has been in several other times. Why didn't Vincenzo bring that up?"

"I can't say. Would Matt have legitimate business with Vincenzo?"

"I doubt it. We buy and sell bonds and securities. Ninety-nine percent of our business is brokering bonds and securities. Vincenzo could do that with us, but I found no transactions for the Mendunis or any of his corporations, other than the eighteen energy companies. Now the FBI said my uncle was skimming bonds and teaching others how to skim bonds at other firms. That eighteen million in bonds I found likely came from skimming."

"So, that money or the bonds was income—commission— for services performed by your firm?"

"Right."

"I was hoping it was just found money and we'd split it up as prize crew like in the old days of the navy," Chief said with a smile.

"Funny. Vincenzo has something on Matt that he's used to get Matt to do things or that someone else has used to get Matt to do things if Vincenzo didn't. My father always protected Matt. Recall I told you the story about my father wanting to go in the army?"

"He did high school ROTC?"

"Yes. He couldn't go in the army because he broke his back in high school. Dad, Matt, and a friend took out the general's car while the general was away. Matt was driving and wrecked it. Dad got hurt. Matt and his friend ran off to get help. My father managed to pull himself into the driver's seat. Dad got cited for driving without a license, broke his back and wrecked the car. Grandma never believed it, but they stuck with the story until a neighborhood kid told his mother the truth. His mother told Grandma Stuart who told Grandma MacKenzie. The Stuarts do not like Matt, but it's more than lying about a car wreck."

"So, your father was disqualified from the army because of Matt. A big deal if you're a general's son."

"Grandpa was a lieutenant colonel then, but you get it."

"Why didn't Matt join the army?"

"Too lazy, out of shape, unmotivated. He'd never finished anything, per my mother."

"Your Aunt Lorraine is cool to your grandfather MacKenzie. I saw Lorraine speaking with Missy and Betsy. It was a heated discussion. When it was over Lorraine hugged Betsy. I think you need to figure out that dynamic and I'll be honest, when Lauren was speaking about your mother and her design talent with Mrs. Schwartz and Haley's mom, Mrs. Schwartz said it was a real shame your mother was gone. Your grandmother MacKenzie shot a look at your grandfather then said, 'Yes. It's a damn shame those two had to die.'"

"What? I mean I heard you, but she said it like that?"

"Yes. She looked at your grandfather and walked off."

"Chief. My grandmother practically gave my mother all of her shares of the firm. Mom paid $1.2 million about six plus years ago for shares valued at nearly $15 million. The shares are now valued at $30 million."

Chief whistled. "That's guilt money, Mark."

"That's not all. When Grandma passes, her remaining shares go to Lorraine."

"Mark, there's more than a car wreck there. Your grandmother knows. Something happened in high school with Matt. Both your grandmothers know what it is."

"Agreed. I need to get to that, but I need to tend to all this other crap. Now I'm meeting Vincenzo's daughter at 1600 today. She wants to tell me the truth about my father's death. She called me earlier to advise that her family was not involved in the killings at Tito's today."

"Do you believe her?"

"I do, for two reasons. One guy killed was her father's man put on Paul's detail to watch him about the chomo thing and to learn whether he took the $60 million. And she's wet-her-pants afraid I'm coming to kill her some night."

"Surfer said you were scary. He said you put the fear of God in them. Okay. You must get organized. We can't help you with Matt. That's all on you. What can we do?"

"The girls want to play on the PWCs before they go shopping. Missy, Lorraine, Haley, Lauren, and Kimberly are going to Riverhead. The grandmas and Betsy are going food and knick-knack shopping nearby. I don't see a chance to cull the grandpas from the herd. However, once the ladies are gone, it will be the grandpas and me."

"Yeah, but they'll be tough to crack. I mean if they don't want you to know, they'll blow you off, *grandson*."

"But at least I can read them."

"Then try. Me, I'd go for Lorraine or Betsy. Lorraine is angry about something, and it has to do with the General. Betsy must know where the bodies are buried even if she played the blind-eyed wife due to Matt's drinking. Look, all those women knew what Cathy was doing before you. They don't keep secrets."

"Thanks. I can't go a week without one of you bringing up Cathy's name."

"Oh, quit whining. We gonna keep this pussy pace or pick it up like we got shit to do?"

"Just waiting for your beer gut to settle."

"Don't forget to bring your shiny shield with you when you meet with Ms. Rapano."

"Why?"

"How'd Perseus beat the Gorgon Medusa?" Chief said

"That's right. He looked at her reflection in his shield."

We took off at a sub five-minute thirty-second pace for the remaining two miles.

#

Chief beat me to the house. I handed him the obligatory twenty dollars. Chief put the bill on the kitchen counter so anyone who asked why the bill was on the counter, he could tell them he out-ran me this morning. I showered outside then snuck into my room to dress. Chief and Talbot would supervise the ladies on the PWCs. By the time I got back to the kitchen, Grandma MacKenzie was starting breakfast.

"Good morning, Mark."

"Good morning, Grandma." She filled my coffee cup just as Chief and Talbot appeared.

"What's that twenty-dollar bill doing on the counter?" Grandma asked.

"Oh. Chief wanted you ladies to have an ice cream cone on him while you shopped today to thank you for your hospitality," I said. Chief was speechless.

"That's very nice of you, Chief. I think we'll do that," Grandma said as she stuffed the bill in her pocket. I stifled a smile. Chief mouthed to me that he'd get even.

Grandma Stuart entered the room. No way to ask questions now. Before long, I was sipping coffee and reading the paper. Lorraine came upstairs followed by Betsy. Missy was putting on her makeup for her breakfast appearance. The grandpas

665

appeared a moment later followed by Missy, Lauren, and Kimberly. LT walked in and nodded me out to the deck.

"You got the news?"

"I did."

"Something else is happening. Carl just sent an email. FBI and Nassau are hunting for two men seen at Nassau County Medical Center. Joe wants you to call him."

"Why do we care?"

"Paul Menduni was moved there this morning from Manhattan."

"I see. As we get settled in here to eat, I will ask about Matt's status, that I'm worried about him. I'm looking for the reactions of Lorraine and my grandparents. You watch my grandfathers. If no one responds or I'm blown off, I'll push it with follow-up questions until something falls from the tree."

"Gotcha."

#

"Hey, Mark. Busy night. LT tell you?" Joe said.

"He did. Why are FBI and Nassau looking for these men?"

"A neighbor next to the Nassau County Medical Center reported seeing two men get out of a black Lincoln Town Car at 5:30 a.m. This neighbor, who lives along the ambulance entrance to the Center, was letting his dog out and he saw the two men, one carrying a hunting rifle with a scope. The man set up and aimed the weapon at the hospital entrance. Paul Menduni was on his way there."

"I think I know the answer to my question. The two guys fit Castellano's and Palami's descriptions."

"Correct."

"They're Romeo Menduni's guys. Are you at the computer?"

"I am."

"What does the GPS on his car show us?"

"You are brilliant."

"Check the video and audio. The unit plugged into the OBDII port should be working. Recall there is cocaine in the glovebox, center console and in his toilet at home."

"Shit. I'm so tired I forgot what we did two weeks ago."

"That's why you called. Let me know what you find. Is Paul at the medical center now?"

"Yes. I'll pass on the information about the Town Car."

"Oh. I'm meeting Alexandra Rapano today. Alone."

"What? This shit is getting out of hand. I'll call you back. Bye."

"Bye."

#

"Lauren. Do you have a game today?" I asked.

"Oh. I forgot to tell you. It's been rescheduled due to a field conflict due to construction on the other fields. Of course, they bumped us girls so the boys could play baseball on our softball field," Lauren said.

"Oh. Okay."

Betsy handed me a plate of eggs, sausage, toast, and hash browns. LT was sitting at the bar opposite my grandfathers. Grandma Stuart was standing next to the stove with Grandma MacKenzie who was cooking some scrambled eggs. Lorraine was sitting with Missy on the lounger in the den area of the former country kitchen using tray tables to set their plates. Lauren and Kimberly sat at the counter, Betsy was floating between the kitchen sink, refrigerator, and counter. Talbot and Chief had taken seats at the table on the kitchen deck. I sat at a chair in the living room with a view to everyone. My grandmothers turned around to eat and talk while they cooked on the stove. I nodded at LT.

"Has anyone heard from Matt? I'm becoming worried."

The talking ceased. Lorraine looked at Aunt Betsy then to the grandmas who, in turn, Grandma Stuart looked back at her plate of food, taking a bite of her eggs and Grandma MacKenzie looked at my grandfathers, then turned back to the stove and busied herself cooking.

"No. I'll try calling him in a bit," Betsy said.

Not getting what I wanted, I pushed it. "I've been calling his cell, the home, and office. Nothing. Can anyone account for that? I mean, why would Matt skip out on Chief like he did?"

Grandma MacKenzie stopped what she was doing. I could see Grandpa Stuart's pained expression, but the General looked at his plate. Lorraine was on high alert. Missy was watching me, bit her lip and nodded her head almost imperceptibly. I looked at Betsy who looked back at me with sorrowful eyes. I pressed.

"Look. I understand drinking. I understand binge drinking. What I don't understand is the wall of silence about it. Betsy, if this hurts, I'm sorry. Lauren, Kimberly, if you would go ready the PWCs, Talbot and Chief will help." Lauren looked at me then to Aunt Missy who nodded.

"Yes, Mark." The girls put down their forks and they walked out to the deck as Talbot and Chief got up to go with them. LT looked at me and I shook him off. I wanted him to stay.

"Lorraine. You look like you might explode. Is there something you'd like to say?"

Lorraine looked at me then to her father, then the General, then back to me. "I do want to say something, but it's so unfair that I have to . . . it seems so . . ."

"It's all right, Lorraine. I know. I've known or suspected for a long time. Matthew is a drunk. He cries and whines when he is drunk—very drunk—and he hates himself for the things that he's done. He could never measure up. He couldn't compete with Will. Will was the athlete, the smart guy, the hero older brother and Matthew couldn't handle it. I'm angry because some of you know things about Matt, things that Matt has done, things that he needed help with. Will covered up for his little brother. He protected him as a boy, and it never stopped. When it should have stopped, it was too late." Betsy paused as she dabbed her eyes with a tissue.

"I love this family. You are all that I have and Matt, but the facade must come down. What did Matt do? What is it that is so bad that it got Will and Liz killed? Liz and Will are gone, and I have this . . . this overwhelming and horrible feeling that

Matt caused their deaths. Why won't we talk about it and save Matt or, failing in that, save the family?"

Grandma MacKenzie turned around. She was angry. Angrier than I'd ever seen before. She'd had enough.

"William . . . tell them! Tell them about Matthew. I told you that one day this would cause a crack in this family, and it would not stop splitting until it was as wide as the Grand Canyon. I warned you in Oceanside and I've warned you over the past several years. Will protected Matt from most of his mistakes, but Will died not knowing . . . not knowing who he was protecting. You knew! William, we're going shopping within the next two hours. Missy, Lorraine, Haley, and the girls are going shopping in Riverhead. In less than two hours we will all be out of here and it will be just Mark, Frank, and you. You will tell Mark what ails this family. It's been kept quiet for too long. And I will say it so there is no mistaking my feelings . . . Will and Liz are dead because of you!" Grandma MacKenzie forcefully tossed her kitchen apron on the counter and stormed off. Grandma Stuart put her plate down and walked off with Grandma MacKenzie. She turned to look at me then she turned to my grandfathers.

"Bill. Make no mistake, I blame you for their deaths, too," and she left the room.

A knock at the front door produced Haley who came into the room. "Hi, everyone. How's . . . what's wrong?" Haley turned to me. I shook my head and beckoned her to me. Missy stood.

"Dad. They're right. It's time Mark knew. It's time for all of us to know. Come on ladies, let's go play on the PWCs for a bit before we go shopping. The tank leaves at 10 a.m." Haley followed Missy out looking at me. I nodded her out. Betsy walked to me.

"Mark, I don't know all that has happened. I fear my husband is much more than a drunk. I fear he is some sort of monster who has done horrible things. I think I know what he is and if I'm correct then, as leader of this family, because all the other men failed us, you do what you must do to protect us. It's what your mother would want," Betsy said, and she walked out.

Grandpa Stuart looked at the General. "You were wrong, Bill, but I've failed, too, by not acting. Mark, Martha, and Emily are correct. We failed and Will and Liz are gone. I," his voice cracked as he wiped his eyes, "hope God takes mercy on our souls." He pulled away from the counter. "You tell him, Bill," he said and walked out of the room.

Haley was still standing there with Missy and Lorraine. I nodded them out the door and pointed LT out of the room. Once all were gone, I looked at my grandfather. He was hunched over, his shoulders sagged, and he wiped his eyes. I was not going to wait for the women to leave. I needed to press my attack. I walked to him, stopping ten feet away.

"Grandpa. I'm close to resolving several matters none of which I'd ever dreamed I'd be involved in, but none more important than my family. It's more than Matt's drinking. It's more than lying about a car wreck in high school that broke my father's back. It's more than Matt skimming from the firm. It's more than Matt teaching others how to skim. It's more than Matt's relationship with the Menduni family or with Rizzo. I know about the false shareholder agreements. Matt and Dad signed off on them. I need to know why the mob almost got twenty percent of the firm. I need to know it all because I will find out.

Mom and Dad left a package for me with attorney Schmidt that I will receive today. It was to be delivered to me when I became president or on my thirty-third birthday. I don't know what it will show me or what it will say, but the mere fact that it was to be delivered to me when I became president is so very wrong because we never discussed me becoming president, ever, before my parents' deaths. Why would we with my father running the show? Not for many years would that have occurred if it occurred at all. Dad knew he would die, and he knew I would step up to take over to protect the family. That breaks my heart that my father knew he might die and there I was, helpless to help him. Had I known I could have done something, even in my condition I could have called someone. Why didn't someone tell me?"

Tears formed in my eyes. I paused then continued.

"I am meeting with Vincenzo's daughter, Alexandra, today. She intends to tell me all she knows about my parents' deaths and Matt's relationship with her family.

A little over a year ago, at my parents' graves, with Lauren's hand in mine, as best I could, I stood, and I said a prayer and I promised my mother, father and Lauren I'd find their killers and that I would avenge their deaths. I suspect that I'm close to fulfilling that promise.

Grandma said to Haley the other day, *'Please don't let him kill them all!'* I now know what Grandma meant. She was telling me that other family members are responsible for my parents' deaths. It's not too difficult to figure out who she's asking me to save by her words. However, I will do what I must do to protect my sister and the rest of my family, even if it means sacrificing the one of us who has hurt the rest. Grandpa, look at me."

He turned to look at me with tears in his eyes.

"I love you, Grandpa. I will protect all of us, but I need to do this. I cannot rest until it is done and settled. You know due to your war experience, and I know due to my long association with war and death that people will die this weekend and this week because of what you and I decide to do or what others try to do to stop me from finding the truth and protecting those women out there. I don't want it to be any of us, but I will give my life to settle this and protect this family if need be if it comes to that . . ."

"NO! NO! NO! NO! How dare you?" Haley screamed. I turned to see Haley, Lorraine and Missy standing on the living room porch.

"No! It's not going to be you, Mark! No one in this family is dying this weekend. We won't let it happen. God, damn you. You almost died and these women, these women who love you, pulled you back from death . . ." her voice cracked, and tears streamed down her face.

My grandmothers, Betsy, Lauren and Kimberly entered the room due to Haley's yelling.

"Someone may go to jail, but you are not dying. Do you understand me?" Haley was crying.

"We're going to have a family! You're going to lead us, and Paulie will have a little brother or sister, and a good man to lead him and teach him. All this death, deceit, and power and . . . I went through it. I won't go through it again. This weekend it's done. Paulie will likely lose his father—I won't let this child lose hers."

I was stunned. "Haley, did I hear . . ."

"Yes, you, big ape, I'm pregnant! You're going to be a father, damn it, so," she paused to think, so angry she couldn't speak, "you better hurry up with that decoder ring!"

I walked to Haley and put my hands on her to pull her too me. She pushed me away.

"You have Lauren, me, and the baby to protect and defend. Oh, Mark, I love you, but sometimes you are so hard-headed."

Haley paused as she collected her thoughts. No one said a word. I looked from Haley, to Lauren, to my grandmothers then to Haley who spun around to my grandfather.

"Grandpa MacKenzie. All I will say to you is fix it. I will not speak to you again until you fix it. None of us will! Shall we go get ready, ladies?"

"Yes!" several of them said in unison.

"Mark. I'll need your credit card in case I see any baby things and the key fob for the tank."

"Anything else?" I said.

"I'll let you know. All this dying talk. I'll keep you so busy you'll have no time to die. Now you men go fix it. Whatever it is, fix it so we can all cry, scream, hit, curse, heal and move on. And another thing, Mark. This is the family's house. You make enough income as president of MacKenzie Securities to put another house there where that old cottage is. I saw the letter on your dresser where they accepted your buy-back offer. I want a house there. Lauren will design the interior for us with my help and it will have enough bedrooms for at least five children, Paulie, Lauren and us. Am I clear?" Haley said.

I looked over at Lauren who smiled at me. "You heard my future sister-in-law. This house is the family's house . . . vacations, family get-togethers—memories. I agree. That point of land is perfect," Lauren said.

I looked at the women of my family. All of them were between anger, sadness, and happiness at what had just transpired. Tears flowed on their faces. I was too primitive to understand it all.

"I'm sorry that I've upset you all." I looked at my grandfathers. "Insensitivity and poor judgement seem to run with the men in this family."

"No, Mark. You are not insensitive. You have your mother's heart, and your father's stubbornness, but, thankfully, not your grandfather's selfishness. Like Haley said, you men go fix what needs to be fixed," Grandma MacKenzie said.

"Yes, ma'am. I'll start with the kitchen. Get going ladies. I'll arrange for dinner tonight. We'll go out to eat. Casual. Is the Soundview okay?" I sheepishly exhorted.

"Yes. That's fine," Missy said as the ladies walked off. My grandfather tapped Grandpa Frank on the shoulder, and they departed the room. I heard the Cadillac start and drive off.

I turned around and it was just me. All I could hear was the sound of the guys out on the bay playing on the PWCs. I was going to be a father!

#

"Mark." I turned at Haley's voice.

"What is your suggested time for dinner?" She said.

"Is 7 p.m. okay?" I ventured.

"Yes. We will be back by 6 p.m. We're just going to the Riverhead outlets and the mall."

"Okay."

"What are you doing?"

"Well, cleaning up and, I guess, looking up house plans."

"Good. Lauren and I have some ideas."

"Yes, ma'am," I said as Haley put out her hand.

"Oh." I gave her my credit card and some cash.

"The key fob?" Haley asked. I looked around and checked my pockets. My grandmother handed it to me, and I passed it to Haley. Haley kissed me.

"Remember what I said."

They walked out together. Five into the SUV and three into the S550.

Now if I could only remember what she said?

I watched the Yukon drive away followed by an FBI sedan with two special agents in it. The S550 went the other direction with a Suburban following with two special agents in it.

My phone buzzed. It was Joe. "Yeah."

"Nothing on the Lincoln. The dot is red and it's in front of the Queens home of Castellano. NYPD checked it and it's his Lincoln."

"Maybe he has two Lincolns like the *Lincoln Lawyer*, we have the *Lincoln Goombahs*."

"We're sharp as a tack today. I ran the data on the GPS. The car has been in and out of the old man's estate several times over the past two weeks. It was last there yesterday morning. It's been to the restaurants in Queens, Freeport, Rockville Center, all over Brooklyn, Newark, Harlem, North Manhattan. He traveled I-95 to Fairfield, Connecticut. Last week it was up I-95 and was in Belle Haven and Fairfield, Connecticut and Rye, New York."

"Were they at Vincenzo's?"

"No."

"Sounds like they work for just the old man."

"It seems so."

"What else have Carl and Ken learned?"

"Well, they're poking around looking for Bonano, Paganelli, Sciortino, Salano, and the rest of the group. They are staying off email and cell phones. None of their cars are out and about either. All their cell phones are off, and batteries removed. It's like they all got whacked and no bodies or they scrambled out of town."

"They're getting around and communicating somehow. Did we get an update on how many the group now consists of?"

"No. We think around fifty to sixty shooters. It's odd. Let me call Stayton and see what the task force knows. So, you're meeting Rapano?"

"Yeah. Oh, my day just got stranger. Something is seriously wrong with the family history and Matt. He's still missing, but he's done a bunch of bad things. We sort of had it out with the family. Grandma MacKenzie read the riot act to the General, blamed him for my parents' deaths. She ordered him to tell me everything or life will be hell for him. My other grandfather shared in the blame, but he went right back at the General. All the women are pissed off at the Grandpas. I'm the leader since the other men screwed up. The women want Matt in jail or worse. I can't die because I must build a house where that drafty, crappy cottage is with enough bedrooms for five kids, Paulie, Lauren, Haley, and me. Oh. I'm going to be a father."

"Are you shitting me?"

"Which part? It's all unbelievable to me. Oh, I must give her a decoder ring."

"That's better than a diamond. With what you'll make now as president, three month's pay makes it a big rock."

"You're depressing me."

"Well, let me go, dad. The agents are out of the house readying for all the busts."

"Joe?"

"Yeah."

"Joe, I don't have a good feeling on this. We're not out of it yet."

"I agree. Rob, Tony, Carl, Ken and all the techs here and in Manhattan are carrying because of the random and violent nature of these guys. You still have that cavalry available?"

"Yes. Six in Manhattan and six in Long Island. Let me give you their 911 codes." I passed the codes to Joe. "What are we missing, Joe?"

"I don't know. I think we'll hear something by this afternoon. I think in Newark first or up in the Bronx. Take good notes with Rapano.

"What of the Invisible Man?"

"Nothing. We quit that to move onto looking for the young guns."

"I'll let you go. I may come by there to pick your brain before I go see Circe."

"Who?"

"Circe. The mythical goddess who imprisoned Odysseus for a year and who turns men into swine. Rapano."

"That's not true. Myra said men are already swine. Anyway. I'll let you go. Time to eat again. I'm going to be overweight when I go back to work."

"Exercise with Surfer."

"I'd die. No thanks. Bye."

"Bye."

#

I had commander's jitters.

"Chief. In the garage are several lengths of nylon line, shovels, chain, and grappling hooks. Same in the Oceanside garage. Load your vehicle with them and ask Surfer to load his vehicle with what he finds there. How much Semtex do we have?"

"We each have eight ounces, igniters, fuse and detcord."

"Okay. Call Surfer. I'm going to the garage to check my car and gear."

I rechecked all my weapons. I wish I had some grenades or an RPG. Alas the government didn't permit civilians to possess those items. I almost forgot Kevlar vests and the plates. I put two vests with plates in the back seat of the car along with my tactical vest/harness. Chief appeared.

"Have the guys check NVGs, Kevlar, swim gear."

"Mark. We're ready, relax. Are you going to Oceanside? It's already 1400."

"I guess not. Well, we're ready. For what, I don't know. I'm going. Follow me out and block them so I can get away."

"Sure."

I put on my comms.

"LT. I'm rolling to Fort Salonga."

"Roger."

I drove out onto the street with Chief right behind me. The FBI guys took my driveway rather than the driveway from the house they were using. Chief stopped and blocked them. They couldn't get around him. I sped east as fast as I safely could. I hoped Chief didn't get arrested. At Riverhead, they'd expect me to get onto the L.I.E., but I'd stay on route 25 to route 25A in Smithtown. My cell phone was off, and the battery pulled. I had my mother's old phone. Joe, LT, and Chief could reach me on it.

I was moving along at sixty miles per hour. I stayed on Route 25 to the Old Country Road bypass got on it then got back onto 25 just past the outlet mall where the ladies were shopping. I passed the Calverton Air Park. I thought I heard the FBI say they had a helicopter there. My ride would take me through several small villages and shopping areas, but that was fine. I'd get to Fort Salonga in about an hour and change.

#

I pulled up to the Rusty Hinge Tavern. Along the north shore of Long Island, beginning at Kings Point and continuing east to Orient Point, are many bays, inlets and freshwater reservoir outlets to Long Island Sound. Old money mansions and multi-acre estates dot the northern quarter of Nassau County. Mixed in were small villages and hamlets where working people live and work. That scheme continues at least as far east as Miller Place, midway in Suffolk County. Many restaurants, bars and taverns dot the coast roads along the harbors, bays, and inlets. The Rusty Hinge, no doubt the name coming to the owner upon entering his recently acquired establishment, has been around a while. It had a hoity-toity crowd that mixed well with the working folks. The food was good and the wildlife usually tame, though a late-night brawl on a Friday or Saturday night wouldn't surprise the regulars.

I parked across the street from the front door. The tavern, surrounding shops and bars in this part of the hamlet were built on a bluff with a view to the Sound over a residential lowland of nice homes. Long Island Sound was five hundred yards from the road. I'd been here several times with other veterans while we were in treatment at North Port VA Medical Center. I put my Kevlar over my console to cover my .44 Magnum as I exited my car. I strode into the tavern and found a seat in a semi-circle booth in the corner near the front of the tavern, but not in the line-of-sight of a drive-by or sniper. I know what you're thinking, why risk it at all?

A well-worn waitress approached me cracking her gum.

"Can I take your order?" Crack-crack.

"Sam Adams draft, please."

"Something to eat?"

"Do you have apple pie?"

"I'll check." She ran off to get my order.

It was 3:47 p.m. I wore sunglasses, so I could scan the room without being obvious. A smattering of locals, tourists, and college kids, perhaps forty people occupied tables or sat at the bar. No one was looking at me. No single men or pairs of men sitting unaccompanied by women nor was anyone standing off in a corner attempting to look inconspicuous. The bartender ignored me, and the busboys and waitresses didn't dawdle. My waitress returned with my beer.

"Your pie will be ready shortly."

"Thank you." I sipped my beer. I picked up the *New York Post* from the booth next to me, opened it and picked up reading where I'd left off earlier. After five minutes of reading, scanning and being unable to concentrate, I laid the paper back on the bench. As I did, I looked up to see Alexandra—Al—enter the tavern. She took five steps in, looked around, taking her time looking.

Trouble finding me or looking for her back-up?

She was dressed in a spring ensemble with dark, I couldn't tell the color, Capri pants, matching high-heeled sandals, a creme-colored blouse, with a sleeveless silk and linen, light green jacket over. Her hair was in a ponytail and pulled through the adjustable band of her crème-colored ball cap that had a frou-frou design on the front. Diamond earrings—two in each ear and a gold cross that wasn't smoldering. She wore a few bracelets and a more sensible sport watch today. She also wore a gold anklet on her left ankle which always drove me wild on a beautiful woman. She tilted her sunglasses to look around and finally decided after two looks I was me. She walked to my table.

Dilemmas, dilemmas—does a man stand for a woman who is a mob underboss who killed his mother? I'd have to write to the *New York Times* ethicist with that question, or would it be to Miss Manners?

I stood as she walked toward me. Alexandra smiled as she approached. She had no weapon. Well, at least not a shooting, stabbing, or cutting weapon. I didn't offer my hand.

"Thank you for seeing me."

She unslung her bag from her shoulder and placed it on the seat. She looked for a place to sit and I nodded for her to sit toward the inside of the semi-circular booth. I sat to her left.

"Put your bag between us, please."

She complied with my order looking confused. I opened her bag and looked for a weapon or another clandestine device. I found her iPhone. Steve Jobs would be thrilled. I found several file folders. The bag was a businesswoman's valise. I closed it and slid it to her. I assumed the folders were for our meeting. I neglected to bring note-taking material, but I had my digital recorder turned on.

"What is it I can get for you?"

"I'll have what you're having," she said as the waitress placed my apple pie in front of me.

Alexandra looked surprised at the pie then at me. "Different. Just a beer. Thank you."

The waitress ran off cracking her gum. We sat in silence for a long minute.

"What is it you wish to tell me?" I asked then I took a bite of my pie.

"Mr. MacKenzie. My father did not order the killing of your father and mother. I don't know what you have that you are relying on to arrive at that . . ." She waited until the waitress set her beer down and departed before continuing. ". . . at that conclusion. There was never any consideration given to harming your mother, ever. Your father's name came up to my father and it was rejected at the first instance, as always. My father does not do those things."

"Who brought up my father's name?"

"Al Rizzo. He'd done some sloppy deals or actual fraudulent deals that your father caught. I cannot speak much on that subject because you are recording me, but the intent of placing people at the firms was to sell bonds of several energy companies and to obtain information on other companies which, as you know, is only illegal if that information is used for insider trading. No discussion ever took place regarding killing your father and mother."

"If I put a document in front of you that discussed killing my father, what would your reaction be if it was addressed from your father?"

"It would be false. If it included any reference to my father considering such action. If Mr. Farina was available, he would confirm what I say. Mr. Pagano can, if you wish to speak to him. My father will tell you directly if you wish. My father, Messrs. Farina and Pagano, and I never condoned nor ordered such activities in our business. If you have something, then it is wrong. We don't do that type of activity. I stake my life on it. I suppose I am as we speak."

I sipped my beer, but I watched her while she spoke. She was either a very good liar or she was telling the truth.

"Who authorized their deaths?"

"If they were authorized, it came from another firm or Romeo Menduni. I would ask you to go back and closely look at your evidence. However, I do not believe your parents deaths were ordered or authorized by anyone."

I ate the last bite of my pie.

"Who killed Rizzo?"

"We don't know. None of the usual sources have shed light on a killer. If I had to guess, my educated guess would be Bonano, Paganelli, the Sciortinos, and that hostile group. We think they did the shootings at Tito's this morning, too."

"What business relationship did my father have with your firm?"

"None, directly. Obviously, through his firm, we got some things done."

"Your hedging on the truth isn't helping you. Lose the edgy professional lawyer . . . I don't mean to be chauvinistic but act like your mother would want you to act and tell me the truth."

Alexandra began to respond, but she seemed to soften, and she looked away from me.

"Do you have children?"

She looked at me surprised by my question then her expression became melancholy.

"No. I don't. My deceased husband could not have children . . ." she again looked off into space.

Did she whack him because she could not have kids with him?

"I've missed a few things in my life, Mr. MacKenzie. You need to know . . ."

"Who in my firm had business with your firm?"

"Rizzo, Train, and Rizzo's assistant and secretary."

"What about Train's staff?"

"No. Rizzo's staff covered him."

"What about the computer tech, Taylor?"

"We did not employ a computer tech at your firm."

"I discovered a tech who was paid cash by mail. He said Train recruited him?"

"We employed no such person. Train must have been using him for other purposes."

"Do you employ a private investigator who photographs our offices or who photographed my father and mother?"

"No."

"What business did you have with my Uncle Matthew?"

That caught her off guard.

"I will tell you what I know. My father, your father and Matthew attended NYU. My father began college several years out of high school. He's fifty-nine years old. I believe three or four years older than your father. Your uncle is three years younger than your father. I believe your father started at NYU two years before my father. Your father was smart, and he helped my father readjust to an academic environment after a few years in the business."

"Sure. I guess he took a break from torching businesses and breaking arms, I take it?" I said and wished I had not.

She looked at me and ignored my jibe.

"Your father was intelligent, and he helped out my father. Your uncle arrived at NYU when your father began his last semester. I am under the impression your father graduated a semester early. The three men lived in the same dorm although your father got an apartment with your mother during his time at college. Matt was introduced to my father. Matt is not as gifted as your father or even my father, but my father felt he owed your father, so he helped Matt with his studies.

Your uncle showed my father how to skim money off various transactions . . ."

"Hold on. You've jumped ahead some years. Tell me about your father's relationship with Matt."

"They were friends. I would not characterize it as good friends. First there was the age and maturity difference. My father is reserved while Matthew is loud, perhaps flamboyant. Second, Matthew almost always drank to excess, and he used drugs. He became obnoxious or very sorrowful when he drank to excess. Matthew had done some bad things as a teenager and while he was at college. My father would not tell me what Matthew did. Anyway, Matthew was out at the house a few times, to our grandfather's home over the years, on the boats and that was the college life they led. My father graduated a year before Matthew since he missed a semester for an injury."

"He was shot as I recall."

"Yes. I was four or five-years-old at the time."

I quickly did the math.

"I'm thirty-eight years old, Mr. MacKenzie."

"And perceptive."

She smiled at me. "Your uncle did different deals or tasks where he worked throughout the 1980s and into the 1990s. If I recall, MacKenzie Securities formed in 1996, and your father moved from a large Wall Street firm to your grandfather's firm. Matt went over a year later. Your father was the muscle and brains behind the firm. It struggled a bit at first, but by the third year it was doing well, and it needed cash to expand. My family provided the funds to finance that expansion."

"Hold on. You're saying my father and grandfather knowingly borrowed funds from your family?"

"No. Matt, as a junior executive without a lot going for him, was going to be fired. Your father told him to find some venture capital funds. Matt went to my father. Your father protected him because Matt told my father that he would be fired if he did not come through with the funds and pull his weight. My father—the firm—set up a venture capital firm. Mr. Farina did the work to form the LLC. It was all legal, tax paid and correct in all respects. Your father's firm, the board, authorized four rounds of funding from VC Venture Capital, LLC which was approved by VC Venture Capital . . ."

"What does VC Venture Capital mean?"

"It's redundant. Venture Capital Venture Capital."

"Aye."

"We loaned $20 million, but no shares of the firm were taken as security. The money was made available like a bank loan. The interest rate was four points over prime with a transaction fee of $1 million. High at the time, but look what your family did? Matt was on the hook for another $5 million at 12%. My father returned the $1 million transaction fee to Matt and loaned him another $3 million for his personal use.

Matt was not paying well at first, then something clicked, and he was ahead. He paid off the debt in 2003. His total payments came to just over ten million dollars. Your firm paid back the VC Venture Capital funds in less than three years. By then the firm was doing very well and your father became vice-president, and the older guys got out of the way. Shortly thereafter your father was named president. Matt moved up to a senior position. I'm not sure what that position was. Matt did okay and your father covered Matt for some mistakes and hiccups. By then Matt was skimming again to pay off another personal debt with my grandfather. By 2009, Matt became so unreliable and his personal conduct so atrocious that my father terminated their relationship. Matt had a falling out with the board. Your grandfather wanted to fire him, but your father didn't permit it. We don't think your father knew of Matt's serious and atrocious criminal conduct. Your grandfather knew of most of it. At least the most serious conduct because he got involved to protect Matt. What do you know of Matt's personal conduct?" she asked.

"He's a drunk, unreliable and has low self-esteem."

"There's more. Much more. While your father protected Matt at the firm, my father or grandfather helped him out of various problems, legal problems such as DUIs, destruction of property, assault and battery and, well, my father called it *date rape*."

"I thought your father didn't tell you what Matt did?"

"He didn't. Mr. Farina, Mr. Pagano, and others did. Matt's conduct became worse and in 2010 he attacked and sexually assaulted a woman at a downtown hotel. He seriously injured the woman. It was fixed by my grandfather because by that time my father had walked away from Matt. Your grandfather sought help from my grandfather, Romeo. An arrangement was made, and Matt was never prosecuted. That's what I know. I'm under the impression the woman was paid over $1 million to keep quiet. Witnesses were paid, too."

I sat there in shock though not showing it. I sipped my second beer.

"Your father was in Matt's office several times, most recently last week."

"Yes. My father is on the NYU Alumni Endowment Committee. Matt had agreed to donate, but over the past several months he did not. My father visited him each month to find out why he did not do what he said he would do. He still has not donated. Check your records. They will show your father gave several hundred thousand dollars each year and increased his giving annually."

"You drifted off talking about the arrangement. What was Matt to do?"

"I don't know exactly, but he and your grandfather were on the hook for a lot of money."

"Please don't let him kill them all . . . I hold you responsible for their deaths." My grandmother wasn't referring to just Matt. I sat there in shock.

"I have emails and memo's involving sixteen people in your organization and others who are involved in the conspiracy to kill my father. I've positively identified fifteen of them. One is unknown. The unknown is Matt.

"Yes."

"The emails authorized the elimination of 'WM.' That's not my father, is it?"

"I told you that."

"'WM' is my grandfather, isn't it?"

She nodded without saying a word. "Mr. MacKenzie I cannot speak to that subject because we're not involved in it. I will tell you that Matt took many bonds in a skimming operation that he ran with Rizzo and Train. Your grandfather knows about some of that. I don't know the exact amount taken, but whatever they took, they walked away with them and did not fulfill their obligation to my grandfather. I do know Matt said it was all your grandfather's doing."

"But this still doesn't explain how my father and mother got killed?"

"Wrong car."

"What?"

"You may not recall, but your father and grandfather drove matching black BMW seven series sedans. Your parents and your grandparents attended a formal affair in the city. They departed at the same time, your grandparents traveling to Rye and your parents to Oceanside. My grandfather's men got the wrong car."

"How do you explain them hitting the car with a wife in it?"

"The men my grandfather relies on are less capable people who may not follow the customs. Mr. MacKenzie, for decades my father has done business without violence. I have pushed that with our associates in agreement with Pagano and Mr. Farina. Business is business. Until Grandpa Romeo Menduni is gone, my father shows him respect, but no more. My father has blocked numerous activities his father has tried to do. Mr. MacKenzie—Mark, my father is now at war with his father. It has been building for months as my father blocked most anything his father wanted to do. We believe and have some evidence that Romeo has instigated Bonano, Paganelli, Salano, the Sciortinos, Rizzo and others. My grandfather has ordered that my father, Mr. Pagano, and I be removed from the organization."

Alexandra removed a folder from her valise. She removed several documents and passed them to me. They were emails, some of which I'd read, but the emails dealing with killing Alexandra and her father, I'd not seen before. I recognized the email addresses of the senders.

"What about Rizzo?"

"We don't think so. We think that's Bonano who did that. Can I call my father? We've gone on longer than I anticipated. He's worried about me. I've left my phone off."

"Yes. Go ahead."

I sipped my beer. Alexandra turned on her phone and tapped an icon.

"Dad. I'm fine. Yes. I'm with him. What? Yes. Who? I . . ." Alexandra looked at me. Her expression had changed to despair. "I don't know if he will. Hold on. He wants to speak with you."

I took the phone as Alexandra began to cry. "What do you want?"

"I know you don't owe me a thing. Paul was killed a little while ago. Mr. MacKenzie, these guys are animals. My daughter explained the background and history to you?"

"Yes."

"I will corroborate all she says and provide you with evidence, if need be, but right now my daughter is out there alone and unarmed. Would you please protect her until I can get there?"

Holy crap. Now I'm going to protect a mob underboss? I looked at my watch. It was 5:15 p.m.

"Yes. Do you know where we are?"

"I have an idea. I've never been there, but we'll find it. Can I speak with my daughter, please? And thank you."

I passed the phone to Alexandra.

"Yes, Daddy? He will," she looked up at me. "I will. I will. Okay. I love you. Bye."

"I guess we'll just wait?"

"No. Get your bag." I tossed money on the table as my mother's phone vibrated.

"Yeah."

"It's Joe. Where are you?"

"The Rusty Hinge."

"Get out! Now! Listen to me. We figured out how they're talking and getting around, satellite communications, CB radio, and marine band VHF, and they're driving sanitation and construction vehicles around the city and Long Island. The FBI just picked up . . ."

I grabbed Alexandra by the hand, and we hurried toward the back of the tavern.

". . . a radio call. They found Alexandra's car."

"Hold on, Joe. Alexandra. Where are you parked?"

"The side lot, by the antique store."

"People are coming here looking for you. They know you're here. Listen to me. I'm parked across the street. There are several bars and stores here, so it will take them a while to find you. I'm in the black Dodge Challenger across the street.

I'll make a U-turn and pull up in front, open the door and you'll jump in. Joe, are you getting this?"

"Yeah. Get out. Now! They're pulling up as we speak. They're in at least three trucks. Get to your car. Nassau PD is moving there now."

"Stay on the line, Joe. Alexandra. They're in sanitation and construction trucks. Go into the lady's room. Count to one hundred then come out to my car. I'll be in front of the bar. If you hear gunfire, remain in the stall in the bathroom until I come get you."

"Okay."

"Go." I hoofed it to the front door. "Joe, you're on speaker. I'll keep talking giving intel on the phone . . ."

"Go. I got her count. Get out."

"I'm going through the door. To my right, east 25A, a green sanitation truck. Further right, east, a white two-and-a-half-ton truck. Three guys. On my left, another sanitation truck. I'm waiting for traffic to cross the street. No one is looking at me."

"Forty, 41, 42 . . ."

"I'm opening my trunk for my shotgun and M-4. I have my SIG on me and a .44 Magnum by my seat."

". . . 59, 60, 61, 62 . . ."

"I have my weapons. I put them in the passenger side. I am walking around the front . . ."

". . . 68, 69, 70, 71 . . ."

"I'm in and starting the car. My shotgun is across my lap. I'm making my . . ."

"... 79, 80, 81, 82 ..."

"... turn. Traffic is in the way."

"... 86, 87, 88, 89 ..."

"I'm turning, Joe. I'm pulling up in front. The sanitation trucks are coming toward me. I'll U-turn out of here and head west."

"... 94, 95, 96 ..."

"Shit! They're out of their vehicles walking toward the tavern. Three guys. They're seventy-five feet away."

"... 99, 100, 101, 102 ..."

"They're looking at me. I'm right in front of the bar."

"... 106, 107, 108 ..."

"Get in!"

Alexandra jumped in the car. The three guys saw Alexandra and ran toward us. I stomped on the gas and turned the wheel just as I saw the first weapon. I spun the wheels as 707 horses connected with the tires and screeched in defiance.

"DUCK!"

Alexandra ducked as I covered her with my Kevlar vest, raised my shotgun, stuck it through the window and pulled the trigger. The blast hit two men, one on his left side and arm, the other on his right side and arm. I backed off the gas as I started to spin to the left. I came off the pedal more and compensated my oversteering. I one-hand pumped the shotgun as a sanitation truck swerved toward me fast from the east on 25A. I fired another shot directly into the driver's side windshield. I dropped the shotgun and yanked the .44 Magnum from between the seat and console. The car continued to spin left; I compensated to slow my turn as I fired the .44 Magnum four times into the oncoming truck as I completed the turn. I straightened out and accelerated west, my ears ringing from the concussion of the shots inside the car.

"Joe. I'm running. I'm clear. I hit at least two with the first shot. Unknown on the others. I'll turn south as soon as I can. They'll expect me to run to Glen Cove. Where's back up?"

"Mark. Are you okay?"

"Yeah. Hey, I'm getting another call?"

"Ignore it, Mark. Mark! LISTEN TO ME, MARK!"

"What is it, Joe?"

"They kidnapped Lauren and Haley."

My world went silent, and my body went numb. At that moment, my world collapsed into the basic emotions God gave me, anger and worry. My heart all but stopped as hate turned my soul black as my automatic response to fight or flight took over.

"How, Joe?" I got out.

"All five of them were kidnapped from the parking lot of the outlet mall. Both FBI agents were killed. They were in their car when two men approached them with a map acting like they needed directions. They shot them through the open map."

I pulled off the highway onto a side street. "They shot them both? Who?"

"Hudson and Wilson."

"Where did they go?"

"They walked them across the lot to a tour van, like a Ford F-550 type of tour van."

"When?"

"A couple of hours ago. We got a call just before I called you. They didn't know until they saw the mall security video. Suffolk thought it was a robbery until they saw the video and FBI car computer panel. Stayton's people are there and at your house. LT buttoned down the house. Your grandmothers, Grandpa Stuart and Betsy are there."

"The General?"

"I don't know where he is. The tour bus drove west. Suffolk County is checking traffic video, and an Amber Alert was issued for the island and the five boroughs."

"God, damn it. What are they doing about finding the bad guys?"

"They put helos in the air and issued the Amber Alert. Nassau, Suffolk, NYPD, and FBI are out looking. Mark. They changed vehicles. They found the tour van at the Park and Ride at the L.I.E."

"Their cell phones?"

"All were left at the scene."

"It's old man Menduni. There's a fight . . . Damn it! Damn it! Damn it!" I yelled and slammed my dashboard. Alexandra startled.

"Mark. Come here. Rob and Tony's techs are all up. They called in more. There are eighteen techs working out of Manhattan looking and listening. Rob, Tony, Kev and Mikey are on their way, Carl just said. Talbot and Chief are on their way."

"How many men are covering my house in Greenport?"

"Four special agents with LT and Southold put ten deputies in the driveway."

"Ask them to pick up the Shores and Paulie and put them at my house too, please. I'm on my way. Call the cavalry and send them to my Greenport house. Tell Stayton they're coming and after they arrive, he should get his agents out investigating. I'm on my way. Out!"

My cell buzzed as I put it down. "Yeah?"

"Stayton here. You know?"

Great. Now he had this number. "Yeah."

"I just heard about your shoot-out. The initial report from Nassau PD is you got four. One dead in the truck that tried to run you over. Nassau and a couple of our guys are responding to the scene and interviewing witnesses. Agents are at your house in Greenport. They're at the outlets, in the air, at your Oceanside house, at the Park and Ride, and at your loft. We've asked NSA to check their birds to see if they caught something. We've set up in our crisis control center in Mineola. Sergeant Cicola and his people are on their way here. NYPD is up. Homeland Security and New York Port Authority Police were ordered to cover the ports, bridges, tunnels and commercial scales. The traffic jams have begun. I'm sorry, Mark. We didn't believe the threat was to your family. We thought it was to you."

"I'm sorry about your agents. I'm going to my Oceanside house. I'll plan from there. I just called in my private security team to secure my Greenport house. Get your agents out investigating. I'll be in touch. Out."

CHAPTER 21

"Mark. What happened?"

"They took my family. Call your father and tell him you're with me."

I thought while she spoke with her father.

"Mark. He wants to speak with you."

I took the phone. "Yeah."

"Thank you very much. Now what happened to your family?"

"They kidnapped Haley, Lauren, Kimberly, Missy, and Lorraine."

"Your mother's sister, Lorraine?"

"Yes."

"I'd like to help. We'll give you the names, addresses, backgrounds, and contact information—everything we have on them. Alexandra told me you know my father and those creeps started a war."

"Where are you?"

"I'm in my car on 106 about to get on 25A."

"Meet me at my house in Oceanside. It's Ross Place. The big white house on the bay-front double lot."

"I know where it is. I was there before your parents redid it. I'm coming in three armored SUVs and an armored limousine."

"Terrific. I'll see you in a little while. Nassau, Suffolk, and FBI are there."

"That's fine. Is my daughter okay?"

"She's scared, but fine. Here she is."

I put the car in gear and drove to my home.

"Mark. I'm sorry. We'll do everything we can. I like Haley. I hope you two have a life together."

"Put this on." I picked up the Kevlar vest. Alexandra put it on and, well, I'm just a little bigger than she is. I increased our speed as I got on the Sagtikos Parkway. I called the Greenport house. Grandma MacKenzie answered the phone.

"Mark. Oh, Mark. What will you do?"

"I'm working on it, Grandma. I'm going to the Oceanside house."

"Mark. You get them back. Do you hear me? You get them back, Mark. Your guys have gone to help. All but LT . . ."

"Stop, Grandma. I can get that from them. Where's Grandpa?"

"I don't know, Mark. I'm worried. He wasn't here when we got back. Frank didn't know where he went. Mark, there's a package here for you from your parents."

"Leave it for me. Grandma, I know. I think I know most of it, now. Why did they cover for him for so long?"

"I don't know, Mark. I should have turned him in myself."

"Which one, Grandma? Matt for his crimes or Grandpa for the cover-up?"

"I'm sorry, Mark, but don't worry about that now. Go get them back—please!"

"Grandma let me speak. I know you're upset. He raped her, didn't he?" My grandmother was crying now.

"Oh, Mark, I'm so sorry. I should have . . . done something back then."

"Answer my question, Grandma. Matt raped my mother and Dad never knew?"

"Yes, Mark, I'm sorry," she said as she cried.

"I'll be in touch. Do what LT says. We'll deal with this when it's over. Bye." I looked ahead as I sped down the parkway. I thought as I turned onto Southern State Parkway. "Did your father know that—about Matt and my mother?"

"Yes. I learned of it from my father's employee like the other crimes. That's how my grandfather, Romeo, first hooked Matt. Mark, I'm very sorry. I never met your mother, but my father said she was a very nice woman, and she was perfect for your father."

I stared ahead as I drove.

"Mark! Mark! Are you all right?"

"Not now, Alexandra."

My phone vibrated. "Yeah."

"It's LT. The Shores are here with Paulie. Mr. Shore is insistent that he help."

"Put him on."

"Mark."

"Yes. This is what I need you to do. LT has weapons, but in my closet and under my bed are tactical shotguns. Write down this address . . . In my closet hanging on my tie rack is a key. It's for the lock on the mini-storage . . . consolidate into as few boxes as you can . . . put the cash in as few boxes as you can . . . take down these numbers . . . enter them in that sequence twice, wait thirty seconds, then enter them again once more . . . the gun safe will open. It will only work once so take everything the first time and the magazines and ammo before you close the door. There are two .45 ACPs in there and several other pistols. Frank is familiar with the .45 ACP so give him one. Betsy gets the over and under shot gun. She's used it often and knows it. Take what you want then . . . I want you and LT to hang tight after you pick up that other stuff. I'll arrange for it to be delivered where I need it. If I need you, it will be by boat. You'll take the center console. I'll know soon. Talk to LT when I'm through speaking with him. Put him on. Mr. Shore . . . , Alexandra, and Vincenzo have joined us to get them back."

"Good, Mark. I'll get this ready then check the boat. Has LT operated the electronics?"

"Yes."

"Good. Here's LT."

"Yeah, Mark."

"Be ready to do the insertion we did last week. I'll call you. If it's a go, we'll rendezvous. I'll have a helo drop us in the Sound and you'll pick us up if need be."

"Roger. We'll be ready. I'll plan the transit for forty knots. I'll use the same way points."

"Very well. LT pass the word. ROE for deadly force. Kill all but those who are unarmed and surrender."

"Mark, if this is a hostage situation and, clearly it is, we can call back to the team under new law to assist civil law enforcement so long as Joe or an FBI guy goes in with us as arresting officer, we're just another Homeland or FBI asset."

"How long to set-up?"

"The FBI or Homeland makes a request to Special Operations Command. Our practiced recall time is two hours loaded and on the ramp. Delta can do this, too."

"I'll call you as soon as we have a location or other idea. Call who you know to grease the skids, so our people get the call."

"Roger. I'm up on both comsets. All of us are."

"Roger. I'll dress out at the house. Are the others there or on their way?"

"They're waiting for you, Mark."

"Roger. Out."

#

I turned onto Ross Place. Uh-oh. That's a lot of media coverage. What's with all the television trucks? I pulled into my driveway which was clear then into the garage through the middle door. Dan was standing on the edge of the lawn asking the television crews to leave or get off the property.

"Alexandra. Stay here. I don't want anyone seeing you yet. I'll be right back." I walked out toward the television crew and reporter Dan was speaking to. They walked toward me.

"Hold on. Let me give you something off the record," I said.

"Go off," the reporter said to the cameraman who released the switch and lowered his camera.

"I'm Mark MacKenzie."

"You are? Then we were right. They kidnapped your family?" The reporter said.

"Hold on. Don't waste my time with questions now. Who are you?"

"Stephanie Phillips, Channel 7 News."

"Come with me. Dan come with me. You two stay here until we call you," I said to the cameraman and tech. I escorted them into my garage, asked Alexandra to follow, and we entered my backyard for privacy.

"This is Alexandra Menduni Rapano." Dan nearly fell over.

"Vincenzo's daughter?" Stephanie asked.

"I am."

"This is the deal. I'll give you the names of every bad guy involved, their home addresses, work addresses, et cetera. I'll give you pictures of my family members and my sister's friend. After Mr. Menduni and I speak, we'll give you a joint statement. I don't know when that will be. I need to keep a lid on what's going on here. Can I get a few hours? I'll get you something for the 10 p.m. news," I said.

"Deal. What are you thinking?" Stephanie said.

"Of killing all the bad guys and getting my family back," I said.

Stephanie looked at me, then to Dan who looked uncomfortable, then to Alexandra.

"I think he's serious. He shot several men saving me earlier," Alexandra said.

I waved Alexandra silent and got Stephanie's attention. "Give me some time. Thanks. Come on in," I said.

"Me, too?" Stephanie said.

"Yes. We have a deal. You do nothing but observe until I say so. If anyone in there asks you to step out of a room for any reason, please do so, but you get full access to this story. Take notes—I don't care, but no pictures inside or of any of us. Tell your producer you're doing this, but that's all you give him," I said.

"Oh, my God! Okay."

"Let's go." We walked into the morning room. "Please excuse the place. We've been busy. Help yourself to coffee or pizza," I said. Joe walked in. "Joe. Please meet Alexandra Menduni Rapano." Joe looked at Alexandra and nodded.

"I see what you mean. Nice to meet you," Joe said.

Alexandra looked up at Joe then smiled after his comment registered.

"This is Stephanie Phillips, Channel 7 News. I'm letting her roam and watch; she will not release anything but what I allow."

"Good," Joe said.

"Vincenzo and his team are enroute here," I said.

"You're kidding?"

"No. Dan, there's a protocol to have part of my old team do an HRT op for civilian agencies. You guys make a request to Special Operations Command. I'm greasing the skids now. Make the request, please. When Special Operations Command gets the request, they will call my old boss. He'll call me because he'll already know. Get it?"

"Okay. So how much time will they need?"

"Two hours onto the airplane ramp. Stayton needs to tell me where we can hide two sixteen-man SEAL platoons packed for hostage rescue," I said.

"Shit! Okay. I'm on it," Dan said as he walked off.

"Joe. Alexandra and her people will identify the people involved. Start her with . . .?"

"Carl is handling that."

"And the locations of property and businesses of all these guys and her grandfather . . ."

"Romeo Guido Menduni. He goes by Rom," Alexandra volunteered as I rolled my eyes.

"All his commercial locations. Who else is here from FBI?" I asked.

"Dana and Wade," Joe said.

"Dana. Come here please," I said as I stuck my head into the family room.

"Yes, Mark," she said as she looked at Alexandra.

"Are we talking with the situation room in Mineola?"

"Yes. On that computer and this cell phone."

"Can I speak with John?"

"Yes." She tapped an icon on the phone.

"John Stayton, please. He's coming," she said unnecessarily. "It's Dana. Mark MacKenzie wants to speak with you. Here he is," Dana said and passed me the phone.

"John."

"Yes, Mark."

"Have we set out a probability chart for their likely locations?"

"Yes. We're filling in likely locations."

"Vincenzo Menduni is going to help us with that. Rob will be on that team, too, since we already have much of that information. What I'd like to do is send a team to each of these locations to probe for intel."

"Mark. We don't have that kind of manpower or the time," John said.

"Just a second, John. Stephanie. How many investigative reporter teams are in the New York City area?" I asked.

"Visual and print media, perhaps four hundred."

"If I sent out a list of locations where bad guys live, would they go out and investigate?" I asked.

"I think so, yes."

"You hear that, John?"

"Yes. Don't do anything yet. Mark, HRT is deployed and stretched thin. We'll have to use our local SWAT, Nassau, and NYPD."

"John. I have an eight-man team here. Did Dan speak with you, yet?"

"He's calling Washington now."

"Where can I land two sixteen-man SEAL platoons and their support crew? They'll be in the air from Virginia Beach in two hours."

"Republic Airport, but we have only one UH-60M tactical helo in the area," John said.

"Joe, can Dave expedite Coast Guard's four MH-60T AUF tactical helos from Cape Cod?"

"I'll call him," Joe said.

"Hear that, John?" I said.

"Coast Guard won't release all their helos for this op. We're gonna be short a helo or two," John said."

"We can clip into anything. What does Nassau, Suffolk or NYPD have? Get them and give us the type and model of helicopter. We train to clip into little birds, too. We just need to know what we're flying. Any contact from the bad guys yet?"

"No. We think they're still moving the women and with you shooting up that group on the North Shore, that surprised them, I'm sure."

"Get back to work. Any ransom, I'll deliver it."

"We'll talk about it, Mark."

"We just did. I will deliver it and my team will cover."

"Okay. Bye," John said.

"Mark?"

"Yeah, Surfer."

"A bunch of goombahs just pulled up in three armored SUVs and an armored limo."

"Yeah. They're going to help us."

"No shit?"

"Mr. Menduni comes all the way back. He'll tell us who else he needs," I said.

"Roger that. Kev, Mikey, Chief, Talbot cover please. No Trojan Horse," Surfer said.

I walked to the door with Stephanie Phillips following. Surfer opened the door, his SIG held at his side. Vincenzo stepped inside and saw the team and nodded.

"You're professional. The short guy outside is my tech guy. What about the rest of them?"

"They stay in the living room, kitchen, back room, and breakfast room. Smoking on the back patio. FBI is here. I have six SEALs with me and other guys hanging around. Are these your trusted men?"

"Yes. They will do as they're told," Vincenzo said.

"Rotate your drivers to watch the vehicles. No one goes into the dining room or family room without one of my team escorting. This is Sergeant Joe Mott, Suffolk PD. That's Special Agent Dan Carter, FBI. That's Stephanie Phillips, Channel 7

News. Those men you don't need to know. If any of your men do something, we'll do what we did to the traitorous Afghanis. Do you understand?"

"What did you do to the traitorous Afghanis?" Vincenzo said.

"You don't want to know," Surfer said.

"Follow me, please. Bring your tech," I said.

#

"Alexandra." She looked up and saw her father.

"Oh, Daddy." She walked to him, and they embraced. Vincenzo nodded at me.

"Thank you, again, for saving my daughter. Now let's get your family back."

"Rob, Tony, Dan, Carl—they're here to help. Get the information they have and pass what is important to John in Mineola. I'll call Lia's Pizza and order more pizzas, sandwiches, and salads. Stephanie. Come with me, please." We walked out to the patio.

"Just a second, let me make a call." I tapped my phone.

"Hello."

"Betsy. Mark."

"Oh, Mark. What's going on?"

"I need recent pictures of the ladies. I can tell . . ."

"We are all ready to go with that. The Schwartzes are on their way here. They have pictures of Kimberly. Where do we email them?" Betsy said.

"Perfect. Write up a short, one-paragraph bio for each of them."

"Okay, Mark. We'll do that now."

"Just a second, Betsy. Stephanie. I need an email," I said.

"Here," she wrote it on her card. "Can I call my producer and tell him they're coming?"

"Yes. Betsy. Email the pics and bios to this email. Get it done in thirty minutes."

"We'll get it done. The Schwartz's just pulled up. Anything else, Mark?" Betsy said.

"Yes. Pray. I'll be in touch. Bye. Stephanie. I want you and your producer to do a breaking news report and to state on-air that Lauren lost her parents in a mysterious, fatal motor vehicle crash and that two reliable sources said that this man, Romeo Menduni, ordered them killed and that these two men, George Castellano and Marco Palami ran them off the road and killed them. Add that two reliable sources have named the two as major cocaine distributors in Queens and Nassau, taking in between fifty and one hundred thousand dollars a week in sales."

"Okay. Who are the reliable sources?" Stephanie asked.

"Alexandra and me for the killing. Joe and me for the drug sales. Come on. They'll tell you. You cannot use our names." We walked into the family room.

"Joe, Alexandra. Come here, please," I said.

"Yeah," Joe said.

"Joe. Can you confirm that Castellano and Palami distribute cocaine and take in between fifty and one hundred thousand a week in sales?" I said.

"Well, it could be as high as two hundred thousand, but yes, I can confirm that," Joe said.

"Alexandra. Who killed my parents?" I asked.

"The two men you just named on orders from Romeo Menduni," she said.

"Thank you. You two go back to work. Stephanie. You have work to do."

"Yes. Thank you."

"Be ready to do the interview for the late news," I said.

"We will be ready."

"Dana. Anything on the location of the hostages?"

"No, Mark, go order the food. You've been going a mile-a-minute since you got here. Let us do our jobs!"

I nodded at her. I walked through the kitchen, poured a double-shot of bourbon over ice. Then asked Chief and Surfer to accompany me to the back patio.

"I figure they're in Nassau, Queens, or Brooklyn. They didn't go over a bridge or leave the island by ferry because of the Amber Alert. I'd say they're in a warehouse or similar in Brooklyn, a warehouse, the funeral home or Menduni's place in Nassau, or at some place in Queens. If one had to go somewhere and all the bridges and ferries are covered . . ."

"You take a boat," Chief said.

"You in the mood to sink a one-hundred-foot yacht?" I asked.

"Give the order and it will be done," Chief said.

"Surfer. You were there with me. How do you want to do it?" I asked.

"If the old man has stirred up all this, coming in by land will be hard. That bay has several ways into his place and several places we can be picked-up from where we can swim in. The usual hull placement, I'd say. You don't necessarily want to destroy the yacht, just disable it," Surfer said.

"We'll need to make sure the hostages are not already aboard the yacht. We'll have to do a snoop first, but placement on the running gear or aft hull is fine. It will sink in just six to eight feet of water. If they're aboard the yacht, then people will be around standing guard. We can still disable the yacht by destroying the running gear," Chief said.

"Our boat is two hours away. LT and Mr. Shore will take it into the bay and get you guys," I said.

"Where's Talbot . . ." Surfer said.

"LT has it. Talbot brought him up-to-speed and Mr. Shore knows a lot more about boats then we do," I said.

"Okay, Mark. Call them in. We need fifteen minutes to check, pack and less than an hour to get there. We'll take one SUV. I'll contact LT while we're on our way there and we'll arrange the pick-up," Surfer said.

"Chief?"

"Easy. Don't worry, Mark. We'll get them out alive," Chief said as he placed his hand on my shoulder.

"How many men?" I asked.

"Five to be sure. House mouse and two swim teams. If they're on the yacht we'll just disable it," Surfer said.

"But if we go in with two, two-man assault teams we need a sniper to cover. We're short on people," Chief said.

"We have Kev and Mikey on long guns, Talbot and you two on one team, LT, Joe and me on the other team," I said.

"Joe's not tested, Mark," Chief said.

"Then we'll put him on a rifle," I said.

"That's even worse. Leave him with you. I want Kev and Mikey on sniper duty. Two teams with SIGs, MP-7s and M-4s," Chief said.

"All right. Plan A, boat insertion, plan B, wet insertion and plan C, we'll make up if needed after we reconnoiter the area. LT has his electronics," I said.

"Let's do this, Mark. Time's a wasting. The faster we get there and sink it, the better for your family," Chief said.

"Okay. Surfer call LT and tell him to launch to the rendezvous point outside Oyster Bay. The plan to sink the yacht is approved for action. Old man Menduni and his people are the hostiles. Thirty-two of our best buddies will join us at some point so you know what we must do. Make sure you wear your IR strobes. I want to disrupt and do intel gathering on them. Square it away with the rest of the team. Let me know when you're in place and ready. Disable any other boats tied up on the property. If you can get a pound of Semtex on the fuel tanks, that would be a pretty display, too," I said.

"If there are no hostages or not too many bad guys aboard, I'll make it happen," Chief said.

"Go. Let me know before you get wet. Once you're in the water watch for a flare from the house mouse cancelling the op. That's only because that yacht is a few million more for the victims. Good luck," I said.

"Roger that. Let's go Chief. I'm stoked. I hope he doesn't order a flare," Surfer said as he and Chief readied to leave.

#

The food from Lia's arrived. The guys quickly and quietly left, though Stephanie noticed them packing and leaving. I listened in as LT and Mr. Shore performed comms checks with the guys as they cruised Long Island Sound at forty-eight knots as they passed through the edge of Smithtown Bay.

I was still sipping the same bourbon on ice, though the ice had melted. I tossed back the rest of the bourbon with four Excedrin from the bottle Haley had given me. Food was aplenty. I'd even sent for pizza for the news crews out in front of my house. Everyone was working hard on finding my family. I was knocked out of my daydream by Joe's voice.

"Mark. We have some ideas. Dan and John just spoke and we're in agreement on several possible locations. We're up on a video conference on the big screen monitor with John's Mineola team and FBI's tactical teams in Melville and Kew Gardens. We want to talk it over. Steve Cicola is there with his men and his SWAT Captain. NYPD has their SWAT Commander there and has three SWAT teams patrolling through Queens and Brooklyn. Nassau just sent a reconnaissance team to the funeral home in Jericho to do a snoop. FBI's SWAT is in standby at the Melville office."

"Let's do this, Joe," I said. I walked into the family room and sat in a chair in front of the big-screen monitor. Joe sat next to me, and Dan, Vincenzo and Alexandra joined us.

"Okay. It's coming up now. We have them," Ken said. I could see John and several uniformed officers and others in suits. Cicola was sitting next to John.

"I see Mark, Joe, Mr. Menduni, Ms. Rapano and Dan. You'll lose me, but still hear me as we go through photos and maps of the locations we'll talk about. Put up the first picture. Thank you. Mark. This is an overhead of a Brooklyn warehouse for a trucking firm. Mr. Menduni knows it well since his father has owned it for about fifty years. It is a possibility because it has lots of room. It has offices and secured storage areas. Why is it not ideal? Too much traffic, lots of security cameras and many female employees around during the work week though it is a twenty-four hour a day operation and some women are always there. It is the site furthest from the kidnap site. Sanitation and food preparation are poor.

Next is an apartment building in Brooklyn. It is only partially occupied. The apartments are being turned into coops or condos . . ."

"Condos," Vincenzo interrupted like it mattered. I gave him a look that silenced him.

"Condos. Several condos are completed and furnished. Problems include residents who will pay attention to rough looking men coming and going who are not contractors. They'd have to isolate the women in an area where no residents lived.

It's a thirty-two-story building with six condos per floor. The top eight floors are framed out. That leaves floors twenty-one to twenty-four with partially completed units. Five women would need to be in the three-bedroom units of which there are two per floor.

Next is an office building in Queens. Lots of offices, about ninety percent occupied. Pluses include lots of offices to hide them in. Minuses are too many people during the day, poor sanitation, food preparation and support.

Fourth on the list is another trucking warehouse for shipping and distribution of big box store items. Problems include lots of people coming and going and it's a twenty-four/seven operation and is loaded with security cameras.

Next is macabre. The funeral home in Jericho. Mr. Menduni rents space there from his father for his people. Mr. Farina works there, but nearly everyone else works for Romeo Menduni. This is a high probability. Small staff, no women, no customers except during viewings. It's three stories over a drive-in garage.

Sixth is the estate on Oyster Bay. It has a thirty thousand plus square foot mansion and many smaller homes and buildings. The property is some seventy-five acres. Mr. Menduni's employees, Mr. Pagano and Mr. Farina, have homes there. What is their status with all that is going on, Mr. Menduni?"

"Mr. Pagano has relocated his wife to a guest home on my estate. We think Mr. Farina has met with foul play. He has been missing for a few days."

"Yes, well, this is a high probability. Last is a couple of the other abandoned estates near the Menduni estate. He bought several of the old estates. They are in disrepair and lack some comforts, but we believe they are sufficiently furnished and have services that would allow them to hold the women there. Food could be prepared there or delivered from elsewhere.

Those are our best bets. The bridges are a no-go for them with the Amber Alert. New York Port Authority Police and Homeland Security Police are stopping and searching each vehicle leaving Brooklyn and Queens. Suffolk County and Homeland Security are checking the ferries. Coast Guard and NYPD are checking all shipping before they leave the Port of New York. We just got better pictures of the women and we sent them to the media."

My phone buzzed. It was Surfer. I stepped away to take it. "Yeah."

"We're all in place. It's quiet over there. LT is coming into the bay now. We'll IR the place and listen for a bit. The yacht has a couple of lights on, but we've been watching it since we arrived. No movement and no guards near it. I don't think anyone is aboard. There is a center console boat and a go-fast boat at the pier. We'll put a few holes in them.

I looked over the main house. Lights are on inside and outside, but I've seen no movement. I got movement at the girlfriend's house and at three other homes. People coming and going. Pagano's and Farina's homes are dark. Lights are on at the rec center and indoor pool. I can see several cars, limos and SUVs coming and going, parked on the property and at each building. Chief will put the charge on the fuel tank."

"Can you see the neighboring estates? Next door, your left from where you're looking from and the two at the end of the dead-end road to the right and west at the end of the street," I said.

"They're dark compared to Menduni's estate. They look empty and seem overgrown."

"They are. Check them out, but don't waste time if you have no indications with your sensors. Look for guards, vehicles, dogs, lights, that kind of thing. They may be alarmed to keep people away since they're abandoned. Menduni owns them."

"I got you, Mark. We'll reconnoiter the area and I'll get back to you. LT is pulling up to the pier we're at. What else?"

"That's it. Go sink that yacht."

"Roger that. Bye."

I stepped back into view of the camera and took my seat.

"Everything okay, Mark?" Stayton said.

"What type of question is that? My sister, her friend, my aunts, and my girlfriend are being held hostage. Until they're home safe nothing will be okay," I said.

"I meant with our probability list. In just over thirty minutes the news will be on, and their pictures published. I like the idea of publishing some of the bad guys' addresses. We're going through which addresses to publish. It'll raise public sentiment."

"It'll do that, I'm sure. John, what if they split them up?" I asked.

"Why would they? If they want to ransom them, it's easier to have them together. It takes more manpower to watch them if they hold them separately. I think they're together. So, does our hostage-negotiations team," Stayton said.

"What if there is no ransom demand? Maybe they're just sending a message?"

"To you? If they didn't want something for the women and just wanted to send a message, they would have killed them and left them. Whether they intended to send a message another way, what would that do for them? You're a young guy; you have some means and you're a former SEAL from a tier one unit. They must know you'd hunt them down. That would be a big problem for them. No, punching you in the nose to send a message is not their main purpose. They took the ladies for a reason. Maybe Matt or your grandfather double-crossed them. They want you to give them something or do something for them."

"John, these guys are involved in the sex slave business," I said.

There was a long pause before John spoke. "Well, by Monday, there will not be many sellers and buyers available," Stayton said.

"Okay. Publish the list of addresses after the news and we'll see what that brings us. Watch the news. It should be interesting," I said.

"We'll be talking, Mark. Nassau and NYPD have been pulling over all sanitation trucks and construction trucks owned by Romeo Menduni and his companies. We've arrested twenty-three men on various charges. We will continue. We're revising

722

the number of men out there. Based on interviews and probability, we think the young guns are comprised of more than two hundred men. Adding Romeo Menduni's men and that brings the total up some."

"More good news. Bye."

"Bye, Mark."

#

"I'd like you all in a few minutes to take a break. Pull-away from the computers and phones and just take a breather, pray, walk around, or exercise. The news with Stephanie will be on soon. Take a break and watch. I'll be going out to give the interview in a little while," I said.

I walked to my old bedroom and into the bathroom to brush my teeth. As I came out as Alexandra walked in.

"What will you do?" She said.

"I'm doing it. Now I'll go on camera and do it."

I walked out to the dining room with Alexandra following me.

"Let's do this, Vincenzo," I said. Vincenzo and Alexandra followed me outside. I would do the talking, but Vincenzo would be next to me and in the shot.

"It will be a few minutes," Stephanie said.

"I will be the only one speaking. Mr. Menduni will stand next to me in part of the video, or your camera guy can come in for a close-up. You have all the pictures, correct?"

"We do. The news starts in just a moment or two. Watch on the truck monitor until we go live," Stephanie said.

I stood behind the cameraman and watched on the flat screen monitor. Vincenzo and Alexandra stood next to me. Four other television news crews were around us, having been tipped off by Stephanie. There would be no questions asked. This was my show. Then it began.

"This is 7 News at Ten. Our top story tonight. Two FBI agents murdered, and five women kidnapped from a suburban mall in Suffolk County today. The FBI has not released the names of the murdered agents, but the five women kidnapped, whose pictures are on our screen, are Lauren MacKenzie, age fifteen, Kimberly Schwartz, fifteen, Haley Shore, thirty, Missy MacKenzie, forty-nine and Lorraine Stuart Collins, fifty-five. Police say the women were last seen getting on a tour bus like the vehicle pictured on our screen. In a 7 News exclusive, our own investigative reporter Stephanie Phillips is with a family member of the women, Mark MacKenzie, at his home in Long Island. Stephanie, what can you tell us?"

"Carol. I'm here at the home of Mark MacKenzie. Some of our viewers might remember Mark as the wounded veteran Navy SEAL who was the subject of our newscast and a story in a Long Island paper last year. Well, he has not taken this attack on his family sitting down. All evening I saw men coming and going to the home behind me. Nassau Police, Suffolk Police and FBI are here. However, I've counted over thirty very rugged and able-bodied men, all with weapons, coming and going all evening. Several vehicles departed earlier, and it is unknown where they were going or who the men were. Additionally, the son of the reputed boss of a local crime family, Vincenzo Menduni, is here with several of his men. Sources have told us that Vincenzo Menduni's father, Romeo Menduni, has ordered the deaths of his son and granddaughter, Alexandra Menduni.

Vincenzo Menduni has allied with Mark MacKenzie in this matter. Mr. MacKenzie has agreed to be interviewed on-camera and he will follow with a short statement. Mr. MacKenzie. Please tell our viewers your relationship to the women."

"Lorraine Stuart is my maternal aunt; Missy MacKenzie is my paternal aunt; Kimberly Schwartz is my sister Lauren's friend; and Haley Shore is my girl . . . my fiancée. These ladies are my family. I want them back!

A little over a year ago my parents, Lauren's parents, were murdered in a motor vehicle collision. This man," I held up a picture, "Romeo Menduni, Mr. Menduni's father, ordered their deaths. These men," I held up another picture, "carried out the order and murdered my parents. Please put those pictures back up so the public may see who these criminals are and may help us. That taller man is George Castellano, age forty-eight. This man, Marco Palami, age forty. Their addresses should be scrolling along the bottom of your screen. I have a list of several more men involved in this case and many other cases. That list will be posted on MacKenzie Securities' website and on Channel 7 News' website. I'm asking the public for any help it can provide. To Romeo Menduni and his men. You have about three hours before I make all this information available to the public. At 1 a.m. it will be done and all of you cowards, beginning with you, Romeo Menduni at the top, all the way down to those punks, Castellano and Palami, at the bottom will be in my sights. To motivate the public to help, I am putting a one-million-dollar bounty on each of you, dead or alive. I will give you until 1 a.m. to release my family or I will hunt you down and kill you. I thank the viewers for their help. Good night." Vincenzo and I spun on our heels and walked to the house.

"An unbelievable turn of events. Mark MacKenzie has just put a one-million-dollar bounty, dead or alive, on the head of the Menduni crime family and the men who kidnapped his family and who killed his parents.

What? Hold on folks. We're getting something. It looks like a yacht. Carol. Are you seeing this?"

"We are. Chopper 7 Eye in the Sky is flying over a bay . . . ."

My phone buzzed. "Yeah, LT."

"We're transmitting. I see the news helicopter circling. It's clear. Our camera is transmitting over the Internet, too. Here we go. One, two, three, K-boom!" LT said.

I watched a nice yacht explode. *Cool.*

"Oh, my God. Did we just see a yacht explode? Yes. We're receiving a report of an explosion on the yacht. The yacht may be owned by Romeo Menduni. We are unable to confirm . . . Hold on. Yes, Channel 7 News Chopper Eye in the Sky has its camera on a large yacht that is ablaze at the pier of Romeo Menduni's sprawling Oyster Bay estate. Carol, do we have Barton?" Stephanie asked.

"Yes, Stephanie. An unbelievable turn of events. We'll go now to our own Channel 7 News Chopper pilot, Barton Williams. Bart what can you tell us?" Carol asked.

"We got a call to fly over Oyster Bay, that a police chase involving the MacKenzie women was in progress. After we'd flown over the Menduni estate I banked west over the bay and hovered with our camera searching for moving boats when the yacht exploded as we approached the marina. It's ablaze now.

726

A police boat is putting water on it, but the yacht has sunk and is sitting on the bottom with the cabin ablaze . . .''

I walked into the house for a glass of water. Everyone was quiet and just looked at me. I filled my glass and walked into the family room. Tony was smiling, Rob was biting his lip to keep from laughing, Joe was shaking his head. Alexandra and Vincenzo looked at me like I was a ghost. Carl and Ken were stifling smiles. The FBI agents were incredulous.

"Good interview, huh? What's taking John so long to call?" I said. Joe walked to me.

"Did you blow up his yacht," Joe whispered.

"Perhaps. How'd you like that whole bounty thing?"

"Nice touch," Joe said.

"Wait until you see the next live, breaking interview where I tell the public all these men were responsible for the child sex murders and slavery ring."

"What are you going to do with those two after all of this?" Joe asked.

"Talk them into coming in. But I have bigger problems. Matt and Grandpa," I said.

"Mark. John is on the phone," Dana said.

"Thanks. Hey, John."

"Mark. We're getting calls from all over the boroughs and Long Island. People are showing up at the homes of mob guys and pulling them out of their houses and beating them in some cases."

"Wow. We haven't even put the list out there yet. I guess the public already knows who the bad guys are."

"Mark. Hold on. We have a call that may be legit," John said.

While I waited for John, Alexandra walked up to me. "My grandfather's boat was blown up," she said.

"Really? I'm sorry to hear that. That was a nice later model Burger, I think," I said.

"Mark. We'll patch the call through a computer to your cell. He wants to talk to you," John said.

"Who does?"

"We don't know, but he knows the facts," John said.

"Mark. LT just called. The SEAL platoons have arrived and they're preparing on six helos. The commander is on the line for you," Joe said.

"I'll speak to Commodore Johnston first."

"Here, Mark," Dana said.

"Commodore."

"Mark. I'm so sorry to hear. FBI and Nassau Police are bringing us up to speed. Lieutenant Evans has painted the picture for us. He says you believe they're most likely holding your family at a North Shore estate."

"Yes, sir. I'm about to speak to the kidnapper for the first time and we're probing a possible location."

"Then go to it. We're here, Mark," Commodore Johnston said.

"Thank you, sir."

I turned on my Satcom microphone. "LT. I'm getting a call. Are you listening?"

"I am. Bye," LT said.

"This is Mark Mackenzie. Who am I speaking to?"

"You think you're so . . ."

"I'm sorry. I didn't catch your name." I motioned for them to turn up the speaker.

"My name is not important."

"What do I call you then? Goombah? Wise guy? Wop? What?"

"Very funny, smart ass. This is what you'll do. We want $30 million in one hundred . . ."

"What do you think this is, a fucking movie? This ain't *Goodfellas*, capisce. What did you think, I'd just put $30 million in a suitcase and carry it to you and, what, you'd let the women go at the end of a dark, deserted road? The money alone weighs over 660 pounds in $100 bills, you moron. First, I need to know your name." I looked at Alexandra, Vincenzo and their tech who were whispering.

"Call me, John."

"What's the matter, John, crime not paying? You gotta kill new FBI agents and kidnap women and children? You know the only way this turns out well for you is to quit now and disappear. Once I post that list at 1 a.m., you'll be torn up by the mob. Sort of apropos, don't you think? My next communication will advise the public in general that you and your men are child molesters and men who have sex with children, kidnap and kill them. I'm betting once your pictures hit the Internet, and we have all your photos, between the $1 million bounty and the chomo thing, I might not have to hunt you down. So, John, what will it be?"

"Mark?"

It was Haley. My skin flushed cold, and my senses went on high alert. "Are you all right, Haley?"

"Yes. He just dragged Lauren away from us. There's four of them plus him. Bald guy. Oh no. Please leave her alone. No! You fucking animal!"

"Haley, tell me about your surroundings."

"Old. Smells like a nursing home. Mold and ammonia smell. Old building. Institutional. I smell the ocean. We heard an explosion. We're in a long . . . No! Don't!"

"Mark. Help me!" Lauren screamed. There was a long pause where I heard only shuffling, screaming, struggling and interference. Then someone got on the phone out of breath.

"How'd you like that, motherfucker?" John said.

"I have your thirty million. I'll have it delivered to you," I said.

"No. You'll bring it, motherfucker. We'll see how tough you are when I get a piece of you. Don't go far from your phone. I will call you at 3 a.m. If you put anything out on the Internet or anywhere else about us, I'll torture your sister to death."

The phone went dead. My gut was in a knot. What did he do to Lauren? What happened to Haley? I looked up to find everyone looking at me. I compartmentalized my emotions. I had a job to do.

"John. Did you get that? She heard the explosion."

"Yes. We believe a North Shore mansion."

"Hold on, John." I put my Satcoms microphone on. "LT. Get anything?"

"I think so. It was weak, so it was from inside a building, but we're nearby. We're moving back in toward the south. Let me look at the chart with an overlay of the properties. I locked the frequency, so I'll hear him even if he doesn't call you. Nice work, Mark. I won't move anyone in until we know exactly where we're going," LT said.

"LT. You guys or the team will rescue my family before anyone else goes in."

"We got it, Mark. We'll find them and get them back," LT said.

"LT. Pass along your intel and impression to Commodore Johnston," I said.

"On it. He's listening to us, Mark."

"Now we wait. I'll be in touch." I clicked off the comset and took it off.

"Mark. John is still on the line," Dana said.

"Yeah, John?"

"You have thirty million?"

"I'm prepared, John."

"We'll go in, too . . ."

731

I cut him off. I wasn't going in to rescue my family with the FBI.

"The description Haley gave tells me old mansion that was used for another purpose. I think she was trying to say *long* building when she was cut off. Not all those mansions are what one would describe as long. I'll bet there are one hundred mansions up there. We're close. LT and his team will plot and triangulate. They'll fix a probable location soon. We have his frequency. Now I need to know what's up there. Where can we stage my friends nearby?" I said.

"We're looking, Mark. How did you find their frequency?" John said.

"The guys are scanning the band with a computer program listening for key words that were programmed into the software. I spoke most of those words during the phone call with the bad guy. Now even if he doesn't call us, we can still find him, and my folks are already working on getting into the phone so we can listen," I said.

"I'll be in touch, Mark. Bye," John said.

I walked to my bedroom to shower and dress. I needed to be ready to save my child, my sister, my fiancée, and family. I quickly showered and put on shorts, an Under Armour shirt and sandals. I'd put on my tactical gear soon enough. I walked to the kitchen and poured an iced tea then out to the patio to sit and think. Vincenzo joined me.

"Mark. I own a few properties nearby my father's place. Just southeast of Mill Neck.

There are three huge mansion estates on the properties and dozens of other buildings and another large parcel. About three hundred acres. One property was part of the Catholic Diocese and it has many buildings on it. It was a place for retired nuns and priests, and for education. My father knows about all those places. They're less than two miles from his property," Vincenzo said.

"Are you serious? That must be where they're at. Why didn't Romeo speak on the phone?"

"I don't know. Maybe he's dead. Maybe he's not fully in command. He's been going nutty and becoming angry all the time. Those guys would put ideas in his head, stories about uniting the families under one don. Paul would see him a lot and bring these guys with him. It's like the general breakdown of values in our country. Everyone wants it for nothing, they don't want to work for it. Paul would bring these guys around to meet the big don. Huge, one hundred plus year old estate, lots of land to take care of, lots of maintenance, lots of staff and he's going broke. I told him to sell or subdivide his properties. He bought all those other places and he's done nothing with them. They're draining him sitting there idle. Mine are set to be knocked down this summer. I'm donating part of the land as a public park, some more land for an equestrian riding facility for special needs children, and a block of old domestic help and servants' homes and workshops to an artist guild so they can have a place to work and sell their art for nothing instead of paying those ridiculous rents in the city. The rest will be developed into homes, small shopping villages and local restaurants," Vincenzo said.

"You trying to buy your way out of prison?" I said.

"If necessary, but Mark, they can't touch us. Alexandra and I spend all our time on legitimate business. All the bad shit, ever since I got shot, has been the old man. We have no common or joint businesses anymore. Ask your lawyers to check. That's why Romeo is going broke. His legit businesses don't do well. He's been doing all manner of crazy things these young guys are doing. Look who I keep around me: lawyers, doctors, PhDs, accountants, contractors, and engineers. If you look at the emails that make you believe Alexandra and I are part of a conspiracy to okay whacking your father, you may have the rest of them, but we had auto replied to most emails from those people with an agreement to abstain—a zero vote. We don't participate. The rest of the families, well, they're into all kinds of crap. Why do you think I was so angry with Paulie? He's into stupid stuff with my father and those other morons. He came to me asking to whack Haley a week ago. He was out of his mind. I told him to leave her alone. He was too stupid to do what I do, what Alexandra does, or what your father, Will, did. By the way, your plan is brilliant. I may lose some property and money because of bad actors, but I'll survive. We'll talk more. Oh, I never killed a guy in my life, ever. Even when I got shot and almost died, I let it go without killing the guy. He got whacked by another family a year later for the stupid shit he was doing. I've never ordered a killing or authorized it. As far as I know, none of my employees have killed anyone. I'm no angel, but I'm not the devil either. Come on. Don't you have some shit to go do to get the girls back?" Vincenzo said.

"Matt told you everything, didn't he?"

"Whatever he knew until you cut off the information. That's why when the other families wanted to meet, I'd agree then I'd disagree and point at an email that they sent, but was created by you. I read all the emails you put out. Excellent work. You had me going for a while. I haven't dealt with those guys in a long time. Everyone thinks what they think. Do you think the FBI or Justice would put out 'Mob boss goes straight?' Do you think they'd ever do a media release that stated they investigated me, and I was legitimate? The FBI and Justice would not exist, at least as large as they are, without us. Check. Most of Title 18, United States Code, is written with us in mind, at least until terrorism and digital child molesters came along. It's all part of the co-opting of our government by people who want to be in power their way. They're state-law matters grown into federal cases to keep the federal government relevant. They thought Alexandra whacked Tommy because he cheated on her. Now I considered beating his ass because of how poorly he treated her and for putting his hands on her, as any father would. Tommy died of an aneurism while taking pills, smoking too much, and drinking too much because he screwed up his life associating with my father and those other guys."

"What about Paul's stuff and the deals made with Rizzo at your father's house?" I asked.

"Haley remembered that? Rizzo was doing stocks with a guy, and they made some money. I didn't like Rizzo, I didn't trust Rizzo, but Farina thought he'd make a good stock and bond guy. Rizzo's grandfather got whacked by the family in the late 1970s. My father liked him and did some deals with him. Matt turned my father onto Rizzo and he introduced Rizzo to the stock guy. I think Rizzo was planning to whack my father and the rest of us as revenge for his grandfather.

Mark, I swear to you, Alexandra and I have done nothing wrong, at least in the manner that you think. No violence. If Farina was here, he'd tell you, God rest his soul." Vincenzo bowed his head and paused for effect then looked up at me and smiled. "Gotcha. He's alive, right? Probably in witness protection. He had to do that. He let himself get sucked into doing bad shit for my father and those shitheads. They would whack him in a second. I got him a nice office in Locust Valley, next door to a terrific Italian deli, a great view and paid him two million a year, cars, and a free house with the best view on Oyster Bay. What does he do, he gets an office at a funeral home in Jericho and hangs out with morons and my father's crew. Pagano will tell you. I considered letting him go, but he kept our work separate and he'd been a loyal guy. I stole him from my father a long time ago and I think he felt he owed Romeo. He can't say shit about me because I've not done anything wrong. You'll see.

I don't want you to worry, Mark. You will get millions, probably billions, from the civil actions Monday. Just not my millions. You'll wipe out my father and much of what the local families have and some. So, can we at least act civil and all? I am sorry about Matt. Did your secretaries tell you I used to visit your father at his office? I'd come see him about the NYU Alumni Association. We were trying to keep some conservative professors and professionals on the school's staff, so the place didn't become too nutty. We had pastrami sandwiches he'd get from Voltz's deli . . ."

I turned to see Alexandra standing there.

"I hope you've changed your opinion about us, but don't you need to do something to rescue Haley and Lauren?" Alexandra said.

"I'm awaiting a call. The SEALs are fine without me. I should pass this information up about your properties. Vincenzo. How did you learn about the civil actions?" I said.

"From Matt. Don't worry. Alexandra, Pagano, and I are the only people who know. Since Matt screwed my father on a deal, I'm the only one he told. Matt is trying to move back into my good graces, but with what I know about Matt there is no chance. If for no other reason than I don't want him near Alexandra. You'll get the rest of the families, but I think the civil actions against me will fail unless liability by association is a cause of action," Vincenzo said.

Alexandra looked on nodding her head.

"Alexandra, if I was wrong, I apologize. Haley said you yelled at and threatened her?"

"Yelled, yes. Breaking up a family and taking a boy from his father is emotional. I'm Italian, I love my nephew. I never threatened to hurt her. I said I'd make sure Paul got as much time with Paulie as she did. That was before Paul got even more stupid. That was almost five years ago, Mark. I'd never help Paul today which is moot now that he is dead."

"Who killed him?"

"I'd guess Bonano or Paganelli ordered it. That voice on the telephone call sounded familiar. We played it for some of our guys and they think it is one of the Sciortinos. They think it is Jerry who said he was John just to confuse you. Haley said he was bald. Jerry frequently shaved his head. There are three Sciortino brothers. I pointed out his picture to Joe and Dan."

"What does he do?"

"He's an enforcer, small-time lieutenant who wants to go big. He's violent. So is his brother John. My brother was impressed with him. They're my distant cousins. I've seen him at my grandfather's home," Alexandra said.

My phone buzzed. "Yeah."

"Put on your satcoms."

"Roger. Excuse me." I walked to my room for my comset and turned it on. "I'm back."

"Mark. He used the phone—same frequency. I have his location based on a four-position fix along a line of position on the west shore of Oyster Bay, just a couple hundred yards west of the shoreline. Roughly three miles from my position now. It appears that he moved southeast from the first fix as he made calls. The distance between the first fix and last fix is one point five miles," LT said.

"LT, that may be Vincenzo's property. He owns several abandoned mansions and an old Catholic Diocese property. I'll get a satellite picture of the building and send it to you. Some of us will join you. Go set up an OP along that line of position. Put out three guys. Listen and report. We'll go fluid from there. Give the guys an east-west line just beyond Westshore Road to work from so we can narrow down the right building. There must be forty buildings, mansions, and mini estates nearby. You must cross Westshore Road and climb a small bluff, so pay attention to civilians. Email me your fixes so we can plot them here. We'll send Commodore Johnston a chart and satellite view, so he has a picture," I said.

"Roger. We'll move there now. The activities at the yacht burning have died down. The fire is out, and the Coast Guard just departed after setting an oil boom. Mr. Shore is an excellent captain. I showed him how to use our programs and he's very good. He's got an H&K-614 and AR-15 that he's familiar with. He'll be our house mouse. He's been very helpful."

"Great. He does not leave the boat—just so that old Marine knows. I'll call back in thirty. Out."

"Joe, Tony, Rob we just got a possible fix along a line of position. I'm having it probed. I'm going to that location."

"Where is it, Mark?" Dan asked.

"Northwest of Romeo Menduni's estate. When that guy *John* calls, put him through to my cell phone. I'll keep him online and we'll fix his exact position. Dan, did those agents deliver those boxes from Greenport?"

"Yes. They're in the garage next to your car."

"Thanks." I asked Joe, Tony, and Rob to come help me put the money, thirty million, into six large, heavy-duty, black nylon sports bags. LT had delivered the money to the mini-storage on the day he picked up my shirts. I smiled thinking about LT carrying $40 million and my laundry around in an SUV. I cut open the boxes and we counted out $30 million. The rest of the cash was placed in my safe and up in the attic. We put the bags of cash in my back seat and on the floor of my Hellcat. I began to dress out and gear up.

Joe opened his Expedition and began dressing out, pulling on his tactical clothing and gear. Rob and Tony assisted us.

"Just like old times when we played as kids, right guys?" I said.

They nodded and smiled but quickly became solemn again. *Except this time someone would likely die.* Vincenzo appeared with Alexandra.

"Where are you going?" Vincenzo said.

"To check out some intel." I said.

"Let me send my best guys with you."

"Sorry. I work with my people. I can't afford not to."

"Then let me do this—leave the driving to us. We'll take you two in two armored SUVs. A driver and you two in one and a back-up SUV and driver in case they order you to drive somewhere alone for the money drop," Vincenzo said.

I looked at Joe who nodded.

"All right. Two SUVs, two drivers. I took out two satcoms headsets and hesitated. I looked at Vincenzo who sensed my hesitation.

"We're on your side, Mark. You can trust us. Alexandra, put on a set and go in the second SUV," Vincenzo said.

"No. She'll go in the first SUV with me until I need to take the SUV alone," I said.

"We're confused. Why are you going in and not the SEAL platoons?" Dan said.

"They're the hammer. If we're correct after we confirm our intelligence, we will assess the situation. Why use a battleship when a fast frigate will do the job? I'll be in touch with Commodore Johnston. Ask John to send the Commodore the site plan and overhead view of the area. Use this as the master to identify the different buildings as Tony has numbered them there. See that building on the northern property—the long building. I think that's what Haley was trying to tell me when she said "long" then was cut off. That building used to belong to the Catholic Diocese, but now Vincenzo owns it. It was a dormitory and sanctuary for retired nuns. It's been empty for fifty years when the diocese built new elsewhere. The first fix on the line of position begins there and moves south to Romeo's estate. We're going to look. The SEAL platoons could do this, too, but that would tie them up needlessly and, if I'm wrong, waste manpower. We'll pinpoint the location. Now we can go in and see what we're up against."

"Got it. How did you learn about this so fast?" Dan asked.

"My expert computer guys, Tony and Rob. Tell the FBI how, guys," I said.

"I looked it up on the county property tax records," Tony said with an amused tone.

Dan considered Tony's statement and smiled, shaking his head. "Should we send some agents with you?" Dan asked.

"For what?" I said.

"To make arrests."

I looked at Dan and shook my head. Joe pulled Dan aside and imparted on him what would happen if we went in.

"Vincenzo. Back up the SUVs to the door here," I said.

"Aye, aye, sir," Vincenzo kidded. His man ran off.

"Rob, Tony, hold down the fort and coordinate comms with FBI, the SEAL Team and us. You both wear your headsets, so you can hear everything. I want you to record it for our protection later. Okay?"

"Got it. You don't want us with you?"

"I need my back covered here. I need you to do this for Lauren, Haley, and my family."

"Got it. Good luck. We'll be waiting on the other side. Mark, what's the all clear and safe code word?" Tony asked.

"My Unborn Angel," I said.

Tony and Rob looked at me then realized what I meant. They gave me *holy shit* looks.

"What code word to send in the cavalry?" Tony said.

"Broken Trident."

Tony gave me a guy-hug. I saluted them and they returned the salute then spun on their heels and went back into my home to work.

Two SUVs backed into my driveway. I put my equipment, weapons and the cash in the back of one. Joe put his gear in on top of the cash. I looked in the other SUV and checked the drivers who watched me.

"You could die tonight," I said.

One big guy looked at me and smiled. "I doubt it. Especially if you got a few more like you waiting for us. I know some of Romeo Menduni's men. You're gonna make them piss their pants when they see you."

I nodded at him. "Let's load up and move," I said. Joe got into the passenger front seat. I sat behind the driver and Alexandra sat next to me. Thankfully, she had changed into black pants and top, lightweight black boots, a lightweight black jacket over top and she wore a black and dark grey ball cap, her ponytail pulled through the band in back.

We drove off, our SUV in lead. We were driving to a point just north of the target property. If I could avoid using the boat, I would, since it was crowded enough with the others on board.

My only fear was that I'd get the call early, but I thought that Sciortino wanted extra time to plan his escape. They needed to devise an escape plan without a boat, or without Romeo Menduni's boats. They'll have to do their escape under cover of darkness since, whether we got the ladies back alive or not, they'd be chased down by us and FBI. We would find them, and they knew it. If I were them and wanted to live, perhaps as a free man on the run, I'd release the women to big fanfare and take off. At least then they'd know I wasn't looking for them.

They couldn't be in a public place to exchange the money for the women. It had to be an abandoned mansion or something like that. Perhaps even Romeo Menduni's mansion. I thought and planned as we drove toward our point at a dead-end road that split Vincenzo's property from the neighbor's property to the north. The road dead-ended at a rocky point that was on a bluff just above Westshore Road and the beach.

"Alexandra. Put on your comset. See this switch? It's the comms to listen only. This switch is to talk. It's like speaking on a cell phone Bluetooth microphone. You will not speak unless spoken to. Understand?"

"Yes."

"I'm making this up as I go along. I suspect that you'll drop Joe and me off here," I indicated a point on the map.

"Then you'll drive away and park here and wait. No talking unless spoken to."

My cell phone buzzed. "Yeah."

"It's John. My people are studying the map and overlay. The estates are connected by a service road running through the several estates. Our analyst caught it. It's just a vehicle width wide so it looks like a wide sidewalk. It begins as a gravel road at the north then becomes aggregate then asphalt."

"Thanks, John. We'll probably use it. Bye."

"Joe. Wake me in twenty-two minutes."

"Right."

Alexandra looked at me with a questioning expression.

"It makes me sharp after a short nap. Why twenty-two minutes? Twenty to nap and two to explain it to you." I closed my eyes and leaned my head back. I heard Joe and the driver snickering.

#

"Mark!" Alexandra said as she pushed my right shoulder.

"Yeah. I'm up. Anything, Joe?"

"No."

"Distance?"

"We're about a mile from the road where we'll leave the other SUV," Joe said.

"Aye."

"Why do you say 'Aye' or 'Aye, aye?' Don't navy sailors say that?"

"Alexandra, I am a navy sailor," I said.

She contemplated my words and resolved the confusion in her mind. I took two Excedrin with a protein water. It would dull the pain and keep me awake. I checked my M-4, the scope, suppressor and magazine. I checked my SIG Sauers on my right thigh and chest harness. My legs were cramped so I stretched them.

"LT. We're in your area. Status?"

"Mark. We've confirmed human activity. No sighting of the hostages. As best we can tell we have twelve bad guys in that building that you suspect they're holding the hostages. It's a long building with many double-hung windows. Kev thought he counted two more men than Surfer and Mikey, moving along to the south about two hundred yards west of Westshore Road.

"Roger. Wait." I looked at the map. Two hundred yards put them on the service road the FBI identified. "LT, all stations. There is a service road running through the various estates near the Menduni estate. When the mansions were built in the late 1800s and early 1900s, domestic help and grounds crews used that road to remain off the regular roads used by the rich people. See it, LT?" I said.

"Got it. Kev, you were probably right. My LOP runs along that road. They likely used it. That's the road the bad guys will use when it goes shitty or when they squirt."

"Roger that," the guys said in unison.

"What else do you have, LT?"

"We smell food, and we hear voices, nothing to stimulate us though. No physical or electronic security. Human security only."

"How are you deployed?"

"Five at one, one, two, and one. I will come in behind two."

"Roger."

I should explain to keep everyone up with the plan. One, one, two, one is the deployment spread of the five SEALs across the target property, dividing the property in quarters from east to west. LT will come in behind the second team, so we'll have a one SEAL, two SEALs, two SEALs and one SEAL spread.

"House mouse will stand off, ready to extract and provide covering fire on command *Normandy*," LT said.

LT always was one to twist history. I'm surprised he didn't label his chart with *Utah, Omaha, Gold, Juno, and Sword* beaches.

"Roger that."

"Mark. Why . . ."

"Not now, Alexandra. This is not training. Distance?" I said.

"Just ahead, two hundred yards," Joe said.

"Roger."

"What did he mean by 'stimulate us?'" Alexandra said.

I wondered if I should just gag her, but I explained. "To men, the sound of a female voice gets our attention or stimulates us. LT and the team did not hear female voices. Now hold your questions, please."

Alexandra nodded. We pulled into and stopped on what amounted to an overgrown lawn between two hedge rows. It was part of the property north of the target estate. Our insertion point was one hundred fifty yards east of our current position near the tip of Mill Neck. We parked and doused the lights.

"Turn off the dome light. Can you drive down that road with the lights off?" I asked the driver.

The driver looked. "Yes," he said.

"Pull the brake lamp fuse and back-up lamp fuse. They're in that box under the left dash," I said as I turned on my LED pen light to red and passed it to him. "Don't put the fuse back in until I tell you in case I need you to pick us up on the run. Let's tell your father what we're doing," I said to Alexandra.

"I'll call him."

"Right. I'll just walk over to the SUV and speak to him." Alexandra gave me a guilty smile. I got out with Joe, and we walked to the second SUV. The window came down.

"Vincenzo."

"Yeah?"

"Put this on." I passed a comm headset to him. "Listen only. How many guns are with you?"

"With me and both drivers, six."

"What type of weapons?"

"Pistols and shotguns."

"All right. Do not enter the estate so you are not killed by accident. I'll use you as a blocker if need be. You have that map I gave you?"

"Yes."

"Know it in case I direct you to a blocking point to stop them from escaping with the women. Joe and I will go in from the northwest side. This may take us some time, perhaps a half hour or more to get to the building if they're watching. No radio, no music, no noise, no smoking outside the vehicle, speak in hushed tones like I am. Post a lookout. Understand?"

"Got it."

#

We got back into the first SUV, the driver backed out and slowly drove toward the drop-off point. I stopped him after one hundred yards. We exited the SUV.

"If for some reason I don't see you again, have a nice life, Alexandra," I said.

"Wait, Mark. Please be careful. Your family needs you," she said as she stepped out of the SUV. She grabbed my left shoulder, reached up and kissed my cheek.

"Thank you for saving my life. Come back with Haley and the girls."

"Yes, ma'am." I turned to Joe. "Let's go. Alexandra. Go back and wait for our call."

"Aye, aye, sir."

Joe and I hurried into the edge of the forest. We waited for the SUV to depart. It was dark, but I could see without my NVGs. We covered our faces with camo grease.

"I'll take point. Walk to my left, behind me. Watch my left hand. If they fire on us, I'll go right. You go right behind me and hit the dirt. Do not shoot back unless I fire, and you have a target. Don't give away your position. Don't get ahead of me. I'm looking for wires and sensors. Ready?"

"Ready."

"LT. I'm going in. Advance to point Charlie and hold."

"Roger. Team. Advance to point Charlie in plus two," LT said.

Joe followed me in. The point of the property we were coming in from was near the mid-point along the north property line. Crossing the property there led to the front entrance to the several buildings serviced by a driveway that extended parallel to the road we'd just come in on. We walked southeast across the forested part of the property. It opened to an overgrown and unkempt lawn that had not seen a mower in my lifetime, but which was springing to life with weeds and wildflowers. We broke through the forest providing us a clear view to the central administration building and the dormitory. Both buildings were red brick and limestone affairs that reminded me of my grammar school. The dormitory was located north of the administration building or to my left as we walked in, but further east toward the water. The dorm once housed living, cooking, and medical facilities for the aging nuns. Hence, Haley's keen observation describing a nursing home smell. The building had entrances at each end and on each side at the middle of the building. The north entrance consisted of two doors for fire escape and services purposes. The south doors were the main entrance, and it was serviced by a semi-circle driveway with a covered, drive-up portico to keep the weather off the elderly ladies as they entered and exited a vehicle. I imagined old Model-T Fords picking up and dropping off the old nuns in their habits. My mind just didn't shut down ever, even on this op. The narrow gravel service road was southeast of my position and on the other side of the building.

We quickly walked to a point just west of the dorm. I held our position and went flat on my gut. Joe did likewise. I looked through my scope into the windows along the first and second floors. After a few scans, I shifted to IR view and looked in each window. It was a two-story dorm with nine windows on the west end. Five on the second floor and four on the first with a set of double doors without windows. All windows were standard double-hung, double-sash type with nine panes in each sash. I saw no human activity.

"Teams, report," I said.

"Heat source. Human. East side of building, first and second floors. The heat plume is concentrated on the first floor with multiple bodies," Surfer reported.

"Weapons?" I asked.

"Second floor. Two large males with long guns," Surfer reported.

"Any humans on the first floor elsewhere?" I asked.

"First floor, south side, window fifteen from the east side. I got heat. Two men or one very large man. I see a long gun," Talbot reported.

"Roger."

The north side of the building has two bump-outs of some fifty feet also constructed of brick and limestone with the same wooden, double-hung windows. The eastern being the dining, kitchen and lounge area, and the western bump-out a small chapel for the elderly nuns unable to ambulate to the small church on the south side of the property. It was distinguished from the dining facility by the arched, stained-glass windows with Biblical scenes rather than the standard double hung windows like the rest of the building. The fifteenth window that Talbot described was directly south of the dining room and sitting area.

"LT. It's dark on this end. Do you have lights showing from the building?"

"Yes. There is a Generac unit on a trailer on the other side of the administration building to the south. It's quiet, but we can hear it and see the heat plume given off by the engine."

"Roger. I'm going to look at the chapel and dining area from the north. Come in closer, but do not cross the service road until I'm ready," I said.

"Roger," LT said.

"Mikey. Can you see through the windows of that bump-out on the north side?" I asked.

"Negative. There is a fence and wall blocking my view. It looks like a service and trash access."

"Roger. I'm going to check it out."

"Roger."

"Joe. We'll creep forward. You'll hold your position at that stand of maple trees. I'll run to the building below the windows to the chapel and go around to the courtyard between the chapel and dining room. Once I hit the north corner, you follow my route, and I'll cover."

"Roger."

"Let's go. We ran forward in the same staggered position. Joe held at the maple trees, and I increased speed and ran to the corner of the building. I hit the building and flattened up against it while Joe dropped to a shooting position by the trees. I dashed along under the windows to the inside corner of the chapel and dorm. I carefully looked through the chapel windows with my scope. Nothing. I flipped to IR and still saw nothing indicating human life. I signaled to Joe, who got up and dashed to the corner of the building and went flat against the wall. I nodded for him to continue, and he ducked and ran low beneath the windows to my position.

The treetops rustled as the light southeast breeze blew. I heard faint man-made noises carried across the bay and Long Island Sound from traffic. A jet passed nearby as it prepared to land at LaGuardia airport. I saw no human activity in the building.

Joe made it to the chapel, and I held him at the inside corner. I looked inside the chapel again, with my IR scope from another window. Nothing. I walked around the north side of the chapel to the courtyard. Nothing. The dining hall had several soft yellow lights on inside and the light filtered out through drapes and old Venetian blinds. I looked through my IR scope through two windows. Bingo! I saw what appeared to be several human forms. I observed for several minutes trying to figure out what I could from the silhouettes. Two shapes walked from north to south and back again. I also saw what looked like a group of humans sitting on some form of furniture as they were elevated above the floor. I could make out three distinct heads, but someone was reclined on what must be a couch. The silhouettes left no doubt as to their gender. I watched a few more minutes to check the rhythm and timing of the two forms walking. I could shoot one guy through the window, I was sure, but what would the other one do? I wondered who were the bodies at the east end of the building? Perhaps sleeping or resting bad guys?

I decided to get closer when I suddenly sensed someone coming up behind me. I swung around, weapon up and I almost killed Joe. I put my finger to my lips. I pointed at the dining hall, indicated two with my fingers and made a penis gesture. Then I showed four fingers and gestured that I had breasts. I pointed at our position on the ground then at Joe, then I pointed at the ground. I handed him my M-4, tapped his shotgun, and shook my head. I showed my hands apart then brought them close together indicating too close. Joe got it.

I removed a SIG and screwed on a suppressor. I hustled to the dining hall west wall. I had a choice of eight windows to view into the room, all with some form of covering partially blocking the view inside. I walked to the north side furthest from the bad guys and looked inside. I saw two men, one middle aged, the other much younger, who stood at the south end of the room. I could clearly see Missy, Lorraine, and Lauren sitting up on couches arranged in a U-shape, the opening of the U to the south toward the men. Seeing Lauren alleviated some of my stress. Missy was sitting on the east couch facing west. Lorraine faced south away from me with Lauren sitting next to her. Someone was on the west couch, but I could not be sure whether it was Kimberly or Haley since they were covered in blankets and lying with pillows.

On a library table behind Lorraine sat two banker desk lights with green glass shades with soft, yellow bulbs casting a golden glow. A coffee table sat between the couches with food containers, Styrofoam coffee cups and magazines.

I moved to the east to a door on the north side of the dining hall. I put my hand on the doorknob and slowly turned it to the right. The mechanicals groaned ever so slightly. I stopped twisting the knob and turned it left until the torsional tension released. I stepped to a window to my right and looked inside. No one had heard the knob twist. I went back to the door and pulled out my tube of lubricant which was made of a penetrating machine oil and rust dissolver. I soaked the knob through the keyhole, each turning surface and the bolt between the door and jamb—anywhere I could squirt it. I turned the knob squirting more oil on the bolt as I twisted it. I twisted it all the way to the right. It would open. Then I recalled the name of the establishment that I'd made a hasty exit from earlier in the day. I slowly let the knob return to the closed position then soaked the three rusty hinges with the oil until it dripped from each hinge. I went back to the window to observe a moment and saw just the younger man in the room. Then I heard a boot scrape a hard surface in the courtyard.

I signaled to Joe with my hand to watch the courtyard. Oops! Even kidnapper goombahs go outside for a smoke in our politically correct world today. I peered around the corner of the building. The man sat in an old wrought-iron chair in front of a wrought-iron table. He was facing south toward the building with his back to me. It hardly seemed fair but fuck him. I came around the corner of the building, weapon up and leveled at his head from ten feet away. I popped him. Part of his face left him as his body slumped forward onto the table. I looked at Joe and gave a thumbs-up. I backed out to Joe's position, and we retreated to the northwest side of the chapel to whisper.

"LT. I just iced one goombah. I have positive ID on three hostages and a fourth is with them. Now only one guy is watching them. Snipers. Prepare to take out the second-floor watchers. The rest of the team take the first-floor men with care. I don't know where our fifth hostage is. Do it like we trained with a hostage amid the bad guys if she is with them. Joe and I will go in and take out remaining hostile with hostages and the one or two bad guys at window fifteen. Copy."

"Roger. Snipers, north and south. One each, on the second floor. One penetrating round. Chief, Talbot, and I will go through the east door and windows. Surfer, through the south window. On my signal, gentlemen, I will call Apache. Snipers take positions. Team move to attack positions," LT said.

"Joe. We're going in the door the smoker came out of. I'll off the other guy with two shots and go directly to the one or two guys in the front office. You heard the plan."

"Roger. I'll cover the girls."

"Correct. We'll exfiltrate out the north door. After I zap that guy, the ladies may become a little queasy. Do not wait for me. Take them out that door and head northwest to the street. We'll order the SUV to pick us up on the run since we don't know their strength. Leave my M-4 on the table if I don't catch you before you run out the door. I will block any squirters trying to get away from the guys and I'll take out anyone who chases you," I said.

They always ran once they knew it was us.

"Ready?"

"Let's go."

We quickly made our way to the door the smoker had recently exited. It was a right-hand door which means its hinged on the left and opened outward with one's right hand. Joe would open the door, and I'd step in, shoot, and turn right to go take out the other guy or guys at window fifteen. We got into position.

"All positions, ready?" I whispered. All five Rogered-up.

"Call it, LT."

"On my count. One, two, three, Apache!" LT said.

Joe yanked the door open, and I stepped inside, leveled my weapon at the guy standing twenty feet away facing the women and shot him twice in the head. I was turning and moving right before his body hit the floor. I heard the ladies scream and Joe say, "Shush. It's Joe."

I quickly moved past the kitchen, headed across to the hall. I opened the door, and a very surprised bad guy caught a bullet between his eyes as I stepped into the hallway toward the door which opened into the room with window fifteen. I kicked the door open and went in. A hat-trick! Three guys, also surprised to see me. I shot the right guy, the center guy, then the left guy following with a security round to each of their heads and I reversed out of the room.

"LT. Six KIA. You need help?"

"No. Eight KIA. No squirters. No hostages."

"Roger. Grab any intel and withdraw to the boat. We'll regroup after we debrief the hostages we grabbed."

"Roger. We're out and moving fast to the boat."

"Roger."

I ran back to the dining hall and saw Joe exiting out the door with the girls. The take-down took about a minute. I holstered my weapon, picked up my M-4 and dashed out the door. I caught the group within seconds.

"Joe. Count?"

"Four, Mark. They took Haley."

The girls were running toward the road. "It's okay, ladies. Slow down. Alexandra. Bring in both SUVs to pick up hostages."

"Okay, Mark. We're coming," Alexandra said.

Lauren burst into tears at the sound of my voice. "Oh, Mark. I prayed that you would come," she sobbed.

"Missy, Lorraine, Kimberly, are you okay?"

"We're okay, Mark," Lorraine said.

"Hold. Stop. They're coming for us. Joe, watch our six. Where's Haley?"

"That sociopath, a short guy with a shaved head, took her after the phone call to you. They took off in a golf cart. The young one you shot in there kept talking on his cell phone wanting food. I think they're getting it from another place nearby because they complained about spilling the minestrone soup and the guy said it was a rough ride. We saw a bright light then heard an explosion earlier tonight just after 10 p.m. Later, we smelled burning diesel fuel," Missy said.

"How did you get here?"

"They took us in a tour van to the Park and Ride lot at the L.I.E. in Riverhead. Then they put us in a white school bus with blacked out windows. Haley had us pull out our hair and spit on the seats to leave a DNA trail in both vehicles," Missy said.

I smiled. Haley was a fighter.

"The windows of the bus were spray-painted black. Haley scratched off some paint and she could tell we were driving on a road along a row of mansions on the Gold Coast. They drove us into a gated place that was all run down. A big mansion. It was just getting dark. They put cloth bags over our heads and put us in golf carts and they brought us here. Haley said it took about seven or eight minutes to get to where you found us. Haley counted seconds as we were driven along in the golf carts on a bumpy and gravel-covered road. Where are we, Mark?" Lorraine said.

"Just about a mile and a half northwest of Romeo Menduni's estate. That was his yacht we blew up to make sure they couldn't move you off the island with it," I said.

"That's where Haley must be," Missy said.

Lauren was wrapped around me while Kimberly was clinging to my other side. I looked at Missy and Lorraine.

"Did they do anything to any of you?" I said looking at Missy and Lorraine for an answer.

"No. Not that. They cut or slashed Lauren's arm which is what caused Haley to go after them," Missy said.

"She what?" I said as I looked at Lauren's arm. It was wrapped with tissues and paper towels. I wrapped it with black duct tape for now and passed her my water.

"Mark, she attacked him. Knocked the little shit down, too. Some of the men knew Haley from being married to Paul Menduni," Missy said.

The SUVs pulled up. We made them get out of the first SUV and we put the girls in, and Joe drove while we debriefed them. We drove back to the wait spot. Joe and I got out and conferenced.

"We got to go in now, Mark. They will soon know what happened in the dorm," Joe said.

"LT. Where are you?" I said.

"One mile off to the southeast."

"How far from the Menduni estate?"

"Less than one thousand yards."

"Go reconnoiter and set up an OP. They have Haley there. Has everyone left following the yacht fire?"

"Yes. It's dead there now," LT said.

"How many hostiles did you estimate appeared after the yacht blew up?" I said.

"More than sixty people, but it became hard to tell after the authorities appeared," LT said.

"We'll do the same deal. Chief, I want you on a long gun, too," I said.

"Roger. We'll spread from north to south along the shoreline," Chief said.

"LT, Talbot. I want you two ready to come in behind us. You know the layout. I suspect Haley is in the main house. I don't know how many bad guys are in there, but Joe and I will go in. You two will come in behind us as best you can. We'll talk it through as things develop. I'm figuring a plan as we go along here," I said.

"Roger, that. Shall I call Commodore Johnston?" LT said.

"Yes. Do that and bring him up to speed and explain to him what we're seeing. I got six KIA you got eight KIA. Report that. Tell him what we did and where we're going. Check the wind, but it seems to me they should come in on their birds from the northwest to the southeast on the north lawn. I'll get back with you in a few minutes. Let me finish debriefing the women."

"Roger, Mark."

The ladies got out of the SUV surprised to see Vincenzo, Alexandra, and their men. I swigged my water.

"Vincenzo. I need this SUV. What else do you have nearby?" I said.

"I have a SUV and limo waiting less than a half mile from here," Vincenzo said.

"Let's go there. I'll call Stayton and brief him, so he and his SWAT are nearby on the next assault. They can contain anyone who runs from the SEALs. Let's go to the other location."

#

We pulled up to a local park. We sat at picnic tables. Vincenzo's men brought sandwiches, cookies, and drinks for the ladies.

"Missy, Lorraine, tell me about the leader," I said.

"Sociopath. Little-guy syndrome. Anger management issues. Violent. He punched Haley a few times, kicked her and slapped her, knocking her down," Lorraine said.

My jaw tightened and my blood pressure rose.

"Mark. He's a nut. I thought he was going to stab Haley," Missy said.

"Joe, you deal with this. What are your thoughts?"

"Bad. He fits the profile of a sociopath and killer. No regard. Look at his plan? He knows things will be going bad for him. If he thinks it's all over for him, he'll likely take as many people with him as he can. I say you and I get on that service path with that armored SUV, gain access to the estate and we go in covered by the snipers. Talbot and LT should come in behind us and the snipers come in behind them after all the bad guys outside are dead. We room-to-room it until we find her. That's a thirty-thousand square foot mansion plus the cellar. Some of those mansions have tunnels that lead to other mansions or into the woods. They've been on good behavior with the authorities around, but with them gone they'll . . ."

"That's it! You're brilliant, Joe. LT, Mark."

"Yeah, Mark."

"I want you to blow up that sport fisherman on the pier next to the Menduni estate. Get the snipers in place and you and Talbot blow it. Call me when you're ready. I'd like to draw as many bad guys as possible out into the open before we go into the mansion. I'll get the guy a new boat. Chief and Surfer, you'll be coming in, too, if you can work it. We're going to assault through the rear of the house after the group comes outside. Joe and I will room-to-room it and we'll see what happens. We'll talk as the situation develops. I'm winging it here, guys, so speak up if you think of something or see something. We can't wait. The leader fits a bad psych profile and combining that with Haley having been married to a mob guy they killed, I doubt they'll hesitate to kill her."

"Roger that. For a guy who likes boats you sure are killing a few tonight. Your plan is good. We're with you. I'll let you know when we're in position," LT said.

"Roger. Joe and I will be going into the mansion in an armored SUV. It'll be epic. Don't shoot us if we must leave the SUV before we get inside."

"Roger, that."

"Vincenzo . . . what?"

"The ladies go in the limo. I'll send it to your Greenport house. The rest of us will go in behind you. Three armored SUVs into that bastard's home might bring it down," Vincenzo said.

"We'll see. Put the bags and gear from that SUV in the trunk of the limo and . . . What Lorraine?"

"Mark. We're not leaving without Haley, Joe, and you. Put us someplace or call Nassau County to watch us, but we'll wait right here with the limo. Right girls?"

They all nodded their heads.

Problems, problems.

"Vincenzo. Leave a driver and Alexandra with them. Here's another comset to listen in with so Alexandra and Missy or Lorraine can hear what goes down. Leave your microphones off unless I call for you. Lead SUV will be me. Joe, I'll drive."

"Why don't I drive?"

"I've trained to take a truck into a building."

"They teach that shit?"

"You take front passenger seat. Vincenzo. I need you two," pointing at his driver, "in the back seat. SUV two and three will not go into the mansion, but will drive up and block the back-patio area where we will go in. Pull the brake light fuses in SUV two and three. The bad guys will be caught almost in a crossfire between the SEALs and you guys. Shoot very carefully. It's poor form to shoot your teammate. The four of us in the lead SUV will start a search of the mansion. LT and Talbot, hopefully, will be able to make it in from the east side of the mansion. We are easy to spot. All of us are over six feet tall and look like me. Only shoot guys who look like Joe," I kidded.

"Thanks. I knew I ate too much this week," Joe said. Vincenzo's guys all laughed.

"I'm calling in the SEAL platoons. When they arrive, and ready to land, drop your weapons and go flat on the ground immediately if you are outside. Here are a couple of IR strobes and duct tape. Turn them on and tape them to the roof of your SUVs. I'll tell the SEAL team the plan, but this is very dangerous. If you can, get into the armored SUV and place your hands on the dashboard or the seat in front of you in plain view. Do it. My guys know what to do and they'll be wearing IR strobes. You men need to understand the danger here. Immediate compliance. If they shout an order, do it. You won't get a second chance. It's not a manhood thing, it's a common-sense thing. Do it and live. These guys are the best our country has serving. Follow their orders. Am I clear?"

"Yes," Vincenzo said as his men nodded.

"Let's go set up on that service road."

My phone buzzed. "Yeah."

"Stayton here. What happened?"

"We got four hostages out. They moved Haley to Menduni's mansion. We're planning to go in. They'll figure out we got the others soon. We killed fourteen rescuing the hostages. We're going in in fifteen minutes. I'm calling in Commodore Johnston to come in behind us. You and your people should get here ASAP to make arrests and secure the scene," I said.

"Where are the ladies?"

"With one of Vincenzo's men and Alexandra Menduni, safe. They're at," I looked at Vincenzo for the answer.

"Elizabeth Park," Vincenzo said.

My heart skipped a beat. "They're at Elizabeth Park. I think you, your SWAT, and Nassau County should head here now to set a perimeter around the estate. You can hear the whole play-by-play. Rob will patch it in to you there. All our comms can be heard. Maybe it will help you if we don't make it. I got to go. Thanks for your help." I clicked on my microphone. "Rob. Let FBI hear what's going on."

"Roger, Mark."

"LT. Status?"

"Snipers are in place. We're approaching the very nice sport fisher you ordered sunk. The Commodore is up to date and listening in. Ready?" LT said.

"Call him in. I say again. Launch the SEAL platoons. All stations it just got serious. Pay attention. Thank you all for what you've done to save my family. I love you all and I hope I see you on the backside of this op. To the men who have served with me and saved my life before, I couldn't serve with a better, more heroic group of heroes than you guys. Thank you. Let's go, LT. Blow it in twelve minutes. We will go in three minutes after you blow the yacht and the crowd forms. Snipers. Armed goombahs only. No women unless they shoot at you. Watch for domestic help and the elderly living on the premises."

"Roger. Blow in twelve."

"Let's go!"

"Mark!" I turned to find Lauren standing there. She hugged me.

"Bring Haley back for Mom and Dad," she said with tears streaming down her face.

"I will, Lauren. I will."

My family hugged Joe and me.

"Let's go."

We got into the vehicles and took off fast. I drove to the estate next to Menduni's and turned into the front entrance and drove along the driveway. Halfway down the drive we passed a white school bus with blacked-out windows. I slowed as I got near the service road. A building blocked our approach and view of the back or north side of the Menduni estate. I stopped and put the transmission in park. Joe and I got out. I put my finger to my lips and looked through my rifle scope. I found two men standing watch at the service road gate to the estate which was fifty to sixty yards away. I walked toward them to close the distance. Then I heard and saw a golf cart coming from the mansion toward the gate. I looked through my scope to see if Haley was on it. She wasn't.

This might be hard.

"Joe. Golf cart with four bad guys coming our way. Snipers. The golf cart has four bad guys. Haley is not on it. It's coming my way to the gate with two bad guys standing watch. Identify a target and on my count of five, take out the guys on the golf cart. I'll take the guys at the gate," I whispered.

"Roger." Came a reply.

"Ready. Five, four, three, two, one, fire." I shot the man furthest from me, swept my weapon to the right and shot the second man. I swept across the golf cart. Four dead on the ground. The cart crashed into a hedge row.

"Six KIA. Good shooting team."

We had less than three minutes until the blow. We got back into the SUV.

"Vincenzo. You know this place. Think. Where would they keep Haley, where the public and domestic help can't see her? Take me there. It's us four and maybe LT and Talbot, but don't count on them getting there in time. As soon as we enter the house Joe and . . ."

"Julio," Julio said.

". . . Julio will toss flash-bangs. Joe show him how on the way in. It's five steps and we're up. Watch yourself. Joe, I think we should open the door, drop a flash-bang, close the door, then do it again. I have one more, a Polish GROM flash-bang. It'll blow six or seven times. Ready?" I looked at my watch. "Okay. Fifteen seconds. Here it goes, watch it! Watch it!"

K-blam! The sport fisher buckled in half as it blew apart in flame and debris. Another explosion followed in the forward part of the yacht, no doubt the gasoline from the tender. I revved the engine. People were running out of the mansion and surrounding houses.

"One minute, guys. One minute." Men were running straight into the snipers who held fire. At least twenty-five people were coming out of the mansion carrying weapons.

"LT. We're going in. Let's go!" I stomped the accelerator as I pressed the button to shift to four-wheel drive. I wanted to be sure we made it all the way inside. The SUV took a hesitant second to accelerate, but we were moving at forty-five miles per hour by the time we went through the fence. A guy looked over at us and fired at us with an Uzi or MAC-10. He emptied his mag at us then his head exploded. Good sniper.

We traveled the distance from the fence line to the mansion's hedge row, about four hundred yards, and we went right through it. We were pushing fifty miles per hour when we went up the hill to the lower patio.

"Hang on!" I yelled as I pressed the accelerator as we approached the steps. More weapons were turned on us as people were dropping as the snipers did their work. We hit the steps and the SUV hesitated momentarily before the four tires grabbed and up we went at thirty-five miles per hour. I pushed the accelerator to the floor as we careened through some patio furniture as the big diesel engine screamed. I took aim at the center of the wall of French doors. We crossed the blue-slate upper patio and slammed into and through the doors. Glass and wood exploded around us.

"Fuck you, you old bastard. Die!" Vincenzo yelled as we came into a huge ballroom, dragging and knocking over furniture. I looked around as I drifted the SUV's rear end to the right, slamming on the brakes. We did a sweeping one-eighty degree turn on the slick marble floor wiping out more furniture and a guy shooting at us with a handgun. The SUV finally stopped.

"Now!" I yelled and covered my ears and closed my eyes. Joe opened his door, dropped a flash-bang and closed his door.

K-blam!

Shit. That hurt.

"Again, and we go. Now!" I yelled as I covered my ears and closed my eyes.

K-blam!

I yanked up the door handle and jumped out, my SIG with suppressor out and up.

"Down those stairs," Vincenzo yelled as he grabbed the back of my harness pushing me forward. We ran toward the staircase. A guy came running at me, raising his weapon. I put him down with two shots. I was alternately running, pulling Vincenzo or he was pushing me, as I slowed to line up a shot. I shot another guy coming up the stairs. We raced down the stairs.

"Joe?" I yelled.

"Behind you!" Came his reply.

We ran down the stairs. Another guy came at us. I shot him twice in the chest. I dropped my magazine on the run and reloaded.

"The wine cellar. The double doors at the end of the hall," Vincenzo yelled.

We veered right and ran to the east, I thought. "We're going in with a flash-bang. We may not hear too well for a bit. Close your eyes when I yell, drop to the floor and cover your ears," I yelled as we ran down the hallway.

We ran toward the wine cellar doors. Castellano turned the corner, his weapon up. Joe and I took his head off with one round each. We ran on past him as he crumbled to the floor.

"Joe. Together. I'll take right. You take left. Here we go!"

I had the flash-bang ready. I'd just toss it as we went in. I had my weapon in my right hand as I hit the right door with my left shoulder, as Joe hit the left door with his right shoulder. The doors exploded open off their hinges as I tossed the flash-bang and yelled, "Now!" As I closed my eyes, covered my ears, and dropped as weapons fired on us.

K-blam! K-blam! K-blam! K-blam! K-blam! K-blam! K-blam!

I opened my eyes and leveled my weapon and shot a guy pointing a weapon at me. I swept left bringing my weapon up as I stood and hesitated as I felt the rounds slam into my chest. I still got a shot off and hit the guy in the head standing to Haley's left. My eyes deceived me as I went down, hit three times in the chest, the Kevlar and plate working, thankfully.

I saw two, short, bald guys. I got up and drew down on the guy with his weapon pointed at Haley's throat while I caught my breath and I stepped forward, halving the twenty-foot distance between us, my weapon trained on the neck of the man with his weapon on Haley.

A group of men and Haley were arrayed in a line in front of us behind a long, narrow wine-tasting table surrounded by leather-backed chairs. Wine racks occupied both walls to my left and right, and shelves of wine bottles filled the area behind the group. Two basement style, eyebrow windows lined each wall to my left and right. Recessed, canister ceiling lights provided lighting to the room. The men were not fully recovered yet. I shot another man before the bald guy with the weapon on Haley screamed, "I'll kill her!"

I shifted my aim back at him. Joe was behind me and to my left on one knee, weapon up and aimed at someone. Vincenzo was behind me and to my right his weapon up and aimed at a target. Julio was further behind us near the doors, his shotgun aimed at someone. Standing in front of me were two bald Italian guys, Romeo Menduni, some big guy with his weapon pointed at me who wore Kevlar, too, as did at least two other men and one of the bald guys. To my left stood Uncle Matt, crying for God's sakes, and then Palami, who killed my mother.

A movement to my left caught my peripheral vision, a weapon coming up toward us. My muscle memory reacted, I swept left, firing two shots into the man and I swung my weapon back at my original target before anyone could react.

"Hold your fucking ground! Don't move! Anyone moves and your fucking dead! Who the fuck are you two guys—Mini-Mes?" I yelled.

Haley was crying. Her lip was swollen, her left eyebrow cut, her face bruised and bloody. Her shirt was ripped and bloodied. She would make it. I winked at her.

"Joe. I'm going to shoot the one with the pistol at Haley's throat. You shoot the fat guy in the head. Vincenzo, shoot Uncle Matt. Julio, shoot Romeo. On a count of three," I said.

Haley's eyes got huge.

"One!"

"Wait, Mark. Don't. Hold on," Matt started to yell and plead.

"Two!"

"Wait, Mark. Stop! Stop! Stop! Don't do it. Let's talk. Wait! Mark. Don't shoot," Matt yelled.

I kept my aim steady. I aimed at the bald guy's neck. I'd explode his vertebrae severing his spinal cord as the round mushroomed through his body. Under twenty feet I never missed. I was twelve feet away—less with my arms extended.

"Hold it, Mark. Let's talk," Matt said.

"What, Matt? What should we talk about? Should we talk about you skimming from the firm? Or how about you hooking up with that old scumbag next to you and wasting Betsy's and your future paying him? How about your criminal behavior, hurting women and beating prostitutes? Is that it? Oh, no? Let's talk about you and Grandpa making a pact with the devil standing next to you to save your neck again. Then you didn't do what you should have done. You blamed Grandpa and let him take the fall for the eighteen million in bonds and two million in cash. You allowed this piece of shit to put a hit on your father, my grandfather, that caused the murders of my mom and dad—your brother and sister-in-law? Or do you want to talk about when you raped my mother in high school? Matt, my father died covering your sorry ass, time and again, and he never knew. She never told him. Matt, my mother is an angel, now. You took her from Lauren and me, and you will answer to me for it.

For the rest of you, let's begin with a fact, Haley will walk out of here alive—I bet my life on it. That's all that matters. You scumbags hurt the mother of my child. You won't live. I might not live, but she will. There is no other way this ends good for you unless you surrender your weapons to me now," I said.

I kept my aim steady on the bald guy, "John" Sciortino was actually Jerry Sciortino who I'd met at my office. His brother John Sciortino stood there shaking like a pussy. I looked at the big guy. He looked worried, sweat ran down his face, but his hand was steady. I knew he'd get off at least one good shot. I scanned to Matt. He looked terrible. Our eyes met and he couldn't hold my gaze. Then I looked back to Jerry Sciortino with the weapon on Haley's throat. His gaze moved from Joe, to Vincenzo, to me. I looked at Haley. Tears streamed down her cheeks as she focused on me. I nodded ever so slightly to her as she looked at me, loving me with her eyes. I smiled at her.

I keyed to a familiar sound. I thought I heard helos coming in, but I couldn't be sure with my hearing damage and tinnitus. Others naturally canted their heads to the sound of the helos. I was right.

"That's two SEAL platoons coming in. The FBI and Nassau County have sealed off the estate. They will not come in to help you until the SEAL Commander says so and that will be after you are all dead. I am talking about serious kill teams who have killed thousands over the past few years. Right now, it's just us. Once that assault team reaches this room, if a sniper doesn't shoot you through that window or that window first, they will come through those doors in one or two, four-man snake lines, each man assigned a kill sector. As they come through the doors they will yell, 'Down! Down!' then shoot all threats standing. All of us men will be dead if we are standing whether holding a weapon or not. A fusillade of hot lead will rip our heads off our necks in chunks and the only one who will be left will be Haley. I'm prepared to die—are you? I don't have to shoot you. All I have to do is wait. What will it be?" I yelled.

I could hear the firefight substantially picking up outside. I heard numerous controlled two and three-shot bursts and the yelling of the squad leaders directing the attack. Flash-bangs and breaching charges exploded as the SEALs gained access to the mansion.

"Hear them? They're coming to kill you. Put your weapons down now! Do it!" I yelled.

Matt went flat on the floor. Old man Menduni looked weak. Fatso was having breathing problems, as sweat poured off him. Palami pissed his pants and cried. The Sciortinos looked at each other and I saw that at that instant an agreement had been made.

I concentrated, I heard her voice, and I yelled, "Everyone down! Now! I love you, Haley!" as I fired my weapon once, twice, then again, and again and again as I ran forward and stepped up onto the table and dove into Haley and the others, just as the windows exploded from all sides—breaching charges, flash-bangs and weapons exploded simultaneously all around me.

CHAPTER 22

"Hi. How was your day?"

"Great. We practiced all our moves and we're ready for our game and competition. Haley, two college scouts, one from the University of Pennsylvania and the other from the University of Michigan want to interview Kimberly and me for athletic scholarships for softball and cheer. They already told us our grades meet their requirements for academic scholarships. They'll hold an initial interview with the coach next week. If we pass the first interview then they'll interview me here at home with you since you're my guardian," Lauren said.

"I'm so proud of you. I'll miss you while you're away at school. Kimberly, too," Haley said.

"It's just for a few weeks at a time. We'll be home often. So, is everyone coming out for the big Columbus Day weekend?" Lauren asked.

"I think so. Aunts Alexandra, Betsy and Lorraine will be here. Betsy will get Lorraine at the train station, and they'll drive out together stopping to get Grandma and Grandpa Stuart at MacArthur Airport.

My parents will be over tomorrow night for dinner. Mom will bring homemade cheesecakes with her."

"Yum. Where's Paulie?"

"He's outside playing with his brother in the sandbox."

"I can't get over how big Markie had grown. How old is he, twenty-one months?"

"Yes. He is a big healthy boy. He sure looks like your brother, too. Go look at the picture collage I put up of Mark when he was a boy in the craft room. So, who else? Grandma and Grandpa MacKenzie decided to drive through the city and they'll pick-up Missy and Marvin.

"Where will we fit everyone?" Lauren said.

"Grandma Rosalie and Grandpa Vincenzo are coming, too. They'll take a few rooms at either the Blue Inn or Soundview Inn."

"The MacKenzie's will stay in their usual room. The Stuarts in the nice second floor suite that turned out beautiful, thank you very much."

"You did a great job on that. Your mother would be very proud of you. You learned well and have become a good designer. Betsy will take downstairs with Lorraine, like usual, or one of them could take your old room, I suppose," Haley said.

"Missy will stay in the master bedroom with Marvelous Marvin, but Grandpa will bitch because they're not married, and it would hurt my delicate young morals."

"You are such a wiseacre—MacKenzie."

"That's the Stuart, German side. Holding my liquor comes from the MacKenzie, Scottish side."

"You better not. I'll have Uncle Joe arrest you."

"Oh, is he coming?"

"Yes, with Myra. You know that he and Myra are getting remarried?"

"I know. It's time for Uncle Joe to settle down now that he can finally sit down. Grandpa Vincenzo said Joe got shot twice in the butt that night. Grandpa Vincenzo said it was the first time he ever grabbed another man's butt when the SEAL corpsman had him hold bandages on Uncle Joe. Those two surprise me at how well they get along."

"I know, right? Well, Grandpa Vincenzo was very lucky he didn't get shot. Mark saved a lot of people that night."

"Do you think about that night, Haley?"

"Yes, Lauren, all the time. In my dreams, I see Mark's face, covered in that camo grease, he's smiling at me as he shoots the bad guys and knocks me down even as he was shot. I think about how unafraid, so absolutely and totally unafraid, Mark was to die that night. Lauren, he stood up to those men and told them that they would all die and that he would die, too, but that he guaranteed that I would make it out alive," Haley said as her voice broke.

"I'm sorry. I didn't mean to upset you, Haley."

"I'm good. I know I've told that story to you before, but it needs to be told. It's part of our family history. Mark knew what was about to happen. He yelled at all of us to get down, then he killed the man who had a gun to my throat, then the man who killed your mother, then old man Menduni, as he ran and jumped onto me, shooting two more men, too. The next thing I saw was a clone of Mark, or Kev or Mikey looking down at me, his weapon pointed at me, my head barely sticking out from under Mark's body. He yelled that I was alive, and they helped me. I was covered with Mark's blood. Your brother is the bravest man I have ever known or will ever know," Haley said as she softly sobbed then paused to collect herself and dry her eyes.

"Can you cut up those tomatoes for me while I start the roast?" Haley said.

"Certainly. Oh. The elevator is stuck, again."

"I know. Paulie showed Markie how to cover the sensor to prevent the door from closing so they can bounce a superball in there. Markie covered the sensor with chewed up animal crackers."

"What a bunch of stinkers."

"Mommy! Aunt Lauren! I love you!"

"We love you, too, sweetheart. Are you alone?" Haley said.

"No. Of course not, Mommy. I'm too little to be alone. I must be with Daddy until I'm thirty, he said."

"Oh, Lizzy, you're so silly!" Haley said.

"That's . . . what . . . Daddy . . . said. Daddy! Yay! I love you, Daddy."

"I love you, too, Lizzy. You're getting fast for such a little one. Come on over here and give your mother a kiss and hug, and don't forget to kiss her belly because your new baby sister or brother is in there."

"Oh, you're silly, Daddy. Babies come from storks."

"If you say so. Well?"

"Oh, all right, Daddy. I love Mommy too much," Lizzy said as she hugged and kissed her mother's belly.

"Hi. What's wrong?" I said as I kissed my wife.

"Nothing. Lauren and I were just talking about a happy moment in my life."

"Probably when you met me," I said smiling at her.

"Something like that," Haley said as she smiled back.

"Can I help?"

"Yes. Just get her passably clean for dinner. Tell Paulie to bring Mark up, too. Why don't you toss them . . ."

"Into the bay!" I said.

"No, Daddy, you're silly. Mommy was going to say *bath*," Lizzy said.

"You are so smart. Come on, let's start the bath. I know you like to take your own."

"I do and Mommy told me I'm smart because I get it from her," Lizzy said.

"Oh, she did, did she?" I said as I glanced at my gorgeous eight-and-a-half-month pregnant wife. Haley stuck her tongue out at me.

"Well, Lizzy, I'll tell you the story about how Mommy got smart."

"Really?"

"Sure. C'mon. I'll tell you while you bathe. It all started when Mommy met me."

"It did?"

"Yes, ma'am. Before Mommy met me, she had slip-on shoes because she couldn't tie her own laces."

"I don't believe you, Daddy, Mommy can tie her laces."

"Now she can because after she met me, she learned how to tie her laces, but you know what I learned?"

"No, Daddy, tell me."

"I learned that your Mommy loves me and now we both love you and Markie. C'mon smarty pants."

"You have to tell Markie that story, Daddy."

"I will, sweetheart," I said.

And my life is beautiful. That night all hell broke loose, but amid all that death, deceit, and betrayal was an angel. At the moment my mother told me to act, I did, and I protected Haley, Lizzy and Mark.

Two SEAL fire teams had chased nine men who were attempting to escape by running for the cellar to get to a tunnel that led to another estate. The men came running through the wine cellar doorway with the SEALs in hot pursuit. As they came through the doorway, Julio fired his shotgun and pistol at them, emptying his weapons, but he was shot and killed.

Vincenzo moved to my right and turned to shoot, but he could see the SEALs coming up behind the bad guys, so he yelled to Joe the SEALs were coming, then dropped his weapon and went flat on the floor with his hands over his head while the nine men or what was left of them fought the SEALs. This happened while two fire teams breached the windows and doors to the wine cellar.

The fat guy, who'd been shot by Joe, and Romeo Menduni, who'd been shot by me, got up with weapons in their hands and were killed by the SEALs. Mini-me, John Sciortino, was buried under his brother Jerry's and my bodies as I slammed into Haley to cover her. That Sciortino made it. He will never see the light of day again.

Joe took two in the ass, bullets that is, and one in his deltoid—just a flesh wound he says—as he shot the big guy then fired at the others. Joe is back at work and has been for more than a year now. Suffolk County and the governor awarded Joe medals for his heroism. He certainly deserved them. Myra was so impressed with Joe's bravery, they spoke, dated, and last I knew they were getting remarried. They must, Myra is pregnant. I think they'll announce the wedding date this weekend.

It's clear that Uncle Matt committed suicide by SEAL. Commodore Johnston said that as the team secured the scene, Matt picked up a weapon he found on the floor, stood up and yelled, "Tell him I'm sorry," as he raised the weapon at the SEALs. No doubt his message was intended for me.

I got shot two more times as I shot Jerry Sciortino and dove into Haley and the others. I managed to kill Dopey Palami, two others and wound two more men. The fat guy who already had a bead on me squeezed off two shots before Joe shot him. One shot hit me between my left clavicle bone and Kevlar vest. It rattled around inside me a tad. The second round hit my right biceps and triceps. I'm all as good as new and fully recovered. My children ask me about the right arm scar, and I tell them their mother got some stretch marks having them, so it was only fair that Daddy got that scar protecting them. I don't know if it makes sense to them, but they seem satisfied that both of us have scars. My angel protected Haley, my children and me that night. I love my mother dearly and her absence has left a hole in my heart that will never scar over, but I'm okay living with that now. I think of her every day.

After the SEALs secured the scene, the FBI, Nassau County, NYPD and all the alphabet agencies descended on the estate, but it was Missy, Lorraine, Lauren, Kimberly, Alexandra, and Haley who descended on Joe and me. They took control and assisted the corpsman and EMTs while they worked on Joe and me at the scene. Despite all Haley went through, she never left my side.

One of the ladies was always with me while I had surgery and all that crap again. I healed much faster this time. My grandmothers joined in helping during those weeks. Each night when it got quiet and they thought I was asleep, one of them talked with Haley telling her about the last time I was shot. It was my mother's actions that they described. This time Haley and Lauren led the charge. My mother would have been proud. The doctors didn't stand a chance.

On the Monday following *The Big Shoot-out*, as my family has taken to calling it, the stocks of the eighteen energy companies collapsed. The stock brokerage houses called the margins due on the crime families and their businesses and froze their trading accounts. At 8 a.m. several hundred civil actions were filed throughout the New York City metropolitan area and by noon all were served on the defendants. My law firm has been ruthless in prosecuting the cases. Of course, it helped that nearly three of every four mobsters were arrested on criminal warrants beginning at the scene of the shoot out and continuing that week.

Fifty-eight bad guys were killed in the shoot-out not counting two of Vincenzo's men. The jury is still out on whether they were criminals, but I am grateful for their help. No one else on our team was seriously hurt beside Joe and me.

Vincenzo and Alexandra were arrested later that week and were given bond. Alexandra came to see me in the hospital, and she asked for my help. I gave it to her. Alexandra and Vincenzo, with Pagano's help, let my attorneys go over their books and accounts and get into their computers. They were fine. They found some tax problems from years back and other minor issues. They handled it all under the tax code. Some late fees and penalties were paid, and the matter resolved. I spoke with Stayton and that Preening Pete guy. Alexandra could assist the prosecutors with information. She is known as CI-2 in the paperwork.

Robert, Tony, Clara, and Barbara supervised all that happened that Monday. They did a terrific job. Rob and Tony's company has grown, and I have them on retainer at MacKenzie Securities. Rob and Audrey are married now. Tony and Clara seem to have hit it off.

I've made a ton of changes at the firm. Marsha is vice-president now and my right-hand woman. She is loved by all the troops, too. She is honest and forthright, and she covers me like my mother would do. Bernice is my administration department head. She was surprised when I moved her up to the position. Clara and Barbara are mid-level executives but remain my primary assistants. We sent them to school for their MBAs. Clara still believes a liberal arts degree is more valuable.

I adjusted the hourly employees' compensation up ten percent and, if they want to, they may become shareholders in MacKenzie Securities. I made twenty percent of the shares available for purchase by the employees. Real dividends are paid quarterly. My employees love it. Clara says I'm a rock star.

Haley and I built our house where the old drafty, crappy cottage was. I commissioned an artist to paint a picture and photographer to photograph the old cottage. Haley and I gave framed paintings and photographs of the cottage to our family and to the guys who stayed there that spring as Christmas gifts.

Our home is rather large. It has seven bedrooms, lots of decks, extra rooms that look like bedrooms, but I'm advised are not, and everything you could want for a basketball team or baseball team or whatever team Haley plans on us fielding. I'm happy to help. I love my children, and I have the best wife a man could want.

I sold my Virginia Beach condo to Lieutenant Commander Evans and his wife Christine. They got a great deal. They love it. They're expecting their first child.

Mikey and Kev decided to leave the navy and start their own security company in New York with reward money they received for apprehending some bad guys, additional investment from me, a line of credit I made available for them, and an employment contract they got with another SEAL friend in New York City.

Surfer also bailed out of the navy. He said he just wasn't senior officer material. He's attending MIT obtaining some computer something or other degree. Surfer has a job with me in IT or selling bonds if he wants, but I think he'll take a job with Rob and Tony when he completes school. Surfer visits us often and he surfs all Long Island's breaks. Sometimes I get to go with him.

Chief is Senior Chief now. He got married and he moved to San Diego to make new SEALs. He will make master chief there and he'll return to the East Coast—the right coast.

Talbot made chief and has his own bunch of knuckle-draggers to lead. He emails me often. He got a Rottweiler to protect his new wife while he's away playing navy. He named the dog Mark. Talbot is another true hero and when he's finished with the danger and adventure, he has a job with me if he wants it.

The attorneys have been very successful in locating more assets and defendants. That venture capitalist and several other well-off child molesters lost most of their assets. The hamlet of Merrick permitted the bulldozing of Monty's home, turning it into a park and memorial. A committee of children volunteers designed and built the landscaping and gardens. Professionals put up the memorial and structures. The names of all the children who died because of these child molesters, are listed on a granite stone wall. Haley and the kids call it "Mark Park" which sounds kind of gay.

The law firm heard I was looking for a yacht and they offered the venture capitalist's yacht seized by the Coast Guard. I turned them down. It's not a place for children.

As far as a yacht goes, we decided that if Missy or I want to take our clients out on a yacht, we'll rent one. I finished the pier extension and put a Sea Ray L590 Fly family cruiser there. It's big enough to allow me to take out family and friends to Martha's Vineyard and to sail to Rye to get my paternal grandparents. I sit on the fly bridge with Lizzy and Markie on my lap, Haley next to me, Paulie and Lauren sitting on either side of us, and we go out after work for sunset cruises, on weekends and on days when I don't feel like doing anything but taking my family out on the boat. Lizzy says we're playing hooky from school. I doubt I'll take it to Florida; I don't have to. Grandparents Stuart visit more often now that the family cottage is back to being a vacation cottage. They spend the summer visiting us and they love having all their great grandchildren around them.

My Aunt Betsy is my close confidant and friend. We were always close, but what happened to our family and how we attacked the problem together brought us closer. She sold her Baldwin waterfront house which was full of bad memories. She found a much smaller house nearer to where she works. I expressed to her that she no longer lived on the water, and she reminded me that we had the Oceanside house and the Greenport house, and that I had three boats which was all she needed. Lauren, Missy, Haley, and I purchased some of Betsy's shares in the firm that she inherited from Matt. Lauren, Missy, Betsy and I gifted shares to Lorraine, the Shores and the children. What Betsy suffered I can only imagine. We're her family and we always will be. The children love her.

We cleaned up the Oceanside home. Lauren and I spent a day there going through our parents' things, old pictures, and art. At dinner time Haley, the children and Kimberly appeared with pizza, salad, apple pie and Oreos for a sleep-over at the "beach" house as the children call it. Lauren and Haley redecorated some of the rooms, the master bedroom for instance. Paulie picked his own room. Lizzy and Markie pick a different room each time they're there. They are like two drunk old people sometimes.

The Parker is on the lift there. Lizzy understands she is named after her grandmother, "the pretty one" she'll tell you in a hushed, conspiratorial tone, she not yet of an age where she can distinguish between great grandparents and grandparents. Lizzy asked Lauren why the Parker didn't have a name? Lauren said she didn't know. Lizzy asked, "Can we name it after Grandma Liz and me so we can always be together?" Lauren asked me, and I agreed. One day, while the boat was in the lift, Lauren and Lizzy painted *Liz & Lizzy* on the boat. It's not too professional, but it's there and readable. The Parker just doesn't seem to care.

The Oceanside house is all finished. It's nearly as roomy as the Greenport house, but it's not our home. It's potential as to what can be a home. Our home is in Greenport. The Oceanside house is Lauren's and my childhood home. What happened there in the first version of the house lingers. I've decided not to tell Lauren about that day. I won't lie to her, and I will tell her one day if she asks.

Looking back there were signs that my mother showed fear of Matt. How she would involuntarily move to my father when Matt was around and, later, when I was older, she'd do the same with me. Her eagerness to not just redo, but to erase the old home and replace it with her creation, something beautiful, full of love and without violence. My mother survived. She ignored her own plight for the good of the family. At least that is how some termed it or sold it at the time. Well, Mom, you were wrong, but your father, my grandfather, failed to protect you. She knew my father, too, and perhaps he would have again acted to protect his brother. I don't want to believe that but look at my grandfather MacKenzie.

And what of my grandfather? Grandma loves him and he is family. As it turns out he was a terrible father who ignored his sons until later in life. Missy and Grandma told me. I love Grandpa, but it's not the same. I don't know that I am yet a good enough person to forgive him. Perhaps someday he will earn it. I have forgiven Grandpa Stuart who sought my forgiveness. He is a better man now that that burden was lifted from him. Grandma and Grandpa Stuart have healed their relationship with Lorraine over what happened to my mother. While he allowed a cover-up of an assault on his daughter to remain secret which goes against nature and every father's being, that was all he did. When he learned of the other horrible acts committed by Uncle Matt—I told him—he and Grandpa MacKenzie had a talk. The General is living in purgatory for his sins.

You may be wondering what became of the General the weekend of the Big Shoot-out? He'd gone to Romeo Menduni to ask him to forgive Matt's debt. Romeo was receptive to the idea for a price and told my grandfather the debt would be forgiven for an immediate payment of $5 million. Grandpa took $5 million of the money I'd stored at the ministorage to pay-off Romeo Menduni for Matt's sins. Grandpa was to meet with Romeo on Sunday about the agreement. Grandpa drove to his home to write up an agreement and to write me a letter because he knew the end was near, that I was about to read letters from my parents, written from the grave, and the letters tell a terribly sad story:

Dear Mark,

Mom and Dad here writing you because our lives are unsettled, too complicated and not easily fixed. While you lie in a hospital bed struggling to survive, it is the two of us who have an overwhelming fear that we will die.

For a long time, something has been wrong in our family, a family cover-up of grand proportions, a cover-up of a painful chapter in our lives, in our history . . . a history of lies, betrayal and deceit are but a few of the words that describe it. There are many reasons for the cover-up—none of them good.

As you can tell by the handwriting it's Mom writing. Your father has contributed to this letter, but I will not permit him to read it. Dad has enclosed his own letter herewith. I will start at the beginning of our problems.

As you know, Dad and I grew up together, neighbors and friends. Because Dad's home was on the water and we lived across the street off the water, much of our time together was spent at the house I sit in as I write to you now. Summers entailed we children going out in the boats to Long Beach and Jones Beach in the 1970s. Our home here was the base of operations. Grandpa MacKenzie was rarely around during our teenage years. Grandma MacKenzie took care of us while some of the other moms worked like Grandma Stuart. It was a neighborhood joke that all the children on the street except Will, Matt and Missy had two homes, their own and the MacKenzies'. Our childhoods were special because of Grandma MacKenzie.

As Dad and them got older, Grandma MacKenzie kept the family in Oceanside. Your father was an athletic and academic superstar and when he entered ninth grade, I fell in love with him. He was a late bloomer emotionally, but he always knew we were special and by tenth grade he recognized it. We did everything together. Dad played football; I cheered. He played basketball and I was there again cheering. Dad played baseball and I was there selling hotdogs, popcorn, and soda for the Glee Club. Your father first kissed me on the dock next to where I had you place the bird bath in the garden. We were in tenth and eleventh grade for that first kiss. I love your father, and he has been with me ever since. He became a good man because of Grandma MacKenzie and Grandma and Grandpa Stuart.

After high school, Dad went to NYU. He stayed in the dorm during the week, coming home on weekends, usually to work. One day during my senior year, after school, I was doing my homework in the old dining room. It was in April of my senior year. Your grandmothers were out together. I don't recall now what they were doing, but as I did my homework and sipped my tea, Matthew came home with a new friend. They'd been drinking and smoking and they'd been in a fight. I told Matt to get cleaned up and go to his room, that Grandma would kill him if she saw him. Matt was always getting into trouble with her, always for something bad that he'd done. Which brings me to the story about Matt, the car wreck and your father's broken back.

You've heard the sanitized version of the story. What occurred was Matt and another friend, both drunk, took Grandpa MacKenzie's car for a joy ride. No joy followed that ride. Will saw the car coming down the street. He was returning from his job. Will waved at Matt to pull over, who slowed down, and your Dad ran up to the driver's side to get Matt to stop. He didn't stop. Matt took off and Dad instinctively reached in to grab the keys. Matt swerved to lose your father, throwing him into a parked car then losing control of the car hitting a tree. Matt and the other boy took off running. Dad picked himself up and crawled to the car and got into the driver's seat. He thought that Matt had gone for help. After a while a neighbor arrived home and saw Dad in the wrecked car. She called the police and an ambulance. They took Dad to the hospital. He was nearly paralyzed. As the tow truck lifted the car, Grandmas MacKenzie and Stuart pulled up. The police told them Dad had wrecked the car. They didn't believe it for a second.

They drove to the hospital. Your father had a broken back. He was lucky though; the paralysis was temporary, and Dad would walk again. Dad lied to Grandmas MacKenzie and Stuart and said he was driving. Dad had a permit but not his license. When both Grandmas pointed out the road rash on his legs and arm, Dad knew he was caught in a lie, but he maintained his story. He could not get a full license for another six months which didn't matter since he would be in traction and a brace for at least that long. Your Uncle Matt left your severely injured father at the scene of the accident. Your father accepted the blame and protected Matt.

For most of his life, Matt has been in trouble. He is a charismatic Jekyll and Hyde. Your father recognized early on that something was wrong with Matt. Your father, not yet mature enough to know, took to covering up for Matt more as he got older. Moving forward.

On that April afternoon, Matt became belligerent to me. His friend, some drug user, picked on Matt for 'taking it from a girl.' I told the guy to leave, and he pushed me against the wall. Matt didn't stand up for me. I hit the guy then, as your father had taught me, kneed him where it hurts. He fell and I ran toward the door. Matt grabbed me and hit me, knocking me down. The other guy kicked me several times where it hurts and walked out. While I laid there on the floor crying in pain, Matt attacked me and raped me. Before he finished, Lorraine walked in. She hit Matt with her pocketbook then she hit Matt several times in the head with a crystal bowl to make him stop. He fell off me and Lorraine beat Matt almost senseless. Then we ran home.

That night we lied to keep your Dad from learning. We lied to Grandmas Stuart and MacKenzie, but it was no use they learned of it the next day. Matt had to get stitches in several places on his head. I never went to the hospital nor told a soul until Lorraine made me tell them—all your grandparents. Grandpas MacKenzie and Stuart thought it best not to report it since Lorraine had so beaten Matt and she was an adult. I didn't participate in the discussion, and I know now it was because I was in shock. Mark, I was still a virgin when Matt attacked me. I just didn't want to lose your Dad. Mark, Dad never knew and with what is going on now I cannot bring myself to tell him after all these years. Grandmas MacKenzie and Stuart were against the decision from the beginning. It was a very frosty year for your grandfathers.

I healed emotionally and devoted myself to my studies in design and to your father. Dad did the same with me. We married young, one month after I graduated high school, and we attended college and worked hard. The happiest day of my life came three years later when you were born. We had a small apartment in the city and your Dad worked his butt off. I did several internships and between Grandmas MacKenzie and Stuart, your aunts Lorraine and Missy, and I'm sure you'll remember my dear friend, Marsha, we raised you and took care of you. The first few years were tough, but with those five women helping us, you had more love than I could ever imagine. You developed into a terrific boy, and an honorable and courageous young man.

During all this time, we carried on and, despite what happened, we became a close family. Lorraine just barely tolerated Matt, and she would avoid him and he her. I acted as if it didn't happen, but there were times when Matt would appear in a room or on the patio, and I would panic. Your father's presence always comforted me and, when you got older, your presence made me feel safe around Matt. During this time, Matt got into more and more trouble. I don't know everything and neither does your father.

While at NYU, both Dad and Matt befriended the son of a mobster. Vincenzo Menduni seemed nice enough when he was out at the house. Lorraine had eyes for him, but he already had a wife and daughter, and he very kindly let her down. Your father was business-like and indifferent with Vincenzo, but Matt became infatuated with him. I'm told Matt had several business dealings with him, but Vincenzo finally ended his relationship with Matt because of things Matt had done. Your father finally stopped covering for Matt after he learned of several violent episodes. Dad will write of them. I don't listen to things about Matt's troubles, but I know now that he has put your father and me in danger because of his dealings with criminals. Dad has begun to carry one of your pistols though he has not fired one since ROTC in high school.

We've spoken to Grandpa MacKenzie. What you don't know is that a long time ago Grandpa and Vincenzo Menduni's father, Romeo Menduni, knew one another. Grandma MacKenzie grew up in New York City a few blocks away from Romeo. Grandma knew Romeo, who was already a wise guy.

Grandpa met Grandma while he attended West Point. At some later time, Romeo befriend Grandpa, but later in their relationship they fought over Grandma. Grandpa won and, as you know, Grandma and Grandpa married when he graduated West Point.

That relationship and its fall-out caused Romeo to become bitter. He never forgot despite having his son, Vincenzo, out of wedlock a few years earlier with the woman he would eventually marry. Once Romeo learned of his son's friendship with Matt, he worked on helping Matt whenever he needed it. Eventually Grandpa MacKenzie asked Romeo for help to protect Matt from a terrible thing he'd done. Romeo got his revenge.

Yet despite this history all I ever wanted was a good life for your father and you. Because of complications during my pregnancy with you and because of the injuries I received in the attack from Matt, the doctors said it was unlikely I could carry again without risking losing the baby or perhaps serious injury to me. My tubes were tied—not very tightly as you so properly observed at the time I got pregnant with Lauren. By then advances in obstetrics informed me that I could safely carry a pregnancy to term, and the second happiest day of my life occurred when Lauren was born. I think you were even happier when I told you I was pregnant.

Lauren was born without complications, and an angel entered our lives. To that point there had been no time in my life that you did not make me smile. After Lauren was born, I did not stop smiling. With you away at school, it was like God gave us a do-over, a second chance. We always wanted several children, but by then we were too old. However, we were overjoyed; a son like you and a beautiful, happy, baby daughter.

You took to your baby sister like I'd never seen a sibling do before. You took her everywhere with you and did everything with her despite your age difference. You taught her to swim before she was two years old! She adores you, her hero big brother, and you love her. She was our family's miracle baby. The old grey and black of poor family choices was wiped away for us by Lauren's birth. Life renewed for all of us, even Lorraine was happier.

Then 9/11 happened. I knew you would go. I knew before the second tower collapsed. The attack was such an affront to your moral precepts and so incited you. When you told us you were going to join the navy and become a SEAL, your father and I had already discussed it. Of course, I didn't want you to go, but I knew you had to. Your father comforted me by saying that by sending the best, it would be a short war and a quick victory, and you would be home soon. You were the best and you proved it time and time again.

Lauren would see the news on television about the various battles in Iraq and Afghanistan and she would tell me, "Don't worry, Mommy, Mark is the bravest Navy SEAL ever. He will protect us," and I would cry, and Lauren would comfort me. Your father's and Lauren's support made it possible for me to support you while you were at war. While I am so very devastated and worried about you now due to your injuries, you are finally improving. It's selfish, but I am glad you will never have to go back. You became mine and Lauren's to keep and take care of again, at least for now. My first-born is home.

There is so much I want to tell you. This letter must seem disjointed.

Whatever your father's concerns are, they are enough for him to have asked me to tell you our family secrets. Dad is worried. He's gone to the police, but they cannot do anything as he doesn't have enough evidence. For the first time, ever, I called your Uncle Matt at work. I asked him to help, to find out what was going on. He said he'd help. If you are reading this, then he didn't help.

"Your father and grandfather MacKenzie have decided you should be president of MacKenzie Securities. I laughed when he told me because I knew he'd not discussed it with you. If you do take the job, do it well. Get rid of the bad and promote the good, but do what you want, Mark. Sometimes I wish your father had spent more time home with us rather than at the firm. Choose family first, Mark. I know you will.

I know what Cathy did hurt you. Don't let that stop you from finding happiness with a woman you love. I have had your father with me since high school. I would not change a thing in our relationship. Go out and find love, get married and have children. You will be a great father, better than your father, I am certain.

If something happens to your father and me, I need you to take care of Lauren. You must raise her, teach her, nurture her and protect her. Your grandparents will be there to help, but she will need you. You have more fortitude, strength, discipline, honor, and integrity than all the other men in our family put together. I say that loving your father with all my heart. You are just a better man. I wish you were of able body now because your father needs you.

I want you to know that your aunts Missy, Betsy, and Lorraine will need you, too, to set the example of male leadership they deserve. I don't expect that Betsy and Matt's marriage will survive much longer. Moreover, I fear that Matt will be in jail or killed. He belongs in jail if what I've heard is true. I have no doubt that your father's problems are a result of Matt's actions. Furthermore, your Grandpa MacKenzie, the same man who convinced my parents and Grandma MacKenzie not to allow Matt to suffer the consequences of his actions all those years ago, has failed us here again by covering for Matt.

Please do what's right and cut out the cancer that infects this family. Protect Lauren and protect your aunts and, above all, protect yourself for without you the rest may not survive, surely, they will not thrive and flourish.

I love you, Mark. You are the embodiment of what every mother would want in a son. I fondly recall our life together. It is very special to me. I just thought about how you would take me fishing and cruising the bays of the North Fork together. I could see then that you would be a good man. I will miss that, our time together.

Having never written a letter like this before, I don't know how to close it.

If you are reading this, then I am no longer of your world and I cry for that as I sit here in my bed writing to you. You should go on in your life, take care of Lauren. Know that I am always with you, a part of you. I am in your heart and in your thoughts as you are in mine. I will come to you when you need me, and I will watch over you and Lauren. Please be well, but most of all, protect your heart and love!

Always, your loving mother,

Mom

#

Dear Mark:

It is with great sadness that we write these letters. As brevity is the hallmark of good writing, I will attempt to do that here.

If you are reading this letter, then your mother and I died of suspicious or criminal circumstances. I won't belabor my concerns as to why I am afraid that I will be killed. Suffice it to say my concerns are real enough such that I have discussed them with your mother, and I asked her to write to you to advise of the many terrible secrets in our family. So as not to upset you unnecessarily, all our concerns pertain to acts of your Uncle Matt and the indifference and cover-up of those acts by your grandfather, my father.

I have recently learned, through a college friend, of the extent of your uncle's acts. There are too many to list. The worst act or crime that I know of committed by Matt was where he beat and raped a call girl in a downtown hotel. She almost died. Through this friend who is a non-participating member of a local crime family, I learned that your grandfather negotiated a deal to protect Matt. There are many instances where Dad has covered for Matt. The sad truth is I have covered for Matt for many years, but never for crimes or violence. Last month I washed my hands of Matt, but Dad would not allow me to dismiss him from the firm. Matt has no job at the firm other than to be there which he frequently is not. Not long ago, Dad wanted to dismiss Matt, and I would not permit it.

798

You need to know that Matt, other people and fraudulent shareholders who work for the mob, led by Rizzo, have threatened to kill me. But I also believe they intend to kill Grandpa. Matt told me that. I informed Grandpa and the police. It went nowhere. Grandpa wrote it off to Matt being drunk and saying stupid things as he has often done in the past. Be as it may, I have taken the threats seriously and taken to carrying one of your pistols with me.

This is a terrible time for our family. I'm sorry I'll miss our time together. I know your mother has been a much better mother to you than I have been a father, but I have always loved you, tried to instill in you good and decent values, honor, and integrity. I am proud to say I was successful, but I am not the only one who may be credited with that accomplishment. Your mother is the better parent. That said, we were a team. We are both very proud of our son. I love your mother and always have as far back as I can remember her. I cherished her and I'd do anything for her that I could do. I feel powerless now and you have only just begun to improve. I've cried nights when I was alone thinking about your injuries over the past few months. Combined, tonight, I feel powerless to protect my family and it is the most emasculating feeling I know because I let it happen. I let the devil remain in my family.

Mark. Your grandfather, my father, has failed as miserably as I have failed. I have enclosed in this package the documents that relate to Matt, Rizzo, Train, and Taylor's betrayal. I think they know I have these documents as I am an idiot on computers. I will place all these documents with our trusted attorney, Mike Schmidt. These are the things you need to know to fix the firm.

Your grandfather got mixed up with Romeo Menduni a long time ago. Fate put Vincenzo, Matt and me together. While Vincenzo is of that family and has done somethings in his youth, I do not believe him to be a sociopath like his father or Matt. He cut off contact with Matt a long time ago. Talk to him. Vincenzo will help you put Matt in prison. I don't know if my father's part in the cover-up is criminal or not, but once you remove Matt from the firm, you will have all power you need to get rid of the rest and cut Grandpa out of anything to do with the business. Any further corroboration you need, speak with Grandma MacKenzie. She will tell you all she knows, and she will help you. Her guilt over the years caused her to sell most of her firm shares to your mother for a fraction of their value. There's a story there, but no one will tell me what it is. Under no circumstances should Lauren ever be left alone with Matt. Your grandmother made that clear to me.

Vincenzo put someone in the firm to report on Matt, Rizzo and the others and to obtain evidence against the mob. I don't know who that person is. I suspect an intern. That person conclusively proved that Matt, Rizzo, Train, and Taylor have been conspiring to skim and have skimmed from the firm. The schemes skimmed some $42 million since Matt worked here. I believe the evidence is included herewith. Follow the money trail, Mark. It will lead to our killers. I so wish you were here sitting with me and of able body.

Love Lauren, take care of her, protect her. I'm sorry Cathy is gone, but while you may not find a woman as good as your mother—no other woman could ever measure up in my opinion—you will find her someday. Love, covet and cherish her and you will have a good life.

I don't know how or I don't want to end this letter, but I must. I love you, Mark. I wish I could have done more. I'm sorry.

Love, your father

♯

I'd read the letters, in the hospital, a few days after I was shot. Haley brought them to me. I read them and initially tried to compartmentalize my emotions, but I broke down and cried while Haley held me. I have mixed emotions about the letters, my parents' thoughts and what they did to help each other. The letter Grandpa wrote to me that weekend I refused to read. I put it away in a safe. He will tell me to my face not in a note.

What strikes me as most bizarre in this whole affair is the fateful intercourse between our family and the Menduni family. My grandmother MacKenzie, before she was a MacKenzie, and Romeo Menduni, then Romec Menduni and my grandfather MacKenzie. Twenty years later, Vincenzo and my father, then Vincenzo and Matt, then thirty years later, Haley and me, which led to Paul and me crossing paths, then Alexandra and me, and now I am Paulie's stepfather.

Haley has asked me to adopt Paulie so we can give him my name. That would end the Menduni dynasty and name at Vincenzo's death. All and all, it sounds like a good deal. The Shores want it to happen. Alexandra has given her blessing. Vincenzo reluctantly concurred not because of any opposition to changing Paulie's name, but acknowledgement of the fact that his family name will terminate with his death.

Paulie looks like Haley and our children look like Haley and me. Perhaps it is best to adopt Paulie and cheat fate from interceding once again to hurt my family. After all, it is my responsibility to protect this family by all means possible.

EPILOGUE

I'd just finished meeting with Ira and our senior broker. We closed out the third quarter with phenomenal numbers. Ira Goldman and Davis Middleton were very pleased.

We'd hired five more brokers and support staff. I have nearly one hundred souls working for MacKenzie Securities, but I still managed the whole deal working two to four days a week, occasionally more. I love my job because I love my employees. I walk around handing out compliments, bonus checks, theater tickets or, to the consternation of my managers, impromptu days off for the hourly employees. I was known to have long lunches with five or six employees in the conference room—my treat.

Late last October, my third child joined the clan. Haley Marie was born the day after my birthday. Like a solar eclipse, the moon blotting out the sun, my birthday will forever be overshadowed by Haley Marie's birthday which is fine with me. She is just over eleven months old and birthday preparations have already begun.

Lizzy and Markie are thirty-two months old and very bright. They love their little sister. Lizzy is the leader of the group, and she gets Markie into everything. Paulie is almost eleven. He loves his siblings and he's been a terrific big brother. Paulie is a MacKenzie now. I adopted him and gave him my name several months ago.

Haley has her hands full, and she loves every minute of it. Amid all the diapers, colds, earaches, and lost sneakers, Haley completed her doctorate in education. Now I must address her as *doctor*. Lizzy said it proves Mommy is smarter than Daddy. I was kidding about having to refer to her as doctor. Anyway.

I hired a childcare something or other, to help with the children during the week with Haley back teaching. I call her a nanny, but I'm told that is a politically incorrect term. I also hired a home cleaning service since the house is so large and the children are so many. I was going to hire a cook or chef, but I was shot down. We—turn that w over to an m—me—will cook our dinners which I love to do. It's just the whole teaching of the clan around hot pans and sharp steel that makes me nervous. Lizzy and Markie climb up on their stools at the counter to help and Haley instigates problems with them just like my mother did with me against my father.

I miss Lauren being in the home every night now that she is in college. Lauren and Kimberly decided to check out the Universities of Michigan, Pennsylvania, and Virginia since all offered them full scholarships on academics, softball and cheer. After two weeks on the road, in her new BMW 4 Series, during which time I was a nervous wreck, they returned and elected to attend the New York School of Design and NYU on a joint program. They got some help from the schools, but not full scholarships like the other schools had offered. No matter, the girls are independently wealthy having collected sizeable settlements due to their ordeal that spring. Together, they purchased a twenty-six hundred square foot double loft one floor below our mother's design loft in SoHo. They use it with their classmates as a palette while they study interior design. Lauren and Kimberly live in our apartment loft while attending school. I stay there a few times each month, but I get lonely for

Haley and the confusion that is bedtime at our home in Greenport.

Lauren has a few gentlemen callers. I've met them all. I keep an eye on my baby sister. I hung an enlarged photograph of the guys and me in full combat gear standing on a mountain in Afghanistan on the wall in the loft because . . . well, you know why.

I love my life. My cell phone buzzed.

"Yes, doctor?"

"Oh, stop it, you. What are you doing?"

"I just finished going over the numbers for the last quarter. We did well. I think I'll be able to pick up a couple extra bundles of diapers at Costco."

"That's good because we'll need them."

That came out a little, well, with extra emphasis. Should I bite?

"So, like I was saying . . ."

"You understood my implication perfectly well, Mr. MacKenzie."

"Really?"

"Yes. I'm almost six weeks along."

"Really?" *I still replied in one-word or monosyllabic answers around Haley most of the time.* "How many is that I can't keep track?"

"Five with Paulie."

"Are we finished?"

"I'm not sure. We'll talk. We could practice abstinence."

Coming from a doctor, I didn't think that was sound advice. "I'll take that under advisement. I'm so happy sweetheart. Naturally, I'm the last to know?"

"No. I haven't told Haley Marie."

"Oh, well, then I'll break the news to her."

"When will you be home, sailor?"

"I was looking at my desk and starting to fade. I think I'll wrap it up. So, who here already knows?"

Silence.

"This is not a constitutional matter. You do not have the right to remain silent."

"I only told Bernice."

"What? It'll be in the Wall Street Journal . . ."

"Surprise!"

"Another child!"

"How terrific!"

"Hold on, folks. Haley, half my staff are standing at my door."

"I may have mentioned to some others. Call me when you leave. Oh. The whole family will be here for dinner and the weekend. Bye. I love you."

"I love you, too. Bye. Okay. Come in if you must." Twenty women came in to congratulate me. After ten minutes of small talk and joking they went back to work.

My desk phone buzzed. "Yes, Margie."

"Jennifer said you have a visitor at reception. A Special Agent John Stayton of the FBI."

I wonder what he wants. "Put him in the small conference room with either a pot of coffee or bottle of bourbon. His choice. I'll be right in. Thanks, Margie."

"Yes, sir."

A few moments later, after wrapping up my computer and desk, I walked to the conference room. Good. He was drinking bourbon. I walked in.

"Hello, SAC Stayton. How are you?" I said as I extended my hand.

"I'm good, Mark. How are you?" He said as he shook my hand.

"Terrific. Haley's pregnant."

"I think I knew that."

"No. Not this one unless you're tapping my phones. I just found out a few minutes ago."

"Great. How many is that?"

"I'm not sure," I deadpanned as I poured myself a shot.

"What brings you to my office all the way from Washington?"

"We're wrapping up the last of the cases and cleaning out the files for all the deceased bad guys before I move into my new job. We took custody of this from Castellano's home."

He placed a small manila envelope in front of me. I opened it and poured the contents onto the table. It was a gold chain necklace with a scrolled plate with a diamond on each end. The scroll was inscribed, *"Mom, All My Love, Mark. Christmas 1993."*

I felt the heat of the tears rush to my eyes.

"Thank you. I really appreciate it, John."

#

I drove home in my now three-year-old, animal cracker-encrusted Hellcat. I was cruising down the expressway at a decent pace for the L.I.E. As I approached the exit for my parents' graves, I got off and drove to the cemetery. I parked in the small lot near their gravestone. My Uncle Matt's grave was several rows away. I walked to my parents' graves and stood before them.

"Mom, Dad, we're all right," I said as I held my mother's necklace in my hand.

"You both would be so proud of Lauren. She is the embodiment of what every parent would want in a daughter. You don't know Haley, but you were both right. I love having a wife and I love my wife. Dad, I know what you meant and Mom, thanks for teaching me. I think I'm a good husband because of you.

You'll be happy to know another grandchild is on his or her way. Your namesake, Lizzy, talks about her grandmother—the pretty one—as if you are here with her. Mom, you were there for me, and you caused me to act that terrible night. That act brought two delightful little humans into the world and saved the life of another beautiful human—my wife. I cannot help but wonder if you don't communicate with Lizzy. Mom, Dad . . . you are both missed. You will never be forgotten."

I brushed some leaves off the ground stone. I noted the silk flowers were faded. Lizzy picked out new each time we visited, and Markie swept the ground stone. It was good for the youngest generation to honor past generations.

"Mom, Dad, we'll make it. You were both right. It's about love."

www.ingramcontent.com/pod-product-compliance
Lightning Source LLC
Chambersburg PA
CBHW071656120626
46550CB00001B/1